Priests of the Bible

Priests of the Bible

Bridging the Gap between God and Man

Incorporating Kings of the Bible

John R. Barber

Priests of the Bible

Bridging the Gap between God and Man

Incorporating Kings of the Bible

Copyright © John R. Barber 2024 – all rights reserved

www.jrbpublications.com

Part 1 – The Priesthood

Part 2 – The Priests

Part 3 – A Priestly People

Part 4 – Kings of the Bible

ISBN 978-0-9537306-5-0

First Edition: June 2024

Published by: John Barber, Southend, England

Cover design: www.greatwriting.org

Book layout and design: www.greatwriting.org

Unless stated otherwise, scripture quotations are taken from the Authorised (King James) Version of the Bible. The book can be freely, electronically downloaded (for personal use only) from the author's website or can be purchased in paper (book) form through Amazon and similar outlets.

Some Relevant Bible Verses

"These [the Bereans] *were more noble than those in Thessalonica, in that they received the word with all readiness of mind, and searched the scriptures daily, whether those things were so"* Acts 17:11.

"As he saith also in Osee [Hosea], *I will call them my people, which were not my people; and her beloved, which was not beloved. And it shall come to pass, that in the place where it was said unto them, Ye are not my people; there shall they be called the children of the living God"* Romans 9:25-26.

"Speaking to yourselves in psalms and hymns and spiritual songs, singing and making melody in your heart to the Lord; giving thanks always for all things unto God and the Father in the name of our Lord Jesus Christ; submitting yourselves one to another in the fear of God" Ephesians 5:19-20.

"All scripture is given by inspiration of God, and is profitable for doctrine, for reproof, for correction, for instruction in righteousness: That the man of God may be perfect, thoroughly furnished unto all good works" 2 Timothy 3:16-17.

"Seeing then that we have a great high priest, that is passed into the heavens, Jesus the Son of God, let us hold fast our profession. For we have not an high priest which cannot be touched with the feeling of our infirmities; but was in all points tempted like as we are, yet without sin. Let us therefore come boldly unto the throne of grace, that we may obtain mercy, and find grace to help in time of need" Hebrews 4:14-16.

"To whom coming, as unto a living stone, disallowed indeed of men, but chosen of God, and precious, Ye also, as lively stones, are built up a spiritual house, an holy priesthood, to offer up spiritual sacrifices, acceptable to God by Jesus Christ. Wherefore also it is contained in the scripture, Behold, I lay in Sion a chief corner stone, elect, precious: and he that believeth on him shall not be confounded. Unto you therefore which believe he is precious: but unto them which be disobedient, the stone which the builders disallowed, the same is made the head of the corner, And a stone of stumbling, and a rock of offence, even to them which stumble at the word, being disobedient: whereunto also they were appointed. But ye are a chosen generation, a royal priesthood, an holy nation, a peculiar people; that ye should shew forth the praises of him who hath called you out of darkness into his marvellous light; Which in time past were not a people, but are now the people of God: which had not obtained mercy, but now have obtained mercy" 1 Peter 2:4-10.

"Knowing this first, that no prophecy of the scripture is of any private interpretation. For the prophecy came not in old time by the will of man: but holy men of God spake as they were moved by the Holy Ghost" 2 Peter 1:20-21.

"*And they* [Christ's followers] *overcame him* [Satan] *by the blood of the Lamb, and by the word of their testimony; and they loved not their lives unto the death*" Revelation 12:11.

"*And hath made us kings and priests unto God and his Father; to him be glory and dominion for ever and ever. Amen ... And hast made us unto our God kings and priests: and we shall reign on the earth ... Blessed and holy is he that hath part in the first resurrection: on such the second death hath no power, but they shall be priests of God and of Christ, and shall reign with him a thousand years*" Revelation 1:6, 5:10, 20:6.

"*Now therefore, if ye will obey my voice indeed, and keep my covenant, then ye shall be a peculiar treasure unto me above all people: for all the earth is mine: And ye shall be unto me a kingdom of priests, and an holy nation. These are the words which thou shalt speak unto the children of Israel*" Exodus 19:5-6.

"*Hear, O Israel: The Lord our God is one Lord: And thou shalt love the Lord thy God with all thine heart, and with all thy soul, and with all thy might. And these words, which I command thee this day, shall be in thine heart: And thou shalt teach them diligently unto thy children, and shalt talk of them when thou sittest in thine house, and when thou walkest by the way, and when thou liest down, and when thou risest up. And thou shalt bind them for a sign upon thine hand, and they shall be as frontlets between thine eyes. And thou shalt write them upon the posts of thy house, and on thy gates*" Deuteronomy 6:4-9.

"*Now therefore fear the Lord, and serve him in sincerity and in truth: and put away the gods which your fathers served on the other side of the flood, and in Egypt; and serve ye the Lord. And if it seem evil unto you to serve the Lord, choose you this day whom ye will serve; whether the gods which your fathers served that were on the other side of the flood, or the gods of the Amorites, in whose land ye dwell: but as for me and my house, we will serve the Lord*" Joshua 24:14-15.

"*For Ezra had prepared his heart to seek the law of the Lord, and to do it, and to teach in Israel statutes and judgments*" Ezra 7:10.

"*The law of the Lord is perfect, converting the soul: the testimony of the Lord is sure, making wise the simple. The statutes of the Lord are right, rejoicing the heart: the commandment of the Lord is pure, enlightening the eyes. The fear of the Lord is clean, enduring for ever: the judgments of the Lord are true and righteous altogether. More to be desired are they than gold, yea, than much fine gold: sweeter also than honey and the honeycomb. Moreover by them is thy servant warned: and in keeping of them there is great reward*" Psalm 19:7-11.

"*Give unto the Lord, O ye mighty, give unto the Lord glory and strength. Give unto the Lord the glory due unto his name; worship the Lord in the beauty of holiness. The voice of the Lord is upon the waters: the God of glory thundereth: the Lord is upon many waters. The voice of the Lord is powerful; the voice of the Lord is full of majesty. The voice of the Lord breaketh the cedars; yea, the Lord breaketh the cedars of Lebanon*" Psalm 29:1-5.

"*Blessed are the undefiled in the way, who walk in the law of the Lord. Blessed are they that keep his testimonies, and that seek him with the whole heart … Let my soul live, and it shall praise thee; and let thy judgments help me. I have gone astray like a lost sheep; seek thy servant; for I do not forget thy commandments*" Psalm 119:1-2, 175-176.

"*The Spirit of the Lord God is upon me; because the Lord hath anointed me to preach good tidings unto the meek; he hath sent me to bind up the brokenhearted, to proclaim liberty to the captives, and the opening of the prison to them that are bound; To proclaim the acceptable year of the Lord, and the day of vengeance of our God; to comfort all that mourn; To appoint unto them that mourn in Zion, to give unto them beauty for ashes, the oil of joy for mourning, the garment of praise for the spirit of heaviness; that they might be called trees of righteousness, the planting of the Lord, that he might be glorified. And they shall build the old wastes, they shall raise up the former desolations, and they shall repair the waste cities, the desolations of many generations. And strangers shall stand and feed your flocks, and the sons of the alien shall be your plowmen and your vinedressers. But ye shall be named the Priests of the Lord: men shall call you the Ministers of our God: ye shall eat the riches of the Gentiles, and in their glory shall ye boast yourselves*" Isaiah 61:1-6.

"*But who may abide the day of his coming? and who shall stand when he appeareth? for he is like a refiner's fire, and like fullers' soap: And he shall sit as a refiner and purifier of silver: and he shall purify the sons of Levi, and purge them as gold and silver, that they may offer unto the Lord an offering in righteousness*" Malachi 3:2-3.

Opening Hymns and Poem

Lord for the years – Timothy Dudley-Smith

1. Lord, for the years
your love has kept and guided,
urged and inspired us,
cheered us on our way,
sought us and saved us,
pardoned and provided:
Lord of the years,
we bring our thanks today.

2. Lord, for that word,
the word of life which fires us,
speaks to our hearts
and sets our souls ablaze,
teaches and trains,
rebukes us and inspires us:
Lord of the word,
receive your people's praise.

3. Lord, for our land
in this our generation,
spirits oppressed by
pleasure, wealth and care:
for young and old,
for commonwealth and nation,
Lord of our land,
be pleased to hear our prayer.

4. Lord, for our world
where men disown and doubt you,
loveless in strength,
and comfortless in pain,
hungry and helpless,
lost indeed without you;
Lord of the world,
we pray that Christ may reign.

5. Lord, for ourselves,
in living power remake us
self on the cross
and Christ upon the throne,
past put behind us,
for the future take us;
Lord of our lives,
to live for Christ alone.

Facing a Task Unfinished – Frank Houghton

1. Facing a task unfinished
That drives us to our knees
A need that undiminished
Rebukes our slothful ease

2. We, who rejoice to know Thee
Renew before Thy throne
The solemn pledge we owe Thee
To go and make Thee known

3. *Where other Lords beside Thee*
Hold their unhindered sway
Where forces that defied Thee
Defy Thee still today

4. *With none to heed their crying*
For life and love and light
Unnumbered souls are dying
And pass into the night

5. *We go to all the world*
With kingdom hope unfurled
No other name has power to save
But Jesus Christ The Lord

6. *We bear the torch that flaming*
Fell from the hands of those
Who gave their lives proclaiming
That Jesus died and rose

7. *Ours is the same commission*
The same glad message ours
Fired by the same ambition
To Thee we yield our powers

8. *We go to all the world*
With kingdom hope unfurled
No other name has power to save
But Jesus Christ The Lord

9. *O Father who sustained them*
O Spirit who inspired

Saviour, whose love constrained them
To toil with zeal untired

10. From cowardice defend us
From lethargy awake!
Forth on Thine errands send us
To labour for Thy sake

11. We go to all the world
With kingdom hope unfurled
No other name has power to save
But Jesus Christ The Lord

12. We go to all the world
His kingdom hope unfurled
No other name has power to save
But Jesus Christ The Lord

Only One Life – C. T. Studd

Two little lines I heard one day, Traveling along life's busy way;
Bringing conviction to my heart, And from my mind would not
depart;
Only one life, 'twill soon be past, Only what's done for Christ will
last.

Only one life, yes only one, Soon will its fleeting hours be done;
Then, in 'that day' my Lord to meet, And stand before His Judgment
seat;
Only one life, 'twill soon be past, Only what's done for Christ will
last.

Only one life, the still small voice, Gently pleads for a better choice
Bidding me selfish aims to leave, And to God's holy will to cleave;
Only one life, 'twill soon be past, Only what's done for Christ will last.

Only one life, a few brief years, Each with its burdens, hopes, and fears;
Each with its days I must fulfill, living for self or in His will;
Only one life, 'twill soon be past, Only what's done for Christ will last.

When this bright world would tempt me sore, When Satan would a victory score;
When self would seek to have its way, Then help me Lord with joy to say;
Only one life, 'twill soon be past, Only what's done for Christ will last.

Give me Father, a purpose deep, In joy or sorrow Thy word to keep;
Faithful and true what e'er the strife, Pleasing Thee in my daily life;
Only one life, 'twill soon be past, Only what's done for Christ will last.

Oh let my love with fervor burn, And from the world now let me turn;
Living for Thee, and Thee alone, Bringing Thee pleasure on Thy throne;
Only one life, 'twill soon be past, Only what's done for Christ will last.

Only one life, yes only one, Now let me say, "Thy will be done";
And when at last I'll hear the call, I know I'll say 'twas worth it all";
Only one life, 'twill soon be past, Only what's done for Christ will last.

Table of Contents

Table of Figures

Preface

Some while back, I tried to answer the question: *"why should a book I write have a preface?"* As I recall, I gave what I felt was an adequate answer, but feel it worth revisiting this time around concerning this book. The main response back then was it was a way for any author to persuade his/her actual and potential readers that his/her "masterpiece" was worth reading, and in my case having also got over any *delusion of grandeur* that comes from expecting all and sundry to defer to my words of wisdom.

As far as **"Priests of the Bible"** goes, I would argue it is to do with an important subject, or rather a related set of subjects, that people, especially serious Christians, ought to know about, and as far as I can make out this has not been adequately covered elsewhere for the *person in the pew* to digest. Looking at it dispassionately, I can understand the argument some might put forward that matters relating to Old Testament priests and the priesthood are hardly relevant for today's God followers, but I hope I can demonstrate, in terms of lessons learned and types and shadows, it is very relevant.

While I can imagine some Bible scholars may want to read what I wrote, I aim it toward ordinary folk. I realise this is not sufficient reason in the eyes of many, especially in a day when people do not read serious books all that much and could probably think of many subjects more worthy of consideration ahead of priests of the Bible. Besides which, the author is a relative nobody, so why read his book?

Having got that off my chest, maintaining as I do that what I am going to put to paper/ether is *imho* so incredibly significant, that people need to know, at least the subject matter, if not my thoughts on the subject, as is evidenced by the strong possibility this might be my last major project before I depart this world. When I say people, while I expect the big majority who read what I write will be Christians of the more earnest variety, I hope Jews with the Berean mentality will also read, given the subject is central to Judaism. This brings me nicely to other reasons why I think writing a Preface is a good idea!

My last major serious work was the Second edition of **"Prophets of the Bible"**, published in 2021. The First edition, which was published in 2020, I referred to as my "Covid lockdown" project. One of the benefits of being put into the old dear category and advised/told to stay at home to *"flatten the curve"* was that it enabled me to write at length concerning every prophet in the Bible (including unknown, unnamed and unrecognised ones), and a good deal of what they prophesied, and that the "Pan(Plan)demic", away from many "normal" distractions, gave me the ideal opportunity to do so.

This brings me to 2021 when, besides producing a significantly added to version of "**Prophets of the Bible**", I also produced a daily "devotional" on the three books of Solomon: Song of Songs, Proverbs and Ecclesiastes. It was around then I came up with the bright idea of producing a trilogy of books, with books on priests and kings, comparable in size to that on prophets. But which to begin with or should I combine the two into one book? As I checked out my writing endeavours for 2022, I found that while I wrote and even preached on these subjects, I still hadn't begun properly to write my book.

Early in 2023, I made up my mind – priests it is, having written on several named priests that would become the core of the book. I had in mind the book would be finished and made available to anyone interested in reading it by the end of 2023. Good progress was made but I did not meet the deadlines I set out. I also found it to be a much bigger subject than I expected, as well as using the opportunity to write about subjects that were on my heart and mind. For, if not included in this book, where?

At the end of 2023 we, Mrs B and I, decided to take a three-month sabbatical, staying in our family home in Trivandrum, India. It meant I could finish what I had begun and also, as an unexpected bonus, write a shortened version of Kings of the Bible, in relative peace and quiet, away from every day distractions. It released me from having to contemplate what might have been a project too far, given my current condition, to write a separate book on the subject of Kings to follow this one on Priests.

I ought to say why the book has taken a lot longer than I had anticipated at the outset, and there are good reasons for this. The main one, maybe, is that there is far more to the subject matter than might first seem to be the case, resulting in a book that has turned out very differently to what I had first imagined. There was a lot more that could be said on subjects like sacrifices and idolatry than I had expected and I was blown away with thoughts pertaining to holiness and glory. I am conscious the book might seem a bit too intense, deep and academic, although these are serious subjects.

Some, when God judges people for not doing the right thing and all the killing taking place (and there is a lot of it to be found) make uncomfortable reading. But we should always be mindful, from the outset and at the end, that God wants to enjoy His people and His people to enjoy Him. For the discerning, Priests of the Bible demonstrates who God truly is and the way to true satisfaction. It doesn't mean us living in holy huddles and playing harps on clouds but, rather, living life to the full.

I also ought to say that while I have long admired the systematic approach to writing adopted by many of the Puritans and their successors and have tried to emulate them with limited success. I do so believing everyone who writes does so with an agenda, even as innocuous as basing what they write on how they truly see "things". I am no exception despite endeavouring to teach what is there in the Bible. I also try to relate this to what I see going on in the church today and, more controversially, what is happening in the world, which is in a great state of flux and there is much we cannot say for sure (which is why spiritually minded Christians fall out). But I have done my best to inform (based on extensive research) and edify (based on my love for the church), and I have laid my cards on the table!

So that's it – besides explaining albeit briefly why, dear reader, you might want to read my book, and how the book came about, I would like to end with one important final point. It is to do with heritage and legacy, also touched on in the "Acknowledgements" section. Now in my dotage, I have come to realise how important a matter this is. There can be no better heritage than a godly one and we leave no better legacy than a God fearing one. Many of my Christian roots are in the Plymouth Brethren, and I recall, going back to my youth, preachers preaching on priests and priesthood related subjects, doing so with gusto. But like probably every other Christian group, the PBs had their strengths and weakness.

One weakness may have been their putting light ahead of life in terms of importance. One strength pertains to the subject matter of this book, and after having been round the block when it comes to engaging with many different types of churches, all with their own interests, emphases, foibles and fixations, other than the messianic types, none of them fully "got" how important priests of the Bible and related matters were. God moves in mysterious ways and even the best of Christian groups did not come to grips with the entire counsel of God. Therefore, take this book as my contribution toward passing the Torch concerning the subjects it addresses to the next generation, should the Lord tarry.

If I have got anything wrong, including when I discuss topics more familiar to Jews than to Gentiles, missed out matters of importance or unduly upset any etc., then please accept my apologies. I write as one who has sought long and hard to find out what the Bible actually teaches and share what I find. I tried to do so free from denominational hang ups or pious platitudes, realising my own axioms. If there is a lesson I have learned in this exercise, it is the importance of serving God whole heartedly.

It is ironic that even in Christian circles that don't recognise priests, a form of clericalism often exists and non-clerics are told to defer to those recognised as in authority in their particular circle, even if theologically speaking they may be wrong, or at least to say nothing and bear the brunt. But then again *"to everything there is a season, and a time to every purpose under the heaven"* Ecclesiastes 3:1, and perhaps our greatest concern should be to obey the Lord God Almighty, irrespective of what others think, and that we remain faithful to Him. Rather than go along with what we are told, we ought to *"buy the truth, and sell it not; also wisdom, and instruction, and understanding"* Proverbs 23:23.

I don't want to stir up trouble, but having lived long enough to have seen many casualties on the way, who thought outside the box and questioned what they were told, and being rebuffed as a result, I can only observe and warn. We all must learn to agree to disagree on matters that are not essential. I have to stick up for folk who question and challenge authority (including respected clergy and Christian leaders, even in my own "camp") over what can be deemed as truth, but it ought to be matched by charity and wisdom, and also humility, recognising there is much we do not and cannot know for sure.

Regarding the notion of a clergy-laity divide (one, unlike many sections of the church, I only endorse to a small extent), I have in mind both as potential readers (should such a divide exist). While I would love it for non-believers, especially those of the sincere seeker variety, to read my book, I am especially aiming what I write at those folk I label as believer-priests, whether clergy or laity, and particularly those in the "humble, nobody" category who take seriously the implications. I am mindful of those who pay the price for going against the societal status quo and/or, as happens in many parts of the world, are persecuted due to their beliefs. I truly believe this book may be my "last hurrah" and I count myself blessed having this opportunity to provide far more substantial content than I had originally envisaged. I have done so in order to inform and encourage the few who choose to read what I wrote.

Whether you read what follows meticulously, and check out what I write, or choose to be more selective in your reading, it matters little. Because what you read has been written over a two-year period and as some of the chapters overlap, there will inevitably be some duplication, so do bear with me. There will be many lessons and applications to be found in what follows, and I put myself at the top of the list of those who need to learn and apply. If you are spurred on to do further study in your search for truth and while at it get closer to God, then I would see that my mission has been a success.

But back to the question raised at the start of this book – the world is full of those who can/do comment on the Bible, ranging from the good/qualified to the bad/unqualified, so why should people read this lengthy treatise when there is so much else that merits study? Moreover, we are reminded: *"be admonished: of making many books there is no end; and much study is a weariness of the flesh"* Ecclesiastes 12:12. I certainly do not claim to be anyone special in terms of why people should read what I write in a world where there are many that seek a readership, whose claims have varying merits. Few, I suspect, would put me high on their "must read" list, but this is my contribution to an important subject which from what I can make out has been woefully neglected. The only affirmation that I really care about these days is that from the God I worship, and it is Him I want to honour.

While I want people to read my book, I would rather they be drawn to Him and what He says through His Word. I hope that what I write supports the wise counsel: "*Stand ye in the ways, and see, and ask for the old paths, where is the good way, and walk therein, and ye shall find rest for your souls*" Jeremiah 6:16, and pray that readers will want to find out for themselves what those "old paths" are.

Most importantly, I would want us to focus on the God of Israel and His Christ, and the fact that everything we read about concerning priests and the priesthood points to Him, which includes the truth found in an old chorus that I recall singing, even before becoming a believer-priest, in my youth.

Oh the love that drew salvation's plan!
Oh the grace that brought it down to man!
Oh the mighty gulf that God did span
At Calvary!

Mercy there was great and grace was free
Pardon there was multiplied to me
There my burdened soul found liberty
At Calvary!

Acknowledgements

Since I can claim truthfully, in writing "**Priests of the Bible**", incorporating as it does (from a late stage) "**Kings of the Bible**", it is all my own work, and I must take full responsibility. Even so, many, including those whose names I don't know or recall, have contributed, going back to the time when I was aged 5 or 6 and attended Sunday School, and later as a young teen attending a Covenanter class, both led by godly folk who knew their Bibles, without which the end product would have been all the poorer.

There have been, down the years, those who have taught me about the subjects addressed by this book, notably in the church I have been long associated with, Coleman Street Chapel, part of the Plymouth Brethren (PB), without whose input I doubt this book would have been written. One brother, Victor Levitt, going way back to my youth, was very much into priest related matters and deserves a mention if only for sowing the seed. I discuss the PB influence in the "**About**" section. There are lots of people, now dead, whose legacy as far as passing on their spiritual insights goes, is still very much alive. I think of great hymn writers, like Isaac Watts, for example, who I sometimes quote in the book.

But practically speaking, there are those who have assisted me who should be named, starting with those helping me to get the words typed into my computer to a form people can read. I am grateful that Una Campbell, someone I got to know soon after becoming a Christian, aged 15, has been a very thorough proof reader and an encourager throughout the long period in which the book evolved. I appreciate her patience, especially given my propensity to want to tinker with what I write. I also have benefitted from the efforts of another friend, Paul Barnes, for helping check out some of what I wrote, and for often challenging me when I come up with what I think is some profound thought.

I am once again grateful to Jim Holmes (*www.greatwriting.org*) for his professional advice, which goes back to when I wrote my two previous books, getting me signed up with Ingram so that people, potentially, anywhere in the world, including booksellers, can order online (the logical way for folk like me to go, given the lack of interest by those who publish "Christian" books). Not only did Jim help me in navigating the process this time around and the final cover design, but he has done what was needed from taking my MS Word document and putting it in a form that Ingram and the like can use.

I do like my NIV study Bible, which I use when on the road in England and in India. I especially like its introductions to each Bible book and find its notes and cross-references helpful as a source for what I write. There is much else on the Internet, where so much "good stuff" can be found, as well as the thoughts of those who give a range of views, to complement that found in dusty old books. I must have listened to hundreds of sermons and read hundreds of articles online preparing for this book. Most come with an agenda, making points, maybe not of interest to what I am writing, but useful even so. I left out notes and references one might expect in an academic treatise as this book is for Joe Bloggs.

I appreciate the resource *biblegateway.com*, where I can read the Bible in many different versions and, if need be, go to a specialist resource for the original language. I recently came across *e-sword* and found being able to lift text and do word searches from the Bible, away from the Internet, to be helpful. I make no apology that I favour the King James Version (KJV). I am not precious on KJV since what really matters is getting the right understanding; and I use other versions too! A complementary resource is the King James Version Audio Bible which can also be accessed from *biblestudytools.com*. On many occasions, I have listened to the Bible being read while reading the text at the same time.

Some of the resources I referred to when I wrote "**Prophets of the Bible**", I have also used here. One is "**A Pathway into the Bible**" by an old friend, Stuart Kimber. While it was not as good on priests, as it was on prophets, it has still proved a great help. I have continued to find invaluable the "**Unlocking the Bible**" audio-visual series by David Pawson. One unlikely online resource, helped by the fact the animated videos that accompany it are short as well as relevant and watchable, is "**The Bible Project**". One surprising and unlikely resource that more often than not gives me that starter for ten I am looking for is **Wikipedia**. Another, and one that is sounder, theologically speaking, is "**Got Questions**". I have often found before going off and shooting from the hip, this has given me solid answers to my questions, or at least confirmed or refuted what I was thinking, concerning which I can then use. I should also mention use of images, of which there are many examples in this book, most having been "borrowed" from elsewhere, for which I am grateful. I discuss use of images in the "**About**" section.

If it were not for the fact this particular book comes with the wow factor that is often missing when I read books of the paper variety, I would likely have said nothing, but "**The Tabernacle – Shadows of the Messiah**" by David M. Levy has proved to be amazing, and I have often drawn upon its contents when writing my own book. What I like about the book is its no nonsense approach and how it cuts to the chase when discussing what might be expected from the cover. It does what some of my Brethren forefathers have been accused of doing and that is to over-spiritualise, often going further than I might want to, but otherwise its content cannot be faulted and more than any other resource this has been the one I have found especially helpful. I love its superb illustrations – just a pity I couldn't use them!

Whilst the PBs have been an important influence, many from quite different stables, theologically speaking, have played a part. My mantra is truth and, when I write, I do so as one beholden to truth and recognise it can be found in many quarters and sometimes champions of truth in certain important areas fail to be so in other areas. But it is frustrating when bastions of Christian orthodoxy subscribe to lies, but that is how it is. Let me go from the sublime to the ridiculous. I confess, I sometimes watch the "show" of Roman Catholic, Latin Mass advocate, Michael Matt (*www.remnant-tv.com*) and I love the way he calls out the attacks on true faith. I must mention the two Lauras (Sanger and Rimmer), not connected, and likely not PB, but whose input and spiritual insights have influenced what I wrote.

So have two of my Israel loving/savvy friends, who are earnest students of the Scriptures: Keith Williams and Carolyn Squire. Talking of Israel, I thank my Israel loving, preacher friend, Stephen Clayden, for sharing his insights. I should also thank Tony Pearce, Jonathan Cahn and Baruch Korman for sharing their thoughts, found online. Recent helpful discoveries also include an Anglican priest: Calvin Robinson. Then there are friends, two that are even older than me, who I have only met online, but who love the Lord and His Word, and are fellow watchmen: Richard Barker and John Hymus; I appreciate their wisdom and encouragement. I should mention two friends who often disagree with me, Paul Fox and Glen Hague, yet are gracious with it, who keep me on my toes. I thank two young in the faith Christians: Stephen and Joanne Evans, who search the Scriptures and ask questions. I thank Paul Slennett, owner of Southend Christian Bookshop, for his friendship, advice and encouragement.

Then there are famous preachers across the ecclesiological spectrum, ranging from Packer to Pawson to Prasch. One preacher, who I hadn't expected would provide the pearls he has, who has helped me to develop some of the thoughts articulated in this book, is John MacArthur. While I agree with much of what these chaps have had to say, there are others I agree with less so and yet I often value the perspectives they do offer. Then there are a number of arch "conspiracy theorist" types, definitely not theologically sound, e.g., Alex Jones, David Icke and Charlie Ward, who have helped in waking me up to what is going on in the world and bridge another gap – that between Bible truth and how we ought to respond. I could go on but, suffice to say, many, unbeknown to themselves, have played their part.

I'm almost at the end. If I have missed anyone out that I should not have, then I apologise. Sometimes a brief encounter or a short word has been enough to spark off a train of thought that then found its way into this book. But I ought to mention my church, Providence Baptist, if for no other reason than bearing with me in my coming to grips with prophets, priests and kings and acting as unwitting guinea pigs for letting me share some of my thoughts. Some have been shared in our church Bible studies and are included in this book. I should especially mention church elders: Roger Ninnis, Ray Birch, Chandi Chirwa and Duncan Briant. An unexpected twist in this long journey from having the idea to arriving at a much lengthier book in terms of number of pages than I had envisaged, was that, in the last three months spent at our family home in India, I wrote some half of the book. There we fellowshipped with folk from the Ponnarakonam Brethren Assembly, who contributed more than they will ever know. Talking of church, while I have been overall disappointed with a lot of church set-ups who have ignored many of the great themes covered in this book, I have also, thankfully, found many who have not.

Then there is my beloved wife, Jolly, who is also my carer. She, more than any, has created the atmosphere, freedom and environment in which I have been able to write. Most importantly, I thank the Lord who has enabled me to write this book. By way of legacy and being able to present my "party piece", I asked Him to allow me to write this book and get it published, and He has. I claim no other authority than that of being a child of God who knows the Bible, who has noted with consternation that many fellow believers have little inkling on these subjects. Whether what I write is the product of my fertile imagination or the result of being quickened by the Holy Spirit, it will be for others to say and for the Lord to judge. But every day, a lot of it to do with my meditating on the words of the Bible, thoughts have come to mind that have later ended up being put into words in this book and throughout this time I have been conscious of a hidden hand leading me, often to places I had not expected to go.

I have sometimes felt like Moses, who had to take off his sandals, when encountering God from out of the midst of the burning bush, revealing Himself as "*I am that I am*", for Moses knew he was treading on holy ground, or Isaiah who, after he saw the Lord, the Holy One of Israel, sitting on His Throne, high and lifted up, declared "*Woe is me! for I am undone ... for mine eyes have seen the King, the Lord of hosts*". More than anything else, I have often found myself touching on amazing, wondrous matters, holy and sublime, and that I was dealing with an awesome God, and yet I have lived to tell the tale.

*1. Now thank we all our God
with heart and hands and voices,
who wondrous things has done,
in whom his world rejoices;
who from our mothers' arms
has blessed us on our way
with countless gifts of love,
and still is ours today.*

*2. O may this bounteous God
through all our life be near us,
with ever joyful hearts
and blessed peace to cheer us,
to keep us in his grace,
and guide us when perplexed,
and free us from all ills
of this world in the next.*

*3. All praise and thanks to God
the Father now be given,
the Son and Spirit blest,
who reign in highest heaven
the one eternal God,
whom heaven and earth adore;
for thus it was, is now,
and shall be evermore.*

Dedication

I have pondered long and hard who to dedicate this work to. On one hand, it is quite easy – it is to you dear reader! Besides reading serious stuff not being the done thing these days, I suspect even among serious Christians "Priests of the Bible" is unlikely to feature on their list of subjects to check out. But you have decided to read some of this lengthy, ever so modest, treatise. Therefore, I salute you!

But the subject is about priests even though many among "my lot" wouldn't recognise this subject as being particularly relevant as far as God is concerned today. I can, however, identify two categories of priest that are relevant. One is what I have come to refer to as believer-priests, those who can refer to themselves as priests because of what the Bible teaches about believers in the Lord Jesus. The other includes what the Bibles refers to as ministers, elders, deacons, pastors, teachers and evangelists, as well as "priest", as being a term claimed by elements of the official church down the ages, all with some sort of oversight responsibility in church related set-ups. It is to those who take on these particular roles, not merely as a paid occupation or some sort of status symbol, but rather seeing it as a call by God to bless His people and who are truly serving Him/them, that I wish to dedicate my book.

There are many that come to mind, most are now dead, who fulfil/fulfilled these criteria, but it is those who are living that I have in mind, including a new generation from which God is calling and will call to exercise this most important priestly role, beginning with where I am presently writing in India, where I come across many who undertake this priestly service at great personal cost, notably in the Brethren set-up that do not believe in priests as such, who I am familiar with. I especially admire those who are not beholden to the approval of their denominational higher ups or those who wield power or money in their own congregations, but rather seek first and foremost the approval of God. We need such folk!

There are many who, without ostentation or given much by way of remuneration or recognition, and who may be opposed by those that hate it when they find Christ is effectively proclaimed, devote their lives to caring for the "flock", going far beyond simply taking services. I use the word "devote" advisedly, having been in set-ups emphasising the need to be called. Methinks, some of that is pious gobbledygook since we are all called if God has chosen us, but at the crux of the matter is something we call dedication. Those who are truly dedicated often have to tread a lonely and difficult path. To be sure, the God who calls also anoints and equips. It is then a matter of being faithful to that calling.

There is Chandi the paid elder from my own church, Steve the minister of the church down the road, Stephen a pastor and evangelist of a nearby messianic leaning congregation; Gwyn, Paul and Ray who faithfully "lay" preach, James who alone has the title "priest" attached, who served at my local "High" Anglican church and, going to the other extreme, because the Exclusive Brethren are loathe to elevate any with a title, Adrian. This is just for starters and in all these cases they do far more than just be the person "up front". I write this in a part of India that enjoys religious freedom but there are many parts of India and in many other countries where that is not the case and where the "priests" have to endure suffering for the sake of the Gospel. I dedicate my book to such folk. All these I wish to encourage.

The Bible says a lot about shepherds and sheep and draws various lessons, particularly concerning the importance of shepherds leading, protecting, guiding the (human) sheep. Ezekiel 34 makes much of the importance of shepherds caring for the sheep. Nowhere is this more shown than in the person of the Lord Jesus Christ, who is our Great Shepherd (John 10:1-18). In one of the encounters Jesus had with His disciples, after rising from the dead, He told Peter that he was to take care of and feed His sheep. Down the ages, there have been those meant to be shepherds who have not done this. But there have been some who have often been unnoticed, unrecognised and, unrewarded who have been diligent in carrying out their solemn calling to be His under-shepherds. Such folk I wish to honour now.

1. In Christ alone, my hope is found
He is my light, my strength, my song
This Cornerstone, this solid ground
Firm through the fiercest drought and storm
What heights of love, what depths of peace
When fears are stilled, when strivings cease
My Comforter, my All in All
Here in the love of Christ I stand

2. In Christ alone, who took on flesh
Fullness of God in helpless babe
This gift of love and righteousness
Scorned by the ones He came to save
'Til on that cross as Jesus died

The wrath of God was satisfied
For every sin on Him was laid
Here in the death of Christ I live, I live

3. There in the ground His body lay
Light of the world by darkness slain
Then bursting forth in glorious Day
Up from the grave He rose again
And as He stands in victory
Sin's curse has lost its grip on me
For I am His and He is mine
Bought with the precious blood of Christ

4. No guilt in life, no fear in death
This is the power of Christ in me
From life's first cry to final breath
Jesus commands my destiny
No power of hell, no scheme of man
Can ever pluck me from His hand
Till He returns or calls me home
Here in the power of Christ I'll stand

About

About the Author

The author is just an ordinary chap who knows his Bible and loves the God of the Bible. He has been studying the Bible for most of his life and is wanting to share what he has found out on his long journey. He has long taught and preached from the Bible and loves to write about what he has found out in that time, mindful there is much he still does not know or has yet to fully experience. He lives with Jolly, his wife, and Matthew, his son, and their one cat (it was until recently three, but two sadly died), in Southend, England, the city where he was born 72 years ago, and has lived for much of his life.

He has three degrees, none majoring in theology. Before "retiring" he had three careers: secondary school science teacher, computer engineer/consultant and community worker. He continues to maintain a "community interest" although these days he is limited due to disability. He is keen to "pass the baton" to the next generation. He has a particular love for and interest in India, the country of Jolly's birth. A lot of this book was written during his recent stay in his Indian family home.

The author has belonged to and been involved with a number of different churches in his time, mostly at the low end of the market, in particular the Plymouth Brethren. These days he joins with the Strict Baptists, although he associates with all sorts of believers, right across the ecclesiological spectrum, and refuses to align with any particular theological stable since none of them "gets it all". He happily describes himself these days as a "Gospel Preaching, Community Activist, Watchman on the Wall".

As for interests not implied from this title, besides reading widely, a lot of those he once had he can no longer do, because of physical limitations. He once participated in a variety of sports, albeit at a modest level; these days the best he can do is spectate. He once travelled the world and walked the great outdoors, but these days he is left with memories. He once got involved in and led a variety of community activities as a volunteer, but these days that involvement is more limited. He once held a number of responsible positions in the workplace but is now officially "retired". He was once an elder in a church, but these days is happy just to serve as a member of the congregation. He still plays chess, participates in church and community ventures, and tries to be a good neighbor with God's help.

Despite now being in his dotage, he continues to write, even when only a few will read his "wisdom". A lot of his writing, including blogs, can be found on his website: *jrbpublications.com*. Prior to writing this book, he wrote "**Prophets of the Bible**" and "**Song of Songs, Proverbs and Ecclesiastes**". As well as his other writings and resources that are still available, these can be freely downloaded from his website. These two mentioned, along with this book, can be purchased from Amazon and the like.

About the Book and the Book's cover

They say "*you can't judge a book by its cover*" and, while that is true, we have designed the cover in such a way to incorporate images that go right to the heart of what the Book is trying to say. This is along with a background of blue (heaven) meeting green (earth) on both front and back covers and is meant to reinforce the thought of priests helping bridge the gap between heaven and earth, i.e., God and man. The various images (front and back cover) relate to specific happenings covered in this Book.

Front:

Top: High Priest upon being dressed in his special garments.

Bottom: Levites carrying the Ark of the Covenant.

Back - Row 1:

Left: Abraham greeted by Melchizedek with bread and wine.

Right: Zadok the priest and Nathan the prophet anointing Solomon the king.

Back - Row 2:

Left: Jehoiada the priest anointing the boy Joash to be king.

Right: Ezra the priest reading the Law from a scroll to the people.

Back - Row 3:

Left: Zacharias the priest encounters an angel in the Holy Place.

Right: The Veil of the Temple is rent in twain.

While I have not done much by way of book promotion, instead relying on word of mouth to pass on the message, I hope there will be folk with influence that like what I do and then go and spread the word about this book. Anyone, anywhere (supposedly) can buy the book online from outlets such as Amazon (I generally advise those wanting to find out how to do a Google search and include in it: book title and author along with ISBN; that usually does the trick). For those who don't wish to buy or want quick access, they can read the book for free as a PDF file from my website (*jrbpublications. com*).

A long time ago I found writing books came at a financial loss but I did so since it is part of my service to the Lord. I don't expect this book to be a best seller, but it is enough if some were to find it helpful. The book is meant for anyone wanting to find out more about its subject and is intent on doing a serious study concerning the wide plethora of issues related to Priests of the Bible, ranging from great scholars to ordinary folk, of all beliefs, and is not about promoting any particular view other than what has come out from doing a lot of in-depth research and study. At the time this was written, there were no plans to promote the book other than within the author's personal network, and he has gone down the self-publishing route, simply because he has been unable to find a publisher he could work with.

In order to find out about the book's contents, might one suggest checking out Chapter 1. As for how and why the book has come about, check out the Preface. While reading from cover to cover is recommended, the book is rather deep and long and unavoidably intense, with a lot of repetition, given chapters often overlap, and the book was written over a two-year period. Some may want to delve into parts that are more of interest to them or even use the book as a reference to support some other venture. Any of the above is ok if readers find what is written to be helpful. It attempts to write about what is suggested on the cover in that it addresses the subject: "*Priests of the Bible – Bridging the Gap between God and Man*", and with an added bonus that came about late on – a consideration of a subject that complements both prophets and priests of the Bible: "**Kings of the Bible**".

It is also worth saying something about the style in which the book is written, referred to "in the trade" as the "house style". Since the author is also the publisher, it is worth making the point that, besides trying to be grammatically correct and writing in English English rather than any other form of English, the style we have ended up with is what the author deems fit, e.g., in the way Scripture is referenced or whether or not to use capital letters, but that he has endeavoured to be consistent when doing so. While he has a propensity to tinker with contents right up to the last moment, as new thoughts come into his head, a lot of effort has been put into proof reading (and he is grateful to those who have helped to do this) but, if there are "typos" etc., left, he is the one to blame and he needs to apologise.

About Referencing and Bible versions

As explained under "Acknowledgements", in producing this book many sources have been studied and sometimes referred to. Some of that content has been adapted for use in this book. If this were a book designed purely for an academic audience, there would be numerous notes and references to back up points that are made, rather than the few that are given, as these could turn people off as well as add to an already large size. But it is for "ordinary folk", even though, given the depth of research that has gone into writing this book, it ought to attract readers with more of an academic interest, e.g., theology teachers and students, and yet not put off those folk who just want to know about the subject this book tries to address. While not academic leaning, the book tries to avoid over spiritualising and resists the temptation of using too many anecdotes of the sort some find off putting, even though the subject matter often lends itself to making spiritual applications. As is often the case, a fine balance is needed.

The one exception, when it comes to assiduously giving references, concerns quoting from the Bible, and then book, chapter and verse are given. Since this book is primarily about what the Bible teaches, there are numerous Bible quotes along with book, chapter and verse. In the vast majority of cases, it is from the King James Version (KJV), which is the version the author prefers and thinks contains the best in the way of quotable quotes. He makes no apology for favoring the KJV and hopes readers will understand and yet may even want in certain cases to check out what other Bible versions have to say.

About Images and Copyright

The issue of images is mildly problematical. The subject matter of the book lends itself to images, especially if in colour (not possible with the present set-up) and there are loads out there that can be lifted from the Internet, although most are unsuitable or contains extra "stuff" that is not of interest. Then there is the matter of copyright and not wanting to transgress on the matter. Even so, in the absence of anything better, I have used several images lifted from the Internet. In a few cases, I have used my limited graphic design abilities to produce my own. I can't help feeling there is a "gap in the market" for specifically providing photo or graphical aids to those who teach the Bible and related subjects at a non-superficial level, and for there to be a comprehensive library of images folk can use.

Choosing the right images to use in this book has been a big deal and a major challenge, along with any copyright implication once suitable images have been found. It has been said a lot: "*One picture is worth a thousand words*", and this was a truth the author had come to appreciate when he wrote "**Prophets of the Bible**" and even more so now when it came to "**Priests** of the Bible". For example, an important subject covered in this book is the Tabernacle in the Wilderness and one cannot but be struck that there may be some 50 chapters in the Bible referring to its layout, and doing so down to the minutest detail, all of which may be significant. Yet even for those who carefully trawl through those chapters and allow their imagination to take over, it is difficult to picture what the Tabernacle actually looked like, and this is but one of many examples of why having suitable pictures helps.

While there are sources for obtaining suitable images to include in order to support what is written, searching for them revealed severe limitations when it comes to finding the right images, and is why the Internet has proven to be a major source. The problem then comes down to copyright and whether to accept the advice that unless written permission has been given – do NOT use. The author has taken the pragmatic approach and sought permission when he could find who owns the copyright (often not possible). If permission is denied then the image is not used and if no response is given then to use the image anyway and apologise in advance should anyone later come forward and take issue that copyright has been infringed. A good example of this approach working was when Pastor Ralph Wilson of Joyful Heart Renewal Ministries (*www.joyfulheart.com*) was asked and he gave his permission for some of his particularly suitable images to be used. The last thing to say, and this as much for practical reasons, these images have been included as Figures in Chapter 2 and referred to throughout the Book.

One discovery made earlier was an online resource that makes freely available images from the Bible, referred to here as "Free Bible Images" (*www.freebibleimages.org*), some I have used, with permission, notably for the cover. This has turned out to be a major provider of images included and referred to in this book. It is a good example of a website making available images from many different sources. In our case, contributors included: Sweet Publishing, Arabs for Christ, James Tissot Collection, Rev. Yves Langevin, Jeremy Park, Jim Padgett, Amy and Carly, Paula Nash Giltner, and David P. Barrett.

A final pedantic yet practical thought concerns size of image in terms of computer byte usage. It is odd but true that while preparing the draft of the book to be handed over to the "experts" to get ready for publication, the author found the images took nearly 20 Mb byte space, while the rest of the book just over 1 Mb. This is no big deal if reading the paper version of the Book but what about folk reading the electronic version on their smart phone where storage space, processor speeds and Internet access is a big deal? This is not something that can be entirely resolved, other than make the point that the images that are used, while readable to even those who share the author's poor eyesight, are not the sharpest, for it is the use of very sharp images that often take up a lot more computer byte storage. The point to make is, while sharp is nice, it is all about making the necessary points and accessibility.

About the Brethren

In this book, I refer to my Plymouth Brethren roots. The PBs were keen to *"rightly divide the word of truth"* 2 Timothy 2:15 and to *"earnestly contend for the faith which was once delivered unto the saints"* Jude 1:3. Since they regarded *"all scripture is given by inspiration of God, and is profitable..."* 2 Timothy 3:16, it should not come as a surprise that this included the less well-known parts of the Bible. The PBs (Open section) have been a major influence on me throughout my Christian life. Going back to my later teens onwards, I can recall lessons on the Law of Moses, Wilderness wanderings, Tabernacle worship, Covenants of YHWH, Feasts and Offerings and a whole raft of subjects from the Old Testament, even down to a fine detail, led by Bible teachers who knew their stuff. Other than with "Messianic leaning" fellowships, I have not had that same experience elsewhere. For readers who care little for "drivers" such as these, I apologise when I sometimes hark back to such times in my book. I do so, not to argue the case for the Brethren being any better overall than any other Christian group (they certainly were not), but when it came to a correct understanding of some of the teachings discussed in this book, they were. Not only is it important to seek out truth, but so are matters to do with heritage and legacy.

About being warned

This book comes with a health warning (although if read in the right way it is a positive one) but then so does the Bible when rightly read with the intention of finding out what is meant by what is written. When the likes of Richard Dawkins, author of **"the God Delusion"**, read the Bible, they might point to instances of God sanctioning genocide as well as lots of violence. Even if, like the author, one takes the view God can only do what is right, one cannot help but be affected by the thought we are dealing with a holy God who cannot be trifled with to help allay such concerns: God (as well as some of the content that is to found in the Bible) does not always make sense and the wished for explanations are not always forthcoming. Then there is the strong possibility that when one seriously studies the Bible, one may come to views that are at odds with one's peers or church leaders but, in this age of deception, even among God's elect, taking an independent line in seeking the truth may be what is needed.

While the author has tried to explain why he covers the subject matter he does, he has not taken the safe option of avoiding controversy altogether and ignoring what might upset those more likely to read this book, but rather, in order to get to the bottom of his subject, it has often meant leaving no stone unturned. It all begs the question, where are the strong Bible teachers today? He concludes that these are too few and even those deemed as solid, sound etc., have "blind spots" and miss what is important. It is for God and others to judge how the author rates as a Bible teacher, but his job is to get folk to study the Bible for themselves and be like the Bereans who "*searched the scriptures daily*" Acts 17:11.

The author has tried to model his writing on the approach of those he has admired over the years who he regards as doctrinally sound and who methodically expound on what the Bible teaches, believing it to be God's Word. He has often checked out what they have to say, even when they are from different camps theologically (as in his experience important insights can often be found in unexpected and unlikely places). The problem often occurs when two people, who hold similar views, come up with different thoughts, conclusions and applications concerning the same subject matter. It could be that both are right and it is a matter of reconciling the two views or that one or even both are wrong. It often comes down to priorities, world views, experiences and fundamental beliefs of the two writers.

While this author claims to take a systematic expository approach in much of his writing (although he gives opinions too), he is not infallible and, besides, the nature of the subjects covered is such that there is always more digging to do and other perspectives that could be legitimately taken into account. It is likely that all his readers will disagree with something he writes, especially in Part 3 of the Book when he offers his personal perspective on "*hot potato*" subjects, such as end time prophecy, Israel, the C(c)hurch, politics, community activism, world events, social justice and "conspiracy theories". He asks for reader forbearance and that we adopt the old adage of "*in essentials unity, in non-essentials liberty, in all things charity*", knowing full well the devil seeks to divide and rule.

The final point is he has tried to do the impossible: produce something "*all singing, all dancing*" in terms of coverage (and quite likely failing to do so), realising that some may find his informal style off-putting. In mitigation, these could be his last words in print and reader indulgence is begged. Also, he may not have got everything right despite his best efforts to provide truth and balance. But he makes no apologies for pushing the narrative of the following Charles Wesley hymn, especially the thought that at the end of our lives we may follow in the footsteps of John the Baptist proclaiming through our lives and words: "*Behold the Lamb of God, which taketh away the sin of the world*" John 1:29.

1. Jesus, the Name high over all,
in hell or earth or sky;
angels and mortals prostrate fall,
and devils fear and fly.
Jesus, the Name to sinners dear,
the Name to sinners giv'n;
it scatters all their guilty fear,
it turns their hell to heav'n.

2. O that the world might taste and see
the riches of His grace!
The arms of love that compass me
would all the world embrace.
Thee I shall constantly proclaim,
tho' earth and hell oppose;
bold to confess Thy glorious Name
before a world of foes.

3. His only righteousness I show,
His saving truth proclaim;
'tis all my business here below
to cry, "Behold the Lamb!"
Happy, if with my latest breath
I may but gasp His Name,
preach Him to all, and cry in death,
"Behold, behold the Lamb!"

Glossary

Wars have been fought because the opposing sides have attached different meanings to terms and acronyms. I have tried to define those I use as I go along but, where these are particularly significant and need further explaining, and are used beyond just a single section, I feel compelled to have a go at defining and explaining what I mean. I tried not to be too radical and more often than not have gone along with what a source, such as Wikipedia (not an obvious friend of the conservative, conspiracy theorist types, some reckon me to be), gives as a definition. So here goes …

AD (and BC): (Used in the context of giving dates) Latin for after Christ and before Christ. Also referred to these days as CE (Christian Era) and BCE (Before Christian Era).

(The) **Apocrypha:** collection of books written in the four centuries between Old and New Testaments.

(The) **Ark:** (of the Covenant) was the ornate, gold-plated wooden chest that housed the tablets of the Law. It rested in the Holy of Holies inside the Tabernacle/Temple and was seen only by the High Priest on the Day of Atonement. YHWH was seen as being enthroned between the cherubim above the Ark.

Atonement: literally meant "to cover," "to take away" in the Old Testament, and is used over 100 times, usually in the context of a sacrifice. The idea is that a person or thing is unclean due to defilement or sin, but with a payment or sacrifice, atonement is made, and he/it is now deemed holy or acceptable.

Believer-priest: is a term often used in this book, referring to Christians doing their "priestly" duties.

(The) **Bible:** is the inspired word of God, consisting of 66 books (39 Old Testament; 27 New Testament).

(The) **Canon:** is a collection of books, which concerning this book, are the 66 books of the Christian Bible that the author and most of the Christian church recognise as being genuine and inspired.

Charismatic: relates to exercising a compelling charm which inspires devotion in others. Often used when referring to the Charismatic Movement, which places special emphasis on the use of spiritual gifts, including prophecy, particularly in the church.

(Real) **Christian:** is a follower of Jesus Christ – by embodying both the beliefs of the Christian faith by believing in Jesus's life, death, and resurrection (orthodoxy), and also by putting that faith into action as true disciples of Christ (orthopraxy).

Church: in Greek *"ekklesia"* – a called-out assembly or congregation (typically of Christians), including universal, but outside of this book is typically used to depict an organisation, building etc. In this book, Church is spelt with a capital 'C' used in a spiritual, mystical sense, and with a small 'c' in other usages.

Clericalism: is the application of the formal, church-based leadership or opinion of ordained clergy in matters of the church and sometimes broader political and sociocultural aspects.

Covenant: a strong, solemn and binding agreement between two parties. The Covenants of interest in this book are the Edenic, Adamic, Noahic, Abrahamic, Mosaic, Davidic and the New Covenant.

Cubit: an ancient measure of length (often used in the Hebrew Scriptures), approximately equal to the length of a forearm. It was typically about 18 inches or 44 cm.

Day of the Lord: refers to an event that takes place at the end of world history, when God deals with humankind, specifically in judgment (an event that is related to Last Days, End Times and Last Things).

Diaspora: the dispersion or spread of a people from their original homeland (typically, the Jews).

Disciple: in Christianity, it is someone who is a dedicated follower of Jesus.

Dispensation: the method or scheme according to which God carries out his purposes towards men.

DV: (Latin: Deo volente) God willing.

Ecclesiology: is the study of the church, derived from two Greek words meaning "assembly" and "word" - combining to mean "the study of the church." The church is the assembly of believers who belong to God. Ecclesiology is crucial to understanding God's purpose for believers in the world today.

Equality and diversity: Equality means ensuring everyone in your setting has equal opportunities, regardless of their abilities, their background or their lifestyle. Diversity means appreciating the differences between people and treating people's values, beliefs, cultures and lifestyles with respect.

Eschatology: is the study of what the Bible says is going to happen in the end times.

(The) Fall: refers to what happened when sin entered the world through one man (Adam). Its effects are numerous and far reaching and includes our lives on earth and our eternal destiny.

Fear: conveys feelings and attitudes ranging from respect and reverence to terror and dread.

Feasts: (or Festivals of the Bible) are: Passover, Unleavened Bread, First Fruits, Weeks (Pentecost), Trumpets, Day of Atonement, and Booths (Tabernacles or Ingathering). Israel's Feasts (later additions: Purim and Hanukkah) were communal and commemorative as well as theological and typological.

Gentile: a noun or adjective that is associated with someone who is not Jewish.

Glory: (of God) pertains to the beauty that emanates from His character concerning all that He is. (Shekinah Glory refers to the visible manifestation of the presence of God.)

Good and bad: in the context, for example when describing a king, and is a relative term that is often used to denote whether a particular king honoured God or not and did what was right or not.

(The) **Gospel:** literally means "good news" and occurs 93 times in the Bible, exclusively in the New Testament. In Greek, it is the word *"euaggelion"*, from which we get our English words evangelist, evangel, and evangelical. The Gospel is, broadly speaking, the whole of scripture; more narrowly, the Gospel is the good news concerning Christ and the way of salvation.

Holy: dedicated or consecrated to God (separate, distinct, perfect). Holiness is one of the attributes of God, encapsulating the notion of absolute perfection. We are called to be a holy people.

Idolatry: the worship of idols (which besides physical images can be anything, even in the mind, that is put before the one, true God), including excessive devotion to and reverence for a person or thing.

Imo, imho: in my opinion; in my humble opinion.

Inter Testament period: is the time between happenings of the Old Testament and the New Testament.

Israel: in the course of the book, it has sometimes come down to a choice between using Israel, Judah or Jews in the text, especially following the divided kingdoms of Israel and Judah. When Israel is used, it usually describes God's Covenant people, although sometimes the term is used to refer to the land that they were promised or have occupied.

Jew: one belonging to, or a continuation through descent or conversion, to the ancient Israelite people and these days could apply to anyone whose religion is Judaism or identifies ethnically as a Jew.

Judgment: (Judgement) opinion or decision given concerning anything, e.g., justice and injustice, right and wrong, good and bad.

King: is the title given in this book to any ruler over a city, country or empire.

KJV: King James Version (the main version of the Bible that is used and referred to throughout this book) – other versions that have also occasionally been used include the Amplified Version (AMP), the English Standard Version (ESV), the New International Version (NIV) and the Message (MSG).

Last days: used in Bible prophecy to refer to future historical events reaching a final climax, culminating in the Second Coming of the Messiah, His Millennial reign and the Final Judgment of humankind (both Testaments); also referred to as "Last Things" and "End Times" and related to the "Day of the Lord".

(The Mosaic) Law: was given to the nation of Israel and is made up of the Ten Commandments, the ordinances, and the worship system, including the priesthood, tabernacle, offerings and feasts.

LBGT: Lesbian, Bisexual, Gay, Transgender.

Levite: a member of the Hebrew tribe of Levi (one of Jacob's sons), especially of that part of it which provided assistants to the priests in the worship in the Jewish temple.

Messiah: the promised deliverer of the Jewish nation prophesied in the Hebrew Bible.

Millennium: a period of a thousand years – as far as the Bible is concerned (according to the author's understanding) this is a period that will be inaugurated with the Coming again of Jesus (the Messiah).

(The) Nazirite/Nazarite vow: is taken by individuals who have voluntarily dedicated themselves to God. The vow is a decision, action, and desire on the part of people whose desire is to yield themselves to God completely. In the Bible, Samson, Samuel and John the Baptist were all Nazirites.

NT: New Testament (also OT: Old Testament).

Palestine: from Latin Palestina (name of a Roman province), from Greek Palaistinē (Herodotus), from Hebrew Pelesheth "Philistia, land of the Philistines". Revived as an official political territorial name in 1920 with the British Mandate. Palestinians include descendants of those who have inhabited the region of Palestine over the millennia, but who today are mostly culturally and linguistically Arab. The Philistines had mostly disappeared from the land they had occupied by the end of the Old Testament.

PB: Plymouth Brethren (comprising "Open" (OB) and "Closed" (XB) sections).

Priest: while in regular usage it is a term associated with a member of the

Christian clergy, in this book it is normally applied as one who represents God (a god) to man and man to God (a god), and also includes "believer-priests" not considered to be members of the clergy.

Prophet: (today and in Bible times) someone who has a teaching and revelatory role, declaring God's truth (heart and mind) on contemporary issues while also revealing details about the future.

(The) **Rapture:** (of the church) is the event in which God takes believers from the earth while making way for His righteous judgment to be poured out on the earth during the Tribulation period.

Repentance: the act of turning away from evil and returning to God, and entails a change in mind.

Replacement theology: (also known as supersessionism and fulfillment theology) essentially teaches that the church has replaced Israel in God's plan.

Righteousness: behavior that is morally justifiable or right. Such behavior is characterised by accepted standards of morality, justice, virtue, or uprightness. The Bible's standard of human righteousness is God's own perfection in every attribute, every attitude, every behavior, and every word.

Sacrifice: is the offering of food items or the lives of animals or humans or even oneself to a higher purpose, in particular divine beings, as an act of propitiation, gratitude or worship.

Salvation: deliverance from danger or suffering; conveying the idea of victory, health, or preservation.

(The) **Samaritans:** occupied the country formerly belonging to the tribe of Ephraim and the half-tribe of Manasseh. The capital of the country was Samaria. When the ten tribes were carried away into captivity to Assyria, the king of Assyria sent people from lands they had conquered to inhabit Samaria.

Satan: (also referred to as the Devil) in the three major Abrahamic religions (Judaism, Christianity, and Islam), the prince of evil spirits and adversary of God. Satan is traditionally understood as an angel who rebelled against God and was cast out of heaven with other "fallen" angels before the creation of man.

Shalom: is a Hebrew word meaning peace and can be used idiomatically as a greeting.

Sin: is the transgression of the law of God and rebellion against God; literally, missing the mark.

Social justice: concept of fair and just relations between the individual and society.

(The) **Synagogue of Satan**: is mentioned in Revelation (2:9 and 3:9) and was opposed to the mission of the church. In this book, the term refers to those who claim to be Jews yet carry out Satan's work.

Tabernacle (and Temple): the Tabernacle is first mentioned in Exodus 25 when God instructed Moses to build one – also referred to as a tent of meeting – to host the presence of the Lord. The Temple in Jewish life refers to the temple built in Jerusalem that was the central place of worship. Associated is the Synagogue, historically and today, that has served as a gathering place for prayer, instruction, and community. It is this that continues to be central to Jewish life today, as it was in the time of Jesus.

(The) **Talmud**: the central text of Rabbinic Judaism and the primary source of Jewish religious law (halakha) and Jewish theology. Until the advent of modernity, in nearly all Jewish communities, the Talmud was the centrepiece of Jewish cultural life and was foundational to "all Jewish thought and aspirations", serving also as "the guide for the daily life" of Jews.

(The) **Torah**: the Law of God as revealed to Moses and recorded in the first five books of the Hebrew Scriptures (the Pentateuch).

(The) **Tribulation**: is a future seven-year period when God will finish His discipline of Israel and finalise His judgment of the unbelieving world. This period is covered in Revelation 6-19.

Truth: telling it like it is; it is the way things really are. The Greek word for "truth" is "*aletheia*", which refers to "divine revelation", related to a word that means "what can't be hidden." It conveys the thought that truth is always there, always open and available for all to see, with nothing being hidden or obscured. The Hebrew word for "truth" is "*emeth*", meaning "firmness," "constancy", "duration".

Watchmen: in the Bible these were guards responsible for protecting and warning towns and military installations of enemy attacks and other potential dangers. Their job was to keep watch and warn the townspeople of threats. It is also used in this book to describe those that watch and warn concerning happenings taking place in the world today.

(The) **Wilderness**: (as a term used in this book) comprises six wildernesses through which the Israelites traveled on their way from Egypt to Canaan, and include: Shur, Etham, Sin, Sinai, Paran, and Zin.

Wisdom: the right use or exercise of knowledge; the choice of laudable ends, and of the best means to accomplish them (in the Bible, God is seen to be the source of true wisdom).

Wokeism: a concern for social justice but concentrating on those issues that society sees as giving rise to injustices, e.g., climate change, critical race theory, immigration, LGBT rights, equal roles for women.

Worship: the feeling or expression of reverence and adoration for a deity (in this book, the deity mostly referred to is YHWH and involves a whole of life and attitude change).

YHWH: (short for Yahweh or Jehovah) is the name often ascribed, especially in the Old Testament, to God (written as G*d by certain pious Jews), and is often translated in the KJV as "The Lord (LORD)".

Part 1
The Priesthood

Chapter 1: Introducing the Priests

"Priests of the Bible" is a sequel to "**Prophets of the Bible**". The latter was a monumental labour of love. While the former is also a labour of love, based on a lifetime of studying the Bible and following those who know what they are talking about when it comes to Priests, it seemed at the beginning it would be unlikely to turn out to be quite so big in terms of number of words written. However, it soon became obvious that this too was a truly huge subject, even when resisting the temptation of going down too many rabbit holes, not over spiritualising and, rather than tackle every detail thrown up on the subject, just provide summaries of many of the pertinent points, and not lose our focus on priests!

A lot of the Prophets' book was to do with setting the scene and providing a historical and cultural context, so to speak, that is often just as applicable when we consider Priests (and Kings when we get to it), and will only be repeated in brief summary form here, and there will also be less going off on tangents and doing deep dives. Also, prophets not only did what prophets were called do, i.e., tell people what God thinks and plans, including prophesying events well into the future that we do well to weigh and apply, but they said much that is notable, applicable for their time but also ours. One of the surprises in preparing this book is how much of what priests did is also relevant for our times. It was also brought home that a major theme of the Bible is God's holiness, we need to be holy and, when it comes to priests, the lessons today's real Christians, not just the clergy, ought to apply.

While priests did speak, their words and even actions outside of carrying out their regular priestly duties, recorded in the Bible, might seem as relatively few, and there are many whose names we don't know, as well as some who are named in order to provide a complete genealogy (something the Bible deems important) but otherwise not much more can be said beyond the obvious that they fulfilled the priestly office, although when it comes to how well we may never know. Ideally, readers of this book should read the Prophets book first, although when it comes to background material particularly pertinent to Priests, especially if not dealt with in the Prophets' book, when this is identified, the author will provide it as best he can or at least state where the information can be found.

As with the Prophets, this Priests' book will be Old Testament focused, and for a very good reason – this was the period when most priests of the Bible operated and records of their activities can be found. Moreover, much of the information concerning priests can only be found in the less studied parts of the Bible, although sometimes supplemented by outside texts. While tribal elders and civil servants had important roles, Prophets, Priests and

Kings dominated. While modern society has its own professional class, such as doctors, teachers, judges and lawyers, one gets the impression that in ancient Israel many of these functions were discharged by Aaronic priests, supported by their Levite associates, and later in Israel's history, those outside the tribe of Levi, and even Israel, were brought in to assist priests. Prophets, Priests and Kings has a nice ring about it, not least because in Jesus all three of these offices wonderfully combined, doing exactly what was required, just as God intended.

While prophets and priests often operated in tandem during Old Testament times, those roles were meant to be complementary, and sometimes they were, although sometimes they were not carried out as harmoniously as one might hope. At least, that was until the New Testament with the arrival of Jesus onto the scene. "*In the beginning was the Word, and the Word was with God, and the Word was God ... the Word was made flesh, and dwelt among us*" John 1:1, 14. The word "dwelt" (Greek, **skēnoō**) pulls us back to the Old Testament wilderness wanderings of Israel, where the glory of God dwelt among the people in a movable tent called the Tabernacle, which as we are to learn was where priests operated and is intrinsic to our understanding. Moreover, we, who have the benefit of hindsight, can remind ourselves: "*He came unto his own, and his own received him not*" John 1:11, for Israel was to reject their prophet, priest and king, the very One who was their longed-for Messiah.

Concerning Abraham, Israel's founding father, we first read about him toward the end of Genesis 11. Israel, through Abraham's descendants Isaac and Jacob, who was later given the name "Israel" (all of which are referred to as the Patriarchs) and Jacob's twelve sons (who between them founded the twelve Tribes of Israel, are often mentioned by name throughout the Old Testament). They first lived in but did not possess the Promised Land, then moving to live in Egypt, until 430 years later, when they numbered around two million. They were led out from Egypt, where they had settled, by Moses, a prophet, to go and settle in the land God promised Abraham, which they did after 40 years. It was early in their 40-year sojourn in the Wilderness that the Priesthood of Israel was instituted, with priests coming from the Tribe of Levi, specifically descendants of Aaron. While all priests were Levites, only a select few Levites were priests, while the rest of the tribe, when qualified, would actually assist the Priests in their duties, provided they met the stringent conditions, which we will get to, in doing so.

The time between when God created the World (if we take the Bible literally) up to the time when the events and writings of the New Testament took place covers a period of 4000 years. The first half is covered in Genesis 1-11 and the other half in the rest of the Bible including the Apocrypha, which covers the Inter Testament period. Understandably, Christians who have been told to take the view that the Apocrypha is not an inspired text could easily ignore that period, but it was one where priests were active and bridges the gap between the Old and New Testaments when, as a whole, priests are often looked on negatively and anti-Jesus. We are living in the remaining 2000 years, the period when the Bible stopped and we await the return of the Messiah. We might divide that middle period into four near equal parts, where at different times Patriarchs, Prophets, Kings and Priests had important parts to play, often operating at the same time, but in terms of who dominated, as far as Israel goes:

- 500 years – Abraham to the Exodus – **Patriarchs**
- 500 years – Exodus to Saul – **Prophets**
- 500 years – Saul to the Exile – **Kings**
- 500 years – Exile to Jesus – **Priests**

It is worth bearing in mind that the Bible is mostly concerned with God (YHWH), what He thinks and feels, and His interaction with His creation and, in particular, the nation of Israel (Old Testament) and the Church (New Testament), although it never replaced Israel. Named individuals were mainly of interest because of the part they played in advancing (or not) God's plans and purposes. We read these scriptures mindful that the lessons we learn from studying the lives of prophets, priests and kings are meant for our spiritual edification, just as "*All scripture is given by inspiration of God, and is profitable for doctrine, for reproof, for correction, for instruction in righteousness: That the man of God may be perfect, thoroughly furnished unto all good works*" 2 Timothy 3:16-17 reminds us.

One of the many wonderful aspects of the Bible is that it tells us what God deems to be important, often revealing what His perspective was, and it does so with outright honesty, such that character flaws in even the best examples of priests etc., can be clearly seen. At the top of God's priority list is holiness and we see why and how when we study Priests of the Bible. It is an easy mistake to make to ignore what the Bible tells us about the religious life of Israel and their genealogies, but if we are to be honest in our studies, we must recognise that such teaching matters. When it comes to named priests, less are named in the Scriptures than in the case of prophets, which is not surprising, for when priests are mentioned it was often in context of them carrying out priestly duties, and they were merely carrying out what the Law and the situation prevailing at the time required them to do.

An attempt at defining what was a true prophet of God (YHWH) was made in "**Prophets of the Bible**" and turned out (at least from this author's attempt) to be a lot more involved than is commonly recognised, but in essence it was about conveying to the people what God was telling them through the prophet, including what was to happen in the future, but not to be ignored is God revealing His thoughts about what was going on. One of the beautiful things about prophets and those who were acting prophetically is they came from all walks of life and the true ones at least told people what they needed to know and heed, although all too often it was not what they wanted to hear and act upon.

When it comes to priests, they were from one tribe – Levi, and moreover one family from that tribe – that of Aaron. When tracing the lineage of individual true priests of YHWH, even up to New Testament times, we find they were descendants of Aaron. The same exercise of defining the priests' role is easier than with prophets, given priests' roles and responsibilities were well defined, as were who qualified to be priests, but we do see developments going from Tabernacle to Temple based worship. The first qualification was through ancestry, although a higher than for others standard of holiness was needed, whereas prophets were divinely appointed from a wide range of backgrounds. Given that God made it clear what he required when He gave Moses the Law, the priests' role was to carry out and help ensure it was carried out by the people the Law applied to, i.e., Israel, and when that did not happen or God had something special to tell the people, the Prophet then had an important part to play.

When seeking a dictionary definition of priest, we find typically words like *"an ordained minister of the Catholic, Orthodox, or Anglican Church, authorized to perform certain rites and administer certain sacraments"* or *"an officer or minister who is intermediate between a bishop and a deacon"* and as for its biblical validity, this is something to discuss, BUT these are NOT priests of the Bible, for as far as we can make out priests went out of business when the Second Temple was destroyed. The more general definition *"a religious leader authorized to perform the sacred rituals of a religion, especially as a mediatory agent between humans and one or more deities"* could include priests of the Bible. The original Hebrew word for priest is "**kohên**" and he is someone who delivers a divine message, stands as a mediator between God and man, and represents one party to the other.

As far as this book is concerned, priests were *"bridging the Gap between God and man"*. To be sure, other words also come to mind, such as mediation, intercession and representation. The Bible, has a lot to say about the Priesthood, and this is part of our main topic, as well as the Levites. Most of the priests in this book were intermediaries between YHWH and those whom the priests were meant to represent. As far as Christians are concerned that intermediary is Jesus, the Eternal, Great High Priest.

The central focus regarding priests in Bible times concerns where the priests operated and what they did at the place where they operated, i.e., at the Temple (and before that, the Tabernacle), with most priests coming into their own (at least as far as Israel and this book are concerned) when there was a Temple and are barely mentioned when not. Unlike with prophets and kings, priests and their Levite associates had clearly defined roles yet, of interest in this book, was when one or other priest said or did something significant that was notable. But what about when there was no Temple, e.g., during the Exile and after AD 70, and will there be a Temple sometime in the future? Who were the priests? What was the relationship between priests and Levites? What about priests who are not of Levi?

All these aspects we will address, including the seeking out of lessons and applications for our own time. Admittedly, however, this will often not cover all the important points or consider many of the spiritual applications that holy and learned commentators of the past have made. One notes with the Tabernacle, Feasts and Offerings, for example, some commentators believe every single feature has a spiritual lesson we can usefully benefit from, such as the placement and significance of each tent peg and curtain hook. This book will also address the priestly function before there were God ordained priests, priests not of the God of the Bible, the marvellous subject of *"the Priesthood of all believers"*, today's priestly equivalent that includes ministers and pastors and the role of the Lord Jesus Christ, sometimes referred to as our *"Great High Priest"*, along with that of His forerunner, Melchizedek.

Due to the way this Book is written, there is a lot of cross referencing, done partly to minimise repetition. Sometimes, repetition is unavoidable in order to provide clarity, and sometimes the same point has already been made in **"Prophets of the Bible"**. It also means readers could, if they so wished, skip over parts and read what interests them most, although reading from beginning to end is recommended. There are several illustrations applicable to more than one chapter and as much for the sake of convenience, most are to be found in Chapter 2, and referred to by their Figure numbers. Figure pages and Chapter pages are found at the beginning of this book. All we ask is to bear with us!

Talking about forbearance, regarding chapter headings, these are purely the result of the author's creative imagination and a long way from what he had in mind at the start of the project. While sixty chapters, three sets of twenty, has a nice ring to it, it was purely a result of deciding how to divide up the presentation. While the ideal may be to keep chapters roughly the same size, some are a lot longer than others. This was almost unavoidable as the requirement was to say what needed saying on each of the important topics identified. There is also a lot of Bible quoting, usually KJV, and while readers who read having a Bible to hand are to be commended, we have done so more to assist the reader.

Then there is the matter of when to spiritualise – the author's own background was such that almost every word in the Bible to do with priests was deemed to have a spiritual significance, although some of it was speculation and unprovable – as always, trying to get the right balance is needed. Also, the temptation was to add more narrative as more thoughts came to mind, but as one wise man faced with a similar conundrum said: "*I decided it was better to write something now than everything never*". This book, for convenience for author and readers, and logistic purposes, is divided into three parts (although, quite late in the day, a fourth part was added to cover the subject "**Kings of the Bible**"):

Part 1 – The Priesthood

This comprises 20 chapters to cover various aspects of the priesthood and things which relate to it. It is important to cover the content of Part 1 before we get to considering named priests in Part 2. We do so to get the necessary background in order to understand why, where and how priests functioned, what their qualifications and duties were and their roles within the communities where they operated.

Chapter 1: Introducing the Priests

Chapter 2: Priests in Context

Chapter 3: Priests from Adam to Moses

Chapter 4: Moses, the Law and the Covenant

Chapter 5: The Tabernacle – An Introduction

Chapter 6: The Tabernacle – The Furniture

Chapter 7: The Aaronic Priesthood – An Introduction

Chapter 8: The Aaronic Priesthood – Readiness for Service

Chapter 9: Sacrifices and Offerings to YHWH

Chapter 10: The Feasts of YHWH

Chapter 11: The Day of Atonement

Chapter 12: The Levites, their Roles and their Legacy

Chapter 13: Categorising Priests of the Bible

Chapter 14: The First Temple

Chapter 15: The Second Temple

Chapter 16: The Inter Testament Period

Chapter 17: Judaism and the New Testament

Chapter 18: The Third Temple

Chapter 19: Jesus our Great High Priest

Chapter 20: The Priesthood: Questions, Praise and Prayer

Part 2 – The Priests

This contains 20 chapters, 17 of which are to do with a named priest, chosen because each did something significant. Interestingly enough, many of these names may not be known to many and are less likely to be preached on, but as Bible students, wanting to dig deep into God's Word, we do well to study these, for we will find therein poignant lessons to be learned from each of them. In selecting each named priest, it was interesting to find that each one had their peculiar characteristics, strengths and weaknesses, all making important contributions, and concerning which we can learn much. The penultimate chapter is a "catch all", concerning priests that were not specifically covered in the preceding chapters. In the final chapter, just as in Part 1, we ask related questions and offer prayers.

Chapter 21: Tracing the Priests

Chapter 22: Melchizedek

Chapter 23: Aaron

Chapter 24: Nadab

Chapter 25: Eleazar

Chapter 26: Phinehas

Chapter 27: Eli

Chapter 28: Abiathar

Chapter 29: Zadok

Chapter 30: Jehoiada

Chapter 31: Azariah

Chapter 32: Hilkiah

Chapter 33: Joshua

Chapter 34: Eliashib

Chapter 35: Ezra

Chapter 36: Zacharias

Chapter 37: Caiaphas

Chapter 38: Ananias

Chapter 39: Unnamed and Lesser-known Priests

Chapter 40: The Priests: Questions, Praise and Prayer

Part 3 – A Priestly People

This contains 20 chapters and addresses topics that have arisen during the author's studies on Priests of the Bible that do not necessarily fit into Part 1 and Part 2. This includes subjects that interest the author that he thinks may interest readers too, useful background information, including some that would otherwise likely not get published, as well as some of his personal perspectives. Much of this content has arisen following the author's earlier, complementary work, **"Prophets of the Bible"**. While Parts 1 and 2 are about priests and the priesthood, Part 3 addresses what could/should interest today's priestly people. Given this more personal approach to writing, we revert to the use of the first-person singular. We should reiterate, in Part 3 especially, that much of what is being shared wasn't planned. But as indicated in the Preface and Acknowledgements, as the author reflected on his subject, new thoughts came to mind, often not specifically to do with priests (although, arguably, could/should be of interest to "A Priestly People"), but is something he would like to share even so and, since without wanting to be unduly dramatic, this could be his last serious book project while he still has the capacity to do so and is still around on planet earth, and what better place to do so than here in this third part?

Chapter 41: The Priesthood of All Believers

Chapter 42: Priests (and Ministers) and the Church

Chapter 43: What I would like to say to the Next Generation

Chapter 44: The Ark, the Glory and Revival

Chapter 45: Jesus' High Priestly Prayer

Chapter 46: The Brethren and the Last Things

Chapter 47: Bible Prophecy and Current Events

Chapter 48: Genesis – The Seedbed of the Bible

Chapter 49: Leviticus – An Unlikely Bible Favourite

Chapter 50: Chronicles – A Book Worth Studying

Chapter 51: "Prophets of the Bible" and "Kings of the Bible"

Chapter 52: Israel – Yesterday, Today and Tomorrow

Chapter 53: The Books of Wisdom

Chapter 54: Relating Old and New Testaments

Chapter 55: Hebrews – The New Testament Book About Priests

Chapter 2: Priests in Context

When "**Prophets of the Bible**" was written, the necessary point was made that understanding the context concerning what we write about and the background to our subject matter was all important. The same consideration and many of the illustrations used that applied to prophets of the Bible are still applicable and are included here. There are additional ones, particularly relating to priests and the priesthood, but those that were specifically to do with prophets are omitted. In preparing to write this book and in exhorting readers when it comes to studying the subject matter, we have come up with comparable points. While it may not be an exhaustive list, it is nevertheless one worth considering:

1. Become familiar with what the Bible has to say about the priests and the priesthood, and what is involved when it comes to being a priestly people.

2. Get to know well all sixty-six books that make up the Bible, for each one of the books has a bearing, and we do well to adopt the practice of comparing scripture with scripture.

3. Even if you favour a particular translation, refer to other translations in order to understand the precise meaning of what is set out.

4. And if still not sure, find out the meaning of the text in the original Hebrew and Greek languages.

5. Study the history of the period in which the priests operated, including non-biblical writings.

6. Study the geography and politics of the period in which the priests operated and be archaeologically aware of the bearing this may have on one getting to know more about the priests.

7. Understand better the Jewish culture and mindset of the time, recognising our own culture may be significantly different and, even if unaware of it, most of us are likely to be products of Greek thinking.

8. Learn from those who know their stuff. There are plenty of examples of those who know, who share their knowledge and insights on the Internet. The challenge comes when deciding what to check out.

9. Realise you don't know it all and you may well hold many views based on your own perspectives and experience, and those of the people around you who are likely to influence your way of thinking.

10. Pray that the Lord will open your eyes and help you to understand. In the final analysis, it is what God thinks that is important and, even when we know a lot, there is a lot we still don't know.

Regarding the illustrations that follow, all of which have been included in order to enhance our understanding of our subject, and will be referred to in the later chapters. Most of these have been lifted from the Internet (with permission sought in order to use them, when we could) and sometimes adapted for our use. Sometimes there were several images to choose from and other times not so. Some illustrations that appeared to be suitable were not included here due to copyright restrictions or they lacked clarity or were produced to make points at odds with those this author wished to make.

Because the content of this book had to be in black and white and many of the illustrations were in colour, adaptation had to be made and, given that use of colour was often significant when it came to priests, we have lost out to an extent. On the face of it, we have been spoilt for choice when there are several illustrations covering the same subject matter, and sometimes, none of what was available was ideal, but we have tried to use what was available as we didn't have the capacity to produce our own. (As an observation, the author can see a "gap in the market" for illustrations that do meet this need.)

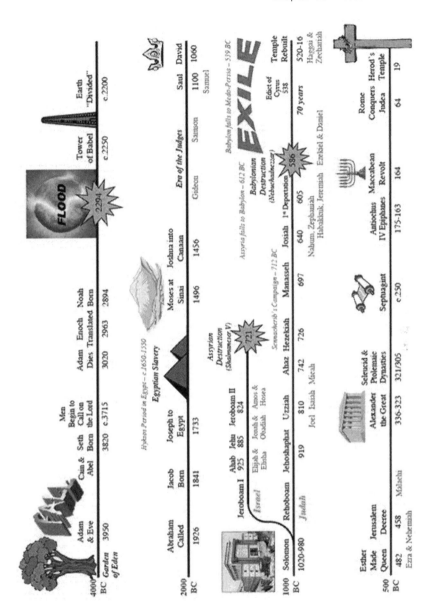

Figure 1. An historical timeline of significant Bible events

While there is a temptation to dive into those parts of the Bible that happen to interest us, we must not lose sight of the fact that the Bible tells the story of humankind, and especially Israel, from the beginning of creation until at the end when there is a new heaven and a new earth, with many significant events in-between, and it does so from the perspective that truly matters – God's.

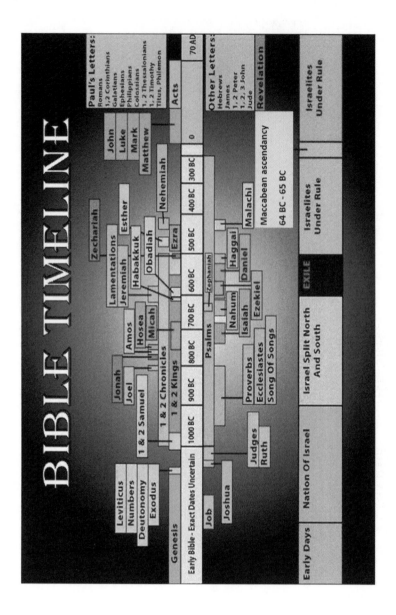

Figure 2. Bible chronology

In this timeline, we arrange all the books of the Bible in what most agree to be chronological order. We relate this to some of the main periods in Bible history. Priests operated during the whole period covered from early on during the Exodus, around 1450 BC, until the destruction of the Temple in 70 AD. From the time of the Babylonian exile around 600 BC until Israel became an independent state in 1948, except for a brief period under the Maccabees, Israel has been under foreign rule. (Correction: the "Maccabean period" (of dominance) is reckoned to be 164 - 65 BC.)

Figure 3. Books of the Bible and the Apocrypha

A major emphasis of this book is to make reference to what the Bible actually says. Most readers will be more familiar with the arrangement of the 66 books of the Bible as found in the Christian Bible. But also of interest is that which is to be found in the Hebrew Bible, where there are significant ordering differences, including differentiating between those books written primarily from a prophetic perspective ("the Prophets") and those written from a primarily priestly perspective ("the Writings"). While not considered to be canonical among most Protestants, we also include the books of the Apocrypha, which among other things help us to better understand the highly significant events that took place during the Inter Testament period.

Figure 4. Babylon to Bethlehem

Of particular interest in this book is the period between a remnant of the exiles returning to the Promised Land to the period covered by the New Testament, when priests particularly came to the fore, and this included the "Silent Years", referred to as the Inter Testament period. It is hoped readers will find helpful the linking of dates and some of the main events during that period.

Kings of Judah and Israel

Saul	1050-1010 BC
David	1010-970
Solomon	970-930

Judah (and Benjamin)				Israel (Ten Northern Tribes)			
King	Reign		Character	Prophets	King	Reign		Character	Prophets
1. Rehoboam	931-913	17 years	Bad	Shemaiah	1. Jeroboam I	931-910	22 years	Bad	Ahijah
2. Abijah	913-911	3 years	Bad		2. Nadab	910-909	2 years	Bad	
3. Asa	911-870	41 years	Good		3. Baasha	909-886	24 years	Bad	
					4. Elah	886-885	2 years	Bad	
					5. Zimri	885	7 days	Bad	
					6. Omri	885-874*	12 years	Bad	Elijah
4. Jehoshaphat	870-848*	25 years	Good		7. Ahab	874-853	22 years	Bad	Micaiah
5. Jehoram	848-841*	8 years	Bad		8. Ahaziah	853-852	2 years	Bad	
6. Ahaziah	841	1 years	Bad		9. Joram	852-841	12 years	Bad	Elisha
7. Athaliah	841-835	6 years	Bad		10. Jehu	841-814	28 years	Bad	
8. Joash	835-796	40 years	Good	Joel	11. Jehoahaz	814-798	17 years	Bad	Jonah
9. Amaziah	796-767	29 years	Good		12. Jehoash	798-782	16 years	Bad	Amos
10. Uzziah (Azariah)	767-740*	52 years	Good		13. Jeroboam II	782-753*	41 years	Bad	Hosea
11. Jotham	740-732*	16 years	Good	Isaiah	14. Zechariah	753-752	6 mo	Bad	
12. Ahaz	732-716	16 years	Bad	Micah	15. Shallum	752	1 mo	Bad	
13. Hezekiah	716-687	29 years	Good		16. Menahem	752-742	10 years	Bad	
14. Manasseh	687-642*	55 years	Bad-repent		17. Pekahiah	742-740	2 years	Bad	
15. Amon	642-640	2 years	Bad	Nahum	18. Pekah	740-732*	20 years	Bad	
16. Josiah	640-608	31 years	Good	Habakkuk Zephaniah	19. Hoshea	732-712	9 years	Bad	
17. Jehoahaz	608	3 mo	Bad		722 BC Fall of Israel / Assyrian Captivity				
18. Jehoiakim	608-597	11 years	Bad	Daniel					
19. Jehoiachin	597	3 mos	Bad	Ezekiel					
20. Zedekiah	597-586	11 years	Bad	Jeremiah					
Destruction of Jerusalem, 9th Av, 586 BC, Babylonian Captivity									

Figure 5. Kings of Israel and Judah

There are many other kings of the Bible that are not of Israel and Judah but the above chart shows all the kings of Israel and Judah from the time the Israelites demanded of Samuel, who was the prophet/judge at the time, that they should have a king, until Israel and Judah went into exile. Many of the priests we will consider operated during the times of these kings, often interacting with them.

PROPHETS OF THE BIBLE			
PROPHETS	PROPHESIED TO/ABOUT	KINGS WHO RULED DURING PROPHET'S TIME	APPROX DATES (B.C.)
Jonah	Nineveh (Assyria)	Jeroboam II	Before Northern Kingdom of Israel Captivity (780-740)
Nahum	Nineveh (Assyria)	Manasseh, Amon, Josiah	Before Southern Kingdom of Judah Captivity (658-615)
Obadiah	Edom	Zedekiah	Before Southern Kingdom of Judah Captivity (590-586)
Hosea	Israel	Jeroboam II, Zechariah, Shallum, Menahem, Pekahiah, Pekah, Hoshea	Before Northern Kingdom of Israel Captivity (780-731)
Amos	Israel	Jeroboam II	Before Northern Kingdom of Israel Captivity (790-779)
Isaiah	Judah	Uzziah, Jotham, Ahaz, Hezekiah, Manasseh	Before Southern Kingdom of Judah Captivity (760-681)
Jeremiah/ Lamentations	Judah	Josiah, Jehoahaz, Jehoiakim, Jehoiachin, Zedekiah	Before Southern Kingdom of Judah Captivity (626-585)
Joel	Judah	Joash	Before Southern Kingdom of Judah Captivity (830-798)
Micah	Judah	Jotham, Ahaz, Hezekiah, Manasseh	Before Southern Kingdom of Judah Captivity (740-695)
Habakkuk	Judah	Jehoiakim, Jehoiachin	Before Southern Kingdom of Judah Captivity (609-597)
Zephaniah	Judah	Amon, Josiah	Before Southern Kingdom of Judah Captivity (640-626)
Ezekiel	Exiled Judah in Babylon	Jehoiachin, Zedekiah (Babylonian Captivity)	During Southern Kingdom of Judah Captivity (593-571)
Daniel	Exiled Judah in Babylon	Jehoiakim, Jehoiachin, Zedekiah (Babylonian Captivity)	During Southern Kingdom of Judah Captivity (605-536)
Haggai	Returned Remnant of Judah	Governor Zerubbabel	After Southern Kingdom of Judah Captivity (520)
Zachariah	Returned Remnant of Judah	Governor Zerubbabel	After Southern Kingdom of Judah Captivity (520-518)
Malachi	Returned Remnant of Judah	Governor Nehemiah	After Southern Kingdom of Judah Captivity (420-415)
Elijah	Israel	Ahab, Ahaziah, Joram	During Northern Kingdom (870-845)
Elisha	Israel	Joram, Jehu, Jehoahaz	During Northern Kingdom (845-800)

Figure 6. Hebrew prophets

This is not an exhaustive list but it does represent what are generally considered to be the main prophets of the Bible and when/where they operated, although there were several others, notably Moses, who often acted in tandem with the priests of the Bible. All except for Elijah and Elisha, concerning whom much was written, are often referred to as "Writing Prophets", with books of the Bible named after them. They prophesied both concerning their own times and times yet to come.

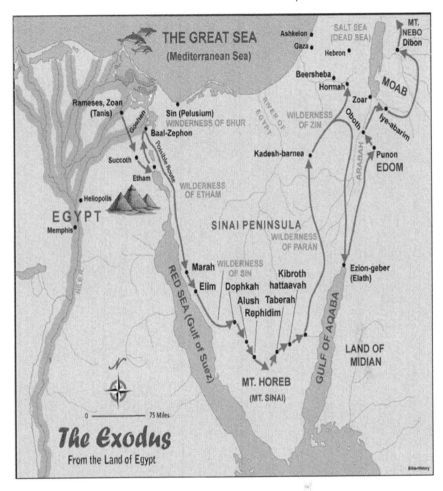

Figure 7. The Exodus Route

The first thing to say is that no-one can know for sure the route taken during the Exodus, when the Israelites spent 40 years wandering in the Wilderness. This is particularly the case when it comes to the location of Mount Sinai, on which Moses received instructions regarding the Law, priests and the Tabernacle, where God's Covenant with Israel was ratified. What is shown is what many scholars believe was the route the Israelites took after leaving Egypt and before entering the Promised Land.

Figure 8. The Ten Commandments

Before we consider the Aaronic priests, the priesthood and the Tabernacle/Temple base from which they operated, we need to consider the Covenant that God made with Israel, in which He made promises to His chosen people and required that they reciprocate by obeying His Law. There have been what many reckon as 613 laws that we can identify from the Torah, but central to all of these are what is very well known and commonly referred to as "the Ten Commandments", along with the "Two Great Commands" that we love God and we love our neighbour.

7 FEASTS

1. **PASSOVER** — 1ST MONTH 14TH DAY
2. **UNLEAVENED BREAD** — 1ST MONTH 15TH-21ST
3. **FIRST FRUITS** — 1ST MONTH DAY AFTER SABATH
4. **PENTECOST** — 50 DAYS AFTER 1ST FRUITS
5. **TRUMPETS** — 7TH MONTH 1ST DAY
6. **DAY OF ATONEMENT** — 7TH MONTH 10TH DAY
7. **TABERNACLES** — 7TH MONTH 15TH-21ST DAY

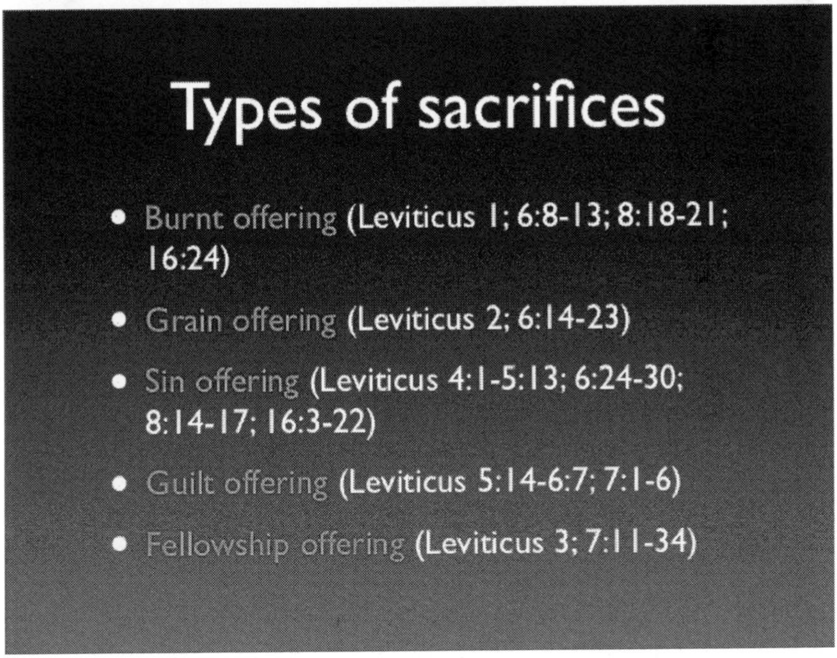

Types of sacrifices

- Burnt offering (Leviticus 1; 6:8-13; 8:18-21; 16:24)
- Grain offering (Leviticus 2; 6:14-23)
- Sin offering (Leviticus 4:1-5:13; 6:24-30; 8:14-17; 16:3-22)
- Guilt offering (Leviticus 5:14-6:7; 7:1-6)
- Fellowship offering (Leviticus 3; 7:11-34)

Figure 9. Feasts and Offerings

Feasts and Offerings (that encompass sacrifices) were a key feature of worship for the Israelites and formed a principal part of priestly duties, which will be discussed in detail in later chapters.

Figure 10. The Tabernacle (two views)

The wonder of the description of the Tabernacle to be found in the Bible is its thoroughness and that this lends itself to making accurate models (as above) and artistic representation (as below).

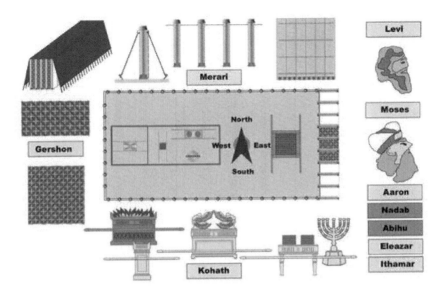

Figure 11. The Tabernacle, Holy Place and Holy of Holies

The most significant feature of the Tabernacle was the Holy Place and the Holy of Holies, the items that were inside these places, and the various duties that were undertaken by priests and Levites. These were the parts of the Tabernacle that could only be seen from the inside and could be entered only by the priests and, in the case of the Holy of Holies, only by the High Priest and then only on one day in the year (the Day of Atonement). All that is on display in the images (above and below) are discussed in various chapters of Part 1 of this book.

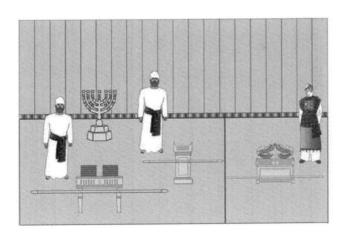

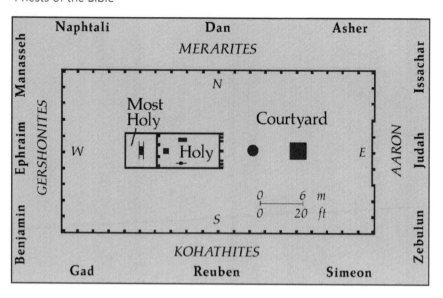

Figure 12. The Tabernacle and its surroundings

With reference to our earlier "Tabernacle" figures, there is much that can be said about the Tabernacle, notable the exactness of what was involved according to what God told Moses. It could be readily set up and dismantled right in the middle of the camp and wherever the camp was during the journey through the Wilderness. Features shown here, not seen in the previous illustrations, include the location, the dimensions and who surrounded the Tabernacle – an inner circle of Aaron and the three Levite clans and an outer circle of the twelve Tribes of Israel (excluding Levi but including the two half tribes: Ephraim and Manasseh).

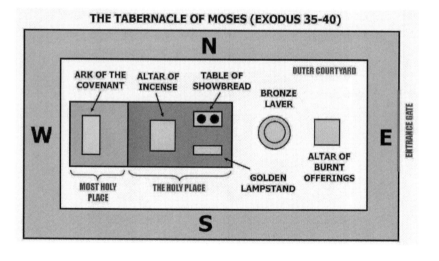

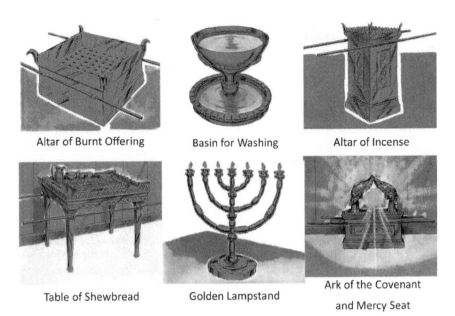

| Altar of Burnt Offering | Basin for Washing | Altar of Incense |

| Table of Shewbread | Golden Lampstand | Ark of the Covenant and Mercy Seat |

Figure 13. The Tabernacle - the Furnishings

An important aspect of the Tabernacle concerned the individual items of furniture contained within it, all of which except for the Basin for Washing we find were carefully specified. As we will see each item is enormously significant and these are shown in the above illustration. Given below is an artist's impression of the three items that were placed inside the Ark of the Covenant.

THE ARK OF COVENANT

- 2 Tablets Commandments
- The manna
- The rod of Aaron

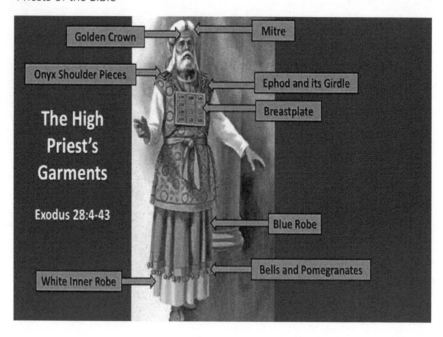

Figure 14. The High Priest's Garments

The details of the garments the priests, especially the High Priest, had to wear in carrying out their duties in the Tabernacle were precisely specified and are discussed in a later chapter. Below is a representation of what the Urim and the Thummim, placed under the breastplate, might look like.

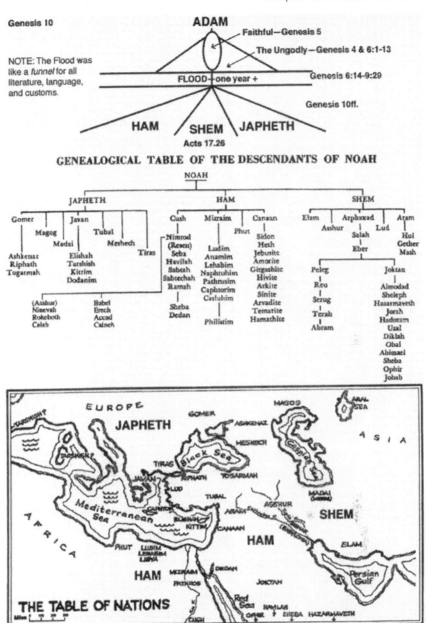

Figure 15. Table of Nations

Following the Flood, we read how the different nations came about. Many we may recognise today.

Figure 16. The Scapegoat

We first come across the Scapegoat when we read about what was to take place on the Day of Atonement, when there were two goats – one to be sacrificed and the other to be released into the wilderness (outside the camp). It also crops up in other contexts (e.g., the author's own testimony). The above image is of the painting that is titled "The Scapegoat" (1854–1856), by the Pre-Raphaelite artist, William Holman Hunt, which was his attempt at depicting "The Scapegoat", as described in Leviticus 16. The image below concerns the author's website, reflecting his attempt at going outside the camp, as Jesus' followers are invited to do, just as the Scapegoat was forced to do.

Abraham's Family Tree

```
                              Terah

Keturah   Hagar   Abraham   Sarah   Nahor            Haran

                                        Milcah  Iscah  Lot
                              Bethuel

Zimran,
Jokshan,  Ishmael   Isaac    Rebekah   Laban
Medan,
Midian,
Ishbak,
Shuah            Esau    Jacob    Rachael   Leah

                    12 Patriarchs + Dinah
```

Figure 17. Genealogy of Abraham

The nation of Israel in Bible times was comprised of the descendants of Abraham through Isaac and Jacob. The family tree (above) shows Abraham's descendants through to Jacob (Ishmael and Esau are also important). The family tree (below) shows Jacob's descendants through to Jesus via David.

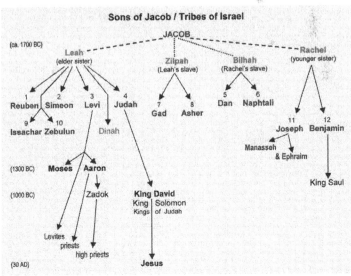

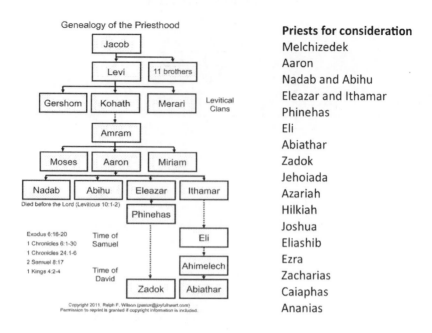

Figure 18. Priests' descendants and Levite clans

The centre piece of **"Priests of the Bible"** is the study of named priests, most of which are of the line of Aaron, who was a descendant of Levi. The Levites were the designated priestly tribe who assisted the Aaronic priests in their duties. Here we provide the beginnings of the Aaronic priest family tree. Also of interest are the Levites and the descendants of the three sons of Levi. See the diagram below, for the marching order led by Judah (and the place of the three Levite clans), when journeying.

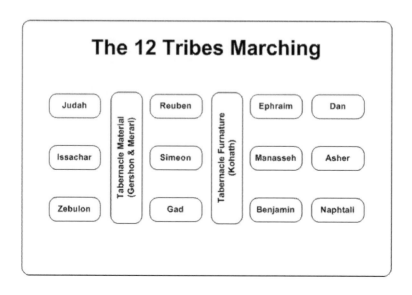

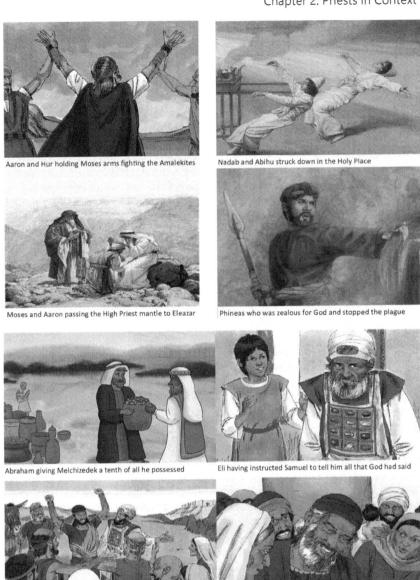

Aaron and Hur holding Moses arms fighting the Amalekites

Nadab and Abihu struck down in the Holy Place

Moses and Aaron passing the High Priest mantle to Eleazar

Phineas who was zealous for God and stopped the plague

Abraham giving Melchizedek a tenth of all he possessed

Eli having instructed Samuel to tell him all that God had said

Solomon with Zadok and Nathan after being anointed king

Zacharias writing down the name "John" for his son to be born

Figure 19. Priests in action

The illustrations above portray eight scenes depicting notable events in the lives of some of the priests that will be covered, and that we will discuss in later chapters.

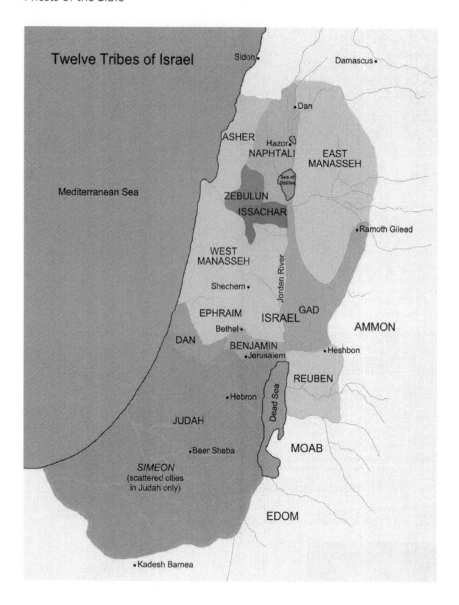

Figure 20. Dividing up the Promised Land

After the Israelites entered the Promised Land, the land was divided up according to tribe. These allocations broadly remained until the time when Israel and Judah were respectively taken into exile.

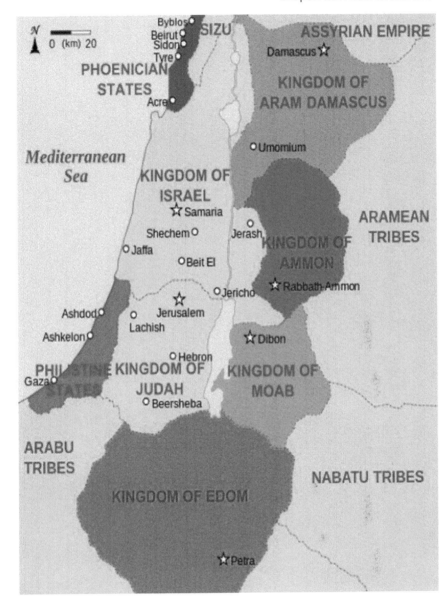

Figure 21. Israel and Judah and the surrounding kingdoms

This is how the region looked, geographically speaking, around the time when Amos prophesied in and to Israel, and not long before Israel was taken into captivity by the Assyrians. Notably, all the countries surrounding Israel and Judah feature (mostly unfavourably) in Amos' prophecies.

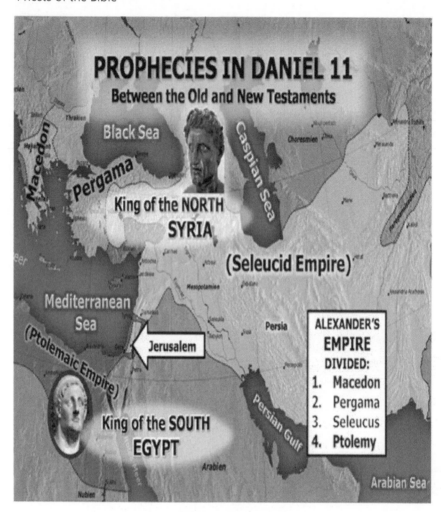

Figure 22. Israel under the Greeks

The Old Testament closes with Israel under Persian rule. The New Testament opens with Israel under Roman rule. Between those times, Greece took over from Persia and Rome took over from Greece. It was Alexander the Great, who conquered much of the known world, who first ruled over the Greek empire. When he died, his kingdom was divided up among his four generals. Firstly, there was Ptolemy who controlled Egypt and also Israel. Secondly, there was Seleucus who controlled Syria and later took over the control of Israel. Wedged between Egypt and Syria was Israel, which was subject to the first and then the other power. Much of what took place was remarkably prophesied by Daniel long before.

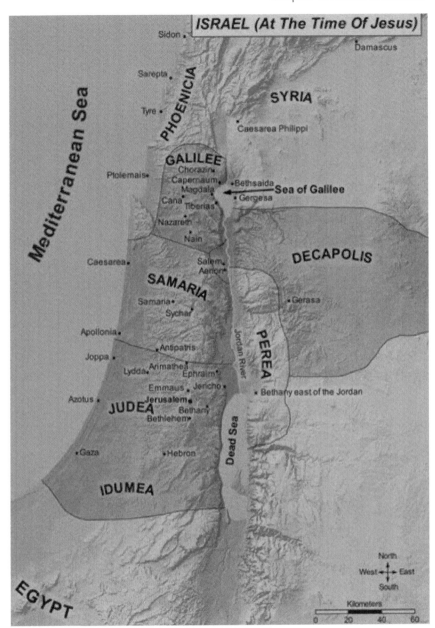

Figure 23. Israel at the time of Jesus

This represents the main geographical area of interest in the Gospels and the early part of Acts. It is interesting to note three areas frequently referred to in the New Testament: Galilee, Samaria and Judea. Jesus had contrasting experiences in each area. Samaria is of particular interest since Jesus had many dealings with the Samaritans. Idumea is of interest since this is where the Edomites, who had an important part to play in Israel's history, were to settle. The whole region was overseen by Roman governors and servient kings that arose out of the Herodian dynasty.

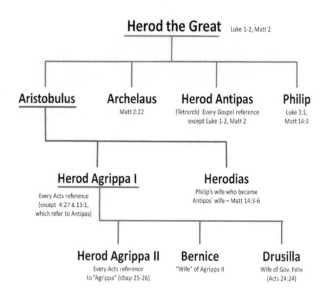

Figure 24. The Herodian dynasty

The Herodian dynasty, beginning with Herod the Great, were under the control of their Roman masters, but held considerable sway over the appointment of priests, especially the High Priest, in New Testament times, and played an important role in the times of Jesus and the early church. It is generally agreed that all the Herods who ruled over Israel were bad kings.

Sadducees *The Compromisers*	Pharisees *The Separatists*
• Mostly comprised of aristocrats • Didn't believe in the resurrection • Only followed the Torah • In the world and of it	• Largest and most popular group • Believed in the resurrection • Strict observance of the Law • In the world but not of it
Essenes *The Monks*	Zealots *The Rebels*
• Monastic group that retreated to the desert • Believed in the resurrection • Held all things in common / celibate • Neither in the world, nor of it	• Violent group opposing Roman rule • Believed in the resurrection • Radical view of Pharisaic beliefs • In the world and against it

Figure 25. Four religious groups in Jesus' time

While the focus of this book is on priests and to a lesser extent Levites, there was the emergence of other religious groupings, particularly following the return from Exile, e.g., the Scribes. During the Inter Testament period, we see the emergence of Pharisees, Sadducees, Essenes and Zealots, of which Pharisees and Sadducees were to play a prominent part in New Testament times. The image above provides a brief summary of what each group stood for, highlighting notable differences.

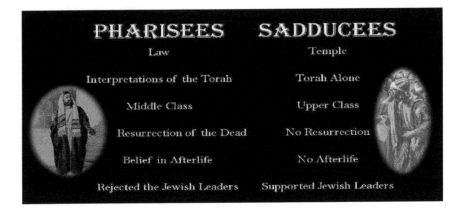

Kingdom	Period	Biggest contribution to spread of Christianity	Comments
Persian Era	539-333 BC	Foreign policy	God used Persia to deliver Israel from the Babylonian captivity and allow the Jewish exiles to return to their land, rebuild it, and worship at the temple in Jerusalem (Ezra 1:1-4).
Greek Era	333-323 BC	Greek language become the common language across	Alexander wanted to create a unified empire by language, custom, and civilization. He enforced unified Greek language; and that language eventually became the language of the land.
Egyptian Era	323-198 BC	The Septuagint - Greek version of old testament	The spread of Greek language resulted in a Greek translation of the Hebrew Bible (the Old Testament) — "the Septuagint"
Syrian Era	198-165 BC	Jewish traditions take a beating	A fight to replace the High priest leads to King's plan to destroy every distinctive characteristic of the Jewish faith
Maccabean Era	165-63 BC	Self-rule	Jews retook Jerusalem, cleansed the temple, and restored biblical worship
Roman Era	63BC - 476AD	Roads to help travel and bring Christianity to different parts	Romans brought peace to the region along with systems, law, stable government and roads. Rome connected their empire together and that was vitally important for the church to fulfil its mission of taking the Gospel across the world.

Figure 26. Reflecting on events in the "Silent years"

Other than what prophets, such as Daniel, foretold, we may well wonder what were the significant events and why these were significant during those Inter Testament years when God appeared to be silent. But as we transition from Old to New Testament, we do well to reflect that much did happen during that 400-year gap that was to have a big impact on the spread of the Christian Gospel.

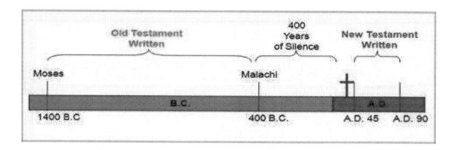

Hebrew vs Greek Thought

HEBREW THINKING

- Starts with FATHER AND FAMILY
- Deals with verbs – ACTION
- Deals with REALITY
- Deals with the CONCRETE
- Deals with EXPERIENTIAL
- Deals with FAMILY AS A UNIT
- Deals with PROSPERITY – Biblical prosperity

GREEK THINKING

- Courts, handling things in a LEGAL WAY
- Nouns – CONCEPTS
- Deals with PHILOSOPHY
- Deals with ABSTRACT
- Deals with THEORY
- Deals with CITY GOVERNMENT
- Deals with DUALISM

Ideas on Wisdom

"Knowing yourself is the beginning of all wisdom" - **Aristotle**

"The fear of the Lord is the beginning of wisdom" - **Solomon**

Much else besides, e.g. the importance of practical work compared to that of leisure; ref. *"De-Greecing the Church"* by *David Pawson*

Figure 27. Greek and Hebrew thinking contrasted

One of the ten points to consider when it comes to context, identified as important at the beginning of this chapter, is understanding the Jewish way of thinking as opposed to the Greek way, which is what influences many in today's western world. The two plates help show why doing this matters.

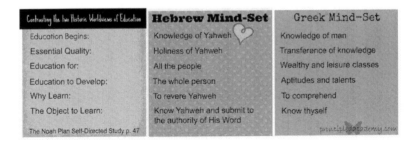

Contrasting the two Historic Worldviews of Education	Hebrew Mind-Set	Greek Mind-Set
Education Begins:	Knowledge of Yahweh	Knowledge of man
Essential Quality:	Holiness of Yahweh	Transference of knowledge
Education for:	All the people	Wealthy and leisure classes
Education to Develop:	The whole person	Aptitudes and talents
Why Learn:	To revere Yahweh	To comprehend
The Object to Learn:	Know Yahweh and submit to the authority of His Word	Know thyself
The Noah Plan Self-Directed Study p. 47		principleacademy.com

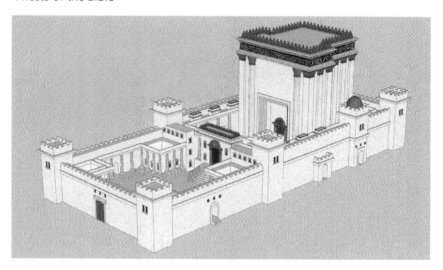

Figure 28. Herod's Temple

In this book we discuss the First, Second and Third Temple. While the First Temple, built under Solomon, was a magnificent affair, yet unlike the Tabernacle we do not have sufficient details to attempt a pictorial depiction. Similarly with the Second Temple, a less ambitious undertaking, built on return from Exile. When King Herod came to power, he undertook to rebuild the Second Temple, which Jesus and the Apostles were familiar with, and which was destroyed by the Romans in AD 70 with no replacement at this time of writing. The prospect of a Third Temple is discussed later in this book. We do have much more detail that is represented above as being Herod's Second Temple, of which all that remains today is what has come to be known as the Western Wall (see below).

Figure 29. Synagogue at Capernaum

From the time of the Babylonian exile up to the destruction of the Temple in AD 70, synagogues played an increasingly significant part in Jewish life. This photo is of the 4th century remains of the synagogue built on the site of the synagogue that Jesus would have been familiar with.

Comparison	Synagogue	Jewish Temple
Definition	The Synagogue is a place in order to assemble and also to study	The Jewish Temple is a religious place to worship for Jews
Who leads	Led by rabbis	Led by priests
Meaning	The Synagogue means "House of assembly"	The Jewish Temple means "House of prayer"
Year Constructed	The first Synagogue was built in 150BC and located in Greece	The first Temple was built in 957BC and located in Jerusalem
Services	Can be used both for prayer and for study purposes	Used for prayers and what is in the Law e.g. re. sacrifices
Numbers Found	There are synagogues to be found all over the world	There has only been one temple in existence at any one time
Destruction	Synagogues tend to last until it has been decided to close or replace	Two temples were destroyed and one has been replaced. After 70AD there was no temple
Architecture	Style can vary between ancient and modern according to taste	Traditionally built as per the norms and needs of the time.

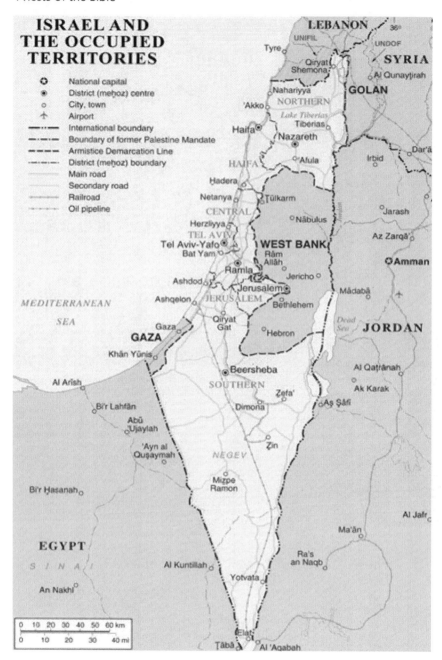

Figure 30. Israel today

Israel today is pivotal to what is happening in the world and in end times prophecy. It is worth reflecting on its territory including the two pockets where Palestinians live, and its near neighbours.

Dominating forces in Human / Jewish History

- 2000 years – Adam to Abraham – *none of the below*
- 500 years – Abraham to the Exodus – *Patriarchs*
- 500 years – Exodus to Saul – *Prophets*
- 500 years – Saul to the Exile – *Kings*
- 500 years – Exile to AD 70 – *Priests*
- 2000 years – AD 70 – 2023 AD – *none of the above*

There was much interaction between prophets, priests and kings. Jesus, who is prophet, priest and king, and much more, alone successfully combined each of these roles.

Figure 31. Prophet, Priest and King

In our study of the Bible, especially the Old Testament, we see the important contributions made by prophets, priests and kings and the interactions between each of them. Each one came to the ascendancy in terms of power at different times. Jesus perfectly combined all three roles. The tragedy is that most Jews in Jesus' time and since rejected Him who was their hoped-for Messiah.

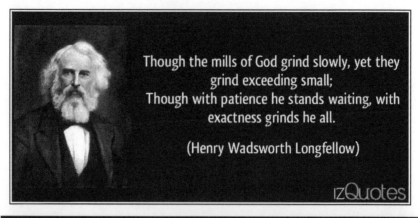

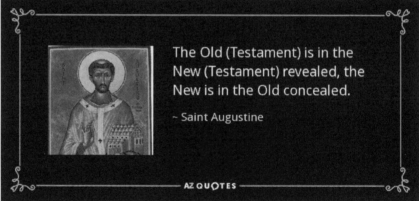

How odd of God to choose the Jews but not so odd as those who choose a Jewish God but spurn the Jews - Unknown

Figure 32. Three wise non-Bible quotes

*

Chapter 1: Daniel and friends obtain favour from the king

Chapter 2: Daniel interprets king's dream

Chapter 3: Shadrach, Meshach, and Abednego in fiery furnace

Chapter 4: Proud king is humbled

Chapter 5: Daniel interprets writing all the wall

Chapter 6: Daniel survives in the lion's den

Figure 33. Images from the first six chapters of Daniel

In "Priests of the Bible", we make frequent references to the Book of Daniel, not just concerning some of the amazing prophecies contained therein but also some of the extraordinary happenings. (Correction: Chapter 5: Daniel interprets the writing on the wall.)

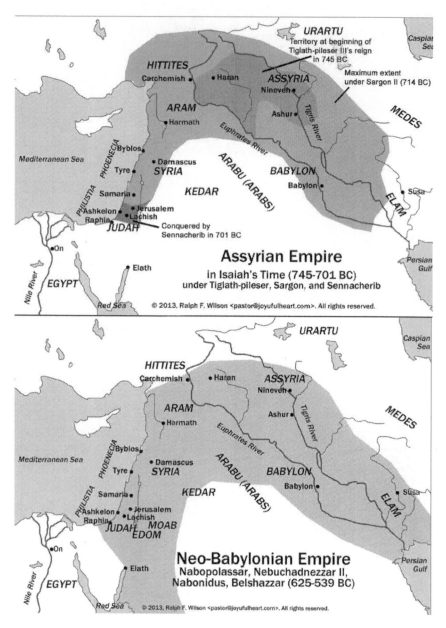

Figure 34. Empires of Assyria and Babylon

When we study events surrounding kings and priests of the Bible, an important consideration is the rising and falling of empires. Here we consider that of Assyria and of Babylon which replaced it.

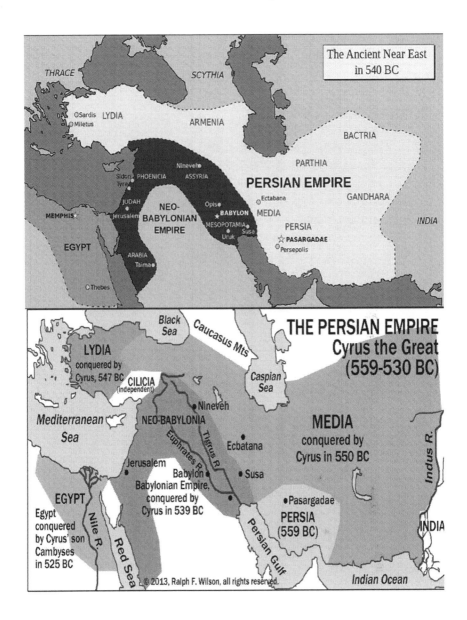

Figure 35. Empires of Babylon and Persia

Further to our illustration of the empires of Assyria and Babylon in the previous map, we now consider that which conquered Assyria, namely Babylon, and then Persia which conquered Babylon.

Significant Babylonian kings

Hammurabi et al. - approximately 1200 BC
- Greatest king of the first Babylonian Empire.
- Wrote the Code of Hammurabi

Nabopolazzar - ?-605 BC
- First king of the Chaldean (or Neo-Babylonian) Empire
- The father of Nebuchdnezzar

Nebuchdnezzar - 605-562 BC
- The greatest king of the Chaldean Empire
- Took Judah into captivity and destroyed the city
- Mentioned 88 times in the Bible

Evil-Merodach - 562-556 BC
- Mentioned in 2 Kings as releasing Jehoiachin king of Judah from prison

Nabonidus and Belshazzar - 556-539 BC
- Father and son co-regents
- Last king of the Chaldeans. Saw handwriting on the wall

Significant Persian Kings

NAME	B.C. DATE	PERSIAN NAME	BIBLE NAME	BIBLE REFERENCE
Cyrus	539-530	Koorush	Cyrus	Isaiah 45, Daniel Ezra 1-3
Cambysses	530-521	Cambujieh	Ahasruerus	Ezra 4-6
Pseudo Smerdis	521	Berooyeh Doroughi	Artaxerxes	Ezra 4:7-23
Darius the Great	521-486	Darryoosh	Darius	Ezra 5-6
Xerxes	486-465	Khashayarshah	Ahasurerus	Esther 1-10
Artixerxes	464-423	Ardeshier Dernaz Dast	Artaxerxes	Neh. 1-13 Ezra 7:10

Figure 36. Babylonian and Persian kings

We note here those kings of Babylon and Persia that played important parts in the Bible story.

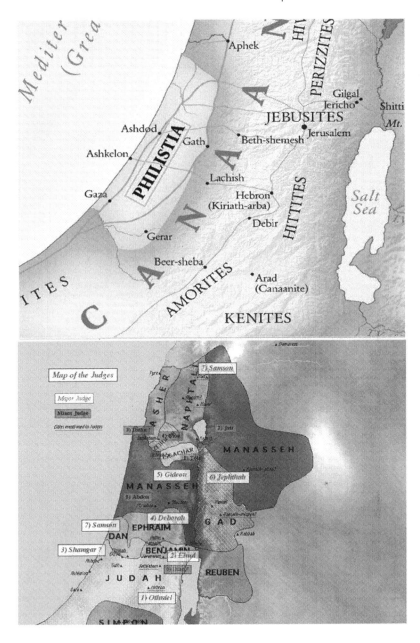

Figure 37. Conquering Caanan (1)

(Top) shows the various inhabitants of the land of Caanan before it was conquered under Joshua. (Bottom) shows the land of Caanan occupied by the tribes of Israel under the Judges.

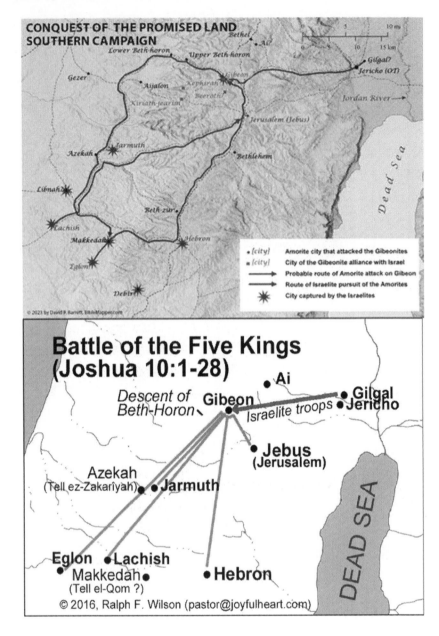

Figure 38. Conquering Caanan (2)

(Top) shows the beginning part of Joshua's campaigns into Caanan's land in order to conquer it. (Bottom) shows the battle against the five Amorite kings, when the sun stood still for a whole day.

Figure 39. The Blood is all important

(Top) High Priest entering the Holy of Holies with the blood of a sacrificed animal on the Day of Atonement. (Middle) Each family had to apply the blood of the Passover lamb that they had killed on the doorposts of their houses. (Bottom) "The Last Supper" – a painting by Leonardo da Vinci.

Figure 40. Abraham and Isaac

The Story of Abraham offering up Isaac is told in Genesis 22 and is very significant.

Before we move on to where these illustrations apply, we pause and ponder who it is we are dealing with through the words of English poet and Anglican hymnwriter, William Cowper (1731-1800):

1. *God moves in a mysterious way*
His wonders to perform;
He plants His footsteps in the sea
and rides upon the storm.

2. *Deep in unfathomable mines*
of never-failing skill;
He treasures up His bright designs,
and works His sov'reign will.

3. *Ye fearful saints, fresh courage take;*
the clouds ye so much dread
are big with mercy and shall break
in blessings on your head.

4. *Judge not the Lord by feeble sense,*
but trust Him for His grace;
behind a frowning providence
He hides a smiling face.

5. *His purposes will ripen fast,*
unfolding every hour;
the bud may have a bitter taste,
but sweet will be the flow'r.

6. *Blind unbelief is sure to err,*
and scan His work in vain;
God is His own interpreter,
and He will make it plain.

Chapter 3: Priests from Adam to Moses

While the Book of Genesis is a particularly significant book of the Bible since it examines origins of so many things, including priests, it says very little about priests *per se*. The Bible only goes to town on the Levitical priests, specifically to do with Aaron and his family, after Israel was camped by Mount Sinai for the giving of the Law, by God, to Moses. Yet, unlike kings, the notion of the priesthood can be seen right at the beginning of God's dealing with humankind, in the Garden of Eden.

The Garden represented heaven on earth, where God and his human creation, Adam and Eve, were freely able to fellowship with God and do so in wonderful harmony, with no need for a priestly intermediary, since direct access was always available and was as God intended. One revered commentator compared the Garden of Eden with the Tabernacle in the Wilderness, in which the priests operated, and in both cases it was about God dwelling with man although, when we come to the Tabernacle, only the High Priest, who represented God's covenant people, could enter the Holy of Holies where God dwelt above the Ark of the Covenant. When we come to the Exodus, and God speaks concerning Israel as being kings and priests, and later still we find this applying to the Church, a similar relationship to that which Adam and Eve once enjoyed in the Garden of Eden was being alluded to.

The very first "priest" reference in the Bible was "*And Melchizedek king of Salem brought forth bread and wine: and he was the priest of the most high God. And he blessed him, and said, Blessed be Abram of the most high God, possessor of heaven and earth: And blessed be the most high God, which hath delivered thine enemies into thy hand. And he gave him tithes of all.*" Genesis 14:18-20, which followed Abraham's involvement in the war fought between the four kings against the five, when he brought Abraham (then named Abram) bread and wine and blessed him and God. We will have a lot more to say concerning Melchizedek when we consider Jesus, the Great High Priest, and Melchizedek himself (in Chapter 22). As we study the Bible, we can see a close association between Jesus and Melchizedek, including not only were they priests of the same order but they were kings too.

The only other "priest" reference in Genesis was when Pharoah gave to Joseph as wife "*Asenath the daughter of Potipherah priest of On*" Genesis 41:45. We know little about this priest other than he was important in Egyptian life. The very fact that Joseph was given the priest's daughter in marriage showed how much Pharoah valued him. Yet the god the Egyptian priest represented was **not** YHWH and is an example of priests in the Bible **not** of YHWH. When Joseph achieved power in Egypt by predicting and was then put in charge of organising the food supply in the light of seven years of famine, he extracted a high price in terms of tribute, in exchange for helping the people but not so with the priests: "*Only the land of the priests bought he not; for the priests had a portion assigned them of Pharaoh, and did eat their portion which Pharaoh gave them: wherefore they sold not their lands ... And Joseph made it a law over the land of Egypt unto this day, that Pharaoh should have the fifth part, except the land of the priests only, which became not Pharaoh's*" Genesis 47:22-26.

While priests were not mentioned before Joseph in Genesis (other than Melchizedek), when later they were we learn that one of the main priestly functions was to make offerings and sacrifices to the Lord. This happened before there were priests appointed for such tasks. We read in Genesis 4 that Cain and Abel both made offerings to the Lord and that God accepted Abel's offering, but not Cain's, and this had much to do with the attitude of the one who was making the offering. We read later of how Noah, Abraham, Isaac and Jacob also offered animal sacrifices, as did Job, who it is reckoned also operated before the Exodus and he did so because he believed his children had sinned and a sacrifice was needed. Just before the Exodus when the Passover lamb needed to be sacrificed, it was likely done by household heads. All this was before the setting up of the Levitical priesthood.

What we see in all these cases is heads of families taking on a priestly role, a lesson worth taking on board today, when it comes to men needing to be good role models and godly examples, taking the lead when it comes to supporting, teaching, blessing etc., their own families. In Abraham's case, he offered up animal sacrifices more than once and when God instructed him to offer up Isaac, who he was not to know would be reprieved at the last moment, and which was a test of obedience, we had a picture of the ultimate sacrifice of God's Son who freely offered himself as an atoning sacrifice for humankind, when he died on the Cross. Offerings and sacrifices represented ways through which man could approach God. It was both a way of saying sorry to God and of saying thank you to God.

One other priest deserves a mention, before we consider the Levitical priesthood that will be the major consideration for this book, and that is Jethro, Moses' father-in-law. The first mention of "*the priest of Midian*" was in Exodus 2:16 (he is called Reuel in 2:18), when Moses was on the run for his life from Pharoah's palace, having earlier killed the Egyptian task master who was oppressing the Hebrews, and when he helped the daughters of this priest of Midian in a dispute around being able to draw water from the well. We are not told whether Jethro was a priest of YHWH or of some unnamed god.

We learn some time later: "*Now Moses kept the flock of Jethro his father in law, the priest of Midian: and he led the flock to the backside of the desert, and came to the mountain of God, even to Horeb"* Exodus 3:1. Then some 40 years after the first meeting, having met God at the site of the burning bush and been given orders to lead the Israelites out of Egypt, we read: *"And Moses went and returned to Jethro his father in law, and said unto him, Let me go, I pray thee, and return unto my brethren which are in Egypt, and see whether they be yet alive. And Jethro said to Moses, Go in peace"* Exodus 4:18. Then the one other time we read of Jethro was soon after embarking on his wilderness journey: *"When Jethro, the priest of Midian, Moses' father in law, heard of all that God had done for Moses, and for Israel his people, and that the Lord had brought Israel out of Egypt; Then Jethro, Moses' father in law, took Zipporah, Moses' wife, after he had sent her back"* Exodus 18:1-2.

We read of two significant actions involving Jethro. Firstly: *"And Jethro rejoiced for all the goodness which the Lord had done to Israel, whom he had delivered out of the hand of the Egyptians. And Jethro said, Blessed be the Lord, who hath delivered you out of the hand of the Egyptians, and out of the hand of Pharaoh, who hath delivered the people from under the hand of the Egyptians ... Jethro, Moses' father-in-law, took a burnt offering and sacrifices for God: and Aaron came, and all the elders of Israel, to eat bread with Moses' father-in-law before God"*. Exodus 18:9-10, 12. Secondly, it was concerning Jethro's wise advice that few would dispute has universal application. Moses was inundated when it came to listening to and judging disputes and how to resolve them. Soon after, we read: *"And Moses let his father in law depart; and he went his way into his own land"*.

Jethro played an important part in Moses' life, especially during his second forty years when Moses, having thought he was a somebody, growing up in Pharoah's palace during his first forty years, then having to live a nomadic existence, living in the Wilderness (all perfect preparation) and with Jethro's support, learning that he was a nobody and then lastly in his final forty years learning how God can use nobodies. Scholars have speculated what exactly was Jethro a priest of, although it is evident, by the time he joined Moses soon after he had crossed the Red Sea, that he was one who reverenced YHWH. One credible explanation was he was a descendant of Keturah, Abraham's second wife, and that the Midian offspring, which Jethro was part of, would have known something of the true God.

For completeness, we need to say a little more about Jethro, starting with his name. Besides also being called Reuel, Jethro is later also referred to as Hobab, when he appears at the end of the Israelites, yearlong stay at Mount Sinai, this time it was likely for the last time: *"And Moses said unto Hobab, the son of Raguel the Midianite, Moses' father in law, We are journeying unto the place of which the Lord said, I will give it you: come thou with us, and we will do thee good: for the Lord hath spoken good concerning Israel. And he said unto him, I will not go; but I will depart to mine own land, and to my kindred. And he said, Leave us not, I pray thee; forasmuch as thou knowest how we are to encamp in the wilderness, and thou mayest be to us instead of eyes. And it shall be, if thou go with us, yea, it shall be, that what goodness the Lord shall do unto us, the same will we do unto thee*" Numbers 10:29-32.

Shortly after Moses' encounter with Jethro, the one a little prior to him reaching Mount Sinai, we come to what might well be seen as the central event during the Exodus when *"In the third month, when the children of Israel were gone forth out of the land of Egypt, the same day came they into the wilderness of Sinai. For they were departed from Rephidim, and were come to the desert of Sinai, and had pitched in the wilderness; and there Israel camped before the mount"* Exodus 19:1, 2.

Moses and the Children of Israel were encamped by Mount Sinai, when the Covenant was established, the Law was given, the building of the Tabernacle and its contents were commissioned, and the Levitical Priesthood established. YHWH tells Moses *"And ye shall be unto me a kingdom of priests, and an holy nation. These are the words which thou shalt speak unto the children of Israel"* Exodus 19:6. Some have argued the privilege of being restricted to the descendants of Aaron was partly as a result of Israel's rebellion, as evidenced in the golden calf incident that occurred not long after.

The theme of priesthood among the laity is also an important theme in the New Testament: *"But ye are a chosen generation, a royal priesthood, an holy nation, a peculiar people; that ye should shew forth the praises of him who hath called you out of darkness into his marvellous light"* 1 Peter 2:9. The Priesthood of all believers is a subject we will consider in Chapter 41. The even more contentious one of priests (and ministers) and the Church we will consider in Chapter 42.

It is worth noting, before Aaron was appointed the first High Priest, priests were already in existence, although we don't know the details: *"And let the priests also, which come near to the Lord, sanctify themselves, lest the Lord break forth upon them"* Exodus 19:22. Also *"And the Lord said unto him, Away, get thee down, and thou shalt come up, thou, and Aaron with thee: but let not the priests and the people break through to come up unto the Lord, lest he break forth upon them"* Exodus 19:24.

Fifty days after leaving Egypt, the miraculous crossing of the Red Sea and early adventures in their Wilderness wanderings, we find Moses and the over two million Israelite escapees from Egypt encamped around Mount Sinai, and Moses being given detailed instructions from YHWH. When it came to the giving and receiving of the Law, many of the laws that were given were to do with the Priesthood and the Priests. Beyond the giving of the Law at Sinai, a significant part of the Old Testament narrative involved activities of named and unnamed priests. Who these priests were and what they did will be an important subject for the rest of this book, where our attention now turns.

Chapter 4: Moses, the Law and the Covenant

In the previous chapter, we ended with the Children of Israel encamped around Mount Sinai, where importantly the Law was given and the Covenant was established and where they would remain for over a year. That period is covered right through the Book of Exodus, onto the Book of Leviticus and into the first ten chapters of the Book of Numbers. Then the Israelites moved on toward their final destination, occupying the Promised Land. The rest of Numbers covers most of the rest of their journey. Deuteronomy, covers the period right at the end of the journey and provides a repetition of the Law and a recap of what the Israelites did and needed to do going forward, along with warnings.

For the story of what happened when possessing the land, we turn to the Book of Joshua. After that we read of Israel under the judges and then ruled by kings, followed by exile and return from exile. That journey should have taken them less than a year but instead it took them 38 and a bit years and meant a whole generation being wiped out, and it was all because of Israel's disobedience.

We can summarise some of the timeline of some salient events during the Wilderness journey:

- Passover (Exodus 12) - (1st year, 1st month, 15th day).
- Arrive at Sinai (Exodus 19:1) - (1st year, 4th month, 1st day).
- Leave Sinai (Numbers 10:11) - (2nd year, 2nd month, 20th day).
- Cross Jordan (Joshua 4:19) - (41st year, 1st month, 10th day).

Moses went up on Mount Sinai several times to meet God and receive instructions, as recorded in Exodus 19 and through to the end of the book. Depending on what we can deduce from the text, Moses climbed Sinai some eight times to meet with the Lord. During which time we read of:

1.   The giving of the Law, which covered principles, such as:
- The rule and norm for God's holiness was God's Law.
- The need for moral purity, actual and ritual.
- Everyone, high and low, was considered as equal under the Law.
- Penalties for breaking the Law.
- Governing all aspects of life for Israel.
- Providing for ways to settle disputes.
- Addressing issues like hygiene, social justice, sexual morality, family

life, dealing with the poor and foreigners.

- How to treat employees who are fellow Hebrews.
- How to deal with people (and animals) who inflict various kinds of personal injury.
- How to deal with thefts and negligence concerning other people's property.
- How to act responsibly towards women, widows, orphans and aliens.
- How to ensure justice, especially for the poor and for foreigners.
- How to celebrate God's involvement in community life by leaving the land uncultivated every seventh year so that the poor could benefit.

2. The establishment of the Covenant, when God promised He would look after, protect and bless His special people – Israel, provided they obeyed the Law that God gave to them, all of which Israel agreed to do: "*And Moses came and told the people all the words of the Lord, and all the judgments: and all the people answered with one voice, and said, All the words which the Lord hath said will we do. And Moses wrote all the words of the Lord, and rose up early in the morning, and builded an altar under the hill, and twelve pillars, according to the twelve tribes of Israel. And he sent young men of the children of Israel, which offered burnt offerings, and sacrificed peace offerings of oxen unto the Lord. And Moses took half of the blood, and put it in basons; and half of the blood he sprinkled on the altar. And he took the book of the covenant, and read in the audience of the people: and they said, All that the Lord hath said will we do, and be obedient*" Exodus 24:3-7.

3. The commissioning of the Tabernacle (elaborated upon in Chapters 5 and 6).

4. The establishment of the Priesthood (elaborated upon in Chapters 7 and 8).

5. Feasts and offerings (elaborated upon in Chapters 9, 10 and 11).

6. Matters pertaining to the Levites (elaborated upon in Chapter 12).

Concerning "covenant", this is a major theme of the Bible. As far as God is concerned, He is always faithful in doing what He has covenanted to do, even though that was often not the case with those who He was in covenant with. As far as the priesthood and priests go, it is the Mosaic Covenant that is of particular interest. It is one that keeps cropping up throughout our journey in the Old Testament, and unlike the Abrahamic Covenant that has ramifications far into the future, the Mosaic Covenant depended on Israel's obedience. It is worth noting the following covenants to be found in the Bible.

1. The Edenic Covenant (Genesis 1:28-30, 2:15-17).

2. The Adamic Covenant (Genesis 3:14-19).

3. The Noahic Covenant (Genesis 8:20-9:17).

4. The Abrahamic Covenant (Genesis 12:1-3).

5. The Mosaic Covenant (Exodus 19-20).

6. The Davidic Covenant (2 Samuel 7:4-17).

7. The New Covenant (Jeremiah 31:31-34, Hebrews 8:7-13).

At the end of Exodus, we read of the glory of God entering the Tabernacle and soon after that, at the beginning of Leviticus, God calls Moses from the Tabernacle, where he received further instructions from God: "*And there I will meet with thee, and I will commune with thee from above the mercy seat, from between the two cherubims which are upon the ark of the testimony, of all things which I will give thee in commandment unto the children of Israel*" Exodus 25:22.

Moses first ascent of Sinai is described in Exodus 19:2-7. He ascends the mountain in verse 3 and comes back down in verse 7. On the mountain God tells Moses that He is offering a Covenant to the people of Israel: if they will keep the covenant, God will make them His own "*treasured possession*" and "*a kingdom of priests and a holy nation*" (verses 5-6). Moses reports this message to the people, and the people respond by saying, "*We will do everything the Lord has said*" (Exodus 19:8).

In his second ascent, Moses returns to the top of Sinai in Exodus 19:8 in order to relay the people's response to the offer of a Covenant. God then tells Moses that He will speak audibly to Moses in a thick cloud so that all the people will put their trust in Moses as God's chosen leader. Moses descends the mountain in verse 9 in order to relay this information to the children of Israel.

In his third ascent, in Exodus 19:10, God is speaking to Moses again. Moses is said to descend the mountain again in verse 14. Moses consecrates the people in preparation for the Lord's appearance on the mountain on the third day (verses 10-11). On the third day, "*there was thunder and lightning, with a thick cloud over the mountain, and a very loud trumpet blast*" (Exodus 19:16). The people of Israel were frightened. Then "*Mount Sinai was covered with smoke, because the Lord descended on it in fire. The smoke billowed up from it like smoke from a furnace, and the whole mountain trembled violently. As the sound of the trumpet grew louder and louder"* (verses 18-19).

Moses' fourth ascent is described in Exodus 19:20-25. God summons Moses to the top of the mountain in order to have him warn the people not to draw near the mountain while His presence is on Sinai. He also tells Moses to bring his brother, Aaron, up the mountain with him. Moses descends the mountain in verse 25. God then delivers the Ten Commandments audibly in Exodus 20:1-17. In fear, the people of Israel plead with Moses not to let God speak directly to them. Instead, they ask Moses to be their intercessor and they would listen to him (verses 18-19). Moses tells them to not be afraid but that God is testing them so that they would fear Him and not sin (verse 20).

In Moses' fifth ascent, he returns to Mount Sinai in Exodus 20:21 as he *"approached the thick darkness where God was."* At this time, God gives Moses various laws, recorded in Chapters 21-23, along with a promise to give the land of Canaan to the children of Israel (Exodus 23:20-33).

In Moses sixth ascent, in Exodus 24:1, Moses is told to bring Aaron, Aaron's sons Nadab and Abihu, and seventy of the elders of Israel with him. The next morning, Moses *"built an altar at the foot of the mountain and set up twelve stone pillars representing the twelve tribes of Israel"* (verse 4). He offered burnt offerings and fellowship offerings and read the Book of the Covenant to the people, who responded, *"We will do everything the Lord has said; we will obey"* (verse 7). To ratify the Covenant, Moses sprinkled the people with the blood of the sacrifice (verse 8).

After the ceremony, Moses, Aaron, Nadab, Abihu, and the elders ascend the mountain, and there they *"saw the God of Israel. Under his feet was something like a pavement made of lapis lazuli, as bright blue as the sky"* (Exodus 24:10). God allows these men to live, even though they had seen God; in fact, they *"ate and drank"* on the mountain (verse 11). God then commands Moses to continue up Sinai in order to receive the stone tablets that God had prepared (Exodus 24:12). Moses takes Joshua with him and sends the others down to the foot of Sinai. While Joshua waits, Moses continues the ascent. For six days, a cloud covers the top of the mountain. On the seventh day, God calls Moses to enter the cloud and approach the top of the mountain.

Moses stays there for 40 days and 40 nights (verse 18). During this meeting on the mountain, God gives Moses much information. This included the Ten Commandments written on tablets of stone by God Himself. Moses also receives complete instructions on how to build the tabernacle, the ark of the covenant, and the altar, specifications for the priestly garments, etc. (Exodus 24-31). At the foot of the mountain, the Israelites had Aaron build the golden calf and were committing idolatry. When Moses and Joshua descend the mountain in Exodus 32:19 and see what the people are doing, Moses breaks the stone tablets in anger. He then destroys the golden calf and disciplines the people.

In his seventh ascent, Moses goes back to the Lord in Exodus 32:31 to intercede on behalf of Israel. Moses offers his own life in exchange for that of Israel (verse 32). God's response was: "*Whosoever hath sinned against me, him will I blot out of my book. Therefore now go, lead the people unto the place of which I have spoken unto thee: behold, mine Angel shall go before thee: nevertheless in the day when I visit I will visit their sin upon them. And the Lord plagued the people, because they made the calf, which Aaron made. And the Lord said unto Moses, Depart, and go up hence, thou and the people which thou hast brought up out of the land of Egypt, unto the land which I sware unto Abraham, to Isaac, and to Jacob, saying, Unto thy seed will I give it*" Exodus 32:33-33:1.

In his eighth (and final) ascent, in Exodus 34:1–2, the Lord says to Moses, "*Chisel out two stone tablets like the first ones, and I will write on them the words that were on the first tablets, which you broke. Be ready in the morning, and then come up on Mount Sinai. Present yourself to me there on top of the mountain.*" Moses is to come alone. On top of the mountain, the Lord reveals Himself to Moses: "*And the Lord descended in the cloud, and stood with him there, and proclaimed the name of the Lord. And the Lord passed by before him, and proclaimed, The Lord, The Lord God, merciful and gracious, longsuffering, and abundant in goodness and truth, Keeping mercy for thousands, forgiving iniquity and transgression and sin, and that will by no means clear the guilty; visiting the iniquity of the fathers upon the children, and upon the children's children, unto the third and to the fourth generation*" (34:5-7). Moses worships the Lord and receives from Him a reaffirmation of the Covenant: "*And he said, Behold, I make a covenant: before all thy people I will do marvels, such as have not been done in all the earth, nor in any nation: and all the people among which thou art shall see the work of the Lord: for it is a terrible thing that I will do with thee*" (34:10).

We then read: "*And the Lord said unto Moses, Write thou these words: for after the tenor of these words I have made a covenant with thee and with Israel. And he was there with the Lord forty days and forty nights; he did neither eat bread, nor drink water. And he wrote upon the tables the words of the covenant, the ten commandments*" (34:27-28). At the end of the Wilderness sojourn, Moses reflects: "*At that time the Lord said unto me, Hew thee two tables of stone like unto the first, and come up unto me into the mount, and make thee an ark of wood. And I will write on the tables the words that were in the first tables which thou brakest, and thou shalt put them in the ark. And I made an ark of shittim wood, and hewed two tables of stone like unto the first, and went up into the mount, having the two tables in mine hand. And he wrote on the tables, according to the first writing, the ten commandments, which the Lord spake unto you in the mount out of the midst of the fire in the day of the assembly: and the Lord gave them unto me"* Deuteronomy 10:1-4.

Moses remains on Mount Sinai for another 40 days and 40 nights, *"without eating bread or drinking water"* (verse 28). When Moses comes back down to the people, *"he was not aware that his face was radiant because he had spoken with the Lord. When Aaron and all the Israelites saw Moses, his face was radiant, and they were afraid to come near him"* (verses 29-30).

Establishing the Law, including that which pertained to the Tabernacle, the Priesthood and the religious and civil life of the Israelites, and the Covenant, was an important pre-requisite before we consider more fully matters concerning the Priesthood.

Chapter 5: The Tabernacle – An Introduction

"*And the Lord spake unto Moses, saying, Speak unto the children of Israel, that they bring me an offering: of every man that giveth it willingly with his heart ye shall take my offering … And let them make me a sanctuary; that I may dwell among them. According to all that I shew thee, after the pattern of the tabernacle, and the pattern of all the instruments thereof, even so shall ye make it*" Exodus 25:1-2, 8-9.

Before we turn to one of the most important aspects of "**Priests of the Bible**", in terms of what was expected of priests and the central place where they carried out many of their duties, readers are invited to check out the pictorial illustrations of what we are about to describe in words concerning the Tabernacle – Chapter 2, Figures 10, 11 and 12, which, while they are artistic representations, accurately portray what actually took place. We can say: since God gave Moses precise instructions concerning the Tabernacle's construction, down to the last tent post/peg and curtain ring, which instructions were carried out to the letter such that, besides setting out what God required of Moses and the Israelites, these all reflect profound spiritual truths, from which many lessons can be drawn.

In our previous chapter, we find Moses and the Children of Israel, encamped around Mount Sinai, where they would remain for a little over a year, and from where they would move on (taking with them the components needed to put up the Tabernacle (Tent) and what was inside it). They would remain in the Wilderness for the next 38 years, before taking possession of the Promised Land under Joshua. In that time, they would have taken down and put up the Tabernacle on numerous occasions. It was eminently designed for such an undertaking, helped by the three Levite putter upper, taker downer clans, all with their well defined duties, who were needed to carry out such operations.

Before we get to the commissioning of the Aaronic Priesthood in Exodus 28-29, to be discussed in later chapters of this book, who were to carry out the various duties that were to take place inside the Tabernacle, we find before then God instructing Moses concerning that which was Tabernacle related, starting in Exodus 25. But it was at Mount Sinai that God began to give Moses the Law and to set out the Covenant. Instructions concerning what God told Moses about building the Tabernacle can be found in Exodus 25-27 and 30-31, and then later on, following the Golden Calf incident, we read in Exodus 35-40 concerning the construction and the making ready and commissioning of the Tabernacle.

When it came to making it ready for use at the end of the Book of Exodus and before God called Moses from inside the Tabernacle in the Book of Leviticus, we read: "*Then a cloud covered the tent of the congregation, and the glory of the Lord filled the tabernacle. And Moses was not able to enter into the tent of the congregation, because the cloud abode thereon, and the glory of the Lord filled the tabernacle. And when the cloud was taken up from over the tabernacle, the children of Israel went onward in all their journeys: But if the cloud were not taken up, then they journeyed not till the day that it was taken up. For the cloud of the Lord was upon the tabernacle by day, and fire was on it by night, in the sight of all the house of Israel, throughout all their journeys.*" Exodus 40: 34-38.

Before we get going, this author would like to make the point that he has had as long a love affair with the Tabernacle, as he has had with the Song of Solomon, going back to the time, when as a young believer, an itinerant Bible teacher came to his church with a scaled down model of the Tabernacle (long before the Internet) and spent a number of nightly sessions talking about the significance of much that was Tabernacle related, down to every tent post/peg and curtain hook/ring, using the opportunity to bring out important spiritual lessons that might well apply to our present situation.

Not just in the Old Testament, but the New Testament too, there are many instances when the Tabernacle is alluded to. Besides which, there are teachings of a heavenly temple (tabernacle), the church being the temple (tabernacle) where God dwells and of Jesus tabernacling among men. While doing research for this book, it became evident Christians that gave particular attention to such details were in a minority, and the majority viewed the Tabernacle in very much broad-brush terms and skipping over and failing to see the significance of the numerous fine details found in the text.

While readers will need to go elsewhere for many of the fine details, the intention in this chapter and the one that follows (that is to do with the furniture inside the Tabernacle) is that we address some of these aspects whilst providing a balance between over and under spiritualisation. What these chapters will not do, if for no other reason than that the task is too big, is to explore every nook and cranny of the Tabernacle, despite being described in the Bible narrative. As for going "elsewhere" to find out more, there are many, typically old, books that go into the details of the Tabernacle, sometimes going further than this author would in seeking out spiritual relevance and application. One book the author often refers to is "**The Tabernacle – Shadows of the Messiah**" by David Levy. As for helpful resources from the Internet, the series on the Tabernacle found on the 119ministries (*www.119ministries.com*) is one he recently stumbled across that makes many important points, but there are several others.

Before we consider Exodus 25 when God tells Moses to build a Tabernacle exactly as instructed so God can dwell among the Israelites for the first time in their history and do so permanently, we should reflect on the previous chapter when He tells Moses to climb the mountain along with Aaron, Nadab and Abihu (Aaron's two eldest sons, who later God punishes with death), and 70 of the elders of Israel to worship God, but only from a distance. We find the people enthusiastic to do all that God commanded them to do and keep their part of the Covenant, after which Moses built an altar and made a burnt offering and a peace offering (the significance of which is explained in Chapter 9).

As Moses and his band climbed the mountain they saw something of the glory of God and were able to enjoy a fellowship meal, as it were, with God. But only Moses, initially accompanied by Joshua, could climb higher and see more of the glory of God. There Moses patiently waited for God to reveal Himself and did so for seven days. It would have been an awesome sight when people could view from a distance the presence of God's glory and as God called Moses from a cloud, into which he entered. We read that Moses was on the mountain 40 days, most of that time alone, and the first thing God told him was concerning the Tabernacle, thus indicating how important this was to God.

We see from the outset what God intended concerning His relationship with the people with which He had made a Covenant, and although they were soon to break it, we see just prior to Moses ascending the mountain that they were initially eager to keep the Covenant. God told Moses exactly what was needed and invited the people to make offerings, whether precious metals or animal skins or a plethora of other necessary items, which were in their possession following their exodus from Egypt. This they willingly and freely gave – more than was needed, and different people who were so gifted by God played their part in the construction work of the Tabernacle and what was placed inside it. Besides materials found in the Wilderness, such as shittim wood, many items taken from Egypt and needed for carrying out the work, most of which were put to good use in making something beautiful.

The wonder of the Tabernacle was that it was where God dwelt and, when we consider the Tabernacle in the Wilderness, it was erected right in the centre of where upwards of two million Israelites were encamped. The glory of the Lord could be physically sensed and there was a cloud hovering over it, which represented God's precence and when that cloud moved so did the Israelites. With reference to Chapter 2, Figure 12, the Tabernacle was surrounded by an inner circle of the Levi clans of Merari, Gershon, and Kohath and finally Aaron and Moses encamped on the North, West, South and East sides respectively. Then there was an outer circle of the remaining tribes: Naphtali, Dan, Asher (North); Benjamin, Ephraim, Manasseh (West); Gad, Reuben, Simeon (South); Zebulun, Judah, Isaachar (East).

We see right away this careful ordering with respect to families was deliberate and typical of every feature of the precise Tabernacle construction that included the pillars/posts that were on the outside of the Tabernacle and the boards around the Holy Place and Holy of Holies and, in all these cases, the curtains around the pillars and boards, along with the sockets and how these were held together and, in the case of the Holy Place and Holy of Holies, the several layers of different animal skins that formed the roof, and especially the curtain (the Veil) separating the Holy Place from the Holy of Holies (the curtain in the Temple would be torn in two from top to bottom, when Jesus died on the Cross).

Precise instructions were given on the curtain design that included blue, scarlet and purple yarn interwoven and with cherubims, along with the intricate needle work (complementing incidentally the design of the High Priest's garments). Much could be made of the significance of blue (the heavenly colour), scarlet (symbolic of blood) and purple (the royal colour) and the cherubim who were part of the angelic protection. The same could be said of how poles and planks were ordered, how curtains were arranged and down to tent pegs and curtain rings – all resulting in a unified whole – suggesting that as well as glory and beauty there was order and unity – all important aspects of God's design.

Because the Tabernacle represented God's holiness, no-one who was in a state of undealt with sin (unless making a guilt offering/sacrifice) or in a state of uncleanness or ritual impurity, as set out in Leviticus, could enter the Tabernacle. If they did enter, it was through the curtain on the East side (the only way in and the only way out) but only priests could enter the Holy Place and only the High Priest, once a year, could enter the Holy of Holies. While what was inside was a holy marvel, none but the priests could see it. In Chapter 6, we consider the six items of furniture: the Brazen Altar and the Brazen Laver in the Outer Court; the Golden Lampstand, the Table of Showbread and the Altar of Incense in the Holy Place and the Ark of the Covenant (along with the Mercy Seat) in the Holy of Holies.

One can see a progression as priests (on behalf of the people drew near to God) and all had to do so in a prescibed way. Before priests could enter the Holy Place, they needed to be justifed by offering sacrifices at the Brazen Altar and sanctified by washing at the Brazen Laver. While what could be seen in the Outer Court was bronze, when we get to the Holy Place it is gold. While a priest's daily duties involved the Golden Lampstand, the Table of Showbread and the Altar of Incense in the Holy Place (all of which, as we will see, were deeply spiritually significant), that was as close as they could get to God whose dwelling was in the Holy of Holies, except on that one occasion that involved the High Priest. As for the rest, providing they were qualified to do so, they could enter the Outer Court and no further.

Much more can be said on the Tabernacle, and what took place inside, led by the priests (which we will consider in later chapters) but for now, besides encouraging readers to check out this subject for themselves, we end with some reasons why studying the Tabernacle and its ministries is important.

1. It is needed for a fuller understanding of God's redemptive program – something that is progressively revealed, starting in Genesis and going right through to Revelation.

2. It informs sinful people (you and me) about the holiness of God and the fear of God.

3. It points to Christ and His all-sufficient work, God's answer to man's sin problem.

4. It shows us how a holy God can exercise His grace and mercy to a sinful people.

5. It shows us how a sinful people can acceptably approach and worship this holy God.

6. It helps us to better understand the Aaronic Priesthood and Christ's priestly ministry.

7. An understanding of how priests operated in and around the Tabernacle can throw further light on what ought to be expected of Christians when they exercise their priestly role.

8. The sacrificial system, one of the main activities inside the Tabernacle, brings home to us the importance of blood sacrifice and of its necessity when it comes to atoning for sin.

9. A greater knowledge of those sacrifices helps us to better understand how God views sin and what pleases God when it comes to showing gratitude and expressing worship.

10. A better understanding of the Tabernacle helps us toward a better understanding of the New Testament and especially the Book of Hebrews.

Chapter 6: The Tabernacle – The Furniture

In our previous chapter, we considered aspects such as the construction of the Tabernacle and its significance in the life of Israel, as well as the numerous lessons that can be drawn from studying the Tabernacle. We now turn to the items of furniture that were to be found inside the Tabernacle. Before we do, readers are invited to refer to Chapter 2, Figure 13, for what these items looked like. These items were designed to be readily transportable, often with rings attached so staves could go through and they could be easily carried as part of the journeying that took place in the Wilderness

Many of the activities recorded that pertain to (the Aaronic) Priests of the Bible were to do with these six items. When we consider their purposes, each item had enormous spiritual significance and as we can later find were types and shadows of what would be revealed when we come to the New Testament. We will consider each item, albeit not in the order that Moses received his instructions concerning their construction, but with reference to the Priests' journey from the outer court (Brazen Altar and Brazen Laver), into the Holy Place (Golden Lampstand, Table of Showbread and Altar of Incense) and that once a year entry by the High Priest into the Holy of Holies (Ark of the Covenant):

The Brazen Altar

"And thou shalt make an altar of shittim wood, five cubits long, and five cubits broad; the altar shall be foursquare: and the height thereof shall be three cubits. And thou shalt make the horns of it upon the four corners thereof: his horns shall be of the same: and thou shalt overlay it with brass. And thou shalt make his pans to receive his ashes, and his shovels, and his basons, and his fleshhooks, and his firepans: all the vessels thereof thou shalt make of brass. And thou shalt make for it a grate of network of brass; and upon the net shalt thou make four brasen rings in the four corners thereof." Exodus 27:1-4.

The first thing anyone saw entering the only way into the Tabernacle would have been the Brazen Altar, used to offer sacrifices, as detailed in Chapters 9 and 11. The altar was effectively a wooden box overlaid with brass, with horns at its four corners and where blood can be applied and collected and so too the ashes as a result of burning the offerings. Along with the altar, there were a number of utensils, such as pans, shovels and flesh hooks, the details of which, as we reflected on in our previous chapter, were carefully prescribed. In Chapter 9, we consider two main categories of sacrifices (offerings), i.e., to show gratitude to God and to receive atonement for sin, through the priests who made the offering for sacrifice on their behalf, and the meaning and details of what took place with each type. It was something open to every Israelite to do as well as those particularly for the priest. The key theme of the sacrificial system was justification, for without it one can go no further with a holy God, who can't stand sin. In the New Testament, such sacrifices are not required because Jesus offered Himself up as an atoning sacrifice, so that we may be justified by faith alone and thereby be able to enter into God's presence, just as the priests did when they entered into the Holy Place.

The Brazen Laver

"And the Lord spake unto Moses, saying, Thou shalt also make a laver of brass, and his foot also of brass, to wash withal: and thou shalt put it between the tabernacle of the congregation and the altar, and thou shalt put water therein. For Aaron and his sons shall wash their hands and their feet thereat: When they go into the tabernacle of the congregation, they shall wash with water, that they die not; or when they come near to the altar to minister, to burn offering made by fire unto the Lord" Exodus 30:17-20.

The next item of furniture one would see when entering the Tabernacle outer court, was the Brazen Laver, situated between the Holy Place and the Brazen Altar. This was for use by the priests alone and is where they would wash. There were two types of washing: when they were ordained for the priesthood and on the Day of Atonement, which was a full body wash and as part of a daily ritual before priests were permitted to make sacrifices on behalf of others, when they would thoroughly wash both hands and both feet. Whereas the Altar represented the need for justification, the Laver represented the need for sanctification. As believer-priests we need to be both justified and sanctified.

While justification is what happens when we put our faith in Christ, sanctification is a continual process and one that is needed for a healthy relationship with God. Unlike other items of Tabernacle furniture, we do not have full details of what was needed in making the Laver, although interestingly it was made from the mirrors the women took with them when leaving Egypt and the reflection of one's image when washing from the basin was a constant reminder of our position before God and the need for holiness. The washing with water throughout the New Testament, whether in baptism or Jesus washing of His disciples' feet, was a continual reminder of the need to be inwardly clean. A salutary reminder for both Old and New Testament believers is *"Who shall ascend into the hill of the Lord? or who shall stand in his holy place? He that hath clean hands, and a pure heart; who hath not lifted up his soul unto vanity, nor sworn deceitfully. He shall receive the blessing from the Lord, and righteousness from the God of his salvation"* Psalm 24:3-5.

The Golden Lampstand

"And thou shalt make a candlestick of pure gold: of beaten work shall the candlestick be made: his shaft, and his branches, his bowls, his knops, and his flowers, shall be of the same. And six branches shall come out of the sides of it; three branches of the candlestick out of the one side, and three branches of the candlestick out of the other side: Three bowls made like unto almonds, with a knop and a flower in one branch; and three bowls made like almonds in the other branch, with a knop and a flower: so in the six branches that come out of the candlestick. And in the candlesticks shall be four bowls made like unto almonds, with their knops and their flowers" Exodus 25:31-34.

Having been justified and sanctified by sacrificing at the Altar and washing at the Laver, the priest was now able to enter into the Holy Place through a curtain, which non priests could only view from the outside but never from inside. There are three items of interest in this 30 feet by 15 feet room and here we begin by considering the Golden Lampstand, which alone provided light. Interestingly, this was made from a single slab of gold and contained seven branches (prongs) comprising clusters of cups, knobs and flowers. The lamp was tended on a daily basis and fuelled by specially prescribed oil.

The word "light" appears 309 times in the Bible. While a study around light would be a profitable one, we will cite just five of the word's usages. The Psalmist could say: *"The Lord is my light and my salvation; whom shall I fear? the Lord is the strength of my life; of whom shall I be afraid"* Psalm 27:1 and *"Thy word is a lamp unto my feet, and a light unto my path"* Psalm 119:105. In introducing the Word that became flesh, we read concerning Jesus: *"That was the true Light, which lighteth every man that cometh into the world"* John 1:9. Jesus claimed to be the Light of the World e.g., *"But as long as I am in the world, I am the light of the world"* John 9:5. As believer-priests we are called to walk in the light: *"But if we walk in the light, as he is in the light, we have fellowship one with another, and the blood of Jesus Christ his Son cleanseth us from all sin"* 1 John 1:7.

The Table of Showbread

"Thou shalt also make a table of shittim wood: two cubits shall be the length thereof, and a cubit the breadth thereof, and a cubit and a half the height thereof. And thou shalt overlay it with pure gold, and make thereto a crown of gold round about. And thou shalt make unto it a border of an hand breadth round about, and thou shalt make a golden crown to the border thereof round about. And thou shalt make for it four rings of gold, and put the rings in the four corners that are on the four feet thereof" Exodus 25:23-26.

The Table of Shewbread (the Bread of the Presence) was just that – a table made out of shittim wood and overlaid with gold and around the top was a gold rim. Associated with the table were two plates on which twelve loaves were placed – each loaf representing one of the tribes of Israel, and spoons. We also learn: "*And thou shalt take fine flour, and bake twelve cakes thereof: two tenth deals shall be in one cake. And thou shalt set them in two rows, six on a row, upon the pure table before the Lord. And thou shalt put pure frankincense upon each row, that it may be on the bread for a memorial, even an offering made by fire unto the Lord. Every sabbath he shall set it in order before the Lord continually, being taken from the children of Israel by an everlasting covenant. And it shall be Aaron's and his sons'; and they shall eat it in the holy place: for it is most holy unto him of the offerings of the Lord made by fire by a perpetual statute*" Leviticus 24: 5-9.

Just as with "light" the word "bread" appears many times throughout the Bible (410 times) and has enormous and manifold significance. When it came to Jesus, we can associate bread with His body, when he offered Himself when He died on the cross, in the Lord's Supper: "*And he took bread, and gave thanks, and brake it, and gave unto them, saying, This is my body which is given for you: this do in remembrance of me*" Luke 22:19. Then there were His claims about being the Bread of Life: "*For the bread of God is he which cometh down from heaven, and giveth life unto the world. Then said they unto him, Lord, evermore give us this bread. And Jesus said unto them, I am the bread of life: he that cometh to me shall never hunger; and he that believeth on me shall never thirst ... I am that bread of life. Your fathers did eat manna in the wilderness, and are dead. This is the bread which cometh down from heaven, that a man may eat thereof, and not die*" John 6:33-35, 48-50.

The Altar of Incense

"*And thou shalt make an altar to burn incense upon: of shittim wood shalt thou make it. A cubit shall be the length thereof, and a cubit the breadth thereof; foursquare shall it be: and two cubits shall be the height thereof: the horns thereof shall be of the same. And thou shalt overlay it with pure gold, the top thereof, and the sides thereof round about, and the horns thereof; and thou shalt make unto it a crown of gold round about. And two golden rings shalt thou make to it under the crown of it, by the two corners thereof, upon the two sides of it shalt thou make it; and they shall be for places for the staves to bear it withal*" Exodus 30:1-4.

We now come to the final item in the Holy Place – the Altar of Incense, significantly placed before the Veil that separated it from the Holy of Holies. Like the Brazen Altar this was a box made from shittim wood but rather than being overlaid with bronze it was overlaid with gold and having on the top a gold rim and horns at each corner. Both morning and evening incense was offered by the priest who took a censer full of burning coals from the Brazen Altar in one hand and specially prepared sweet incense in the other and ignited the incense by sprinkling it over the burning coals (Leviticus 16:12-13). Offering the right incense was crucial as Nadab and Abihu found to their cost, and by the right person as King Uzziah found to his cost. A thick cloud of smoke curled upward filling the Tabernacle, symbolic of Israel's prayers to God. It is a salutary thought and a sacred privilege to be reminded that this was the closest the priest could get to God, other than on the Day of Atonement, but today's believer-priest through Jesus our Great High Priest can go inside the Veil and commune with God, anytime, anywhere.

Once again, we are reminded of the importance of prayer, for us and to God, and on top of sacrifice (justification) and washing (sanctification) there is the important part played by prayer in today's believer-priest relationship with and approach to God: "*And when he had taken the book, the four beasts and four and twenty elders fell down before the Lamb, having every one of them harps, and golden vials full of odours, which are the prayers of saints*" Revelation 5:8.

We might well want to pause and reflect here on the importance of prayer in our dealings with God:

1. Sweet hour of prayer
Sweet hour of prayer
That calls me from a world of care
And bids me at my Father's throne
Make all my wants and wishes known
In seasons of distress and grief
My soul has often found relief
And oft escaped the tempter's snare
By Thy return, sweet hour of prayer

2. Sweet hour of prayer
Sweet hour of prayer
The joys I feel, the bliss I share
Of those whose anxious spirits burn

With strong desires for Thy return

With such I hasten to the place

Where God my Savior shows His face

And gladly take my station there

And wait for Thee, sweet hour of prayer

The Ark of the Covenant

"And they shall make an ark of shittim wood: two cubits and a half shall be the length thereof, and a cubit and a half the breadth thereof, and a cubit and a half the height thereof. And thou shalt overlay it with pure gold, within and without shalt thou overlay it, and shalt make upon it a crown of gold round about. And thou shalt cast four rings of gold for it, and put them in the four corners thereof; and two rings shall be in the one side of it, and two rings in the other side of it" Exodus 25:10-12.

Our final item of furniture is the most important (discussed further in Chapter 44) – the Ark of the Covenant (a box overlaid with gold) along with the Mercy Seat (Atonement Cover) (the lid to the box that was all gold, along with two cherubim that faced each other with wings touching and which formed part of the Mercy Seat), all of which was placed inside the 30 feet by 15 feet Holy of Holies. It was the place where Moses communed with God after the Tabernacle had been built and centuries later where the likes of King Hezekiah prayed toward, since it was there that God dwelt between the two cherubim. As we discuss in Chapter 11, the Mercy Seat was where the High Priest brought the blood of the bull and goat that had been slain on the Day of Atonement and where it was sprinkled.

Inside the Ark of the Covenant were three items. Firstly, there were the replacement tablets on which were written the Ten Commandments. Secondly, there was a pot with manna sent from God to feed the Israelites during their journey in the Wilderness. Thirdly, there was Aaron's rod that budded, proof that God had chosen Aaron to minister before Him and not those who wished to usurp his authority. Above all, the Ark of the Covenant represented the glory of God and His dwelling among men, which was fully realised in Jesus: *"In the beginning was the Word, and the Word was with God, and the Word was God. The same was in the beginning with God. All things were made by him; and without him was not any thing made that was made … And the Word was made flesh, and dwelt among us, (and we beheld his glory, the glory as of the only begotten of the Father,) full of grace and truth"* John 1:1-3, 14.

Chapter 7: The Aaronic Priesthood – An Introduction

" *At Mount Sinai, God designated Aaron and his descendants to serve as priests (Exodus 28:1, 29:44; 30:30; 40:13-15; Numbers 3:3-4). One of the twelve tribes of Israel, Levi, was assigned priestly duties, although not all Levites were priests. Only those designated could perform priestly duties, not other Levites (Numbers 16:1-3; 17:1-10; 18:1-3), not Moses or his descendants (1 Chronicles 23:13). The Levites who served had to be between 30 and 50 years old (Numbers 4:3), unblemished – e.g. not lame (Leviticus 21:16-23), have a proper marriage (Leviticus 21:9, 14) – i.e. not married to a harlot or a divorced woman or a widow other than a priest's widow (Ezekiel 44:22). While the other tribes of Israel were given an inheritance, when it came to dividing up the land, this was not so for the tribe of Levi, for the Lord was their inheritance (Deuteronomy 10:9). The standards of ritual holiness and actual holiness among priests were high, and when two of Aaron's sons offered unauthorized fire before the Lord (Leviticus 10:1), without further ado, God struck them down dead.*

Among the duties of the priests was to teach the people (Leviticus 10:8-11), serve as judges to resolve controversy (Deuteronomy 21:5), offer sacrifices (Exodus 29:38-42), assess impurity (Leviticus 13-15), burn incense (Exodus 30:7-8), bless the people (Numbers 6:22-27), bless God (Deuteronomy 10:8), keep the tabernacle (Numbers 3:38; 4;16), take care of the altar (Leviticus 6:8-13), the lamps, and the showbread (Leviticus 24:1-9), prepare the holy things for each day's journey (Numbers 4:5-15), continue the sacred fire (Leviticus 6:12-13), and blow the trumpets (Numbers 10:1-10). As for the high priest, he was God's leader over the priests. Aaron served as the first high priest (Exodus 40:12-13). Aaron's son, Eleazer, replaced him as high priest when he died (Numbers 20:26-28). The position of high priests continued through the time of Christ (Matthew 26:3) until the destruction of the temple by the Romans in 70 AD. Their duties included: direct the work of the priests and Levites (Numbers 3,4), inquire of the Lord (Judges 20:28), consecrate other priests (Exodus 29:1-37), maintain the golden candlestand with its fire (Leviticus 24:1-4), burn incense daily (Exodus 30:7-8), and offer sacrifices on the Day of Atonement (Hebrews 5:1, Leviticus 16, 23) the one day he could enter the Holy of Holies" quoted from **"Prophets of the Bible"**.

We are still at Mount Sinai and having considered *"Moses, the Law and the Covenant"* (Chapter 4), *"The Tabernacle – An introduction"* (Chapter 5) and *"The Tabernacle – The furniture"* (Chapter 6) we now turn our attention to priests whose main duty, at least at this time in Israel's history, was to carry out various services inside the Tabernacle, doing all the duties required of them concerning which God had instructed Moses. As our quote reminds us, there were other functions that would develop, such as teaching the people that which was clean and unclean and the difference between holy and unholy. In Part 2, we consider the main named priests of the Bible and how they fared in these matters.

When it comes to priests of the Bible, there are several categories, as discussed in "Chapter 13: *Categorising Priests of the Bible*" but in this chapter our focus is on Aaron and his descendants. We are well aware of Aaron, ever since Moses had his "burning bush" encounter with God in Exodus 3 as being in effect Moses' right-hand man from that point on and up to the end of the wilderness journey, playing a significant part (good and sometimes bad) in many of the adventures. As for character and what they did etc., we consider further Aaron and his four sons in Chapters 23, 24 and 25.

Our introduction to the Aaronic priesthood begins "*And take thou unto thee Aaron thy brother, and his sons with him, from among the children of Israel, that he may minister unto me in the priest's office, even Aaron, Nadab and Abihu, Eleazar and Ithamar, Aaron's sons*" Exodus 28:1. What was required of the priests, and particularly concerning their garments, presented in great detail, would be elaborated on in Exodus 28, 29 and 39. The ordination of priests and the start of a priest's ministry is described in Leviticus 8 and 9. The sacredness of what priests were meant to do with respect to God's holiness can be seen in God's judgement over Aaron's sons, Nadab and Abihu, who offered unauthorised fire, in Leviticus 10. Leviticus 8 and 9 details what took place when Aaron and his sons were ordained. Leviticus 21 and 22 gives rules governing priests (all further discussed in Chapter 9).

It should be re-emphasised that it is only after instructions are received regarding the Tabernacle, that we are introduced to the Aaronic priesthood. As we have already discussed, there was a considerable amount of priestly activity prior to then. Nowhere is God's perspective concerning priests more evident than at the beginning of Israel's encampment at Mount Sinai, when God declared: "*Now therefore, if ye will obey my voice indeed, and keep my covenant, then ye shall be a peculiar treasure unto me above all people: for all the earth is mine: And ye shall be unto me a kingdom of priests, and an holy nation. These are the words which thou shalt speak unto the children of Israel*" Exodus 19:5-6.

Whilst it might be rather stretching it to deduce the reason for the Aaronic priesthood was because Israel who God had wanted to be a "*kingdom of priests*" did not obey God's voice and keep His Covenant, it is nevertheless instructive of where the heart of God lay and is a theme picked up in the New Testament (1 Peter 2:9). We pick up on the theme of today's believer-priests in Chapter 41.

But the Tabernacle (where God chose to dwell) and Priests of the line of Aaron (that ministered in the place God chose to dwell) are two of the big ideas that God has put forward in order that He can dwell with His people and His people can enjoy fellowship with Him, just as was the case in the Garden of Eden and will be the case in the new heaven and the new earth. As we have already seen, what the priests had to do was a solemn undertaking as well as an enormous privilege.

The term priest (Hebrew **kohen**) means one who officiates. In the case of Aaron and the priests that followed and officiated in the Tabernacle and later the Temple, they were not or were not meant to be self-appointed or appointed by men but rather they were appointed by God. While having unique access to God in that they could offer sacrifices and attend to the duties that were required in the Holy Place, they were also mortal men and, like those they represented, were subject to the weakness of the flesh. But because of that they were expected to show compassion toward those they served.

As we will see in the next chapter, there were several pre-requisites that needed to be put in place before they were able to serve. Moreover, as we will consider in Chapter 19, all this pointed to Jesus, the Great High Priest and because He was perfect in every way and because He gave His own life as an atoning sacrifice, for US, is able to be the perfect intermediary on behalf of today's believer-priests, who repent of their sins and put their trust in Jesus as their Lord and Saviour.

The importance of priests as leaders of the Israelite community cannot be overstated, not just spiritually as we might expect but in all aspects of Israel's life. When we consider 17 named priests in Part 2, we may well reflect how varied were their duties and contributions, and how well they responded to their sacred calling. The Old Testament ends on a sorry note and it was all too evident that God was no longer revered as He should have been. This is well documented in the last book of the Bible – Malachi, and central to the prophet's (God's) condemnation were the priests.

One often overlooked example of why priests, especially the High Priest, was important, concerns his role as seen in the teachings concerning the Cities of Refuge: *"That the slayer that killeth any person unawares and unwittingly may flee thither: and they shall be your refuge from the avenger of blood. And when he that doth flee unto one of those cities shall stand at the entering of the gate of the city, and shall declare his cause in the ears of the elders of that city, they shall take him into the city unto them, and give him a place, that he may dwell among them. And if the avenger of blood pursue after him, then they shall not deliver the slayer up into his hand; because he smote his neighbour unwittingly, and hated him not beforetime. And he shall dwell in that city, until he stand before the congregation for judgment, and until the death of the high priest that shall be in those days: then shall the slayer return, and come unto his own city, and unto his own house, unto the city from whence he fled"* Joshua 20:3-6. One application could be when it comes to the death of Jesus, the Great High Priest, for as a consequence of the High Priest's death, the person who offended (in this case it is the person who had committed manslaughter) was able to be fully exonerated following his offence.

As Israel were about to enter the 400-year "Silent years" period, where the returning exiles would be oppressed first by the Greeks and then by the Romans, while the worship of false gods that dominated before the Exile were not present, what was present was the opposite to the whole-hearted devotion God had sought from the people, and what was so tragic was that this spiritual malaise was priest led.

"And now, O ye priests, this commandment is for you. If ye will not hear, and if ye will not lay it to heart, to give glory unto my name, saith the Lord of hosts, I will even send a curse upon you, and I will curse your blessings: yea, I have cursed them already, because ye do not lay it to heart. Behold, I will corrupt your seed, and spread dung upon your faces, even the dung of your solemn feasts; and one shall take you away with it. And ye shall know that I have sent this commandment unto you, that my covenant might be with Levi, saith the Lord of hosts. My covenant was with him of life and peace; and I gave them to him for the fear wherewith he feared me, and was afraid before my name. The law of truth was in his mouth, and iniquity was not found in his lips: he walked with me in peace and equity, and did turn many away from iniquity. For the priest's lips should keep knowledge, and they should seek the law at his mouth: for he is the messenger of the Lord of hosts. But ye are departed out of the way; ye have caused many to stumble at the law; ye have corrupted the covenant of Levi, saith the Lord of hosts. Therefore have I also made you contemptible and base before all the people, according as ye have not kept my ways, but have been partial in the law" Malachi 2:1-9.

Two priests we don't include in that 17-priest list in Part 2 are Zechariah and Uriah, one acting out of righteous indignation and holy zeal, in accordance with that same high calling and paying the price, and one too readily succumbing (as all too easy it would have been) to the evil dictates of the one who was ruling at the time, and no doubt thus able to live the easy life. Zechariah had seen that King Joash had turned from worshipping the true God to a false god and publicly called him out for doing so and was killed, on the instructions of the king, in retaliation. King Ahaz, having seen and liked an altar that was dedicated to one of the false gods on his travels, instructed Uriah the priest to build something similar to be placed inside the Temple. All we know is Uriah complied and did so without objecting.

In closing this chapter, we wanted first to draw attention to one of those jumped out of the page verses that comes when one reads the Bible, from one of the Songs of Ascent: "*Let thy priests be clothed with righteousness; and let thy saints shout for joy*" Psalm 132:9. Possibly above everything else, the Aaronic priests were significant, along with their splendid priestly attire, because they were meant to be exemplars of God's righteousness. As for the saints, who would witness all this, their response would be to shout for joy. Secondly, we wanted to end with the priestly blessing – widely used today: "*Speak unto Aaron and unto his sons, saying, On this wise ye shall bless the children of Israel, saying unto them, The Lord bless thee, and keep thee: The Lord make his face shine upon thee, and be gracious unto thee: The Lord lift up his countenance upon thee, and give thee peace*" Numbers 6:23-26.

But by way of an unexpected "extra" and partly because there seemed nowhere else especially suitable to fit these thoughts in, although some are touched on elsewhere, concerns that period covered in the Book of Numbers that begins in Chapter 10, when the Israelites leave Sinai to continue their wilderness journey and ends toward the end of that journey, in Chapter 20, where we read about the deaths of Miriam and Aaron. A lot of what we read concerns the people complaining and rebelling against both God and Moses and invariably ends in some sort of divine reprimand. As interesting and important as these happenings are, we will not dwell on them given we are meant to be focusing on priests.

In Chapter 10, we read about the part played by the silver trumpets as a means of alerting the people (10:1-10) and then how the people set out as a well-marshalled host, including the precise order according to tribal division. The Chapter ends: "*And they departed from the mount of the Lord three days' journey: and the ark of the covenant of the Lord went before them in the three days' journey, to search out a resting place for them. And the cloud of the Lord was upon them by day, when they went out of the camp. And it came to pass, when the ark set forward, that Moses said, Rise up, Lord, and let thine enemies be scattered; and let them that hate thee flee before thee. And when it rested, he said, Return, O Lord, unto the many thousands of Israel*" 10:33-36. In Numbers 33, we read of 42 stages in Israel's journey, when each time they would have followed the pattern we find set out in Chapter 10.

In Chapter 12 we read of Miriam and Aaron opposing Moses, and here we find Aaron exceeding his priestly authority and being rebuked by God (in Miriam's case, she was struck with leprosy). God summons the two at the entrance of the Tabernacle and speaks: "*If there be a prophet among you, I the Lord will make myself known unto him in a vision, and will speak unto him in a dream. My servant Moses is not so, who is faithful in all mine house. With him will I speak mouth to mouth, even apparently, and not in dark speeches; and the similitude of the Lord shall he behold: wherefore then were ye not afraid to speak against my servant Moses? And the anger of the Lord was kindled against them; and he departed"* (12:6-9).

The other occasion in this section when Aaron fell short of what was expected of him as a priest was his complicity, along with Moses, in the striking of the rock incident and how God responded: *"And the Lord spake unto Moses and Aaron, Because ye believed me not, to sanctify me in the eyes of the children of Israel, therefore ye shall not bring this congregation into the land which I have given them. This is the water of Meribah; because the children of Israel strove with the Lord, and he was sanctified in them"* (20:12-13). In this chapter we also read about Aaron's death and the High Priest mantle being passed on to his son, Eleazar: *"And Moses did as the Lord commanded: and they went up into mount Hor in the sight of all the congregation. And Moses stripped Aaron of his garments, and put them upon Eleazar his son; and Aaron died there in the top of the mount: and Moses and Eleazar came down from the mount. And when all the congregation saw that Aaron was dead, they mourned for Aaron thirty days, even all the house of Israel"* (20:27-29).

The other incident, or rather series of incidents, in our Numbers 10-20 survey, concerns Korah (a Levite) and his group of co-conspirators, and the budding of Aaron's staff. The story is a peculiar one and is unlikely to resonate with modern sensibilities, but it is nevertheless important when it comes to one having more understanding of God's ways, including His holy character and the significance of the Aaronic priesthood. We read: *"Now Korah, the son of Izhar, the son of Kohath, the son of Levi, and Dathan and Abiram, the sons of Eliab, and On, the son of Peleth, sons of Reuben, took men: And they rose up before Moses, with certain of the children of Israel, two hundred and fifty princes of the assembly, famous in the congregation, men of renown: And they gathered themselves together against Moses and against Aaron, and said unto them, Ye take too much upon you, seeing all the congregation are holy, every one of them, and the Lord is among them: wherefore then lift ye up yourselves above the congregation of the Lord? And when Moses heard it, he fell upon his face"* (16:1-4).

The culmination of this act of rebellion was each of the 250 were required to stand before the Lord with a censor with fire and burning incense. We read of the ground opening up and swallowing the men alive. But the rebellion did not stop there. We read *"But on the morrow all the congregation of the children of Israel murmured against Moses and against Aaron, saying, Ye have killed the people of the Lord"* (16:41). And yet again, God shows His displeasure by sending a plague that was stopped because of Aaron, for it was with God's authority that He made atonement for the people by burning acceptable incense. *"And Moses said unto Aaron, Take a censer, and put fire therein from off the altar, and put on incense, and go quickly unto the congregation, and make an atonement for them: for there is wrath gone out from the Lord; the plague is begun. And Aaron took as Moses commanded, and ran into the midst of the congregation; and, behold, the plague was begun among the people: and he put on incense, and made an atonement for the people. And he stood between the dead and the living; and the plague was stayed. Now they that died in the plague were fourteen thousand and seven hundred, beside them that died about the matter of Korah. And Aaron returned unto Moses unto the door of the tabernacle of the congregation: and the plague was stayed"* (16:46-50).

Which brings us to the budding of Aaron's staff: *"And the Lord spake unto Moses, saying, Speak unto the children of Israel, and take of every one of them a rod according to the house of their fathers, of all their princes according to the house of their fathers twelve rods: write thou every man's name upon his rod. And thou shalt write Aaron's name upon the rod of Levi: for one rod shall be for the head of the house of their fathers. And thou shalt lay them up in the tabernacle of the congregation before the testimony, where I will meet with you. And it shall come to pass, that the man's rod, whom I shall choose, shall blossom: and I will make to cease from me the murmurings of the children of Israel, whereby they murmur against you. And Moses spake unto the children of Israel, and every one of their princes gave him a rod apiece, for each prince one, according to their fathers' houses, even twelve rods: and the rod of Aaron was among their rods. And Moses laid up the rods before the Lord in the tabernacle of witness. And it came to pass, that on the morrow Moses went into the tabernacle of witness; and, behold, the rod of Aaron for the house of Levi was budded, and brought forth buds, and bloomed blossoms, and yielded almonds"* (17:1-8). This was again proof that God had chosen Aaron to be His priest. His rod would then be placed inside the Ark of the Covenant as a continual reminder.

We end this survey of Numbers 10-20 (and also this chapter) with what God says concerning the duties of priests. This is also about the duties of Levites and how all this ties in with the duties of those Levites who were also priests: *"And the Lord said unto Aaron, Thou and thy sons and thy father's house with thee shall bear the iniquity of the sanctuary: and thou and thy sons with thee shall bear the iniquity of your priesthood. And thy brethren also of the tribe of Levi, the tribe of thy father, bring thou with thee, that they may be joined unto thee, and minister unto thee: but thou and thy sons with thee shall minister before the tabernacle of witness. And they shall keep thy charge, and the charge of all the tabernacle: only they shall not come nigh the vessels of the sanctuary and the altar, that neither they, nor ye also, die. And they shall be joined unto thee, and keep the charge of the tabernacle of the congregation, for all the service of the tabernacle: and a stranger shall not come nigh unto you. And ye shall keep the charge of the sanctuary, and the charge of the altar: that there be no wrath any more upon the children of Israel. And I, behold, I have taken your brethren the Levites from among the children of Israel: to you they are given as a gift for the Lord, to do the service of the tabernacle of the congregation. Therefore thou and thy sons with thee shall keep your priest's office for every thing of the altar, and within the vail; and ye shall serve: I have given your priest's office unto you as a service of gift: and the stranger that cometh nigh shall be put to death"* (18:1-7).

The rest of Numbers 18 is also relevant, as it talks about offerings to priests and Levites, but we will leave it there and move on. But before we do, let us ponder on the ways of God that are past finding out, as this old hymn reminds us. One "mystery" concerns descendants of Korah, who God slew. Of all of the psalms in the Bible, eleven are attributed to the sons of Korah. These beautiful psalms express a spirit of great gratitude and humility to an awesome, mighty God. They express a longing for God and deep devotion. These poetic songs include Psalms 42, 44-49, 84-85, and 87-88.

1. Guide me, O Thou great Jehovah,

Pilgrim through this barren land.

I am weak, but Thou art mighty;

Hold me with Thy powerful hand.

Bread of heaven,

Feed me now and evermore;

Bread of heaven,

Feed me now and evermore.

2. Open now the crystal fountain,

Whence the healing waters flow;

Let the fire and cloudy pillar

Lead me all my journey through.

Strong Deliverer,

Be Thou still my Strength and Shield.

Strong Deliverer,

Be Thou still my Strength and Shield.

3. When I tread the verge of Jordan,
Bid my anxious fears subside;
Death of death, and hell's destruction,
Land me safe on Canaan's side.
Songs of praises, I will ever give to Thee;
Songs of praises, I will ever give to Thee.

[Ending]
Land me safe on Canaan's side
Bid my anxious fears, bid my anxious fears
Land me safe on Canaan's side
Bid my anxious fears, bid my anxious fears, goodbye

Chapter 8: The Aaronic Priesthood – Readiness for Service

Having considered God instructing Moses regarding Aaron and his descendants and their roles as related to the priesthood, we turn our attention to what needed to happen to the priests before taking up their duties, in particular concerning their ordination. But before that we need to consider what they had to wear, for right after calling Aaron and his four sons to serve Him as priests, God gave very specific instructions as to what His requirements and expectations were.

Concerning the priestly garments, Moses was told: "*And thou shalt make holy garments for Aaron thy brother for glory and for beauty. And thou shalt speak unto all that are wise hearted, whom I have filled with the spirit of wisdom, that they may make Aaron's garments to consecrate him, that he may minister unto me in the priest's office*" Exodus 28:2-3. The garments were holy, for they were set apart for use only in the Tabernacle. They were glorious because of exalting the priestly office before the people. They were beautiful because the colours harmonised with the furnishings found inside the Tabernacle, and moreover matched the priestly function of worshipping God in the beauty of holiness.

The rest of Exodus 28 provides in great detail how God instructed Moses on how each item of the High Priest's garment should be. With reference to our Chapter 2, Figure 14 which shows how that garment looked, with each item labelled: "*And these are the garments which they shall make; a breastplate, and an ephod, and a robe, and a broidered coat, a mitre, and a girdle: and they shall make holy garments for Aaron thy brother, and his sons, that he may minister unto me in the priest's office. And they shall take gold, and blue, and purple, and scarlet, and fine linen.*" (28:4-5). As discussed in Chapter 5, all these colours had a profound spiritual significance relating to the purpose of the Tabernacle.

Ephod and its Girdle

"*And they shall make the ephod of gold, of blue, and of purple, of scarlet, and fine twined linen, with cunning work. It shall have the two shoulderpieces thereof joined at the two edges thereof; and so it shall be joined together. And the curious girdle of the ephod, which is upon it, shall be of the same, according to the work thereof; even of gold, of blue, and purple, and scarlet, and fine twined linen*" (28:6-8). "Ephod" denotes a garment of special religious significance and one that we were to come to see as especially relating to the priestly office. There were two pieces, front and back, carefully joined by gold braided straps, clasped together on the shoulders of the priest (28:13-14). The ephod was held close to the body by a girdle, with colours that blended with the ephod.

Onyx Shoulder Pieces

"And thou shalt take two onyx stones, and grave on them the names of the children of Israel: Six of their names on one stone, and the other six names of the rest on the other stone, according to their birth. With the work of an engraver in stone, like the engravings of a signet, shalt thou engrave the two stones with the names of the children of Israel: thou shalt make them to be set in ouches of gold. And thou shalt put the two stones upon the shoulders of the ephod for stones of memorial unto the children of Israel: and Aaron shall bear their names before the Lord upon his two shoulders for a memorial" (28:9-12). These two stones that were laid on the shoulders of the priest powerfully represented what the priest was meant to do. After all, his main duty was to act as an intermediary between the people and God and their names were in effect laid upon his shoulders. There is an obvious application here for believer-priests today when we intercede on behalf of others.

Breastplate *"And thou shalt make the breastplate of judgment with cunning work; after the work of the ephod thou shalt make it; of gold, of blue, and of purple, and of scarlet, and of fine twined linen, shalt thou make it. Foursquare it shall be being doubled; a span shall be the length thereof, and a span shall be the breadth thereof. And thou shalt set in it settings of stones, even four rows of stones: the first row shall be a sardius, a topaz, and a carbuncle: this shall be the first row. And the second row shall be an emerald, a sapphire, and a diamond. And the third row a ligure, an agate, and an amethyst. And the fourth row a beryl, and an onyx, and a jasper: they shall be set in gold in their inclosings. And the stones shall be with the names of the children of Israel, twelve, according to their names, like the engravings of a signet; every one with his name shall they be according to the twelve tribes"* (28:15-21). Verses 22-28 details how the breastplate was to be fastened to the rest of the garments. Like the stones on the High Priest's shoulders, the breastplate held an enormous significance as he went about his regular duties (their names were on his heart as well as his shoulders): *"And Aaron shall bear the names of the children of Israel in the breastplate of judgment upon his heart, when he goeth in unto the holy place, for a memorial before the Lord continually"* (28:29).

Urim and Thummim

"And thou shalt put in the breastplate of judgment the Urim and the Thummim; and they shall be upon Aaron's heart, when he goeth in before the Lord: and Aaron shall bear the judgment of the children of Israel

upon his heart before the Lord continually" (28:30). The Urim (Hebrew: "lights") and the Thummim (Hebrew: "perfections") are elements associated with the breastplate used when making judgement, although we can't say for sure what they looked like and how these were used, although later indications are they continued to be used, e.g., Ezra 2:63. They are a set of two objects used by the High Priest to answer a question or to reveal the will of God.

Robes, Bells and Pomegranates

"*And thou shalt make the robe of the ephod all of blue. And there shall be an hole in the top of it, in the midst thereof: it shall have a binding of woven work round about the hole of it, as it were the hole of an habergeon, that it be not rent. And beneath upon the hem of it thou shalt make pomegranates of blue, and of purple, and of scarlet, round about the hem thereof; and bells of gold between them round about: A golden bell and a pomegranate, a golden bell and a pomegranate, upon the hem of the robe round about. And it shall be upon Aaron to minister: and his sound shall be heard when he goeth in unto the holy place before the Lord, and when he cometh out, that he die not*" (28:31-35). Commentators have suggested spiritual significance behind the alternating bells and pomegranates at the hem of the robe, which might on first sight be a surprising addition to the High Priest's attire. The bell ringing was how the people could follow his movements in the Holy Place. The word "pomegranate" appears three times in the Song of Songs when it was used in the context of love. Pomegranates were a significant feature in the design of Solomon's Temple. As for their significance, different reasons are given including to show fruitfulness, blessing and prosperity.

Golden Crown and Mitre

"*And thou shalt make a plate of pure gold, and grave upon it, like the engravings of a signet, HOLINESS TO THE LORD. And thou shalt put it on a blue lace, that it may be upon the mitre; upon the forefront of the mitre it shall be. And it shall be upon Aaron's forehead, that Aaron may bear the iniquity of the holy things, which the children of Israel shall hallow in all their holy gifts; and it shall be always upon his forehead, that they may be accepted before the Lord. And thou shalt embroider the coat of fine linen, and thou shalt make the mitre of fine linen, and thou shalt make the girdle of needlework*" (28:36-39). The inscribed plate on the forefront of the turban is significant in that those holy things referred to were the gifts the people were to bring and the High Priest was to carry away their sins by virtue of offering atoning sacrifices on their behalf.

Garments of other priests

"*And for Aaron's sons thou shalt make coats, and thou shalt make for them girdles, and bonnets shalt thou make for them, for glory and for beauty*" (28:40). While most of our attention in this chapter has been on the garments to be worn by the High Priest, what the other priests wore was also important and these garments, while a simpler affair, were still meant for glory and beauty. About simplicity, on that one occasion in the year when the High Priest entered the Holy of Holies he did not wear the elaborate garb that has been detailed but his garments were plain and simple, for he was coming into God's presence as a sinner, on behalf of the sinners he represented.

Breeches and Undergarments

"*And thou shalt put them upon Aaron thy brother, and his sons with him; and shalt anoint them, and consecrate them, and sanctify them, that they may minister unto me in the priest's office. And thou shalt make them linen breeches to cover their nakedness; from the loins even unto the thighs they shall reach: And they shall be upon Aaron, and upon his sons, when they come in unto the tabernacle of the congregation, or when they come near unto the altar to minister in the holy place; that they bear not iniquity, and die: it shall be a statute for ever unto him and his seed after him*" (28:41-43). So we finish this chapter on a note that includes "anoint", "consecrate" and "sanctify", all of which were needed to fulfil the priests' office. But so as not to overlook any items, we also read here concerning the priests' undergarments, needed to maintain modesty and decency. While one's underwear would normally be seen to be of interest to the wearer alone, the fact it is carefully specified here tells us that it mattered to God concerning the priest's garments. If there is a wider application, the part of us (our inner self) that no-one sees besides God matters much.

"*And the Lord spake unto Moses, saying, Take Aaron and his sons with him, and the garments, and the anointing oil, and a bullock for the sin offering, and two rams, and a basket of unleavened bread; And gather thou all the congregation together unto the door of the tabernacle of the congregation*" Leviticus 8:1-3.

Having set out in detail the requirements for the priests' garments in Exodus 29, we then read what needed to happen regarding the priests' ordination in Exodus 30. When everything came to be in place, in particular the building of the Tabernacle and what took place inside it, we then read about what actually happened in Leviticus 8 and 9, following descriptions of the various sacrifices that were to take place, as detailed in Chapter 9, precisely implementing what had been set out in Exodus 28 and 29.

It was to be a public event such that all the congregation would be able to witness what went on. It involved a number of different stages, each one of which could lend itself to a spiritual application, given that today's followers of Jesus are also believer-priests and need to be made ready for service. We will refer to each of the appropriate sections of Leviticus 8 and 9, in describing the different stages. We begin with Moses addressing the assembly: *"And Moses did as the Lord commanded him; and the assembly was gathered together unto the door of the tabernacle of the congregation. And Moses said unto the congregation, This is the thing which the Lord commanded to be done"* (8:4-5).

Cleansed for service (8:6) This involved Moses giving the priests a full body wash, thus depicting the need for them to be cleansed in order to be fit to serve. Thereafter, priests washed themselves, but only their hands and feet, as part of their daily routine when serving in the Tabernacle.

Clothed for service (8:7-9) This involved Moses clothing Aaron with the garments that we have already described.

Anointed for service (8:10-13) This involved Moses in applying a specially prepared concoction that was for the exclusive use of priests inside the Tabernacle to pour on the Altar and then over Aaron's head (followed by dressing the other priests). The need to anoint is a recurring theme throughout the Bible as it is for today's believer-priests, with oil often representing the Holy Spirit. We do well to recognise that we can only satisfactorily serve God through the power of His Holy Spirit, rather than our own. The anointing oil would also have been of a sweet-smelling fragrance, as should be our own lives. We note later on an intriguing oil related reference: *"Behold, how good and how pleasant it is for brethren to dwell together in unity! It is like the precious ointment upon the head, that ran down upon the beard, even Aaron's beard: that went down to the skirts of his garments"* Psalm 133:1-2. The author recalls as a young Christian the matter of "haves" and "have nots" in terms of Christians being baptised in or filled with the Holy Spirit was a divisive one. While discussing the points of view of opposing parties may be an interesting one, it is not one for this book, other than to make the point that serving God in the power of the Holy Spirit is an important and necessary factor for us as believer-priests.

Sin offering (8:14-17) This involved the sacrifice of a bull, and this was about dealing with guilt, as we discuss in (our) Chapter 9.

Burnt offering (8:18-21) This involved the sacrifice of a ram, and was about showing gratitude and giving of ourselves to God, as (once again) we discuss in (our) Chapter 9.

Ordination offering (8:22-32) This offering involved sacrificing another ram and was specifically to do with the priests' ordinations. It had many facets and involved applying blood, mingled with anointing oil, to different parts of the priests' bodies, all pointing to the need of both the blood and the Spirit.

Repeat of offerings (8:33-36) The three offerings (above) were to be repeated each day for seven days, during which time Aaron and his sons were required to remain inside the Tabernacle.

Priests begin their ministry (9:1-21) Having been ordained, the priests were now deemed ready to serve and it was the start of carrying out business as usual, which is what followed. Making a morning and evening burnt offering would henceforth be carried out every day.

Ordination completed "*And Aaron lifted up his hand toward the people, and blessed them, and came down from offering of the sin offering, and the burnt offering, and peace offerings. And Moses and Aaron went into the tabernacle of the congregation, and came out, and blessed the people: and the glory of the Lord appeared unto all the people. And there came a fire out from before the Lord, and consumed upon the altar the burnt offering and the fat: which when all the people saw, they shouted, and fell on their faces*" Leviticus 9:22-24.

This process of consecrating Aaron and his sons so that they could serve as priests went as God had intended and having carried out all the above it was near the end. But there were still some awesome happenings, albeit not necessarily part of the script. We read how Moses and Aaron blessed the people and the glory of the Lord appeared for the people to see. Then there was fire sent from the Lord to consume the burnt offering that was on the altar, followed by people falling on their faces in awe.

But that was not the end of the story of consecrating the first priests, although perhaps it should have been. While life for the priests was able to proceed in doing all those things that needed to take place in the Tabernacle, as detailed between Exodus 25 and Leviticus 8, as they took on their duties, we read of an incident that would have shaken many, especially since it involved Aaron's two eldest sons: "*And Nadab and Abihu, the sons of Aaron, took either of them his censer, and put fire therein, and put incense thereon, and offered strange fire before the Lord, which he commanded them not. And there went out fire from the Lord, and devoured them, and they died before the Lord*" Leviticus 10:1-2. We can make of it what we will when making any connection, but one thing is clear – the consecration of the priests was long and drawn out and appeared to have taken place successfully, but what followed soon after was disobedience, with Nadab and Abihu paying a terrible price as a result of their folly.

We could end our chapter here as we have got down to the details when it comes to "making ready for service", but there is more to come when we consider conduct in service, for priests were to be, as we have already seen, exemplars when it came to showing God's holiness. The way in which they conducted themselves, as seen in the Nadab and Abihu incident, was important and is a salutary reminder that it is one thing to follow faithfully all that was needed in the ordination process but another to live in accordance with all that this represented. Leviticus 21 and 22, which we might title "*Holiness and the Priests*" considers some of these aspects, even though a lot of what we find set out here is unlikely to resonate with modern culture and sensibilities.

Rather than attempting the impossible and try to apply some of these strange impositions and restrictions, we summarise what these were, and leave it for readers to make of it what they will.

- Keep away from dead bodies that are not of close family (21:1-4, 11).
- No trimming beards, or tattoos (21:5-6).
- Don't marry an immoral woman or divorcee (21:7-8).
- The immoral daughter of a priest is to be killed (21:9).
- Not to be unkempt or to tear hair or clothes e.g., in order to mourn (21:10).
- Wife to be a virgin from his own people (21:13-15).
- Cannot have physical blemishes (21:17-23).
- Separate from and treat with respect the holy things of the people (22:2-3).
- Be without disease e.g., leprosy, gonorrhoea (22:4-6).
- Cannot touch anything unclean (22:5-7).
- Eat only food deemed to be holy (22:8-9).
- Not to allow food deemed holy to be eaten outside his family (22:10-16).
- Make only acceptable offerings (22:17-30).

One lesson we can take away is that we, who are believer-priests, just like the Aaronic priests, are called to a life of holiness, not so that we can impress others but rather as part of our devotion to God, taking heed of the exhortation: "*walk worthy of the vocation wherewith ye are called, with all lowliness and meekness, with longsuffering, forbearing one another in love*" Ephesians 4:1-2.

We end this section with the Lord's instruction to Moses, as particularly applying to priests: "*Therefore shall ye keep my commandments, and do them: I am the Lord. Neither shall ye profane my holy name; but I will be hallowed among the children of Israel: I am the Lord which hallow you, That brought you out of the land of Egypt, to be your God: I am the Lord*" Leviticus 22:31-33.

*1. Take my life and let it be
consecrated, Lord, to thee.
Take my moments and my days;
let them flow in ceaseless praise.*

*2. Take my hands and let them move
at the impulse of thy love.
Take my feet and let them be
swift and beautiful for thee.*

*3. Take my voice and let me sing
always, only, for my King.
Take my lips and let them be
filled with messages from thee,*

*4. Take my silver and my gold;
not a mite would I withhold.
Take my intellect and use
every power as thou shalt choose.*

*5. Take my will and make it thine;
it shall be no longer mine.
Take my heart it is thine own;
it shall be thy royal throne.*

*6. Take my love; my Lord, I pour
at thy feet its treasure store.
Take myself, and I will be
ever, only, all for thee.*

Chapter 9: Sacrifices and Offerings to YHWH

There can be little argument that as far as the Old Testament is concerned, sacrifices to YHWH were a big deal and were mandated, according to a prescribed criterion, typically when there had been sin, as well as those that were free will offerings. Following the setting up of the Aaronic priesthood and while there was a Tabernacle or Temple, offering sacrifices on behalf of the people was one of the principal activities of the priests, and while we read of exceptions, for example Manoah, Samson's father, offered a burnt offering to the Lord (Judges 13), and also Samuel, it was something priests did.

Sacrifices and offerings, terms that appeared to be used synonymously were typically animals. Five types were identified: bulls, goats, lambs, turtle doves and pigeons, and in some cases those making the offering could choose which animal they offered, according to their means, and it could involve agricultural produce in the case of the grain offering. We read, for example, how Mary and Joseph, following the birth of Jesus, offered two turtledoves at the Temple in Jerusalem, in Luke 2:21-24.

When we come to later in the New Testament, such sacrifices were no longer required. This is because Jesus is the ultimate sacrifice as discussed in "Chapter 19: Jesus our Great High Priest" and "Chapter 55: Hebrews – the New Testament Book about Priests". As for followers of Jesus, they were expected to offer themselves up as living sacrifices (Romans 12:1) to God, to offer sacrifices of praise (Hebrews 13:15) and as a holy priesthood they were to offer spiritual sacrifices (1 Peter 2:5).

Sacrifice/Offering	Significance	References
Burnt	Gratitude – Surrender	Leviticus: 1; 6:8-13,
Meat (Meal, Grain)*	Gratitude – Service	Leviticus: 2; 6:14-23
Peace (Fellowship, Thanksgiving)*	Gratitude – Serenity	Leviticus: 3; 7:11-21
Sin	Guilt – Substitute	Leviticus: 4:1-5:13; 6:24-30
Trespass (Guilt, Reparation)*	Guilt – Satisfaction	Leviticus: 5:14-6:7; 7:1-6

We refer to the offerings by the names given in the KJV, noting the offerings may be referred to by different names in other Bible versions.

There are the five sacrifices/offerings which are described in Leviticus chapters 1 to 7, which is followed by discussion on "Eating Fat and Blood Forbidden" (7:22-27) and "The Priests' Share" (7:28-38), before attention is turned to the consecration of priests in chapters 8 and 9, during which there is the presenting of a sin offering (8:14-17) and a burnt offering (8:18-21), which was discussed earlier, in "Chapter 8: The Aaronic Priesthood – Readiness for Service".

Before we discuss these five sacrifices/offerings, let us consider general principles behind sacrifices and offerings and what went on before Moses received these instructions from the Lord, further to the setting up of the Tabernacle in the Wilderness. For that we need to go back right to the beginning, when God created the heavens and the earth, and Adam, followed by Eve, were installed in the Garden of Eden, where they were able to enjoy a harmonious relationship with God.

Up to the point when they ate of the forbidden fruit, just as no priestly intermediary was needed between Adam and God, given there was perfect fellowship, neither were sacrifices. Sacrifices with the assistance of a priest came some 2600 years later for the godly line through Seth, Shem and Abraham, and any sacrifice that was made before that would have been without priest involvement. We get a hint of sacrifices beginning to happen when, prior to being expelled from Eden, following their sin of eating the forbidden fruit, God clothed Adam and Eve with animal skins (Genesis 3:21).

As for explicit references to offerings and sacrifices, the first we read of concerns those offered by Cain and Abel, when we read: "*Cain brought of the fruit of the ground an offering unto the Lord. And Abel, he also brought of the firstlings of his flock and of the fat thereof. And the Lord had respect unto Abel and to his offering: But unto Cain and to his offering he had not respect*" Genesis 4:3-5.

Before Moses, we read of Noah, Abraham, Isaac, Jacob and Job (and his three comforters) making offerings to the Lord, usually coinciding with significant events in their lives. We read the first thing Noah did when he stepped out of the Ark as the flood subsided: "*Noah builded an altar unto the Lord; and took of every clean beast, and of every clean fowl, and offered burnt offerings on the altar. And the Lord smelled a sweet savour; and the Lord said in his heart, I will not again curse the ground any more for man's sake; for the imagination of man's heart is evil from his youth; neither will I again smite any more every thing living, as I have done. While the earth remaineth, seedtime and harvest, and cold and heat, and summer and winter, and day and night shall not cease*" Genesis 8:20-22.

Another example of a significant event was in Abraham's life when a sacrifice was made following God reaffirming His Covenant, in Genesis 15.

We do not read of sacrifices being made while Israel was in Egypt prior to Moses. Before we come to the specific instructions given to Moses concerning the offerings in Leviticus, we read of occasions in the time of Moses when sacrifices were offered, notably in the killing of the Passover Lamb and applying the blood to doorposts and when the Israelites were encamped around Mount Sinai, sacrifices were made.

It is worth noting that offerings and sacrifices were a feature of most religions, and not just with the descendants of Abraham. The main reason for doing so was to gain the favour of their deity, notably in times of calamity or when the help of that god was wanted. Sometimes it even involved human sacrifice, a practice that even Israel and Judah in their apostasy had sometimes succumbed to. The only time a human sacrifice was sanctioned by God was when He tested Abraham and told him to offer up his son, Isaac, but was given a last-minute reprieve.

When it comes to sacrifices and offerings to YHWH, as we will see, this covers making atonement for one's sins and it was also a way of thanking Him for all that He had done and as a means of enjoying fellowship with Him. At the end of Exodus, after the Tabernacle was ready to be used, we find that the glory of the Lord had come down and no-one was able to enter in until, at the start of Leviticus, God calls Moses from inside the Tabernacle. The first thing God instructed Moses concerning was to do with offerings, indicative of their central role in Tabernacle worship.

While offering sacrifices was done according to a prescribed pattern, it is worth noting the attitude of the offerer was as, if not more, important than following all the requirements God specified. In David's Psalm of penitence, we read: *"For thou desirest not sacrifice; else would I give it: thou delightest not in burnt offering. The sacrifices of God are a broken spirit: a broken and a contrite heart, O God, thou wilt not despise"* Psalm 51:16-17. It is salutary to note Samuel's words to King Saul: *"Hath the Lord as great delight in burnt offerings and sacrifices, as in obeying the voice of the Lord? Behold, to obey is better than sacrifice, and to hearken than the fat of rams"* 1 Samuel 15:22. Such sentiments are expressed by the prophets, e.g., *"To what purpose is the multitude of your sacrifices unto me? saith the Lord: I am full of the burnt offerings of rams, and the fat of fed beasts; and I delight not in the blood of bullocks, or of lambs, or of he goats"* Isaiah 1:11.

We now consider each offering God commanded Moses, mindful of the depth and significance of every detail, concerning which it is unlikely we can do it full justice. While we read of other types of offerings, such as when ordaining the priests, these are the main ones and these are frequently referred to throughout the Bible, notably on feast days, and also on other special occasions.

The Burnt Offering

"And the Lord called unto Moses, and spake unto him out of the tabernacle of the congregation, saying, Speak unto the children of Israel, and say unto them, If any man of you bring an offering unto the Lord, ye shall bring your offering of the cattle, even of the herd, and of the flock. If his offering be a burnt sacrifice of the herd, let him offer a male without blemish: he shall offer it of his own voluntary will at the door of the tabernacle of the congregation before the Lord. And he shall put his hand upon the head of the burnt offering; and it shall be accepted for him to make atonement for him. And he shall kill the bullock before the Lord: and the priests, Aaron's sons, shall bring the blood, and sprinkle the blood round about upon the altar that is by the door of the tabernacle of the congregation" Leviticus 1:1-5.

It is likely that the Burnt Offering was the most common of all the offerings that had been made before these words were spoken and also after. There was no compulsion behind making this offering and it was to be burnt whole and as a sweet-smelling aroma to the Lord. While the carrying out of the sacrifice as with the other offerings was to be done by the priest, the person making the offering would lay his hand on the animal before it was killed by way of identifying with the sacrifice. It is an example of an offering when any of the animals mentioned earlier could be offered, and it was, just as with the animals in the other offerings, to be without blemish (a criticism in Malachi's day was this was not done) and with suitable preparation, including the washing and arrangement of body parts.

Also significant was the priest taking off his garments and putting on other garments and carrying the ashes outside the camp to a clean place after the animal had been completely burnt. Concerning the fire on the altar, it needed to be kept burning and was not to go out, suggesting when it came to burnt offerings the life of whoever was to present the offering needed to be fully surrendered to God irrespective of the time, season and circumstance. It should be noted that the priests were to perpetually offer burnt offerings both at the start and at the end of the day.

The Meat (Meal, Grain) Offering

"And when any will offer a meat offering unto the Lord, his offering shall be of fine flour; and he shall pour oil upon it, and put frankincense thereon: And he shall bring it to Aaron's sons the priests: and he shall take thereout his handful of the flour thereof, and of the oil thereof, with all the frankincense thereof; and the priest shall burn the memorial of it upon the altar, to be an offering made by fire, of a sweet savour unto the Lord: And the remnant of the meat offering shall be Aaron's and his sons': it is a thing most holy of the offerings of the Lord made by fire" Leviticus 2:1-3.

When it comes to word usage, in particular in giving a title to convey what this offering is for, the KJV use of meat is somewhat confusing as unlike the four other offerings no meat was involved. A better word is meal (Hebrew: **minchah** – meaning gift), and in the usage here it was in the context of a response by the Israelites by way of thanksgiving to God for His love and goodness toward them. The NIV and ESV translate the word used as "grain", which was the central feature of the cocktail of ingredients which were offered, and is the word we will use here as it is one that may be least likely to create confusion among readers when it comes to distinguishing between the different offerings.

As with all the offerings there is a lot of detail given and along with that a lot of spiritual significance – much of which we will not do justice to in this brief summary. As with the burnt offering and the peace offering that follows it was to be burnt as a sweet-smelling savour to the Lord and was offered freely, and this offering was one that the offerers, and in particular Aaron and his family, could partake of as only a part was to be an offering to the Lord made by fire. There appear to be three types of grain offerings. Firstly, there is the offering of fine flour with oil and frankincense put on it. Secondly, there is the offering of cakes of fine flour unleavened, mingled with oil, baked in a pan. Thirdly, there was the offering of the first fruits of green ears of corn dried by the fire served with oil, frankincense and salt, all of which were symbolic of the sort of relationship the people were meant to have with God, with salt symbolic of the Covenant. It was also an offering the priests made daily.

The Peace (Fellowship) Offering

"And if his oblation be a sacrifice of peace offering, if he offer it of the herd; whether it be a male or female, he shall offer it without blemish before the Lord. And he shall lay his hand upon the head of his offering, and kill it at the door of the tabernacle of the congregation: and Aaron's sons the priests shall sprinkle the blood upon the altar round about" Leviticus 3:1-2.

When the offerer makes this offering, he first lays hands on the animal to be sacrificed, by way of identification and then it is slaughtered at the entrance to the tent of meeting. The priest then sprinkles the blood around the altar and carefully lays the kidney and liver along with the fat of the animal to be burnt on the altar. This offering is made as an expression of thankfulness, along with thick loaves made without yeast and brushed with oil. What is not burnt is divided between the priest and his family and the offerer, along with his family and associates, who as it were enjoy a meal with God. They were not to eat any of the fat or any blood. The peace offering is also made in fulfilment of vows, e.g., the vow of the Nazirite. The food needed to be consumed within a given time period.

The Sin Offering

"And the Lord spake unto Moses, saying, Speak unto the children of Israel, saying, If a soul shall sin through ignorance against any of the commandments of the Lord concerning things which ought not to be done, and shall do against any of them: If the priest that is anointed do sin according to the sin of the people; then let him bring for his sin, which he hath sinned, a young bullock without blemish unto the Lord for a sin offering" Leviticus 4:1-3.

Having considered three offerings made by way of gratitude, we turn to the remaining two that were made because of guilt due to sin. We often find in our reading of the Old Testament that more than one type of sacrifice was offered and it was important to deal with guilt before showing gratitude. Unlike the "gratitude" offerings, the "guilt" offerings were not offered as a sweet-smelling savour. Firstly, we consider the sin offering. Here it is clear it was for sin due to ignorance, i.e., unintentional, begging the question, as well we know, that often when we sin it is anything but unintentional.

A number of offerer groups were identified: priests, whole communities, leaders of communities and individuals and slightly different instructions were given in each case, starting with the type of animals that could be offered. The one presenting the offering needed first to place his hands on the head of the animal being offered as a way of identifying with the sin that the animal was taking upon itself. In all cases blood was applied to the horns of the altar and what was left poured out at the base of the altar. In the first two cases blood was also sprinkled inside the Tent of Meeting and the part of the bull (in this case) that was not burnt on the altar was burnt outside the camp. The purpose of the offerings was to make atonement for sin. A number of scenarios where making such offerings was required were identified. Regarding individuals, a number of alternatives were given for choice of animals, and for the very poor this could be as modest as a tenth of an ephah of fine flour.

The Trespass Offering

"And the Lord spake unto Moses, saying, If a soul commit a trespass, and sin through ignorance, in the holy things of the Lord; then he shall bring for his trespass unto the Lord a ram without blemish out of the flocks, with thy estimation by shekels of silver, after the shekel of the sanctuary, for a trespass offering. And he shall make amends for the harm that he hath done in the holy thing, and shall add the fifth part thereto, and give it unto the priest: and the priest shall make an atonement for him with the ram of the trespass offering, and it shall be forgiven him" Leviticus 5:14-16.

There is much in common between the Sin and Trespass offerings. Both were made as a result of guilt on the part of the offerer in order to receive atonement. A number of different scenarios were given, when it comes to sinning against God and man (which also in effect was a sin against God). But there was one further significant aspect when it came to the Trespass offering. The one who was guilty needed to make restitution to the one he sinned against. It is a salutary reminder for those who are under the New Covenant that while we know that *"If we confess our sins, he is faithful and just to forgive us our sins, and to cleanse us from all unrighteousness"* 1 John 1:9, if we are truly penitent and, if applicable and we are in a position to do so, then we need to make restitution to those we wrong.

In Conclusion

From a Gentile Christian perspective, especially for those not well versed in the Hebrew Scriptures, one might be tempted to see "Sacrifices and Offerings to YHWH", like much else that concerned the Aaronic priests, as nigh irrelevant, especially if (rightly) taking the view that, when Jesus died for our sins as a willing, atoning sacrifice, He did all that was needed in order for us to be reconciled with a holy God. Before Christ, such may have, at best, seemed to be a remote prospect and how one might become right with God was a crucial question that needed to be answered. The sacrificial system, especially the five offerings discussed in the first seven chapters of Leviticus, was God's answer and pointed to what was later to come about through the only begotten Son of God.

For today's believer-priests, not beholden to follow the Mosaic Law, the matter of making offerings and sacrifices as laid out in that law is not something that should concern the way we conduct ourselves. But making offerings to the Lord should be, about which much could be said. All we will do here is pass on as a timely reminder what God requires of us: *"I beseech you therefore, brethren, by the mercies of God, that ye present your bodies a living sacrifice, holy, acceptable unto God, which is your reasonable service"* Romans 12:1 and *"Ye also, as lively stones, are built up a spiritual house, an holy priesthood, to offer up spiritual sacrifices, acceptable to God by Jesus Christ"* 1 Peter 2:5.

Moreover, this sacrificial system highlighted two important truths: having a right relationship with God (which was always God's desire) and, before that, the need to deal with sin in the light of scriptures like *"the soul that sinneth, it shall die"* Ezekiel 18:20, 23, *"for all have sinned, and come short of the glory of God"* Romans 3:23 and *"the wages of sin is death"* Romans 6:23, concerning which we have a remedy given Jesus was and is the perfect and all-sufficient sacrifice: *"Christ died for our sins according to the scriptures"* 1 Corinthians 15:3 and *"This is a faithful saying, and worthy of all acceptation, that Christ Jesus came into the world to save sinners; of whom*

I am chief" 1 Timothy 1:15. Rather than theologise further on such matters, which we will do later, we might do well to reflect on the words of the old hymn, that tells us a lot concerning what we need to know:

1. No blood, no altar now,
The sacrifice is o'er!
No flame, no smoke ascends on high,
The lamb is slain no more,
But richer blood has flow'd from nobler veins,
To purge the soul from guilt, and cleanse the reddest stains.

2. We thank Thee for the blood,
The blood of Christ, Thy Son:
The blood by which our peace is made,
Our victory is won:
Great victory o'er hell, and sin, and woe,
That needs no second fight, and leaves no second foe.

3. We thank Thee for the grace,
Descending from above,
That overflows our widest guilt,
Th'eternal Father's love.
Love of the Father's everlasting Son,
Love of the Holy Ghost, Jehovah, Three in One.

4. We thank Thee for the hope,
So glad, and sure, and clear;
It holds the drooping spirit up
Till the long dawn appear;
Fair hope! with what a sunshine does it cheer
Our roughest path on earth, our dreariest desert here.

5. We thank Thee for the crown
Of glory and of life;
'Tis no poor with'ring wreath of earth,
Man's prize in mortal strife;
'Tis incorruptible as is the throne,
The kingdom of our God and His incarnate Son.

Chapter 10: The Feasts of YHWH

"And the Lord spake unto Moses, saying, Speak unto the children of Israel, and say unto them, Concerning the feasts of the Lord, which ye shall proclaim to be holy convocations, even these are my feasts" Leviticus 23:1-2.

FEAST	REFERENCE	DATE	PROPHETIC SIGNIFICANCE
Sabbath	Leviticus 23:3	7th day of every week	God's people at rest
Feast of Passover	Leviticus 23:4-11	1st month, 14th day	Jesus dies for sinners
Feast of Unleavened Bread	Leviticus 23:4-11	1st month, 15th - 21st day	Jesus is buried
Feast of First Fruits	Leviticus 23:11-14	1st month, day after Sabbath	Jesus is resurrected
Feast of Pentecost	Leviticus 23:15-22	50 days after First Fruits	Holy Spirit is given
Feast of Trumpets	Leviticus 23:23-25	7th month, 1st day	Jesus comes back
Day of Atonement	Leviticus 23:26-32	7th month, 10th day	Jesus judges sin Israel turns to Jesus
Feast of Tabernacles	Leviticus 23:33-44	7th month, 15th - 21st day	Jesus reigns on earth Gentiles worship God

In this chapter we will concentrate on Leviticus 23 and what it has to say concerning the seven Feasts of YHWH (eight if you include the Sabbath) that God ordained to be "holy convocations" (as opposed to holidays as typically understood today as times of relaxation and leisure) for the Children of Israel. We will consider for each of the feasts, when they took place, what was required and took place on each occasion, the part played by priests, where the Feasts are mentioned outside the Torah and the prophetic aspects of each feast, trying to maintain a healthy balance between spiritualising every tiny aspect of each feast and ignoring spiritual aspects altogether, as many do.

For each feast, an offering was required, or more than one type of offering in some cases, including some that did not involve blood sacrifice. Other than what was offered on the Day of Atonement these are the same offerings as detailed in Leviticus 1-7 and discussed in Chapter 9. Given it was the priest who made these offerings, this shows why the part played by priests during these feasts was significant. We later read: "*Three times in a year shall all thy males appear before the Lord thy God in the place which he shall choose; in the feast of unleavened bread, and in the feast of weeks, and in the feast of tabernacles: and they shall not appear before the Lord empty*" Deuteronomy 16:16. Given "*the place*" would become the Temple in Jerusalem, where the priests operated, it is easy to see how the priests would play an important role. Given the dates of the other four feasts, it is likely when the men made that pilgrimage, they would have celebrated these other feasts too.

Those "three times" represented the time of the barley harvest (Unleavened Bread – Spring), wheat harvest (Weeks – Spring) and fruit harvest (Tabernacles – Autumn) respectively, illustrating the importance of remembering God's provision at harvest time. Prophetically, we will argue the Spring feasts (Passover, Unleavened Bread, First Fruits, Pentecost) looked forward to Jesus' first coming (death, burial, resurrection, coming of the Holy Spirit) and the Autumn feasts (Trumpets, Day of Atonement, Tabernacles) looked forward to Jesus' second coming (announcing His return, Israel seeing their crucified Messiah and weeping, Jesus dwelling with Israel during the Millennium).

It should be noted that the months in which the Jewish feasts fell are based on the lunar calendar rather than the solar calendar we use today. It means the actual days the feasts fall on, by today's reckoning, will be different each year. It is further noted that in addition to the Seven Feasts of YHWH there are other feasts Jews today celebrate, notably Purim and Hanukkah, which we will discuss at the end of the chapter. Given there is now no longer a temple or priests, it follows there are no longer sacrifices but what was practised in Old Testament times has been replaced by a quite different set of traditions and just as the Christian feasts, e.g., Christmas and Easter, are celebrated quite differently, often having little or nothing to do with Christianity, the same could be said for the Jewish feast celebrations having little or nothing to with Judaism. While outside the scope of this book, in current Judaism the Talmud, which is the central text of Rabbinic Judaism as laid out by Jewish Rabbis over a long period, is the primary source of Jewish religious law (*halakha*) and Jewish theology, and often deferred to more than the Torah. As interesting as a study on how Jews today celebrate the feasts might be, this is outside the author's experience and the scope of this book.

The Sabbath (23:3)

"*Six days shall work be done: but the seventh day is the sabbath of rest, an holy convocation; ye shall do no work therein: it is the sabbath of the Lord in all your dwellings*".

While we can trace the Sabbath back to the time of creation, when we read "*Thus the heavens and the earth were finished, and all the host of them. And on the seventh day God ended his work which he had made; and he rested on the seventh day from all his work which he had made*" Genesis 2:1-2, we cannot find it being mandated on people until the Israelites got to Sinai in Exodus 19, and when it was one of the Ten Commandments to: "*Remember the sabbath day, to keep it holy*" Exodus 20:8. There are other sabbaths too, notably the seventh year one when the land was given a rest from growing crops. Moreover, after seven times seven years, there would be a year of Jubilee when people would be freed from debts and if indebted in any way given their freedom. Back to the Sabbath, the importance of observing God's command and consequences of non-observance is illustrated in Numbers 15:32-36 when we learn that a young man was stoned for gathering sticks on the Sabbath.

We might reflect on how Sabbath observance in earlier Old Testament times compares with attitudes to be found in contemporary Christianity. Notably, Jesus and the first Christians (all Jews) observed the Sabbath but not with the extra rules imposed by the religious leaders of the time. Most Christians today do not do anything differently on the Sabbath (seventh) day to that on other days (other than often seeing it as part of a weekend break). Many do things differently on the Sunday (first) day, with some even referring to it as the Lord's Day, when no work is done and time given to attending Christian services and reflection. There is considerable variance, including a lackadaisical attitude by many. There may be a biblical mandate for Gentile believers not observing the Sabbath in the same way as their Hebrew brethren, but there is none for substituting Sunday for Saturday as a special day, which was done at the behest of church authorities after the New Testament period.

The Bible talks about a "sabbath rest". With reference to "*Forty years long was I grieved with this generation, and said, It is a people that do err in their heart, and they have not known my ways: Unto whom I sware in my wrath that they should not enter into my rest*" Psalm 95:10-11, we read: "*Let us therefore fear, lest, a promise being left us of entering into his rest, any of you should seem to come short of it. For unto us was the gospel preached, as well as unto them: but the word preached did not profit them, not being mixed with faith in them that heard it. For we which have believed do enter into rest, as he said, As I have sworn in my wrath, if they shall enter into my rest: although the works were finished from the foundation of the world. For he spake in a certain place of the seventh day on this wise, And God did rest the seventh day from all his works. And in this place again, If they shall enter into my rest. Seeing therefore it remaineth that some must enter therein, and they to whom it was first preached entered not in because of unbelief: Again, he limiteth a certain day, saying in David, Today, after so long a time; as it is said, Today if ye will hear his voice, harden not your hearts. For if Jesus had given them rest, then would he not afterward have spoken of another day. There remaineth therefore a rest to the people of God. For he that is entered into his rest, he also hath ceased from his own works, as God did from his. Let us labour therefore to enter into that rest, lest any man fall after the same example of unbelief"* Hebrews 4:1-11.

Before we turn our attention to the Seven Feasts of YHWH, we might reflect on some underlying principles concerning the Sabbath, some of which apply to these various feasts, particularly the importance of recognising that we follow a holy God who also wishes to bless us. In this day of the rich and powerful exploiting the poor and disempowered, and a world that is anything but being at rest, God's solution is better than Marxist or other alternatives, and comes with a blessing: *"Only if thou carefully hearken unto the voice of the Lord thy God, to observe to do all these commandments which I command thee this day. For the Lord thy God blesseth thee, as he promised thee: and thou shalt lend unto many nations, but thou shalt not borrow; and thou shalt reign over many nations, but they shall not reign over thee. If there be among you a poor man of one of thy brethren within any of thy gates in thy land which the Lord thy God giveth thee, thou shalt not harden thine heart, nor shut thine hand from thy poor brother: But thou shalt open thine hand wide unto him, and shalt surely lend him sufficient for his need, in that which he wanteth"* Deuteronomy 15:5-8.

As for entering into the rest, whatever that is, part of the Christian hope is reflecting on what the Sabbath foreshadows and can be further seen in the Millennial reign of Christ and their final state.

The Passover and the Feast of Unleavened Bread (23:4-8)

"These are the feasts of the Lord, even holy convocations, which ye shall proclaim in their seasons. In the fourteenth day of the first month at even is the Lord's passover. And on the fifteenth day of the same month is the feast of unleavened bread unto the Lord: seven days ye must eat unleavened bread. In the first day ye shall have an holy convocation: ye shall do no servile work therein. But ye shall offer an offering made by fire unto the Lord seven days: in the seventh day is an holy convocation: ye shall do no servile work therein".

Of all the feast of YHWH, the Passover is the one that many Christians particularly identify with, because it was when Jesus celebrated it with His disciples that he instituted the Lord's Supper (Communion) that Christians ever since and across all denominational strands have celebrated.

The first Passover coincided with the tenth and final plague of Egypt, after which Pharoah let the Israelites go in order to journey into the Wilderness and eventually possess the land that God had promised to Abraham. It was a terrible occasion when the firstborn son of every Egyptian family and of every animal was slain by God and the Israelites were only spared because they had sacrificed a (Passover) lamb and applied the blood to the side posts and upper door posts of their houses.

We are given a full account of what was required in Exodus 12, when we read: *"And the Lord spake unto Moses and Aaron in the land of Egypt saying, This month shall be unto you the beginning of months: it shall be the first month of the year to you"* (12:1-2). While Jews today equate their new year *Rosh Hashanah* with the Feast of Trumpets, it is at Passover time that the new year truly begins because of its enormous significance in the life of the nation and was its major turning point.

While this author has tried not to give too many personal anecdotes, he hopes readers with bear with him for sharing this one ... The building that the church fellowship he was associated with for much of his life had little of the religious paraphernalia that typically went along with many places of worship. The exception was texts embedded into the walls. At the back of the Hall where we met was the text *"When I see the blood, I will pass over you"* Exodus 12:13. It could be clearly seen by the preacher at the front and was meant to serve as a reminder that when he preached, he was not to forget the Blood – which is something that Christians are meant to do whenever they drink from the communion cup: *"For this is my blood of the new testament, which is shed for many for the remission of sins"* Matthew 26:28. Our two texts are related insofar that Jesus is our Passover Lamb.

It is notable that mention is made of keeping the Passover and encouraging God's people to celebrate it at the appointed place, including those in Israel after it had separated from Judah, and for priests to be sanctified in order to officiate, under the last two good kings of Judah (Hezekiah – 2 Chronicles 30, and Josiah – 2 Chronicles 35) and also on the return from exile (Ezra 6).

In the passage covering the Passover, coverage is given of the Feast of the Unleavened Bread, which began as soon as the Feast of Passover had ended just before the Feast of First Fruits begins. It appears the practical reason for unleavened bread is that it needed to be prepared in haste as the people needed to leave Egypt in haste. Some commentators point to the Bible association of leaven with evil, e.g., *"Your glorying is not good. Know ye not that a little leaven leaveneth the whole lump? Purge out therefore the old leaven, that ye may be a new lump, as ye are unleavened. For even Christ our passover is sacrificed for us: Therefore let us keep the feast, not with old leaven, neither with the leaven of malice and wickedness; but with the unleavened bread of sincerity and truth*" 1 Corinthians 5:6-8. And the people needed to disassociate from that which is evil. If we are to associate First Fruits with Jesus rising from the dead as argued in the next section and Passover with Jesus' death on the Cross, in this, then what comes in-between is Jesus' burial, when He descended into Hell. It is a time of sober reflection preceding a time of triumphal jubilation when Jesus rose from the dead.

Offering the First Fruits (23:9-14)

"*And the Lord spake unto Moses, saying, Speak unto the children of Israel, and say unto them, When ye be come into the land which I give unto you, and shall reap the harvest thereof, then ye shall bring a sheaf of the firstfruits of your harvest unto the priest: And he shall wave the sheaf before the Lord, to be accepted for you: on the morrow after the sabbath the priest shall wave it. And ye shall offer that day when ye wave the sheaf an he lamb without blemish of the first year for a burnt offering unto the Lord. And the meat offering thereof shall be two tenth deals of fine flour mingled with oil, an offering made by fire unto the Lord for a sweet savour: and the drink offering thereof shall be of wine, the fourth part of an hin. And ye shall eat neither bread, nor parched corn, nor green ears, until the selfsame day that ye have brought an offering unto your God: it shall be a statute for ever throughout your generations in all your dwellings*".

The Feast of First Fruits served as a reminder to the Israelites of God's provision in the Promised Land. Ultimately, the Israelites were to acknowledge that God had rescued them from slavery in Egypt and provided them a place to live and grow crops (Deuteronomy 26:1-11).

As its name suggests, the Feast of First Fruits required the Israelites to bring "*a sheaf of the first grain*" they harvested each year to the priest. The priest would then take the sheaf and wave it before the Lord the day after the Sabbath. On the same day, all the Israelites were to sacrifice a year-old lamb without defect as a burnt offering and give a food offering of grain, oil, and wine. The Israelites were not allowed to eat any of the crop until the day the first portion was brought before the priest. The first fruits belonged to God, and was when the people of Israel acknowledged God as the source of their crops and the one who provided for them.

The Feast of First Fruits marked the first harvest of the year, heightening the symbolism that reminded the Israelites of God's provision. The first thing the Israelites did after a long and laborious season of growing crops was express their thankfulness to God for meeting their needs. And because ancient Israel was an agriculturally based society, the Israelites were acknowledging God's provision for both their food and their income. Like the other Jewish feasts in the Old Testament, the Feast of First Fruits prophetically foreshadowed the coming Messiah and His ministry. Paul links Christ and His resurrection to first fruits: *"But now is Christ risen from the dead, and become the firstfruits of them that slept. For since by man came death, by man came also the resurrection of the dead. For as in Adam all die, even so in Christ shall all be made alive. But every man in his own order: Christ the firstfruits; afterward they that are Christ's at his coming"* 1 Corinthians 15:20-23.

Just as the first portion of the harvest in the Old Testament anticipated the full harvest still to come, Jesus' resurrection anticipated the full resurrection to come for all those who are in Christ. His resurrection signals the very beginning of a brand-new creation promised in the Old Testament (Isaiah 43:18–19; 65:17). We are reminded *"For we know that the whole creation groaneth and travaileth in pain together until now. And not only they, but ourselves also, which have the firstfruits of the Spirit, even we ourselves groan within ourselves, waiting for the adoption, to wit, the redemption of our body"* Romans 8:23. For believers today, it is a foreshadowing and reminder of what Christ has done in redeeming creation and what He will do when He finally returns.

The Feast of Weeks (Pentecost) (23:15-22)

"And ye shall count unto you from the morrow after the sabbath, from the day that ye brought the sheaf of the wave offering; seven sabbaths shall be complete: Even unto the morrow after the seventh sabbath shall ye number fifty days; and ye shall offer a new meat offering unto the Lord. Ye shall bring out of your habitations two wave loaves of two tenth deals; they shall be of fine flour; they shall be baken with leaven; they are the firstfruits unto the Lord. And ye shall offer with the bread seven lambs without blemish of the first year, and one young bullock, and two rams: they shall be for a burnt offering unto the Lord, with their meat offering, and their drink offerings, even an offering made by fire, of sweet savour unto the Lord. Then ye shall sacrifice one kid of the goats for a sin offering, and two lambs of the first year for a sacrifice of peace offerings. And the priest shall wave them with the bread of the firstfruits for a wave offering before the Lord, with the two lambs: they shall be holy to the Lord for the priest. And ye shall proclaim on the selfsame day, that it may be an holy convocation unto you: ye shall do no servile work therein: it shall be a statute for ever in all your dwellings throughout your generations. And when ye reap the harvest of your land, thou shalt not make clean riddance of the corners of thy field when thou reapest, neither shalt thou gather any gleaning of thy harvest: thou shalt leave them unto the poor, and to the stranger: I am the Lord your God".

The Feast of Weeks is the second of the three "solemn feasts" that all Jewish males were required to travel to Jerusalem to attend (Exodus 23:14–17; 34:22–23; Deuteronomy 16:16) and offer sacrifices. This important feast gets its name from the fact that it starts seven full weeks, or exactly 50 days, after the Feast of First Fruits. Since it takes place exactly 50 days after the previous feast, this feast is also known as "Pentecost" (Acts 2:1), which means "fifty." Commentators differ on the importance they attach to the significance of the likelihood that, when God gave the Law to Moses on Mount Sinai, it was 50 days after the Children of Israel had celebrated their first Passover feast.

In all three of the feasts that Jewish males were required to attend, "first-fruit" offerings would be made at the Temple as a way of expressing thanksgiving for God's provision. Just as the Feast of Firstfruits included the first fruits of the barley harvest, the Feast of Weeks was in celebration of the first fruits of the wheat harvest. Since the Feast of Weeks was one of the "harvest feasts," the Jews were commanded to "present an offering of new grain to the Lord". This offering was to be "two wave loaves of two-tenths of an ephah" which were made "*of fine flour . . . baked with leaven.*" This is also the only feast where leavened bread is used.

The offerings were to be made of the first fruits of that harvest. Along with the "wave offerings" they were also to offer seven first-year lambs that were without blemish along with one young bull and two rams. Additional offerings are also prescribed in Leviticus and the other passages that outline how this feast was to be observed. Another important requirement of this feast is that, when the Jews harvested their fields, they were required to leave the corners of the field untouched and not gather "any gleanings" from the harvest as a way of providing for the poor and strangers.

To the Jews, this time of celebration is known as Shavuot, which is the Hebrew word meaning "weeks." This is one of three separate names that are used in scripture to refer to this important Jewish feast. Each name emphasises an important aspect of the feast as well as its religious and cultural significance to both Jews and Christians. Besides being called the Feast of Weeks in Leviticus 23, this special feast celebration is called the "Day of the First Fruits" in Numbers 28:26 and the "Feast of Harvest" in Exodus 23:16, and among Christians is more commonly known as Pentecost.

Like other Jewish feasts, the Feast of Weeks is important in that it foreshadows the coming Messiah and His ministry. Following His resurrection, Jesus spent the next 40 days teaching His disciples before ascending to heaven (Acts 1). Fifty days after His resurrection and after ascending to heaven to sit at the right hand of God, Jesus sent the Holy Spirit as promised (John 14:16–17) to indwell the disciples and empower them for ministry. The promised Holy Spirit arrived on the Day of Pentecost.

On the Day of Pentecost or the Feast of Weeks, the "first fruits" of the church were gathered by Christ as some 3,000 people heard Peter present the Gospel after the Holy Spirit had empowered and indwelt the disciples as promised (Acts 2). With the promised indwelling of the Holy Spirit, the first fruits of God's spiritual harvest under the New Covenant began. Today that harvest continues as people continue to be saved, but there is also another coming harvest whereby God will again turn His attention back to Israel so that *"all of Israel will be saved"* (Romans 11:26). Looking back to Joel's prophecy (Joel 2:28–32) and forward to the promise of the Holy Spirit in Christ's last words on earth before His ascension into heaven (Acts 1:8), Pentecost signals the beginning of the church age.

The Feast of Trumpets (23:23-25)

"And the Lord spake unto Moses, saying, Speak unto the children of Israel, saying, In the seventh month, in the first day of the month, shall ye have a sabbath, a memorial of blowing of trumpets, an holy convocation. Ye shall do no servile work therein: but ye shall offer an offering made by fire unto the Lord".

The Feast of Trumpets marked the beginning of ten days of consecration and repentance before God. It is one of seven Jewish feasts or festivals appointed by the Lord and the first of the three feasts that occur in the autumn. The Feast of Trumpets began on the first day (at the new moon) of the seventh month. Its name comes from the command to blow trumpets (Leviticus 23:24; Numbers 29:1-6). It is also referred to as *Rosh Hashanah*, which means "Head of the Year," because it marks the beginning of the Jewish civil calendar. During this celebration, no kind of work was to be performed, but burnt offerings and a sin offering were to be brought before the Lord.

In the Leviticus passage, the words "trumpet blasts" are a translation of the Hebrew word **teruah**, which means "a shout" or "a blowing." It appears that the **shofar** (ram's horn) was to be blown at this time, as it was on the other new moons (Psalm 81:3). Jewish tradition indicates that both the ram's horn and the priestly silver horns (**hazozerah**) were used in the Feast of Trumpets.

The Feast of Trumpets was important for several reasons. First, it commemorated the end of the agricultural and festival year. Also, the Day of Atonement fell on the tenth day of this month, and the Festival of Booths began on the fifteenth day and represent a progression of thought beginning with repentance on the Festival of Trumpets, forgiveness on the Day of Atonement and rest on the Festival of Booths, all being bound up with the Second Coming of Christ. The blowing of the trumpets on the first day of the month heralded a solemn time of preparation for the Day of Atonement;

this preparation time was called "Ten Days of Repentance" or the "Days of Awe." The trumpet sound was an alarm of sorts and can be understood as a call to introspection and repentance.

The prophets linked the blowing of trumpets to the future Day of Judgment: *"Blow the trumpet in Zion; sound the alarm on my holy hill. Let all who live in the land tremble, for the day of the Lord is coming. It is close at hand"* (Joel 2:1; also Zephaniah 1:14, 16). In the New Testament, we see that the Lord's Second Coming will be accompanied by the sound of a trumpet (1 Corinthians 15:51-52; 1 Thessalonians 4:16-17). Each of the judgments in Revelation 8-9 is signalled by a trumpet. Just as the shofar called the Jewish nation to turn their attention to the Lord and ready themselves for the Day of Atonement, so will the "trump of God" call us to heaven and warn the world of coming judgment.

The Day of Atonement (Yom Kippur) (23:26-32)

"And the Lord spake unto Moses, saying, Also on the tenth day of this seventh month there shall be a day of atonement: it shall be an holy convocation unto you; and ye shall afflict your souls, and offer an offering made by fire unto the Lord. And ye shall do no work in that same day: for it is a day of atonement, to make an atonement for you before the Lord your God. For whatsoever soul it be that shall not be afflicted in that same day, he shall be cut off from among his people. And whatsoever soul it be that doeth any work in that same day, the same soul will I destroy from among his people. Ye shall do no manner of work: it shall be a statute for ever throughout your generations in all your dwellings. It shall be unto you a sabbath of rest, and ye shall afflict your souls: in the ninth day of the month at even, from even unto even, shall ye celebrate your sabbath".

All the feasts mentioned are significant and complementary, but given the special relevance of the Day of Atonement to some of the central themes of "Priests of the Bible" we present our thoughts on this particular feast in a separate chapter (Chapter 11) that is devoted to *Yom Kippur*.

The Feast of Tabernacles (Sukkot, Booths) (23:33-44)

"And the Lord spake unto Moses, saying, Speak unto the children of Israel, saying, The fifteenth day of this seventh month shall be the feast of tabernacles for seven days unto the Lord. On the first day shall be an holy convocation: ye shall do no servile work therein. Seven days ye shall offer an offering made by fire unto the Lord: on the eighth day shall be an holy convocation unto you; and ye shall offer an offering made by fire unto the Lord: it is a solemn assembly; and ye shall do no servile work therein. These are the feasts of the Lord, which ye shall proclaim to be holy convocations, to offer

an offering made by fire unto the Lord, a burnt offering, and a meat offering, a sacrifice, and drink offerings, every thing upon his day: Beside the sabbaths of the Lord, and beside your gifts, and beside all your vows, and beside all your freewill offerings, which ye give unto the Lord. Also in the fifteenth day of the seventh month, when ye have gathered in the fruit of the land, ye shall keep a feast unto the Lord seven days: on the first day shall be a sabbath, and on the eighth day shall be a sabbath. And ye shall take you on the first day the boughs of goodly trees, branches of palm trees, and the boughs of thick trees, and willows of the brook; and ye shall rejoice before the Lord your God seven days. And ye shall keep it a feast unto the Lord seven days in the year. It shall be a statute for ever in your generations: ye shall celebrate it in the seventh month. Ye shall dwell in booths seven days; all that are Israelites born shall dwell in booths: That your generations may know that I made the children of Israel to dwell in booths, when I brought them out of the land of Egypt: I am the Lord your God. And Moses declared unto the children of Israel the feasts of the Lord".

The Feast of Tabernacles, also known as the Feast of Booths and Sukkot, is the seventh and last feast that the Lord commanded Israel to observe and one of the three feasts that Jews were to observe each year by going to *"appear before the Lord your God in the place which He shall choose"* (Deuteronomy 16:16). The importance of the Feast of Tabernacles can be seen in how many places it is mentioned in scripture, sometimes called the Feast of the Ingathering, the Feast to the Lord, or the Feast of Booths (Exodus 23:16; Deuteronomy 16:13). Many important events in Israel's history have taken place at the time of the Feast of Tabernacles. It was at this time when Solomon's Temple was dedicated to the Lord: *"And all the men of Israel assembled themselves unto king Solomon at the feast in the month Ethanim, which is the seventh month"* 1 Kings 8:2.

It was at the Feast of Tabernacles that the Israelites, who had returned from exile to rebuild the temple, gathered to celebrate under the leadership of Joshua and Zerubbabel (Ezra 3). Later, the Jews heard Ezra read the Word of God to them during the Feast of Tabernacles (Nehemiah 8). Ezra's preaching resulted in a great revival as the Israelites confessed and repented of their sins. It was also during this Feast that we read: *"In the last day, that great day of the feast, Jesus stood and cried, saying, If any man thirst, let him come unto me, and drink. He that believeth on me, as the scripture hath said, out of his belly shall flow rivers of living water. (But this spake he of the Spirit, which they that believe on him should receive: for the Holy Ghost was not yet given; because that Jesus was not yet glorified.)"* (John 7:37-39).

The Feast of Tabernacles began five days after the Day of Atonement and at the time the autumn harvest had just been completed. It was a time of joyous celebration as the Israelites celebrated God's continued provision for them in the current harvest and remembered His provision and protection during the 40 years in the wilderness. It was the last of the three feasts that all "native born" male Jews were commanded to participate in. As one of the pilgrim feasts, it was also the time when they brought their tithes and offerings: *"Thou shalt observe the feast of tabernacles seven days, after that thou hast gathered in thy corn and thy wine: And thou shalt rejoice in thy feast, thou, and thy son, and thy daughter, and thy manservant, and thy maidservant, and the Levite, the stranger, and the fatherless, and the widow, that are within thy gates. Seven days shalt thou keep a solemn feast unto the Lord thy God in the place which the Lord shall choose: because the Lord thy God shall bless thee in all thine increase, and in all the works of thine hands, therefore thou shalt surely rejoice"* (Deuteronomy 16:13-15). Following the building of the Temple, with the influx of people coming to Jerusalem in order to celebrate the three feasts, we can only imagine what the scene must have been like. Thousands of people coming together to remember and celebrate God's deliverance and provision, all living in temporary shelters or booths. During the eight-day period, many sacrifices were made. It required all 24 divisions of priests to be present to assist in the sacrificial duties.

God's instructions for celebrating the Feast of Tabernacles were given soon after God had delivered Israel from bondage in Egypt. The feast was to be celebrated each year on "the fifteenth day of this seventh month" and was to run for seven days. Like all feasts, it begins with a "holy convocation" or Sabbath day when the Israelites were to stop working to set aside the day for worshipping God. On each day of the feast they were to offer an "offering made by fire to the Lord" and then after seven days of feasting, again the eighth day was to be "a holy convocation" when they were to cease from work and offer another sacrifice to God (Leviticus 23). Lasting eight days, the Feast of Tabernacles begins and ends with a Sabbath day of rest. During the eight days of the feast, the Israelites would dwell in booths or tabernacles that were made from the branches of trees. The Feast of Tabernacles, like all the feasts, was instituted by God as a way of reminding Israelites in every generation of their deliverance by God from Egypt and His care for His people. The feasts are significant for they foreshadow the work and actions of the coming Messiah. Much of Jesus' public ministry took place in conjunction with the Feasts. Ironically, the people waved palms when Jesus entered Jerusalem for the last time, expecting their king was coming to save them and reign, but this was not yet the time.

The Feast of Tabernacles is symbolic of Christ's Second Coming when He will establish His earthly kingdom. It is the one feast that Gentiles are required to observe, during Christ's Millennial reign. *"And it shall come to pass, that every one that is left of all the nations which came against Jerusalem shall even go up from year to year to worship the King, the Lord of hosts, and to keep the feast of tabernacles. And it shall be, that whoso will not come up of all the families of the earth unto Jerusalem to worship the King, the Lord of hosts, even upon them shall be no rain. And if the family of Egypt go not up, and come not, that have no rain; there shall be the plague, wherewith the Lord will smite the heathen that come not up to keep the feast of tabernacles"* Zechariah 14:16-18.

The Feast of Tabernacles is unique, insofar as the nations also were invited in ancient times to come up to Jerusalem at this season to worship the Lord alongside the Jewish people. This tradition first arose from the command given to Moses that Israel should sacrifice seventy bulls at this time, which were offered for the seventy nations descended from Noah (see Numbers 29:12-35). The entire Numbers 29 chapter is taken up with the various sacrifices offered on each day of the Feast. When Solomon later dedicated his Temple during the Feast of Tabernacles, he also called on the Lord to hear the prayers of all the foreigners that would come there to pray (2 Chronicles 6:32-33). Thus, Jerusalem and the Temple itself were destined from the start to be a *"house of prayer for all nations"* (Isaiah 56:7; Matthew 21:13). Another unique aspect of Sukkot is that it is a feast of joy. It is an autumn harvest feast to be marked with great rejoicing in the ingathering of the fruit of the land. Israel also was called to instruct the nations in the laws of God and the people were to take joy in this task. Thus, Sukkot also serves as a harbinger of the joyous last-days ingathering of the nations. Interestingly, after times of difficulty we read of Tabernacles celebrated in Ezra and in Nehemiah.

Again, we see these as being joyous occasions: *"They kept also the feast of tabernacles, as it is written, and offered the daily burnt offerings by number, according to the custom, as the duty of every day required"* Ezra 3:4 and *"And all the congregation of them that were come again out of the captivity made booths, and sat under the booths: for since the days of Jeshua the son of Nun unto that day had not the children of Israel done so. And there was very great gladness. Also day by day, from the first day unto the last day, he read in the book of the law of God. And they kept the feast seven days; and on the eighth day was a solemn assembly, according unto the manner"* Nehemiah 8:17-18.

Some argue Jesus was born at the time of the Feast of Tabernacles as seen in the words of John when he wrote: *"And the Word became flesh and dwelt among us, and we beheld His glory, the glory as of the only begotten of the Father, full of grace and truth"* John 1:14. The word John chose to speak of Jesus "dwelling" among us is the word tabernacle, which means to "dwell in a tent."

The Feast of Tabernacles begins and ends with a special Sabbath day of rest. During the days of the feast all native Israelites were "to dwell in booths" to remind them that God delivered them out of the "land of Egypt" and to look forward to the coming Messiah, who would deliver His people from the bondage of sin. This feast, like all of the feasts of Israel, reminded the Jews and should remind Christians that God has promised to deliver His people from the bondage of sin and deliver them from their enemies. Part of God's deliverance for the Israelites was His provision and protection of them for the 40 years they wandered in the Wilderness, cut off from the Promised Land. The same holds true for Christians today. God protects us and provides for us as we go through life in the wilderness of this world. While our hearts long for the Promised Land (heaven) and to be in the presence of God, He preserves us in this world as we await the world to come and the redemption that will come when Christ returns again to "tabernacle" or dwell among us in bodily form.

"He that dwelleth in the secret place of the most High shall abide under the shadow of the Almighty. I will say of the Lord, He is my refuge and my fortress: my God; in him will I trust. Surely he shall deliver thee from the snare of the fowler, and from the noisome pestilence. He shall cover thee with his feathers, and under his wings shalt thou trust: his truth shall be thy shield and buckler. Thou shalt not be afraid for the terror by night; nor for the arrow that flieth by day; Nor for the pestilence that walketh in darkness; nor for the destruction that wasteth at noonday. A thousand shall fall at thy side, and ten thousand at thy right hand; but it shall not come nigh thee. Only with thine eyes shalt thou behold and see the reward of the wicked. Because thou hast made the Lord, which is my refuge, even the most High, thy habitation; There shall no evil befall thee, neither shall any plague come nigh thy dwelling. For he shall give his angels charge over thee, to keep thee in all thy ways. They shall bear thee up in their hands, lest thou dash thy foot against a stone. Thou shalt tread upon the lion and adder: the young lion and the dragon shalt thou trample under feet. Because he hath set his love upon me, therefore will I deliver him: I will set him on high, because he hath known my name. He shall call upon me, and I will answer him: I will be with him in trouble; I will deliver him, and honour him. With long life will I satisfy him, and shew him my salvation" Psalm 91:1-16.

Feast of Purim

Purim is the first of the feasts not ordained by YHWH that is celebrated still by Jews today. We read about the origins of this feast in the Book of Esther. *"Wherefore they called these days Purim after the name of Pur. Therefore for all the words of this letter, and of that which they had seen concerning this matter, and which had come unto them, The Jews ordained, and took upon them, and upon their seed, and upon all such as joined them-selves unto them, so as it should not fail, that they would keep these two days according to their writing, and according to their appointed time every year; And that these days should be remembered and kept throughout every generation, every family, every province, and every city; and that these days of Purim should not fail from among the Jews, nor the memorial of them perish from their seed. Then Esther the queen, the daughter of Abihail, and Mordecai the Jew, wrote with all authority, to confirm this second letter of Purim. And he sent the letters unto all the Jews, to the hundred twenty and seven provinces of the kingdom of Ahasuerus, with words of peace and truth, To confirm these days of Purim in their times appointed, according as Mordecai the Jew and Esther the queen had enjoined them, and as they had decreed for themselves and for their seed, the matters of the fastings and their cry. And the decree of Esther confirmed these matters of Purim; and it was written in the book"* Esther 9:26-32. It is a time of celebration recalling how the Jews were spared from annihilation, as recorded in the Book of Esther.

Feast of Hanukkah

Hanukkah is the second of the feasts not ordained by YHWH that is cel-ebrated by Jews today, often in the way many Gentiles celebrate Christmas. But it is not found in the Bible, although some argue it is a feast Jesus cele-brated, e.g., *"And it was at Jerusalem the feast of the dedication, and it was winter. And Jesus walked in the temple in Solomon's porch"* John 10:22,23.

Hanukkah (Chanukah – "dedication") is the Jewish eight-day, winter-time "festival of lights," celebrated with a nightly menorah lighting, special prayers and fried foods. It is thus named because it celebrates the rededi-cation of the Temple. In the second century BCE, Israel was ruled by the Seleucids (Syrian-Greeks), who tried to force the Jewish people to accept Greek culture and beliefs rather than of God. Against all odds, a small band of faithful but poorly armed Jews, led by Judah the Maccabee, defeated and drove the Greeks from the land, reclaimed the Temple and rededicated it to the service of God. According to tradition, when they sought to light the Temple's Menorah (the seven-branched candelabrum), they found only a single cruse of olive oil that had escaped contamination by the Greeks. Miraculously, they lit the menorah and the one-day supply of oil lasted for eight days, until new oil could be prepared under conditions of ritual purity. It has been suggested that Jesus celebrated Hanukkah but there is insufficient evidence to prove this.

As we come to the end of our consideration of the Jewish feasts, let us consider one of the psalms that may well have been sung on feast days, and which, as was often the case, was sung on a note of celebration because of who God is and what He has done:

"O give thanks unto the Lord; for he is good: because his mercy endureth for ever. Let Israel now say, that his mercy endureth for ever. Let the house of Aaron now say, that his mercy endureth for ever. Let them now that fear the Lord say, that his mercy endureth for ever. I called upon the Lord in distress: the Lord answered me, and set me in a large place. The Lord is on my side; I will not fear: what can man do unto me? The Lord taketh my part with them that help me: therefore shall I see my desire upon them that hate me. It is better to trust in the Lord than to put confidence in man. It is better to trust in the Lord than to put confidence in princes. All nations compassed me about: but in the name of the Lord will I destroy them. They compassed me about; yea, they compassed me about: but in the name of the Lord I will destroy them. They compassed me about like bees: they are quenched as the fire of thorns: for in the name of the Lord I will destroy them. Thou hast thrust sore at me that I might fall: but the Lord helped me. The Lord is my strength and song, and is become my salvation. The voice of rejoicing and salvation is in the tabernacles of the righteous: the right hand of the Lord doeth valiantly. The right hand of the Lord is exalted: the right hand of the Lord doeth valiantly. I shall not die, but live, and declare the works of the Lord. The Lord hath chastened me sore: but he hath not given me over unto death. Open to me the gates of righteousness: I will go into them, and I will praise the Lord: This gate of the Lord, into which the righteous shall enter. I will praise thee: for thou hast heard me, and art become my salvation. The stone which the builders refused is become the head stone of the corner. This is the Lord's doing; it is marvellous in our eyes. This is the day which the Lord hath made; we will rejoice and be glad in it. Save now, I beseech thee, O Lord: O Lord, I beseech thee, send now prosperity. Blessed be he that cometh in the name of the Lord: we have blessed you out of the house of the Lord. God is the Lord, which hath shewed us light: bind the sacrifice with cords, even unto the horns of the altar. Thou art my God, and I will praise thee: thou art my God, I will exalt thee. O give thanks unto the Lord; for he is good: for his mercy endureth for ever" Psalm 118:1-29.

Chapter 11: The Day of Atonement

Having in Chapter 10 considered the various Jewish feasts mandated in Leviticus 23, along with others that came about since, i.e., Purim and Hanukkah, along with their prophetic significance and links with the Aaronic Priesthood, in this chapter we consider one them – The Day of Atonement (Yom Kippur) in greater depth, concentrating on Leviticus 16, which details what happened on that day. It is not that the other feasts do not merit special attention but Yom Kippur is especially important here given it is at this feast more than any other that the High Priest has such a prominent role. A deeper understanding of the significance of this feast helps us to better understand Jesus, our Great High Priest, and the plan of salvation God had in mind ever since (and even before) the creation of man.

Before we draw lessons from our study of this subject, we must do a detailed examination of what took place on the Day of Atonement, doing so based on what is written in Leviticus 16, and the writings of those (and there have been many) who have insights into what happened, as well as the traditions.

Sacrifices for the Day of Atonement (16:1-11)

- God spoke to Moses following the death of Aaron's two sons in the Tabernacle (Leviticus 10) and told him to instruct Aaron not to enter the Most Holy Place except under specific conditions.

- When the time came for Aaron to enter the Most Holy Place, he was to clothe himself in the priestly garments that were specified and take a bull for a sin offering and a ram for a burnt offering to the Tabernacle.

- That priestly garment was not the beautiful attire described in our Chapter 6, which would be worn on all other occasions when ministering in the Tabernacle, but rather a plainer affair, indicative that Aaron was one sinner entering God's presence on behalf of other sinners.

- From the people, he was to take two male goats, one of which was for a sin offering, and a ram for a burnt offering.

- The bull was to be offered as a sin offering for Aaron's house.

- Aaron was then to take the two goats and cast lots over them.

- The goat which was selected by the lot was used as a sin offering.

- The other was presented to the Lord to make atonement and then set free into the wilderness.

The High Priest enters the Most Holy Place (16:12-28)

- Aaron was to take fire from the bronze altar and burn two handfuls of incense in front of the Most Holy Place so that the smoke covered the mercy seat.

- He was then to take some of the bull's blood on his finger and sprinkle it on and in front of the mercy seat.

- The goat for the sin offering was to be killed and its blood sprinkled in the same way.

- By doing this the High Priest made "atonement" for the sins of himself, his house, and all the people of Israel. The fact the High Priest was not killed by God, indicated God's acceptance.

- No one but the High Priest was allowed in the Tabernacle while this was happening.

- When this was complete, Aaron was to put some of the blood on the bronze altar to atone for it, just as he had atoned for the Most Holy Place and the rest of the Tabernacle.

- Then Aaron was to take the second goat, the one on which the lot had not fallen, and confess all the sins of Israel over it while his hands were on its head.

- God said: "*The goat shall bear all their iniquities on itself to a remote area, and he shall let the goat go free in the wilderness.*"

- Following this, Aaron was to bathe himself and put on his regular High Priestly garments and offer the burnt offering for himself and the burnt offering for the nation. As discussed in Chapter 9, the burnt offering indicated gratitude and full surrender to YHWH – a fitting end!

- The man who took the goat out into the wilderness was to bathe himself before he was permitted to re-enter the camp.

A statute forever (16:29-34)

- This day of atonement (known today as Yom Kippur) was to be observed by the Jews every year on the 10th day of the 7th month.

- They were to "afflict" themselves and become sad and mourn for all past wrong doings.

- They were to abstain from ordinary work on that day.

- The word afflict (Hebrew **anah**) means to be bowed down or humbled (often associated with fasting), a recurring theme in

Jewish life (e.g., Deuteronomy 8:1-3, Ezra 8:21, Psalm 35:13) and something that Gentile believers have tended to downplay to their cost.

• The day was dedicated to their cleansing from sin.

It is worth mentioning the Scapegoat (see Chapter 2, Figure 16). The Scapegoat is referred to in other chapters of this book. Just like the goat chosen by lot is a type of Christ (a sacrifice for sin) so is the goat released into the wilderness having had the sins of the people transferred to it. Jesus was literally made the scapegoat for our sins when He was sentenced to die. We follow Christ when we obey – "*Let us go forth therefore unto him without the camp, bearing his reproach*" Hebrews 13:13.

As we reflect on how we might apply the lessons taught in Leviticus 16, which are reinforced throughout the Bible, it is worth reflecting on the psalm that David wrote when the prophet Nathan came and confronted him after David had committed adultery with Bathsheba and murdered her husband, Uriah the Hittite: "*Have mercy upon me, O God, according to thy loving-kindness: according unto the multitude of thy tender mercies blot out my transgressions. Wash me throughly from mine iniquity, and cleanse me from my sin. For I acknowledge my transgressions: and my sin is ever before me ... For thou desirest not sacrifice; else would I give it: thou delightest not in burnt offering. The sacrifices of God are a broken spirit: a broken and a contrite heart, O God, thou wilt not despise. Do good in thy good pleasure unto Zion: build thou the walls of Jerusalem*" Psalm 51:1-3; 16-18.

If we need an example of what to do and what to pray as we consider these matters, we do well to consider the prayer of the prophet Daniel that he prayed as an old man: "*And I set my face unto the Lord God, to seek by prayer and supplications, with fasting, and sackcloth, and ashes: And I prayed unto the Lord my God, and made my confession, and said, O Lord, the great and dreadful God, keeping the covenant and mercy to them that love him, and to them that keep his commandments; We have sinned, and have committed iniquity, and have done wickedly, and have rebelled, even by departing from thy precepts and from thy judgments: Neither have we hearkened unto thy servants the prophets, which spake in thy name to our kings, our princes, and our fathers, and to all the people of the land. O Lord, righteousness belongeth unto thee, but unto us confusion of faces, as at this day; to the men of Judah, and to the inhabitants of Jerusalem, and unto all Israel, that are near, and that are far off, through all the countries whither thou hast driven them, because of their trespass that they have trespassed against thee. O Lord, to us belongeth confusion of face, to our kings, to our princes, and to our fathers, because we have sinned against thee. To the Lord our God belong mercies and forgivenesses, though we have rebelled against him; Neither have we obeyed the voice of the Lord our God, to walk in his laws, which he set before us by his servants the prophets. Yea, all Israel have transgressed thy law, even by departing, that they might not obey thy voice; therefore the curse is poured upon us, and the oath that is written in the law of Moses the servant of God, because we have sinned against him. And he hath confirmed his words, which he spake against us, and against our judges that judged us, by bringing upon us a great evil: for under the whole heaven hath not been done as hath been done upon Jerusalem. As it is written in the law of Moses, all this evil is come upon us: yet made we not our prayer before the Lord our God, that we might turn from our iniquities, and understand thy truth"* Daniel 9:3-13.

It is a mistake of much of contemporary Christianity that we do not mourn over all the things going on in the world that are not what God has intended, even though He allows it and we wonder why He does. There is much else we could and ought to mourn over, e.g., broken relationships and our part in them. It is true that followers of Jesus are under Grace rather than under Law, but we would be remiss if we did not **anah** ourselves for what we see going on around us, seeing where this leads (like Daniel) and it is probably a reason why we do not see the Shekhinah Glory and the power of the Holy Ghost today. And of course, it goes beyond affliction, prayer and fasting, for it should lead us into action.

There is no requirement for Christians, especially Gentiles, to recognise the Day of Atonement in their own practice, but when the Day of Atonement comes round (and this chapter was purposefully written on that day in 2023), even though our sins may not fall into the category of adultery and murder, it is nigh certain, nevertheless (and while this is not the place to list them, this author can think of many he has committed), we have sinned and we need to repent and ask for forgiveness. We do well to reflect and do all that is implied in **anah** (afflicted, humbled).

The wonderful news is that while the celebration of this feast, which is anything but a feast in the commonly understood sense, is not mandated, our Great High Priest (Jesus – assuming we are one of His followers) fully atones for our sins (something we remember when we take communion). It is why we have written a chapter that is dedicated to this feast in particular, since it sets the scene for when we come to "Chapter 19: Jesus our Great High Priest", who amazingly is both priest and sacrifice. *"And if any man sin, we have an advocate with the Father, Jesus Christ the righteous: and he is the propitiation for our sins: and not for our's only, but also for the sins of the whole world"* 1 John 2:1-2.

Throughout writing **"Priests of the Bible"** it has been evident that even among genuine Christians there is a range of views, from antipathy and indifference to enthusiasm and interest, and nowhere is this more evident than when it comes to the Feats of YHWH. Some hardly know or care about Yom Kippur or the other feasts, arguing they are New Testament people. Others pay careful attention, including being afflicted and humbled on Yom Kippur and celebrating the other Feasts of YHWH and ignoring traditional "Christian" feasts, e.g., when it comes to celebrating Christmas, Easter etc. It is not the author's intention to persuade readers where on the spectrum of interest/indifference their actions should lie. Yet for this author, especially in the light of researching this book, it has been a time of sober reflection, not just lamenting his own sins committed since last Yom Kippur but also those of people in his orbit, including those who have hurt and wronged him and others, and his own culpability, doing so in the spirit of forgiveness and desire for reconciliation. Additionally, the manifold evil that is so evident in the world is recognised which, while he may not have been able to stop, he might have played a bigger part in resisting it – which could/should give rise to **anah** (afflicted).

In closing this chapter, we turn our attention to those to whom the Feast of Atonement, along with other feasts, was directed – the Jewish people. Without wanting to be over simplistic, it appears that, on this their most sacred day of the year, most celebrate Yom Kippur with the *Yom* (Day) but without the *Kippur* (Atonement). In the eyes of many thoughtful onlookers this might render whatever they put in place of what would have once taken place in the Temple, which hasn't been around for almost 2000 years, somewhat meaningless. Which brings us to the prophet, Hosea. We argued in Chapter 10 that the Feasts had a prophetic significance. Again, without wanting to be simplistic, when considering the prophetic significance of the seven identified Feasts of YHWH, the first four, (Spring) Feasts: Passover, Unleavened Bread, First Fruits and Pentecost, were more to do with Jesus' first coming, and the last three, (Autumn) Feasts: Trumpets, Day of Atonement and Tabernacles, with His second coming. In the passage we now quote, we are reminded how Hosea was told to love his wife who had betrayed him by her promiscuity (just as Israel had betrayed God), but looking forward to the future, a time that can only occur with the Second Coming of Israel's Messiah, when Israel will return to YHWH their God. They will do so initially with weeping, as they come to realise how they have rejected their Messiah, which will be replaced with joy when they are reconciled and fall in love with Him.

"Then said the Lord unto me, Go yet, love a woman beloved of her friend, yet an adulteress, according to the love of the Lord toward the children of Israel, who look to other gods, and love flagons of wine. So I

bought her to me for fifteen pieces of silver, and for an homer of barley, and an half homer of barley: And I said unto her, Thou shalt abide for me many days; thou shalt not play the harlot, and thou shalt not be for another man: so will I also be for thee. For the children of Israel shall abide many days without a king, and without a prince, and without a sacrifice, and without an image, and without an ephod, and without teraphim: Afterward shall the children of Israel return, and seek the Lord their God, and David their king; and shall fear the Lord and his goodness in the latter days" Hosea 3:1-5.

On the face of it, the prophetic fulfilment of Yom Kippur happened when Jesus died on the Cross and the Veil of the Temple was torn from the top to the bottom and so confirmed that His once and for all sacrifice had made full atonement for sin, for all those who believe on him. But most of Israel fail/failed to see it, and for the religious substitute all sorts of non-prescribed religious practices as part of their religion, but one day they will see it, in their time of greatest need. About this, we read: *"In that day shall the Lord defend the inhabitants of Jerusalem; and he that is feeble among them at that day shall be as David; and the house of David shall be as God, as the angel of the Lord before them. And it shall come to pass in that day, that I will seek to destroy all the nations that come against Jerusalem. And I will pour upon the house of David, and upon the inhabitants of Jerusalem, the spirit of grace and of supplications: and they shall look upon me whom they have pierced, and they shall mourn for him, as one mourneth for his only son, and shall be in bitterness for him, as one that is in bitterness for his firstborn ... In that day there shall be a fountain opened to the house of David and to the inhabitants of Jerusalem for sin and for uncleanness."* Zechariah 12:8-10, 13:1.

Could this be the time when we see the full prophetic fulfilment of Yom Kippur? Yet that is not the end – for when we read further in Zechariah and consider Israel's blessings in Christ's Millennial reign, it is not the sixth Feast of YHWH (Yom Kippur) that will be celebrated but the seventh (Tabernacles) and whatever some may think about celebrating feasts, this is one feast that all will celebrate: *"And it shall come to pass, that every one that is left of all the nations which came against Jerusalem shall even go up from year to year to worship the King, the Lord of hosts, and to keep the feast of tabernacles. And it shall be, that whoso will not come up of all the families of the earth unto Jerusalem to worship the King, the Lord of hosts, even upon them shall be no rain"* Zechariah 14:16-17.

It is by design that the three Autumn Feasts of YHWH were very close to each other timewise and just as there is a sequence with the four Spring feasts this is also the case with the three Autumn feasts.

- Trumpets (Rosh Hashanah) – 7th Month, 1st Day – Repentance.
- Day of Atonement (Yom Kippur) – 7th Month, 10th Day – Forgiveness.
- Tabernacles (Sukkot) – 7th Month, 15th – 21st Day – Messiah.

The great theme of Rosh Hashanah is repentance, and the overarching theme is that of forgiveness. The first day of Rosh Hashanah begins a ten-day season of repentance, often called the Ten Days of Awe by the Jewish people. These ten days conclude with the observance of the Day of Atonement.

But let us end, not on a note of affliction and mourning but rather on one of joy and jubilation as we consider what John saw in his Revelation as he looked into the future and what is to happen in the heavenly realm: "*After this I beheld, and, lo, a great multitude, which no man could number, of all nations, and kindreds, and people, and tongues, stood before the throne, and before the Lamb, clothed with white robes, and palms in their hands; And cried with a loud voice, saying, Salvation to our God which sitteth upon the throne, and unto the Lamb. And all the angels stood round about the throne, and about the elders and the four beasts, and fell before the throne on their faces, and worshipped God, Saying, Amen: Blessing, and glory, and wisdom, and thanksgiving, and honour, and power, and might, be unto our God for ever and ever. Amen. And one of the elders answered, saying unto me, What are these which are arrayed in white robes? and whence came they? And I said unto him, Sir, thou knowest. And he said to me, These are they which came out of great tribulation, and have washed their robes, and made them white in the blood of the Lamb. Therefore are they before the throne of God, and serve him day and night in his temple: and he that sitteth on the throne shall dwell among them. They shall hunger no more, neither thirst any more; neither shall the sun light on them, nor any heat. For the Lamb which is in the midst of the throne shall feed them, and shall lead them unto living fountains of waters: and God shall wipe away all tears from their eyes*" Revelation 7:9-17

Chapter 12: The Levites, their Roles and their Legacy

Not that writing other chapters does not present challenges, but this could be particularly seen to be the case when writing about the Levites. The word "Levite" appears 262 times in the Old Testament and crops up throughout, often in the context of complementing what priests did. Perhaps surprisingly, the word appears only twice in Leviticus and yet is used 48 times in Numbers, which is where we learn much about their roles, especially concerning the Tabernacle. The word is used 93 times in Chronicles, particularly when considering Temple worship and the various activities taking place in Israel's life, and then 58 times in the Books of Ezra and Nehemiah as they consider the worship of God following the return from Exile. Levites also have a significant part to play in some of the Old Testament prophecies.

Levites are only mentioned three times in the New Testament, begging the question whether the role of the Levite had diminished, maybe in the light of all the other religious offices that by then had become evident, yet one of the usages is in the Parable of the Good Samaritan as told by Jesus, when rather than the priest or Levite helping the man who had been mugged, it was a Samaritan. Jesus was evidently making the point that true devotion to God demanded more than mere religion.

We have already made the point that, of the twelve tribes, the descendants of Levi (the third son of Jacob through Leah), which we refer to as Levites, were the priestly tribe and it came with special privileges and responsibilities. Only descendants of Aaron, himself one of the descendants of Levi, could serve as priests. Throughout this book, we have used the phrase "*Aaronic priesthood*" to hammer home the fact that, while all priests were Levites, only Aaron's descendants can be priests, although we also find references made to the "*Levitical priesthood*", for example in Hebrews 7:11.

One thing that stands out about Levi, and is a reason some argue that makes Levi's descendants suitable for priestly functions is a story when, along with his brother Simeon, Levi brought violent retribution on the family of the person who had raped their sister (Genesis 34:25). When at the end of his life Jacob blesses his sons, he is scathing concerning Levi: "*Simeon and Levi are brethren; instruments of cruelty are in their habitations*" Genesis 49:5.

The Levites come to prominence during the Israelite's journey in the Wilderness, when Moses was up Mount Sinai, communing with God, while the people down below were worshipping the Golden Calf. We read what happened after a righteously indignant Moses came down from the mountain:

"Then Moses stood in the gate of the camp, and said, Who is on the Lord's side? let him come unto me. And all the sons of Levi gathered themselves together unto him. And he said unto them, Thus saith the Lord God of Israel, Put every man his sword by his side, and go in and out from gate to gate throughout the camp, and slay every man his brother, and every man his companion, and every man his neighbour. And the children of Levi did according to the word of Moses: and there fell of the people that day about three thousand men" Exodus 32:26-28. That propensity for violence, along with a zeal for God, could be seen in the grandson of Aaron, Phinehas, who also dispensed similar justice (see Chapter 26).

But we have to wait until we get to the Book of Numbers in order to find out about the special role and requirements the Lord had for non-Aaronic Levites. One commentator has suggested that while in Egypt the Levites had assumed certain priestly functions, based in part on the premise that Moses and Aaron, as Levites, were recognised by Pharoah as being of the priestly class, which was why he allowed them access to him, while the rest of the Hebrews were not allowed that privilege since they were slaves. We have already noted mention of priests, e.g., Exodus 19:22, 24, and that was before Moses received his instructions from YHWH on the matter while he was on Mount Sinai.

But back to Numbers, we read: *"But thou shalt appoint the Levites over the tabernacle of testimony, and over all the vessels thereof, and over all things that belong to it: they shall bear the tabernacle, and all the vessels thereof; and they shall minister unto it, and shall encamp round about the tabernacle. And when the tabernacle setteth forward, the Levites shall take it down: and when the tabernacle is to be pitched, the Levites shall set it up: and the stranger that cometh nigh shall be put to death. And the children of Israel shall pitch their tents, every man by his own camp, and every man by his own standard, throughout their hosts. But the Levites shall pitch round about the tabernacle of testimony, that there be no wrath upon the congregation of the children of Israel: and the Levites shall keep the charge of the tabernacle of testimony"* Numbers 1:50-53.

Levi had three sons, Gershon, Kohath, and Merari. When transporting the Temple, each clan had different and well-defined duties. Kohath would transport the Holy Ark and other accoutrements, Gershon carried the curtains, Merari carried the beams, sockets, and bars. In later generations, as the population grew, and worship came to be centred round the Temple and the Tabernacle became redundant, the Levites would be divided into 24 mishmarot (guards) (similar to what went on with priests). Each group served a stint in the Temple undertaking a large range of duties (including new ones) specific to Temple activities before relinquishing their place to the next one on the roster.

As for the Gershonites, Kohathites, and Merarites serving under Aaron to assist him and other priests in their responsibilities and to guard the tabernacle, they were not allowed to intrude upon those functions exclusive to priests. The Kohathites were in charge of the Ark of the Covenant, the Table of Showbread, and other holy items (Numbers 10:21; 1 Chronicles 9:32). These items were carried on staves on their shoulders when the sanctuary was moved (Numbers 7:9; 4:15; Exodus 25:26-28). The Gershonites were in charge of the curtains, ropes, and coverings (Numbers 4:24-26). The Merarites were in charge of taking care of and carrying the pillars, bases, frames, pegs, and cords that formed the structure of the tent of meeting. The Levites were able to readily set up and take down the Tabernacle while on the move in their Wilderness journey, since everyone knew and did his duty.

A Levite, between the ages of 25 and 50 years, was to carry on the services of the Tabernacle and later the Temple. At the age of 50 years, he was freed from his responsibilities. He had the honour of taking care of minor services on a voluntary ground (Numbers 8:25-26). The Levites were exempt from military service; consequently, they were not counted with the tribal forces (1 Chronicles 9:33). In addition to those duties laid out from the outset pertaining to the Tabernacle and to be replaced by those duties pertaining to the Temple, there were other duties that were not entirely Tabernacle and Temple related although this started to be evident, even before the Temple project was mooted.

In Chapter 7, we touched on some of the many duties the Aaronic priests undertook besides that which were to do with the six specified items of furniture found inside the Tabernacle, albeit supported by the Levites. We also considered those duties applicable to Levites as well as that of priests and the relationship between the two that were given in Numbers 18:1-7. That same interaction and consideration concerning the duties of Priests and Levites applied as we transition to the First and Second Temple periods of Israel's history. In many instances, when Levites are mentioned, it was often along with priests when it came to carrying out these various duties.

One gets the impression that many of these duties today would be undertaken by professionals in their respective fields. However, as far as the Hebrew Scriptures are concerned it was invariably in the context of service to God, the restraints of His Law and in obedience to His commands, and at least until toward the end of the Old Testament, that they appeared to make up most of the professional class as well as taking on other functions. Levites as worship leaders, singers, prophets, musicians, finance officers, administrators, civil servants, medical professionals, guards, law enforcers, judiciary members (judges and lawyers) and teachers come to mind but invariably those Levites not from the line of

Aaron and thus not priests, often worked alongside and under the direction of those who were.

There was something especially noteworthy concerning Levites insofar they were given to God in exchange for the firstborn of other tribes, and since there was some excess, these all had to be redeemed with money: "*And thou shalt take the Levites for me (I am the Lord) instead of all the firstborn among the children of Israel; and the cattle of the Levites instead of all the firstlings among the cattle of the children of Israel ... Take the Levites instead of all the firstborn among the children of Israel, and the cattle of the Levites instead of their cattle; and the Levites shall be mine: I am the Lord. And for those that are to be redeemed of the two hundred and threescore and thirteen of the firstborn of the children of Israel, which are more than the Levites; Thou shalt even take five shekels apiece by the poll, after the shekel of the sanctuary shalt thou take them*" Numbers 3:41, 45-47.

Soon after, these instructions concerning the setting apart of the Levites were further reinforced: "*And the Lord spake unto Moses, saying, Take the Levites from among the children of Israel, and cleanse them. And thus shalt thou do unto them, to cleanse them: Sprinkle water of purifying upon them, and let them shave all their flesh, and let them wash their clothes, and so make themselves clean. Then let them take a young bullock with his meat offering, even fine flour mingled with oil, and another young bullock shalt thou take for a sin offering. And thou shalt bring the Levites before the tabernacle of the congregation: and thou shalt gather the whole assembly of the children of Israel together: And thou shalt bring the Levites before the Lord: and the children of Israel shall put their hands upon the Levites: And Aaron shall offer the Levites before the Lord for an offering of the children of Israel, that they may execute the service of the Lord. And the Levites shall lay their hands upon the heads of the bullocks: and thou shalt offer the one for a sin offering, and the other for a burnt offering, unto the Lord, to make an atonement for the Levites. And thou shalt set the Levites before Aaron, and before his sons, and offer them for an offering unto the Lord. Thus shalt thou separate the Levites from among the children of Israel: and the Levites shall be mine. And after that shall the Levites go in to do the service of the tabernacle of the congregation: and thou shalt cleanse them, and offer them for an offering. For they are wholly given unto me from among the children of Israel; instead of such as open every womb, even instead of the firstborn of all the children of Israel, have I taken them unto me. For all the firstborn of the children of Israel are mine, both man and beast: on the day that I smote every firstborn in the land of Egypt I sanctified them for myself. And I have taken the Levites for all the firstborn of the children of Israel*" Numbers 8: 5-18.

As Levites, the Kohathites, Gershonites, and Merarites did not get specific territory in the Promised Land. God commanded that they be given cities and pastureland from among the lands of the other tribes (Joshua 21:2) and that they should be well provided for (Numbers 35:1, 2). The distribution of the cities of Israel was decided by the drawing of lots (Joshua 21:1-8). The Gershonites received 13 cities; the Kohathites, more in number, received 23; the Merarites were the smallest in number, so they received only 12 cities. Among these cities were 6 cities of refuge to which a manslayer may flee (Numbers 35:6). There were three cities in Canaan, and three on the east side of Jordan (Numbers 35:14; Deuteronomy 4:43; Joshua 20:7-8). The Levites received no territorial inheritance in the Land as did the other tribes (Numbers 18:20). They received tithes from non-Levites, and also gave tithes.

"And the Lord spake unto Aaron, Thou shalt have no inheritance in their land, neither shalt thou have any part among them: I am thy part and thine inheritance among the children of Israel. And, behold, I have given the children of Levi all the tenth in Israel for an inheritance, for their service which they serve, even the service of the tabernacle of the congregation. Neither must the children of Israel henceforth come nigh the tabernacle of the congregation, lest they bear sin, and die. But the Levites shall do the service of the tabernacle of the congregation, and they shall bear their iniquity: it shall be a statute for ever throughout your generations, that among the children of Israel they have no inheritance. But the tithes of the children of Israel, which they offer as an heave offering unto the Lord, I have given to the Levites to inherit: therefore I have said unto them, Among the children of Israel they shall have no inheritance. And the Lord spake unto Moses, saying, Thus speak unto the Levites, and say unto them, When ye take of the children of Israel the tithes which I have given you from them for your inheritance, then ye shall offer up an heave offering of it for the Lord, even a tenth part of the tithe. And this your heave offering shall be reckoned unto you, as though it were the corn of the threshingfloor, and as the fulness of the winepress. Thus ye also shall offer an heave offering unto the Lord of all your tithes, which ye receive of the children of Israel; and ye shall give thereof the Lord's heave offering to Aaron the priest. Out of all your gifts ye shall offer every heave offering of the Lord, of all the best thereof, even the hallowed part thereof out of it. Therefore thou shalt say unto them, When ye have heaved the best thereof from it, then it shall be counted unto the Levites as the increase of the threshingfloor, and as the increase of the winepress" Numbers 18:20-30.

The need to look after the Levites would be re-iterated: *"And the Levite that is within thy gates; thou shalt not forsake him; for he hath no part nor inheritance with thee. At the end of three years thou shalt bring forth all the tithe of thine increase the same year, and shalt lay it up within thy gates:*

And the Levite, (because he hath no part nor inheritance with thee,) and the stranger, and the fatherless, and the widow, which are within thy gates, shall come, and shall eat and be satisfied; that the Lord thy God may bless thee in all the work of thine hand which thou doest" Deuteronomy 14:27-29.

We have touched on the part Levites played in the First Temple (Chapter 14) and the Second Temple (Chapter 15). While mentioned many times in scriptures covering those periods we will not consider further, other than refer to an incident recorded in the Book of Nehemiah, as we near the end of the period in Israel's history that is covered by the Old Testament. The reason for doing so is to illustrate yet again that right from the time of Moses and until we come to the end of the Hebrew Scriptures as they concern Israel, the part played by Levites (both of Aaron and not of Aaron) was very important.

"So they read in the book in the law of God distinctly, and gave the sense, and caused them to understand the reading. And Nehemiah, which is the Tirshatha, and Ezra the priest the scribe, and the Levites that taught the people, said unto all the people, This day is holy unto the Lord your God; mourn not, nor weep. For all the people wept, when they heard the words of the law. Then he said unto them, Go your way, eat the fat, and drink the sweet, and send portions unto them for whom nothing is prepared: for this day is holy unto our Lord: neither be ye sorry; for the joy of the Lord is your strength. So the Levites stilled all the people, saying, Hold your peace, for the day is holy; neither be ye grieved. And all the people went their way to eat, and to drink, and to send portions, and to make great mirth, because they had understood the words that were declared unto them. And on the second day were gathered together the chief of the fathers of all the people, the priests, and the Levites, unto Ezra the scribe, even to understand the words of the law. And they found written in the law which the Lord had commanded by Moses, that the children of Israel should dwell in booths in the feast of the seventh month" Nehemiah 8:8-14.

We end though on a note that might come as a surprise if we consider Levites merely from the perspective of them only being relevant when there was a Tabernacle or Temple. It is the part they will play in yet to be fulfilled prophecy, as can be seen in the words of five of the Hebrew prophets.

Looking far into the future concerning a regathered Israel, Isaiah writes: *"And they shall bring all your brethren for an offering unto the Lord out of all nations upon horses, and in chariots, and in litters, and upon mules, and upon swift beasts, to my holy mountain Jerusalem, saith the Lord, as the children of Israel bring an offering in a clean vessel into the house of the Lord. And I will also take of them for priests and for Levites, saith the Lord"* Isaiah 66:20-21.

One of Jeremiah's prophecies, written around the time of the last king of Judah, concerns the future of the Davidic line and the future Messiah. At the same time, he sees a part that will be played by the Levites: *"For thus saith the Lord; David shall never want a man to sit upon the throne of the house of Israel; Neither shall the priests the Levites want a man before me to offer burnt offerings, and to kindle meat offerings, and to do sacrifice continually. And the word of the Lord came unto Jeremiah, saying, Thus saith the Lord; If ye can break my covenant of the day, and my covenant of the night, and that there should not be day and night in their season; Then may also my covenant be broken with David my servant, that he should not have a son to reign upon his throne; and with the Levites the priests, my ministers. As the host of heaven cannot be numbered, neither the sand of the sea measured: so will I multiply the seed of David my servant, and the Levites that minister unto me"* Jeremiah 33:17-22.

The word Levite appears ten times in the Book of Ezekiel and each of these references were linked to what in Chapter 18 we identify as concerning the Third Temple. In many of these references the Levites Ezekiel had in mind were descendants of Zadok the priest, e.g., *"But the priests the Levites, the sons of Zadok, that kept the charge of my sanctuary when the children of Israel went astray from me, they shall come near to me to minister unto me, and they shall stand before me to offer unto me the fat and the blood, saith the Lord God"* Ezekiel 44:15.

As discussed elsewhere, Zechariah 10-12 is significant in that it looks forward to the last battle when all the nations of the world gang up on Israel, but God (alone) saves them, and in this quote, we see that in the future there is a part to be played by the Levites: *"In that day shall there be a great mourning in Jerusalem, as the mourning of Hadadrimmon in the valley of Megiddon. And the land shall mourn, every family apart; the family of the house of David apart, and their wives apart; the family of the house of Nathan apart, and their wives apart; The family of the house of Levi apart, and their wives apart; the family of Shimei apart, and their wives apart"* Zechariah 12:11-13.

Humanly speaking, man may be done with Levites but as far as Malachi was concerned, God isn't: *And he shall sit as a refiner and purifier of silver: and he shall purify the sons of Levi, and purge them as gold and silver, that they may offer unto the Lord an offering in righteousness"* Malachi 3:3.

Chapter 13: Categorising Priests of the Bible

While "**Priests of the Bible**" will likely strike only a few as a worthwhile subject for an author, yet as has been already argued, this subject is enormously relevant to the situation we find ourselves in today. In this chapter, we try to categorise who were the Priests of the Bible, and in doing so have come up with several categories. The intention here is to discuss each of those we identify:

No need for priests (Adam before the Fall)

At the very beginning of the Bible (Genesis 1 and 2) we read of God's wonderful creation that included the idyllic Garden of Eden, in which He placed our first ancestors – Adam and Eve. There was no need for priests as Adam and Eve enjoyed perfect fellowship with God. Then came the Fall, as described in Genesis 3, with the rest of the Old Testament to be taken up with man trying to communicate with God or their chosen deity using the office of Priest in various guises, and the New Testament telling us about the promised Messiah, who among other things is, for those who believe, the Great High Priest.

Melchizedek

Righteous Melchizedek was the King of Salem (Jerusalem). He was both a king and a priest, laying the foundations of the city where the Messiah would appear. Since he is only being covered in just a few verses (Genesis 14:17-24) he might thereafter be ignored but for the reference in Psalm 110, where we read: "*The Lord said unto my Lord, Sit thou at my right hand, until I make thine enemies thy footstool ... The Lord hath sworn, and will not repent, Thou art a priest for ever after the order of Melchizedek*" Psalm 110:1, 4 and in several places in the Book of Hebrews when it refers to Jesus. Melchizedek is a hugely significant Bible character, as discussed elsewhere in this book.

Priests of God but before the Aaronic priests

These include: Abel, Noah, Abraham, Isaac, Jacob and Job, who exercised one of the main functions of priests, which was to offer up sacrifices to God. These and others who fitted the bill of acting as some sort intermediary between the true God and those they represented are discussed in Chapter 3.

Aaron and his descendants (and also Levites)

This is the main subject of this book, which is introduced in Chapters 6 and 7 and is discussed at length in several places after that. Priests, along with prophets, played a big role in the life of Israel, although they would be too often ignored and, in the case of priests, too easily gave in when this happened. The Levites were known as the priestly tribe and are discussed in Chapter 12. The Aaronic priests were of the tribe of Levi. While the non-Aaronic Levites could not serve as priests, they complemented what priests did, e.g., when it came to serving in the Tabernacle or Temple.

Priests not of YHWH or not of the Aaronic line

The Bible makes many mentions of other gods and what went on regarding their worship and what was done in order to appease and serve those gods and to gain their favour. We first encounter priests, not of YHWH, when Joseph was in Egypt (Genesis 41). What we can find out from reading between the lines is limited concerning the priests that operated in these systems (sometimes alongside false prophets, e.g., the Prophets of Baal in Elijah's times). We know in Israel's case, following the dividing of the unified Kingdom (Judah under Rehoboam and Israel under Jeroboam) that king Jeroboam was faced with a dilemma in that the Temple and the priests were in Judah. He set up his own false "golden calf" system based at centres in Bethel and Dan, installing his own priests. Tragically, both Israel and Judah were to turn to other gods prior to their exiles. It was this false worship, more than anything else, that led to Israel and later Judah being sent into exile. It is worth mentioning that back in the days of the Judges (Judges 18) the tribe of Dan set up a graven image and appointed a non-Levitical priest to oversee worship of that image and this worship continued until the time of Israel's captivity.

This false worship even found its way into the Temple, with priests not of Aaron and not of YHWH administering such false religion, and we even find examples of Aaronic priests being drawn in to support false religion (e.g., Uriah under Ahaz). Interestingly, while we may have had priests not of YHWH or Aaron in the Inter Testament period, two of the priests (Zacharias and Caiaphas) that can be found in New Testament times can trace their lineage back to Aaron, even though the priesthood had become compromised with Rome, and their puppet kings, e.g., Herod, deciding who can serve as priest, and especially who was to become the influential High Priest. There were cases when kings tried to usurp the role of the priest, e.g., Saul and Uzziah. Both were to pay a heavy price for doing so.

Jesus, the Great High Priest

Besides Melchizedek, Jesus was the only king that could legitimately serve as priest of the Most High God (YHWH). We consider in depth Jesus our Great High Priest in Chapter 19. Unlike the Aaronic priesthood that serves as a valuable lesson, when it comes to types and shadows, Jesus alone took on that crucial role of High Priest, thus enabling Christian believers to enter into God's holy presence.

The Priesthood of all believers

An important aspect of New Testament teaching, although it can be traced back to Mount Sinai in Exodus 19, is that of the Priesthood of all Believers, which is discussed in Chapter 41 and we refer to as believer-priests. It is good to be reminded: "*Ye also, as lively stones, are built up a spiritual house, an holy priesthood, to offer up spiritual sacrifices, acceptable to God by Jesus Christ ... But ye are a chosen generation, a royal priesthood, an holy nation, a peculiar people; that ye should shew forth the praises of him who hath called you out of darkness into his marvellous light*" 1 Peter 2:5-9.

Priests and ministers today

Much of what many recognise as church history sees the church as being typically led by three offices: bishops, presbyters (that include priests) and deacons (often seen as some form of hierarchy). That notion has come to be increasingly challenged, although some form of priest equivalent was usually practised. Coming from the Plymouth Brethren and later being involved with other Christian set-ups that tended to be anti-Catholic and therefore anti-priest, the author felt it appropriate that in order to gain a fair balance he should devote a chapter (42) considering the important part played by priests (and their Low Church equivalent) today. Whatever one wants to call what the "moderns" may refer to as "*the leadership*", many of the things today's leaders do or are meant to do are not so dissimilar to what would have been expected from the Hebrew priests, and therefore warrant a deeper consideration, and while not into sacrificing animals etc., we can derive important lessons from them.

Priests of the future

The Bible is a book of prophecy. While the Tabernacle and what are commonly referred to as the First and Second Temples (discussed in Chapters 5, 14 and 15), there is also a yet to be built Third Temple (discussed in Chapter 18), whether one that is being planned right now or Ezekiel's Temple (the author believes this will happen during the Millennial reign of Christ) that we read about in Ezekiel 40-48. We know that in the latter there will be priests of the line of Aaron, specifically of Zadok. There is also a place for the Levites, also prophesied in Jeremiah 33:21-22. The last consideration of Bible end times prophecy concerns the New Heaven and the New Earth, where John writes: "*I did not see a temple in the city, because the Lord God Almighty and the Lamb are its temple*" Revelation 21:22. One can picture a scene that takes us back to the Garden of Eden, when priests as such were not needed.

Chapter 14: The First Temple

The challenges that face us when considering matters relating to priests include where to begin and end, what to include or miss out, how deep we ought to go with our subject matter and when to use one's own words or simply quote from the Bible, which often says what needs saying better than we might anyway. Nowhere is this more pronounced than when we consider the subject of the First Temple (also referred to as Solomon's Temple). Another aspect to ponder is how big a deal the Temple is to our story. After all, the time that elapsed between God calling Abraham to be the Father of a great nation and that nation having its own Temple was a thousand years. For half that time, Israel made do with the Tabernacle (covered in Chapters 5 and 6) and we do not read of God requiring that they build Him a Temple, being quite satisfied merely to dwell in the midst of His people within the Tabernacle.

The two main persons involved in the "Temple project", who laid out the plans and did some of the important preparatory work, were King David and his son, Solomon, who implemented those plans and ensured the Temple was built with no expense spared. When we began the "Priests" project, we had not expected as a late "add on" to be writing about kings, but we have, and readers can read about David and Solomon in Part 4, especially Chapters 63 and 64. Following Solomon, were all the kings of Judah, from Rehoboam to Zedekiah. The First Temple was to play a part in their stories, and for some of them significantly so (positive and negative). As for YHWH, it goes without saying He does not need a temple to live in (something Solomon was all too well aware of). As for blessing the Temple and what went on inside or coming from it, God said He would do so if His people would honour Him. Given that turned out not to be the case, the First Temple was later destroyed by the Babylonians, in 586 BCE, and the Second Temple, built to replace it, was later destroyed by the Romans in 70 CE.

But it is to David we must first turn in order to find out about Solomon's Temple. We learn that he became king at the age of 30 after several years on the run from Saul, despite having been anointed as the king to replace him. We learn he reigned 40 years, 7 years in Hebron and 33 years in Jerusalem, which henceforth became known as the City of David. He captured Jerusalem from the Jebusites and fought several battles, in particular against the Philistines and was able to make the city and the nation secure against its enemies, with God's help. It became evident from the outset that true worship of God was his priority, seen for example in the return of the Ark to Jerusalem.

It was related to this background that David set his heart on building the

Temple: "*And it came to pass, when the king sat in his house, and the Lord had given him rest round about from all his enemies; That the king said unto Nathan the prophet, See now, I dwell in an house of cedar, but the ark of God dwelleth within curtains. And Nathan said to the king, Go, do all that is in thine heart; for the Lord is with thee*" 1 Chronicles 17:1-2. But soon after God revealed to Nathan that it was not what He wanted and, while He would establish a covenant so descendants of David would always sit on the throne, it would not be David that would build God's house (not that God needed one anyway). One reason given was that David had shed too much blood, but it would be one of his sons (which later was named as Solomon). When told by Nathan, who simply passed on what God had told him, David accepted that decision without objecting, and ended by speaking words of thanksgiving and worship to God.

While David could not build the Temple, he did all he could to ensure that everything was in place for the Temple to be built ranging from securing the finances and materials needed to organising the duties of the priests, Levites, singers and gatekeepers who would serve in the Temple. It is worth noting that music and song would be a feature of Temple worship, although it is likely this was a feature of worship relating to the Tabernacle. This was one of the many aspects David paid attention to and many of his psalms were designed to be sung: "*And David spake to the chief of the Levites to appoint their brethren to be the singers with instruments of musick, psalteries and harps and cymbals, sounding, by lifting up the voice with joy*" 1 Chronicles 15:16. Music became an important feature under David and was even linked to musicians prophesying. When David led the return of the Ark to Jerusalem (a necessary pre-requisite), it was with musical accompaniment: "*And David was clothed with a robe of fine linen, and all the Levites that bare the ark, and the singers, and Chenaniah the master of the song with the singers: David also had upon him an ephod of linen. Thus all Israel brought up the ark of the covenant of the Lord with shouting, and with sound of the cornet, and with trumpets, and with cymbals, making a noise with psalteries and harps*" 1 Chronicles 15:27-28.

We read how David secured the Temple site, which according to tradition was where Abraham went to offer his son as a sacrifice (Genesis 22). This was following God's judgement after David had commissioned a census that was not in God's will: "*And Gad came that day to David, and said unto him, Go up, rear an altar unto the Lord in the threshingfloor of Araunah the Jebusite. And David, according to the saying of Gad, went up as the Lord commanded. And Araunah looked, and saw the king and his servants coming on toward him: and Araunah went out, and bowed himself before the king on his face upon the ground. And Araunah said, Wherefore is my lord the king come to his servant? And David said, To buy the threshingfloor of thee, to build an altar unto the Lord, that the plague may be stayed from the people. And Araunah said unto David, Let my lord the king take and offer up what seemeth good unto him: behold, here be oxen for burnt sacrifice, and threshing instruments and other instruments of the oxen for wood. All these things did Araunah, as a king, give unto the king. And Araunah said unto the king, The Lord thy God accept thee. And the king said unto Araunah, Nay; but I will surely buy it of thee at a price: neither will I offer burnt offerings unto the Lord my God of that which doth cost me nothing. So David bought the threshingfloor and the oxen for fifty shekels of silver. And David built there an altar unto the Lord, and offered burnt offerings and peace offerings. So the Lord was intreated for the land, and the plague was stayed from Israel"* 2 Samuel 24:18-25.

We read that when Solomon did build the Temple, he *"began to build the house of the Lord at Jerusalem in mount Moriah, where the Lord appeared unto David his father, in the place that David had prepared in the threshingfloor of Ornan the Jebusite"* 2 Chronicles 3:1. Just like his father, at the beginning of his reign at least, even if not at the end, worshipping God in an appropriate and prescribed manner was Solomon's priority. It began with carrying the Ark of the Covenant and continued in making sacrifices. Solomon began as he was to continue while the Temple was built: *"So Solomon, and all the congregation with him, went to the high place that was at Gibeon; for there was the tabernacle of the congregation of God, which Moses the servant of the Lord had made in the wilderness. But the ark of God had David brought up from Kirjathjearim to the place which David had prepared for it: for he had pitched a tent for it at Jerusalem. Moreover the brasen altar, that Bezaleel the son of Uri, the son of Hur, had made, he put before the tabernacle of the Lord: and Solomon and the congregation sought unto it. And Solomon went up thither to the brasen altar before the Lord, which was at the tabernacle of the congregation, and offered a thousand burnt offerings upon it"* 2 Chronicles 1:3-6.

Before attending to building the Temple, Solomon received the first of two visitations from the Lord, who asked him what it was he wanted that He could give him. The exchange that followed was a revealing one concerning Solomon's priorities: *"Give me now wisdom and knowledge, that I may go out and come in before this people: for who can judge this thy people, that is so great? And God said to Solomon, Because this was in thine heart, and thou hast not asked riches, wealth, or honour, nor the life of thine enemies, neither yet hast asked long life; but hast asked wisdom and knowledge for thyself, that thou mayest judge my people, over whom I have made thee king: Wisdom and knowledge is granted unto thee; and I will give thee rich-*

es, and wealth, and honour, such as none of the kings have had that have been before thee, neither shall there any after thee have the like" 2 Chronicles 1:10-12.

In embarking on the building project, Solomon sought help from the King of Tyre, who had been friends with his father: *"And Solomon sent to Huram the king of Tyre, saying, As thou didst deal with David my father, and didst send him cedars to build him an house to dwell therein, even so deal with me. Behold, I build an house to the name of the Lord my God, to dedicate it to him, and to burn before him sweet incense, and for the continual shewbread, and for the burnt offerings morning and evening, on the sabbaths, and on the new moons, and on the solemn feasts of the Lord our God. This is an ordinance for ever to Israel. And the house which I build is great: for great is our God above all gods. But who is able to build him an house, seeing the heaven and heaven of heavens cannot contain him? who am I then, that I should build him an house, save only to burn sacrifice before him?"* 2 Chronicles 2:3-6. The king responded generously and gave Solomon all that he needed and more, and even a master craftsman to supervise some of the work. Solomon responded by giving him supplies and cities.

The project would require a very large number of workmen. We read: *"And Solomon numbered all the strangers that were in the land of Israel, after the numbering wherewith David his father had numbered them; and they were found an hundred and fifty thousand and three thousand and six hundred. And he set threescore and ten thousand of them to be bearers of burdens, and fourscore thousand to be hewers in the mountain, and three thousand and six hundred overseers to set the people a work"* 2 Chronicles 2:17-18. The project was huge and the result would be breath taking. Details of what was involved, which included attention to the finest detail and the use of the costliest of materials (often gold), are given in the text and after seven years of intense work, at a cost that by today's standards would be considered astronomical, the Temple was ready to be commissioned, where the Ark of the Covenant would be brought once more into the Holy of Holies:

"Thus all the work that Solomon made for the house of the Lord was finished: and Solomon brought in all the things that David his father had dedicated; and the silver, and the gold, and all the instruments, put he among the treasures of the house of God. Then Solomon assembled the elders of Israel, and all the heads of the tribes, the chief of the fathers of the children of Israel, unto Jerusalem, to bring up the ark of the covenant of the Lord out of the city of David, which is Zion ... And it came to pass, when the priests were come out of the holy place: (for all the priests that were present were sanctified, and did not then wait by course: Also the Levites which were the

singers, all of them of Asaph, of Heman, of Jeduthun, with their sons and their brethren, being arrayed in white linen, having cymbals and psalteries and harps, stood at the east end of the altar, and with them an hundred and twenty priests sounding with trumpets:) It came even to pass, as the trumpeters and singers were as one, to make one sound to be heard in praising and thanking the Lord; and when they lifted up their voice with the trumpets and cymbals and instruments of musick, and praised the Lord, saying, For he is good; for his mercy endureth for ever: that then the house was filled with a cloud, even the house of the Lord; So that the priests could not stand to minister by reason of the cloud: for the glory of the Lord had filled the house of God" 2 Chronicles 5:1-2, 11-14.

Solomon then blesses the people and offers his prayer of dedication, before the people, which is not just pertinent to the occasion and the place the Temple was to have in the life of Israel, but is one of the most outstanding prayers we find recorded in the entire Bible, as found in 1 Kings 8:23-55, and is preceded by: *"And Solomon stood before the altar of the Lord in the presence of all the congregation of Israel, and spread forth his hands toward heaven"* (8:22). While what we read is Solomon's prayer, we note he makes references to future prayers offered in the Temple, but more so away from the Temple. When we read Jonah's prayer, while in the belly of the fish, in Jonah 2:1-9, and Hezekiah's prayer in response to the Assyrian threat, in Isaiah 37:14-20, we find both prayed toward the Temple, for that is where God dwelt. The content of Solomon's prayer is also found in 2 Chronicles 6:12-42. Given the prayer's importance, let us consider each section in turn, with reference to that passage:

1. God is to be worshipped for who He is and as one who keeps His covenant. Solomon reminds God of His promises to David concerning the Throne and his successors (6:14-17).

2. While recognising God is far bigger than the Temple, it is still where He has chosen to dwell and, accordingly, He is asked to hear and respond, including to forgive, to prayers offered in and toward the Temple (6:18-21).

3. God is invited to judge with respect to neighbours' disputes and grievances in terms of one party doing wrong, and oaths made accordingly at the altar (6:22-23).

4. When the people are defeated in battle because of their sin, God is asked to forgive and restore when they return to Him (6:24-25).

5. When there is drought because of Israel's sin, and they turn from their sin, God is asked to send the rain (6:26-27).

6. When there is famine or plague, or enemies besiege them because

of Israel's sin, and they then turn from their sin, God is asked to forgive and restore the people and that they may fear Him and walk in His ways (6:28-31).

7. God is asked to hear and respond to the prayer of the foreigner who turns to Him (6:32-33)

8. God is asked to hear the people's prayer when they go to war against enemies (6:34-35).

9. Looking far ahead to a time when the people are taken captive by their enemies because of their sin and then in their plight they repent and pray toward the Temple, God is asked to hear their prayer and uphold their cause (6:36-39)

10. The prayer ends: "*Now, my God, let, I beseech thee, thine eyes be open, and let thine ears be attent unto the prayer that is made in this place. Now therefore arise, O Lord God, into thy resting place, thou, and the ark of thy strength: let thy priests, O Lord God, be clothed with salvation, and let thy saints rejoice in goodness. O Lord God, turn not away the face of thine anointed: remember the mercies of David thy servant*" (6:40-42).

To get what happened next, we need to consider both the Kings and Chronicles accounts, for both provide powerful perspectives. In Kings, we read of Solomon's final, gripping benediction and his exhortation to the people: "*And it was so, that when Solomon had made an end of praying all this prayer and supplication unto the Lord, he arose from before the altar of the Lord, from kneeling on his knees with his hands spread up to heaven. And he stood, and blessed all the congregation of Israel with a loud voice, saying, Blessed be the Lord, that hath given rest unto his people Israel, according to all that he promised: there hath not failed one word of all his good promise, which he promised by the hand of Moses his servant. The Lord our God be with us, as he was with our fathers: let him not leave us, nor forsake us: That he may incline our hearts unto him, to walk in all his ways, and to keep his commandments, and his statutes, and his judgments, which he commanded our fathers. And let these my words, wherewith I have made supplication before the Lord, be nigh unto the Lord our God day and night, that he maintain the cause of his servant, and the cause of his people Israel at all times, as the matter shall require: That all the people of the earth may know that the Lord is God, and that there is none else. Let your heart therefore be perfect with the Lord our God, to walk in his statutes, and to keep his commandments, as at this day*" 1 Kings 8:54-61.

Following Solomon's prayer and blessing, there was a dramatic response: "*Now when Solomon had made an end of praying, the fire came down from heaven, and consumed the burnt offering and the sacrifices; and the glory of the Lord filled the house. And the priests could not enter into the house of the Lord, because the glory of the Lord had filled the Lord's house. And when all the children of Israel saw how the fire came down, and the glory of the Lord upon the house, they bowed themselves with their faces to the ground upon the pavement, and worshipped, and praised the Lord, saying, For he is good; for his mercy endureth for ever"* 2 Chronicles 7:1-3. It was followed by seven days of music and great celebration, as well as an enormous number of animal sacrifices to do with the dedication of the altar, after which Solomon *"sent the people away into their tents, glad and merry in heart for the goodness that the Lord had shewed unto David, and to Solomon, and to Israel his people"* (7:10).

We end this episode of dedicating the Temple on a great high, perhaps the greatest one seen under the kings of Israel and Judah, and along with it a great promise and a great warning, all of which we will see being played out with the kings, even beginning with Solomon himself, for in his later years he drifted away from God: *"Thus Solomon finished the house of the Lord, and the king's house: and all that came into Solomon's heart to make in the house of the Lord, and in his own house, he prosperously effected. And the Lord appeared to Solomon by night, and said unto him, I have heard thy prayer, and have chosen this place to myself for an house of sacrifice. If I shut up heaven that there be no rain, or if I command the locusts to devour the land, or if I send pestilence among my people; If my people, which are called by my name, shall humble themselves, and pray, and seek my face, and turn from their wicked ways; then will I hear from heaven, and will forgive their sin, and will heal their land. Now mine eyes shall be open, and mine ears attent unto the prayer that is made in this place. For now have I chosen and sanctified this house, that my name may be there for ever: and mine eyes and mine heart shall be there perpetually. And as for thee, if thou wilt walk before me, as David thy father walked, and do according to all that I have commanded thee, and shalt observe my statutes and my judgments; Then will I stablish the throne of thy kingdom, according as I have covenanted with David thy father, saying, There shall not fail thee a man to be ruler in Israel. But if ye turn away, and forsake my statutes and my commandments, which I have set before you, and shall go and serve other gods, and worship them; Then will I pluck them up by the roots out of my land which I have given them; and this house, which I have sanctified for my name, will I cast out of my sight, and will make it to be a proverb and a byword among all nations"* 2 Chronicles 7:11-20.

But life moves on. As far as the Bible goes, what comes next is life under Solomon and the kings that followed, until there were no more kings and, for a period, no Temple either. About the kings' activities, the Temple may feature but generally only to support a more pressing narrative. Following Solomon, and to be considered further in Chapter 64, we find that according to how individual kings who followed Solomon responded to God's requirements and, most importantly, whether or not they and the people kept to the Covenant, so did what went on in the Temple along with its associated activities.

Solomon's Temple would be plundered several times. In the fifth year of his son Rehoboam's reign, the Egyptian pharaoh Shishak took away treasures of the Temple and the king's house, as well as shields of gold that Solomon had made; Rehoboam replaced them with brass ones (1 Kings 14:25; 2 Chronicles 12:1-12). A century later, Jehoash, king of the northern Kingdom of Israel, advanced on Jerusalem, broke down a portion of the wall, and carried away the treasures of the Temple and the palace (2 Kings 14:13-14). Later, when Ahaz of Judah was threatened by defeat at the hands of Rezin of Aram-Damascus and Pekah of Israel, he turned to King Tiglath-Pileser IV for help. To persuade him, he *"took the silver and gold that was found in the house of Yahweh, and in the treasures of the king's house, and sent it for a present to the King of Assyria"* (2 Kings 16:8). At another critical juncture, Hezekiah cut off the gold from the doors and doorsteps of the temple he himself had overlaid, and gave it to king Sennacherib (2 Kings 18:15-16). The ultimate plunder occurred at the end, under King Nebuchadnezzar, who not only took all that was of value, but he also destroyed the Temple.

Besides plunder, worship of other gods was introduced and was even found taking place inside the Temple. But also the opposite occurred when the Temple was restored to how it should have been, typically under good kings. We read, for example, in 2 Kings 12:1-17 and 2 Chronicles 24:1-14 how King Joash and the priests of the temple organised a restoration programme funded from popular donations. The temple was restored to its original condition and further reinforced. Similarly, under the last good king: Josiah, money was raised to restore the Temple: *"And they put it in the hand of the workmen that had the oversight of the house of the Lord, and they gave it to the workmen that wrought in the house of the Lord, to repair and amend the house"* 2 Chronicles 34:10.

Sadly, it was too little, too late. The downward spiral away from God continued under four further kings, concerning all of which, their reigns were short lived and they all did evil despite being repeatedly told by the Lord's prophets to repent. The final destruction of the Temple, which God warned Solomon would happen as a result, in His last visitation, did happen. For the next 70 years, Israel was without a temple, but then it once more had one. That is the subject of our next chapter.

But we end on a positive note, of which there were many during the First

Temple period. The Temple, was primarily about worshipping God. That was also the purpose of the Tabernacle that preceded it but the focus appeared to be on those activities to do with the items of furniture that were inside it: Altar of Sacrifice, Bronze Laver, Golden Candlestick, Table of Showbread, Altar of Incense and Ark of the Covenant. Even then, worship in the sense modern Christians understand, i.e., hymns and prayers, still featured. We read concerning one of the principle functions of the Levites, Moses reminding the Israelites: *"the Lord separated the tribe of Levi, to bear the ark of the covenant of the Lord, to stand before the Lord to minister unto him, and to bless in his name, unto this day"* Deuteronomy 10:8. But praise and worship, with musical accompaniment, including stringed instruments and choirs, led by priests and Levites, became more prominent and was evident from the time of David onward.

As to what exactly comprised worship is a matter of conjecture. It is likely Psalms were said and more likely sung. Half of the Psalms are reckoned to have been composed by David, although the whole of the Psalms came together during the Inter Testament period. Psalms that were sung likely included the Songs of Ascent. The Songs of Ascent are a special group of psalms comprising Psalms 120-134. They are also called Pilgrim Songs. Four of these songs are attributed to David (122, 124, 131, 133) and one to Solomon (127). It is worth considering "Solomon's Song" insofar it places the Temple in a proper context as a place of worship: *"Except the Lord build the house, they labour in vain that build it: except the Lord keep the city, the watchman waketh but in vain"* Psalm 127:1.

The city of Jerusalem is situated on a high hill and Jews travelling to Jerusalem for one of the three main annual Jewish festivals (discussed in Chapter 10) traditionally sang these songs on the "ascent" or the uphill road to the City and on to the Temple. According to some traditions, the Jewish priests also sang some of these Songs of Ascent as they walked up the steps to the Temple in Jerusalem.

We will end our chapter with another Psalm of David (103) that one can imagine being sung as part of Temple worship and being of relevance to those who did worship, but with the reminder that just as God rejected sacrifices that didn't glorify him, the same applies to other forms of worship: *"I hate, I despise your feast days, and I will not smell in your solemn assemblies. Though ye offer me burnt offerings and your meat offerings, I will not accept them: neither will I regard the peace offerings of your fat beasts. Take thou away from me the noise of thy songs; for I will not hear the melody of thy viols. But let judgment run down as waters, and righteousness as a mighty stream"* Amos 5:21-24. But let us turn to Psalm 103, and because it helps and relates to the music, we will set it out verse by verse:

1 Bless the Lord, O my soul: and all that is within me, bless his holy name.

2 Bless the Lord, O my soul, and forget not all his benefits:

3 Who forgiveth all thine iniquities; who healeth all thy diseases;

4 Who redeemeth thy life from destruction; who crowneth thee with lovingkindness and tender mercies;

5 Who satisfieth thy mouth with good things; so that thy youth is renewed like the eagle's.

6 The Lord executeth righteousness and judgment for all that are oppressed.

7 He made known his ways unto Moses, his acts unto the children of Israel.

8 The Lord is merciful and gracious, slow to anger, and plenteous in mercy.

9 He will not always chide: neither will he keep his anger for ever.

10 He hath not dealt with us after our sins; nor rewarded us according to our iniquities.

11 For as the heaven is high above the earth, so great is his mercy toward them that fear him.

12 As far as the east is from the west, so far hath he removed our transgressions from us.

13 Like as a father pitieth his children, so the Lord pitieth them that fear him.

14 For he knoweth our frame; he remembereth that we are dust.

15 As for man, his days are as grass: as a flower of the field, so he flourisheth.

16 For the wind passeth over it, and it is gone; and the place thereof shall know it no more.

17 But the mercy of the Lord is from everlasting to everlasting upon them that fear him, and his righteousness unto children's children;

18 To such as keep his covenant, and to those that remember his commandments to do them.

19 The Lord hath prepared his throne in the heavens; and his kingdom ruleth over all.

20 Bless the Lord, ye his angels, that excel in strength, that do his commandments, hearkening unto the voice of his word.

21 Bless ye the Lord, all ye his hosts; ye ministers of his, that do his pleasure.

22 Bless the Lord, all his works in all places of his dominion: bless the Lord, O my soul.

Chapter 15: The Second Temple

By way of recap and according to Wikipedia, we read: "*The Siege of Jerusalem (circa 589–587 BC) was the final event of the Judahite revolts against Babylon, in which Nebuchadnezzar II, king of the Neo-Babylonian Empire, besieged Jerusalem, the capital city of the Kingdom of Judah. Jerusalem fell after a 30-month siege, following which the Babylonians systematically destroyed the city and Solomon's Temple. The Kingdom of Judah was dissolved and many of its inhabitants were exiled to Babylon ... The destruction of Jerusalem and its temple led to a religious, spiritual and political crisis, which left its mark in prophetic literature and biblical tradition. The Kingdom of Judah was abolished and annexed as a Babylonian province with its center in Mizpah. The Judean elite, including the Davidic dynasty, were exiled to Babylon. After Babylon had fallen to Cyrus the Great, founder of the Persian Achaemenid Empire, in 539 BC, he allowed the exiled Judeans to return to Zion and rebuild Jerusalem. The Second Temple was completed in 516 BC*".

By way of further recap and according to Britannica, we read: "*Cyrus II, founder of the Achaemenian dynasty of Persia and conqueror of Babylonia, in 538 BCE issued an order allowing exiled Jews to return to Jerusalem and rebuild the Temple. Work was completed in 515 BCE. There is no known detailed plan of the Second Temple, which was constructed as a modest version of the original building. It was surrounded by two courtyards with chambers, gates, and a public square. It did not include the ritual objects of the First Temple; of special significance was the loss of the Ark itself. Ritual, however, was elaborate and was conducted by well-organized families of priests and Levites. During the Persian and Hellenistic (4th–3rd century BCE) periods, the Temple generally was respected, and in part subsidized, by Judaea's foreign rulers. Antiochus IV Epiphanes, however, plundered it in 169 BCE and desecrated it in 167 BCE by commanding that sacrifices be made to Zeus on an altar built for him. This final act touched off the Hasmonean revolt, during which Judas Maccabeus cleansed and rededicated the Temple; the event is celebrated in the annual festival of Hanukkah. During the Roman conquest, Pompey entered (63 BCE) the Holy of Holies but left the Temple intact. In 54 BCE, however, Crassus plundered the Temple treasury. Of major importance was the rebuilding of the Second Temple begun by Herod the Great, king (37 BCE–4 CE) of Judaea. Construction began in 20 BCE and lasted for 46 years ... The Herodian Temple was again the centre of Israelite life. It was not only the focus of religious ritual but also the repository of the Holy Scriptures and other national literature and the meeting place of the Sanhedrin, the highest court of Jewish law during the Roman period. The rebellion against Rome that began in 66 CE soon focused on the*

Temple and effectively ended with the Temple's destruction on the 9th/10th of Av, 70 CE. All that remained of the retaining wall surrounding the Temple Mount was a portion of the Western Wall (also called the Wailing Wall), which continues to be the focus of Jewish aspirations and pilgrimage. Made part of the wall surrounding the Muslim Dome of the Rock and Al-Aqsā Mosque in 691 CE, it returned to Jewish control in 1967".

All that we have quoted is interesting and relevant, but since our focus is on Priests of the Bible it is to priests we return and, in particular, Ezra the priest and the book that bears his name. As far as re-building the Temple goes, the key figures were Zerubbabel the governor, Joshua the High Priest and the prophets Haggai and Zechariah. While Ezra was the one who wrote about what happened and would play an important part in this post-exile period, he does not appear on the scene until much later (those mentioned were part of the first return from exile in 537 BCE; Ezra led the second return in 458 BCE. The first return is covered in Ezra 1-6; the second return is covered in Ezra 7-10).

The Book of Ezra begins where the Book of Chronicles ends – with the Cyrus edict and adding that in returning to their homeland the Israelites would be given the help and provisions needed, particularly with the aim to rebuild the Temple (returning what was left of Temple treasures that had been taken by the Babylonians): *"Now in the first year of Cyrus king of Persia, that the word of the Lord by the mouth of Jeremiah might be fulfilled, the Lord stirred up the spirit of Cyrus king of Persia, that he made a proclamation throughout all his kingdom, and put it also in writing, saying, Thus saith Cyrus king of Persia, The Lord God of heaven hath given me all the kingdoms of the earth; and he hath charged me to build him an house at Jerusalem, which is in Judah. Who is there among you of all his people? his God be with him, and let him go up to Jerusalem, which is in Judah, and build the house of the Lord God of Israel, (he is the God,) which is in Jerusalem. And whosoever remaineth in any place where he sojourneth, let the men of his place help him with silver, and with gold, and with goods, and with beasts, beside the freewill offering for the house of God that is in Jerusalem"* Ezra 1:1-4.

Ezra records the return and those who were returnees, including priests, Levites, gatekeepers, singers and Temple servants, in Chapters 1 and 2. The people under their civil and spiritual leaders set about the task of restoring religious life soon upon return and before the rebuilding got going: *"And when the seventh month was come, and the children of Israel were in the cities, the people gathered themselves together as one man to Jerusalem. Then stood up Jeshua the son of Jozadak, and his brethren the priests, and Zerubbabel the son of Shealtiel, and his brethren, and builded the altar of the God of Israel, to offer burnt offerings thereon, as it is written in the law of Moses the man of God. And they set the altar upon his bases; for fear was upon them because of the people of those countries: and they offered burnt offerings thereon unto the Lord, even burnt offerings morning and evening. They kept also the feast of tabernacles, as it is written, and offered the daily burnt offerings by number, according to the custom, as the duty of every day required"* Ezra 3:1-4.

In the rest of Ezra 3, we read how soon after that the work of rebuilding the Temple began, and it was done in an organised and systematic way, accompanied by much weeping and joy, for there were some who could remember the First Temple. But soon after the work began so did the opposition, which we read about in Ezra 4. It came in many and often subtle ways and provides a salutary lesson to any doing the Lord's work, which the devil objects to. It can be by flattery along the lines "we want to help" by those non-Jews who had been repatriated to the land. They continued by causing mischief and then writing to the kings of Persia that followed Cyrus saying these were rebels that needed to be stopped. We read that ploy was successful: *"Then ceased the work of the house of God which is at Jerusalem. So it ceased unto the second year of the reign of Darius king of Persia"* (4:24).

The work continued after a possible fifteen-year lapse, and much of it had to do with the encouragements and warnings given by the two prophets: Haggai and Zechariah: *"Then the prophets, Haggai the prophet, and Zechariah the son of Iddo, prophesied unto the Jews that were in Judah and Jerusalem in the name of the God of Israel, even unto them. Then rose up Zerubbabel the son of Shealtiel, and Jeshua the son of Jozadak, and began to build the house of God which is at Jerusalem: and with them were the prophets of God helping them"* Ezra 5:1-2. While being forbidden by the Persian king was a good enough reason to stop work, another was that the people had lost enthusiasm.

The Book of Haggai is the second shortest, after Obadiah, of the prophetic books of the Bible, but a lot of what was said was Temple related. His message was direct and it was a rebuke. He also made the point that because they had not made God their priority they lost His blessing e.g., experiencing bad harvests: *"In the second year of Darius the king, in the sixth month, in the first day of the month, came the word of the Lord by Haggai the prophet unto Zerubbabel the son of Shealtiel, governor of Judah, and to Joshua the son of Josedech, the high priest, saying, Thus speaketh the Lord of hosts, saying, This people say, The time is not come, the time that the Lord 's house should be built. Then came the word of the Lord by Haggai the prophet, saying, Is it time for you, O ye, to dwell in your cieled houses, and this house lie waste? Now therefore thus saith the Lord of hosts;*

Consider your ways. Ye have sown much, and bring in little; ye eat, but ye have not enough; ye drink, but ye are not filled with drink; ye clothe you, but there is none warm; and he that earneth wages earneth wages to put it into a bag with holes" Haggai 1:1-6. They needed to get back to work, and so they did ...

"Then Zerubbabel the son of Shealtiel, and Joshua the son of Josedech, the high priest, with all the remnant of the people, obeyed the voice of the Lord their God, and the words of Haggai the prophet, as the Lord their God had sent him, and the people did fear before the Lord. Then spake Haggai the Lord 's messenger in the Lord's message unto the people, saying, I am with you, saith the Lord. And the Lord stirred up the spirit of Zerubbabel the son of Shealtiel, governor of Judah, and the spirit of Joshua the son of Josedech, the high priest, and the spirit of all the remnant of the people; and they came and did work in the house of the Lord of hosts, their God" Haggai 1:12-14.

In Haggai 2, the prophet looks far ahead, beyond even the immediate aftermath following when the Temple is built and in giving certain prophecies that are yet to be fulfilled, possibly even beyond our own times. He tells those involved in the re-building: *"Yet now be strong, O Zerubbabel, saith the Lord; and be strong, O Joshua, son of Josedech, the high priest; and be strong, all ye people of the land, saith the Lord, and work: for I am with you, saith the Lord of hosts"* 2:4. As for that more distant future, we read: *"And I will shake all nations, and the desire of all nations shall come: and I will fill this house with glory, saith the Lord of hosts. The silver is mine, and the gold is mine, saith the Lord of hosts. The glory of this latter house shall be greater than of the former, saith the Lord of hosts and in this place will I give peace, saith the* Lord *of hosts. (2:7-9).*

When we consider the *"desire of nations"* we think of two beautiful incidents when Jesus was being presented at the Temple. He was welcomed by Simeon: *"And, behold, there was a man in Jerusalem, whose name was Simeon; and the same man was just and devout, waiting for the consolation of Israel: and the Holy Ghost was upon him. And it was revealed unto him by the Holy Ghost, that he should not see death, before he had seen the Lord's Christ. And he came by the Spirit into the temple: and when the parents brought in the child Jesus, to do for him after the custom of the law, Then took he him up in his arms, and blessed God, and said, Lord, now lettest thou thy servant depart in peace, according to thy word: For mine eyes have seen thy salvation"* Luke 2:25-30. He was also welcomed by Anna: *"And there was one Anna, a prophetess, the daughter of Phanuel, of the tribe of Aser: she was of a great age, and had lived with an husband seven years from her virginity; And she was a widow of about fourscore and four years, which departed not from the temple, but served God with fastings and prayers night and day. And she coming in that instant gave thanks likewise unto the Lord, and spake of him to all them that looked for redemption in Jerusalem"* Luke 2:36-38.

Concerning Zerubbabel, we read: *"I will shake the heavens and the earth; And I will overthrow the throne of kingdoms, and I will destroy the strength of the kingdoms of the heathen; and I will overthrow the chariots, and those that ride in them; and the horses and their riders shall come down, every one by the sword of his brother. In that day, saith the Lord of hosts, will I take thee, O Zerubbabel, my servant, the son of Shealtiel, saith the Lord, and will make thee as a signet: for I have chosen thee, saith the Lord of hosts"* (2:21-23).

Zechariah is considerably longer than Haggai and touches on several subjects not directly to do with the rebuilding of the Temple and without the specific condemnation seen in Haggai. But Zechariah does prophesy at around the same time and he also urges a change in attitude: *"The Lord hath been sore displeased with your fathers. Therefore say thou unto them, Thus saith the Lord of hosts; Turn ye unto me, saith the Lord of hosts, and I will turn unto you, saith the Lord of hosts. Be ye not as your fathers, unto whom the former prophets have cried, saying, Thus saith the Lord of hosts; Turn ye now from your evil ways, and from your evil doings: but they did not hear, nor hearken unto me, saith the Lord"* Zechariah 1:2-4. But he does have encouraging words, specifically for Joshua and Zerubbabel.

In Zechariah 3, we see a picture of Satan accusing Joshua before God but the Lord standing with him and cleansing him from any sin. The regulation for the maintenance of the priesthood had fallen into disuse, and they had neither robes, vessels, nor proper provision of offerings. Probably also, the spiritual life of the priests was at a low ebb. But there is One who pleads, who says *"The Lord rebuke thee"*. Like Joshua, we too might be as brands scorched and charred with the burning, but have been plucked out of the consuming flame and are now being kept for some high and useful purpose.

In Zechariah 4, Zerubbabel was to learn the lesson that what he was to do was *"not by might, nor by power, but by my spirit, saith the Lord"*. He had faltered in the great work of reconstruction and had practically lost heart. Here he is encouraged to renew his efforts and persevere to the top-stone. He might be weak and flexible as a wick but none of his deficiencies could hinder him from finishing his life-work, if only his spirit was kindled with the divine fire and fed by the grace of the Holy Spirit.

Back to Ezra 5 and on to Ezra 6, we see the to and fro in correspondence between the Persian authorities in the land and the Jewish leaders, and the new king. The way the Jewish operatives responded during this delicate phase was a lesson in due decorum and God honouring confidence: "*We are the servants of the God of heaven and earth, and build the house that was builded these many years ago, which a great king of Israel builded and set up. But after that our fathers had provoked the God of heaven unto wrath, he gave them into the hand of Nebuchadnezzar the king of Babylon*" Ezra 5:11-12. The outcome was the positive one they had hoped for. Darius found and read the Cyrus edict and as a result gave his blessing and support for the work to proceed, even asking they pray for him!

The king's response included: "*Let the work of this house of God alone; let the governor of the Jews and the elders of the Jews build this house of God in his place. Moreover I make a decree what ye shall do to the elders of these Jews for the building of this house of God: that of the king's goods, even of the tribute beyond the river, forthwith expenses be given unto these men, that they be not hindered. And that which they have need of, both young bullocks, and rams, and lambs, for the burnt offerings of the God of heaven, wheat, salt, wine, and oil, according to the appointment of the priests which are at Jerusalem, let it be given them day by day without fail: That they may offer sacrifices of sweet savours unto the God of heaven, and pray for the life of the king, and of his sons*" Ezra 6:7-10.

And the work did continue until it had been completed. The Temple was dedicated and the religious life traditionally connected with the Temple resumed in the ways that had been long ago set out: "*the children of Israel, the priests, and the Levites, and the rest of the children of the captivity, kept the dedication of this house of God with joy*" (6:16). The Passover was celebrated, and it was an occasion when their God fearing Gentile neighbours could participate. "*And the children of the captivity kept the passover upon the fourteenth day of the first month. For the priests and the Levites were purified together, all of them were pure, and killed the passover for all the children of the captivity, and for their brethren the priests, and for themselves. And the children of Israel, which were come again out of captivity, and all such as had separated themselves unto them from the filthiness of the heathen of the land, to seek the Lord God of Israel, did eat, And kept the feast of unleavened bread seven days with joy: for the Lord had made them joyful, and turned the heart of the king of Assyria unto them, to strengthen their hands in the work of the house of God, the God of Israel*" Ezra 6:19-22.

The Temple and activities around it would continue, including in the later rebuilt temple under King Herod that would finally be destroyed by the Romans in 70 CE. We are now coming toward the end of the Old Testament, and we can see the Temple being used in the remaining chapters of Ezra and Nehemiah. Religious life continued to be topsy turvy with highs and lows, although from the last prophet (Malachi), right at the end of the Old Testament record, devotion to God was at a generally low state, especially among the priests. While worship of false gods did not seem to be the issue, there was the Old Testament equivalent of the Laodicean spirit talked about in Revelation 3.

But always there is hope, for there remained a remnant of those who feared the Lord: "*Then they that feared the Lord spake often one to another: and the Lord hearkened, and heard it, and a book of remembrance was written before him for them that feared the Lord, and that thought upon his name. And they shall be mine, saith the Lord of hosts, in that day when I make up my jewels; and I will spare them, as a man spareth his own son that serveth him*" Malachi 3:16-17.

We now enter the Inter Testament period (discussed in Chapter 16), with the spiritual life of the priests and others responsible for Temple worship seeming to be more at a low than a high, and the sort of compromise with the ungodly, sometimes seen in the First Temple period, now common place. There were also times of Temple desecration by Greek and Roman occupiers. Toward the end of that period, the Temple was rebuilt over a period of several years, under King Herod, and was a magnificent edifice. This building too is often referred to as the Second Temple.

Then we come to the New Testament period (discussed in Chapter 17). What is perhaps surprising is the number of references made to the Temple in the New Testament and the significant part the Second Temple continued to play in the life of Jesus and the church. Despite the Temple being seen as under the control of a corrupt and compromised religious hierarchy with priests that had abandoned the godly ideals we already noted at the start of the Aaronic priesthood, both Jesus and the Apostles visited the Temple on several occasions, often using the opportunity to teach and minister.

Just with reference to Matthew's Gospel alone, we come across texts, such as: "*Then the devil taketh him up into the holy city, and setteth him on a pinnacle of the temple*" (4:5), "*And Jesus went into the temple of God, and cast out all them that sold and bought in the temple, and overthrew the tables of the moneychangers, and the seats of them that sold doves*" (21:12), "*And the blind and the lame came to him in the temple; and he healed them*" (21:14), "*And when he was come into the temple, the chief priests and the elders of the people came unto him as he was teaching, and said, By what authority doest thou these things? and who gave thee this authority?*" (21:23), "*And, behold, the veil of the temple was rent in twain from the top to the bottom; and the earth did quake, and the rocks rent*" (27:51). And in all these cases, we are referring to the Second Temple.

Following the destruction of the Second Temple, there has been no Temple since then, even though the prospect of a Third Temple remains a likely one and is something we discuss in Chapter 18. It is worth noting what is named the Western (or Wailing) Wall, in the Old City of Jerusalem today, is a place of prayer and pilgrimage sacred to the Jewish people. It is all that remains of the retaining wall surrounding the Temple Mount, the site of the First and Second Temples of Jerusalem.

Just as we ended our chapter on the First Temple with a Psalm, we will do so with this chapter, and likely also a Psalm of David (45), which could well have been sung, perhaps in the context of honouring an earthly king, but since it comes under the "messianic" category it is more about a king that is coming to reign, the very king those involved with Second Temple worship would be looking forward to:

1 My heart is inditing a good matter: I speak of the things which I have made touching the king: my tongue is the pen of a ready writer.
2 Thou art fairer than the children of men: grace is poured into thy lips: therefore God hath blessed thee for ever.
3 Gird thy sword upon thy thigh, O most mighty, with thy glory and thy majesty.
4 And in thy majesty ride prosperously because of truth and meekness and righteousness; and thy right hand shall teach thee terrible things.
5 Thine arrows are sharp in the heart of the king's enemies; whereby the people fall under thee.
6 Thy throne, O God, is for ever and ever: the sceptre of thy kingdom is a right sceptre.
7 Thou lovest righteousness, and hatest wickedness: therefore God, thy God, hath anointed thee with the oil of gladness above thy fellows.
8 All thy garments smell of myrrh, and aloes, and cassia, out of the ivory palaces, whereby they have made thee glad.
9 Kings' daughters were among thy honourable women: upon thy right hand did stand the queen in gold of Ophir.
10 Hearken, O daughter, and consider, and incline thine ear; forget also thine own people, and thy father's house;
11 So shall the king greatly desire thy beauty: for he is thy Lord; and worship thou him.
12 And the daughter of Tyre shall be there with a gift; even the rich among the people shall intreat thy favour.
13 The king's daughter is all glorious within: her clothing is of wrought gold.

14 She shall be brought unto the king in raiment of needlework: the virgins her companions that follow her shall be brought unto thee.
15 With gladness and rejoicing shall they be brought: they shall enter into the king's palace.
16 Instead of thy fathers shall be thy children, whom thou mayest make princes in all the earth.
17 I will make thy name to be remembered in all generations: therefore shall the people praise thee for ever and ever.

And also, since this is also relevant to Temple worship, yet another Song of Ascent (Psalm 122):

1 I was glad when they said unto me, Let us go into the house of the Lord.
2 Our feet shall stand within thy gates, O Jerusalem.
3 Jerusalem is builded as a city that is compact together:
4 Whither the tribes go up, the tribes of the Lord, unto the testimony of Israel, to give thanks unto the name of the Lord.
5 For there are set thrones of judgment, the thrones of the house of David.
6 Pray for the peace of Jerusalem: they shall prosper that love thee.
7 Peace be within thy walls, and prosperity within thy palaces.
8 For my brethren and companions' sakes, I will now say, Peace be within thee.
9 Because of the house of the Lord our God I will seek thy good.

Chapter 16: The Inter Testament Period

Given this book is about Priests of the Bible, we might be tempted to overlook a 400-year period that according to Protestant tradition is not covered by the Bible, although in the Roman Catholic tradition it is, i.e., in the Apocrypha. Given our argument in Chapter 2, however, that for a proper understanding of a subject such as Priests this requires one digging deep into the context and background of whatever our subject is, we need to study this Inter Testament period for reasons that include our better understanding the New Testament set-up for priests. Having knowledge of the priesthood and religious environment in which Jesus and the Apostles operated, understanding why this was significantly different to how we left it under the newly returned exiles from Babylon under the likes of Ezra and Nehemiah, is achieved partly as a result of studying "the Silent years". The events of this period, along with how these years impacted the Jewish people, gives us important insights into what Jesus was up against and further highlights why His priesthood is far superior to that which preceded it.

While this period is often referred to as the Silent years, given there was no prophet after the last Old Testament prophet, Malachi, until the prophet whom Malachi prophesied was to come, identified in the New Testament as John the Baptist, much was happening in the world with the rise and fall of great empires: Persian, Greek and Roman. The last book of the Old Testament contains some sorry reading as to what the situation was and should have been from God's perspective. While there had been some mini-revivals among the returnees from exile, it was far from enough and the general trajectory as far as devotion to God went was a downhill spiral and also most Jews did not return.

"Isn't it true that a son honors his father and a worker his master? So if I'm your Father, where's the honor? If I'm your Master, where's the respect?" God-of-the-Angel-Armies is calling you on the carpet: "You priests despise me! "You say, 'Not so! How do we despise you?' "By your shoddy, sloppy, defiling worship. "You ask, 'What do you mean, "defiling"? What's defiling about it?' "When you say, 'The altar of God is not important anymore; worship of God is no longer a priority,' that's defiling. And when you offer worthless animals for sacrifices in worship, animals that you're trying to get rid of—blind and sick and crippled animals—isn't that defiling? Try a trick like that with your banker or your senator—how far do you think it will get you?" God-of-the-Angel-Armies asks you. "Get on your knees and pray that I will be gracious to you. You priests have gotten everyone in rouble. With this kind of conduct, do you think I'll pay attention to you?" God-of-the-Angel-Armies asks you. "Why doesn't one of you just shut the Temple

doors and lock them? Then none of you can get in and play at religion with this silly, empty-headed worship. I am not pleased. The God-of-the-Angel-Armies is not pleased. And I don't want any more of this so-called worship!" Malachi 1:6-10 (The Message).

An important factor not to overlook is the expectation of the promised Messiah to restore Israel's fortunes, but before things got better they seemed to first get a whole lot worse and, as it turned out, God's response (the coming of Jesus) at the end of these Silent years, while welcomed by some Jews, was not welcomed by most, although it did wonderfully bring the Gentiles into the equation.

A study of what took place during the Inter Testament period is fascinating and in preparing this section the author was spoilt for choice when it came to what to check out, prioritising that which is more applicable to Priests of the Bible. With reference to Chapter 2, Figure 4, we are reminded of the Books of the Bible that detail the Exile of the Northern Kingdom of Israel by the Assyrians, later followed by the Southern Kingdom of Judah into Exile by the Babylonians. Then there are accounts of what occurred following the Exile in books like Ezra, Nehemiah and Esther along with that of the three prophets: Haggai, Zechariah and Malachi. There the Hebrew Bible ends with more spiritually awake Jews looking forward to their coming Messiah of the lineage of their greatest king, David.

Of particular interest from a scriptural perspective is that besides the Apocrypha, regarded by most of the theologians the author has had most to do with, as non-canonical and often ignored, there is the Book of Daniel, in particular Chapters 2 and 7-12. Here, especially in Chapter 11 (see Chapter 2, Figure 22), we find considerable detail of some of the important happenings in this period. Following the, on the whole, benevolent Persian rule, was that of the Greeks under Alexander the Great, who was taught by perhaps the greatest philosopher of his time, Aristotle. Alexander managed to conquer a large part of the then known world, which, upon his death, was divided into four areas under four of his generals. Israel, strategically placed in the crossroads of the world, first came under the "Egyptian" rule under Ptolemy and his successors and then under "Syrian" rule, under Seleucus and his successors.

One of the significant things the Greek rule did was to impose Greek culture, which while considered superior by Alexander the Great and those who followed him, clashed with the Hebrew culture in several ways and has ramifications to this day in the way Christianity is perceived by its adherents. It is notable that the Hebrew Bible was translated into Greek (the Septuagint) in this period and was the version referred to by New Testament writers. This culture clash came to a head under Antiochus IV Epiphanes whose notable achievement was to cruelly subjugate the Jewish people and antagonise them by imposing pagan worship, often on pain of death if they did not comply. Again, Daniel has a lot to say in advance on these matters (although many liberal scholars argue these predictions were added with the benefit of hindsight). Daniel was also looking far into the future, including the yet to happen Second Coming of Jesus. Some of this is covered in the author's book "**Prophets of the Bible**" but, even so, there is much more that could be usefully said concerning "Daniel's prophecies".

This brings us to the Maccabean revolt, a Jewish rebellion led by the Maccabees (the father was a priest and he had five sons, one notably was Judas, a brilliant military strategist and a freedom fighter – whose attitude toward Judaism might be seen as "fundamentalist" given his ruthless zeal), against the Seleucid Empire and against the Hellenistic influence on Jewish life and its attempts to impose a false worship on the Jewish people. The main phase of the revolt lasted from 167–160 BCE and ended with the Seleucids in control of Judea, but the conflict between the Maccabees, Hellenised Jews, and the Seleucids continued until 134 BCE, with the Maccabees eventually attaining independence. That independence was relatively short lived as one great empire (the Greeks) was overtaken by another one (the Romans) around 65 BCE, which brings us to the time of Jesus. This independence won against huge odds is celebrated to this day, each year by Jews at Hanukkah time.

Before we turn our attention to the New Testament situation, there is much worth pointing out that is pertinent to the main themes of this book, and strangely resonates with issues and attitudes we can see today, often causing difference of opinion and approach, even among Christians, e.g., most groups celebrating Christmas and Easter but some preferring to celebrate the Jewish feasts, unlike those that are much more widely followed in church circles these are Bible based. On the Jewish side, nominal Judaism matches that of nominal Christianity. As far as religious observance goes, often this is governed more by the Talmud rather than the Torah. We will therefore use the opportunity to make a number of pertinent points that pertain to our having a fuller understanding.

1. While we are talking about the 400 "Silent years", with the promised Messiah tarrying his coming in order to liberate his people and set up His kingdom, much was happening that was highly significant but, as always, the Almighty bides His time for when the time is right.

2. While there was resistance among the priests to their new rulers, notably from the Maccabees, there is every indication that many priests initially welcomed their new Greek and Roman masters and made compromises in order not to incur their displeasure.

There was considerable divergence in the way different priests accommodated their new rulers.

3. While the Aaronic priesthood was to continue, as demonstrated in Chapter 17, much adaptation could be seen, including priests being appointed by the new rulers on the basis of their willingness to toe the official line rather than their spiritual and hereditary credentials. Some of the Maccabees exercised both priestly and kingly roles e.g., one often referred to is John Hyrcanus who was a Hasmonean (Maccabean) leader and Jewish High Priest of the 2nd century BCE (born 164 BCE, reigned from 134 BCE until his death in 104 BCE).

4. While the Greeks brought in a culture that was in conflict with Judaism and the teaching of the Law, and the Romans imposed a rule that was often harsh, both did things that were later to be beneficial in the spreading of the Christian Gospel. Taking the Gospel to both Greeks and Romans, or at least to those under their sway, was a major occupation of the early church.

5. One of the defining factors of Judaism was a mindset that was meant to be more in tune with that of YHWH God than that of the nations around Israel. While Jews have remarkably maintained their unique identity, we see in the process, especially with the forced spreading of Greek culture, this being challenged during the period, and having a long-term effect, including the challenge faced by this author of having been indoctrinated by Greek thinking.

6. We see during this period the importance attached to the office of scribe and paying more attention to the rules (often over and above that set out in the Torah), the significance of the Jewish council, referred to as the Sanhedrin, the emergence of the Pharisees and Sadducees, often clashing with Jesus and mentioned by New Testament writers, as well as Zealots and Essenes as important religious groups to emerge at the end of this period, the spread of synagogue worship to surpass that of the Temple for religious practice, the Samaritans while mentioned in the Old Testament who are given important new significance by Jesus in the New, the beginnings of the puppets of Rome, the Herodian dynasty, and the replacing of Zerubbabel's Temple with that built by Herod.

7. While we have said a lot about Greek occupation, it is worth saying a little more about that of the Romans, who also exercised similar cruelty. The siege of Jerusalem (63 BC) occurred during Pompey the Great's campaigns in the East, shortly after his successful conclusion of the Third Mithridatic War. Pompey had been asked

to intervene in a dispute over inheritance to the throne of the Hasmonean Kingdom, which turned into a war between Hyrcanus II and Aristobulus II. His conquest of Jerusalem, however, spelled the end of Jewish independence and the incorporation of Judea as a client kingdom of the Roman Republic. The Maccabean revolt that began with hope ended with all sorts of compromise and capitulation. The Hasmonean dynasty ended in 37 BCE when the Idumean (related to Edom) Herod the Great became king of Israel, designated "King of the Jews" by the Roman Senate.

8. The Jewish diaspora, the dispersion of Israelites out of their ancient ancestral homeland (the Land of Israel) and their subsequent settlement in other parts of the globe is a phenomenon that began voluntary before the two forced exiles (the Northern Kingdom by the Assyrians and the Southern Kingdom by the Babylonians), which we have discussed. This process continued during the Inter Testament period and throughout the Christian era. It is a long and fascinating subject but not one for detailed coverage in this book. By the time we get to the modern era and, specifically, the founding of the State of Israel in 1948, we find Jewish communities that have been scattered all over the world. In many ways they managed to keep their cultural identity, if not their religious one. They have been both welcomed and despised by their host communities. The bringing back of sections of the Jewish diaspora to their traditional homeland, especially in the light of the World War 2 Holocaust (and other persecutions throughout their history) is a huge subject we can only touch on in this book.

As we move from between the Testaments toward the New Testament and the coming into the world of Jesus, Israel's Messiah, which is where the Priesthood should be leading us, it seems only appropriate to end with an Advent hymn that looks forward to and invites such a coming:

1. O come, O come, Immanuel,

and ransom captive Israel

that mourns in lonely exile here

until the Son of God appear.

[Refrain]

Rejoice! Rejoice! Immanuel
shall come to you, O Israel.

2. *O come, O Wisdom from on high,*
who ordered all things mightily;
to us the path of knowledge show
and teach us in its ways to go. [Refrain]

3. *O come, O come, great Lord of might,*
who to your tribes on Sinai's height
in ancient times did give the law
in cloud and majesty and awe. [Refrain]

4. *O come, O Branch of Jesse's stem,*
unto your own and rescue them!
From depths of hell your people save,
and give them victory o'er the grave. [Refrain]

5. *O come, O Key of David, come*
and open wide our heavenly home.
Make safe for us the heavenward road
and bar the way to death's abode. [Refrain]

6. *O come, O Bright and Morning Star,*
and bring us comfort from afar!
Dispel the shadows of the night
and turn our darkness into light. [Refrain]

7. *O come, O King of nations, bind*
in one the hearts of all mankind.
Bid all our sad divisions cease
and be yourself our King of Peace. [Refrain]

Chapter 17: Judaism and the New Testament

We have come a long way from the time of Adam in the Garden of Eden, when there was no need for priests and he could access God directly. We have considered the time before God instructed Moses to set up the priestly system overseen by the tribe of Levi, when the likes of Noah, Job, Abraham, Isaac and Jacob all offered animal sacrifices and while there was a brief mention of the Melchizedek priesthood, the main focus as far as the Old Testament is concerned was Aaron and his descendants who served as priests in the Tabernacle and later in the Temple, along with the Levites.

While priests and the priesthood dominated the Jewish religion, it had undergone huge changes by the time we get to the New Testament. When we began our priesthood journey, having considered the Law and the Covenant (Chapter 4), we find in Chapters 5 through to 11 that things appeared to be simpler and more straightforward during the time when Israel travelled in the Wilderness and settled in Canaan under the leadership of Joshua, with the Priests who were assisted by the Levites being the central "religious" figures and the Tabernacle being the principal place of worship.

Then there was the building of the First Temple (Chapter 14) and, after a period of exile with the priesthood temporarily suspended (given there was no Temple), that of the Second Temple (Chapter 15) when there was a lot more to take note of when it came to religious practice and the way priests and Levites operated and new players, such as Scribes and various religious factions. There is also the prospect of a to be built Third Temple (Chapter 18). The various extensions to ways Judaism was carried out and the divergence seen from the end of the Old Testament continued during the Inter Testament period (Chapter 16), bringing us to the time of Jesus, of whom we read: *"But when the fulness of the time was come, God sent forth his Son, made of a woman, made under the law, to redeem them that were under the law, that we might receive the adoption of sons"* Galatians 4:4-5.

The first thing that might strike us was Jesus, all of His disciples and most of His followers while on earth were faithful Jews who did what was required by the Jewish Law, starting with his parents: Joseph and Mary. We read concerning Simeon, soon after Jesus birth and circumcision on the eighth day *"And it was revealed unto him by the Holy Ghost, that he should not see death, before he had seen the Lord's Christ. And he came by the Spirit into the temple: and when the parents brought in the child Jesus, to do for him after the custom of the law, Then took he him up in his arms, and blessed God, and said, Lord, now lettest thou thy servant depart in peace, according to thy word: For mine eyes have seen thy salvation, Which thou hast prepared before the face of all people. A light to lighten the Gentiles, and the glory of thy people Israel*" Luke 2:26-32. When Jesus was 12, He went with His parents to Jerusalem to celebrate the Passover: "*And it came to pass, that after three days they found him in the temple, sitting in the midst of the doctors, both hearing them, and asking them questions*" Luke 2:46.

Concerning Jesus' followers, after Jesus ascended into heaven and the pouring out of the Holy Spirit on the Day of Pentecost we read: "*And they, continuing daily with one accord in the temple, and breaking bread from house to house, did eat their meat with gladness and singleness of heart*" Acts 2:46 and "*Now Peter and John went up together into the temple at the hour of prayer, being the ninth hour*" Acts 3:1. Notwithstanding that synagogues were to have a greater role, a trend that began when the Jews were in exile in Babylon, the Temple was still the main place of religious devotion, at least until the time it became clear Christ followers were no longer welcomed.

One point that we will return to in Chapter 54, for example, is that in order to have a complete understanding of the purposes of God, we need to be familiar with the contents of both Old and New Testament and take up the counsel offered in Chapter 2 concerning background and context. While somewhat simplistic, there is nevertheless certain truth in the claim that the Old Testament is a Jewish book and the New Testament is a Christian book. While Jews are encouraged to study the New Testament, not just because it tells us things necessary for salvation, but it answers many of the questions raised in the Old Testament; similarly, for Christians to come to a fuller understanding and appreciation of the Gospel, they do well to go back to its root that is found in the Old Testament.

But getting back to the question of what had changed by the time we get to the New Testament, we do well to consider changes listed under "Point 6" at the end of Chapter 16, touching on this subject:

Priests

While Priests like Caiaphas and Ananias are given a bad press because of their opposition to Jesus and Paul respectively, others such as Zacharias (father of John the Baptist) can be looked on more positively as discussed in Part 3 of this book. Moreover, we read that "*a great company of the priests were obedient to the faith*" Acts 6:7. Because of the power exercised by secular authorities, such as King Herod, to appoint priests, they chose those they could control. Those who became High Priest were generally of a low calibre spiritually or being aligned with the will of God, for they were often political appointees. Chief priests, along with scribes, like Pharisees and Sadducees, not only tended to oppose Jesus and His disciples that followed later, but they had the political clout to carry out their threats.

Scribes

The organisation of scribes, referred to several times in the New Testament, can be seen as far back as the time of Ezra (who is referred to both as a priest and scribe). Baruch, Jeremiah's faithful assistant, was also a scribe (Jeremiah 36:32). They were highly educated men, trained to write. At first, they were merely transcribers of God's law and synagogue readers, but later they became interpreters of God's law whose responsibility was to teach the Torah and they received prominence as Judaism became more pre-occupied with applying the Law rather than the system of Tabernacle or Temple worship laid out in the Books of Exodus and Leviticus and later Chronicles. Scribes produced legal documents, recorded deeds, and acted as notary public and court secretary.

Rome

Judah, after having been under the control of Babylon, Persia and Greece, ended up under the control of Rome. While Rome could be ruthless when it came to putting down rebellion and insisting its subjects adhere to its laws, e.g., paying taxes (something we find Jesus, Peter and Paul exhorting Christ followers to do) Rome, in the main, allowed its Jewish subjects considerable freedom when it came to the practice of their religion, and delegated certain powers to Jewish religious authorities when it came to regulating their own affairs. They also brought in a measure of peace and stability, along with roads and major engineering and infrastructure projects, which proved beneficial in spreading the Word.

The Herodian dynasty

While Israel was ruled from Rome, under a succession of Roman governors, notably Pontius Pilate, who condemned Jesus to death, they also installed their own puppet kings, who were given power and authority over the people and land they reigned over – as long as they were in line with their Roman overlords. This was done through the Herodian dynasty, beginning with Herod the Great (72 BC – 4 BC). The Herodian dynasty were Edomites who had converted to Judaism and were able to gain favour with the Romans. There are several Herods mentioned in the Bible and all undertook acts of wickedness, starting with killing baby boys when Jesus was born. While not trusted by the Jewish inhabitants, they undertook several building projects, notably the re-building of the Second Temple, which took place during the period 20 BC to 63 AD, in order to help to placate their subjects. Chapter 2, Figure 24 shows the family tree of the Herods of the Bible, starting with Herod the Great.

The Sanhedrin

The term Sanhedrin is from a Greek word that means "assembly" or "council" and dates from the Hellenistic period, but the concept is one that goes back to the Torah when God commanded Moses: "*Gather unto me seventy men of the elders of Israel, whom thou knowest to be the elders of the people, and officers over them; and bring them unto the tabernacle of the congregation, that they may stand there with thee*" Numbers 11:16. Also, "*Judges and officers shalt thou make thee in all thy gates, which the Lord thy God giveth thee, throughout thy tribes: and they shall judge the people with just judgment*" Deuteronomy 16:18. Within the land there were local courts, also referred to as Sanhedrin. The Great Sanhedrin was the supreme court during the Second Temple period, made up of 70 men and the High Priest. In the Second Temple period, the Great Sanhedrin met in the Temple in Jerusalem. The court convened every day except festivals and on the Sabbath. As far of the New Testament is concerned, this Sanhedrin played a major role in the condemnation of Jesus and later Stephen.

Religious groupings

In Chapter 16, we identified the emergence of four groupings within Judaism (check out Chapter 2, Figure 25 for what each of these stood for): Pharisees, Sadducees, Zealots and Essenes. We read in the New Testament Jesus often coming in contact with two of these groups. While certain contact was positive, e.g., in the case of Nicodemus, much of it was antagonistic, both groups seeing Jesus as a threat despite strongly disagreeing theologically and eventually ganging up together to see Jesus removed. One cannot help but see parallels with today's religious situation and see their emergence as a response to successively being ruled by Babylon, Persia, Greece and Rome. While not much is said about the Zealots and Essenes, these two groups played an important part in Judaism at that time.

The Temple

Despite many religious activities going on, the Temple was still the centre of Jewish religious life and the priests still continued to make a very important contribution to that life, including doing all the activities God told Moses should happen. The New Testament records several occasions when Jesus and His disciples entered the Temple and took part in the services held there. The rebuilt Second Temple under the Herodian dynasty was a magnificent construction, although its destruction by the Romans in AD 70, in response to a Jewish led revolt, proved a major turning point in the way Judaism operated. The Priesthood and the sacrificial system ceased, although other religious leaders continued. Prayer took the place of sacrifice, and worship was rebuilt around rabbis who acted as teachers and leaders of individual communities, often based around the synagogues. The Talmud became a major influence in Jewish religious life, often ahead of that of the Torah.

The Synagogue

According to one definition, a synagogue is a building in which Jewish people worship and study their religion, in much the same way that churches are seen to do in Christianity and mosques in Islam. We see the emergence of synagogues during the period of Exile when there was no Temple and their numerical growth on return from exile and during Inter Testament times, which brings us to New Testament times. We see several accounts of Jesus and His disciples, notably Paul, preaching the "Good News" in synagogues and engaging with the people. While this was an opportunity to share the Gospel message, there was also sometimes a hostile reaction. We read in Luke 4:16-30 how early on in Jesus' ministry, when he preached on Isaiah 61 at his home synagogue in Nazareth, this caused an angry reaction from among those who listened, who sought to throw Him out of the city. We considered what a typical synagogue from Jesus' time looked like and compared synagogue and temple worship in Chapter 2, Figure 29, noting that today synagogues around the world are many and varied.

The Samaritans

According to Wikipedia: "*Samaritans are an ethnoreligious group who originate from the ancient Israelites. They are native to the Levant and adhere to Samaritanism, an Abrahamic and ethnic religion similar to Judaism, but differing in several important aspects. Samaritan tradition claims the group descends from the northern Israelite tribes who were not deported by the Neo-Assyrian Empire after the destruction of the Kingdom of Israel. They consider Samaritanism to be the true religion of the ancient Israelites and regard Judaism as a closely related but altered religion. Samaritans also regard Mount Gerizim (near both Nablus and biblical Shechem), and not the Temple Mount in Jerusalem, to be the holiest place on Earth*".

We will touch on Samaritans with respect to those Jews returning from exile to settle back in their land, also occupied by Samaritans, when we consider Eliashib in Chapter 34 and Ezra in Chapter 35. When it comes to the New Testament, there are many references to Samaritans and these are not accidental, especially in the light of the antipathy Jews and Samaritans had for one another.

Three incidents involving Jesus show us how He reached out to Samaritans when fellow Jews failed to do so. There was his encounter with the woman at the well, which begins "*Then cometh he to a city of Samaria, which is called Sychar, near to the parcel of ground that Jacob gave to his son Joseph. Now Jacob's well was there. Jesus therefore, being wearied with his journey, sat thus on the well: and it was about the sixth hour"* John 4:5-6. Then there was the Parable of the Good Samaritan (Luke 10:29-37).

It wasn't the priest or Levite who helped the chap who had been mugged but rather the Samaritan. Then there was the healing of the ten lepers (Luke 17:11-19), when it was the Samaritan that gave thanks. It is noteworthy that when Jesus told His disciples: *"But ye shall receive power, after that the Holy Ghost is come upon you: and ye shall be witnesses unto me both in Jerusalem, and in all Judaea, and in Samaria, and unto the uttermost part of the earth"* (Acts 1:8) that between telling the good news to the Jews and other Gentiles they needed to go to Samaria – which the disciples did!

A Personal Perspective

We have deliberately written chapters in this Part 1 and Part 2 to follow in the third person so as not to personalise matters and help us focus on God and what He thinks. Having elaborated on those points raised in Chapter 16, the author requests reader forbearance when it comes to sharing his personal perspective. When the Preacher declared *"there is nothing new under the sun"* Ecclesiastes 1:9, it seems in a strange way many of these observations could apply to today's church and world.

Consider the four stand-out religious groupings: Pharisees, Sadducees, Zealots and Essenes. We see their like today. As a "conservative" Christian, it is easy to be dismissive of the Sadducee liberal equivalent that have both compromised by following the way of the world and dismissed essential beliefs and, if it weren't for the fact Pharisees are also portrayed as the bad guys, we would admire their sticking to their guns regarding fundamental doctrine. Their problem and one that also helps to give today's conservatives a bad press is they were legalistic and unloving, including adding stuff not in the Scriptures and neglecting the Spirit of the Law as seen in the summation of the Law – *"Love Thy Neighbour"*. When we consider Jesus and interactions He had with the Pharisees and Sadducees of His day, His biggest complaint was their replacing the more important Spirit of the Law with the Letter of the Law, and adding laws on trivial matters, not in the Torah, to the point of obsession.

As for today's zealots, many have been rightly accused of being overzealous when a more winsome approach might be more appropriate but, even so, zeal (for God's glory) is much lacking and needed. But arguably a more serious form of Christianity, such as practised by the Puritans, is preferable and needed to replace the anything goes variety we see today. As for the Essenes, the history of the church contains many accounts of their Christian equivalent – monks and the like, who chose a life of quiet contemplation and withdrawal from worldly pre-occupations and often included celibacy. At the same time, they were able to serve the poor and vulnerable in their communities. But as in all things, while spirituality is better than worldliness, we are left in the world in order to do good and yet to live life.

In order to apply the lessons to today's fractured Christian community, we could conclude that nearly every faction has something of merit to offer and none of them get everything right, whether it be those more conservatively in-clined with their entrenched positions in the light of an anti-God culture and a church establishment intent on appeasing the powers that be, along with those zealous, even more conservative types, or today's Essenes who withdraw from the world, or Liberals types, including those once labelled Evangelical, who adopt a religion of pick and mix, which is not the way to go!

"In for a penny, in for a pound" – having ventured a personal perspective, another pertinent one that is related to the subject matter of this chapter is that of Jewish versus Greek mindset. David Pawson, who has already been cited as a helpful source for research purposes, even though there will be points that the author and some readers would rightly take issue with, often lamented concerning the extent of Greek influence on today's church, and this to the detriment of Jewish influence. The seed had already been sown prior to the church, when the Greek empire emerged during the Inter Testament period. The object as far as this particular personal perspective goes is not to go into the ins and outs of what the author recognises as being a valid concern but rather to make two main points.

Firstly, while it is regrettable that Jews, especially those of the Orthodox leaning variety, who go to great pains to keep their cultural identity, being prepared and having had to pay the price for maintaining that identity, have also been barking up the wrong tree when it comes to their fixation on prac-tices not mandated by the Torah and failing to recognise their Messiah, as identified in Isaiah 53.

Secondly, there is understandably a backlash by those in the minority Messianic, Evangelical Christian camp against those in the majority, who typically do not give Israel and its religious observances much credence, who uncritically take on board an assortment of Hellenistic influences and some-times tend to take the pro-Palestine position when it comes to who is right in the current Israel/Palestine conflict. YHWH is more interested that we adopt His ways and there is nothing in the Bible to insist men, for example, wear Kippah/Yarmulke head caps or adopt Jewish speak in their commu-nications. As for Christmas/Easter versus Passover/Tabernacles, freedom of choice ought to be the watchword. As for the Israel/Palestine conflict, this is a complex and controversial subject we discuss in Chapter 52.

Transitioning from Judaism to Christianity

We end this chapter by considering the question that the Early Church needed to deal with and one which Paul wrestled with, for example in his letter to the Galatians: whether or not in order to become a Christian one first needs to become a Jew? This question has huge ramifications and it would be easy to go off on several tangents. To prevent doing so, we need to be brought back to the main focus of this book: The Priesthood (Part 1), The Priests (Part 2) and A Priestly People (Part 3).

When the Church was supposed to have begun, on that first Day of Pentecost, following Jesus' Ascension, it was almost exclusively Jewish in composition. But Jesus had commanded His disciples to preach the Gospel to the whole world, which was almost all Gentile. Peter needed a vision from God in order to get on with the task and make his first Gentile convert, Cornelius, as detailed in Acts 10. But controversy soon followed when it was argued that in order to be a faithful Christian one needed to first be a faithful Jew. Even today, the extent to which Gentile believers need to adopt Jewish ways has remained a contentious one and as with all subjects a right balance is needed, remembering Paul's words on the subject: *"Stand fast therefore in the liberty wherewith Christ hath made us free, and be not entangled again with the yoke of bondage"* Galatians 5:1 but also *"For though I be free from all men, yet have I made myself servant unto all, that I might gain the more"* 1 Corinthians 9:19.

It is the author's belief that a lack of understanding of "Jewish ways" (as well as the Hebrew Scriptures), and adapting to a culture more in line with Greek thinking, has been to the church's overall detriment. But back to that early controversy. This led to the Council of Jerusalem, as detailed in Acts 15, which following prayerful deliberation, culminated in a declaration by the Apostles and leaders of the church, followed by a letter to "whoever it may concern", which included the words *"For it seemed good to the Holy Ghost, and to us, to lay upon you no greater burden than these necessary things; That ye abstain from meats offered to idols, and from blood, and from things strangled, and from fornication: from which if ye keep yourselves, ye shall do well"* Acts 15:28-29.

The trend from then onward was instead of the Church comprising predominantly Jewish believers, it would become dominated by Gentile believers, and increasingly those having little connection with Jewish culture and the Hebrew Scriptures, which is overwhelmingly the position today. Also, from early in church history there was a move toward leading church figures, e.g., Justin Martyr, Marcion and Augustine of Hippo advocating replacement theology, the Church has replaced Israel. This is not the platform to reflect deeply on Israel other than to refer readers to the author's book

"**Prophets of the Bible**", which includes several examples of yet to be fulfilled prophecy concerning Israel and to declare Israel has not been replaced and still has an important place in God's plans, especially when it comes to "Last Things" prophecy and events (and is also discussed in Chapter 46).

Attitudes to Israel vary considerably among Christians, including a view of perhaps the majority of Christendom that Israel has been replaced by the Church. How this author sees things is that the Church is distinct from Israel but has not replaced it. There are Jews who follow Jesus, and might be seen as being in both camps, but most do not. Others are religious, but often it is an empty shell that is unacceptable to YHWH, and all need the Gospel (Romans 1:16). As for the good and bad guys on the world stage, the situation is complex – neither is it Israel can do no wrong as some have us believe, especially given the unprovoked onslaughts it has had to face from many of the world powers, nor is it that Israel are purely targets/victims given their oppression of the Palestinians.

While outside the scope of this book, the author has argued in his other writings, such as the blog section of his website, that world affairs are often orchestrated by a satanically inspired, tiny, cabal, some of whom are highly placed Jews (in name only, in the mould of King Herod). His belief is that while unbelieving Israel will be subject to even more trials and tribulations (e.g., "*the time of Jacob's trouble*" Jeremiah 30:6-8) its future is nevertheless a bright one and he shares Paul's concern, who wrote: "*my heart's desire and prayer to God for Israel is, that they might be saved*" Romans 10:1.

Related to this and partly covered in "**Prophets of the Bible**" is the place of Israel in today's world. The author has noted a range of views among thoughtful, sincere Christians, ranging from Israel being replaced by the church to Israel occupying centre stage in God's plans and purposes, especially after the Church has been raptured. Another consideration where there are extremes of views is that at one extreme there are those who hold to the notion that Israel can do no wrong, to others who when it comes to contentious questions, such as the Palestinian one, see Israel as the wrong doers.

The author can only re-iterate his views and concerns that most of today's Jews are unsaved and like unsaved Gentiles they are sinners needing to repent or face God's judgment, for they have also rejected *Yeshua* their *Mashiach*, who "*came unto his own, and his own received him not*" John 1:11. As well as corrupt elements who pass as Jews but are more like those who we read of who are the modern day equivalent to "*the synagogue of Satan*", Revelation 2:9, 3:9, there are many non-believing Jews who seek to do the right thing, inspired by their religious traditions and the Hebrew Scriptures. Jews have both had to suffer unspeakable and undeniable persecution down the last two millennia and, while antisemitism still exists, some accused of being antisemitic for political reasons have merely criticised Israel (often for valid reasons), in the same way others might concerning other nations.

Besides believing there will yet be a *time of Jacob's trouble* on top of all the other troubles Israel has had to face throughout its 4000-year history, the author believes the rebirth of Israel as a nation in 1948 was a fulfilment of prophecy that opened the way for many other end time prophecies to be fulfilled. Israel's ability to withstand aggression, typically from surrounding Arab nations, often against great odds, was in part as a result of divine protection. Israel taking centre stage in future wars to take place before Jesus returns and their suffering under the Antichrist are to be expected. As for present day Israel, the author's observation is that it is largely characterised by unbelief.

When it comes to religious observance, it is not God's Law (the Torah) that the religiously inclined Jew typically gravitates toward but rather it is man's flawed interpretation of that Law, led by the post-Temple replacement to the priests (rabbis) – the Talmud. The system in place today is not so dissimilar to the one that Jesus encountered – religion without YHWH or a distorted view of Him. As far as most of today's Jews are concerned, a spiritual blindness has fallen on them and the historical tragedy has been that many elements of the professing church have failed to reach Jews for Jesus.

Besides looking forward to the fulfilment of Paul's *"that they might be saved"* prayer there are the words of the prophet *"And I will pour upon the house of David, and upon the inhabitants of Jerusalem, the spirit of grace and of supplications: and they shall look upon me whom they have pierced, and they shall mourn for him, as one mourneth for his only son, and shall be in bitterness for him, as one that is in bitterness for his firstborn"* Zechariah 12:10. And of course, there is Israel taking centre stage during Jesus' Millennial reign, which will bring in a time of peace, righteousness and justice to all the earth and, for the first time following the Fall (of Adam), the good guys will be in the ascendancy.

In winding up this particular section, we point to the teaching of Paul to the Romans. Having, in chapters 1 to 8, brilliantly set out many of the great doctrines of the Christian faith that were beloved of the Reformers, for example, he turns his attention to Israel, something many of those same Reformers tended to downplay and even rationalise with notions of "Replacement theology", as do many Christians today. While we live in the time of the Gentiles, God has not forgotten or replaced the descendants of Abraham or reneged on His promises, and their time will surely come.

While God's covenant with Abraham applies today just as much to believers in Jesus (Jew and Gentile), e.g., *"Know ye therefore that they which are of faith, the same are the children of Abraham. And the scripture, fore-*

seeing that God would justify the heathen through faith, preached before the gospel unto Abraham, saying, In thee shall all nations be blessed. So then they which be of faith are blessed with faithful Abraham" Galatians 3:7-9, there is still a special place for the physical descendants of Israel (discussed in Chapter 52), where among other things we will consider the Abrahamic Covenant: *"And I will make of thee a great nation, and I will bless thee, and make thy name great; and thou shalt be a blessing: And I will bless them that bless thee, and curse him that curseth thee: and in thee shall all families of the earth be blessed"* Genesis 12:2-3 (but also check out Genesis 15:18-21).

"Boast not against the branches. But if thou boast, thou bearest not the root, but the root thee. Thou wilt say then, The branches were broken off, that I might be grafted in. Well; because of unbelief they were broken off, and thou standest by faith. Be not highminded, but fear: For if God spared not the natural branches, take heed lest he also spare not thee. Behold therefore the goodness and severity of God: on them which fell, severity; but toward thee, goodness, if thou continue in his goodness: otherwise thou also shalt be cut off. And they also, if they abide not still in unbelief, shall be grafted in: for God is able to graft them in again. For if thou wert cut out of the olive tree which is wild by nature, and wert grafted contrary to nature into a good olive tree: how much more shall these, which be the natural branches, be grafted into their own olive tree? For I would not, brethren, that ye should be ignorant of this mystery, lest ye should be wise in your own conceits; that blindness in part is happened to Israel, until the fulness of the Gentiles be come in. And so all Israel shall be saved: as it is written, There shall come out of Sion the Deliverer, and shall turn away ungodliness from Jacob: For this is my covenant unto them, when I shall take away their sins" Romans 11:18-27.

The point to make here is that those of us who are Gentile believers have been grafted into the olive tree that represents Israel and are partakers of the promise God made to Abraham, Isaac and Jacob while having NOT replaced them and we look forward to the day when *"all Israel shall be saved"*. How all this pans out in the future requires a deeper discussion beyond the remit of this book, albeit addressed partly in **"Prophets of the Bible"** and touched on in Chapters 46 and 52. The next big event in God's calendar, that we can look forward to, is the Second Coming of the Lord Jesus Christ and after that a physical Millennium, when Israel plays a major part. The future of Israel is positive, for after suffering more trials and tribulations, after which they turn to their Messiah (Zechariah 12-14), the promises made to Abraham 4000 years ago will be fully fulfilled and for that we give God all the glory.

We can reflect of the words of the hymn writer, when considering a time yet to come when Israel's true king (Jesus) reigns supreme and we can truly pray *"Thy Kingdom Come"*:

1. *Sing we the King who is coming to reign,*
   Glory to Jesus, the Lamb that was slain;
Righteousness, peace then His empire shall bring,
   Joy to the nations when Jesus is King.

[Refrain]
Come let us sing: Praise to our King,
   Jesus our King, Jesus our King:
This is our song, who to Jesus belong:
   Glory to Jesus, to Jesus our King.

2. *All men shall dwell in His marvelous light,*
   Races long severed His love shall unite,
Justice and truth from His scepter shall spring,
Wrong shall be ended when Jesus is King. [Refrain]

3. *All shall be well in His kingdom of peace,*
   Freedom shall flourish and wisdom increase,
Foe shall be friend when His triumph we sing,
Sword shall be sickle when Jesus is King. [Refrain]

4. *Knowledge and fear of the Lord then shall be*
   As the deep waters that cover the sea;
   All things shall be in the splendor of spring
And all harmonious when Jesus is King. [Refrain]

5. *Kingdom of Christ, for thy coming we pray,*
   Hasten, O Father, the dawn of the day
   When this new song Thy creation shall sing,
Satan is vanquished and Jesus is King. [Refrain]

Chapter 18: The Third Temple

When we began this project, which was principally to consider Priests of the Bible, it seemed pretty clear we needed to devote chapters to the First and Second Temples, for not only is there much written about these temples in the Bible but a lot of it is related to priests and the priesthood. As for a Third, yet to be built, Temple, much less is found in the Bible and scholars are divided as to what to make out of it and faithful Christians differ on how to respond to the building of such a Temple.

When the author did his customary Google search on the subject, there was a lot to be found, much of it related to the desire of certain Jews, mostly of the Orthodox variety, for such a Temple to be built. Nor is this a mere pipe dream but plans have been drawn up and preparations are being made for such a Temple to be built on the ancient Temple site, and this includes breeding the red heifers needed for making sacrifices to God. Many reasons are given for supporting "the Third Temple project" (see *thirdtemple.org*) starting with *"to restore the oneness of G-d, the one G-d for all humanity at the site where His home is to be built"*. In attracting supporters of those seeking to peacefully build the Third Temple of Jerusalem on the Temple Mount, promoting ideas such as it being used to make a transition from hatred and conflict to love and peace, certain Christians, often of the Messianic, Fundamentalist variety, are sympathetic toward and supportive of such an undertaking, seeing it as being needed to fulfil Bible prophecy, prior to Christ's Second Coming, and in standing in solidarity with Israel.

Wikipedia gives us the following helpful information: *"The "Third Temple" refers to a hypothetical rebuilt Temple in Jerusalem. It would succeed Solomon's Temple and the Second Temple, the former having been destroyed during the Babylonian siege of Jerusalem in c.587 BCE and the latter having been destroyed during the Roman siege of Jerusalem in 70 CE. Although it remains unbuilt, the notion of and desire for the Third Temple is sacred in Judaism, and particularly in Orthodox Judaism; it is anticipated as the most sacred place of worship for Jews. The Hebrew Bible holds that Jewish prophets called for its construction to be fulfilled prior to, or in tandem with, the Messianic Age. The building of the Third Temple also plays a major role in some interpretations of Christian eschatology. Among religious Jews, the anticipation of an ultimate future project centred around building the Third Temple at the Temple Mount in the Old City of Jerusalem has been a running theme that, in Israel, is also espoused as an ideological motive."*

During the two millennia that have elapsed since the destruction of the Second Temple, there have been no serious attempts to build a third temple, despite it being the dream of many. Instead, during the times the Muslims were in control of Jerusalem they have erected mosques on the site of the Second Temple, which remain and are in use today. While a matter of contention, Israeli authorities have not dared to do anything about replacing the Al Aqsa mosque and the Dome of the Rock that are currently on the Temple mount site with a Jewish temple, knowing that if they did it would likely give rise to an unwinnable holy war. All that is left of the Second Temple is the part remains of its outer walls, which continue to be a place of pilgrimage for visitors and those wanting a restored temple alike.

Whether there was a call for the people to build the Third Temple is a contentious point, although there was a call, notably by Haggai and Zechariah, to build the Second Temple soon upon their return from exile. Most of those leading the move for a third Temple can hardly be considered as being in tune with the mind of God, given they have rejected His Son, leaving one to wonder how God can bless any project that would be born in an atmosphere of unbelief and which He has not blessed. Yet we cannot ignore scriptures such as to be found in the Book of Revelation that more than imply that BEFORE Jesus returns and after the Second Temple was destroyed there will be a further Temple.

Looking at an undefined future, Zechariah sees another temple *"Behold the man whose name is The Branch; and he shall grow up out of his place, and he shall build the temple of the Lord: Even he shall build the temple of the Lord; and he shall bear the glory, and shall sit and rule upon his throne; and he shall be a priest upon his throne: and the counsel of peace shall be between them both. And the crowns shall be to Helem, and to Tobijah, and to Jedaiah, and to Hen the son of Zephaniah, for a memorial in the temple of the Lord. And they that are far off shall come and build in the temple of the Lord, and ye shall know that the Lord of hosts hath sent me unto you"* Zechariah 6: 12-15.

When we consider the prophet Jeremiah, and one of the many Old Testament prophecies looking forward to a coming Messiah, we read concerning the Lord's Eternal Covenant with David: *"Behold, the days come, saith the Lord, that I will perform that good thing which I have promised unto the house of Israel and to the house of Judah. In those days, and at that time, will I cause the Branch of righteousness to grow up unto David; and he shall execute judgment and righteousness in the land.*

In those days shall Judah be saved, and Jerusalem shall dwell safely: and this is the name wherewith she shall be called, The Lord our righteousness. For thus saith the Lord; David shall never want a man to sit upon the throne of the house of Israel; Neither shall the priests the Levites want a man before me to offer burnt offerings, and to kindle meat offerings, and to do sacrifice continually. And the word of the Lord came unto Jeremiah, saying, Thus saith the Lord; If ye can break my covenant of the day, and my covenant of the night, and that there should not be day and night in their season; Then may also my covenant be broken with David my servant, that he should not have a son to reign upon his throne; and with the Levites the priests, my ministers" Jeremiah 33:14-21. Of interest here is not just a future king but future priests, begging the question where they operate. As for the prophet Daniel, it can be argued, e.g., the Abomination of Desolation made at the Temple, was only partially fulfilled under the rule of Antiochus Epiphanes but to be fully fulfilled by a yet to appear Antichrist.

Disappointingly but unsurprisingly, when doing Google searches on the subject, hardly any reference was made to the most significant passage in the Bible concerning a not yet built temple – Ezekiel 40-48. Also unsurprisingly, the text lends itself to varied interpretations, including among otherwise sound Bible scholars who struggle to see how this could be fulfilled under a future Messiah given references to sacrifices etc. If one were to take the more literal approach to interpretation and a belief in a future Millennium, not only is such a temple yet to be built, but much of what is described in these verses cannot happen before the return of the Messiah, most likely during His Millennial kingdom reign, although the question is begged, why is such a temple needed along with its sacrificial system, given Jesus has already dwelt (tabernacled) among us and lives in His Church. Moreover, He made the ultimate sacrifice, sufficient to atone for all sin, which means no more sacrifices are required?

Since God's glory is an important consideration in our book, it is worth highlighting that the glory of the Lord went up from the midst of the city and it was the symbol of God's presence, which had departed from the Temple (Ezekiel 10:18), but also 2600 years later, and we are still waiting (unless, like some Christian commentators, we were to apply this in purely spiritual terms), just as God's glory had departed to the east, it would return to the Temple from the east (Ezekiel 43:4). Interestingly, Ezekiel received his vision of the future Temple around 570 BC, some half way through the Babylonian exile, which along with its messianic associations would have raised hopes and expectations of what might happen when the Jews would return from Exile. Zerubbabel's Second Temple, completed some 50 years later, was nothing like the Temple seen in Ezekiel's vision. Neither was Herod's rebuilt Second Temple or any temple being planned or suggested as possible today.

"Prophets of the Bible" highlights the following concerning the Temple, as well as the City and Land:

1. The precise measurements and detail given of the Temple construction.

2. Similarities with the First and Second Temples but significant differences too.

3. Animal sacrifices are regularly offered.

4. No mention of the Veil, the Holy Place furniture or the Ark of the Covenant.

5. Everyone had and knew their place in the well-ordered life of the Temple.

6. The sense of order and purpose; divine peace and blessing.

7. The sense of righteousness and justice.

8. No High Priest; he has been replaced (it seems) by the Prince.

9. The priests of Zadok, the Levites under the Prince to supervise activities.

10. The glory of God that left the Temple in Ezekiel Chapters 10 and 11, returns in 43.

11. The river that flows from the Temple in Chapter 47 that gives life to all.

12. The Dead Sea now fertile with the surrounding area teeming with life.

13. The unusual apportionment of the Land.

14. *"The name of the city from that day shall be, The Lord is there"* (48:35).

15. All this is central to what we can expect to see in the Millennial Kingdom.

This brings us back to the question of a yet to be built temple before Jesus returns to earth. In the Book of Revelation, there are 13 references to "temple" but most of them are to a heavenly temple. One is with reference to the New Jerusalem, after the Millennium, where we read: *"And I saw no temple therein: for the Lord God Almighty and the Lamb are the temple of it"* (21:22). Another reference appears to be what takes place in a period referred to as the Great Tribulation, a little prior to Christ's coming again in glory in Chapter 19. We also read *"And there was given me a reed like unto a rod: and the angel stood, saying, Rise, and measure the temple of God, and the altar, and them that worship therein. But the court which is without the temple leave out, and measure it not; for it is given unto the Gentiles: and the holy city shall they tread under foot forty and two months. And I will give power unto my two witnesses, and they shall prophesy a thousand two hundred and threescore days, clothed in sackcloth. These are the two olive trees, and the two candlesticks standing before the God of the earth. And if any man will hurt them, fire proceedeth out of their mouth, and devoureth their enemies: and if any man will hurt them, he must in this manner be killed"* (Revelation 11:1-5).

Concerning Daniel's Abomination of Desolation prophecy (see also Matthew 24) and the prospect of a yet to be built temple prior to Jesus' return, the other applicable New Testament reference is: *"Now we beseech you, brethren, by the coming of our Lord Jesus Christ, and by our gathering together unto him, That ye be not soon shaken in mind, or be troubled, neither by spirit, nor by word, nor by letter as from us, as that the day of Christ is at hand. Let no man deceive you by any means: for that day shall not come, except there come a falling away first, and that man of sin be revealed, the son of perdition; Who opposeth and exalteth himself above all that is called God, or that is worshipped; so that he as God sitteth in the temple of God, shewing himself that he is God"* 2 Thessalonians 2:1-4. It is evident Paul is not writing about Antiochus Epiphanes, who did something similar during the Inter Testament period, but one yet to come. The "man of sin" is often equated with the future Antichrist.

In conclusion, thoughtful believers will hold different views and there is a lot yet to be unravelled concerning "The Third Temple", whether it is the one that was meant to be built following Judah's return from captivity in Babylon or one we might expect to be built prior to Christ's return or one that is entirely different to all other temples built before it or even possible humanly speaking, which the author believes to be the case and will be built during the Millennium, after Christ returns. The point of this chapter is not to be controversial or distracting, but rather to encourage readers to check out for themselves what the Bible says on the subject of "The Third Temple" and to write in the interests of attempting to provide readers a comprehensive coverage of the subject of "Priests of the Bible".

It is unlikely the writer of the following hymn had the Third Temple in mind when penning these words, but since all the temples we have discussed are/were meant for the purpose of blessing the Lord, these words are applicable. Moreover, it is also evident that the words of this song are based, at least loosely, on Psalm 103, which is where we ended our chapter that discussed the First Temple. Evidently, King David and Matt Redman had something in common when it came to the worship of God!

[Refrain]
Bless the Lord oh my soul
Oh my soul
Worship his holy name
Sing like never before
Oh my soul
I worship your holy name

1. The sun comes up
Its a new day dawning
Its time to sing your song again
What ever may pass and whatever lies before me
Let me be singing when the evening comes [Refrain]

2. You're rich in love and you're slow to anger
Your name is great and your heart is kind
For all your goodness I will keep on singing
10,000 reasons for my heart to find [Refrain]

3. And on that day when my strength is failing
The end draws near and my time has come
Soon my soul will sing your praise un-ending
10,000 years and there forever more [Refrain]

Chapter 19: Jesus our Great High Priest

In the Bible, especially the Old Testament, prophets, priests and kings played an important part and often interacted with and complemented one another. Jesus alone combined all three offices and did so perfectly, despite being rejected by His own people. He continues to do so. In both **"Prophets of the Bible"** and **"Priests of the Bible"**, "prophets, priests and kings" as relating to Jesus has been a recurring theme but in this chapter our focus is on priests, specifically Jesus our Great High Priest.

As a Prophet, Jesus called the world, particularly Israel, to turn from sin and return to God, and He was put to death for doing what all true prophets were called by God to do, and did – which was to present the truth which God deemed to be important, to the people, declaring what God thought and felt about what truly mattered, even when listeners found it to be unpalatable, and then went on to reject both message and messenger. Crowds identified Him as *"Jesus the prophet"* (Matthew 21:11). He spoke of Himself as being a Prophet: *"No prophet is accepted in his own native place"* (Luke 4:24). Among His prophecies, we find that a few days before His death He foretold His death and resurrection (Matthew 16:21-28). The Olivet discourse in Matthew 24, which included predicting the destruction of the Temple, was pure prophecy. Whenever Jesus foretold the future, what he said always came to pass. Peter cited Moses when he preached Christ: *"For Moses truly said unto the fathers, A prophet shall the Lord your God raise up unto you of your brethren"* (Acts 3:22).

As a King, Jesus is spoken of as such in the Gospels. Gabriel announced to Mary that the Lord God would give to her son the Throne of David His father, and He would rule over the house of Jacob for ever. Magi looked for a newborn King of the Jews, leading to Herod killing the baby boys in a fit of rage. When Jesus last entered Jerusalem, He fulfilled the prophecy *"thy King cometh unto thee: he is just, and having salvation; lowly, and riding upon an ass"* (Zechariah 9:9), as crowds hailed Him as their King. He was arrested and killed for declaring Himself to be King, and the soldiers mocked Him because of it. When Pilate asked if He was King of the Jews, Jesus replied, *"You say so"*. He clarified, *"My kingdom does not belong to this world"* (John 18:36). The charge written against Jesus was *"Jesus the Nazarene, the King of the Jews"*. Jesus announced the Kingdom of God. He is foretold as King: *"In thy majesty ride prosperously because of truth and meekness and righteousness"* (Psalm 45:4). His return is anticipated: *"King of kings, and Lord of lords"* (Revelation 19:16). When He returns to planet earth, we read *"He shall rule them with a rod of iron"* (Revelation 2:27).

In the New Testament, while we see glimpses of Jesus as Priest, for example in His prayer in John 17 that has been referred to as His High Priestly prayer, and there was another occasion a little prior to His death when Jesus prayed in the Garden of Gethsemane, we find, except for the Book of Hebrews, there is little explicitly that associates Jesus with the Priesthood. Therefore, it is to Hebrews we need to turn if we want to find out more. Here, He is presented as the Great High Priest and, through Him, believers are given direct access to God because of what He did by giving Himself as the all-sufficient, atoning sacrifice. Because of Him, man needs no other intermediary in order to approach God.

The letter to the Hebrews was written by an author unknown, to an audience unknown, although we know this was specifically to Jews who were well familiar with the Hebrew Scriptures, which are frequently referred to. Hebrews can be looked upon as the New Testament counterpart to the Old Testament Book of Leviticus. The main theme of the letter is that you name it (e.g., angels, Moses) we find Jesus is better/superior. The main concern of the author of the letter was of readers falling away from their faith in Jesus, in the light of actual and threatened persecution, tempted by the prospect that if they were to renounce their faith and go back to Judaism things would become easier for them. While there are many topics covered in the letter, our focus will be on Jesus our Great High Priest, about which the epistle's author has much to say. We will do so by considering each chapter in turn and what it has to say on the subject. Bear in mind, when making the case, the arguments used by the author are more likely to appeal to the Jewish way of thinking than to that of the Greek.

Chapter 1

Jesus is better – God's final word.

1 God, who at sundry times and in divers manners spake in time past unto the fathers by the prophets,

2 Hath in these last days spoken unto us by his Son, whom he hath appointed heir of all things, by whom also he made the worlds;

3 Who being the brightness of his glory, and the express image of his person, and upholding all things by the word of his power, when he had by himself purged our sins, sat down on the right hand of the Majesty on high:

4 Being made so much better than the angels, as he hath by inheritance obtained a more excellent name than they.

Hebrews hits the ground running as it begins by elevating Jesus as far above anyone or anything else, He is God's Son, and by first making the point that Jesus, through whom God has spoken, is not an angel as might have been expected but, rather, someone who is better than the angels.

Chapter 2

The Salvation pioneer – Jesus made fully human.

17 Wherefore in all things it behoved him to be made like unto his brethren, that he might be a merciful and faithful high priest in things pertaining to God, to make reconciliation for the sins of the people.

18 For in that he himself hath suffered being tempted, he is able to succour them that are tempted.

Jesus is fully human and can identify with His brethren. He is thus able to take on the responsibilities of the High Priest. Given He has been tempted, He is able to help others who have been tempted.

Chapter 3

The centrepiece of all that we believe – Jesus is greater than Moses.

1 Wherefore, holy brethren, partakers of the heavenly calling, consider the Apostle and High Priest of our profession, Christ Jesus;

2 Who was faithful to him that appointed him, as also Moses was faithful in all his house.

3 For this man was counted worthy of more glory than Moses, inasmuch as he who hath builded the house hath more honour than the house.

Of all the characters of the Old Testament, Moses was probably considered the greatest among Jews, and for good reason, for it was through Moses the Covenant was given and the Law was received, yet Jesus is even greater, by virtue of Him being the Son, the ever-faithful High Priest.

Chapter 4

Jesus the Great High Priest.

14 Seeing then that we have a great high priest, that is passed into the heavens, Jesus the Son of God, let us hold fast our profession.

15 For we have not an high priest which cannot be touched with the feeling of our infirmities; but was in all points tempted like as we are, yet without sin.

16 Let us therefore come boldly unto the throne of grace, that we may obtain mercy, and find grace to help in time of need.

We need to see that we have a Great High Priest and take care to hold fast in matters pertaining to the faith and not to fall away. It is pertinent that Jesus can identify with our weakness but when doing so it is always without sin. As a result, we can always boldly approach the Throne of Grace.

Chapter 5

The High Priest who cried out in pain.

1 For every high priest taken from among men is ordained for men in things pertaining to God, that he may offer both gifts and sacrifices for sins:

2 Who can have compassion on the ignorant, and on them that are out of the way; for that he himself also is compassed with infirmity.

3 And by reason hereof he ought, as for the people, so also for himself, to offer for sins.

4 And no man taketh this honour unto himself, but he that is called of God, as was Aaron.

5 So also Christ glorified not himself to be made an high priest; but he that said unto him, Thou art my Son, to day have I begotten thee.

6 As he saith also in another place, Thou art a priest for ever after the order of Melchisedec.

7 Who in the days of his flesh, when he had offered up prayers and supplications with strong crying and tears unto him that was able to save him from death, and was heard in that he feared;

8 Though he were a Son, yet learned he obedience by the things which he suffered;

9 And being made perfect, he became the author of eternal salvation unto all them that obey him;

10 Called of God an high priest after the order of Melchisedec.

Among the features of the Aaronic priesthood, was the need for priests to make offerings for their own sins as well as for the sins of the people. Since they themselves were sinful by nature, they could empathise with those they served, whilst having been called to the priesthood by God. Jesus was ordained a Melchizedec priest (as foretold in Psalm 110). We are reminded how Jesus prayed "*let this cup pass from me*" when praying in the Garden of Gethsemane, just prior to His arrest.

Chapter 6

God gave His Word – the certainty of God's Promise.

16 For men verily swear by the greater: and an oath for confirmation is to them an end of all strife.

17 Wherein God, willing more abundantly to shew unto the heirs of promise the immutability of his counsel, confirmed it by an oath:

18 That by two immutable things, in which it was impossible for God to

lie, we might have a strong consolation, who have fled for refuge to lay hold upon the hope set before us:

19 Which hope we have as an anchor of the soul, both sure and stedfast, and which entereth into that within the veil;

20 Whither the forerunner is for us entered, even Jesus, made an high priest for ever after the order of Melchisedec.

We who have run for our very lives to God have every reason to grab the promised hope with both hands and never let go. It's an unbreakable spiritual lifeline, reaching past all appearances right to the very presence of God where Jesus, running on ahead of us, has taken up his permanent post as High Priest for us, that of the order of Melchizedek. We can base this sure and steadfast hope on the fact that God has so promised and God never breaks his promises.

Chapter 7

Jesus is likened to Melchizedek, a permanent priest of God.

21 (For those priests were made without an oath; but this with an oath by him that said unto him, The Lord sware and will not repent, Thou art a priest for ever after the order of Melchisedec:)

22 By so much was Jesus made a surety of a better testament.

23 And they truly were many priests, because they were not suffered to continue by reason of death:

24 But this man, because he continueth ever, hath an unchangeable priest-hood.

25 Wherefore he is able also to save them to the uttermost that come unto God by him, seeing he ever liveth to make intercession for them.

26 For such an high priest became us, who is holy, harmless, undefiled, separate from sinners, and made higher than the heavens;

27 Who needeth not daily, as those high priests, to offer up sacrifice, first for his own sins, and then for the people's: for this he did once, when he offered up himself.

28 For the law maketh men high priests which have infirmity; but the word of the oath, which was since the law, maketh the Son, who is conse-crated for evermore.

In so many ways, the priesthood Jesus represents is better than the Aaronic priesthood. Firstly, there was one oath and that was enough – that of Jesus being a priest of the order of Melchizedek. Secondly, His priesthood is perma-nent – Jesus never dies and always intercedes on our behalf. Thirdly, His once and for all sacrifice was all sufficient for us to be able to come before God.

Chapter 8

The High Priest of a new covenant – a new plan for Israel.

1 Now of the things which we have spoken this is the sum: We have such an high priest, who is set on the right hand of the throne of the Majesty in the heavens;

2 A minister of the sanctuary, and of the true tabernacle, which the Lord pitched, and not man.

3 For every high priest is ordained to offer gifts and sacrifices: wherefore it is of necessity that this man have somewhat also to offer.

4 For if he were on earth, he should not be a priest, seeing that there are priests that offer gifts according to the law:

5 Who serve unto the example and shadow of heavenly things, as Moses was admonished of God when he was about to make the tabernacle: for, See, saith he, that thou make all things according to the pattern shewed to thee in the mount.

6 But now hath he obtained a more excellent ministry, by how much also he is the mediator of a better covenant, which was established upon better promises.

We are reminded that Jesus is the mediator of the better covenant. There was nothing wrong with the one given to Moses, who faithfully followed all God's instructions, in the setting up of an earthly tabernacle from where the priests ministered, along with gifts and offerings. But this was a mere example and shadow of the better covenant with better promises that Jesus was the mediator of.

Chapter 9

A visible parable pointing to the realities of Heaven.

11 But Christ being come an high priest of good things to come, by a greater and more perfect tabernacle, not made with hands, that is to say, not of this building;

12 Neither by the blood of goats and calves, but by his own blood he entered in once into the holy place, having obtained eternal redemption for us.

13 For if the blood of bulls and of goats, and the ashes of an heifer sprinkling the unclean, sanctifieth to the purifying of the flesh:

14 How much more shall the blood of Christ, who through the eternal Spirit offered himself without spot to God, purge your conscience from dead works to serve the living God?

15 And for this cause he is the mediator of the new testament, that by

means of death, for the redemption of the transgressions that were under the first testament, they which are called might receive the promise of eternal inheritance.

24 For Christ is not entered into the holy places made with hands, which are the figures of the true; but into heaven itself, now to appear in the presence of God for us:

25 Nor yet that he should offer himself often, as the high priest entereth into the holy place every year with blood of others;

26 For then must he often have suffered since the foundation of the world: but now once in the end of the world hath he appeared to put away sin by the sacrifice of himself.

27 And as it is appointed unto men once to die, but after this the judgment:

28 So Christ was once offered to bear the sins of many; and unto them that look for him shall he appear the second time without sin unto salvation.

The all sufficiency of what Jesus did was when he shed His own precious blood. When we consider the Tabernacle, the various items of furniture and what went on there concerning gifts and sacrifices, including, importantly, what took place on the Day of Atonement, all this is relevant when it comes to our reflecting on what it was that Christ has done, but what took place then was never enough. His sacrifice was God's solution to the sin problem and in making the way open for our salvation.

Chapter 10

The Sacrifice of Jesus – once and for all.

19 Having therefore, brethren, boldness to enter into the holiest by the blood of Jesus,

20 By a new and living way, which he hath consecrated for us, through the veil, that is to say, his flesh;

21 And having an high priest over the house of God;

22 Let us draw near with a true heart in full assurance of faith, having our hearts sprinkled from an evil conscience, and our bodies washed with pure water.

23 Let us hold fast the profession of our faith without wavering; (for he is faithful that promised;)

In the light of all that has been said concerning Jesus our Great High Priest, it is imperative that we hang in there. Moreover, we can do what only the High Priest could do under the Old Covenant and that is to enter into the Holy of Holies. We can do so boldly because all the requirements of the Law were met by Jesus, who is our Great High Priest.

Chapter 11

Faith in action.

1 Now faith is the substance of things hoped for, the evidence of things not seen.

2 For by it the elders obtained a good report.

3 Through faith we understand that the worlds were framed by the word of God, so that things which are seen were not made of things which do appear.

Chapter 12

Discipline in a long-distance race and an unshakable kingdom.

12 Wherefore lift up the hands which hang down, and the feeble knees;

13 And make straight paths for your feet, lest that which is lame be turned out of the way; but let it rather be healed.

14 Follow peace with all men, and holiness, without which no man shall see the Lord:

Chapter 13

Concluding exhortations, encouragements and a final benediction.

12 Wherefore Jesus also, that he might sanctify the people with his own blood, suffered without the gate.

13 Let us go forth therefore unto him without the camp, bearing his reproach.

14 For here have we no continuing city, but we seek one to come ...

20 Now the God of peace, that brought again from the dead our Lord Jesus, that great shepherd of the sheep, through the blood of the everlasting covenant,

21 Make you perfect in every good work to do his will, working in you that which is well pleasing in his sight, through Jesus Christ; to whom be glory for ever and ever. Amen.

What we have done is, at best, to offer a brief exposition of a profound doctrine that has enormous practical implications. While Chapters 11-13 say little about Jesus the Great High Priest *per se*, the outstanding doctrine is covered in the preceding chapters, and we refer to these in order to present a complete albeit brief coverage of every chapter contained in the Letter to the Hebrews. The Hall of Faith chapter (11), and those giving exhortations and encouragement (12, 13), and especially those words concerning going Outside the Camp, which is a subject that will be covered in Chapter 56 and is a part of the author's own testimony, are some of the applications we can find in the light of what had been written prior to then – all lessons we can take away because of Jesus our Great High Priest.

We end on a note of praise, giving the Anglican, Irish-American, lady hymn writer, Charitie Lees Bancroft (1841–1923), the last word on this amazing subject of Jesus our Great High Priest:

1. Before the throne of God above
I have a strong and perfect plea,
a great High Priest whose name is "Love,"
who ever lives and pleads for me.
My name is graven on His hands;
my name is written on His heart;
I know that while in heav'n He stands,
no tongue can bid me thence depart;
no tongue can bid me thence depart.

2. When Satan tempts me to despair,
and tells me of the guilt within,
upward I look and see Him there
who made an end of all my sin.
Because the sinless Savior died,
my sinful soul is counted free;
for God the Just is satisfied
to look on Him and pardon me;
to look on Him and pardon me.

3. Behold Him there, the risen Lamb!
My perfect, spotless Righteousness;
the great unchangeable I AM,
the King of glory and of grace!
One with Himself I cannot die;
my soul is purchased with His blood;
my life is hid with Christ on high,
with Christ my Savior and my God;
with Christ my Savior and my God!

Chapter 20: The Priesthood: Questions, Praise and Prayer

In this final chapter of Part 1, we will consider each one of the preceding Part 1 chapters and ask a question readers might like to ponder or, if part of a group, to discuss. We end each section with a word of prayer and praise, which relates to the aspect of the priesthood that is under consideration.

Chapter 1: Introducing the Priests

As we set out on our "Priests of the Bible" journey, why do you think such a study matters?

We thank you Lord for the Priests who serve you in order to serve others, doing so mindful of your holiness and wanting to give you glory.

Chapter 2: Priests in Context

When studying priests and any subject found in the Bible, we have argued that it is important to get the context right. Why is this necessary and in what ways have you found the illustrations helpful?

Dear Lord, we thank you for your holy Word. May we be good stewards of it and please give us a better understanding of who you are and what your purposes are for us, Israel and this world.

Chapter 3: Priests from Adam to Moses

God has always been seeking to communicate with man. One way to do so was through priests. How did he do this before instructing Moses concerning the Levitical Priesthood.

We thank you Lord it was always your intention to have a relationship with man whom you have created, and you continued to do so after Adam fell and before you instituted the priesthood.

Chapter 4: Moses, the Law and the Covenant

Before giving detailed instructions concerning the priests and the Tabernacle, we read of God giving the Law to Israel and making a Covenant with them. Why was doing this so important?

Thank you, Lord, that your Law is perfect and you are a Covenant keeping God. May we be those who obey your Law and keep you Covenant whenever these apply to us.

Chapter 5: The Tabernacle – An Introduction

Why was the Tabernacle so important in the life of Israel and why should we study this today?

We thank you Lord that you have chosen to dwell with your believing people. May we not be those who abuse this wonderful privilege but rather avail ourselves of it.

Chapter 6: The Tabernacle – The Furniture

What significance does the furniture that was placed inside the Tabernacle have for us today?

We marvel at your wisdom Lord, at your instructions concerning the altar of sacrifice, the wash basin, the showbread, the lampstand, the altar of incense and the ark, and thank you for what it teaches us.

Chapter 7: The Aaronic Priesthood – An Introduction

What were the reasons behind establishing the Aaronic Priesthood and what lessons can we learn?

Thank you, Lord, for giving Israel the Levitical (Aaronic) Priesthood and for what this teaches us today.

Chapter 8: The Aaronic Priesthood – Readiness for Service

What significance can we attach to the garments the priests had to wear and what they had to do before they were allowed to serve as priests?

We realise, Lord, that to serve you as a priest was an enormous undertaking given that you are a holy God. May we not treat lightly what you expect from us who are believer-priests.

Chapter 9: Sacrifices and Offerings to YHWH

What were the main sacrifices to YHWH and what significance can we attach to each one of them?

We know from your Word, Lord, how important sacrifices and offerings were. May we be those who offer spiritual sacrifices that are acceptable to you.

Chapter 10: The Feasts of YHWH

In what ways are the Feasts of YHWH still relevant?

Thank you, Lord, for each one of the feasts that you ordered your people to celebrate and for the meaning that was behind them.

Chapter 11: The Day of Atonement

Why was making atonement for Israel's sin necessary and why is it necessary still for us?

Thank you, Lord, that you provided a way for your people of old and today to atone for their sins.

Chapter 12: The Levites, their Roles and their Legacy

Why is the role of Levites in Bible times so important and how would you sum up their legacy?

Thank you, Lord, for setting apart the Tribe of Levi for your service. May we be those who are dedicated to your service ahead of any other interest.

Chapter 13: Categorising Priests of the Bible

We have identified several categories of priest. Which ones do you reckon to be the most important?

We thank you Lord, in your wisdom, you have ordained ordinary people to serve you as priests. As believer-priests may we too be dedicated to your service.

Chapter 14: The First Temple

What was the purpose of the First Temple. In which ways did it serve the purpose for which it was built and in which ways did it fail to serve that purpose?

Thank you, again, Lord, that you deem to dwell with man and may we be those who offer acceptable prayers to you in your heavenly Temple and as you dwell among us today.

Chapter 15: The Second Temple

Why was it necessary to build a Second Temple?

We thank you for the folk who put your work and interests ahead of their own. May we be such people.

Chapter 16: The Inter Testament Period

In what ways is the term "Silent years" appropriate and what ways inappropriate when it comes to considering the events that took place in the Inter Testament Period?

We thank you, Lord, even when you appear silent, you are always working and you do work your purposes out perfectly, even in ways we cannot predict or understand.

Chapter 17: Judaism and the New Testament

How would you describe the state of Judaism in the times of Jesus? How does it compare with now?

We thank you, Lord, even when your specially chosen people have rejected you and your Covenant, your love for them remains and your purposes will not be thwarted.

Chapter 18: The Third Temple

How do you understand the meaning and significance of the Third Temple and why do you think that?

We thank you, Lord, that Jesus shall reign and it will be wondrous beyond all comprehension.

Chapter 19: Jesus our Great High Priest

In what way did Jesus (our Great High Priest) achieve what the Priests of Aaron could not?

We thank you, Lord, that because Jesus is our Great High Priest we can freely come to you.

Finally

We conclude Part 1 with a hymn. The lyrics further reminds us of some of the reasons why learning about the Priesthood is something worth doing, in that priests ordained by God demonstrated that He wanted to relate to humankind, showing us how that could be achieved. Before Jesus came, what we had were types and shadows, all important, but when He came we were able to find a way back to God. Jesus is the sacrificial lamb that Isaiah prophesied concerning over 700 years beforehand:

"He is despised and rejected of men; a man of sorrows, and acquainted with grief: and we hid as it were our faces from him; he was despised, and we esteemed him not. Surely he hath borne our griefs, and carried our sorrows: yet we did esteem him stricken, smitten of God, and afflicted. But he was wounded for our transgressions, he was bruised for our iniquities: the chastisement of our peace was upon him; and with his stripes we are healed. All we like sheep have gone astray; we have turned every one to his own way; and the Lord hath laid on him the iniquity of us all. He was oppressed, and he was afflicted, yet he opened not his mouth: he is brought as a lamb to the slaughter, and as a sheep before her shearers is dumb, so he openeth not his mouth" Isaiah 53:3-7.

1. O teach me what it meaneth,
That cross uplifted high,
With One, the Man of Sorrows,
Condemned to bleed and die!
O teach me what it cost Thee
To make a sinner whole;
And teach me, Savior, teach me
The value of a soul!

2. O teach me what it meaneth,
That sacred crimson tide,
The blood and water flowing
From Thine own wounded side.
Teach me that if none other
Had sinned, but I alone,
Yet still Thy blood, Lord Jesus,
Thine only, must atone.

3. O teach me what it meaneth,
Thy love beyond compare,
The love that reacheth deeper
Than depths of self-despair!
Yes, teach me, till there gloweth
In this cold heart of mine
Some feeble, pale reflection
Of that pure love of Thine.

4. O teach me what it meaneth,
For I am full of sin,
And grace alone can reach me,
And love alone can win.
O teach me, for I need Thee,
I have no hope beside—

The chief of all the sinners
For whom the Savior died!

5. *O teach me what it meaneth*
The rest which Thou dost give
To all the heavy-laden
Who look to Thee and live.
Because I am a rebel
Thy pardon I receive
Because Thou dost command me,
I can, I do believe.

6. *O infinite Redeemer!*
I bring no other plea;
Because Thou dost invite me
I cast myself on Thee.
Because Thou dost accept me
I love and I adore;
Because Thy love constraineth,
I'll praise Thee evermore!

Part 2
The Priests

Chapter 21: Tracing the Priests

Having established a lot of what is relevant concerning the Priesthood in Part 1, from a Bible perspective, we now turn to the priests, specifically named priests who did something noteworthy. A list of several of the priests to be covered, including family relationships, can be found in Chapter 2, Figure 18. A consideration of the different categories of Priests of the Bible is given in Chapter 13.

As far as the Levitical priesthood, through Aaron, is concerned, from Chapter 23 on, the rest of Part 2 is devoted to Aaronic priests. This is not an exhaustive list but all the priests we discuss have not only been mentioned by name in the Bible, but so were certain of their acts that we identify as significant. A lot of what priests did was simply carrying out the duties laid out, particularly in Exodus and Leviticus, and as far as the Bible account went names of priests doing this did not usually merit mention.

In Chapter 38, we will use the opportunity to cover as best we can those priests, named but often unnamed, that feature in the Bible account and do so with the intention that was there when we began this project, to at least try to address every priest of the Bible. We even include priests in the Inter Testament period, notably those from the Maccabean dynasty, that illustrate if nothing else the variety of experiences that we encounter when it comes to reading about priests of the Bible.

With reference to Chapter 2, Figure 18, which also provides some of the ancestry of named priests we identify, we consider some of the significant named priests of the Bible, notably of the two important orders as far as the Bible is concerned: Melchizedek and Aaron. Of Aaron's four sons, two of them, Nadab and Abihu, died without having an heir. It meant the remaining priests were descendants of one or other of Aaron's remaining two sons, Eleazar or Ithamar and right up to the destruction of the Temple in AD 70 the ancestry of the priests could usually be traced all the way back to Aaron.

When we considered Ezekiel's Temple, described in Ezekiel 40-47, which this author argues is yet to be established during the Millennium following Jesus coming back (see Chapter 18), the priests identified are from the line of Zadok, a descendent of Aaron, through his son, Eleazar. Following the destruction of the Temple in AD 70, the Aaronic priesthood ceased to operate. Remarkably, we found during our studies, evidence that almost every named priest was from the line of Aaron.

The ancestry of Priests of the Bible is yet another example of where as far as God and the Bible is concerned, family matters. But just as with the kings of Judah that can all be traced back to David, those who occupied the position of priest could be anywhere on the scale between very good and very bad. We see a range of characters from heroic to tragic, although the ability of priests to carry out the priestly office in the way God intended, as laid out in the Torah, as the needs of the time demanded, often depended on who was ruling at the time, whether under Joshua and the Judges, one of the Kings of Israel or Judah (after the Kingdom divided) or, following return from the Exile, under foreign rule.

Chapter 22: Melchizedek

As we begin our journey through the Bible in order to identify priests that did something significant, we begin with the first one that is mentioned, Melchizedek, who was a king as well as a priest. He was the only priest in our list that was from a different order to all the others, where an important distinction can be made. From a Christian perspective, he is the most significant of all the priests.

"And Melchizedek king of Salem brought forth bread and wine: and he was the priest of the most high God. And he blessed him, and said, Blessed be Abram of the most high God, possessor of heaven and earth: And blessed be the most high God, which hath delivered thine enemies into thy hand. And he gave him tithes of all" Genesis 14:18-20.

Other than these three verses in Genesis 14, when Melchizedek comes on the scene and soon after disappears, it might be easy upon first reading to conclude, while intriguing, there is not much more to say other than what we read. Interestingly, Melchizedek combined being a priest of the *Most High God* with that of King of Salem (Jerusalem). He met Abraham after the war fought between the four kings and the five, when Abraham and his small army played a significant part, including involvement in rescuing Lot. After being blessed, Abraham gave Melchizedek a tenth of all he had. There is much more to Melchizedek, who centuries later is mentioned in the Psalms and then the New Testament, perhaps surprisingly, attaching a significance that makes him someone highly important and relevant.

The chapter in Genesis in which Melchizedek appears in person, for the one and only time in the Bible, would seem to be more about Abraham (then named Abram) rescuing his nephew Lot, a casualty in a war that had taken place, about which it is written: *"Then the king of Sodom, the king of Gomorrah, the king of Admah, the king of Zeboyim and the king of Bela (that is, Zoar) marched out and drew up their battle lines in the Valley of Siddim gainst Kedorlaomer king of Elam, Tidal king of Goyim, Amraphel king of Shinar and Arioch king of Ellasar – four kings against five"* Genesis 14:8-9.

In the verses before and after Melchizedek was mentioned we read of the King of Sodom, who had benefitted from Abram's timely intervention, offering him a reward, which he flatly refused. From the exchanges that took place we sense his understandable contempt for the King of Sodom: *"But Abram said to the king of Sodom, "With raised hand I have sworn an oath to the Lord, God Most High, Creator of heaven and earth, that I will accept nothing belonging to you, not even a thread or the strap of a sandal, so that you will never be able to say, 'I made Abram rich.'"* Genesis 14:22-23.

It was in stark contrast to Abram's deference shown to Melchizedek, who had given him only bread and only wine (reminds the author of the words often spoken by his Brethren mentors when celebrating the Lord's Supper, back in the day) and added the words *"Blessed be Abram by God Most High, Creator of heaven and earth. And praise be to God Most High, who delivered your enemies into your hand"*, to which Abram responded: *"Then Abram gave him a tenth of everything"* Genesis 14:19-20. A lot can be made of why Abram chose to respond in the way he did.

A surprise reference perhaps is the one Psalm mentioning Melchizedek: *"The Lord said unto my Lord, Sit thou at my right hand, until I make thine enemies thy footstool. The Lord shall send the rod of thy strength out of Zion: rule thou in the midst of thine enemies. Thy people shall be willing in the day of thy power, in the beauties of holiness from the womb of the morning: thou hast the dew of thy youth. The Lord hath sworn, and will not repent, Thou art a priest for ever after the order of Melchizedek. The Lord at thy right hand shall strike through kings in the day of his wrath. He shall judge among the heathen, he shall fill the places with the dead bodies; he shall wound the heads over many countries. He shall drink of the brook in the way: therefore shall he lift up the head"* Psalm 110:1-7.

Many see Melchizedek as a type of Christ, or even Christ himself, given the words of Psalm 110, which can be taken as a prophecy, when David looked forward to the coming of the Messiah who is to gloriously reign. If it wasn't for this, and the connection made in the Book of Hebrews, which we will get to, it is unlikely most would give Melchizedek a second thought. What is remarkable is that David made a connection that one doubts, humanly speaking, anyone would have seen, unless there was more that had been recorded about the encounter that we do not know about, but for the fact he did so as he was inspired by the Holy Spirit and, as with all recorded prophecies, it was for a good reason.

But clearly this mystery man of the Bible, the one it is said who had no father or mother or beginning or end of days, who enters and leaves the stage ever so quickly that proverbially you would miss it if you just blinked, is of great significance because of the huge respect Abraham gave to Melchizedek, evidenced by Abraham giving him a tenth of all that he had. The story illustrates that worship of the one true and living God was happening, through the godly line of Seth and later Shem, even before Abraham was given instructions to found a great nation (Israel) to be God's special possession.

"As he saith also in another place, Thou art a priest for ever after the order of Melchisedec ... Called of God an high priest after the order of Melchisedec" Hebrews 5:6, 10.

"Which hope we have as an anchor of the soul, both sure and stedfast, and which entereth into that within the veil; Whither the forerunner is for us entered, even Jesus, made an high priest for ever after the order of Melchisedec" Hebrews 6:19-20.

"For this Melchisedec, king of Salem, priest of the most high God, who met Abraham returning from the slaughter of the kings, and blessed him … For he was yet in the loins of his father, when Melchisedec met him. If therefore perfection were by the Levitical priesthood, (for under it the people received the law,) what further need was there that another priest should rise after the order of Melchisedec, and not be called after the order of Aaron? … And it is yet far more evident: for that after the similitude of Melchisedec there ariseth another priest … For he testifieth, Thou art a priest for ever after the order of Melchisedec … (For those priests were made without an oath; but this with an oath by him that said unto him, The Lord sware and will not repent, Thou art a priest for ever after the order of Melchisedec:)" Hebrews 7:1, 10-11, 15, 17, 21.

The theme of Melchizedek and why this was a better priesthood than the one much of this book concentrates on, that of Aaron, was picked up in the New Testament (Hebrews 5, 6 and 7) and is discussed in Chapter 19, when we consider Jesus, our Great High Priest. We are reminded that we (who follow Christ) have a great High Priest, who is of the order of Melchizedek, who is perfect and eternal, unlike those under the Aaronic priesthood, which began under Moses.

Perhaps the most important lesson of all is that Jesus, our Great High Priest, ever intercedes for us and we can approach the Father God at any time through Him and, because of his priestly office, he ever pleads on our behalf before His Father. This thrilling prospect and huge privilege, makes the Genesis 14 story highly relevant since Melchizedek was at least a type of and forerunner of Jesus, who combines the offices of prophet, priest and king, and is the eternal Son of God.

As a final thought, the name Melchizedek means "King of Righteousness" and he was also king of Jerusalem, which means "City of Peace". Our Jesus who is the embodiment of righteousness and peace is an everlasting priest of the Order of Melchizedek.

Chapter 23: Aaron

We now come to the first High Priest of Israel, Aaron, whose descendants, right down to New Testament days, occupied the priest's office, for no member of any other family was qualified to enter the priesthood. He appears on the scene soon after Moses' burning bush experience, when God called Moses to be the one to lead the Israelites out of Egypt into the Promised Land. His job was to be Moses' spokesman when dealing with Pharoah, requesting he let the Israelites go.

At the time, Moses was aged 80 and Aaron was 83. Their older sister, Miriam, had had the presence of mind to find a way for baby Moses to escape Pharoah's slaughter of Hebrew baby boys. The three siblings had a close relationship and were together for most of the next 40 years throughout their wilderness journey, before they all died just before Israel were to enter the land that was promised to Abraham. Aaron did not resent his younger brother taking the limelight as leader over Israel and as we read in the accounts of what took place, invariably Aaron was there supporting his brother.

While there were blemishes, such as in the matter of the golden calf, when he agreed to the people's demand to build an idol despite being explicitly forbidden, his rebellion against Moses' authority, and his complicity, along with Moses, when it came to wrongly striking the rock at Meribah, instead of speaking to it, Aaron served God, Moses and the people well and did all that was required of his office. Besides his important role in dealing with Pharoah, we read, for example, of Aaron holding up Moses' arms, when early on in their wilderness journey the Israelites fought the Amalekites and prevailed.

"And Moses said unto Joshua, choose us out men, and go out, fight with Amalek: tomorrow I will stand on the top of the hill with the rod of God in mine hand. So Joshua did as Moses had said to him, and fought with Amalek: and Moses, Aaron, and Hur went up to the top of the hill. And it came to pass, when Moses held up his hand, that Israel prevailed: and when he let down his hand, Amalek prevailed. But Moses hands were heavy; and they took a stone, and put it under him, and he sat thereon; and Aaron and Hur stayed up his hands, the one on the one side, and the other on the other side; and his hands were steady until the going down of the sun. And Joshua discomfited Amalek and his people with the edge of the sword" Exodus 17:9-13.

But now we come to the time when the office of priest is instigated by God and from now on this will be our focus: *"And take thou unto thee Aaron thy brother, and his sons with him, from among the children of Israel, that he may minister unto me in the priest's office, even Aaron, Nadab and Abihu, Eleazar and Ithamar, Aaron's sons. And thou shalt make holy garments for Aaron thy brother for glory and for beauty. And thou shalt speak unto all that are wise hearted, whom I have filled with the spirit of wisdom, that they may make Aaron's garments to consecrate him, that he may minister unto me in the priest's office. And these are the garments which they shall make; a breastplate, and an ephod, and a robe, and a broidered coat, a mitre, and a girdle: and they shall make holy garments for Aaron thy brother, and his sons, that he may minister unto me in the priest's office"* Exodus 28:1-4.

As far as we can tell, Aaron carried out all the priestly duties that were laid down in the Law, and which we have detailed in Chapter 5. Moreover, he was the first to do so and thus he set a precedent. When his two sons, Nahab and Abihu, were slain by God for offering *"strange fire"*, he accepted this as being God's righteous judgment. When it was his time to die, just prior to that he passed the High Priestly mantle on to one of his two remaining sons, Eleazar, after which Israel mourned his passing for 30 days, which if nothing else showed how importantly he was regarded by the Israelites.

The big blot on Aaron's tenure as Moses' right-hand man and Israel's High Priest for the best part of 40 years was the part he played in "the golden calf" incident which, but for Moses' intercession, might have put an end to any hope Israel had of becoming a great nation, dwelling securely in the land God promised. While Moses was on Mount Sinai, receiving the Law from God and establishing the Covenant that He was to have with His chosen people, Israel, Aaron was left in charge down below. The people grew impatient and demanded of Aaron that he would make them a golden calf as an object of worship. Rather than resist, Aaron gave in to those demands.

Then toward the end of their wilderness journey, Aaron sided with his strong-minded sister against Moses, in speaking against Moses and thus incurring God's displeasure, when we read *"And Miriam and Aaron spake against Moses because of the Ethiopian woman whom he had married: for he had married an Ethiopian woman. And they said, Hath the Lord indeed spoken only by Moses? hath he not spoken also by us? And the Lord heard it"* Numbers 12:1-2. A final blot was when Moses struck the rock at Meribah, instead of speaking to it, to bring forth water for the complaining Israelites to drink. While the main person that is attributed blame is Moses, Aaron was complicit when it came to not giving God the glory and, along with Moses, God did not allow him to enter the Promised Land.

Arguably, Aaron's most important high priestly duty took place on the Day of Atonement (detailed in Chapter 10). The fact this had to be done every year was an important reason why the writer to the Hebrews could argue the priesthood of the Order of Melchizedek, the one which Jesus was part of, is superior to that of the Order of Aaron, yet that order was significant as it was a precursor to and shadow of what was to come. While caution is needed when attaching spiritual significance, much of what Aaron did while carrying out his priestly duties was spiritually highly significant. All the duties relating to worship in the Tabernacle, which we read about in Exodus, Leviticus and Numbers, were overseen and undertaken (with the help of his sons and the Levites) by Aaron the High Priest.

It is worth re-iterating that Aaron and his descendants, alone, were allowed to minister inside the Tabernacle (and later Temple), and that remained the case while the Old Covenant was operating and there was a temple or tabernacle. We read of a sober account when Korah, a Levite, supported by *"two hundred and fifty princes of the assembly, famous in the congregation, men of renown and they gathered themselves together against Moses and against Aaron, and said unto them, Ye take too much upon you, seeing all the congregation are holy, every one of them, and the Lord is among them: wherefore then lift ye up yourselves above the congregation of the Lord?"* Numbers 16:2-3.

The outcome was that God judged in the matter and the ground opened up and swallowed the rebels. When later the people complained and God sent a plague, it was Aaron and his censor of burning incense that made atonement. After this, a test was made for each of the tribes to present a rod in the Tabernacle along with Aaron's rod in order to demonstrate who it was that God had chosen. *"And it came to pass, that on the morrow Moses went into the tabernacle of witness; and, behold, the rod of Aaron for the house of Levi was budded, and brought forth buds, and bloomed blossoms, and yielded almonds. And Moses brought out all the rods from before the Lord unto all the children of Israel: and they looked, and took every man his rod. And the Lord said unto Moses, Bring Aaron's rod again before the testimony, to be kept for a token against the rebels; and thou shalt quite take away their murmurings from me, that they die not"* Numbers 17:8-10. We later read of *"the ark of the covenant overlaid round about with gold, wherein was the golden pot that had manna, and Aaron's rod that budded, and the tables of the covenant"* Hebrews 9:4. The placement of the rod in the Ark of the Covenant was to be a perpetual reminder of the authority YHWH had given to Aaron alone.

Regarding Aaron's death and the passing on of the office of High Priest to his son, Eleazar, we read: *"And the children of Israel, even the whole congregation, journeyed from Kadesh, and came unto mount Hor. And the Lord spake unto Moses and Aaron in mount Hor, by the coast of the land of Edom, saying, Aaron shall be gathered unto his people: for he shall not enter into the land which I have given unto the children of Israel, because ye rebelled against my word at the water of Meribah. Take Aaron and Eleazar his son, and bring them up unto mount Hor: And strip Aaron of his garments, and put them upon Eleazar his son: and Aaron shall be gathered unto his people, and shall die there. And Moses did as the Lord command-*

ed: and they went up into mount Hor in the sight of all the congregation. And Moses stripped Aaron of his garments, and put them upon Eleazar his son; and Aaron died there in the top of the mount: and Moses and Eleazar came down from the mount. And when all the congregation saw that Aaron was dead, they mourned for Aaron thirty days, even all the house of Israel" Numbers 20:22-29.

Overall, Aaron was faithful in what he did; he carried out his duties supporting Moses and serving as Israel's High Priest diligently and well, and did not seek the limelight. He demonstrated what was best practice and set an example for future High Priests to follow. The duties Aaron and other priests carried out in the Tabernacle were highly significant as we have shown, as were their roles as spiritual leaders in Israel. Behind all the carefully laid out activities, the one that was the most significant, was Aaron as High Priest representing the people to God and God to the people. All the legitimate priests of YHWH that followed, up to the time of Jesus, were descendants of Aaron.

Aaron is referred to on several occasions in the Bible following his death, notably in the Book of Psalms and this is usually done in positive terms.

"Thou leddest thy people like a flock by the hand of Moses and Aaron" Psalm 77:20.

"Moses and Aaron among his priests, and Samuel among them that call upon his name; they called upon the Lord, and he answered them" Psalm 99:6.

"He sent Moses his servant; and Aaron whom he had chosen" Psalm 105:26.

"They envied Moses also in the camp, and Aaron the saint of the Lord" Psalm 106:16.

"O house of Aaron, trust in the Lord: he is their help and their shield" Psalm 115:10.

"The Lord hath been mindful of us: he will bless us; he will bless the house of Israel; he will bless the house of Aaron" Psalm 115:12.

"Let the house of Aaron now say, that his mercy endureth for ever" Psalm 118:3.

"Behold, how good and how pleasant it is for brethren to dwell together in unity! It is like the precious ointment upon the head, that ran down upon the beard, even Aaron's beard: that went down to the skirts of his garments" Psalm 133:1-2.

"Bless the Lord, O house of Israel: bless the Lord, O house of Aaron" Psalm 135:19.

Chapter 24: Nadab

We first find mention of Nadab, soon after we are introduced to Aaron: "*And Aaron took him Elisheba, daughter of Amminadab, sister of Naashon, to wife; and she bare him Nadab, and Abihu, Eleazar, and Ithamar*" Exodus 6:23. The one thing anyone who recognises the name is likely to know about Nadab, along with Abihu, his brother, concerns their shocking and untimely death: "*Nadab and Abihu died before the Lord, when they offered strange fire before the Lord, in the wilderness of Sinai, and they had no children: and Eleazar and Ithamar ministered in the priest's office in the sight of Aaron their father*" Numbers 3:4 and "*Nadab and Abihu died, when they offered strange fire before the Lord*" Numbers 26:61. There is little else known about Nadab other than he did what many sons of High Priests did following Aaron and that was to assist their fathers in their priestly duties and along with it enjoy the privileges as well as taking on the responsibilities that came with priests. These duties were grave and highly important, for they were ministering on behalf of a holy God who must not be dishonoured.

As for other Bible mentions of Nadab (and Abihu), besides in the Books of Moses (Exodus, Leviticus, Numbers), we only have what is said in the Book of Chronicles regarding chronology, and notably when looking back on the strange fire incident: "*But Nadab and Abihu died before their father, and had no children: therefore Eleazar and Ithamar executed the priest's office*" 1 Chronicles 24:2. While alive, the two times he is spoken of are "*And he said unto Moses, Come up unto the Lord, thou, and Aaron, Nadab, and Abihu, and seventy of the elders of Israel; and worship ye afar off*" Exodus 24:1, (indeed a privilege and one Eleazar and Ithamar did not share) and "*And take thou unto thee Aaron thy brother, and his sons with him, from among the children of Israel, that he may minister unto me in the priest's office, even Aaron, Nadab and Abihu, Eleazar and Ithamar, Aaron's sons*" Exodus 28:1.

What is striking about Nadab and Abihu is the matter-of-fact description of their death and, in doing so, the attention given to the seriousness of their sin and the importance of God's holiness: "*And Nadab and Abihu, the sons of Aaron, took either of them his censer, and put fire therein, and put incense thereon, and offered strange fire before the Lord, which he commanded them not. And there went out fire from the Lord, and devoured them, and they died before the Lord. Then Moses said unto Aaron, This is it that the Lord spake, saying, I will be sanctified in them that come nigh me, and before all the people I will be glorified. And Aaron held his peace. And Moses called Mishael and Elzaphan, the sons of Uzziel the uncle of Aaron, and said unto them, Come near, carry your brethren from before the sanctuary out of the camp. So they went near, and carried them in their coats out of the camp; as Moses had said. And Moses said unto Aaron, and unto Eleazar and unto Ithamar, his sons, Uncover not your heads, neither rend your clothes; lest ye die, and lest wrath come upon all the people: but let your brethren, the whole house of Israel, bewail the burning which the Lord hath kindled. And ye shall not go out from the door of the tabernacle of the congregation, lest ye die: for the anointing oil of the Lord is upon you. And they did according to the word of Moses"* Leviticus 10:1-7.

In the Leviticus 10 account of Nadab's death, there is no explanation of what "strange fire" was (the Amplified version adds *"unauthorized, unacceptable"*) and it has led scholars to try to figure out what it was they did that the Lord *"commanded them not"* such that as a result *"there went out fire from the Lord, and devoured them, and they died before the Lord"*. It is salutary to note that Aaron was not allowed to (and did not) mourn the death of his first two sons and neither could his two remaining sons, Eleazar and Ithamar, although non priests could. The lesson is clear: God is holy and is not to be trifled with. There are many Old Testament examples of what happened when God was displeased, especially when people failed to worship Him in the right way, and in the New Testament, the story of Ananias and Sapphira springs to mind. It is a lesson we do well to learn, particularly for those who profess to follow the Lord and especially if having ministerial responsibility. When God does visit us in revival as opposed to today's mediocrity, it is something we do well to remember and take heed.

Chapter 25: Eleazar

Before preparing for this Priests of the Bible series, we could have taken the view that covering one son of Aaron (Nadab) would have been enough, and all we needed was to mention his three brothers in passing when considering Nadab. But as we read on, it becomes clear that another son of Aaron (Eleazar), quite a different proposition to the two brothers who were slain by God, was significant too, not just by the number of times he is mentioned but that he did well upon taking on the role of assisting his father, Aaron, in his priestly duties, early in the Wilderness journey after the priesthood was begun at Mount Sinai, and taking on extra responsibilities following the deaths of Nadab and Abihu.

Toward the end of 40 years in the Wilderness, Eleazar became High Priest in his father's stead. Along with Aaron and Moses, Eleazar went to Mount Hor, when the High Priest's garments were stripped from Aaron and put on Eleazar (Numbers 20: 22-29). Eleazar continued in that office the whole 25 years while Joshua led Israel. Right at the end of the Book of Joshua and soon after Joshua died, we read: *"And Eleazar the son of Aaron died; and they buried him in a hill that pertained to Phinehas his son, which was given him in mount Ephraim"* Joshua 24:33.

Please bear with us for quoting Wikipedia at length but here it does provide an excellent summary concerning Eleazar: *"Eleazar played a number of roles during the course of the Exodus, from creating the plating for the altar from the firepans of Korah's assembly, to performing the ritual of the red heifer. After the death of his older brothers Nadab and Abihu, he and his younger brother Ithamar were appointed to the charge of the sanctuary. His wife, a daughter of Putiel, bore him Phinehas, who would eventually succeed him as High Priest. Leviticus 10:16–18 records an incident when Moses was angry with Eleazar and Ithamar, for failing to eat a sin offering inside the Tabernacle in accordance with the regulations set out in the preceding chapters of Leviticus regarding the entitlement of the priests to a share of the offerings they made on behalf of the Israelite people. As the Israelites moved through the wilderness during the Exodus journey, Eleazar was responsible for carrying the oil for the lampstand, the sweet incense, the daily grain offering and the anointing oil, and also for oversight of the carriage of the Ark of the Covenant, table for showbread, altar and other tabernacle fittings which were transported by the Kohathite section of the Levite tribe. Following the rebellion against Moses' leadership recorded in Numbers 16, Eleazar was charged with taking the rebels' bronze censers and hammering them into a covering for the altar, to act as a reminder of the failed rebellion and the restriction of the priesthood to the Aaronid dynasty. On Mount*

Hor he was clothed with the sacred vestments, which Moses took from his father Aaron and put upon him as successor to his father in the high priest's office, before Aaron's death. Eleazar held the office of high priest for more than twenty years. He took part with Moses in numbering the people, and assisted at the inauguration of Joshua. He assisted in the distribution of the land after the conquest. When he died, he "was buried at Gibeah, which had been allotted to his son Phinehas in the hill country of Ephraim" ... The high-priesthood remained in the family of Eleazar until the time of Eli, into whose family it passed. Eli was a descendant of Ithamar, Eleazar's brother. The high priesthood was restored to the family of Eleazar in the person of Zadok after Abiathar was cast out by Solomon."

Eleazar is mentioned by name eight times in the Book of Joshua, whereas the term "priest" is used 36 times. The point being that the function of the priests, e.g., making offerings and carrying the Ark of the Covenant, was more important than individual personalities, and the work of the priests as intermediaries between God and the people, under the supervision of the High Priest, when it came to taking possession of the Promised Land, as led by Joshua, was very important. Except for a strange incident soon after the slaying of Nadab and Abihu: *"And Moses diligently sought the goat of the sin offering, and, behold, it was burnt: and he was angry with Eleazar and Ithamar, the sons of Aaron which were left alive, saying, Wherefore have ye not eaten the sin offering in the holy place, seeing it is most holy, and God hath given it you to bear the iniquity of the congregation, to make atonement for them before the Lord?"* Leviticus 10:16-17, we read of no other complaint (and it could be Moses was wrong in this case) against Eleazar during the whole of the 60 plus years that he served as priest, which as far as can be made out was done with distinction.

Eleazar had been through a lot including seeing God's judgment against two of his brothers and his own father and Moses and several instances of God dispensing justice on those who transgressed, and on Israel's enemies, as well as sharing in the hardships of 40 years spent in the Wilderness. But throughout that period, he just got on and carried out his duties and the fact little attention was paid to him as a person suggests it was without fuss. Unlike many other characters of the Bible who we deem to be good, we can discern no character flaw. He is portrayed as a worthy successor to Aaron, the one to whom future High Priests would later be traced back. It is also worth noting later on when special praise is given to Zadok, that Zadok was Eleazar's descendant.

Before we move on, we should mention the fourth of Aaron's sons: Ithamar. We read that the first two sons, Nadab, and Abihu *"had no children: and Eleazar and Ithamar ministered in the priest's office in the sight of Aaron their father"* Numbers 3:4. While our focus has been on Eleazar, Ithamar too played an important part exercising the priestly office, sharing many of the duties. A number of priests that followed, including High Priests were descendants of Ithamar. When we consider priests right up to New Testament times, we can trace they were descendants of either Eleazar or Ithamar.

Chapter 26: Phinehas

As we continue on with our journey where we are looking out for named priests of the Bible who did something significant and/or from which we can learn important lessons, we come to Phinehas, grandson of Aaron, son of Eleazar and nephew of Nadab. We first come across Phinehas early on in the Exodus account, even before the Wilderness journey began: "*And Eleazar Aaron's son took him one of the daughters of Putiel to wife; and she bare him Phinehas: these are the heads of the fathers of the Levites according to their families*" Exodus 6:25.

According to Wikipedia: "*Phinehas was the grandson of Aaron and son of Eleazar, the High Priests (Exodus 6:25). He distinguished himself as a youth at Shittim with his zeal against the heresy of Peor. Displeased with the immorality with which the Moabites and Midianites had successfully tempted the Israelites (Numbers 25:1–9) to inter-marry and to worship Baal-peor, Phinehas personally executed an Israelite man and a Midianite woman while they were together in the man's tent, running a javelin or spear through the man and the belly of the woman, bringing to an end the plague sent by God to punish the Israelites for sexually intermingling with the Midianites. Phinehas is commended by God in Numbers 25:10-13, as well as King David in Psalms 106:28–31 for having stopped Israel's fall into idolatrous practices brought in by Midianite women, as well as for stopping the desecration of God's sanctuary. After the entry to the land of Israel and the death of his father, he was appointed the third High Priest of Israel, and served at the sanctuary of Bethel (Judges 20:28)*".

It was therefore toward the end of that 40-year Wilderness journey when Phinehas comes to our attention. The stand out quality Phinehas showed was zeal, although not one particularly regarded by a modern culture that sees "qualities" like tolerance as far more important. But as far as God is concerned, Phinehas was to be commended for turning away His wrath and was promised a blessing for his descendants in the generations to come. Not long after and just prior to Moses' death, God told him to take vengeance on the Midianites, where Phinehas again played a key role: "*And Moses sent them to the war, a thousand of every tribe, them and Phinehas the son of Eleazar the priest, to the war, with the holy instruments, and the trumpets to blow in his hand*" Numbers 31:6.

Phinehas was later given a place of honour in the Psalms "*Thus they provoked him to anger with their inventions: and the plague brake in upon them. Then stood up Phinehas, and executed judgment: and so the plague was stayed. And that was counted unto him for righteousness unto all generations for evermore*" Psalm 106:29-31. The story behind what happened began in Numbers 22 when we read "*And the children of Israel set forward, and pitched in the plains of Moab on this side Jordan by Jericho*" (22:1) and there followed a behind the scenes account of the (false) prophet Balaam being asked to curse Israel by the king of Moab and ending up blessing Israel.

What Baalam failed to do through sorcery, he almost succeeded, as the historian Josephus pointed out, because of the Moabites infiltration with forbidden practices, and this in what was to become a recurring theme in Israel's history: idolatry and sexual immorality, and one that was later to spill over even into the church, as evidenced by Jesus' words "*But I have a few things against thee, because thou hast there them that hold the doctrine of Balaam, who taught Balac to cast a stumblingblock before the children of Israel, to eat things sacrificed unto idols, and to commit fornication*" Revelation 2:14.

"*Praise ye the Lord. O give thanks unto the Lord; for he is good: for his mercy endureth for ever. Who can utter the mighty acts of the Lord? who can shew forth all his praise? Blessed are they that keep judgment, and he that doeth righteousness at all times ... They joined themselves also unto Baalpeor, and ate the sacrifices of the dead. Thus they provoked him to anger with their inventions: and the plague brake in upon them. Then stood up Phinehas, and executed judgment: and so the plague was stayed. And that was counted unto him for righteousness unto all generations for evermore ... Save us, O Lord our God, and gather us from among the heathen, to give thanks unto thy holy name, and to triumph in thy praise. Blessed be the Lord God of Israel from everlasting to everlasting: and let all the people say, Amen. Praise ye the Lord*" Psalm 106:1-3, 28-31, 47-48.

The obvious lesson we can draw from the life of Phinehas is the importance of zeal for God. One of his important jobs at the time he summarily executed the two high ranking lovers and thereby put an end to God's plague of judgment was that of a doorkeeper at the Tabernacle. Centuries later, we are told: "*In earlier times Phinehas son of Eleazar was the official in charge of the gatekeepers, and the Lord was with him*" 1 Chronicles 9:20. This couple had violated the sanctity of that sacred area in flagrant defiance. This caused him to be righteously indignant for the Lord and take on implementing the remedy in the harshest of ways, something no-one else did, including Moses and Eleazar.

Zeal rightly exercised (e.g., in doing good works) is to be commended, but it can be misplaced, sometimes for laudable reasons. Some of the 26 Bible usages are to do with misdirected zeal, e.g., Paul before his conversion. Understandably, many today are suspicious and wary when they come across people particularly zealous (often an attribute of those dealing excess judgment or terror in the name of religion). In the account found in Joshua

22, Phinehas played a key role in sorting out a dispute that could have led to much bloodshed. We read of the tribes of Reuben and Gad, and the half tribe of Manasseh, after conquering the land west of the Jordan, returning to live in the land east of the Jordan that had been allocated to them and building an altar as a way of commemorating what God had done (but not in order to sacrifice). This angered the remaining tribes, construing it as an act of idolatry, and ready to go to war over the matter. Given his track record on dealing with matters concerning idolatry, we might have expected Phinehas to side with the outraged nine tribes, but when he came to a correct understanding, after listening to what the three tribes had to say, was satisfied and peace was restored.

As we consider Phinehas, who we were introduced to early in the Book of Exodus and find a lot more about in Numbers, we find he continued serving as priest, often behind the scenes, throughout the Book of Joshua, when at the end he becomes High Priest upon the death of his father, Eleazar. He also crops up again in Judges: "*And the children of Israel enquired of the Lord, (for the ark of the covenant of God was there in those days, And Phinehas, the son of Eleazar, the son of Aaron, stood before it in those days,) saying, Shall I yet again go out to battle against the children of Benjamin my brother, or shall I cease? And the Lord said, Go up; for tomorrow I will deliver them into thine hand*" Judges 20:27-28. The back story begins in Judges 19 and is a terrible one involving murder and civil war, but Phinehas, now old, and how old we don't know, is here showing his true mettle, once again taking a lead, doing what was needed. If there is a lesson, may it be so for us that we show a right zeal for God.

As we conclude, it is worth considering God's covenant of peace of an everlasting priesthood: "*And the Lord spake unto Moses, saying, Phinehas, the son of Eleazar, the son of Aaron the priest, hath turned my wrath away from the children of Israel, while he was zealous for my sake among them, that I consumed not the children of Israel in my jealousy. Wherefore say, Behold, I give unto him my covenant of peace: And he shall have it, and his seed after him, even the covenant of an everlasting priesthood; because he was zealous for his God, and made an atonement for the children of Israel*" Numbers 25:10-13. It is called a covenant of peace with respect to the effect of Phinehas' heroic action, whereby he effected peace between God and his people, and with regard to the principal end of the priestly office, which was constantly to do that which Phinehas now did, even to mediate between God and men, in order to achieve peace and reconciliation with Him, e.g., through making offerings.

Chapter 27: Eli

We first come across Eli in the often-recounted story of a barren woman, Hannah, on her annual family visit to the Tabernacle at Shiloh to make an offering to God, pouring out her heart to Him in bitterness due to her not being able to conceive. In her prayer, she told God she would dedicate any son she would have to Him, vowing the vow of a Nazirite: "*then I will give him unto the Lord all the days of his life, and there shall no razor come upon his head*" 1 Samuel 1:11b. There in the midst of her anguish she was spotted by Eli, who at first thought she was drunk but, when told the reason for her grief, Eli blessed her and she went on her way, after which she conceived. Eli was the High Priest and a judge in Israel, where he was following in the footsteps of those in the Book of Judges.

Hannah dedicated the son who was born to her to the Lord. When old enough, he was taken to Eli and put in his charge, for Samuel had been set apart for God's service. For all intents and purposes, despite often being given an unsympathetic press because of his wayward sons, who assisted in the priestly duties (as was the custom), who he failed to sufficiently reprimand, Eli was likely a good priest when it came to carrying out his duties and as we see at the end of his life his concern was for God's glory. He appeared to be a good mentor to Samuel, who was to play an important part in Israel's history as a prophet and Israel's last judge before they had a king. However, Eli failed to take the needed action, allowing his sons to bring dishonour to God's name while they were ministering in the Tabernacle.

"*And there came a man of God unto Eli, and said unto him, Thus saith the Lord, Did I plainly appear unto the house of thy father, when they were in Egypt in Pharaoh's house? And did I choose him out of all the tribes of Israel to be my priest, to offer upon mine altar, to burn incense, to wear an ephod before me? and did I give unto the house of thy father all the offerings made by fire of the children of Israel? Wherefore kick ye at my sacrifice and at mine offering, which I have commanded in my habitation; and honourest thy sons above me, to make yourselves fat with the chiefest of all the offerings of Israel my people? Wherefore the Lord God of Israel saith, I said indeed that thy house, and the house of thy father, should walk before me for ever: but now the Lord saith, Be it far from me; for them that honour me I will honour, and they that despise me shall be lightly esteemed. Behold, the days come, that I will cut off thine arm, and the arm of thy father's house, that there shall not be an old man in thine house. And thou shalt see an enemy in my habitation, in all the wealth which God shall give Israel: and there shall not be an old man in thine house for ever. And the man of thine, whom I shall not cut off from mine altar, shall be to consume thine eyes, and to grieve thine heart: and all the increase of thine house shall die in the flower of their age. And this shall be a sign unto thee, that shall come upon thy two sons, on Hophni and Phinehas; in one day they shall die both of them. And I will raise me up a faithful priest, that shall do according to that which is in mine heart and in my mind: and I will build him a sure house; and he shall walk before mine anointed for ever. And it shall come to pass, that every one that is left in thine house shall come and crouch to him for a piece of silver and a morsel of bread, and shall say, Put me, I pray thee, into one of the priests' offices, that I may eat a piece of bread"* 1 Samuel 2:27-36.

As we can see from this text, Eli was warned by an unnamed prophet of God's displeasure due to his sons' disgraceful conduct which he had allowed to continue and by doing so had honoured his sons before God, where his priorities ought to be. Besides the rebuke, which is to be expected, there is the salutary reminder that one's actions (good or bad) could impact future generations and we must take heed. The prophecy was clear and specific. There would be a judgment coming that would affect future generations of his family and this would include the premature deaths of his two miscreant sons.

Likely a period of years elapsed before Samuel received the call of God and was given the same message that the prophet had earlier given to Eli but was apparently ignored. The way Eli conducted himself during the call of Samuel was to be commended. But later we come to a series of events happening in a short period, including the death of Eli and his two wayward sons and, in the eyes of Eli, what was most significant, the loss of the Ark of the Covenant. As for Samuel, he had by this time grown up to be a well renowned prophet and he did so under Eli's tutelage.

"Whatever Samuel said was broadcast all through Israel. Israel went to war against the Philistines. Israel set up camp at Ebenezer, the Philistines at Aphek. The Philistines marched out to meet Israel, the fighting spread, and Israel was badly beaten—about four thousand soldiers left dead on the field. When the troops returned to camp, Israel's elders said, "Why has God given us such a beating today by the Philistines? Let's go to Shiloh and get the Chest of God's Covenant. It will accompany us and save us from the grip of our enemies." So the army sent orders to Shiloh. They brought the Chest of the Covenant of God, the God-of-the-Angel-Armies, the Cherubim-Enthroned-God. Eli's two sons, Hophni and Phinehas, accompanied the Chest of the Covenant of God. When the Chest of the Covenant of God was brought into camp, everyone gave a huge cheer. The shouts were like thunderclaps shaking the very ground. The Philistines heard the shouting and wondered what on earth was going on: "What's all this shouting

among the Hebrews?" Then they learned that the Chest of God had entered the Hebrew camp. The Philistines panicked: "Their gods have come to their camp! Nothing like this has ever happened before. We're done for! Who can save us from the clutches of these supergods? These are the same gods who hit the Egyptians with all kinds of plagues out in the wilderness. On your feet, Philistines! Courage! We're about to become slaves to the Hebrews, just as they have been slaves to us. Show what you're made of! Fight for your lives!" And did they ever fight! It turned into a rout. They thrashed Israel so mercilessly that the Israelite soldiers ran for their lives, leaving behind an incredible thirty thousand dead. As if that wasn't bad enough, the Chest of God was taken and the two sons of Eli—Hophni and Phinehas—were killed. Immediately, a Benjaminite raced from the front lines back to Shiloh. Shirt torn and face smeared with dirt, he entered the town. Eli was sitting on his stool beside the road keeping vigil, for he was extremely worried about the Chest of God. When the man ran straight into town to tell the bad news, everyone wept. They were appalled. Eli heard the loud wailing and asked, "Why this uproar?" The messenger hurried over and reported. Eli was ninety-eight years old then, and blind. The man said to Eli, "I've just come from the front, barely escaping with my life." "And so, my son," said Eli, "what happened?" The messenger answered, "Israel scattered before the Philistines. The defeat was catastrophic, with enormous losses. Your sons Hophni and Phinehas died, and the Chest of God was taken." At the words, "Chest of God," Eli fell backward off his stool where he sat next to the gate. Eli was an old man, and very fat. When he fell, he broke his neck and died. He had led Israel forty years. His daughter-in-law, the wife of Phinehas, was pregnant and ready to deliver. When she heard that the Chest of God had been taken and that both her father-in-law and her husband were dead, she dropped to her knees to give birth, going into hard labor. As she was about to die, her midwife said, "Don't be afraid. You've given birth to a son!" But she gave no sign that she had heard. The Chest of God gone, father-in-law dead, husband dead, she named the boy Ichabod (Glory's-Gone), saying, "Glory is exiled from Israel since the Chest of God was taken." 1 Samuel 4:1-22 (The Message)

God's judgment was swift and decisive and was dispensed at the hands of the Philistines, who beat Israel in battle, slew Eli's two sons and captured the Ark of the Covenant, which Israel under the two brothers had taken into battle as if it were a good luck charm. When news of what had happened was brought back to Eli, it was the taking of the Ark that was to prove the greatest shock. Eli's story is a tragic one, given his privileged position and responsibilities. As for his own service, he himself appeared to carry out his duties faithfully. But he was weak and cowardly. He failed to rightly honour God by allowing his sons' disgraceful conduct to go unchecked. The words of the unnamed prophet are poignant and ones we do well to take to heart when it comes to performing our own service for the Lord, while at the same time taking responsibility for disciplining any children we happen to have. Later (1 Kings 2:27) we read of King Solomon removing Abiathar (Eli's descendant) as the Lord's priest and this was the final fulfilment of the prophet's word at Shiloh concerning Eli's family.

Chapter 28: Abiathar

We first come across Abiathar, after his father, Ahimelech the High Priest, and the rest of his family were killed by Doeg the Edomite on the orders of King Saul because he had assisted David who was fleeing from him. He alone escapes, while the rest of his family were slain. He then joined David's band of outlaws and discontents and was with him right up to David's death, serving as a priest, teacher of the Law and trusted counsellor, including the time when David, who was by then well established as king, had again to flee. But this time it was from his son, Absalom, who wanted to steal the throne and almost succeeded in doing so. Abiathar's priestly duties included wearing the High Priestly garments, and this included using the Urim and the Thumin that was used to find out God's will.

Another priest later appears on the scene, Zadok, who we will discuss in the next chapter. It is not clear in David's time who was the High Priest, but we do not read of any conflict between the two and both carried out their priestly duties faithfully and were both loyal to King David. The parting of the ways occurred when David was about to die and the question arose who would take over as king – Solomon (David's named successor) or Adonijah (who strictly speaking was next in line). While Zadok sided with Solomon, Abiathar supported Adonijah. But it was Solomon, understandably upset that Abiathar had supported his brother rather than him, who eventually prevailed, and so Abiathar was removed from his priestly duties. As far as the line of priests from Eli to Abiathar went, this was the end of the line: "*So Solomon thrust out Abiathar from being priest unto the Lord; that he might fulfil the word of the Lord, which he spake concerning the house of Eli in Shiloh*" 1 Kings 2:27.

Abiathar was referred to by Jesus: "*And the Pharisees said unto him, Behold, why do they on the sabbath day that which is not lawful? And he said unto them, Have ye never read what David did, when he had need, and was an hungred, he, and they that were with him? How he went into the house of God in the days of Abiathar the high priest, and did eat the shewbread, which is not lawful to eat but for the priests, and gave also to them which were with him?*" Mark 2:24-26. Commentators have pointed out that it was Ahimelech, who was High Priest at that time. They differ concerning Abiathar's character, for in the end he had supported the "wrong" candidate for king, although some point out Adonijah was the legal heir and, as a stickler for the Law, Abiathar would have understood this.

One lesson we can take from this story is that Abiathar was a good example of someone who carried out his duties diligently. He was part of a family that had paid a terrible price for doing the right thing, and was able to adapt to changing circumstances when this was needed. Other than in the case of the succession as King of Israel, everywhere else when Abiathar had a part to play we find he was a faithful priest and was a loyal supporter of God's choice for king: David, including sharing in David's many hardships. His departing was sad given his years of dedicated service. As we will see, when we consider Zadok, who Solomon named High Priest to replace Abiathar, the prophecy given by the unnamed prophet in the time of Eli, even if one today's readers might overlook, was highly significant.

Chapter 29: Zadok

Z adok and Abiathar were the priests that served during the time of David, sharing priestly duties once David became king. As we noted earlier, the parting of the ways for the two came toward the end of David's life, when Adonijah tried to become king instead of Solomon, and was supported by Abiathar, although it was Solomon who was the one David and also God (according to the records) intended to follow him as king when he died, and here Solomon was supported by Zadok. With his help, Solomon overcame the coup, Abiathar was deposed in disgrace and Zadok became the High Priest.

Zadok, which appropriately means "*righteous*", "*just*", traces his ancestry back to Aaron, through Eleazar and Phinehas (all of which have been discussed in previous chapters) and from what we can work out many of the High Priests that followed him, until after the return from the Exile with later infiltration of Greeks and Romans were descendants of Zadok. Zadok first appears on the scene while David was exiled but was soon to take the throne, upon Saul's death (assuming it was this Zadok): "*And these are the numbers of the bands that were ready armed to the war, and came to David to Hebron, to turn the kingdom of Saul to him, according to the word of the Lord … And Zadok, a young man mighty of valour, and of his father's house twenty and two captains*" 1 Chronicles 12:23, 28.

We don't get the impression of Zadok taking much of the limelight, at least not until the time of transition from David to Solomon (when he is called upon, along with Nathan the prophet, to anoint Solomon as king), but from all that we read it suggests Zadok carried out his duties faithfully and was loyal to David and then to Solomon. He played his part bringing the Ark of the Covenant to Jerusalem, when David danced before the Lord, and thereafter played an important part in the worship of YHWH centred around the Tabernacle (and later the Temple): "*And Zadok the priest, and his brethren the priests, before the tabernacle of the Lord in the high place that was at Gibeon*" 1 Chronicles 16:39 and "*And David distributed them, both Zadok of the sons of Eleazar, and Ahimelech of the sons of Ithamar, according to their offices in their service*" 1 Chronicles 24:3.

During the time of Absolam's rebellion, Zadok supported David, especially during his time of trial when his help was needed most. Other than mention of Zadok's priestly duties, there seems not much more we can find out concerning Zadok the man, when it came to his words and deeds, that is until toward the time of David's death when along with Nathan he played his part in ensuring the kingly crown was passed on to Solomon, and anointing him king, rather than to his older brother, Adonijah. "*So Zadok the priest, and Nathan the prophet, and Benaiah the son of Jehoiada, and the Cherethites, and the Pelethites, went down, and caused Solomon to ride upon king David's mule, and brought him to Gihon. And Zadok the priest took an horn of oil out of the tabernacle, and anointed Solomon. And they blew the trumpet; and all the people said, God save king Solomon. And all the people came up after him, and the people piped with pipes, and rejoiced with great joy, so that the earth rent with the sound of them"* 1 Kings 1:38-40. Regarding the transition from Tabernacle worship (under David) to Temple worship (under Solomon), we can't say for sure what Zadok's part was other than that he appeared to have faithfully carried out his priestly duties, which is confirmed by references to him after his death.

It is worth noting, as we look far into the future, to Ezekiel's vision of the Temple (Ezekiel 40-48) during the period of the Exile of Judah to Babylon, Zadok is referenced by name four times as he looks ahead at a Temple yet to come, with the priests being Zadok's descendants. As always, when we study the Scriptures, what we find matters and in God's sight Zadok was significant. There is debate among scholars as to what this Temple that has never been built refers to and whether literal or actual, and if actual when it is meant to happen, and this is something we considered in **"Prophets of the Bible"**, where the conflicting views are considered, as well as in Chapter 18.

One stand out feature is the importance of holiness and the role of the Zadok priesthood when it came to *"teach my people the difference between the holy and profane, and cause them to discern between the unclean and the clean"* Ezekiel 44:23. In wrapping up, we refer again to the prophecy the unnamed prophet gave to Eli, in particular: *"And I will raise me up a faithful priest, that shall do according to that which is in mine heart and in my mind: and I will build him a sure house; and he shall walk before mine anointed for ever"* 1 Samuel 2:35. The prophet was looking far into the future and was merely passing on the words of the Lord, and even when doing so it was with limited understanding.

Footnote 1

As part of researching Zadok, there are several helpful videos and articles. One that drew the attention of this author was titled: **"Zadok and Abiathar Priesthoods – David Wilkerson"**. Wilkerson made the distinction between two anointed priests but the former, Abiathar, lost that anointing evidenced by his actions in siding with Adonijah, the unrighteous candidate, in the matter of the kingly succession, whereas Zadok made the righteous choice and maintained that anointing, as evidenced by the Ezekiel references. His point is that many a Christian leader (and he included himself) can begin well and one can be used by God yet fall away from enjoying the blessing of

God due to sin. Unlike Abiathar, Zadok continued in the blessing. In another sermon, "**A Remnant Priesthood**", Wilkerson argued that God seeks such among His people today, a righteous remnant, a holy people, functioning in the Zadok mould. It should be noted that another commentator was more sympathetic toward Abiathar, who had after all served well as priest when times were hard, and all he was doing was applying the custom as he saw it that was to do with kingly succession, even if ignoring what God thought on the matter.

Footnote 2

While writing this, the coronation of King Charles III took place. One of the anthems played during that event was "**Zadok the Priest**". According to Wikipedia: "*Zadok the Priest is a British anthem that was composed by George Frideric Handel for the coronation of King George II in 1727. Alongside The King Shall Rejoice, My Heart is Inditing, and Let Thy Hand Be Strengthened, Zadok the Priest is one of Handel's coronation anthems. One of Handel's best-known works, Zadok the Priest has been sung prior to the anointing of the sovereign at the coronation of every British monarch since its composition and has become recognised as a British patriotic anthem. Part of the traditional content of British coronations, the texts for all four anthems were picked by Handel—a personal selection from the most accessible account of an earlier coronation, that of James II in 1685. The text is a translation of the traditional antiphon, Unxerunt Salomonem, itself derived from the biblical account of the anointing of Solomon by the priest Zadok (1 Kings 1:38-40). These words have been used in every English, and later British, coronation since that of King Edgar at Bath Abbey in 973*". Sadly, in this author's view, the religious symbolism on show, epitomised by anointing the King in a similar way to what happened with Zadok and Solomon, was overshadowed by the anti-God, Masonic symbolism and the sense that what was being witnessed represented the state of the church today, i.e., religious ritual with God left out.

Chapter 30: Jehoiada

Jehoiada is one priest of the Bible that many, including serious students, may not be aware of, but as far as this author is concerned is toward the top of the list when it comes to unsung heroes. The relevant sections of the Bible when considering Jehoiada are 2 Kings 9-12 and 2 Chronicles 22-24. We give here a lengthy quote from the Chronicles account as it provides the powerful account of what Jehoiada did to restore the throne to its rightful heir, an action that had important ramifications when we consider the coming Messiah, who would be from the line of David, as the prophets had foretold.

"And in the seventh year Jehoiada strengthened himself, and took the captains of hundreds, Azariah the son of Jeroham, and Ishmael the son of Jehohanan, and Azariah the son of Obed, and Maaseiah the son of Adaiah, and Elishaphat the son of Zichri, into covenant with him. And they went about in Judah, and gathered the Levites out of all the cities of Judah, and the chief of the fathers of Israel, and they came to Jerusalem. And all the congregation made a covenant with the king in the house of God. And he said unto them, Behold, the king's son shall reign, as the Lord hath said of the sons of David. This is the thing that ye shall do; A third part of you entering on the sabbath, of the priests and of the Levites, shall be porters of the doors; And a third part shall be at the king's house; and a third part at the gate of the foundation: and all the people shall be in the courts of the house of the Lord. But let none come into the house of the Lord, save the priests, and they that minister of the Levites; they shall go in, for they are holy: but all the people shall keep the watch of the Lord. And the Levites shall compass the king round about, every man with his weapons in his hand; and whosoever else cometh into the house, he shall be put to death: but be ye with the king when he cometh in, and when he goeth out. So the Levites and all Judah did according to all things that Jehoiada the priest had commanded, and took every man his men that were to come in on the sabbath, with them that were to go out on the sabbath: for Jehoiada the priest dismissed not the courses. Moreover Jehoiada the priest delivered to the captains of hundreds spears, and bucklers, and shields, that had been king David's, which were in the house of God" 2 Chronicles 23:1-9.

And he set all the people, every man having his weapon in his hand, from the right side of the temple to the left side of the temple, along by the altar and the temple, by the king round about. Then they brought out the king's son, and put upon him the crown, and gave him the testimony, and made him king. And Jehoiada and his sons anointed him, and said, God save the king. Now when Athaliah heard the noise of the people running and praising the king, she came to the people into the house of the Lord: And she looked, and, behold, the king stood at his pillar at the entering in, and the princes and the trumpets by the king: and all the people of the land rejoiced, and sounded with trumpets, also the singers with instruments of musick, and such as taught to sing praise. Then Athaliah rent her clothes, and said, Treason, Treason. Then Jehoiada the priest brought out the captains of hundreds that were set over the host, and said unto them, Have her forth of the ranges: and whoso followeth her, let him be slain with the sword. For the priest said, Slay her not in the house of the Lord. So they laid hands on her; and when she was come to the entering of the horse gate by the king's house, they slew her there. And Jehoiada made a covenant between him, and between all the people, and between the king, that they should be the Lord's people. Then all the people went to the house of Baal, and brake it down, and brake his altars and his images in pieces, and slew Mattan the priest of Baal before the altars. Also Jehoiada appointed the offices of the house of the Lord by the hand of the priests the Levites, whom David had distributed in the house of the Lord, to offer the burnt offerings of the Lord, as it is written in the law of Moses, with rejoicing and with singing, as it was ordained by David. And he set the porters at the gates of the house of the Lord, that none which was unclean in any thing should enter in. And he took the captains of hundreds, and the nobles, and the governors of the people, and all the people of the land, and brought down the king from the house of the Lord: and they came through the high gate into the king's house, and set the king upon the throne of the kingdom. And all the people of the land rejoiced: and the city was quiet, after that they had slain Athaliah with the sword" 2 Chronicles 23:10-21.

Like any study of the Bible, knowing the context is all important, and before we get to Jehoiada and two important figures linked to him: Joash, the king, and Athaliah, the queen (mother of the previous king, Ahaziah), it is worth setting the scene. Recapping: following the death of Solomon, Israel was divided into the northern kingdom (ten tribes) and southern kingdom (two tribes). They were at different times at war with each other and allied against a common enemy (at the time Joash comes onto the scene that enemy was Syria). We pick up the story after good king Jehoshaphat ruled over Judah and bad king Ahab ruled over Israel and even then we read there were alliances. When Ahab died, he was followed by Ahaziah, Joram and Jehu (all bad kings). Jehoshaphat's descendants: Jehoram and Ahaziah were also bad. The story around these characters was tragic. When Ahaziah (the Judah one) was killed, his mother, Athaliah, took over, a truly wicked woman, who sought to kill any of royal descent which might have any claim to the throne. The one who escaped was Joash, then only one year old, who was rescued by Jehoshabeath, daughter of Jehoram and wife of Jehoiada.

What was so remarkable about our story was that were it not for Jehoiada's wise and courageous actions, things would have ended tragically for Judah, bearing in mind it was God's intention to perpetuate the line of David, from which the Messiah would come. He hid the boy Joash in the Temple for six years and carefully orchestrated events resulting in Joash becoming king and Athaliah deposed and executed. He became Joash's mentor, renewing the holy Covenant, and while Jehoiada was alive Joash was a good king. We later see the important part priests played as teachers, and here Jehoiada was a great example. Under Joash, the people returned to God; the Temple was restored, true worship took place, and false worship, including that of Baal was stopped, even though as often happened in Judah's history the High Places were not removed, and the people prospered. The repair of the Temple and raising the money to do so was a major undertaking, but under Jehoiada it all happened.

We are told that Jehoiada was 130 years old when he died, "full of days", and was buried with the kings, which demonstrated the esteem in which he was held. Given his service as priest went back a long time, he was likely the beneficiary of the reforms instigated under kings Asa and Jehoshaphat, which we discuss later. Amazingly, that meant he was around 90 when he began the work for which he was best remembered and showing by example that however old we might be we can still make a difference. While godly offspring is no guarantee for fathers who live righteous lives, it was so here as Zechariah, his son, succeeded him as priest but acted more like a prophet when confronting Joash concerning the errors of his ways and warning him of the consequences of his disobedience.

When Jehoiada died, Joash took foolish advice and turned from the counsel of his former mentor. Judah turned from God, with disastrous consequential results, just as was warned about when God gave the Law to Moses. Joash did not remember Jehoiada's kindness for he killed his son, Zechariah, for speaking out publicly, as a prophet would have done, concerning his unrighteous actions, and paid the same price as did many a prophet after him when speaking truth to power. Joash was himself murdered by way of revenge not long after and Judah suffered under the hands of Syrian invaders.

It is a sobering reminder that despite all his efforts rescuing and mentoring Joash, things ended up the way they did. After being rescued and mentored by Jehoiada, we might expect better, but we can count on the Bible telling it as it is. As far as our account goes, we can take heart from the life of Jehoiada, an old man who made a difference. He joins the illustrious company of priests of the Bible who functioned well in their appointed office, whose focus was to do right in God's eyes, reminding us once again there were outstanding priests, just as there were outstanding kings and prophets.

Chapter 31: Azariah

Given there are a number of Azariahs in the Bible (indeed, different people with the same name is a common feature of the Bible), it is therefore important to make clear who we are talking about.

Our Azariah (the priest) is he who served as High Priest during the reign of king Uzziah, tenth king of the (divided) kingdom of Judah. Uzziah came to the Throne aged 16 and reigned 52 years and *"did that which was right in the sight of the Lord"* 2 Kings 15:3. Uzziah is discussed in 2 Kings 15:1-7 and 2 Chronicles 26:1-23 and given a brief but pertinent reference in Isaiah 6:1 (*"In the year that king Uzziah died I saw also the Lord sitting upon a throne, high and lifted up, and his train filled the temple"*). In the Kings account, Uzziah is (confusingly) called Azariah and Azariah the priest is not mentioned by name, and neither is the incident that led to Uzziah's tragic (given all his past good deeds) demise. To find more about these, we have to turn to the Chronicles account.

"Then all the people of Judah took Uzziah, who was sixteen years old, and made him king in the room of his father Amaziah. He built Eloth, and restored it to Judah, after that the king slept with his fathers. Sixteen years old was Uzziah when he began to reign, and he reigned fifty and two years in Jerusalem. His mother's name also was Jecoliah of Jerusalem. And he did that which was right in the sight of the Lord, according to all that his father Amaziah did. And he sought God in the days of Zechariah, who had understanding in the visions of God: and as long as he sought the Lord, God made him to prosper. And he went forth and warred against the Philistines, and brake down the wall of Gath, and the wall of Jabneh, and the wall of Ashdod, and built cities about Ashdod, and among the Philistines. And God helped him against the Philistines, and against the Arabians that dwelt in Gurbaal, and the Mehunims. And the Ammonites gave gifts to Uzziah: and his name spread abroad even to the entering in of Egypt; for he strengthened himself exceedingly. Moreover Uzziah built towers in Jerusalem at the corner gate, and at the valley gate, and at the turning of the wall, and fortified them. Also he built towers in the desert, and digged many wells: for he had much cattle, both in the low country, and in the plains: husbandmen also, and vine dressers in the mountains, and in Carmel: for he loved husbandry. Moreover Uzziah had an host of fighting men, that went out to war by bands, according to the number of their account by the hand of Jeiel the scribe and Maaseiah the ruler, under the hand of Hananiah, one of the king's captains. The whole number of the chief of the fathers of the mighty men of valour were two thousand and six hundred. And under their hand was an army, three hundred thousand and seven thousand and five hun-

*dred, that made war with mighty power, to help the king against the enemy.
And Uzziah prepared for them throughout all the host shields, and spears,
and helmets, and habergeons, and bows, and slings to cast stones. And he
made in Jerusalem engines, invented by cunning men, to be on the towers
and upon the bulwarks, to shoot arrows and great stones withal. And his
name spread far abroad; for he was marvellously helped, till he was strong"*
2 Chronicles 26: 1-15.

But first let us check out Uzziah the king for it is he rather than Azariah the priest that people will be more likely drawn to when reflecting on
these passages. Other than not getting rid of the High Places (an omission
of some of the other good kings of Judah), and the incident we will get to
that involved Azariah, Uzziah could not be faulted in these accounts and he
did much good. He came under a godly influence and honoured God from
early on and was blessed accordingly, with the land enjoying peace and prosperity, undertaking public works projects, loving the soil and overcoming
Judah's enemies: *"And he sought God in the days of Zechariah, who had
understanding in the visions of God: and as long as he sought the Lord, God
made him to prosper"* 2 Chronicles 26:5. Ironically, given his run in with
priests, Uzziah continued to empower priests and support the activities of
the Temple.

*"But when he (Uzziah) was strong, his heart was lifted up to his destruc-
tion: for he transgressed against the Lord his God, and went into the temple of the Lord to burn incense upon the altar of incense. And Azariah the
priest went in after him, and with him fourscore priests of the Lord, that
were valiant men: And they withstood Uzziah the king, and said unto him, It
appertaineth not unto thee, Uzziah, to burn incense unto the Lord, but to the
priests the sons of Aaron, that are   consecrated to burn incense: go out of
the sanctuary; for thou hast trespassed; neither shall it be for thine honour
from the Lord God. Then Uzziah was wroth, and had a censer in his hand to
burn incense: and while he was wroth with the priests, the leprosy even rose
up in his forehead before the priests in the house of the Lord, from beside
the incense altar. And Azariah the chief priest, and all the priests, looked
upon him, and, behold, he was leprous in his forehead, and they thrust him
out from thence; yea, himself hasted also to go out, because the Lord had
smitten him. And Uzziah the king was a leper unto the day of his death, and
dwelt in a several house, being a leper; for he was cut off from the house of
the Lord: and Jotham his son was over the king's house, judging the people
of the land"* 2 Chronicles 26: 16-21

The tragedy though was Uzziah taking it upon himself, out of pride, to
burn incense in the Temple, which as we discussed earlier was a service that
was forbidden to any who were not priests and if the doing so was not in

the prescribed manner as laid out in the Law. It was here Azariah the priest comes onto the scene and, along with the priests who were under him, confronted the king for his misdeed. This was a brave and right act and Uzziah could have retaliated harshly. As it happened, God had the last word. Uzziah was struck with leprosy by God and he lived as a leper for the rest of his days. If there is a lesson we can draw from this incident and, in particular that of Azariah's response, it is that as we have seen previously, God is holy and He must not be trifled with.

Secondly, and something pertinent down through history when the nearest equivalent to Hebrew priests, Christian priests, ministers, pastors etc., have compromised with earthly authorities in order to gain favour or in order to live a quiet life or to be seen as good law-abiding citizens is that we should obey God rather than man. Compromise and acquiescence was NOT something Azariah did, and instead he confronted and rebuked King Uzziah for his wrong doing. He put God first and can be held up as an example to follow by today's Christian leaders. There is nothing in the Bible record to say Azariah was rewarded for his righteous act, but doing the right thing has its own reward. Azariah will be remembered as one who stood against misplaced authority for the cause of righteousness.

Chapter 32: Hilkiah

As with our previous Bible priest (Azariah), the priest we are looking at here (Hilkiah) will be remembered (if he is remembered at all) for just one thing and something that will be seen in the eyes of some as not being that big a deal. Hilkiah was the person who found the Book (the Book of the Law) when repairing the Temple and, as we will see, this was a pretty significant deal.

"For in the eighth year of his reign, while he (Josiah) was yet young, he began to seek after the God of David his father: and in the twelfth year he began to purge Judah and Jerusalem from the high places, and the groves, and the carved images, and the molten images ... Now in the eighteenth year of his reign, when he had purged the land, and the house, he sent Shaphan the son of Azaliah, and Maaseiah the governor of the city, and Joah the son of Joahaz the recorder, to repair the house of the Lord his God. And when they came to Hilkiah the high priest, they delivered the money that was brought into the house of God, which the Levites that kept the doors had gathered of the hand of Manasseh and Ephraim, and of all the remnant of Israel, and of all Judah and Benjamin; and they returned to Jerusalem ... And when they brought out the money that was brought into the house of the Lord, Hilkiah the priest found a book of the law of the Lord given by Moses. And Hilkiah answered and said to Shaphan the scribe, I have found the book of the law in the house of the Lord. And Hilkiah delivered the book to Shaphan. And Shaphan carried the book to the king, and brought the king word back again, saying, All that was committed to thy servants, they do it. And they have gathered together the money that was found in the house of the Lord, and have delivered it into the hand of the overseers, and to the hand of the workmen. Then Shaphan the scribe told the king, saying, Hilkiah the priest hath given me a book. And Shaphan read it before the king. And it came to pass, when the king had heard the words of the law, that he rent his clothes" 2 Chronicles 34:3, 8-9, 14-19

Also, as with Azariah's significant story, the main character, or at least the one that people who do know it, remember, is not the priest but the king, in this case King Josiah, the last good king of Judah. Josiah followed two bad kings: Manasseh and Amon that left the land, including worship of God, in a sorry state, and after him came Jehoahaz, Jehoiakim, Jehoiachin and Zedekiah, after which there were no more kings following the Exile of Judah to Babylon. We read the story, which is but part of the Josiah record, in 2 Kings 22 and 2 Chronicles 34. Both begin with words to the effect: *"Josiah was eight years old when he began to reign, and he reigned in Jerusalem 31 years and he did that which was right in the sight of the Lord,"* and continue to give an account of his good works that back up this statement.

Finding the Book of the Law, and some scholars think it was Deuteronomy where it talks of blessings that follow obedience to God and cursing that follows disobedience, was to have a huge impact on the fortunes of the Southern kingdom of Judah (the Northern kingdom, Israel, was already in exile) and we have Hilkiah to thank for finding it. He knew how important his find was and ensured that his discovery was made known, which once in the hands of Josiah led to a time of national repentance, for under his leadership the requirements of the Law were put into practice. Besides his discovery, we note that Hilkiah could be trusted as he faithfully and effectively oversaw the works restoring the Temple, long neglected, and led the initiative of consulting Huldah, the prophetess, to find out God's perspective on the whole matter. The positive outcome is these actions led to a national revival and the judgment God had intended was halted, for at least a time. The negative outcome is that the revival was short lived, for the national downward trend toward apostasy resumed after Josiah died.

Hilkiah means "Yah (short for Yahweh) is my portion" of which there are a number in the Hebrew Scriptures with that name but, given what Hilkiah in our story did, is a fitting name for Hilkiah the Priest. We read in Ezra 7:1-5: "*Now after these things, in the reign of Artaxerxes king of Persia, Ezra the son of Seraiah, the son of Azariah, the son of Hilkiah, The son of Shallum, the son of Zadok, the son of Ahitub, The son of Amariah, the son of Azariah, the son of Meraioth, The son of Zerahiah, the son of Uzzi, the son of Bukki, The son of Abishua, the son of Phinehas, the son of Eleazar, the son of Aaron the chief priest*" and we are reminded that Hilkiah is part of a long line of faithful priests. If there is a lesson, it is the importance of God's Word (Deuteronomy plus the other 65 books of the Bible), the importance of hearing and heeding what it says and thus to be aligned to God's will and using whatever influence we have to encourage others to read that Word for themselves and act accordingly.

Chapter 33: Joshua

Joshua the High Priest appears on the scene as part of the first wave of Jews to return to Judah after Babylonian exile and as a result of the edict by Cyrus the Great who had authorised and supported the return of the Jews from their Babylonian exile, after 70 years of captivity, all of which had been prophesied by the prophets: Isaiah and Jeremiah. It is worth noting that the Temple had been destroyed at the start of the captivity and during that period priests were not able to function.

Joshua is mentioned by name in Ezra and Nehemiah (there he is referred to as Jeshua) as well as the two prophets operating at the time of the first wave of returnees: Haggai and Zechariah, both of whom were urging the rebuilding of the Temple. Notably, most of the exiles who settled in Babylon, preferred staying put where they were comfortably well off rather than face an uncertain future. No doubt, Joshua's role in the rebuilding project was crucial and it was a far from smooth undertaking.

"And he shewed me Joshua the high priest standing before the angel of the Lord, and Satan standing at his right hand to resist him. And the Lord said unto Satan, The Lord rebuke thee, O Satan; even the Lord that hath chosen Jerusalem rebuke thee: is not this a brand plucked out of the fire? Now Joshua was clothed with filthy garments, and stood before the angel. And he answered and spake unto those that stood before him, saying, Take away the filthy garments from him. And unto him he said, Behold, I have caused thine iniquity to pass from thee, and I will clothe thee with change of raiment. And I said, Let them set a fair mitre upon his head. So they set a fair mitre upon his head, and clothed him with garments. And the angel of the Lord stood by. And the angel of the Lord protested unto Joshua, saying, Thus saith the Lord of hosts; If thou wilt walk in my ways, and if thou wilt keep my charge, then thou shalt also judge my house, and shalt also keep my courts, and I will give thee places to walk among these that stand by. Hear now, O Joshua the high priest, thou, and thy fellows that sit before thee: for they are men wondered at: for, behold, I will bring forth my servant the Branch. For behold the stone that I have laid before Joshua; upon one stone shall be seven eyes: behold, I will engrave the graving thereof, saith the Lord of hosts, and I will remove the iniquity of that land in one day. In that day, saith the Lord of hosts, shall ye call every man his neighbour under the vine and under the fig tree" Zechariah 3:1-10.

In all five of the references (by name) to Joshua in the Book of Haggai, he is mentioned alongside Zerubbabel the governor of Judah, who was the grandson of Jehoiachin the penultimate king of Judah. In his prophecy, Haggai was encouraging both Joshua and Zerubbabel to get on with the job of overseeing the building of the Temple, which after the work enthusiastically began had stopped for a period of years due to discouragement and distraction – but, despite setbacks, they did get on with the building project, just as the Lord had instructed them to do through His prophets.

As far as this account of Joshua goes, our focus needs to be on Zechariah Chapters 3 and 6, which describe a series of visions that Zechariah had, many of which relate to Last Day events and the Messiah that was to come, but in these two chapters Joshua played a significant role. In Chapter 3, we see a picture of Joshua dressed in filthy garments being accused by Satan on one side and the Angel of the Lord standing on the other, as it were the Advocate for the Defence.

Satan is the chief protagonist to the Almighty throughout scripture, Genesis to Revelation. Concerning Satan, we read *"Now is come salvation, and strength, and the kingdom of our God, and the power of his Christ: for the accuser of our brethren is cast down, which accused them before our God day and night. And they overcame him by the blood of the Lamb, and by the word of their testimony; and they loved not their lives unto the death"* (Revelation 12:10-11). Accusing is what Satan did in Zechariah's vision and he continues to do today. We note that Satan was not being withstood by AN angel but THE ANGEL which has led some commentators to speculate as to his identity, some taking a view that along with other "The Angel" references in the Old Testament this was the pre-incarnate Jesus Christ.

"And the word of the Lord came unto me, saying, Take of them of the captivity, even of Heldai, of Tobijah, and of Jedaiah, which are come from Babylon, and come thou the same day, and go into the house of Josiah the son of Zephaniah; Then take silver and gold, and make crowns, and set them upon the head of Joshua the son of Josedech, the high priest; And speak unto him, saying, Thus speaketh the Lord of hosts, saying, Behold the man whose name is The Branch; and he shall grow up out of his place, and he shall build the temple of the Lord: Even he shall build the temple of the Lord; and he shall bear the glory, and shall sit and rule upon his throne; and he shall be a priest upon his throne: and the counsel of peace shall be between them both. And the crowns shall be to Helem, and to Tobijah, and to Jedaiah, and to Hen the son of Zephaniah, for a memorial in the temple of the Lord. And they that are far off shall come and build in the temple of the Lord, and ye shall know that the Lord of hosts hath sent me unto you. And this shall come to pass, if ye will diligently obey the voice of the Lord your God" Zechariah 6:9-15.

In any case, the role of Jesus in His first coming is pertinent to this story. We don't know the details of why Joshua was arrayed in filthy garments and what he was being accused of, other than to take note that Satan is the master of accusing people, especially those who are closest to God, when it comes to their sins and failures. As High Priest, Joshua had the sacred job of representing the people to God, e.g., on the Day of Atonement. Looking throughout history as recorded in the Bible, we find it is something that Satan hates, seeing how he seeks to discourage and crush the people of God through making his accusations. But there was a way out, and we are reminded Jesus' main work in His First Coming was that of redemption. Also, *"There is therefore now no condemnation to them which are in Christ Jesus, who walk not after the flesh, but after the Spirit"* Romans 8:1.

In this vision, we see Joshua cleansed of his sin and his filthy garments being replaced with clean ones, and being charged by God to do the work of a priest. At the end of this particular vision, we see mention of "the Branch" (Zechariah 6:12), which we can take to be the Messiah that is to come: *"And there shall come forth a rod out of the stem of Jesse, and a Branch shall grow out of his roots"* Isaiah 11:1, and *"Behold, the days come, saith the Lord, that I will raise unto David a righteous Branch, and a King shall reign and prosper, and shall execute judgment and justice in the earth"* Jeremiah 23:5.

In the Zechariah 6 vision, both the Branch and Joshua are mentioned along with a crown combining both the priestly and kingly functions being placed on Joshua's head. Other than the exceptional case of Melchizedek (seen as a forerunner to Jesus) the offices of priest and king could not be joined. But in the person of Jesus they were. We remember what many sections of the church celebrate as Palm Sunday when Jesus rode into Jerusalem on a donkey, fulfilling yet another of Zechariah's prophecies. The Second Coming of the Messiah will be preceded by battles (depicted by horses and chariots) with Joshua being a type of that which is to come: *"Then take silver and gold, and make crowns, and set them upon the head of Joshua the son of Josedech, the high priest; And speak unto him, saying, Thus speaketh the Lord of hosts, saying, Behold the man whose name is The Branch; and he shall grow up out of his place, and he shall build the temple of the Lord: Even he shall build the temple of the Lord; and he shall bear the glory, and shall sit and rule upon his throne; and he shall be a priest upon his throne: and the counsel of peace shall be between them both"* Zechariah 6:11-13.

Joshua the Priest is remembered as the one Satan accused but, whatever the sin he was being accused of, he was cleansed and restored. We who know God may also humbly declare we are mere *"brands plucked from the fire"*, *"and hath made us kings and priests unto God and his Father; to him be glory and dominion for ever and ever ... and we shall reign on the earth"* Revelation 1:6, 5:10. As believer-priests, we can take heart that however wretched and filthy we are or feel, there is one who is prepared to stand alongside us, cleanses us through His blood and make it possible for us to serve as priests.

Chapter 34: Eliashib

Some of the priests mentioned previously did one significant thing to qual-ify for a mention. Eliashib the High Priest, who was serving in the time of Nehemiah, and was also the grandson of Joshua, discussed in the previous chapter, did at least two, and these were quite contrasting. We would be wrong to place Bible characters into either a wholly good category or a wholly bad one, for most, if not all, were mixtures of good and bad, albeit in differing proportions. Concerning the two things that Eliashib did, which we are about to consider, one was clearly good and one was clearly bad.

In 444 BC, Nehemiah led the return of the third wave of returnees from Babylon (a few craftsmen), around 14 years after the second wave of returnees under Ezra (mostly priests and Levites) and around 93 years after the first wave under Joshua and Zerubbabel. The hoped for renewal in the land had not happened and those who had returned from exile were in a sorry state. While the Temple had been built, there was much other building that needed to be done, notably that concerning the walls round Jerusalem, that were needed to provide security for the city dwellers. This much concerned Nehemiah. With the blessing and support of Artaxerxes the king, Nehemiah was commissioned to go to Jerusalem and supervise the building work. This he quickly undertook with resolve, ingenuity and passion.

Here we meet Eliashib for the first time, although little is said about his priestly activities. *"Eliashib the high priest and his fellow priests went to work and rebuilt the Sheep Gate. They dedicated it and set its doors in place, building as far as the Tower of the Hundred, which they dedicated, and as far as the Tower of Hananel"* Nehemiah 3:1. While many others were involved in this important building project, the fact that Eliashib, who was the recognised spiritual leader, led the way by doing his bit, was significant, and no doubt inspired others, especially given it was hazardous activity as they were opposed in a variety of ways. We read about the three who were the main opposition, who were to play a part in Eliashib's second notable action: *"But when Sanballat the Horonite, and Tobiah the servant, the Ammonite, and Geshem the Arabian, heard it, they laughed us to scorn, and despised us, and said, What is this thing that ye do? will ye rebel against the king?"* Nehemiah 2:19.

Sanballat, Tobiah and Geshem continued to do mischief against the Jews who had returned from exile. It is not clear what time had elapsed but Nehemiah had temporarily disappeared from the scene, likely to return to serve the Persian king, where he resumed his duties as the king's cupbearer. We do not know what led up to all that happened, but Eliashib gave Tobiah a room in the Temple and we learn that one of Eliashib's grandsons married the daughter of Sanballat. When he found out about it, upon his return, Nehemiah was angry, not just because of what Tobiah and Sanballat had done earlier to thwart the purposes of God but Eliashib had broken God's command by consorting with the enemy:

"Now it came to pass, when they had heard the law, that they separated from Israel all the mixed multitude. And before this, Eliashib the priest, having the oversight of the chamber of the house of our God, was allied unto Tobiah: And he had prepared for him a great chamber, where aforetime they laid the meat offerings, the frankincense, and the vessels, and the tithes of the corn, the new wine, and the oil, which was commanded to be given to the Levites, and the singers, and the porters; and the offerings of the priests. … and came back to Jerusalem. Here I learned about the evil thing Eliashib had done in providing Tobiah a room in the courts of the house of God … One of the sons of Joiada son of Eliashib the high priest was son-in-law to Sanballat the Horonite. And I drove him away from me" Nehemiah 13:3-5, 7, 28.

We can take both encouragement and warning from these two actions. Firstly, re-building whatever is the spiritual equivalent of the walls of Jerusalem has to be the right priority for today's people of God, especially for those in position of leadership, and Eliashib's example is one worth following.

Secondly, in our daily activities, there is often temptation to compromise for some perceived gain and all too often this means making deals with those who are enemies of God. The people of God are under huge pressure to adopt the status quo and naturally we want to engage positively with those among whom we find ourselves placed. While we do well to live peaceably with our ungodly neighbours and even look to find common ground in order to work for the greater good, we are also called to pursue holiness, which requires worldly separation and maybe rejection by those around us.

Instead of being remembered as one of the main heroes in the much-needed building of the wall, helping to inspire others and lead the way, which helped to ensure that God's people were kept protected from outside intruders, Eliashib will forever be remembered as one who supported those who had no interest in advancing God's cause but, rather, they were intent on undermining it. It could be so for many who served God down the ages, who did good but what is remembered are the bad things that they have done. While the goal ought to be that we are those who do the will of God, it is sad when the legacy that we leave behind is one where the opposite is the case.

Chapter 35: Ezra

We come now to Ezra, the last of our priests mentioned in the Old Testament who we have identified as being significant priests. He is far from being the last Priest of the Bible, which continued as far as Judaism goes up to the destruction of the rebuilt Herodian dynasty, Second Temple, in AD 70. A lot could be said about changes to how priests operated after Ezra, notably in the Inter Testament period when priests continued to play a significant role, up to significant New Testament priests, namely: Zechariah, Caiaphas, and Ananias, more than 400 years later. For now, we focus on Ezra. One of his legacies was that he showed how future priests might best be able to operate following the Exile.

Returning from exile:

"537 BC, comprising fifty thousand from the tribes of Judah and Benjamin, led by Zerubbabel, under King Xerxes / Cyrus (rebuilding the social life).

458 BC, comprising eighteen hundred, mainly priests and Levites, led by Ezra, under King Artaxerxes (concerned with rebuilding the religious life).

444 BC, comprising a few craftsmen, led by Nehemiah, under King Artaxerxes (concerned with rebuilding the physical life)." **Prophets of the Bible**, page 76.

"Much of what we know about life after return from exile can be found in the Books of Ezra (meaning "help") and Nehemiah (meaning "comfort"); although it is just one book in the Hebrew Bible, with perhaps Ezra as author. One commentator, noting remarkable similarities in approach between the two books, divides Ezra chapters as 1-2 return (1), 3-6 rebuild, 7-8 return (2) and 9-10 reform; and Nehemiah chapters as 1-2 return (3), 3-7 rebuild, 8-10 renew and 11-13 reform; with chapter 9 in both confessing of national sins. (The numbers 1,2 and 3 in brackets refer to the first, second and third returns from exile.)" **Prophets of the Bible**, page 77.

Ezra is somewhat different in what he did compared with other priests, and he wasn't the High Priest, although he was certainly qualified by virtue of tracing his ancestry to Aaron. It is worth noting that in line with the observation that the Bible is primarily about God and His dealings with humankind, while Ezra is mentioned by name in the two books (Ezra and Nehemiah) it is said he had written (as well as in a third, the Book of Chronicles, which he may have written), more important is the subject of God, how He related to the Exiles and how the Exiles responded to Him, after they returned home following the Babylonian captivity. Ezra stands out, not because of his direct contribution to Temple worship but as a scribe, teacher, organiser and someone who was zealous that YHWH be honoured in the right way.

"Now after these things, in the reign of Artaxerxes king of Persia, Ezra the son of Seraiah, the son of Azariah, the son of Hilkiah, The son of Shallum, the son of Zadok, the son of Ahitub, The son of Amariah, the son of Azariah, the son of Meraioth, The son of Zerahiah, the son of Uzzi, the son of Bukki, The son of Abishua, the son of Phinehas, the son of Eleazar, the son of Aaron the chief priest: This Ezra went up from Babylon; and he was a ready scribe in the law of Moses, which the Lord God of Israel had given: and the king granted him all his request, according to the hand of the Lord his God upon him. And there went up some of the children of Israel, and of the priests, and the Levites, and the singers, and the porters, and the Nethinims, unto Jerusalem, in the seventh year of Artaxerxes the king. And he came to Jerusalem in the fifth month, which was in the seventh year of the king. For upon the first day of the first month began he to go up from Babylon, and on the first day of the fifth month came he to Jerusalem, according to the good hand of his God upon him. For Ezra had prepared his heart to seek the law of the Lord, and to do it, and to teach in Israel statutes and judgments" Ezra 7:1-10.

Chapters 1 to 6 of the Book of Ezra is an account of what took place starting from 80 years previously. While the Temple had been built, things were far from what should have been and overall morale was low. In Ezra 7 and onward, we read of Ezra and a small group of returnees, including priests and Levites and those who assisted in that pertaining to religious life among the returning Jews, now entering our story. Ezra had been granted favour by the Persian king. A lot of what needed to be done was done under Ezra's enthusiastic leadership and with the king's support. A serious issue though was that the people were not following the Law of God, and this included inter-marriage with those residents in the land, who were not Jewish and were not following the God of Israel.

"Now when Ezra had prayed, and when he had confessed, weeping and casting himself down before the house of God, there assembled unto him out of Israel a very great congregation of men and women and children: for the people wept very sore. And Shechaniah the son of Jehiel, one of the sons of Elam, answered and said unto Ezra, We have trespassed against our God, and have taken strange wives of the people of the land: yet now there is hope in Israel concerning this thing. Now therefore let us make a covenant with our God to put away all the wives, and such as are born of them, according to the counsel of my lord, and of those that tremble at the commandment of our God; and let it be done according to the law. Arise; for this matter belongeth unto thee: we also will be with thee: be of good

courage, and do it. Then arose Ezra, and made the chief priests, the Levites, and all Israel, to swear that they should do according to this word. And they sware. Then Ezra rose up from before the house of God, and went into the chamber of Johanan the son of Eliashib: and when he came thither, he did eat no bread, nor drink water: for he mourned because of the transgression of them that had been carried away. Then all the men of Judah and Benjamin gathered themselves together unto Jerusalem within three days. It was the ninth month, on the twentieth day of the month; and all the people sat in the street of the house of God, trembling because of this matter, and for the great rain. And Ezra the priest stood up, and said unto them, Ye have transgressed, and have taken strange wives, to increase the trespass of Israel" Ezra 10:1-10.

As we can see, Ezra is mentioned by name several times in Ezra 10 and it was to do with a show down involving the people who had married foreign wives, contrary to what the Law prescribed. That same principle applies to Christians: *"Be ye not unequally yoked together with unbelievers"* 2 Corinthians 6:14. Following Ezra's actions was a time of prayer, confession and penitence and this was led by Ezra and resulted in those who had married outside of Judaism divorcing their wives.

"And all the people gathered themselves together as one man into the street that was before the water gate; and they spake unto Ezra the scribe to bring the book of the law of Moses, which the Lord had commanded to Israel. And Ezra the priest brought the law before the congregation both of men and women, and all that could hear with understanding, upon the first day of the seventh month. And he read therein before the street that was before the water gate from the morning until midday, before the men and the women, and those that could understand; and the ears of all the people were attentive unto the book of the law. And Ezra the scribe stood upon a pulpit of wood, which they had made for the purpose; and beside him stood Mattithiah, and Shema, and Anaiah, and Urijah, and Hilkiah, and Maaseiah, on his right hand; and on his left hand, Pedaiah, and Mishael, and Malchiah, and Hashum, and Hashbadana, Zechariah, and Meshullam. And Ezra opened the book in the sight of all the people; (for he was above all the people;) and when he opened it, all the people stood up: And Ezra blessed the Lord, the great God. And all the people answered, Amen, Amen, with lifting up their hands: and they bowed their heads, and worshipped the Lord with their faces to the ground" Nehemiah 8:1-6.

We see again Ezra being mentioned in the Nehemiah account, and this was concerning his dedication to studying the Law. His desire was for others to know and follow it. We see an example in Nehemiah 10 when he opened the Book of the Law and read it to the people. Ezra is described as both priest and scribe, those who were defined as a member of a learned class in ancient Israel through New Testament times as studying the Scriptures and serving as copyists, editors, teachers, and jurists. Ezra's actions led to a mini revival and while all too short lived (as we will see in the Book of Malachi, the final prophet of the Old Testament, in that it revealed God's displeasure) it showed what could and should have been taking place as we enter the 400-year Inter Testament period.

"O that my ways were directed to keep thy statutes! Then shall I not be ashamed, when I have respect unto all thy commandments. I will praise thee with uprightness of heart, when I shall have learned thy righteous judgments ... With my whole heart have I sought thee: O let me not wander from thy commandments. Thy word have I hid in mine heart, that I might not sin against thee. Blessed art thou, O Lord: teach me thy statutes ... My lips shall utter praise, when thou hast taught me thy statutes. My tongue shall speak of thy word: for all thy commandments are righteousness. Let thine hand help me; for I have chosen thy precepts" Psalm 119: 5-7, 10-12, 171-173.

Some commentators suggest Ezra wrote Psalm 119 (extracts above are pertinent). While Judaism as practised by the priests would become corrupted, as was evident when Jesus came onto the scene, Ezra showed how following the tenets of the Law could be practised during this post-Exile period, although a series of foreign rulers, led by the Greeks and Romans, provided a challenge that Jewish inhabitants of Israel failed to rise to, albeit with notable exceptions. As for Ezra, he will be forever remembered as a man of prayer and the Word, and one who had first and foremost a heart for God. There can be no better epitaph and example to follow than: *"For Ezra had prepared his heart to seek the law of the Lord, and to do it, and to teach in Israel statutes and judgments"* Ezra 7:10.

Chapter 36: Zacharias

As we come to the New Testament, we can reflect on many changes in the priesthood since our last mentioned (Old Testament) priest, Ezra, over 400 years previously. Given the rather negative press found in the New Testament to priests, because of their unsympathetic response to Jesus and His ministry, the promised Messiah that Israel had been looking forward to, it might be easy to dismiss all as being corrupt. But it is well to note that shortly after Jesus' ascension to heaven and when His disciples began preaching the Gospel that *"the word of God increased; and the number of the disciples multiplied in Jerusalem greatly; and a great company of the priests were obedient to the faith"* Acts 6:7. The first priest named in the New Testament was Zacharias (also referred to as Zechariah) and he was decidedly of the non-corrupt variety. He is mentioned in only one place in the Bible – Luke 1.

"There was in the days of Herod, the king of Judaea, a certain priest named Zacharias, of the course of Abia: and his wife was of the daughters of Aaron, and her name was Elisabeth. And they were both righteous before God, walking in all the commandments and ordinances of the Lord blameless. And they had no child, because that Elisabeth was barren, and they both were now well stricken in years. And it came to pass, that while he executed the priest's office before God in the order of his course, According to the custom of the priest's office, his lot was to burn incense when he went into the temple of the Lord. And the whole multitude of the people were praying without at the time of incense. And there appeared unto him an angel of the Lord standing on the right side of the altar of incense. And when Zacharias saw him, he was troubled, and fear fell upon him" Luke 1: 5-12.

One significant, often overlooked, aspect concerning Zacharias, was that he was *"of the course of Abia"* or *"to the priestly division of Abijah"* (NIV). If we want to find out more about the course/division of Abia/Abijah, we need to refer to when David was preparing for the building of the Temple and to how he organised the priests: *"Now these are the divisions of the sons of Aaron. The sons of Aaron; Nadab, and Abihu, Eleazar, and Ithamar. But Nadab and Abihu died before their father, and had no children: therefore Eleazar and Ithamar executed the priest's office. And David distributed them, both Zadok of the sons of Eleazar, and Ahimelech of the sons of Ithamar, according to their offices in their service"* 1 Chronicles 24:1-3. There were 24 divisions of priests and, as well as serving during festivals, each was assigned a date/time slot to do temple duty, thus covering the whole year. Zechariah was in the eighth, the division of Abijah. It was while doing one of the duties, offering incense, symbolic of the prayers of the people, that the angel Gabriel appeared to him. While on the subject of lineage, it is worth noting that Zacharias' wife, Elisabeth, was also descended from Aaron, the first High Priest of Israel. Always, we should bear in mind, it is these and other aspects of the story God deemed as being significant.

"But the angel said unto him, Fear not, Zacharias: for thy prayer is heard; and thy wife Elisabeth shall bear thee a son, and thou shalt call his name John. And thou shalt have joy and gladness; and many shall rejoice at his birth. For he shall be great in the sight of the Lord, and shall drink neither wine nor strong drink; and he shall be filled with the Holy Ghost, even from his mother's womb. And many of the children of Israel shall he turn to the Lord their God. And he shall go before him in the spirit and power of Elias, to turn the hearts of the fathers to the children, and the disobedient to the wisdom of the just; to make ready a people prepared for the Lord. And Zacharias said unto the angel, Whereby shall I know this? for I am an old man, and my wife well stricken in years. And the angel answering said unto him, I am Gabriel, that stand in the presence of God; and am sent to speak unto thee, and to shew thee these glad tidings. And, behold, thou shalt be dumb, and not able to speak, until the day that these things shall be performed, because thou believest not my words, which shall be fulfilled in their season. And the people waited for Zacharias, and marvelled that he tarried so long in the temple. And when he came out, he could not speak unto them: and they perceived that he had seen a vision in the temple: for he beckoned unto them, and remained speechless. And it came to pass, that, as soon as the days of his ministration were accomplished, he departed to his own house" Luke 1:13-23.

Before we consider what Gabriel revealed to Zacharias, we note other significant points. The first is the couple *"were both righteous before God, walking in all the commandments and ordinances of the Lord blameless"*. While our attention is usually drawn to the son that the two were to have, God chose Zacharias and Elisabeth to be the parents of John the Baptist, just as He chose Joseph and Mary to be the parents of Jesus, and that choice played a part in who John was to become. The second point was that Elisabeth was barren and past child bearing age, and we learn from the words of Gabriel that followed they had prayed for a child and God had heard their prayer. Sometimes the 400-year period between Old and New Testaments is referred to as "the Silent years" and the hopes following the return of some of the Jews from exile appeared dashed and those who ruled over Israel after the Persians, the Greeks and the Romans, were less than sympathetic toward them. Through all this time there were the faithful, who among other things prayed to God and, as we see in the case of Zacharias, God heard and answered prayer. The main hope for most Jews was the coming of the Messiah to set up His kingdom. As we see reading on in Luke 1, all that was about to happen.

"And his father Zacharias was filled with the Holy Ghost, and prophesied, saying, Blessed be the Lord God of Israel; for he hath visited and redeemed his people, And hath raised up an horn of salvation for us in the house of his servant David; As he spake by the mouth of his holy prophets, which have been since the world began: That we should be saved from our enemies, and from the hand of all that hate us; To perform the mercy promised to our fathers, and to remember his holy covenant; The oath which he sware to our father Abraham, That he would grant unto us, that we being delivered out of the hand of our enemies might serve him without fear, In holiness and righteousness before him, all the days of our life. And thou, child, shalt be called the prophet of the Highest: for thou shalt go before the face of the Lord to prepare his ways; To give knowledge of salvation unto his people by the remission of their sins, Through the tender mercy of our God; whereby the dayspring from on high hath visited us, To give light to them that sit in darkness and in the shadow of death, to guide our feet into the way of peace. And the child grew, and waxed strong in spirit, and was in the deserts till the day of his shewing unto Israel" Luke 1:67-80.

When Christians consider the Christmas story, often overlooked is the part played by Zacharias, although mention may be given to Elisabeth and the birth of John. It must have been an alarming experience encountering the Angel Gabriel and even more so the message that Zacharias received concerning the birth of John. It is hard not to feel sympathy with Zacharias for not believing Gabriel's message but the consequence of his unbelief was being struck dumb. But it all happened as Gabriel said it would and this was followed by Mary, Elisabeth's cousin, also becoming pregnant. Perhaps one of the most heart-warming stories in the whole Bible concerns John, who while still in his mother's tummy, leaped in her womb when the two pregnant ladies met and Elisabeth, recognising who was being carried in Mary's womb (incidentally, here is good biblical evidence the baby in the mother's womb is sacrosanct to God), blessed God, Mary and her child to be. So it was, that John concerning whom Jesus was to speak: *"Among them that are born of women there hath not risen a greater than John the Baptist"* Matthew 11:11 was born and Zacharias would once again be able to speak.

The first words on Zacharias' lips once speech was restored were praise followed by a remarkable prophecy concerning John the Baptist, all of which came to pass during John's life and consistent with both the words of the Angel and what the Scriptures predicted. After that, we read no more about Zacharias, yet the part he played in the Bible narrative and his positive legacy, however, were huge. We are reminded too that at a time when the priesthood had been compromised and priests fell short of the high standards laid out in the Law, there were faithful priests like Zacharias.

Chapter 37: Caiaphas

According to Wikipedia: "*Joseph ben Caiaphas ... was the Jewish high priest who, according to Josephus was high priest of the Jews during the years of Jesus' ministry, and according to authors of the Gospels, Matthew, Luke and John, was organizer of the plot to kill Jesus. He famously presided over the Sanhedrin trial of Jesus. The primary sources for Caiaphas' life are the New Testament, and the writings of Josephus. Josephus records that he was made high priest by the Roman procurator Valerius Gratus after Simon ben Camithus had been deposed*".

In most Christian traditions, Caiaphas, unlike Zacharias, looked at previously, was considered one of the bad guys. Before we look at the Bible record, we should consider the question posed in an online article titled: "*Was Caiaphas a Descendant of Aaron?*" With the exception of Melchizedek, all the priests considered in Part 2 up to now were. From around the Maccabean period, around 160 BC, we find that the priesthood had been compromised and corrupted (discussed in Chapter 14). The article begins: "*the office of high priest became politicized in the Maccabean period, and by the time of the New Testament the position of high priest was treated like a political appointment. According to Josephus, Herod the Great appointed no less than six high priests*".

The writer continues to set the scene: "*Caiaphas himself was appointed by the Roman procurator Valerius Gratus. Josephus describes Valerius Gratus as follows: "This man deprived Ananus of the high priesthood, and appointed Ismael, the son of Phabi, to be high priest. He also deprived him in a little time, and ordained Eleazar, the son of Ananus, who had been high priest before, to be high priest: which office, when he had held for a year, Gratus deprived him of it, and gave the high priesthood to Simon, the son of Camithus; and, when he had possessed that dignity no more than a year, Joseph Caiaphas was made his successor. When Gratus had done those things, he went back to Rome, after he had stayed in Judea eleven years, and Pontius Pilate came as his successor*" This can be checked out for Josephus account "**Antiquities of the Jews, 18:34-35**".

The writer helpfully points out the recent discovery of ossuaries containing the remains of Caiaphas and members of his family. Ossuaries were boxes carved from a block of limestone, intended to hold the bones of the deceased in a rock-cut tomb. One such ossuary contained an inscription that identified Caiaphas as coming from the priestly course of Ma'aziah. Ma'aziah was the 24th and final priestly family appointed by David for service in the temple (1 Chronicles 24:18) (we have earlier identified our previous priest, Zacharias, as belonging to the eighth course).

In another article, based on these same archaeological finds, the author posed the question "*Did Caiaphus Regret Killing Jesus? – Mysteries Of The Bible Unlocked – Caiaphas Good Guy Or Bad Guy*". In Caiaphas' tomb were found two nails, of the sort used to hang people being crucified to the cross. He concludes that maybe he did and the nails gave the evidence. We will not know one way or other this side of eternity if that was so but, in any case, it was evident that Caiaphas was motivated more by religious and political considerations than by the pursuit of truth and justice.

There were two persons referred to as High Priests at the time Jesus was brought to trial and eventually executed: Caiaphas and his father-in-law, Annas. According to Josephus, Caiaphas was the High Priest at the time and central to the plot to bring Jesus to trial, presiding over it and calling for his death. "*And they led Jesus away to the high priest: and with him were assembled all the chief priests and the elders and the scribes ... And the high priest stood up in the midst, and asked Jesus, saying, Answerest thou nothing? what is it which these witness against thee? But he held his peace, and answered nothing. Again the high priest asked him, and said unto him, Art thou the Christ, the Son of the Blessed? And Jesus said, I am: and ye shall see the Son of man sitting on the right hand of power, and coming in the clouds of heaven. Then the high priest rent his clothes, and saith, What need we any further witnesses? Ye have heard the blasphemy: what think ye? And they all condemned him to be guilty of death*" Mark 14:53, 60-64.

While the charges were that Jesus had committed blasphemy, the real reason for wanting Jesus out of the way was political and Jesus posed a significant threat. Not only were the religious establishment keen to hold on to power, especially given that they had been sharply criticised when Jesus spoke and likely felt undermined, they were afraid that a popular leader, which Jesus was, would come to the attention of the Romans who could (and eventually did) destroy the Temple. Caiaphas remained as High Priest for a short time following Jesus' death and he continued to oppose this new Way.

We later read: "*And Annas the high priest, and Caiaphas, and John, and Alexander, and as many as were of the kindred of the high priest, were gathered together at Jerusalem*" Acts 4:6.

It is worth pondering some of Caiaphas' words, recorded (only) in John's Gospel. What he spoke was truth of the most profound kind. The tragedy is he did not follow Him who is The Truth, and the one that he more than any would have known about – Israel's promised Messiah. "*Then gathered the chief priests and the Pharisees a council, and said, what do we? for this man doeth many miracles. If we let him thus alone, all men will believe on him: and the Romans shall come and take away both our place and nation.*

And one of them, named Caiaphas, being the high priest that same year, said unto them, Ye know nothing at all, nor consider that it is expedient for us, that one man should die for the people, and that the whole nation perish not. And this spake he not of himself: but being high priest that year, he prophesied that Jesus should die for that nation; And not for that nation only, but that also he should gather together in one the children of God that were scattered abroad. Then from that day forth they took counsel together for to put him to death" John 11:47-53.

Chapter 38: Ananias

Sadly, our last two named priests of the Bible, Caiaphas and now Ananias, were on the wrong side when it came to doing the will of God. Notwithstanding human disobedience, God is sovereign and, we are often reminded, despite man's worst efforts, God's purposes prevail, even using man's wrong actions to further His plans. In Caiaphas' case, it was his attitude toward and designs to entrap Jesus that led to His arrest and execution.

In Ananias' case, it was his hostile attitude toward Paul that led to him being put under house arrest, which in our first text (that follows) included ordering Paul to be struck, and from our second text, the opposition of which Ananias appeared to be the primary instigator eventually led to Paul being shipped off to Rome for trial under Caesar. Ananias the priest is referred to by name twice in the Bible: *"And the high priest Ananias commanded them that stood by him to smite him on the mouth"* Acts 23:2 and *"And after five days Ananias the high priest descended with the elders, and with a certain orator named Tertullus, who informed the governor against Paul"* Acts 24:1.

According to Wikipedia (and backed up by extra biblical sources): *"Ananias son of Nedebeus was a high priest who, according to the Acts of the Apostles, presided during the trials of the apostle Paul at Jerusalem (Acts 23:2) and Caesarea (Acts 24:1). Josephus, Antiquities xx. 5. 2, called him "Ananias ben Nebedeus". He officiated as high priest from about AD 47 to 52. A. C. Hervey described him as "a violent, haughty, gluttonous, and rapacious man, and yet looked up to by the Jews".*

In the narrative recorded in the Acts of the Apostles, Paul was called to appear before the Sanhedrin, on the instructions of the commander of the Roman garrison in Jerusalem. Ananias heard Paul's opening defence and commanded those who stood by him *"to strike him on the mouth"*. Paul described him as a *"whitewashed wall"* declaring that God would strike Ananias for this unlawful act.

Those who stood by accused Paul of reviling or insulting the High Priest, to which Paul replied that he did not know that he was the High Priest. Seeing that there were both Pharisees and Sadducees on the Sanhedrin (see Acts 23:4-9 for the context), Paul saw an opportunity. Which side Ananias was on we cannot say for sure but both sides had compromised with the authorities, although discussed elsewhere, especially the Sadducees. Therefore, when Paul perceived that one part were Sadducees and the other Pharisees, he cried out in the council, *"Men and brethren, I am a Pharisee, the son of a Pharisee; concerning the hope and resurrection of the dead I am being judged!"* (Acts 23:6, NKJV).

In other sources we later read that Quadratus, governor of Syria, accused Ananias of being responsible for acts of violence. Ananias was sent to Rome for trial (52 CE), but was acquitted by the emperor Claudius. He continued to officiate as High Priest until 58 CE. Being a friend of the Romans, Ananias was murdered by the people at the beginning of the First Jewish-Roman War.

Having begun our series on named priests who were significant on a high: Aaron and Melchizedek, we end it on a low: Caiaphas and Ananias, even though their office demanded respect as was required by scripture, and as the Apostle Paul clearly recognised. While the Bible account concentrated on the facts, both these priests had been compromised and it was evident they were more intent on holding onto their positions of power and maintaining the status quo rather than doing what Priests of YHWH were meant to do and represent Him to the people and do whatever God would have wanted of them.

Chapter 39: Unnamed and Other Named Priests

We have named and discussed 17 priests in greater detail and referred to some other priests. But many more priests functioned up to the time of the Exile and after that up to the destruction of the Temple in AD 70. Many, we don't know by name (far more so than in the case of the prophets)!

An attempt to consider every priest in detail from the time the Levitical priesthood was instituted during the Exodus from Egypt to Canaan until the destruction of the Temple in AD 70 would be beyond the scope of this book. However, it is a matter worth reflecting on; not just the priests of Israel that were of YHWH and from the Aaronic line, right up to New Testament times, as far as we can make out, but also the Levites, who duties complemented those of the priests. What we will do here is consider some of those priests functioning from the time of King David until the time of King Jehoshaphat.

Our period is covered in the Books of Samuel, Kings and Chronicles. While matters pertaining to priests are included in the Samuel and Kings accounts, most of the information we need is to be found in the Books of Chronicles. This is unsurprising as one of the main differences between the Books of Kings and Chronicles was the former was written from a prophet's viewpoint and focused on how Israel came to be in the position they were in while the latter was from a priest's viewpoint, looking both a long way back in religious Israel's history, way before there were priests, and looking forward to the coming of its future Messiah from David's line, and it included details concerning genealogies and religious life. In doing so, we bridge the gap between Zadok and Jehoiada who, as we have already discussed, were outstanding priests and exemplars of how priests should be. In this period, priests were very active.

One feature, often overlooked when studying the life of David, whose life was fraught with conflict and war, was the priority he gave to the religious life of Israel in a way that honoured the God with whom they were in Covenant, and promoted the worship of YHWH, the one true God, evidenced already when describing the prominent roles of Abiathar and Zadok, the High Priests of his time. The bringing back to Jerusalem of the Ark of the Covenant was one notable act where David played a leading role. Among his significant acts was detailed preparation for the building of the Temple (he was disqualified from building it) helping to ensure the carrying out of what needed to happen, e.g., regarding the duties of the Priests and Levites once the Temple had been built. Moreover, he also contributed through the writing of his Psalms; many were meant to be sung and were sung as part of

Temple worship. (In other chapters, we reflect on the words of some of the Psalms sung at the Temple.)

A lot of coverage is given in 1 Chronicles to how David planned to use and organise Priests and Levites and their important contribution to the life of Israel, not just religious but other functions. In the reigns of the kings who followed, it was in the judiciary, as teachers, civil servants, musicians and gatekeepers, supported by the Levites who were organised according to their lineage corresponding to the sons of Levi: Gershon, Kohath and Merari. Something picked up centuries later in our New Testament studies of Zacharias and Caiaphas were the 24 divisions of priest, led by the descendants of the two surviving sons of Aaron (16 from the line of Eleazar and 8 from the line of Ithamar), who operated what could be seen as a shift system when it came to carrying out their duties in the Temple.

- The Ark Brought to Jerusalem (Chapter 15).
- Ministering Before the Ark (Chapter 16).
- Preparation for the Temple (Chapter 22).
- The Levites (Chapter 23).
- The Division of Priests (Chapter 24).
- The Rest of the Levites (Chapter 24).
- The Musicians (Chapter 25).
- The Gatekeepers (Chapter 26).
- The Treasurers and Other Officials (Chapter 26).
- David's Plans for the Temple (Chapter 28).

When we consider the kings between David and Jehoshaphat, we begin with Solomon, David's son, who began well, and this included following the blueprint that was set out by David when it came to the building of the Temple, Temple activities and the functions of priests, but he finished badly. This laid the way open for many of the troubles that followed, starting with the division of the Kingdom into the two tribes to the South (Judah), under his son, Rehoboam, and the ten tribes to the North (Israel), under Jeroboam, who like all the kings of Israel that were to follow was considered bad.

The Book of Chronicles, unlike Kings, focuses just on Judah, for it is there the true worship of YHWH, along with priests, can be mostly found, even though there were always those in the Northern Kingdom, even after the Fall to Assyria in 722 BC that as God had to remind Elijah *"Yet I have left me seven thousand in Israel, all the knees which have not bowed unto Baal, and every mouth which hath not kissed him"* 1 Kings 19:18. And not just Elijah, we find that Elisha, Amos and Hosea were also prophets that spoke the word of YHWH to Israel and sought to turn the people back to Him. But we also find whenever YHWH was not worshipped in the right way this invariably brought about the introduction of priests that were not of YHWH, which we consider in Chapter 9.

Both Rehoboam and his son, Abijah, would be seen as bad kings of Judah, in contrast to the two kings that followed them: Asa and Jehoshaphat, seen as good kings. But it is never that straightforward for even these two bad kings did good things and these two good kings did bad things (thoughts we will develop when we get to **"Kings of the Bible"**). The good thing that all four kings did was to encourage the true priests, who appeared to have flourished in that period and from what we can make out did all that was required of them carrying out their duties as they were allowed.

It was not just Israel that strayed from the Covenant God made with them at Mount Sinai, but it was to be a recurring theme with Judah too. We read under Rehoboam: "*And Judah did evil in the sight of the Lord, and they provoked him to jealousy with their sins which they had committed, above all that their fathers had done. For they also built them high places, and images, and groves, on every high hill, and under every green tree*" 1 Kings 14:22-23, and even under the good kings we find that the High Places, often dedicated to the worship of false gods, continued to operate.

Another aspect of Rehoboam's reign, however, was that following the ten to two tribal division, the true Priests and Levites, intent no doubt on the true worship of YHWH, were prepared to relocate from the Northern to the Southern Kingdom, a move that cost them materially: "*And the priests and the Levites that were in all Israel resorted to him out of all their coasts. For the Levites left their suburbs and their possession, and came to Judah and Jerusalem: for Jeroboam and his sons had cast them off from executing the priest's office unto the Lord*" 2 Chronicles 11:13-14.

We read concerning Abijah (Abijam) "*Now in the eighteenth year of king Jeroboam the son of Nebat reigned Abijam over Judah. Three years reigned he in Jerusalem. and his mother's name was Maachah, the daughter of Abishalom. And he walked in all the sins of his father, which he had done before him: and his heart was not perfect with the Lord his God, as the heart of David his father. Nevertheless for David's sake did the Lord his God give him a lamp in Jerusalem, to set up his son after him, and to establish Jerusalem*" 1 Kings 15:1-4.

Other than its negative portrayal, the Book of Kings says little about Abijah's deeds, but Chronicles devotes a whole chapter to the war between Abijah and Jeroboam, with priests playing an important part: "*Have ye not cast out the priests of the Lord, the sons of Aaron, and the Levites, and have made you priests after the manner of the nations of other lands? so that whosoever cometh to consecrate himself with a young bullock and seven rams, the same may be a priest of them that are no gods. But as for us, the Lord is our God, and we have not forsaken him; and the priests, which minister unto the Lord, are the sons of Aaron, and the Levites wait upon their business ... And when Judah looked back, behold, the battle was before and behind: and they cried unto the Lord, and the priests sounded with the trumpets ... And Abijah and his people slew them with a great slaughter: so there fell down slain of Israel five hundred thousand chosen men. Thus the children of Israel were brought under at that time, and the children of Judah prevailed, because they relied upon the Lord God of their fathers"* 2 Chronicles 13:9-10, 14, 17-18.

When Abijah died, Asa, his son, reigned in his stead. The best thing that can be said about Asa is: *"And Asa did that which was right in the eyes of the Lord, as did David his father"* 1 Kings 15:11, although toward the end, he made wrong alliances rather than trust in the Lord and it proved to be his undoing. There is one significant mention of priests during his 41 years: *"And the Spirit of God came upon Azariah the son of Oded: And he went out to meet Asa, and said unto him, Hear ye me, Asa, and all Judah and Benjamin; The Lord is with you, while ye be with him; and if ye seek him, he will be found of you; but if ye forsake him, he will forsake you. Now for a long season Israel hath been without the true God, and without a teaching priest, and without law. But when they in their trouble did turn unto the Lord God of Israel, and sought him, he was found of them"* 2 Chronicles 15:1-4. We see here the importance of the role of the priest as a teacher, and this was to continue under Jehoshaphat, his son, and later, as we have already considered, under the priests: Jehoiada and Ezra.

When Asa died, Jehoshaphat, his son, reigned in his stead. Again, the commentary on his reign was a positive one despite, as with his father, he instigated some acts of folly toward the end of his reign and he was duly rebuked: *"And Jehoshaphat his son reigned in his stead, and strengthened himself against Israel ... And the Lord was with Jehoshaphat, because he walked in the first ways of his father David, and sought not unto Baalim; But sought to the Lord God of his father, and walked in his commandments, and not after the doings of Israel"* 2 Chronicles 17:1, 3-4. The priest as teacher was a priority that continued under Jehoshaphat: *"And with them he sent Levites, even Shemaiah, and Nethaniah, and Zebadiah, and Asahel, and Shemiramoth, and Jehonathan, and Adonijah, and Tobijah, and Tobadonijah, Levites; and with them Elishama and Jehoram, priests. And they taught in Judah, and had the book of the law of the Lord with them, and went about throughout all the cities of Judah, and taught the people. And the fear of the Lord fell upon all the kingdoms of the lands that were round about Judah, so that they made no war against Jehoshaphat"* 2 Chronicles 17:8-10.

Another role of priests that came to the fore during Jehoshaphat's reign was that of judges, and while we know little else about him, the part that Amariah, the chief priest, played was an important one, and in doing so courageously this had its own rewards: *"Moreover in Jerusalem did Jehoshaphat set of the Levites, and of the priests, and of the chief of the fathers of Israel, for the judgment of the Lord, and for controversies, when they returned to Jerusalem. And he charged them, saying, Thus shall ye do in the fear of the Lord, faithfully, and with a perfect heart. And what cause soever shall come to you of your brethren that dwell in your cities, between blood and blood, between law and commandment, statutes and judgments, ye shall even warn them that they trespass not against the Lord, and so wrath come upon you, and upon your brethren: this do, and ye shall not trespass. And, behold, Amariah the chief priest is over you in all matters of the Lord; and Zebadiah the son of Ishmael, the ruler of the house of Judah, for all the king's matters: also the Levites shall be officers before you. Deal courageously, and the Lord shall be with the good"* 2 Chronicles 19:8-11.

After Jehoshaphat, Priests and Levites continued to be mentioned often, particularly in Chronicles, even if not by name, especially under the good kings of Judah, where they received encouragement to carry out their priestly office. With reference to Chapter 2, Figure 5, there were according to this, following Jehoshaphat, ten bad kings and six good kings, but we need to bear in mind all kings were a mixture of good and bad but usually when a king was bad he introduced or allowed the worship of gods that were not YHWH and thereby there was limited scope for priests to function as they ought. An example of what goes wrong when it comes to priests functioning can be seen under King Ahaz. Jehoshaphat was followed by three mostly bad kings and four mostly good kings, and then came Ahaz.

"In the seventeenth year of Pekah the son of Remaliah Ahaz the son of Jotham king of Judah began to reign. Twenty years old was Ahaz when he began to reign, and reigned sixteen years in Jerusalem, and did not that which was right in the sight of the Lord his God, like David his father. But he walked in the way of the kings of Israel, yea, and made his son to pass through the fire, according to the abominations of the heathen, whom the Lord cast out from before the children of Israel. And he sacrificed and burnt incense in the high places, and on the hills, and under every green tree. Then Rezin king of Syria and Pekah son of Remaliah king of Israel came up to Jerusalem to war: and they besieged Ahaz, but could not overcome him. At that time Rezin king of Syria recovered Elath to Syria, and drave the Jews from Elath: and the Syrians came to Elath, and dwelt there unto this day.

So Ahaz sent messengers to Tiglathpileser king of Assyria, saying, I am thy servant and thy son: come up, and save me out of the hand of the king of Syria, and out of the hand of the king of Israel, which rise up against me. And Ahaz took the silver and gold that was found in the house of the Lord, and in the treasures of the king's house, and sent it for a present to the king of Assyria. And the king of Assyria hearkened unto him: for the king of Assyria went up against Damascus, and took it, and carried the people of it captive to Kir, and slew Rezin. And king Ahaz went to Damascus to meet Tiglathpileser king of Assyria, and saw an altar that was at Damascus: and king Ahaz sent to Urijah the priest the fashion of the altar, and the pattern of it, according to all the workmanship thereof. And Urijah the priest built an altar according to all that king Ahaz had sent from Damascus: so Urijah the priest made it against king Ahaz came from Damascus. And when the king was come from Damascus, the king saw the altar: and the king approached to the altar, and offered thereon. And he burnt his burnt offering and his meat offering, and poured his drink offering, and sprinkled the blood of his peace offerings, upon the altar. And he brought also the brasen altar, which was before the Lord, from the forefront of the house, from between the altar and the house of the Lord, and put it on the north side of the altar. And king Ahaz commanded Urijah the priest, saying, Upon the great altar burn the morning burnt offering, and the evening meat offering, and the king's burnt sacrifice, and his meat offering, with the burnt offering of all the people of the land, and their meat offering, and their drink offerings; and sprinkle upon it all the blood of the burnt offering, and all the blood of the sacrifice: and the brasen altar shall be for me to enquire by. Thus did Urijah the priest, according to all that king Ahaz commanded" 2 Kings 16:1-16.

As far as this book goes, with its focus on priests, the point of interest in this account was not just that Ahaz introduced false worship into the Temple in order to curry favour with the Assyrians, but that he involved Urijah the priest in implementing his ungodly directives, and Urijah complied.

Regarding good kings Uzziah and Josiah, these have already been referred to when we considered Azariah and Hilkiah the Priests respectively. But we end with one of the outstandingly good kings, Hezekiah, concerning whom much is written and, as far as Chronicles goes, large portions of Chapters 28-31. This included reversing the decline in religious observance to the true God wrought by his father, Ahaz, encouraging and enabling Temple worship, supporting the office of Priests and Levites (including ensuring they were adequately provided for), and this happened throughout his reign.

Once more, upon his death and Manasseh becoming king, idolatry became the norm (although later in his reign he repented) as also happened with Amon his son. True worship was restored under Josiah, but it was all too little too late. After four more bad kings: Jehoahaz, Jehoiakim, Jehoia-chin and Zedekiah, the Temple was destroyed and Judah went into Exile, with the office of priest suspended during the Exile, to be restored on return-ing from Exile under Zerubbabel and Joshua and to an extent it flourished. Priests continued to play an important part in the life of those who had re-turned to Israel throughout the Inter Testament period and right up to New Testament times.

We should mention a priest who is not found in the Protestant Bible but is in the Catholic Bible (The Apocrypha) – Mattathias (who was the head of a family of priests commonly known as the Maccabees), a priest of the line of Aaron who had five sons. His third son, Judas, along with his band of freedom fighters, led a revolt against Greek rule. The Maccabees were a group of Jewish rebel warriors who took control of Judea, which at the time was part of the Seleucid Empire. They founded the Hasmonean dynasty, which ruled from 167 BCE to 37 BCE, being a fully independent kingdom from about 110 to 63 BCE. They reasserted the Jewish religion including restoring Temple worship, expanded the boundaries of Judea by conquest, and reduced the influence of Hellenism and Hellenistic Judaism.

The Maccabees, and notably Judas, are remembered for their zeal and in achieving, not just a period of Jewish independence against a cruel, formi-dable foe, but doing so in the light of the acquiescence and compromise by most Jews living in Israel, including their leaders, to foreign rule, and restor-ing the worship of YHWH and the Temple. To this day, some of these events are recalled whenever the Feast of Hanukkah is celebrated. One Maccabean priest often referred to is John Hyrcanus, a Hasmonean (Maccabean) leader and Jewish High Priest of the 2nd century BCE (born 164 BCE and reigned from 134 BCE until his death in 104). John Hyrcanus acted like a king (some-thing that was never intended) and sought political alliances to hold on to power. The Maccabees are discussed in Chapter 16.

Chapter 40: The Priests: Questions, Praise and Prayer

In this final chapter of Part 2, just as we did in Part 1, we will consider each of the preceding Part 2 chapters and ask a question readers might like to ponder or, if part of a group, to discuss. We end each section with a word of prayer and praise, which relates to each of the priests under consideration.

Chapter 21: Tracing the Priests

What were the two main categories of priests that have been identified in Part 2 and what were their main functions?

We thank you Lord that you have always wanted a relationship with your people and that you established the priesthood so that the priests could be intermediaries between you and the people.

Chapter 22: Melchizedek

We read very little about Melchizedek while he was alive but, from what we read later, why did Abraham decide to give him a tenth of everything he had and why is Melchizedek still significant today?

We thank you Lord for Melchizedek, who was a priest of the most High God as well as being a righteous king, and especially do we thank you for Jesus who is forever a priest of the Order of Melchizedek.

Chapter 23: Aaron

Why was Aaron such an important figure in the Bible and how would you sum up his legacy?

We thank you Lord for giving Aaron and the Levitical Priesthood to Israel. Help us who are believer-priests to carry out our priestly duties faithfully and help us not to stumble others along the way.

Chapter 24: Nadab

Why was Nadab's end such a shocking one? What does this teach us about God and how we ought to approach Him?

We worship you, Lord. You are the thrice holy God. May we not take your holiness for granted and may we ever respond to your call for us to be holy.

Chapter 25: Eleazar

Why was Eleazar's elevation to the priesthood unexpected and how well did he fare in that role?

We thank you Lord that Eleazar stepped up to the plate when he was called to do so. As we go about our daily tasks, may we be among those found faithful.

Chapter 26: Phinehas

What is the one thing Phinehas will be ever remembered for? Why was this one action so important and significant, and how do we know God approved of what he did?

May we ever be zealous for the things that you regard as important Lord, as did Phinehas, and may our zeal not be misplaced.

Chapter 27: Eli

We see in the life of Eli both the good and the bad. How might we sum up that life?

We thank you for your glory dear Lord. May we be concerned for your glory and may we not be afraid to confront that which is evil, even among those who are close to us.

Chapter 28: Abiathar

What was the tragedy that caused Abiathar to enter the limelight? In what ways did he do the right things and in what way did he do what was wrong?

We thank you Lord for Abiathar that championed the right cause when all seemed to be lost. Give us discernment to know what is right and wisdom and courage to do what is right and turn from wrong.

Chapter 29: Zadok

How did Zadok enter the scene; how did he rise to prominence and why is he so commended?

May we faithfully serve you as believer-priests Lord, as did Zadok.

Chapter 30: Jehoiada

How were Jehoiada's actions concerning King Joash so significant?

We pray that when it comes to a need or crisis we will respond in the right way and, when it comes to mentoring others, may we do so faithfully and well.

Chapter 31: Azariah

Why was Azariah's action confronting King Uzziah both brave and necessary?

May we not take liberties when it comes to doing what you require and keep us from doing those things that you have forbidden.

Chapter 32: Hilkiah

Why was Hilkiah's discovery so important when it came to King Josiah's attempts at leading the people back to the true worship of God?

We thank you for the Law, and we are mindful of blessings for those who obey and cursing for those who don't. May we learn to treasure your Word, Lord, and incline our hearts so that we obey it.

Chapter 33: Joshua

Why was Joshua a brand plucked from the fire and why was that affirmation necessary and important?

Thank you, Lord, that when Satan accuses us when we fail or do wrong, that we can look to our Lord Jesus Christ, our Great High Priest, who continues to plead our cause.

Chapter 34: Eliashib

Can you identify one good thing and one bad thing Eliashib did?

Lord, may we be ever ready to build whatever it is that needs building and may we not consort with those who seek to thwart your will and purposes.

Chapter 35: Ezra

Why was Ezra's role and contribution so vital for the returning exiles?

Lord, may we be those who prepare our hearts to seek and to do what you would have us do, and may we be found among those who can teach others what are your statutes and judgements.

Chapter 36: Zacharias

In what way was Zacharias in for a shock and what was his vision in the Temple all about and how was it to prove to be so significant?

We thank you Lord for those of whom it can be said they *"are righteous before God, walking in all the commandments and ordinances of the Lord blameless"*. May we be such people.

Chapter 37: Caiaphas

What was Caiaphas' role in the trial and execution of Jesus?

There is so much temptation to compromise with the world Lord. May we be among those who remain faithful to you and be on the side of truth and right, even if it incurs the displeasure of the world.

Chapter 38: Ananias

In what ways did Ananias oppose Paul?

Lord, help us to be a blessing that helps rather than be a stumbling block that hinders, especially when it comes to those who desire to know you better and want to serve you.

Chapter 39: Unnamed and Other Named Priests

Of all the unnamed and lesser-known priests we have identified, which ones strike you as being particularly significant and why?

You are the God we adore and serve. Help us to do so without fuss so that you get all the glory. Thank you too for the privilege of being your believer-priests.

Finally

In ending Part 2, we do well to remind ourselves that one of the principle functions of the Levitical priesthood was to worship God. Above the Mercy Seat over the Ark of the Covenant was seen as where God dwelt, but He could not be approached, except on that one occasion on the Day of Atonement, and then only by the High Priest; notwithstanding the fact that He inhabits eternity and is worshipped by myriads of heavenly beings and redeemed saints that have passed from this life. We close with the following hymn that is all about worshipping our wonderful, majestic, beautiful, dreadful, holy God.

1. My God, how wonderful Thou art,

Thy majesty how bright,

How beautiful Thy mercy seat,

in depths of burning light!

2. How dread are Thine eternal years,

O everlasting Lord;

by prostrate spirits, day and night,

incessantly adored.

3. How wonderful, how beautiful,
the sight of Thee must be,
Thine endless wisdom, boundless pow'r,
and awful purity.

4. O how I fear Thee, Living God,
with deepest, tend'rest fears,
and worship Thee with trembling hope,
and penitential tears.

5. Yet I may love Thee too, O Lord,
Almighty as Thou art;
for Thou hast stooped to ask of me
the love of my poor heart.

6. No earthly father loves like Thee,
no mother e'er so mild,
bears and forbears, as Thou hast done
with me, Thy sinful child.

7. Father of Jesus, love's reward,
what rapture will it be,
prostrate before Thy throne to lie,
and ever gaze on Thee!

Part 3
A Priestly People

Chapter 41: The Priesthood of all Believers

When we think about the Protestant Reformation, viewing it through the lens of some of its most prominent leaders, such as Luther and Calvin, it is likely that the doctrine of justification by faith will stand out in terms of significant factors concerning how theological outlooks were affected. This is pertinent to **Priests of the Bible** when we think of Jesus as being a Priest of the order of Melchizedek and Him being the one whose atoning sacrifice, along with His continuous High Priestly intercession, is of paramount importance in the way we can approach God. The good news is that this applies to all those who have repented of their sin and put their trust in Christ irrespective of their church affiliation.

We can see why such a doctrine is so important, especially as prior to the Reformation people were often bound by what the Roman Catholic Church and its priests said one had to believe and do in order to have a right relationship with God, which invariably had to be through or with the approval of a church-ordained priest, and involved any number of things that the church insisted people had to have happen in order to be justified. It should be added that with respect to the need to be holy, most of the Reformers would have also recoiled from any notion that once having been justified by faith one can then do what one pleases. The issue at stake for them was the Roman Catholic church insisting that whatever they said, regardless of whether or not it was in the Bible, had to be adhered to.

Related to the belief in the doctrine of justification by faith is that of the *priesthood of all believers*. I agree with what my first "Google hit" came up with: "*The doctrine of the priesthood of all believers states that all believers in Christ share in his priestly status; therefore, there is no special class of people who mediate the knowledge, presence, and forgiveness of Christ to the rest of believers, and all believers have the right and authority to read, interpret, and apply the teachings of Scripture. In contrast to the beliefs of the medieval church, the Protestant doctrine of the priesthood of all believers holds that there is no longer a priestly class of people within God's people, but that all believers share in Christ's priestly status by virtue of their union with Christ.*"

Central to the notion of a priestly people (and I hope, dear reader, you are one) is that of the priesthood of all believers, which is the logical continuation of Part 1 (The Priesthood) and Part 2 (The Priests). Priests of the Bible, specifically the Levitical (Aaronic) priesthood, gave the means God laid out for His people (Israel) to approach Him, the Holy One of Israel, prior to Christ. Given what Christ accomplished by dying and rising from the dead, this no longer applies to those who have turned from their sin and have put their faith in Christ for salvation. We note that "*It is Christ who died, yea rather, who is risen again, who is even at the right hand of God, who also maketh intercession for us"* Romans 8:34.

Given that Jesus is our Great High Priest, we can claim His promise as believer-priests: *"Verily I say unto you, Whatsoever ye shall bind on earth shall be bound in heaven: and whatsoever ye shall loose on earth shall be loosed in heaven. Again I say unto you, That if two of you shall agree on earth as touching any thing that they shall ask, it shall be done for them of my Father which is in heaven. For where two or three are gathered together in my name, there am I in the midst of them"* Matthew 18:18-20.

In a lifetime of observation among the different denominations, I have seen a wide variation as to what is implied by the priesthood of all believers, ranging from "everything needs to be done under the authority of or through the priest or minister" to the whole idea of a clergy/laity divide being an affront to the Almighty and the plain teaching of Scripture. It is not my intention to go down numerous doctrinal rabbit holes to offer the correct answer (a matter I also touch on in the next chapter) but rather to share my understanding of the ramifications of being part of the priesthood of all believers.

My own Plymouth Brethren background might put me in the latter camp, although I recognise things are not always that simple. For example, and without wanting to take Scripture out of context, with reference to Korah's rebellion (detailed in Numbers 16), as has been earlier discussed, and with reference to New Testament teaching, such as *"Obey them that have the rule over you, and submit yourselves: for they watch for your souls, as they that must give account"* Hebrews 13:17, I would counsel folk that it is beholden on believer-priests to submit to those who look after the Lord's people. Moreover, we are also told *"let every soul be subject unto the higher* [i.e., secular] *powers"* Romans 13:1. Being a priest does not excuse us from our need to be accountable to other humans. While we are accountable firstly to God and are beholden to do what is true and right, we must not ignore this.

I would like to share an experience going back to my PB roots and something I miss that I saw practised (especially when practised well, which was often not the case). This was typically seen in the way the PB Breaking of Bread meetings were conducted. It demonstrated how the priesthood of all believers could be seen in the context of congregational worship; although this typically excluded women, based on the belief that women should maintain silence when it came to teaching and leading worship. I for one have cause to appreciate that I was encouraged from an early age to preach and teach and to take responsibility in many aspects of Christian ministry but with the proviso that I lived a godly life and I needed to be doctrinally sound, and at the same time: *"submit yourselves to your elders"* 1 Peter 5:5.

We met in accordance with the teaching "*How is it then, brethren? when ye come together, every one of you hath a psalm, hath a doctrine, hath a tongue, hath a revelation, hath an interpretation. Let all things be done unto edifying …*" 1 Corinthians 14:26 (but without the speaking in tongues). A typical meeting involved different brethren doing just that, plus prayer, praise and worship and culminating with any brother who was in fellowship officiating over the Lord's Supper (as "led by the Spirit"). There is a lot more to the priesthood of believers than the way meetings/services are run, of course, and that which was often practised in PBism. My own observation is that when it comes to meetings (services), especially the Lord's Supper, every group has its own peculiar views on how meetings should be conducted. This should not be a falling out matter – despite my preferring the PB way of doing things!

In order to ascertain what the priesthood of all believers involves, we should consider what was expected of priests of the Bible, a subject considered in earlier chapters, and remember that priests were about helping to bridge the gap between God and man and act in a mediation capacity. It is something we should treat with due reverence as is becoming those who have direct access to God, within the Veil into the Holy of Holies, and to recognise that this huge privilege comes with huge responsibilities. In our own humble capacities and unique circumstances, we are called to be His representatives on earth: "*Now then we are ambassadors for Christ*" 2 Corinthians 5:20a.

When I checked out what preachers had to say about the subject of the priesthood of all believers, I found many began by referring to the teachings of Peter: "*To whom coming, as unto a living stone, disallowed indeed of men, but chosen of God, and precious, Ye also, as lively stones, are built up a spiritual house, an holy priesthood, to offer up spiritual sacrifices, acceptable to God by Jesus Christ. Wherefore also it is contained in the scripture, Behold, I lay in Sion a chief corner stone, elect, precious: and he that believeth on him shall not be confounded. Unto you therefore which believe he is precious: but unto them which be disobedient, the stone which the builders disallowed, the same is made the head of the corner, And a stone of stumbling, and a rock of offence, even to them which stumble at the word, being disobedient: whereunto also they were appointed. But ye are a chosen generation, a royal priesthood, an holy nation, a peculiar people; that ye should shew forth the praises of him who hath called you out of darkness into his marvellous light*" 1 Peter 2:4-9.

Often the point was made relating these verses to how God began to speak to Moses on Mount Sinai: "*Now therefore, if ye will obey my voice indeed, and keep my covenant, then ye shall be a peculiar treasure unto me above all people: for all the earth is mine: And ye shall be unto me a kingdom of priests, and an holy nation. These are the words which thou shalt speak unto the children of Israel"* Exodus 19:5-6. Soon after, it led to the giving of the Law, establishing of the Covenant, the ordering of the Tabernacle, and the setting up of the Aaronic priesthood. It was 2600 years after God had created man that included the time of the Great Flood that killed all but eight of earth's inhabitants.

As we have already pointed out, in the beginning, Adam communed with God in the Garden of Eden, and there was no need of any "middle man". Later, we find individuals, typically heads of households (e.g., Noah, Job, Abraham, Isaac and Jacob), exercising the priestly role by offering sacrifices. When it came to Israel being called a "kingdom of priests", we can ponder how this would be fulfilled. Given their propensity to disobey God, it is easy to see how priestly mediation would have been needed.

At the end of the Bible, a description is made of a scene in heaven of believers around the Throne of God and the Lamb, which is Christ, for we read: *"And they sung a new song, saying, Thou art worthy to take the book, and to open the seals thereof: for thou wast slain, and hast redeemed us to God by thy blood out of every kindred, and tongue, and people, and nation; And hast made us unto our God kings and priests: and we shall reign on the earth"* Revelation 5:9-10. These believers could include today's believers, referred to in these verses as kings and priests. We refer to them as believer-priests. If that is us, the prospect of reigning with Him upon earth should cause us to respond in holy awe.

We ought to rejoice in the prospect of The Marriage Supper of the Lamb: *"Let us be glad and rejoice, and give honour to him: for the marriage of the Lamb is come, and his wife hath made herself ready. And to her was granted that she should be arrayed in fine linen, clean and white: for the fine linen is the righteousness of saints"* Revelation 19:7-8. We are to *"shew forth the praises of him who hath called you out of darkness into his marvellous light"* 1 Peter 2:9, that being the pretty amazing expectation concerning those to whom Peter wrote his letter. Put in another way: *"But you are the ones chosen by God, chosen for the high calling of priestly work, chosen to be a holy people, God's instruments to do his work and speak out for him, to tell others of the night-and-day difference he made for you – from nothing to something, from rejected to accepted"* 1 Peter 2:9-10 (The Message).

Those who lay claim to the "priest" label have a considerable responsibility as well as a wonderful privilege, given we are to reign with Christ on earth in a time yet to come. But it all begins now, and we can do so in the light of the glorious truth: *"Therefore if any man be in Christ, he is a new creature: old things are passed away; behold, all things are become new. And all things are of God, who hath reconciled us to himself by Jesus Christ, and hath given to us the ministry of reconciliation; To wit, that God was in Christ, reconciling the world unto himself, not imputing their trespasses unto them; and hath committed unto us the word of reconciliation. Now then we are ambassadors for Christ, as though God did beseech you by us: we pray you in Christ's stead, be ye reconciled to God. For he hath made him to be sin for us, who knew no sin; that we might be made the righteousness of God in him."* 2 Corinthians 5:17-21. We are His representatives here on earth now, whose responsibilities include pleading with others to be reconciled to God. It is a salutary thought that many to whom the prophecy of Revelation was addressed would soon after suffer great persecution. The contrast between being despised and rejected by men and given a place of honour by God was a huge one. In such times, believers often show their true mettle, and we need to be prepared for such times.

I would like to close with a passage from Isaiah, that Jesus claimed was fulfilled through Him: *"The Spirit of the Lord God is upon me; because the Lord hath anointed me to preach good tidings unto the meek; he hath sent me to bind up the brokenhearted, to proclaim liberty to the captives, and the opening of the prison to them that are bound; To proclaim the acceptable year of the Lord, and the day of vengeance of our God; to comfort all that mourn; To appoint unto them that mourn in Zion, to give unto them beauty for ashes, the oil of joy for mourning, the garment of praise for the spirit of heaviness; that they might be called trees of righteousness, the planting of the Lord, that he might be glorified. And they shall build the old wastes, they shall raise up the former desolations, and they shall repair the waste cities, the desolations of many generations. And strangers shall stand and feed your flocks, and the sons of the alien shall be your plowmen and your vinedressers. But ye shall be named the Priests of the Lord: men shall call you the Ministers of our God: ye shall eat the riches of the Gentiles, and in their glory shall ye boast yourselves"* Isaiah 61:1-6.

When we read the Luke 4 account of Jesus reading from the scroll at the synagogue in His home place, Nazareth, He stopped reading at: *"to proclaim the acceptable year of the Lord"*, adding the statement: *"this day is this scripture fulfilled in your ears"* Luke 4:21. Many would argue that some of Isaiah's prophecy contained in the rest of this passage, including *"the day of vengeance of our God"*, is yet to be fulfilled. Usually overlooked, but pertinent when it comes to our subject, is *"ye shall be named the Priests of the Lord: men shall call you the Ministers of our God"* Isaiah 61:6, which tells us of a bright future for the people of God, including being recognised in and fully able to execute their priestly role.

Whilst, in this chapter, we have considered the subject of the "Priesthood of all Believers" more in an individualist sense, we should also reflect on the subject in the corporate sense, as applying to the Church, with a capital

"C", noting the church, with a small "c" has often disappointed, not just by becoming "woke", i.e., bowing to cultural, often anti-gospel, norms, but by refusing to stand up against the evil, which includes deception, that is threatening and succeeding to take over society. As believer-priests, who belong to His Church, this we must withstand even if there is a price to pay. Not to do so will incur both the displeasure and judgement of Him who we are called to and have pledged to serve. If this book teaches us anything, it is the sacred responsibilities that come when called to be priests.

A final thought is, if what we have written appears to be unduly heavy and rather off putting to those who have been put off by *"holier than thou"* Christians who seem to lack understanding or empathy concerning life's toils and struggles, we must look to Jesus, *"the friend of sinners"*, who gladly mixed with the low and high of society, from those thinking they were holy to those who knew they were not. His example is one we do well to follow. We can and must do so without compromising our witness and resisting the *"pendulum swinging too far the other way"* tendency, in a culture that exalts the "virtues" of tolerance, equality and diversity, sometimes ending up by calling good evil and evil good.

1. Here comes Jesus, see Him walking on the water,
He'll lift you up and He'll help you to stand;
Oh, here comes Jesus,
He's the Master of the waves that roll.
here comes Jesus, let him take your hand.

2. Here comes Jesus, see Him feed the hungry people,
He'll fill your life till you hunger no more;
Oh, here comes Jesus,
He's the answer to your every need.
Here comes Jesus, He will your life restore.

3. Here comes Jesus, see him cleanse the leper,
He'll heal your heart and will give you His aid;
Oh, here comes Jesus,
He's the great Physician;
Here come Jesus, don't be afraid.

4. Here comes Jesus, see Him walking up to Calvary,
He's going to die for you and me;
Oh, here comes Jesus,
He's the ransom for the guilty one;
Here comes Jesus, to set us free!

Chapter 42: Priests (and Ministers) and the Church

I hope readers will forgive me for shooting from the proverbial hip and for a lack of systematic Bible exposition. Almost 2000 years ago, the Temple in Jerusalem was destroyed, and that marked the end of the Aaronic priesthood. Yet many today carry the title of priest, even in Christian circles, and this despite, strictly speaking, there being no biblical mandate to call such people priests, other than in the context of the priesthood of all believers, which we considered in the previous chapter.

Church government, in particular who should be in leadership in churches and what their roles and responsibilities are/should be, is a contentious subject. It is one where there is a wide range of views. Historically, it has caused major fallings-out among churches and, pertinently, denominations. I would like to start with a caveat that I have a view concerning some of the finer points of this debate, and to an extent will be sharing my perspectives; but it is not my intention to push my views other than relate to what is taught in the Bible and the subject of this part of my book: "A Priestly People".

Before I reflect on the subject of priests today, including under that umbrella, not just those given the title "priest" in Catholic, Orthodox and High Anglican set-ups, but also ministers, elders, deacons, pastors and evangelists in non-conformity, with groups such as among the Exclusive Brethren that do not push any of these offices when it comes to church leadership. I would like first to refer to what Paul taught. While other New Testament writers also wrote on the subject, Paul wrote by far the most.

Regarding the offices existing in the church in New Testament times, Paul identified five when he wrote: "*And he gave some, apostles; and some, prophets; and some, evangelists; and some, pastors and teachers; For the perfecting of the saints, for the work of the ministry, for the edifying of the body of Christ: Till we all come in the unity of the faith, and of the knowledge of the Son of God, unto a perfect man, unto the measure of the stature of the fulness of Christ*" Ephesians 4:11-13. Often, when it comes to priests and ministers today, they may be expected to combine roles of pastor and teacher, and sometimes evangelist, although many churches recognise these all to be specialist roles.

Most churches today do not recognise the office of *apostle*, although many have bishops and senior ministers that ordain other ministers and those who plant churches, two of the functions that were specifically undertaken by apostles in New Testament times. Most do not recognise the office of *prophet* as present in today's church although some, notably those labelled Charismatic or Pentecostal, attach significance to the gift of prophecy, especially when related to exercising the gifts of the Spirit. One of the weaknesses in church life, in my view, and a reason for writing "**Prophets of the Bible**", is that while the priest role may be elevated, the opposite is often true of the prophet role. One lesson from the Old Testament is that Israel enjoyed more of God's blessings when priests and prophets operated in tandem. Disappointingly, some churches do not promote the office of *evangelist*, given it was to preach the Gospel to all nations that Jesus' disciples were especially commissioned to do.

When we read of Paul's missionary journeys, we find he appointed elders (referred to as bishops in the KJV) in some of the churches he established, and in doing so he recognised that these new fellowships needed to have suitable spiritual oversight. As for qualifications, he wrote: "*This is a true saying, if a man desire the office of a bishop, he desireth a good work. A bishop then must be blameless, the husband of one wife, vigilant, sober, of good behaviour, given to hospitality, apt to teach; Not given to wine, no striker, not greedy of filthy lucre; but patient, not a brawler, not covetous; One that ruleth well his own house, having his children in subjection with all gravity; (For if a man know not how to rule his own house, how shall he take care of the church of God?) Not a novice, lest being lifted up with pride he fall into the condemnation of the devil. Moreover he must have a good report of them which are without; lest he fall into reproach and the snare of the devil*" 1 Timothy 3:1-7.

The office of *deacon* came about in Acts 6, when it became evident as the churches grew that there was a need to appoint deacons to assist in some of the more practical matters. As for the qualifications expected of a deacon, Paul makes it clear that spiritual gifts and personal qualities are just as needed for deacons as they are with elders, besides practical abilities or helper type qualifications, when he wrote: "*Likewise must the deacons be grave, not double tongued, not given to much wine, not greedy of filthy lucre; Holding the mystery of the faith in a pure conscience. And let these also first be proved; then let them use the office of a deacon, being found blameless. Even so must their wives be grave, not slanderers, sober, faithful in all things. Let the deacons be the husbands of one wife, ruling their children and their own houses well. For they that have used the office of a deacon well purchase to themselves a good degree, and great boldness in the faith which is in Christ Jesus*" 1 Timothy 3:8-13.

An insight into Paul's expectations when it comes to eldership can be seen in one of his missionary journeys, after summoning elders to meet him, sharing his story and what he deemed important: "*And from Miletus he sent to Ephesus, and called the elders of the church ... Take heed therefore unto yourselves, and to all the flock, over the which the Holy Ghost hath made you overseers, to feed the church of God, which he hath purchased with his own blood. For I know this, that after my departing shall grievous wolves enter in among you, not sparing the flock. Also of your own selves shall men arise, speaking perverse things, to draw away disciples after them … I have shewed you all things, how that so labouring ye ought to support the weak, and to remember the words of the Lord Jesus, how he said, It is more blessed to give than to receive"* Acts 20:17, 28-30, 35.

Some church groups, especially at the high end of the ecclesiological spectrum, teach apostolic succession whereby the successors to apostles in the New Testament appoint clergy. Others, in many non-conformist groups, appoint their ministers by democratic vote from the church members, often with the one who is appointed having had the "right" theological training and approved by the denominational hierarchy. Within Brethren circles (with which I am particularly familiar), some groups, notably among the Exclusives, do not appoint ministers, following the lead of their founder, J.N.Darby, who taught that since the church is in ruins there can be no apostolic succession. As for democracy, it was regarded as a worldly concept that the "saints" (assembly members) should steer clear of.

While it was expected in XB set-ups for members to come to a consensus on how to proceed, often one person came to the fore and then dominated assembly life with his views, with those who dissented being told to shut up or be excommunicated. Often in OB assemblies, once established, new elders were appointed by the existing elders, which, according to one respected elder, who shared with me how things were done, often led to nepotism. "Heavy shepherding", whereby those deemed to be "in charge" directed members of the church on what they should or should not do, is not only to be found among the Exclusives but has often been present in Pentecostal and Charismatic set-ups.

I mention this, not to make a case on how I think elders/pastor-teachers should be appointed, but rather to write on what takes place in various set-ups I have knowledge of, and to put forward a view that this should not determine whether or not we associate with a particular church, and that there are often many different issues (e.g., do they preach and practise the Gospel?), besides how they practise church government. I do so with a sense of pain and sadness for too many true believers have given up on church. There are many reasons for this, besides losing enthusiasm for the things of God.

One of the reasons is down to how churches are led. Often, I have seen people with justifiable concerns that are ignored and dismissed by the leaders, and they leave. Personality conflicts have ever been a recurring theme. Splits are often more about personality rather than process and both these are often seen as being more of an issue than doctrinal correctness. Before I give my response to such folk (who I can often sympathise with), I would like to consider the roles and responsibilities of our post-New Testament priest equivalent and return to the qualities I would like to see. Given this part of my book is about a priestly people, such considerations are relevant if we are going to find God's best.

One of the strengths of the Brethren movement I have found (arguably there were weaknesses too) was their belief in the plurality of elders, a practice we have seen being increasingly taken on board by other denominations, as different members of the leadership team take on complementary roles in the running of the church, according to gifting, etc. The Brethren, but this is true elsewhere, were keen on missionary enterprise, where every member was seen as being a missionary. They were also keen to encourage their young men to be preaching the Gospel as opportunities arose. Fulfilling the Great Commission was vital: *"Go ye therefore, and teach all nations, baptizing them in the name of the Father, and of the Son, and of the Holy Ghost: Teaching them to observe all things whatsoever I have commanded you: and, lo, I am with you always, even unto the end of the world"* Matthew 28:19-20.

My own observation has been that too often, much that was done of significance in church life was initiated through the priest/minister. He (and, these days, she also) took on those functions of the Aaronic priesthood that are still applicable: such as leading worship, pastoral oversight and teaching/preaching. In addition, he/she would often be responsible for things like finance, fabric, administration, home and overseas mission and finding ways to reach out to a wide and diverse community, and even taking on the role as *"chief cook and bottle washer"*. While this may work after a manner for small and fledgling congregations, with larger ones something needs to give. Addressing the issue of doing all that needs doing and involving and equipping each member to contribute remains a challenge that faces each church congregation, and is too often ignored, as is the important one concerning how individual churches can/ought to cooperate with and support other churches. The matter of women priests/ministers remains a contentious one, although increasingly accepted in many churches. I know and honour many gifted lady priests, but believe that those who lead should be male.

Then there is the teaching of the Body of Christ (1 Corinthians 12), where each member is part of the Body (with Christ as the Head), with each having a part they could and should play, which, if ignored, would be to the detriment of the church as a whole. Using the Old Testament example of the priests and Levites, where these were dedicated to the service of YHWH, but with the onus on members of the non-Levite tribes to support priests and

Levites, as they did not have other income sources. Often priests/ministers are put on pedestals and expected to cope alone, with "the flock" ignoring their responsibilities when it comes to support. Cases of priest/minister burn out or falling because of some sin that has come to light are many and, while it may be argued some of these were not truly called, one wonders how many fruitful ministries have been nipped in the bud due to poor support.

I return to the subject of "priest" qualities that matter in the church context. It is true that our faith is in God rather than any priest, however gifted, but with reference to the subtitle of this book (Bridging the gap between God and Man) while Christ has bridged that gap through His atoning death on the Cross, any priest worth his/her salt will do no better service than that of empowering members of the congregation to draw closer to God. Sadly, some enter the ministry for the wrong reasons and fail to do this. Some are more beholden to the fear and praise of men than that of God. Many churches look no further than theological qualifications by a denomination approved institution when deciding to appointment their priest/minister. What I have observed is that those who truly shepherd the flock are of great value and do a great service and we need more of such people to be priests/ministers.

Many theological training colleges fail to equip those they are meant to train in this regard. As one who loves to dig deep into matters theological, I am aware that too often study, rather than drawing the student closer to God, sometimes has the opposite effect, especially if uncritically reading or hearing what those who do not believe have to say, when seeking to rationalise deep spiritual truths. Please don't get me wrong for, as my approach has shown, getting meaning, background and context is essential. I have experienced in my attempt to dig deep and refusing to be beholden to any one school of thought that my faith has been shaken to the core – but then I also see that as a positive. Some enter ministry with good intentions yet fall away. Always, there is the temptation to compromise. The trials and distractions that priests/ministers have to face are formidable. They often have to face pressures those in the church are often barely aware of and if they are they choose to ignore. While priests/ministers do not always "get it right", it is clear that they need our support and prayers. Encouraging priests/ministers in fulfilling their calling is one of the most worthwhile things we can do.

Just as well-meaning politicians might be bought by powerful interests who have them do what they want, the same can apply to preachers. Without wanting to sound sanctimonious, we need preachers and priests who fear God and do not fear man, knowing full well there will be a price to pay for taking that route. Going back to the dedication of this book, I have named some who, while far from perfect (and some are in churches I would not join), have gone some way in fulfilling this bridging-the-gap role. My prayer is that God will raise up those with a priest's heart, who truly have His anointing and do what Paul urged the elders of Ephesus to do: "*Take heed therefore unto yourselves, and to all the flock, over the which the Holy Ghost hath made you overseers, to feed the church of God, which he hath purchased with his own blood*" Acts 20:28, and that they will be supported by those they minister to.

Now, I would like to offer some words of exhortation to those who are disillusioned with, thinking of or having given up on church. For one thing, God has not given up on both church and the Church (with a Big 'C' – His *ekkelisa*, the remnant that comprises all true believers) and neither should we. Christian fellowship ought to be very important for a priestly people, regardless of who is or appears to be "in charge" (although, in truth, it should be Christ). I am not saying go to a church where Christ or His word is dishonoured or important truths denied, but my reading of the New Testament is that Christians did meet regularly and worked together to extend the Kingdom. While there is a time to speak and not to speak, I support anyone who is calling out those who call evil good or turn to lies rather than the truth.

There is no such thing as a perfect church and all churches have strengths and weaknesses. It was the great preacher, C.H.Spurgeon, who said: "*If I had never joined a church till I had found one that was perfect, I should never have joined one at all; and the moment I did join it, if I had found one, I should have spoiled it, for it would not have been a perfect church after I had become a member of it. Still, imperfect as it is, it is the dearest place on earth to us.*" Sometimes we need to go back to adopting the "*a time to speak and time not to speak*" adage, and to maintain a discrete silence when we disagree. I suppose I have been fortunate that I have spent most of my Christian life operating in a very small number of imperfect churches and have kept with them despite sometimes profoundly disagreeing. I recall as a young Christian being impressed by an illustration that was shared at the time – a coal in a fire alongside other coals will burn brightly but remove it from the fire and that will not be the case. I realise some do not have a good experience and, in the end, give up on church. While every experience is different and I cannot generalise, I would normally counsel – hang in there and if you still cannot find a church to join, seek fellowship with other believer-priests for the purpose of fellowship and service.

We are called to love, forgive and forbear with one another and that the church comprises all those who are redeemed to God by Christ's blood *out of every kindred, and tongue, and people, and nation.* The Church is a mystery: "*And to make all men see what is the fellowship of the mystery, which from the beginning of the world hath been hid in God, who created all things by Jesus Christ: To the intent that now unto the principalities and powers in heavenly places might be known by the church the manifold wisdom of God"* Ephesians 3:9-10 and is God's instrument to reach the world with the Gospel and oppose the powers of darkness. She is Christ's holy bride that He will be wedded to when He returns: *"This is a great mystery: but I speak concerning Christ and the church"* Ephesians 5:32.

Much of this book is about the Tabernacle/Temple where the Levitical priests operated on behalf of God and the people. We are reminded *"Ye also, as lively stones, are built up a spiritual house, an holy priesthood, to offer up spiritual sacrifices, acceptable to God by Jesus Christ"* 1 Peter 2:5. While God no longer dwells in the Holy of Holies, He does dwell in His Church, His Temple and spiritual home. Despite feeling sad at the state of today's church, I am optimistic for the Church and believe God is far from done with it and He will have His way, even if it means she will have to endure much shaking, trials and tribulations. The Church remains His instrument to reach a lost world. It is not about denominations or egos, and this means that each member has an important part to play in God's grand design.

We must look to God to raise up priests/ministers to lead His Church; those concerned with His holiness and glory above all other consider- ations, fearing only Him, caring little for man's approval, intent on em- powering, serving and working with those who have been wounded and discouraged, and for the "unsaved" to be brought into His Church. While having different duties to that of priests in Bible times, we need their priest- ly equivalent *"who can have compassion on the ignorant, and on them that are out of the way; for that he himself also is compassed with infirmity"* Hebrews 5:2.

Sadly, as I survey the hierarchy within church circles, I see many at the top, notably in the Anglican communion (as far as the UK goes) who have turned away from the essential truth of Scripture (although over the years I have seen that trend in many of the mainstream denominations). It is not a matter of High Church versus Low Church, but rather adherence to the Word of God and being committed to proclaiming that truth, even if going against the tide of expectations of those who have the power to hire and fire. Seeing so many disaffected believers, sheep who are scattered because there is no shepherd to lead them, it seems we need those at the top and the bottom that can follow the example of the Good Shepherd and gather the very sheep that have been scattered and lead others within the flock to bring in those outside the flock to be followers of Jesus. As a non-Anglican, this is evident whatever the ecclesiology that is adhered to – we need priests of the right, godly calibre (and it really does not matter what title you give them as long as you let them do what needs doing). I sense too, when God really starts to move in power, along with persecution, most have not seen, we may also see a radical realignment of "church", including true believers meeting in their own homes. I am hopeful that God will raise up those priests in our day that will lead His Church as God intends.

I end this chapter with mixed feelings, beginning with a sense that some thoughtful believers who read what I have written may misunderstand what I am trying to say and why I am saying it despite my efforts to explain myself. One of the tragedies of church life is that too often people have got on their spiritual high horses and put down those who see things differently before considering other perspectives that may be valid. Sometimes it comes with a hidden, underlying message: *"this is how we do things and it is non-negotiable"*, with the implication: *"take it or leave it"*.

This chapter is about priests/ministers, recognising that across the church spectrum there is a wide range of opinions as to who they are, how they should be appointed and recognised, and their roles and responsibilities, especially if adopting a clergy-laity paradigm. The implications of what happens when we do see things differently are huge and while forgive and forbear are often the right things to do, I have seen too many church splits not to realise that it is easier to say than to do. But our deciding to leave a fellowship of fellow believers or allowing for others who are dissatisfied or have a grievance to leave without seeking reconciliation and restitution, should be looked upon only as a last resort.

I will leave the relevant debate as to what to do for the best for others to conduct, given the wide range of scenarios. Speaking personally, I try to adopt the "agree to disagree" approach with anything that is not essential, and recognise I must try to fit into where God has placed me as best I can. The doctrine of the Church (with a capital "C"), the mystical company of Christ's elect, is important. Only God knows who that comprises. Whilst the church (with a small "c"), the organisation, that may or may not meet in a building, that often comes with a denominational label, is also important, I find these days that my greater concern is for the true Church, ranging across the church spectrum from Catholic to Brethren, and increasingly includes those who do not identify with or belong to churches of any denomination. It is why I end with two hymns; the first is new and views the church in lofty terms; the second is old and is about the Bride of Christ; it was sung at my wedding all those years ago.

1. *O Church of Christ, invincible,*
   The people of the Lord,
   Empowered by the Spirit's breath
   And nourished by his word.
   His covenant of grace will be
   Our portion evermore,
   For He who called us will not change,
   Our help and our reward.

2. *O chosen people called by grace,*
   The sons of Abraham,
   Who walk by faith and things unseen,
   And on His promise stand,
   That every nation of the earth
   Will hear about this love
   That causes broken hearts to heal
   And pays our debts with blood.

3. *O Church of Christ in sorrow now,*
   Where evil lies in wait;
   When trials and persecutions come
   This light will never fade.
   For though the hordes of hell may rage,
   Their power will not endure;
   Our times are in the Father's hand,
   Our anchor is secure.

4. *O Church of Christ, upon that day*
   When all are gathered in,
   When every tear is wiped away
   With every trace of sin;
   Where justice, truth and beauty shine,

And death is passed away,
Where God and man will dwell as one
For all eternity.

And

1. The church's one foundation
is Jesus Christ, her Lord;
she is His new creation,
by water and the word.
From heav'n He came and sought her
to be His holy bride;
with His own blood He bought her,
and for her life He died.

2. Elect from every nation,
yet one o'er all the earth,
her charter of salvation:
one Lord, one faith, one birth.
One holy name she blesses,
partakes one holy food,
and to one hope she presses,
with every grace endued.

3. Though with a scornful wonder,
men see her sore oppressed,
by schisms rent asunder,
by heresies distressed,
yet saints their watch are keeping,
their cry goes up, "How long?"
and soon the night of weeping
shall be the morn of song!

4. The church shall never perish!
Her dear Lord to defend,
to guide, sustain, and cherish,
is with her to the end;
though there be those that hate her,
and false sons in her pale,
against the foe or traitor
she ever shall prevail.

5. 'Mid toil and tribulation,
and tumult of her war,
she waits the consummation
of peace forevermore;
till with the vision glorious
her longing eyes are blest,
and the great church victorious
shall be the church at rest.

6. Yet she on earth hath union
with God the Three in One,
and mystic sweet communion
with those whose rest is won;
O happy ones and holy!
Lord give us grace that we,
like them, the meek and lowly,
on high may dwell with Thee.

Epilogue

I had not intended to write an epilogue to this chapter, and have only done so toward the end of my writing endeavours because I still felt the need to hammer home what was really on my heart, clear up potential misunderstandings and try to fill in any important gap I might have missed. We have gone from "The Priesthood" (Part 1) and "The Priests" (Part 2) to "A Priestly People" (Part 3 – this part).

In both this chapter and the previous one, we have considered (arguably) two of the most important aspects concerning today's priestly people, who I identify as being true followers of Jesus. *"The Priesthood of All Believers"* (Chapter 41) and *"Priests (and Ministers) and the Church"* (Chapter 42 – this chapter) could be seen as two sides of the important proverbial coin. One side concerns all of us and the other side concerns a small minority, if we are to adopt the majority view found in Christendom that there is a clergy-laity divide (I have already given my view on such a "divide" so I won't say more).

It is written: *"But when he [Jesus] saw the multitudes, he was moved with compassion on them, because they fainted, and were scattered abroad, as sheep having no shepherd. Then saith he unto his disciples, The harvest truly is plenteous, but the labourers are few; Pray ye therefore the Lord of the harvest, that he will send forth labourers into his harvest"* Matthew 9:36-38. I find this verse bothersome, for what Jesus saw happening in His day I am seeing today, not just in the world at large but also in the church, which should be providing the very response that Jesus was calling for.

Sadly, too often "the flock" is misled and people like me, clergy or no, have our work cut out. If going back to our key "priesthood of all believers" text: *"But ye are a chosen generation, a royal priesthood, an holy nation, a peculiar people; that ye should shew forth the praises of him who hath called you out of darkness into his marvellous light"* 1 Peter 2:9, we should be those Jesus had in mind to: *"send forth labourers into his harvest"*. There should be leaders of stature and authority (clergy) helping us do so.

Sadly, "the flock" is often in disarray because of the way churches are led. Of course there is a need for forbearance, love that covers a multitude of sins, to deal with our own sins before criticising the sins of others and all too often "the disaffected" who leave a church have a wrong attitude or have grown cold concerning the things of God. But as I have already indicated, I have seen too many legitimate grievances not to be concerned and that often when someone sincere leaves one set-up there is not an alternative he/she can join. There are many reasons I have noted but here are some: promoting false doctrine, failing to preach the Gospel, insisting that members go along with views not mandated in the Bible, either extreme when it comes to rigid orthodoxy or excessive liberalism, a tolerance of and not dealing with sin within the congregation, heavy shepherding or bullying, a leaning toward excessive wokeness rather than bold righteousness, the rejection of those calling out evil in our society and branding them as "conspiracy theorists", a lack of genuine love. While it can be argued that we can and should function in churches where these things happen, a wise priest will want to make changes. It is why entreating the Lord about these things should be something we need to pray over.

My call to "the clergy" is that you do what should be your job, and that is what Paul told a group of clergy in his day to do: *"Take heed therefore unto yourselves, and to all the flock, over the which the Holy Ghost hath made you overseers, to feed the church of God, which he hath purchased with his own blood"* Acts 20:28. My call to "the laity" is to take heed of the exhortation to: *"Obey them that have the rule over you, and submit yourselves: for they watch for your souls, as they that must give account, that they may do it with joy, and not with grief: for that is unprofitable for you"* Hebrews 13:17, which should also include prayer, support and encouragement for our leaders. But I want to add a caveat ...

One of the societal shifts I have observed from when I was a child until now that I am an old man, is we do not respect authority in the way we once did. Automatic deference toward our elders is not there as it once was and nor is it for authority figures, including "the clergy" – the tendency nowadays is not to do something simply because some authority figure has told us to do so, with even the more submissive among us emboldened to follow suit. This can be a bad thing for, as painful as this could be for us, we are told: *"Render therefore to all their dues: tribute to whom tribute is due; custom to whom custom; fear to whom fear; honour to whom honour"* Romans 13:7 and: *"Put them in mind to be subject to principalities and powers, to obey magistrates, to be ready to every good work"* Titus 3:1.

Withstanding authority can sometimes be a good thing as too often those in authority have been shown up to be wrong and they need to be challenged, especially (for us) given we should be about pursuing truth and doing the right thing. Having seen the propensity of people to look up to heroes, including among Christians – charismatic leaders, and having lived long enough to see the folly when doing so, I urge readers to find balance, exercise humility, go labour in the harvest field and take our orders from our commander in chief, the Lord Jesus Christ, ahead of leaders, secular or spiritual. Also:

"The first of all the commandments is, Hear, O Israel; The Lord our God is one Lord: And thou shalt love the Lord thy God with all thy heart, and

with all thy soul, and with all thy mind, and with all thy strength: this is the first commandment. And the second is like, namely this, Thou shalt love thy neighbour as thyself. There is none other commandment greater than these" Mark 12:29-31.

As a final thought, bringing together the need for ordinary men and women today to "shepherd" the "flock" (the people of God) and the expectation of the Great Shepherd, who has already come but who is coming again – the Lord Jesus Christ, who will certainly do so, we note the words of the prophet, Jeremiah: "Woe to the shepherds who are destroying and scattering the sheep of my pasture!" declares the Lord. Therefore this is what the Lord, the God of Israel, says to the shepherds who tend my people: "Because you have scattered my flock and driven them away and have not bestowed care on them, I will bestow punishment on you for the evil you have done," declares the Lord. "I myself will gather the remnant of my flock out of all the countries where I have driven them and will bring them back to their pasture, where they will be fruitful and increase in number. I will place shepherds over them who will tend them, and they will no longer be afraid or terrified, nor will any be missing," declares the Lord. "The days are coming," declares the Lord, "when I will raise up for David a righteous Branch, a King who will reign wisely and do what is just and right in the land. In his days Judah will be saved and Israel will live in safety. This is the name by which he will be called: The Lord Our Righteous Savior. "So then, the days are coming," declares the Lord, "when people will no longer say, 'As surely as the Lord lives, who brought the Israelites up out of Egypt,' but they will say, 'As surely as the Lord lives, who brought the descendants of Israel up out of the land of the north and out of all the countries where he had banished them.' Then they will live in their own land.'" Jeremiah 23:1-8.

Chapter 43: What I Would Like to Say to the Next Generation

It was a little over five years ago when I blogged concerning the "words of wisdom" I would like to pass on to members of the next generation on how to live a fuller, more productive life and not make the same mistakes I made. A lot has happened since then, including changing views on life. I continue to learn, and recognise I still have a long way to go in truly learning important lessons. I thought, with the desire to share such thoughts with my readers, and since we are considering stuff that could and should interest a priestly people, that it would be a good idea to adapt what I wrote back then.

One thing I have noticed about getting old is that while one's faculties may be in decline, compared with yesteryear, one would have picked up a lot in the preceding years concerning how best to live one's life and contribute to the common good; which, if these lessons had been taken on board earlier, it could have lessened one's own pain, and one could have made an even bigger difference in terms of doing good in the world. Not that we can turn the clock back and do what we should have done in the first place or expect a sympathetic audience, but we can pass on the wisdom we have learned to those who come after us; although this is best done by setting an example and gently encouraging, rather than bludgeoning one's thoughts on to others regardless of whether or not they are ready to listen.

In no particular order, these are some of the more important lessons I have learned and am still learning that I would like to pass on to the next generation, especially any young person who will give me an ear, bearing in mind that my experience is not exactly the same as others, and those whom we may want to encourage operate under quite different circumstances, and will have different abilities and interests, and different hopes and aspirations. I am also mindful that this is not a definitive list and others might add valid suggestions which are also helpful. Some of the lessons learned have been painful ones, yet as I look back, I can see the benefits, not least, that of being able to help others.

1. Being kind is more important than being successful.

2. As a youngster, the qualities of humility, kindness, faithfulness and godliness would have been low down in my list of those things that I value; these days they are right at the very top.

3. It is better to give than to receive; to serve rather than be served, and become like the unprofitable servant Jesus spoke about in His parables.

4. Honour your mother and father; love your spouse.

5. Remember the poor and those who cannot give back what you might have given to them.

6. Be someone who doesn't just say you are going to do something; rather do what you say.

7. Look after your health – physical, mental, social and spiritual.

8. Set boundaries – work, family, friendships and, while you are at it, any other relationship, ever mindful of our limitations and the human tendency to exploit and do mischief. Be aware that there are many time-wasters out there, some of whom you can't help and are better to avoid.

9. Having good character is better than having good anything else; being honourable is worthwhile even if it costs you and making truth your guiding principle in a world that is full of deceit is something that ought to be enthusiastically pursued.

10. Rather than be seen as one who does good, it is better to do good, even when no-one sees it.

11. Deferred gratification generally reaps benefits in the long run.

12. There is often a case to keep our own counsel; and when we do find opportunity to speak to first ask the questions: is it true, is it necessary and is it kind?

13. Nothing is for certain in this life (except death and taxes).

14. Things rarely stay the same in this life; be prepared for change, ever ready to adapt.

15. Life really is short – ask any oldie; most will clearly recall their vigorous youth.

16. Value your loved ones while they are still alive (and show them that you do).

17. The things that are most precious in life are invariably the simplest, and are often free.

18. Good manners cost little and invariably reap great dividends.

19. Don't be a respecter of persons; whether their status is high or low or, more poignantly, can give you something you want; all are deserving of our respect, especially those who can't give back – in fact, helping those who can't repay is often where most blessings can be found.

20. Try to learn practical skills; you never know when these will come

in useful – and while I am thinking on this point in a country where I don't speak the language – learn other languages.

21. Never look down on those whose giftings and interests are more practical than intellectual. I have discovered that the older I get the more I value the contributions of those folk who are able to make stuff, get things to work, fix what is broken, and work with inferior materials etc.

22. The vagaries of life are such that one day you may be rich, the next day poor; you may be well, the next day sick; you may be the one to go to for advice, the next day no-one wants to know; you may be honoured and recognised, the next day ignored; you are alive, the next day you are dead; moreover, eternity is an infinitely long time and you do well to prepare for it now.

23. Get a well-rounded education, even though a lot of it may be indoctrination; observe well; read widely; keep learning right up to the end, realising even then you will know just a little; and, whatever your learning level, try to use your abilities to contribute to the common good.

24. Develop a career and ideally one you can do best in and if it benefits others that is a bonus.

25. Start to invest in the future, including financially – there is wisdom in the John Wesley maxim "*earn all you can, save all you can, and give all you can*".

26. Follow your dreams but don't let dreams be your master or ignore the realities of the present.

27. The world can be said to be divided into three groups: fools, villains and the good guys (or mixtures thereof), and who can be sure which is which?

28. When I was young, I broadly believed what politicians, media and the elites told me; but I don't anymore and, given that is the case, I need to find alternatives and respond accordingly.

29. The more I see, the more I am convinced the world is run by bad people under the control of Satan; making it necessary not only that we recognise this is so but find ways to deal with it.

30. Recognise that little is what it seems and you will likely be biased anyway, even inadvertently, and since you do not possess all the facts, and are often unlikely to have taken in other valid perspectives, you would do well to be circumspect when making judgments.

31. Try to understand the other person's point of view, even if you strongly disagree with them, for you might still learn something; try to live in peace with all and treat all respectfully.

32. Everyone is on a journey, even those who are most disagreeable, so be careful not to judge or react prematurely towards those you might take exception to, especially when not knowing all the facts. There is a lot to say for adopting St. Paul's approach of being all things to all men.

33. There will be times when we feel we are hard done by and unfairly treated. It could leave us with chips on our shoulders. Yet some are worse off than us and life is not fair. We do well to make what happens in life to be not about us and, instead, let us consider others. Take heed what the Bible teaches about one being a new creation – it means we can/must ditch the past.

34. Take each day as it comes; neither expect too little nor too much; make the most of it; don't dwell on the past or put off until tomorrow what could/should be done today.

35. Learn to be humble and avoid being proud, for pride does come before a fall; but if you do fall you can be picked up and then it is a matter of taking the time to take stock and move on.

36. Try to complete those tasks that you have begun.

37. Learn to forgive others – you will be unjustly dealt with in life and let down and betrayed by those you least expect, but it is better to forgive than carry an unforgiving burden.

38. Learn to forgive yourself – you will make mistakes, sometimes big ones; try to see these as opportunities to learn from them and grow; and to press on in order to realise your life's goals.

39. See all of life as a learning curve; learn from the past and use the lessons you learn in the process to help you to prepare for the future.

40. Triumph and disaster (and who can say what will come next) are two imposters to be treated just the same (just as Kipling said).

41. Be happy: but holiness should be sought firstly, ahead of happiness.

42. Memorise the Bible – the fount of so much true wisdom; for we do well to make it a priority to "*get wisdom, get understanding*" Proverbs 4:5.

43. Learn to love God – therein lies the secret to what truly matters; reflect how wonderful it is to be a child of God, loved by Him. His desire is toward you, even when you have blown it.

44. Remember the other great command is to love your neighbour, whoever he/she is.

45. Better to fear God than to fear man; stop trying to impress or please man but instead focus your efforts on pleasing God; don't take umbrage when you are spurned or ignored.

46. Cultivate a spirit of thankfulness rather than that of complaint – it is usually better to view a glass as being half full rather than half empty, to look on the positive rather than the negative.

47. Hang-ups, hurts, disappointments, rejections and failures will come to us all but we do well not to dwell on them and to move on; for if you are a Christian, you are part of God's new creation. We can put the past behind us and plead the precious blood of Jesus when doing so.

48. Things are often not what they seem, so learn to question (almost) everything and do not be taken in, even if your information / perception source appears ever so credible, and given those who run the planet do not like being questioned, that is all the more reason to do so.

49. Long ago, I learned the truth of Murphy's law: anything that can go wrong will go wrong – and not to assume anything; and, having seen it played out on countless occasions, I have concluded that, while we may hope for the best, we do well also to prepare for the worst.

50. *"Remember now thy Creator in the days of thy youth, while the evil days come not, nor the years draw nigh, when thou shalt say, I have no pleasure in them ... Fear God, and keep his commandments: for this is the whole duty of man. For God shall bring every work into judgment, with every secret thing"* Ecclesiastes 12:1, 13-14.

51. When we read the Bible, we find several warnings concerning idolatry and following false gods. The temptation, often subtle, is to succumb, and this needs to be constantly resisted.

52. We will be continually bombarded with new ways of doing things, when sometimes the old ways may still be better. We should be looking to adopt the ways (old and new) that are best.

53. All of us are affected by those closest to us when coming to a view or setting out priorities. As you mix with those whose views and priorities differ, brace yourself that these may be better.

54. As we contemplate there is a powerful "Unholy Trinity" (politicians, media and societal elites) calling the shots, don't get taken in, especially as most of them do lie and don't fear God.

55. Your life may turn out to be one that is full of pain and suffering, which may or may not be as a result of your own foolishness, but do not despair because there is a bountiful hidden hand who has your back and He is wanting to turn bad experiences into something that is beautiful.

56. Live in the hope of the blessed return to planet earth of our Lord Jesus Christ.

Some concluding thoughts

Like many, I have taken inspiration from the poem 'IF' by Rudyard Kipling, and it is pertinent here:

If you can keep your head when all about you
Are losing theirs and blaming it on you,
If you can trust yourself when all men doubt you,
But make allowance for their doubting too;
If you can wait and not be tired by waiting,
Or being lied about, don't deal in lies,
Or being hated, don't give way to hating,
And yet don't look too good, nor talk too wise:

If you can dream—and not make dreams your master;
If you can think—and not make thoughts your aim;
If you can meet with Triumph and Disaster
And treat those two impostors just the same;
If you can bear to hear the truth you've spoken
Twisted by knaves to make a trap for fools,
Or watch the things you gave your life to, broken,
And stoop and build 'em up with worn-out tools:
If you can make one heap of all your winnings
And risk it on one turn of pitch-and-toss,

And lose, and start again at your beginnings
And never breathe a word about your loss;
If you can force your heart and nerve and sinew
To serve your turn long after they are gone,
And so hold on when there is nothing in you
Except the Will which says to them: 'Hold on!'

If you can talk with crowds and keep your virtue,
Or walk with Kings—nor lose the common touch,
If neither foes nor loving friends can hurt you,
If all men count with you, but none too much;
If you can fill the unforgiving minute
With sixty seconds' worth of distance run,
Yours is the Earth and everything that's in it,
And—which is more—you'll be a Man, my son!

And we close with some apt quotes from my missionary pioneer, cricketing hero, C.T.Studd, for there is no better task for believers of any age than to bring the Gospel to the unreached and the unsaved:

1. *Some wish to live within the sound of church or chapel bell, I want to run a rescue shop within a yard of hell.*

2. *Only one life, 'twill soon be past, only what's done for Christ will last.*

3. *If Jesus Christ be God and died for me, then no sacrifice can be too great for me to make for Him.*

4. *The light that shines farthest shines brightest nearest home.*

5. *God's real people have always been called fanatics.*

6. *The "romance" of a missionary is often made up of monotony and drudgery; there often is no glamor in it; it doesn't stir a man's spirit or blood. So don't come out to be a missionary as an experiment; it is useless and dangerous. Only come if you feel you would rather die than not come. Don't come if you want to make a great name or want to live long. Come if you feel there is no greater honor, after living for Christ, than to die for Him.*

7. *The best cure for discouragement or qualms is another daring*

plunge of faith.

8. *Christ wants not nibblers of the possible, but grabbers of the impossible by faith in the omnipotence, fidelity, and wisdom of the Almighty Savior.*

And now in my old age, I can both look back and look forward: "*For thou art my hope, O Lord God: thou art my trust from my youth. By thee have I been holden up from the womb: thou art he that took me out of my mother's bowels: my praise shall be continually of thee. I am as a wonder unto many; but thou art my strong refuge. Let my mouth be filled with thy praise and with thy honour all the day. Cast me not off in the time of old age; forsake me not when my strength faileth ... I will go in the strength of the Lord God: I will make mention of thy righteousness, even of thine only. O God, thou hast taught me from my youth: and hitherto have I declared thy wondrous works. Now also when I am old and greyheaded, O God, forsake me not; until I have shewed thy strength unto this generation, and thy power to every one that is to come. Thy righteousness also, O God, is very high, who hast done great things: O God, who is like unto thee! Thou, which hast shewed me great and sore troubles, shalt quicken me again, and shalt bring me up again from the depths of the earth.*" Psalm 71:5-9, 16-20.

Chapter 44: The Ark, the Glory and Revival

In the iconic 1981 film "**Raiders of the Lost Ark**", the central plot was around the hero seeking to stave off attempts by the baddies to find and acquire the long-lost Ark of the Covenant in order to give them powers of invincibility. At the end, it appeared the baddies had succeeded in their quest but it came with terrible consequences. When they opened and looked into the Ark, we find the film's hero telling his companion NOT to look. While the film is fiction, and not altogether biblically accurate, there is enough in the film to demonstrate the significance of the Ark and, if not treated with the reverence that was warranted by this most holy of artifacts, there would be a heavy price to pay: one's own life.

An Internet search will reveal much that has been said concerning the location of the Ark and attempts to find it. While this makes fascinating reading/watching, that is not the subject of this chapter. The last time the Ark, which God had commissioned Moses to make, is mentioned in the Bible, was in the times of King Josiah, the last good king of Judah, at the time he restored the Temple that had hitherto been allowed to descend into ruin: "*And said unto the Levites that taught all Israel, which were holy unto the Lord, Put the holy ark in the house which Solomon the son of David king of Israel did build; it shall not be a burden upon your shoulders: serve now the Lord your God, and his people Israel*" 2 Chronicles 35:3. Less than 100 years after this, the Temple was ransacked and destroyed by King Nebuchadnezzar and there is no more mention of the Ark of the Covenant, other than "*And the temple of God was opened in heaven, and there was seen in his temple the ark of his testament: and there were lightnings, and voices, and thunderings, and an earthquake, and great hail*" Revelation 11:19.

Regarding the construction, features and purpose of the Ark of the Covenant (or "Testimony") and the Mercy Seat with its two cherubim, which was in effect the lid laid on top of the Ark, along with the other items of furniture that were placed inside the Tabernacle; I refer readers to Chapter 6. The Ark continued to play an important part in Jewish worship right up to the time when Solomon's Temple was destroyed. While the God who inhabits the Universe and exists throughout eternity does not live in a box, that box (Ark), or just above it (between the two cherubim), was where God was believed to dwell. Concerning King Hezekiah's prayer, when faced with the Assyrian threat, we read: "*And Hezekiah prayed before the Lord, and said, O Lord God of Israel, which dwellest between the cherubims, thou art the God, even thou alone, of all the kingdoms of the earth; thou hast made heaven and earth*" 2 Kings 19:15. This notion of God being between the two cherubim above the Ark of the Covenant is re-echoed in at least two other places in the Bible: 1 Samuel 4:4 and 2 Samuel 6:2.

There are many references to the Ark following its construction and Israel's journey in the wilderness. Notably the Ark was carried by the priests when Israel crossed the River Jordan prior to entering the Promised Land (Joshua 3 and 4) and when encircling Jericho prior to the walls of the city falling and the Israelites taking the city (Joshua 6). If nothing else, it represented that it was God that was going before and with the Israelites, ensuring their endeavours were successful. A huge error of judgment occurred when Eli's sons, Hophni and Phinehas, took the Ark into battle against the Philistines, seeing it as a good luck charm, but the Ark was captured, the Israelite army was defeated and Hophni and Phinehas were killed because they had been disobedient to God. But then the tables were turned on the Philistines who had placed the Ark in the temple of Dagon, their god, and the idol was found on the floor, smashed in pieces. The Philistines were afflicted by a plague and quickly returned the Ark.

Later we read of events to do with the Ark coming to Jerusalem and God striking Uzzah dead for having the presumption to handle the Ark in order to steady the ox cart, and God blessing the house of Obededom the Gittite in whose house the Ark remained for a period. We also have the account of David dancing before the Lord when the Ark finally ended up in Jerusalem. Later, under Solomon, David's son, the Ark played a central part in the dedication of the Temple: *"And all the elders of Israel came; and the Levites took up the ark. And they brought up the ark, and the tabernacle of the congregation, and all the holy vessels that were in the tabernacle, these did the priests and the Levites bring up. Also king Solomon, and all the congregation of Israel that were assembled unto him before the ark, sacrificed sheep and oxen, which could not be told nor numbered for multitude. And the priests brought in the ark of the covenant of the Lord unto his place, to the oracle of the house, into the most holy place, even under the wings of the cherubims: For the cherubims spread forth their wings over the place of the ark, and the cherubims covered the ark and the staves thereof above. And they drew out the staves of the ark, that the ends of the staves were seen from the ark before the oracle; but they were not seen without. And there it is unto this day"* 2 Chronicles 5:4-9. My point is that the Ark is related to my other main subject of this chapter, that relating to glory, specifically the Shekhinah glory.

The Hebrew word "**kavod**" translates as "importance", "weight", "deference", or "heaviness", but primarily **kavod** means "glory", "respect", "honor", and "majesty". There are 488 references to the word "glory" or related words, such as "glorify", in the KJV, many of which are not to do with God and more to do with mundane, man related matters. For example, the first time the word "glory" appears is: "*And he heard the words of Laban's sons, saying, Jacob hath taken away all that was our father's; and of that which was our father's hath he gotten all this glory*" Genesis 31:1. Our interest, however, is to do with God's glory, sometimes referred to as "*Shekhinah glory*". It was what occurred in both the commissioning of the Tabernacle under Moses and the Temple under Solomon. In both cases, no-one was able to enter these places because they had been filled with God's Shekhinah glory. We read, for example, at the end of the Book of Exodus: "*And Moses was not able to enter into the tent of the congregation, because the cloud abode thereon, and the glory of the Lord filled the tabernacle. And when the cloud was taken up from over the tabernacle, the children of Israel went onward in all their journeys: But if the cloud were not taken up, then they journeyed not till the day that it was taken up. For the cloud of the Lord was upon the tabernacle by day, and fire was on it by night, in the sight of all the house of Israel, throughout all their journeys*" Exodus 40:35-38.

My first Google hit, trying to get a succinct definition of this term, helpfully stated: "*This concept is found in Judaism. The Hebrew Bible mentions several places where the presence of God was felt and experienced as a Shekhinah, including the burning bush and the cloud that rested on Mount Sinai. The Shekhinah was often pictured as a cloud or as a pillar of fire and was referred to as the glory of God*". There were other examples of Moses being exposed to God's glory, before the Tabernacle had been built. We read, for example: "*And he said, I beseech thee, shew me thy glory. And he said, I will make all my goodness pass before thee, and I will proclaim the name of the Lord before thee; and will be gracious to whom I will be gracious, and will shew mercy on whom I will shew mercy. And he said, Thou canst not see my face: for there shall no man see me, and live. And the Lord said, Behold, there is a place by me, and thou shalt stand upon a rock: And it shall come to pass, while my glory passeth by, that I will put thee in a clift of the rock, and will cover thee with my hand while I pass by: And I will take away mine hand, and thou shalt see my back parts: but my face shall not be seen*" Exodus 33:18-23.

It would be a fruitful exercise to go through our 488 "glory" references, even if focusing only on those which applied to God; but, having thought about it, I decided not to go there, not just because of the time and effort needed but rather in knowing what instances to address or not, and still do the subject justice. Instead, I would like to focus on the here and now, and reflect on how God's glory might apply to our current situation. After all, many a prayer that is prayed e.g., along the lines: "*For of him, and through him, and to him, are all things: to whom be glory for ever*" Romans

11:36 (and I include those prayed by me) that includes words to the effect that whatever is done, along with the outcome, needs to be for God's glory (alone), as we yearn for and look forward to the day when "*the earth shall be filled with the knowledge of the glory of the Lord, as the waters cover the sea*" Habakkuk 2:14.

Some who read this will have experienced the tangible presence of God that has similarities to what Moses experienced and have seen His hand at work in the area of the supernatural and miraculous. Some like me have seen glimpses of these things, but I long for more and look forward to life beyond the grave, mindful that: "*Eye hath not seen, nor ear heard, neither have entered into the heart of man, the things which God hath prepared for them that love him*" 1 Corinthians 2:9. The problem I face, and one that many have had before me, is when I am unwilling to pay the price, along the lines: "*Except a corn of wheat fall into the ground and die, it abideth alone: but if it die, it bringeth forth much fruit*" John 12:24. Whether or not God shows His glory akin to what Moses experienced is up to God. Yet all of us who follow Christ have had a foretaste of God's glory: "*And the Word was made flesh, and dwelt among us, (and we beheld his glory, the glory as of the only begotten of the Father,) full of grace and truth*" John 1:14. Moreover, aspects of God's glory are things all of us can see if we look for them: "*The heavens declare the glory of God; and the firmament sheweth his handywork*" Psalm 19:1.

I would like now to turn our attention to the subject of revival. It is one that over the years has been discussed by Christians on my wavelength, with varying conclusions as to what is needed, with many examples cited of past revivals. Sometimes that longing is matched by disappointment in the face of spiritual mediocrity. One helpful perspective on revival is that it is to recover, repair or restore: "*Sow to yourself in righteousness, reap in mercy; break up your fallow ground; for it is time to seek the Lord till He come and reign righteousness upon you*" Hosea 10:12. Most agree that revival is desirable and we should long for it, but what is it in real terms? Examples include the first Day of Pentecost after Jesus ascended into heaven, up to the recent "Asbury revival", although some will put that, and other examples that may be cited, down to hot air and emotionalism rather than the work of the Holy Spirit.

Besides drawing readers' attention to two books that I have found helpful in the past: "**Lectures on Revival**" by Charles Finney (albeit recognising some of his views on how churches should operate are not ones I share, yet I am finding how up to date and pertinent are his observations) and another "classic": "**Why Revival Tarries**" by Leonard Ravenhill, I want to share these thoughts of my own:

1. I have little doubt there have been numerous examples of revival, when God has been working in extraordinary ways, throughout church history (as well as in Old Testament Israel).

2. Real revival can take place in many different ways, involve people from many different theological perspectives and, since we are considering "glory", it is God and not man glorified. I have noted that often before revival there is brokenness and contrition among God's people.

3. We cannot be prescriptive in the way God is to work, e.g., whether or not it is accompanied by sign gifts, when/where it takes place, the people He uses as His instruments (often it is with those people many consider to be the least likely or qualified, given: "*God hath chosen the foolish things of the world to confound the wise … that no flesh should glory in his presence*" 1 Corinthians 1:27, 29) in bringing about revival and how long revival lasts, from hours to years.

4. We should not despise the day of small things. As I have stated elsewhere, qualities like godliness, faithfulness and kindness are things the least of us can practise, and so we must.

5. I agree with the person who listed the following as signs of revival happening, which was seen soon after Peter's sermon on the Day of Pentecost, and is recorded in the Book of Acts:

- Emphasis on Jesus (2:36).
- Repentance (2:37-38).
- A passion for prayer (2:42).
- Hunger for the Word (2:42).
- A burden for the lost (2:40).
- Increase in numbers saved (2:41, 47).
- A surge in callings to ministry and missions (4:20).
- The manifest presence of God (2:43).

6. It is right, proper and desirable (even essential) for the people of God to long and pray for revival, but in doing so they need to be prepared to count the cost and pay the price. Some of our brothers and sisters are already suffering for their faith and God has not forgotten them.

I would like to give a last word to Isaiah: "*Oh that thou wouldest rend the heavens, that thou wouldest come down, that the mountains might flow down at thy presence, As when the melting fire burneth, the fire causeth the waters to boil, to make thy name known to thine adversaries, that the nations may tremble at thy presence! When thou didst terrible things which we looked not for, thou camest down, the mountains flowed down at thy presence. For since the beginning of the world men have not heard, nor perceived by the ear, neither hath the eye seen, O God, beside thee, what he hath prepared for him that waiteth for him*" Isaiah 64:1-4. Surely, that should be something which resonates with all of us!? Words are cheap but, notwithstanding, I would like to end with the words of two hymns. The first is a desire of the heart (which we do well to have) and the other is a prayer (which we do well to pray):

1. Jesus, Thine all-victorious love
Shed in my soul abroad;
Then shall my heart no longer rove,
Rooted and fixed in God,

2. Oh, that in me the sacred fire
Might now begin to glow;
Burn up the dross of base desire,
And make the mountains flow.

3. He, who at Pentecost didst fall,
May He my sins consume;
Thy Holy Ghost, for Him I call;
Thy burning Spirit, come.

4. Refining fire, go through my heart,
Illuminate my soul;
Scatter Thy life through every part,
And sanctify the whole.

5. *My steadfast soul, from falling free,*
Shall then no longer move,
While Christ is all the world to me,
And all my heart is love.

And

1. *Search me, O God, and know my heart today*
Try me, O Savior, know my thoughts, I pray
See if there be some wicked way in me
Cleanse me from every sin, and set me free.

2. *Lord, take my life, and make it wholly Thine;*
Fill my poor heart with Thy great love divine;
Take all my will, my passion, self and pride;
I now surrender: Lord - in me abide.

3. *O Holy Ghost, revival comes from Thee;*
Send a revival - start the work in me.
Thy Word declares Thou wilt supply our need;
For blessing now, O Lord, I humbly plead.

Chapter 45: Jesus' High Priestly Prayer

" *These words spake Jesus, and lifted up his eyes to heaven, and said, Father, the hour is come; glorify thy Son, that thy Son also may glorify thee: As thou hast given him power over all flesh, that he should give eternal life to as many as thou hast given him. And this is life eternal, that they might know thee the only true God, and Jesus Christ, whom thou hast sent. I have glorified thee on the earth: I have finished the work which thou gavest me to do. And now, O Father, glorify thou me with thine own self with the glory which I had with thee before the world was. I have manifested thy name unto the men which thou gavest me out of the world: thine they were, and thou gavest them me; and they have kept thy word. Now they have known that all things whatsoever thou hast given me are of thee. For I have given unto them the words which thou gavest me; and they have received them, and have known surely that I came out from thee, and they have believed that thou didst send me. I pray for them: I pray not for the world, but for them which thou hast given me; for they are thine. And all mine are thine, and thine are mine; and I am glorified in them. And now I am no more in the world, but these are in the world, and I come to thee. Holy Father, keep through thine own name those whom thou hast given me, that they may be one, as we are. While I was with them in the world, I kept them in thy name: those that thou gavest me I have kept, and none of them is lost, but the son of perdition; that the scripture might be fulfilled. And now come I to thee; and these things I speak in the world, that they might have my joy fulfilled in themselves. I have given them thy word; and the world hath hated them, because they are not of the world, even as I am not of the world. I pray not that thou shouldest take them out of the world, but that thou shouldest keep them from the evil. They are not of the world, even as I am not of the world. Sanctify them through thy truth: thy word is truth. As thou hast sent me into the world, even so have I also sent them into the world. And for their sakes I sanctify myself, that they also might be sanctified through the truth. Neither pray I for these alone, but for them also which shall believe on me through their word; That they all may be one; as thou, Father, art in me, and I in thee, that they also may be one in us: that the world may believe that thou hast sent me. And the glory which thou gavest me I have given them; that they may be one, even as we are one: I in them, and thou in me, that they may be made perfect in one; and that the world may know that thou hast sent me, and hast loved them, as thou hast loved me. Father, I will that they also, whom thou hast given me, be with me where I am; that they may behold my glory, which thou hast given me: for thou lovedst me before the foundation of the world. O righteous Father, the world hath not known thee: but I have known thee, and these have known that thou hast sent me.*

And I have declared unto them thy name, and will declare it: that the love wherewith thou hast loved me may be in them, and I in them" John 17:1-26.

For the sake of clarification, the prayer we know so well that is regularly prayed in churches, which begins: *"Our Father which art in heaven ..."* (Matthew 6:9-13, Luke 11:2-4), I will refer to as the disciples' prayer, since this is what Jesus taught His disciples to pray when they asked Him: *"teach us to pray"*. The prayer Jesus prayed for His disciples, including those who follow Him today, just prior to Him being taken, tried and crucified, and which takes up the whole of John 17, and is reproduced in full above, is what I will refer to as the real Lord's Prayer and, given what is one of the central themes of this book, can be rightly referred to as Jesus' High Priestly Prayer, since Jesus did precisely what the Aaronic High Priests were meant to do – represent the (His) people before God (His Father).

One of the many remarkable things about this prayer is that it was prayed just hours before Jesus was arrested, which He knew beforehand was going to happen, knowing too that it would lead to His execution. Rather than make His escape or call on the Angels to come to His aid, He went through it all – and He did so for us. As a priest of the Order of Melchizedek, not only did He offer a sacrifice like the Aaronic priests, but He was that sacrifice, made in order to redeem us. What is remarkable is that He was thinking of His followers, which include those of us who would believe through their preaching, recognising He was leaving them in a hostile world and praying they be kept by God and be His fruitful followers, and especially that they will be united in His love, the best way to convince unbelievers of the truth. One might say this relates to the Christian calling concerning the priesthood of all believers.

Given our Great High Priest has departed from this earthly scene, we are his representatives. From the time I became a Christian in my teens, until the present day, I have been intrigued by two texts that I came to see as being particularly important: *"A new commandment I give unto you, That ye love one another; as I have loved you, that ye also love one another"* John 13:34 and: *"Neither pray I for these alone, but for them also which shall believe on me through their word; That they all may be one; as thou, Father, art in me, and I in thee, that they also may be one in us: that the world may believe that thou hast sent me"* John 17:20-21. It seemed to me that if Christians really did love one another, people who weren't Christians would be able to identify those who were based on the way they see Christians conduct themselves and, moreover, they would come to believe as a result. While I have seen many good examples of Christians (often unassumingly) loving each other and being, spiritually speaking, united as one, I have lived long enough to have noted countless examples of this not being the case. Here, I am talking about real Christians and not just those in name only. It has long bemused me why this is so because, if love and unity were the norm, people would be able to identify who the real Christians are and they may become true believers – but I recognise that I'm guilty too!

My own introduction to the faith, and with which I was associated for a good part of my life, was through the Plymouth Brethren (PB). I learned early on that there were three main groupings of Christians: Evangelical, Liberal and Catholic – and, arguably, a fourth one – the sects, who reject historical Christianity. The PBs were firmly in the Evangelical group, although many were suspicious of other Evangelicals, let alone those other groupings who some might not even have regarded as truly Christian. But even in this tight circle, love and unity were often missing. Having been around a long time, I have seen too many examples of avoidable disunity among professing Christians, including among those whose Christian commitment I have no reason to doubt. Sometimes it can be put down to doctrinal disagreement but often it was down to personalities. I have seen examples of those who get the significance of Jesus' High Priestly prayer but are part of the problem. This could include me! It can be perplexing given that the prospect of this prayer being answered seems as far away as ever.

Many of those I have associated with believed in the Pre-Tribulation "Rapture", when Jesus comes in "secret" to whisk away true Christians, before coming again openly such that all eyes will see Him; not this time as a suffering servant but rather as the King of glory. Among other things, He will sit down at His "marriage supper" (described in Revelation 19) with His prepared Bride, the true Church (comprising His faithful followers): *"Let us be glad and rejoice, and give honour to him: for the marriage of the Lamb is come, and his wife hath made herself ready. And to her was granted that she should be arrayed in fine linen, clean and white: for the fine linen is the righteousness of saints"* (19:7-8).

But I make the point that, since when Jesus prayed His prayer, we would rightly expect it would be answered and His Bride would be indeed ready for His return – yet things may have got worse unity wise and many elements of today's church would seem to resemble that of the church at Laodicea, to whom Jesus addressed His letter in Revelation, concerning its lukewarmness, and that it needed to take to heart His words: *"I counsel thee to buy of me gold tried in the fire, that thou mayest be rich; and white raiment, that thou mayest be clothed, and that the shame of thy nakedness do not appear; and anoint thine eyes with eyesalve, that thou mayest see"* Revelation 3:18. Jesus' words: *"sanctify them through thy truth: thy word is truth"* are particular pertinent in a day when we can see a lack of sanctification and a lack of truth among those Jesus prayed for, which we need to be exemplars of.

We can easily think of reasons for this lack of unity; and, arguably, in the case of our (all of us) inability to agree on what truly matters and to put aside lesser differences, it is difficult to see how significant, meaningful, progress can be achieved, given the division is sometimes masqueraded with respectability. As far as many of my early PB mentors were concerned, how can we be united with those who teach a false gospel? I feel, I have gone full circle. By this, and as discussed in "Chapter 56: Returning to "Outside the Camp"", I began by going along with the counsel of some of my early PB mentors and steered clear of those deemed to be unsound. But later I found myself associating with non PB types and trying to distinguish between beliefs that were essential (and trying to be flexible when possible) and those that were not. I later went out of my way to engage with those not in my theological camp, mindful of this prayer and the need to work together for the common good, as well as wanting to make the effort in order to answer Jesus' prayer for His true followers to be one in Him.

While my current pessimism is partly borne out of hopes dashed, disillusionment with institutional church and personal fallings-out, including with those who are seen as leaders in the church, I see many signs of life, sometimes among Christians who are not to be found in my own theological "camp" and, dare I say it, it is often so in some "third world" countries, and especially in times of persecution. Nowadays, I resonate more with those who see themselves among the remnant, which respectable Christians might wrongly dismiss as being troublesome, etc. While I can't say the institutional church is irrelevant, what is much more relevant is the Church, which comprises real Christians.

Now I see the whole shebang as rather more complex and do not wish to claim special spiritual superiority, for no Christian, ever, has got things totally correct. Sometimes it is down to people having different spiritual journeys, perspectives, differences in gifting, experiences, circumstances and personalities. It is not that we should dismiss differences when it comes to preaching on sin, righteousness and judgment (three things the Holy Spirit was sent into the world to convict people of), noting some wrongly argue we should ignore differences because it is more important to be united. Yet there are all sorts of issues Christians see differently that are not strictly speaking essential as far as salvation and real fellowship is concerned. True fellowship doesn't happen as a result of dotting the i's and crossing the t's when it comes to adherence to sound doctrine but rather our preparedness to be the answer to Jesus' prayer, seeking to live in unity with our brothers and sisters who are in Christ.

It should not be about any of those issues coming under the social justice umbrella – LBGTQ rights, racial justice, climate change, to name but three, and how to get involved in our wider communities. Neither is it three of the biggies that have got Christians worked up and falling out over in recent years: Brexit, Trump and things to do with Covid-19 and, more recently, who is right in the wars in Ukraine and Israel, and the old chestnut of how we respond to what the powers that be dismiss as conspiracy theories and can Christians have true fellowship when there is a faction that believes the world is run by psychopaths. I have no compunction to **not** speak on such matters (and if you read my blogs you will see several instances when I have) but these should not divide Christians as all too often they do. Before people think I am into self-justification, I confess I have been at fault for not responding well enough to the challenge of doing what Jesus would do, thinking it is more about me than Him, and taking exception to being called out for adopting the positions I have. It is **not** about me. At best, I am merely His unprofitable servant, whose job is to serve and to get that right balance between truth and grace. The Christians I admire most are the worshippers that seek to live their lives honouring the Lord.

The upshot is that Jesus prayed for one thing and that is what we should be looking for now. This should not detract from some of the remarkable setting for the real Lord's prayer. He prayed it hours before He was arrested, fully knowing what lay ahead, yet ever thinking of those He prayed for. He had done all He was meant to do, barring being that ultimate sacrifice, which was about to happen, followed by rising from the dead in triumph – evidence that His prayer had been heard. Then there were the things He prayed for. What He wanted to see was *"that the world may believe that thou hast sent me"*. We need to remind ourselves that our Great High Priest continues to intercede for us and, as if it were, willing us on in advance to be effective, having been sent by Him into an all too often hostile world. But the big question for us is: what do we do about it (with the Lord's help)? It is a mistake to ignore or fail to respond biblically to what is going on in the world. It is a mistake to lose our nerve in order to appease a loud group of God haters, and ignore our commission to make true disciples of Jesus, and that involves gospel proclamation. It is a mistake to think that the only part of "church" that matters is the section we belong to (assuming we do). Our concern should be for all our brothers and sisters in Christ, to help them be that radiant Bride for when He returns to planet earth.

It is a mistake to elevate many areas of minor disagreement as matters to irrevocably fall out over – but then, what is minor? Christians who give the matter thought differ on which way the world is heading. All of this is in the Lord's hand and if the Book of Revelation meant anything at the time it was written, it was to prepare recipients for tribulation, in the assurance that in patient endurance there will be great reward, and God wins in the end. While I believe and hope for revival, I see true believers coming under more attack but also being an answer to Jesus' prayer. Whichever way the world is heading, we are called to put our trust in the Lord and heed the call for unity with our brethren.

Finally, and to reiterate, it is a mistake to let egos get in the way. In the final analysis we should be God's servants, first and foremost. It involves our serving His Church and not taking umbrage with people we disagree with or things that upset us. While pragmatism is necessary given present realities, including focusing on what we can/should do/change, let's leave the rest with the Lord. There is much in the words of the following scripture that we would do well to dwell upon and practise. We might care to sing one of the songs often associated with the Jesus Movement of the 1960s and 70s (still applicable), with all its hopes and optimism: *"They'll know we are Christians by our love"*.

We are one in the Spirit, we are one in the Lord;
We are one in the Spirit, we are one in the Lord;
And we pray that all unity will one day be restored.

Chorus: And they'll know we are Christians by our love, by our love,
yes, they'll know we are Christians by our love.

We will walk with each other, we will walk hand in hand;
We will walk with each other, we will walk hand in hand;
And together we'll spread the news that God is in our land.

We will work with each other, we will work side by side;
We will work with each other, we will work side by side;
And we'll guard each man's dignity and save each man's pride.

All praise to the Father, from whom all things come;
And all praise to Christ Jesus, His only Son.
And all praise to the Spirit who makes us one.

On a related note, we might also ponder these words, which while they are to do with our having the mind of Christ, they tell us of Him who came from the highest place to the lowest place to save us: *"If there be therefore any consolation in Christ, if any comfort of love, if any fellowship of the Spirit, if any bowels and mercies, Fulfil ye my joy, that ye be likeminded, having the same love, being of one accord, of one mind. Let nothing be done through strife or vainglory; but in lowliness of mind let each esteem other better than themselves. Look not every man on his own things, but every man also on the things of others. Let this mind be in you, which was also in Christ Jesus: Who, being in the form of God, thought it not robbery to be equal with God: But made himself of no reputation, and took upon him the form of a servant, and was made in the likeness of men: And being found in fashion as a man, he humbled himself, and became obedient unto death, even the death of the cross. Wherefore God also hath highly exalted him, and given him a name which is above every name: That at the name of Jesus every knee should bow, of things in heaven, and things in earth, and things under the earth; And that every tongue should confess that Jesus Christ is Lord, to the glory of God the Father"* Philippians 2:1-11.

Chapter 46: The Brethren and the Last Things

What follows is a paper with minor amendments that I presented at a Brethren history conference, in July 2023, with the title "**Coleman Street Chapel and the Last Things (1966 – 1977)**". While not about Priests of the Bible as such, it does come under the category of being something I wrote that I consider important enough to want to put in print and believe it may be of interest to *a priestly people* …

In this presentation, I want to consider the subject of the Brethren and Last Things, based on my own experiences and observations inside Brethren Assembly circles, and its relevance today. In particular, I want to focus on a 12 year period concerning the assembly that I was mostly connected with, that was founded in 1900 – Coleman Street Chapel, Southend-on-Sea (see image above). In its heyday, it had some 300 people "in fellowship" and a Sunday School of 500, and was instrumental in establishing several Gospel Halls and missions, both at home and abroad.

I would like to begin with two quotes and, at the end, reflect on the accuracy of what is quoted:

Firstly: "*The beginnings of the Brethren movement were attended by a* *keen interest in the fulfilment of Biblical prophecy, and many of them are still characterized by this eschatological awareness. Their hymnology gives quite a prominent place to the Second Advent of Christ. But no single line of prophetic interpretation is held or imposed by them. Indeed, one of the many features which many people find attractive is the spiritual and intellectual liberty which is enjoyed there in an atmosphere of brotherly love"*, from a paper titled "**Who are the Brethren?** by F.F. Bruce" (1962).

Secondly: *"But the most significant figure to adopt a form of futuristic premillennialism was J.N.Darby, the fertile mind behind another Adventist sect, the Brethren ... He steadily advocated the view that the predictions of Revelation would be fulfilled after believers had been caught up to meet Christ in the air, the so-called 'rapture'"*, from the section to do with Millennial beliefs, from a book entitled "**Evangelicalism in Modern Britain**" by David Bebbington (1989).

I began to be actively involved in Coleman Street Chapel, Southend, a "middle of the road" Brethren assembly, soon after my conversion as a Christian in 1966, aged 15, and remained involved until I moved away in 1977. I wish to concentrate on this period. While based on my personal memories, perspectives and earlier research, I sought corroboration where I could. I re-joined the Assembly in 1988, when I came back to live in Southend, and remained a member, and later an elder, until we decided to close in 2013. That period also has a bearing. Besides the chapel, I was associated with other differing Brethren set-ups, ranging from "tight" to "progressive", in the UK and also in India.

In the first period, the Assembly held two mid-week meetings, one for prayer and one for ministry, which was in effect solid Bible teaching. My first visit to a ministry meeting was a defining experience insofar as in recent years it helped inspire me to write my book, "**Prophets of the Bible**". The brother teaching on that occasion was Winston Chilcraft. His subject for the evening was the prophet Elijah and Naboth's vineyard, and what was happening in the region. I got to know Brother Chilcraft in later years. He was known as the "go to" man when it came to Bible prophets. Rather than talk much about Last Things, it was more about the prophets' rebukes regarding idolatry, sexual immorality, dealing unjustly with the poor and needy, and the relevance of their message to their day and to our own.

Coleman Street Chapel had a long history of inviting well known (in Brethren circles) speakers in order to minister. One big name was Mark Kagan and I recall him teaching on Ezekiel's temple, found in Ezekiel 40-48. Brother Kagan was clearly of the view that this was a prophecy yet to be fulfilled, and it would happen during Christ's Millennial reign. When it comes to more controversial aspects, such as the Third Temple where the Zadok priests ministered, including the offering of animal sacrifices, he viewed this as part of God's plan in order to teach the Jewish people, who had been anticipating the coming of their Messiah ever since Ezekiel's day, the prophetic significance of the Hebrew Scriptures.

While I don't recall them making a big deal over it, when it came to theology, the Chapel's leading lights in this period were into Dispensationalism rather than the Covenant Theology subscribed to by some of my Strict Baptist associates, who I am involved with now. One exponent of this was Victor Levitt, a well-respected Bible teacher, known as the "go to" man when it came to the first five books of the Bible. Just as Brother Chilcraft helped inspire me to write my **"Prophets of the Bible"** book, Brother Levitt helped inspire me to do this with my current writing project: **"Priests of the Bible"**. I recall one short but significant exchange when Brother Levitt tried to put me right, insisting that the "Gospel of the Kingdom", found for example in Matthew's Gospel, was different to the "Gospel of the Grace of God", found in Paul's epistles, as regularly preached at the Sunday evening Gospel meetings.

This exchange was significant because another brother contributed to the conversation, who saw the Gospel of the Kingdom and that of the Grace of God as being in effect the same. His name was Paul Bullivant, and he had his own teaching and evangelistic ministry and attracted round him some of the young people with the camps he organised and meetings in his own home. He had shortly prior to that a healing experience and was referred to by a member of the Oversight, who later had his own Charismatic experience, as someone who had just crossed Jordan and was still dripping wet. Brother Bullivant expressed the view that, rather than see the Kingdom in futuristic terms, it is something that ought to be experienced in the here and now. Not long after, he decided to leave the Chapel and was later to join the band that Neil Summerton labelled as *"were Brethren"* (**"Local Churches for a New Century"**, Partnership, 1996), and became a leader in one of these new expressions of church.

"Last Things" were not the main concerns of the Oversight during this period and neither was refuting the "errors" of Catholics, Liberals and many Evangelicals, nor urging members not to succumb to the dangers that would arise from being too worldly, but rather it was the teachings that arose out of the new Charismatic Movement, notably concerning the "Second Blessing" and Speaking in Tongues.

While most members of the Chapel did not have a complete view concerning how events detailed in the Book of Revelation would pan out in the days to come, my recollection is that those, who thought they nearly did usually believed that after the scenes set in heaven, in Chapters 4 and 5, the rest of the book is about happenings in a yet to take place future, including the Great

Tribulation, in which period the Antichrist emerges. Two notable occurrences in that period are the forcing of humanity to take the Mark of the Beast (Chapter 13) and the Mystery and Fall of Babylon (Chapters 17 and 18).

Fifty years on, arguably, we can now see more clearly how both of these could happen. At the end of the Tribulation period, there will be a great battle and then Christ returns in glory (in Chapter 19). Then the Marriage Supper of the Lamb is followed by the binding of Satan and the Millennium. Then, after one final battle, following Satan being released and deceiving the nations, there will be the Last Judgement when humankind has to appear before God at the Great White Throne and will be judged and, along with Satan, cast into the Lake of Fire should their names not be written in the Book of Life.

One emphasis should be noted, since it reinforced the necessity of being ready for the Lord's return. Many Brethren believed the Judgment Seat of Christ (1 Corinthians 3:10-15), with rewards handed out based on our works, is for true believers only, and is different to that of the Great White Throne Judgement (Revelation 20:12) that is for everyone else. The final big events will see the new heaven and the new earth established. In Chapters 6 to 19, attention switches to Israel and its saints, as the Church has been raptured. It was thought that that event could happen at any time. In coming to this understanding, many Old Testament scriptures were studied; for example, the Book of Daniel.

The Pre-Tribulation Rapture, when the "saints" (all true followers of Christ) will suddenly meet Him in the air, was a cherished belief. This could happen at any time and the subject was often brought up during the Sunday evening Gospel preaching meetings and other times, when the main emphasis was calling on people to turn to Christ (even though often it was a matter of preaching to the converted). One consequence of those not responding to the Gospel call was, in the words of the popular 2000 series, they would be Left Behind. I don't recall any dissenting voices to this view at that time (nor in other Brethren set-ups). If there were, these would likely not have been looked upon favourably.

An even more important meeting than that taking place on Sunday evenings for Gospel preaching was the "Morning Meeting" for the "Breaking of Bread", when considering the Lord's return took only second place to that of His atoning sacrifice. When I first began to attend meetings, the "Believers Hymn book" was used on Sunday mornings and "Sankeys" on other occasions, with both containing several hymns to do with the Lord's return. A popular "Breaking of Bread" hymn, has the title: "For the Bread and for the Wine", and was often sung on such occasions. What follows are all eight verses:

1. For the bread and for the wine,
For the pledge that seals Him mine,
For the words of love divine,
We give Thee thanks, O Lord.

2. Only bread and only wine,
Yet to faith, the solemn sign
Of the heav'nly and divine!
We give Thee thanks, O Lord.

3. For the words that turn our eye
To the cross of Calvary,
Bidding us in faith draw nigh,
We give Thee thanks, O Lord.

4. For the words that fragrance breathe
These plain symbols underneath,
Words that His own peace bequeath,
We give Thee thanks, O Lord.

5. For Thy words in Spirit, shown,
For Thy will to us made known,
"Do ye this until I come,"
We give Thee thanks, O Lord.

6. **Till He come** we take the bread,
Type of Him on whom we feed,
Him who liveth and was dead!
We give Thee thanks, O Lord.

7. **Till He come** *we take the cup;*
As we at His table sup,
Eye and heart are lifted up!
We give Thee thanks, O Lord.

8. **For that coming,** *here foreshown,*
For that day to man unknown,
For the glory and the throne,
We give Thee thanks, O Lord.

My final brother of note in that era, concerning "Last Things", was Anton Campbell. He was the "go to" man when coming to an understanding of the Book of Revelation, due to his extensive study of that subject. I recall him taking a series with the young people on this Book. One thing I remember him telling us was that man would not get to the moon! Listening to him speak on other occasions, my belief is that he took the standard Brethren view when interpreting the Book of Revelation, as outlined above, and part of his prophetic understanding was that the true church would simply disappear as raptured, meeting the Lord in the air, before most of the events described in Revelation took place, and was distinct from the Lord's Second Coming, when *"every eye shall see him"* (Revelation 1:7).

I ran an earlier draft of this paper by Una, Mr. Campbell's daughter, requesting she confirm or refute the above observations, particularly as relating to her father and also inviting her to share her own thoughts concerning the period in question. I am glad that she concurred with my observations, making this significant point: *"The rapture was an even more vivid part of the Gospel in the late 40s and early 50s than I remember at Coleman Street in the 60s. I think that was because having emerged from WW2 and been made aware of the horrors of the concentration camps, and also the re-birth of Israel as a nation, believers were expecting the Lord to intervene at any moment as surely iniquity had come to the full?"* The following is what Una Campbell wrote concerning the main subject of this paper.

"My memories of Coleman Street date from the early 1960s until 1972. It was a very happy time, marked by the great interest all the older folk took in the children and young people's activities. Looking back, I believe the Christ-centred Breaking of Bread meeting on Sunday mornings was at the heart of all the service at Coleman Street. With regard to Last Things, I would say that the Dispensational, futuristic view was held by the major-

ity. I hesitate to say 'all', but I never heard other views put forward during my younger days. Two things in particular stand out: First, that the second coming of the Lord was often spoken of in the Gospel meeting with the emphasis on not delaying to come to Jesus for salvation. This was, of course, a reference to the Rapture and not the Lord's Second Coming at the end of the Tribulation. By the mid-60s, I had stopped teaching in Sunday School and was holding meetings for young folk at home and inviting friends from work, old school friends etc., but the aim was always to bring as many as possible to the Gospel meeting on Sunday evening. From time to time Peter Brandon visited Coleman Street for a gospel campaign and his emphasis was always the Lord's return. Second, a notable speaker on Last Things was Mark Kagan, as you have already mentioned. He had one great enthusiasm; to speak about Israel and her coming Messiah. Mark Kagan stayed in our home during his visit to Coleman Street and he spent a long time talking to me about Israel and pointing out many things from the Scriptures. Undoubtedly, it was more of a privilege than I realised at the time. In later years I have read other views, such as replacement theology, but have never found any scriptural reason to change my mind".

When returning to the Chapel in 1988, I found numbers had sharply declined, as was the case with many UK Brethren assemblies; including the sort of old men once active in Assembly life, like I may have become, who assiduously studied not yet fulfilled prophecy, and also interest in Last Things had considerably lessened. There was, for example, little mention of the Pre-Tribulation rapture of the Church in the preaching, although the basic beliefs that I encountered as a 15-year-old still held. One likely reason is that those who preached were no longer exclusively members of the Brethren who were deemed to be doctrinally sound, and those who did preach were likely to be of the view that this was too complex and controversial a subject on which to preach. Interestingly, I found this was not the case with many Indian assemblies I visited, where the preachers were often "old school" Brethren.

But the emphasis *"Ye should earnestly contend for the faith which was once delivered unto the saints"* (Jude 1:3) continued at the Chapel. In 1999, I published **"Coleman Street's Children"**, a history of the Chapel through the lens of its leading lights, including their beliefs, which may be seen as mainstream Evangelical. In its Doctrines and Practices, as taken from the Trust Deeds of Coleman Street Gospel Hall, when it came to Last Things, we read: *"That He will come again to receive them* [them being true followers of Christ] *unto Himself and to set up His kingdom".*

In my research, it was often confirmed that members tended not to be involved in the community or politically. But there was lots of evidence of them helping the poor, done either as well-meaning individuals, without ostentation, or as part of the natural outworking of assembly life, although this did not take precedence over gospel proclamation. Political activism did not happen as a rule (although members tended to vote Conservative, even if closeted, if they voted at all). It should be noted though, whether it was as professionals or tradesmen, those so engaged took their work responsibilities seriously, as well as the need to be good neighbours. When I interviewed David Iles, who was the Correspondent during the period I was first involved, he confirmed that the focus was on the world to come, rather than today's world (which, in accordance with Darbyite eschatology, was on a downward spiral); and the priority, through mission and evangelism, was to get people saved. [*Note: from this point on, I go from making observations to inferences that some may disagree with.*]

When applying "Last Things" prophecy to world events, this was what Brethren students of prophecy often did, but two things stuck out: Firstly, Israel becoming a sovereign state in 1948, the first time since around 600 BC when the Southern Kingdom of Judah went into Babylonian captivity; for, besides a short period under the Maccabees, up to 1948 it was always under foreign rule. It made possible the fulfilment of many prophecies where Israel would occupy centre stage. Concerning the Jews and Israel, they broadly supported them in control of the land promised to Abraham and there remained for them a special place in God's plans as promised to Abraham. Secondly, regarding the Common Market, later known as the European Union, many Brethren were against the UK joining (the UK did join in 1973 but left in 2020), because they saw this as related to the ten-nation confederacy that was prophesied in the Books of Daniel and Revelation, that would become allied with the Antichrist.

In 2020 and 2021, my Covid lockdown project was to search the scriptures and what had been said about the prophets and their prophecies, noting it is reckoned that 27% of the Bible is of a predictive nature, culminating in writing my book "**Prophets of the Bible**", where I attempted to consider the lives, times and prophecies of every prophet in the Bible, including those that are generally not seen as prophets, noting much unfulfilled prophecy is interpreted differently by even doctrinally sound Christians. In a Web article, "**Fulfilled Prophecy: Evidence for the Reliability of the Bible**" by Hugh Ross - August 22, 2003, it was argued: "*Unique among all books ever written, the Bible accurately foretells specific events in detail many years, sometimes centuries, before they occur. Approximately 2,500 prophecies appear in the pages of the Bible, about 2,000 of which already have been fulfilled to the letter – no errors*". That means there are four times as many fulfilled prophecies as unfulfilled.

I tried to provide balanced, sound exegesis, but was up front concerning my axioms and the influence of my early Brethren upbringing. I took the view that the Bible should be considered literally unless that was clearly not the case, that there will be a future, physical Millennium and, unlike much of Christendom, Israel has not been replaced by the church, and there is a distinct role for Israel, apart from the Church, all in accordance with Darby's system but, unlike Darby, I was not convinced when it came to his views on the Pre-Tribulation Rapture and his dispensational approach to interpreting "Last Things". In the Second Edition, I considered two controversial subjects:

Firstly, I questioned if there are prophets prophesying now, bearing in mind that the gift of prophesy was widely practised in the Early Church and the exercise of that gift was actively encouraged. I was particularly concerned with what is happening in the world today, noting many *"were Brethren"* Charismatic prophets took strong issue with what some political prophets who prophesied about current events have said, such as concerning the Trump Presidency and him being anointed by God in order to "drain the swamp"; noting too that many traditionalist Brethren took the view that, once the Bible canon was complete, there was no office of prophet and no further prophetic word.

Secondly, I did what Brethren prophecy students of old did: consider world events in the light of "Last Things" and how the world was heading, studying how current events were reported and misreported by mainstream and alternative media. This included trying to come to terms with notions like *"Great Reset"*, *"Great Awakening"* and *"Great Deception"*; and coming to a view we are now seeing all of these being played out and that the Devil is most effective operating as an Angel of Light rather than as the Prince of Darkness. As interesting and pertinent as my findings may be, it is outside the scope of a paper that is to do with what the Brethren I have come across thought about Last Things.

But with arguably so much pointing to prophecy being or about to be fulfilled before our very eyes, one might expect, if they were around today, that they might have a field day reconciling prophecy and world events. [*Since presenting this paper, one respected "Brethren watcher" put forward the view that those I discuss were of a generation that was a lot more trusting of people in authority, and would have not have been carried away like many of their ilk (i.e., people like me) today who are ever seeking to "connect the dots", and so end up putting authority figures in a bad light. Someone else made the point that the semblance of "Christian consensus" existing 50 years ago is clearly no longer the case. As fascinating as this may be, we may never know how the "old Brethren" might have responded. Moreover, even in the period discussed there would have been various views held within the Brethren.*]

Arguably, many of the "Last Things" enthusiasts in the Brethren circles that I was long ago acquainted with asked many of the right questions, even though, and depending on one's views of eschatology, they may not have always come up with the right answers. It was evident though that even among the most saintly and scholarly there was a wide range of views. If there is a major criticism, in my view, it is the escape mentality that many had that, given evil was going to get worse, and at some point before the Antichrist is revealed they would be raptured, they did little to confront evil – partly too as a consequence of seeing the Kingdom in futuristic terms and not something for the present. It is worth noting that many who were interested in "Last Things" realised when it came to the Book of Revelation, for example, a true understanding required a thorough study of the Old Testament (partly explaining why Brethren sometimes ended up as professors of the Old Testament at theological institutions).

While we cannot say for certain how the Brethren between when the movement emerged in the 1830s and 50 years ago would have responded to today's crazy, messed-up world; yet it is likely since they questioned what one was told one should believe, doing so in the light of scripture, they might have been less likely to be misled – for example, regarding the Corona Plandemic, the Climate Emergency and the War in Ukraine; and would not have been too carried away with the social justice concerns that have beset modern evangelicalism. We must not forget too the place and role of Israel in world events, which students of prophecy would have seen as being significant in these End Times.

While my recollection of the Brethren 50 years ago is that they were pro-Israel, albeit prioritising the conversion of the Jews, their views on Christian Zionism, Anti-Semitism, Messianic congregations and the Palestinian perspective were probably not unanimous. It is notable that many Brethren gave much attention to studying the Pentateuch (which I discuss in **"Priests of the Bible"**). In studying Brethren writings on matters such as the Tabernacle, we often find a considerable amount of these attempting to apply this teaching to today. They tended to over-spiritualise, a Greek rather than Jewish tendency, although this is something, unlike most churches, they tended to do because of their recognition of "types" and "shadows" in the Old Testament having fulfilment in the New Testament. The Brethren were into "Last Things" because it formed a major part of the Old Testament scriptures. It was intrinsic to their theology. While the promised Messiah has come, much needs to happen around His Second Coming, in which both the Church and, mostly unbelieving, Israel still have important parts to play.

Today's make-up of the Brethren, in the UK at least, is a lot different to that of 50 years ago, partly as a result of a steep decline. It has resulted in a lot of polarisation and separation of ways between the more progressive (usually ditching the term "assembly") and the more traditionalist assemblies. The number of UK traditionalist leaning assemblies operating may these days be in a minority, and along with retaining the distinctive traits of Brethrenism, it is these that would have taken most interest in "Last Things". As for the rest, many would take from non-Brethren traditions and likely go along with whatever Evangelical consensus they are more inclined toward, with some having ditched their Brethren roots altogether and, more likely than not, interest in Last Things does not feature highly.

If the Brethren were right and the world will get even worse, which, following the emergence of the movement 200 years ago, has arguably been the case, we must take note, recalling their emphasis on holiness, mission and walking with God in obedience, and be like the five wise virgins who had their lamps trimmed while waiting for the bridegroom. We must prepare for the worst (mindful that the world will only get truly better after the return of Christ) and hope for the best (the physical return of Christ: this time it will be in glory, righting what is wrong); and that has to remain our blessed hope.

In the period 1966-1977, while we note much interest in "Last Things" by members of Coleman Street Chapel, yet it was one that was already declining, and that included the expectation of the imminent rapture of the Church, and has continued until this day. Likely, what we have seen was typical for the Brethren movement as a whole, at least in the UK. We now live in extraordinary times (maybe our Brethren forefathers would have said the same about their times), where Christians, including today's Brethren, have differing views on where the world is heading. Besides the views that were traditionally held, these include not having any view or to go along with the narratives mainstream media, politicians and societal elites would have us believe or for there to be a great awakening as evil is exposed and dealt with, believed by a mixture of political prophets, new agers and conspiracy theorists; or what is seen by some as an Orwellian, dystopian nightmare being promoted by the likes of Klaus Schwab and Yuval Noah Harari, endorsed by many world leaders, including King Charles, which scenario many early Brethren believed would play out and lead up to the Great Tribulation.

Another view is that whichever way it goes, the onus is on their successors today to be faithful to God, remembering He is in control and, if we read to the end of our Bibles, we find that He has already triumphed. While we are at it, we do well to draw lessons from what our Brethren forefathers believed.

Going back to the Bruce quote, he was right, although maybe a little too generous when declaring Brethren could and would graciously agree to disagree regarding different interpretations to those that were most widely accepted; i.e., Darby's and those of his ilk, when it came to "Last Things".

As for Bebbington, he too was essentially correct, given my own experience when it came to Brethren eschatology. Yet he was too dismissive when it came to labelling them as *"another Adventist sect"*, since they had many other preoccupations besides that of Adventism, notably their primary concern to faithfully carry out the Great Commission (Matthew 28:19-20) and to be holy (1 Peter 1:16). But let us give Mr. Darby the last word; sentiments my early Brethren mentors would have resonated with:

1. This world is a wilderness wide—

I have nothing to seek or to choose;

I've no thought in the waste to abide;

I've nothing to regret or to lose.

2. The path where our Savior is gone

Has led up to His Father and God—

To the place where He's now on the throne,

And His strength shall be mine on the road.

3. With Him shall our rest be on high,

When in holiness bright I sit down—

In the joy of His love ever nigh—

In the peace that His presence shall crown.

4. 'Tis the treasure I've found in His love,

That has made me now pilgrims below;

And 'tis there, when I reach Him above,

As I'm known, all His fulness I'll know.

5. And, Savior, 'tis Thou from on high,

I await till the time Thou shalt come

To take him Thou hast led by Thine eye,

To Thyself in Thy heavenly home.

Chapter 47: Bible Prophecy and Current Events

In Chapters 46 and 51, I consider the subject of Bible prophecy but, in this chapter, I would like to relate Bible prophecy to what I see taking place in the world right now, where I believe the world may be heading as a result and how the people of God ought to respond. But brace yourself and fasten your seat belts as what I am about to write will take you out of your comfort zone, will be controversial, even among Christians who normally share my views, and it is unlikely you will agree with all I write.

I have seen big fall outs among Christians when it comes to sizing up what is going on in the world and how we should respond. Besides doing deep dives on subjects like priests of the Bible, it takes up a lot of my time when it comes to finding out the truth about these matters, watching and praying, testing and weighing, and if I have lacked winsomeness and wisdom on this journey, I can only apologise, but not being a watchman is not an option, noting God's displeasure trumps man's (Ezekiel 33 relates).

I recall in my youth a popular preacher (I think it was Billy Graham) coming out with the statement "*You preach with the Bible in one hand and the newspaper in the other*". I believe this is an idea that originated from Karl Barth, one of the most influential theologians of the 20th century. Barth put it this way: "*Take your Bible and take your newspaper, and read both. But interpret newspapers from your Bible.*" While broadly in agreement, I have come increasingly to the view that newspapers from mainstream media cannot, on the whole, be trusted (my first of many controversial statements).

This book is about priests of the Bible. Having considered the subject of the priesthood in Part 1 and priests in Part 2, we come to a priestly people in Part 3. As well as the people of God being called to be a priestly people, they are also called to be a prophetic people, insofar as their existence reveals God's purposes for humanity and through them God's will can be shown. We are told, for example, "*the testimony of Jesus is the spirit of prophecy*" Revelation 19:10. While we may argue that to be a prophet requires a divine calling, all of us are told by Jesus to "*watch and pray*". As A. W. Tozer said: "*We desperately need seers who can see through the mist ... Christian leaders with prophetic vision*".

Part of my contribution to watching and praying is regularly blogging about what I see to be going on in the world, what to make out of it and how best to respond. I am also being quickened to pray more, realising that while I must still do "my bit", God is the key. I do so while mindful that many of my own Christian associations have been with those with a quietist mindset, which is to do with having a calm acceptance of things as they are without attempting to resist or change them, albeit, as I show in Chapter 46, some have a heightened awareness of what is going on because of their interest in and study of yet to be fulfilled Bible prophecy. This remains another contentious subject among Christians.

How one sees what is taking place in the world has been a major cause of division and it begs the question of how Christians ought to respond. Even among the more learned and spiritual, views range from believing what we are told from "official" sources, ignoring what is happening and not getting involved, obedience to those "in charge" and taking on board the opinions of those who are "in charge" who dismiss what "conspiracy theorists" and "trouble makers" have to say and avoid them. I take as my role model "*the children of Issachar, which were men that had understanding of the times, to know what Israel ought to do*" 1 Chronicles 12:32, noting with regret there are too few of such folk around.

I recognise that throughout the history of the church, Christians have had to suffer, having to patiently endure bad people who were calling the shots, knowing they can manipulate "the system" such that they are able to get away with it. As a result, many choose to focus their attentions, laudably, on carrying out the Great Commission and living holy lives. But if we truly love our neighbour and make a difference that meets with the approval of Him whose views are what truly matter, we cannot just sit idly by and let things happen, even if it leaves us in a quandary when it comes to knowing what to do.

I have come to a view that ignorance is no excuse and while sometimes, often even, there is little we can do by way of prevention when we see the world going down a wrong path, led by fools and villains, we should at least try to form a right response. I lament that those we recognise as leaders in the church do too little to guide the flock on such matters, and even go along with what they are told. Sadly, the same too often goes for "my lot" when they hide behind texts like: "*Let every soul be subject unto the higher powers*" Romans 13:1, believe what they are told by "the Unholy Trinity" (government, media and elites), who often lie, and point out that, given we are in the world but not of it, there is little the child of God could/should do when it comes to responding to the bad goings on in the world.

Before I return to Bible prophecy, which is where I think our focus should be, I would like to revisit one of my blogs, posted on the last day of 2022: "**Looking back at 2022; looking forward to 2023**". I included 12 points of significance, developing points I raised a year earlier in my updated "**Prophets of the Bible**" book. It is not an exhaustive list and I am often reminded that in my enthusiasm to see justice done now, it takes longer (sometimes never) to come to a satisfactory resolution or definitive view, let alone convince others. I reflected on these points, noting developments, when I wrote six months later, in July 2023, and included my thoughts in brackets [] after each point. I revisited these points six months later, in February 2024, just prior to publishing, adding more thoughts in brackets {}.

In making these "final" thoughts on the thoughts I had a year ago, which were on the thoughts I had a year before that, I confess there is still much I don't know for sure and I am far from confident when it comes to predicting how things I observe will finally resolve. I am reminded that, while I am called to be a watchman, I am not called to research every nook and cranny. When having done one's research and come to a view, the big question is how to respond? I had thought to spend a good deal of quality time checking out the "12 points" and deciding what my response should be before "going to press", but have decided not to and it will remain work in progress. I'd rather share broadly how I see things.

I am also mindful that some of what I say can be construed as "conspiracy theory" and earns the rebuke of certain Christian leaders concerning Christians they feel need to brought to heel, who have the temerity to question the "official narrative" and have the presumption of trying to "wake up" fellow Christians, including priests and ministers. While we must be beholden to the truth (not conjecture), knowing that without it we cannot be truly free, we must recognise there is much we do not and often cannot know, yet all too often we find conspiracy theories later being proven to be conspiracy facts. Sadly, divisions among Christians on the matter continue and for those who, like me, are vexed at the way our culture is being taken over by Satan and his minions (arguably, it has ever been thus) but just as vexed at how churches respond, we must continue to put our trust and hope in God (just as the Psalmist did who recognised similar in his own day), speak and live truth, yet still love our detractors.

For example, I have little doubt the official accounts given concerning "the JFK assassination" and "9/11", as well as some relating to some of the "12 points" raised in my article that I am about to share are not only false but rather part of Satan's agenda to take over the planet and subjugate humanity, often using deception and division as his means, effectively employing his minions to do his bidding.

"We began 2022 coming out of Covid-19 lockdown. While not dismissing Covid-19 is for real (I had it, supposedly, in 2022), my belief that the pandemic was a plan/scamdemic was reinforced."

[And even more so as evidence is coming to light. It is a scary thought but all round the world governments have used draconian methods to lock down populations – and it was all based on a lie.]

{We are far from out of the woods and we continue to see people wear masks "just in case". One hears rumours the next plandemic is just round the corner and it is well to be prepared for such a possibility. If you believe as I do that this is an important way to control the masses, it cannot be discounted. Given the huge damage more are seeing due to lockdowns etc., this is not an issue likely to go away soon. Meanwhile, there are whispers of another "pandemic" in the offing, so we need to be prepared. *"Disease X: Scientists, leaders prepare for a possible virus"* is a present reality. One day, the whole scandalous truth will come out and, while I hope it will be sooner, I cannot say assuredly when.}

"At the start of 2022, many had been jabbed because of Covid-19, often more than once. Reports of the net harm done due to taking the jab have escalated and many now believe this is so."

[And even more so as more evidence is coming to light. Rather than protecting people against "the virus", we are seeing that the net harm done by taking the jab has outweighed the purported benefits.]

{We continue to find evidence being presented concerning the net harm of "vaccines" and that evidence is being ignored by the powers that be. For example, when there was debate in the UK Parliament recently concerning unexplained and excess deaths possibly as a result, few MPs attended. Such is the price to pay for challenging the status quo, and we should not be surprised too few do so. The possibility/probability there has been a concerted effort by some to kill many should shock us all.}

"Early in 2022 Russia invaded Ukraine and were held up as the villains, but more villainous were the Ukraine authorities and their western backers. Who can say what the final outcome will be, but it remains a daunting prospect."

[Further escalation has been attempted, urged on by the power brokers and, at the same time, more acts of villainy revealed, especially on the side of Ukraine and Zelensky's puppet masters. If anything, Russia appears to be winning and with no attempt by those who have the power to do so to admit to wrong doing and pursue peace. One feels that the conflict is really about who controls Ukraine as long as it isn't Russia, and a lot of it is to cover up the nefarious activities and interests of the Deep State players, and those pushing the war care little about those who suffer and die as a result.]

{The conflict continues, and even more is it evident that the Russians are winning. Those anti-Russian elements, including the UK government, that have poured money into propping up the "Zelensky regime" and making also sorts of noises about how bad Putin is and how they intend to oppose him, seemed to have switched interest to the Israel/Gaza situation. As always, it has been the innocent who suffer. It should be added, none of this makes

Putin/Russia "the good guys", but then who is good and bad? Having been tempted to the view that the world's interest has moved on from Ukraine, after hearing recent speeches coming out of the World Economic Forum and UK government, I am less sure. The situation in Ukraine is tragic, with avoidable deaths etc., and people in my country are being lied to and led by a political class that will do all it takes to bring to heel those pesky Ruskies. In the recent Tucker Carlson interview with Putin it is evident history matters and yet this and what appear to be legitimate Russian grievances are being ignored. It is not for me to say who is right and wrong and to what extent but it is evident there are evil forces afoot against the truth coming out, and people suffer! Even Christian pundits I respect continue to have it in for Putin and maybe for good reason, but I can't help feeling they ignore the fact that cowards will be cast into the Lake of Fire on Judgement Day.}

"The transhuman agenda advances as pushed by certain elites, whether it is a matter of persons including youth changing their sexual identity or the merging of humans with machines."

[That agenda continues and more are being sucked into it, including the Church of England, although seeing some of its members strongly object-ing. Close to home, a family has taken their child out of a CofE school due to concerns over transgender indoctrination. Pertinent to this book is the seed war taking place ever since Genesis 1-11, along with the Nephilim and its perversion of human genetics.]

{From what I can make out, that agenda continues to be pushed, and those who take the Bible view that there can be only two genders and are prepared to take issue with those who insist otherwise, will suffer the conse-quences. As for merging humans and machines, I have little doubt the tech-nology continues to be developed and the question is how is the transhuman agenda going to be advanced? When it comes to connecting dots, I have little doubt the roll out of 5G is a further factor. What "Sons of God" attempted in Genesis 6 their successors are attempting today through transhumanism.}

"The Climate Emergency narrative is back again, dominating the think-ing of many, including government, and having profound, detrimental im-plications as to how things are done."

[We have seen the ante upped, including BBC reports about excessive temperatures in countries such as Greece. It was an argument used by gov-ernments, e.g., the Dutch, to destroy traditional farming, push for 15-minute cities in order to move to zero carbon emissions and penalise dissent. The "science" about climate change that we are told to accept is increasingly be-ing seen as not scientific. What is unsurprising yet regrettable is alternative perspectives can hardly be found in mainstream media.]

{The UK Energy Act 2023 was recently passed by the UK Parliament, which indicates where their priorities lie. The Act is a landmark piece of legislation detailing the UK's approach to achieving energy independence and its 'net zero' obligations, and is likely to have big implications for personal freedoms. While there may be a sense of lull, I have no doubt the Climate Change hoax continues to be pushed. As I write, I read of German farmer protests that have widespread ramifications over planned cuts to "climate-damaging" subsidies in the agriculture sector. (Since writing this, I note the German farmers have been joined by those from other countries in their protesting.) What we cannot ignore is the changes being forced on how food is produced, and other changes, are part of the UN Agenda 2030.}

"More evidence is coming out that the 2020 US Presidential election was stolen as were the 2022 US mid-terms, and elections in other countries, e.g., Brazil, but more people are waking up, to the damage done by the election stealers."

[From soon after the last US presidential election was over, I had little doubt massive fraud took place but with attempts to overturn the result ignored or worse, corruption in the seats of power has become more evident. As I write, Trump faces his third indictment this year accused of helping to instigate the January 6th riots while more evidence of corruption in the Biden family has been ignored.]

{Biden is being increasingly seen as a liability. It will be interesting to see who will stand for the Democrats in 2024. While neither Republican nor Democrat, the Biden regime is as insidious as they come. They still continue to go after Trump, e.g., through raising law suits. Meanwhile, more are raising the issue of fraud, pointing to irrefutable evidence it took place, and more "ordinary folk" believing that this was the case, but what will give and when? The latest Trump related news on the BBC website is about two US states refusing to let Trump onto their 2024 Presidential election ballot (and Trump responding by making legal challenges), all down to his alleged incitement of the 2021 US Capitol riot. Yet looking at the GOP presidential candidates, it is Trump who is way ahead as the front runner. He continues to be demeaned by fine Christians as well as the bad people in power, but I still see him as a key player in the good versus evil paradigm we are clearly in, who fits the bill as the Lord's anointed. But so was King Jehu, whose story we have told – and look how he turned out. The lesson is to trust in God alone. Seeing the stand-off between certain US states and the Biden regime over the uncontrolled (some say deliberate) stream of those coming illegally into the country begs the question: will this be what will awaken the American people that they have been had, and there I will leave it.}

"2022 has seen significant moves toward mandatory digital ids, such that

people can be controlled and these are often related to their social credit score, the intended financial reset and a cashless society."

[Moves toward this end continue, using China as a model. There have been many cases, often not reported, of banks closing or being bailed out. The stealing of money from the people by a tiny elite that might benefit from their fraud, with those who comply with their plans benefitting, and the system of money being printed that is not backed by assets, and debt enslavement are the issues at stake. As I write, it is unclear whether the outcome will be a continuation of the status quo or a new system based on the true value of money, including the eventual dismantling of the US Federal Reserve.]

{While little is said about a financial reset in mainstream media, there are all sorts of reports of radical changes in the world financial sector and a monetary realignment. I have little doubt something huge is soon to happen that will be for all to see. I sense that the days of a world money system based on the US dollar and fiat currency are numbered. I have no doubt that those in power continue to push their mandatory digital ids and cashless society agenda, yet there are forces at work to oppose this.

Pertinent to these discussions is the BRICS currency replacing the US dollar as the major world trading currency. BRICS is an intergovernmental organisation comprising Brazil, Russia, India, China, South Africa, Egypt, Ethiopia, Iran and the United Arab Emirates. There is a lot that could be said about BRICS and what appears to be a paradigm shift with power going from west to east and, to be welcomed, a reversal to the propensity of the US to print money not backed up by physical assets and its ability to enslave poorer nations through a nefarious agenda that cares little for the people affected, but it is beyond the scope of this book despite this being of enormous significance. While continuing to watch with interest, I urge people not to get carried away even if all this might appear to be a good thing. It could be that the perpetrators of evil are switching tack from hard sell to soft sell but still with its ultimate goal of enslavement. Two factors to consider are China, who is at the centre of this shift and is also the most advanced in adopting social credit scoring and related draconian measures to control its citizens, and Elon Musk, hailed as a hero in standing up against the bad guys, who also controls the technology that makes these changes possible and is likely not someone acting with altruistic intent.}

"The UK, having got rid of Boris and seen off Liz, now have an unelected globalist puppet, Rishi, as their Prime Minister."

[My disappointment with the British political system continues, e.g., a party expelling an MP who spoke against vaccines, giving huge amounts of aid to the corrupt Ukraine government, moving to curtail free speech and those questioning wrongs in our society, and with too few speaking out about the sort of concerns I raise in this chapter. While some stand out in the political arena concerning these issues, the system is a broken one, with people having to choose between unsatisfactory alternatives and with Labour and the LibDems being if anything worse than the Conservatives.]

{I have seen little to alter my pessimism but am hopeful that good people, who are waking up to what is really happening in the world, will become MPs. Sadly, besides an election system that does little to encourage minority parties, I am far from convinced as to the viability of the alternatives. Yet what I am seeing is people wanting to make a difference, including through political activism. It is true that some/much of it is to do with social injustice, but at least people are seeing things are bad. Going back to Liz, her recent remarks on the Farage show about the UK Deep State, confirm why she was ousted. George Galloway winning the latest by-election suggests more voters are rejecting the establishment.}

"The Unholy Trinity (media, politicians and elites) have in 2022 increasingly shown their true colours and their lies have been found out, and this has given rise to an empowered alternative media and now many whistle blowers coming forward."

[This is ongoing. The good news is more whistle blowers are coming forward. A picture is emerging that monumental corruption has been taking place, just as the conspiracy theorists have said.]

{This continues to be ongoing and I have no reason to change my views. From reports I am getting, typically not picked up by the Unholy Trinity, whistle blowers still have to pay a price for doing so. While there are instances of mainstream media reporting villainy, we have a long way still to go. Meanwhile, we are continuing to see more whistle blowers bravely come forward, inspired by those before them.}

"The move to shut down and penalise free speech continues to escalate, especially now as the baddies are getting called out."

[It seems ludicrous but moves, including those to change the law, supposedly to protect people from falsehoods, and penalising people for simply seeking and speaking the truth, are ongoing.]

{I haven't checked out developments but would be surprised if the global trend to shut up those who expose State sanctioned wrong doings and tell the truth were to reverse in the near future. As I write I listen to the US media presenter, Owen Shroyer, who has just come out of prison for his part in the January 6th 2021 attack on the US Capitol. My point is not to discuss the rights and wrongs of what happened but to echo the point Shroyer made that many wrongly suffer for speaking truth to power. Meanwhile, leaders of the globalist elite push the idea that "disinformation" is our biggest threat. It is bizarre in a sick way when we hear world leaders cite "disinformation" in current threats on humanity. The latest example is the kickback seen arising out of Tucker Carlson interviewing Vladimir Putin.}

"Children continue to go missing and be trafficked with evil intent."

[The newly released film "Sound of Freedom" shows but the tip of the iceberg of this heinous crime.]

{This remains a huge issue that is largely ignored by mainstream media. In checking out this issue, I noted an article posted on **UK Column** that documents all sorts of paedophilia related crimes under the auspices of the United Nations and those associated with the UN. But how to stop these crimes? I might be wrong, but I suspect child trafficking is a major factor in today's ginormous cover up.}

"Before 2020, I would not have reckoned on this; in 2021 I began to see this was so; in 2022 I was convinced – Planet Earth is run by a tiny, globalist, elite cabal, beholden to Satan, who have many of the world's politicians and those who run its institutions in their pockets. They have been pushing much that has been referred to above, to depopulate and enslave humanity with ideas of "new normal", "build back better" and its Great Reset agenda."

[The more I do my research, and as improbable as this seems, the more I am convinced this is the case. Given they are being exposed, I won't put it past them to continue to stage false flag events.]

{While I do not have much to add since I wrote last time, I remain of this view and am also of the view that some good Christians vehemently oppose me because they do NOT believe *Planet Earth is run by a tiny, globalist, elite cabal, beholden to Satan* and my suggesting such is the case is way too out-landish and divisive. I do not have the energy or the calling to check out what is happening on the world stage amidst the mixed reporting I do listen to and watch. Humanly speaking, when I do, I am filled with horror and foreboding at the unchecked evil and amount of deception, especially among Christian leaders. We can hope for change – due to the efforts of awake pagans, God fearing people and God.

There are those who herald a bright future as evil is exposed, as well as those who see a dark future ahead of the Lord's return. If Balaam and his donkey can speak among the profoundest of truths ever spoken, then so can the least likely and always we must test and weigh what we hear. We must not "cherry pick" who it is we are to believe. First and foremost, we must be seekers after the truth. While I hope that the good guys will win and the bad given their just desserts, the only "bright" future I can expect, besides a temporary respite because God is gracious, is concerning the true Church;

a harvest of souls for the Kingdom and of our Lord's return. Much as I hope there will be a golden age of truth, justice and righteousness, I cannot entertain such an inviting prospect, given my study of history, the Bible and human nature, other than after Jesus returns. It is why we (the people of God) must not be distracted from the task entrusted to us of preaching the Gospel. Besides taking the appropriate action in the light of world events and connecting dots when we can, we must remain faithful to Him.}

There is a lot more I could add concerning observations resulting from my watchman on the wall activities, including an angry "right wing" nationalistic backlash taking place to counter the current woke, socialist, globalist agenda that we have been seeing in recent years, but I will desist and invite readers who are interested to read my blogs. Before I move on to Bible prophecy, I want to consider one of my seminal blogs of 2022, that I revisited in 2023, where I asked the question where are the people living on this planet heading: is it for a Great Reset, a Great Awakening or a Great Deception?

The term "Great Reset" is one used by the likes of Klaus Schwab who heads the World Economic Forum, supported by leaders all around the globe, and is linked to UN Agendas 2021 and 2030. Those championing the Great Reset include Britain's King Charles and this is hailed by elements of the Unholy Trinity and those who go along with what they say. It used to be called the New World Order and it invariably involves the common people giving up certain rights and property to big government and those working in collusion with them, such as big corporations, in exchange for security when it comes to countering climate change, pandemics and war. Those wanting a Great Awakening include people with New Age beliefs, the "deplorables" who question the status quo, and "political" prophets.

In essence, those hoping for and/or expecting a Great Awakening are often of the view that the evil, elite cabal will not only be exposed but will be overturned by something more wholesome that will empower the common folk and bring in a version of the Millennium, albeit one that more often than not is at odds with my understanding of what the Bible teaches. The term Great Deception could apply to anyone of us (including me) and, given what Jesus taught about the elect being deceived, no-one is immune. Many who believe the lies pushed by the Unholy Trinity, include those in leadership positions in churches, as well as those who ignore what is going on or who don't care. I see all three, the Great Reset, Great Awakening and Great Deception, playing out right now. While God wins in the end (the Bible tells us so), Satan is even more effective as an Angel of Light than he is as the Prince of Darkness. While I have no time for the "Great Resetters", I am far from convinced by the "Great Awakeners".

I would like to end this chapter by stating how I see this all tying in with

Bible prophecy, a subject I touched on in my **"Prophets of the Bible"** book and continue to study. The first thing to do is reiterate my understanding that there are around 2500 prophecies in the Bible, about 2000 of which have been precisely and literally fulfilled, leaving 500 yet to be fulfilled but with little doubt they will be sometime in the future, although timing as always is something for the Almighty. While I could refer to a number of Old Testament books, I would like to focus on the Book of Revelation, reiterating my belief that Chapters 6 to the end are about future events, including the Millennium after Jesus returns.

Three subjects spring to mind that seem closer to fulfilment today, especially in the light of so many developments and more non-mainstream media coverage than 50 years ago when I began my journey as a Christian. These were at the top of the list of subjects on which prophecy students in my church had views. While I cannot say how they would react to today's situation, I suspect they would be even more sceptical on what the powers that be would have us believe when it comes to what is really going on. One difference between now and 50 years ago is that we have moved a lot further away from the Christian consensus that once existed. There has also been a marked acceleration in momentous happenings and who can say how these will finally resolve? But we have to leave it there and consider these three subjects that are all to do with things yet to happen before we do a final wrapping up.

The Mark of the Beast: relates to the number "666" and is linked to the emergence of the Antichrist, hailed by many as someone who can bring about the sort of society envisaged by supporters of the Great Reset. Without that mark, people cannot buy or sell. It is quite easy to see how technological advances linked to agendas like transhumanism, and a cashless society that is linked to a social credit score controlled by some powerful entity, having the tools at their disposal, can make this happen. How the Antichrist manages to come to power and is even welcomed is an intriguing question.

The Mystery of Babylon: (whose Fall is predicted) is a system that goes all the way back to the Tower of Babel and epitomises man's rebellion against God. It combines commercial, political and religious systems. Big corporations controlled by asset managers like Blackrock and Vanguard, linked to Big Pharma that have members of the Unholy Trinity under their control, are all part of the Babylonian system which, even if people are unaware of it, has huge control and influence over all our lives. The question remains: who are the true powers, even behind these powerful entities.

The Final Battle: We are seeing a realignment of nations and different alliances being formed, partly as an outcome of the Ukraine and Israel conflicts, noting that what is presently taking place, just as in Bible times, has Israel at the centre. Then there is the currently in-progress global financial reset taking place, which if the baddies have their way will include a cashless society and centralised control on how we spend our money and how much. It is also looking like there will be a ditching of dependence on the US dollar, which many African nations have also shown an interest in, as well as countries like China allying with Russia, and is likely to have huge implications for us all. It is easy to imagine how the way nations are lining up could lead to such a Battle (the Bible declares there will be one and probably more than one, in several places, and is a subject I reflect on in "**Prophets of the Bible**"), although it appears from what the Bible teaches on the subject that in the Ezekiel 38/39 Gog-Magog battle/war Israel will be standing alone and it is God who alone will rescue them. Also to consider is the Battle of Armageddon, which appears to happen near the end of the tribulation period (Revelation 16:12-16).

Even as I write (November 2023), there are major happenings in the world such as coups in Niger and Gabon and fires in Maui, on top of developments in many of the situations already touched on, and I cannot help feeling these are not altogether unrelated and are a precursor to end times events spoken of in the Bible, including the opening of "the seals" which is described in Revelation 6. I further write in February 2024 and in doing so re-visit what I wrote previously. Many of the issues I have raised and will no doubt concern readers (even those who see things a lot differently to me) continue without being resolved, one wonders whether changes will be for better or worse. For example, the gap between the "haves" and "have nots" continues to widen and the mass migrations we have seen the world over continue unabated. I still see lots of alarming things happening all round the world, led by powerful, globalist agencies like the UN, NATO, WEF and WHO, that lead me to wonder what the outcome will be and what our response ought to be, but let what I have said suffice for now. Again, I reiterate there is much I do not know for sure and yet suspect the picture of what is really going on in the world that falls in the "evil" category may be even worse and more outlandish than I thought.

I have sometimes been given the label "truther", a term often used in the pejorative sense to describe someone who doubts the generally accepted account of an event, believing that an official conspiracy exists to conceal the true explanation; a conspiracy theorist. Having been through the mill for speaking my mind, sometimes in lacking grace and wisdom, I can recognise the stigma that comes from being so accused. In mitigation, I would point out my heart's desire is for God and His glory, righteousness and truth. I have yet to find a "conspiracy theorist" or Bible preacher who gets everything right and only God has the complete big picture. I regret that those in Christian leadership have often fallen way short when coming to terms with these matters. The best I can counsel is to seek after God and to follow the wisdom of the Psalms and hymns, with which I end this chapter, putting our confidence in and commitment to God alone, living in accordance with the two Great Commands to do with loving God and loving our neighbour. I am conscious the above may be rather a lot to take in, but I did warn readers at the start of this chapter that reading all this will take you out of your comfort zone.

I do not apologise for writing as I do, mindful of the importance of knowing the truth, which sets us free, and warning people of what is going on. While what I say will upset some Christians at a time when we need unity, we cannot be oblivious to how things are, even if we are unclear what to do when we are aware. We all need God's wisdom on what to do and His grace to do what needs to be done. Inaction is not an option if we are to take seriously the command to love our neighbour. Moreover, we must be careful not to succumb to media-driven fear or Satan's strategy to divide (God's people) and rule, and recognise even the best among Christian leaders can get things significantly wrong. Neither must we latch onto this or that person in seeking to "come to a view" (something in my experience even the best of us do). Rather, our remit is seeking truth, recognising it can be found in many different quarters, even unlikely ones, and that in doing so it can be a lonely path we tread, for even the best of us do not like being contradicted. Sometimes, because of the deception that pervades our world, there is much we cannot know for sure but, even more than that, it is about honouring the Lord and loving Him.

I would like to return to the subject of "*are there true prophets operating today*", a subject that I raised in "**Prophets of the Bible**". While, unlike some/ many Christians I have associated with, who take a particular interest in yet to be fulfilled Bible prophecy, but also believe that at best today's prophets are no more than inspired preachers, and the gift of prophecy spoken of in the New Testament no longer applies to today's church, I have dissented from that view because it is unscriptural. I believe the gift of prophecy is still applicable and there are, according to the definitions I gave in that book, true prophets who have continued to operate, from soon after New Testament times until now.

One dilemma I have faced is coming to terms with the differences in views expressed by my charismatic friends, e.g., restricting the use of the gift to what takes place in the church, and those cited by the likes of **Elijah Streams** and **Richards Watch** (both of which I check out from time to time) that I label as "political prophets" that speak concerning world events and significant personalities on the world stage. We find members of that former group objecting to what those in the latter group claim as coming from the Lord. I should add that both of these "watcher" groups have included prophecies I question are from God, yet they are to be commended for giving prominence to the prophetic voice.

Regrettably and unsurprisingly, a prophetic understanding, including a desire for the people of God to have one, is largely absent in today's church, and this is made worse when they are listening to today's secularists instead. If they did what the Bible says, they would be encouraging true prophets to prophesy, testing and weighing what is said and expecting to see the fulfilment of true prophecies, such as we are led to believe when reading Joel 2:28-32. St. Paul's counsel: "*Quench not the Spirit. Despise not prophesyings. Prove all things*" 1 Thessalonians 5:19-21 is always applicable.

I confess, while I am sympathetic to the notion there are prophets of the Lord prophesying today, I continue to adopt my "*test and weigh*" approach out of necessity, mindful that our reading of the Bible shows us in many places that there have always been false prophets among us. Yet I recognise the importance of the gift of prophecy today (and it is one we need to covet), along with Bible prophecy, in understanding the world etc., sensing such are the days that we are living in we will yet see an outpouring of the Holy Spirit, including a greater manifestation of the gift of prophecy through many.

Yet it has ever been the case that, even among the best of us, we gravitate toward those who prophesy what we think ought to be said or what we want to see or think should happen, and we need to be both Word and Spirit based in our thinking. Often when studying Bible prophecy, it is not clear exactly what was intended, nor the time scales that are involved. Moreover, all of us, believer in Jesus or not, believer in future prophecy and/or prophecy today or not, we have to face the possibility we may be wrong when it comes to identifying who are the fools, villains and good guys operating in our world today, and find out that we have been duped, and that is why me must continuously look to God.

In trying to reach out to all Christians, I recognise we often see things quite differently. I am reminded we are called to be Jesus' disciples, and there is a cost for us all in doing so. Jesus said: "*If any man will come after me, let him deny himself, and take up his cross, and follow me. For whosoever will save his life shall lose it: and whosoever will lose his life for my sake shall find it*" Matthew 16:24-25. The big question for me and any wannabe follower of Jesus is: will we take up our cross? I often have to remind myself: I am an "unprofitable servant" (of the Lord) and as such it is not my place, if people object to and reject what I have to say (and me), to take exception and react. My calling is simply to serve Him as best I can and it is my privilege to do so, even if at the end of the day I am still unprofitable.

When it comes to end times prophecy and current events, a lot more could be said. We might rightly ask how what we are seeing being played out on the world stage ties in with what the Bible and the prophets would have us expect, and that study remains an ongoing one. But we must draw things to a close, and we need to consider other subjects that should be of interest to a priestly people. But let us end by quoting the words of two Psalms, 2 and 37, penned in the light of bad people doing bad things and good people suffering, and the frustrating realisation, as expressed by the Psalmist, that they appear to have got away with it, yet we, like him, know we can put our entire trust in the Lord:

"Why do the heathen rage, and the people imagine a vain thing? The kings of the earth set themselves, and the rulers take counsel together, against the Lord, and against his anointed, saying, Let us break their bands asunder, and cast away their cords from us. He that sitteth in the heavens shall laugh: the Lord shall have them in derision. Then shall he speak unto them in his wrath, and vex them in his sore displeasure. Yet have I set my king upon my holy hill of Zion. I will declare the decree: the Lord hath said unto me, Thou art my Son; this day have I begotten thee. Ask of me, and I shall give thee the heathen for thine inheritance, and the uttermost parts of the earth for thy possession. Thou shalt break them with a rod of iron; thou shalt dash them in pieces like a potter's vessel. Be wise now therefore, O ye kings: be instructed, ye judges of the earth. Serve the Lord with fear, and rejoice with trembling. Kiss the Son, lest he be angry, and ye perish from the way, when his wrath is kindled but a little. Blessed are all they that put their trust in him" Psalm 2:1-12.

"Fret not thyself because of evildoers, neither be thou envious against the workers of iniquity. For they shall soon be cut down like the grass, and wither as the green herb. Trust in the Lord, and do good; so shalt thou dwell in the land, and verily thou shalt be fed. Delight thyself also in the Lord: and he shall give thee the desires of thine heart. Commit thy way unto the Lord; trust also in him; and he shall bring it to pass. And he shall bring forth thy righteousness as the light, and thy judgment as the noonday. Rest in the Lord, and wait patiently for him: fret not thyself because of him who prospereth in his way, because of the man who bringeth wicked devices to pass. Cease from anger, and forsake wrath: fret not thyself in any wise to do evil. For evildoers shall be cut off: but those that wait upon the Lord, they shall inherit the earth. For yet a little while, and the wicked shall not be: yea, thou shalt diligently consider his place, and it shall not be. But the meek shall inherit the earth; and shall delight themselves in the abundance of peace. The wicked plotteth against the just, and gnasheth upon him with his teeth. The Lord shall laugh at him: for he seeth that his day is coming. The wicked have drawn out the sword,

Priests of the Bible

and have bent their bow, to cast down the poor and needy, and to slay such as be of upright conversation. Their sword shall enter into their own heart, and their bows shall be broken. A little that a righteous man hath is better than the riches of many wicked. For the arms of the wicked shall be broken: but the Lord upholdeth the righteous. The Lord knoweth the days of the upright: and their inheritance shall be for ever." Psalm 37:1-18.

And finally with two hymns, seemingly unrelated to this deep dive into trying to understand prophecy and current events yet pertinent by way of providing much needed balance and giving us reassurance, especially to encourage those who, like me, are drawn to and could get lost going down rabbit holes:

1. When peace like a river attendeth my way,
When sorrows like sea billows roll;
Whatever my lot Thou hast taught me to say,
"It is well, it is well with my soul!"

It is well with my soul!
It is well, it is well with my soul!

2. Though Satan should buffet, though trials should come,
Let this blest assurance control,
That Christ hath regarded my helpless estate,
And hath shed His own blood for my soul.

3. My sin—oh, the bliss of this glorious thought—
My sin, not in part, but the whole,
Is nailed to His Cross, and I bear it no more;
Praise the Lord, praise the Lord, O my soul!

4. For me, be it Christ, be it Christ hence to live;
If dark hours about me shall roll,
No pang shall be mine, for in death as in life
Thou wilt whisper Thy peace to my soul.

And

1. O soul, are you weary and troubled?
No light in the darkness you see?
There's light for a look at the Savior,
And life more abundant and free!

[Refrain]
Turn your eyes upon Jesus,
Look full in His wonderful face,
And the things of earth will grow strangely dim,
In the light of His glory and grace.

2. Thro' death into life everlasting,
He passed, and we follow Him there;
O'er us sin no more hath dominion--
For more than conqu'rors we are! [Refrain]

3. His Word shall not fail you--He promised;
Believe Him, and all will be well:
Then go to a world that is dying,
His perfect salvation to tell! [Refrain]

Epilogue

When I wrote **"Prophets of the Bible"** and the part to do with working out what to make of and how to respond to ongoing events in the world that I deemed significant, of which there was a great number, I recognised at the very end it remained very much work in progress and I was far from figuring out all the right answers despite doing more testing and weighing, watching and praying than most. The same conundrum faces me this last day of February 2024 when it comes to current events, when out of necessity I must draw a line to changing or adding to what I have written, or else this book will never be completed and go to publishing. Strangely, some of the same events I pondered while writing about prophets are the same ones now I am writing about priests, which tells me things are often less straightforward to figure out than I might have thought originally. Moreover, the challenges faced by what should be a "prophetic people" are the same ones now faced by that same "priestly people".

As I pondered in both books, I reckon when it comes to deciding whether we are heading for *"A Great Reset"*, *"A Great Awakening"* or *"A Great Deception"*, it will be a mixture of all three, with a view, articulated in this chapter and in **"Prophets of the Bible"**, of how Bible, End Times prophecy will play out, as well as a recognition that there is a lot I don't know and can't say for sure. I don't feel too bad about this, firstly because the same is evident with almost every Christian pundit I have followed and maybe the Lord only requires me to know so much and instead focus on being His faithful servant. What I do know is there is an *"Unholy Trinity"* of media, politicians and societal elites who lie to us and who "control the narrative". As the people of God, we are called to follow His narrative, work to extend His Kingdom (souls saved and godly input) and be His salt and light. Ignoring what is going on or not responding as God would have us respond is not an option and the prospect of being raptured from Planet Earth anytime soon must not be an excuse for our not pursuing truth and acting righteously (which goes far beyond our regular every day dealings to bringing God's goodness into a bad world). As I have discovered, finding alternatives to the Unholy Trinity to inform us aright is not always easy given the amount of misinformation "out there" and, besides which, getting to the bottom of all that is really going on is unlikely what any of us are called to do, but we do need to find the right balance.

People of my ilk are often called "conspiracy theorists", something I have already unapologetically recognised and responded to. I won't repeat my thoughts here other than cite the text that jumped out of the pages when I thought about how to deal with my conspiracy antipathetic detractors (and deciding between fact and fiction and how best to respond) in **"Prophets of the Bible"**: *"Do not call conspiracy everything this people calls a conspiracy; do not fear what they fear, and do not dread it. The Lord Almighty is the one you are to regard as holy, he is the one you are to fear, he is the one you are to dread"* Isaiah 8:12-13 (NIV). A lot of my watching continues to be that which those labelled as "conspiracy theorist" have pointed out, if for no other reason than, unlike the majority (sadly), I don't trust the Unholy Trinity, but I do take the prophet's warning seriously, including the need to fear God.

I daresay when, dear reader, you get to read this, the world will appear a different place to the one I am seeing now and there will be surprises (or maybe not, given most changes appear to take place slowly and we are often only aware of them happening when it is clearly evident). Even as I write I note developments in what could still turn into war between the NATO alliance and the Russian Federation as well as what appears to be a humanitarian crisis in Gaza and a continuation of an anti-Israel backlash. Then the crisis at the USA Southern border with what is in effect an invasion by military age men while at the same time Trump's popularity continues to grow as the Deep State and "the swamp" do all they can to eliminate him and those who do not toe the line. I expect that at the right time we must be prepared for a shock, especially if not sharing my view that the world is controlled by a tiny elite beholden to Satan, as to what is really going on that can be placed in the nefarious, wicked category is revealed. The best I can do as I wrap up this chapter is to exhort you to decide completely, whole heartedly to worship the God of Israel, who knows all, hear from Him and do what He says.

A long time ago, I realised that Bible savvy old men who were active as young men "serving the Lord", when they got old often became obsessed with End Times Bible prophecy and over critical of the next generation with their endeavours in the Lord's service. Later, I saw how tempting it was to spend time figuring out what was going on in the world and like the Psalmist become despondent because the wicked seemed to prevail and the righteous had to look on with consternation and suffer for being righteous. I make this observation: firstly, to confess in my old age I have fitted that bill, secondly, to warn against getting the wrong balance in life and thirdly, to affirm the Lord keeps us around to serve Him and bless others. By all means do what the Lord requires of us who are in active service in His army, but allow Him to sort out the world, the church and other people in ways He sees fit. The Bible is full of wise counsel to those who face the predicament I have often found myself in and this book has fully and freely quoted from the Bible. It is now up to me and others like me to put into practice what the Bible teaches. As I pondered on what verse to finish this chapter with, the word "delight" came to mind. It occurs 24 times in the Psalms and what better way to end than with the Psalmist's exhortation: *"Delight thyself also in the Lord: and he shall give thee the desires of thine heart"* (37:4).

We are now at the end of March 2024 and the point of no return has come. Proof reading is now over, including my toning down certain controversial bits that might upset some of the nice folk reading this and could have put them off from reading further, and the next step really is no more tinkering with what I wrote and to go to publishing. Since I am not Elisha, who knew what the king said in his bedroom, I cannot offer with 100 per cent certainty the fully rounded picture of what is really going on in today's runaway world. And lots is going on! "Conspiracy theorists" and "political prophets" agree this is the case and that monumental things are about to happen, which may also relate to the "Tribulation period" spoke off in Revelation 6-19, where the war between God and Satan, began even before Genesis, reaches a climax. I am thinking of the Moscow Concert Hall attack, the big ship crashing into the Baltimore Bridge, Taiwan earthquakes, assorted happenings in the British Royal Family, further developments in the Ukraine and Gaza wars, an eclipse, a huge financial crash/reset, more revelations concerning the Covid "death jab", deep underground tunnels, startling happenings in Trump land, all of which have occurred since writing at the end of February. Some have suggested, that a lot of the above, concerning which news reporting outlets continue to present half-truths, may be distractions from what is really happening. While many recoil when they hear people put forward the argument that much of what we see of a concerning nature is related and orchestrated by an evil cabal, I believe, unapologetically, this to be the case, as can be demonstrated should anyone care to check this out. As for who, prominent on the world stage, are the good and bad guys, the more I study, the less I am sure.

Long ago, I realised there are limits to doing one's "own research", especially when it comes to taking the time and effort needed to get to the bottom of what is going on, not that I don't value those who do, who I often see as the true heroes, especially when they speak truth to power despite it costing them when they do so (and more are waking up to the fact they "have been had"). Thinking of the day when certain earnest Christians used to wear "WWJD" (What Would Jesus Do) wristbands, I concur that especially in the light of the above, and given the limitations of what ordinary folk (including most of my readership) can do to make a significant dent in our current craziness, this is an important, maybe the most important, question to respond to. Without being over-simplistic and noting that I cringe when pious platitudes are banded around, let me make an attempt, speaking to myself before preaching to others. Besides the Two Great Commandments to do with loving God and loving our neighbour, there are four things it has taken me to getting into my dotage to making as my top priorities: humility, kindness, faithfulness and godliness. Then there are (and please excuse me) some rhyming couplets I sometimes add at the end when I write serious stuff: "Watch and Pray", "Test and Weigh" and "Trust and Obey". I end with a salutation I find myself using a lot these days – "Shalom".

Chapter 48: Genesis – The Seedbed of the Bible

In this book, "**Priests of the Bible**", the focus, as far as the Old Testament (we have to add the 400-year Inter Testament period too), and in particular the nation of Israel, is concerned, has been on the 2000 years following the Call of Abraham, when one or other office: prophet, priest or king, dominated, with priests of YHWH continuing to operate up to New Testament times, at least up to the destruction of the Temple in AD 70. It begs the question concerning the first 2000 years, covered by the first eleven chapters of the Book of Genesis (according to Bishop Ussher, planet earth began on October 23, 4004 BC, when God created "*the heavens and the earth*" (Genesis 1:1)).

The Book of Genesis, especially the first eleven chapters, can be rightly looked upon as the seedbed of what is to follow, and a true understanding of what the Bible teaches, right up to the end of the Book of Revelation, starts with a consideration of these chapters, albeit the ones in the Bible most argued over. The age of the earth, the details of creation, including how these fit in with notions of evolution, and the Flood narrative, to name but three, all have proved to be controversial and much debated subjects, where many have tried to allegorise or label as myth what we find in these chapters. It is not my intention to continue that debate in these pages, which I acknowledge is a huge subject, but my own position is: if God said it (and I have no doubt that Genesis was divinely inspired) then it is not for me to put my own interpretation on what is written, especially given that there is much I do not know.

Most of our thoughts regarding priests arise from long after God called Abraham (Genesis 12) to be the Father of a great nation, and especially 500 years later, after Moses led Israel out of Egypt, through the Wilderness, but died before Israel took possession of the Promised Land under Joshua. Israel remains God's specially chosen nation, which will play an important part in the unravelling events and, while there is much to interest Gentile believers, the main focus of the Old Testament is on Israel. Even in the New Testament, Israel still has an important place but here the main focus turns to the Gentiles who, along with the Jews, share the blessings God intended right from the time he created our planet and He said: "*Let us make man in our image, after our likeness*" Genesis 1:26.

As far as this book goes, besides the exceptional case of Melchizedek (starting with Abraham's encounter with him), discussed at length elsewhere, the priests that are of most interest are those who came into being after Moses received the Law and Covenant from God on Mount Sinai and continued until the destruction of the Second Temple in AD 70, when they abruptly ceased to operate, yet noting, following the "Fall", there have always been priests, including those of gods other than the true God, those who nowadays do exercise priestly functions (some given that title and others not) and the priesthood of believers that we are invited to join, with Jesus being our Great High Priest.

I count myself fortunate that from an early age (even going back to when I was a junior in Sunday School) I was encouraged to study the Bible for myself and from then on that is what I did. In the years that followed, I read the Bible through several times, notably the Book of Genesis. In 2022, I led a series of Bible studies at my church on Genesis, and did so viewing the Book through the lens of seven of its main characters. Slides of the seven 45 minutes studies can be accessed from my website:

1. Part 1: Adam (Chapters 1-3) – the creation story and man's fall.

2. Part 2: Enoch (Chapters 4-6) – from Abel to Methuselah.

3. Part 3: Noah (Chapters 6-11) – from the Great Flood to the Tower of Babel.

4. Part 4: Abraham (Chapters 11-24) – God calls a man to found a great nation.

5. Part 5: Isaac (Chapters 24-27) – God keeps His promises.

6. Part 6: Jacob (Chapters 27-37) – God's unlikely choice.

7. Part 7: Joseph (Chapters 37-50) – God calls a man to preserve His chosen people.

While it would be profitable to discuss the second half of Genesis (Chapters 12-50), the focus as far as this chapter is concerned is on Genesis 1-11. Much that is pertinent to Priests of the Bible concerning Genesis 12-50 has been covered elsewhere in this book and, rightly so, because it is necessary to our understanding of priests. Regarding those first eleven chapters of Genesis, that are not to do with Israel *per se*, these are important because they tell us the origins of much that we now see as significant, e.g., the universe, earth, life, man, sex, sin, death, decay, redemption, marriage, culture, music, nations, war and much else that is pertinent to the days in which we live. While I am not a strict creationist, I am leaning to that position as it best tackles the issue of origins. I note in studying recent church history and the rise of the cult of doubt, these are the chapters that come under most attack.

The one important origin we are not told about, however, is that of God, for "*In the beginning God*" Genesis 1:1a. The most significant origin outside these early chapters concerns Israel, where we read: "*Now the Lord had said unto Abram, Get thee out of thy country, and from thy kindred, and from thy father's house, unto a land that I will shew thee: And I will make of thee a great nation, and I will bless thee, and make thy name great; and thou shalt be a blessing: And I will bless them that bless thee, and curse him that curseth thee: and in thee shall all families of the earth be blessed"* Genesis 12:1-3.

Concerning three of the 'hot' topics of our present age, these early chapters, notably the first two, provide helpful guidance on how we ought to respond to the secular rationale we are continually being subjected to, noting that what followed in Chapter 3 was the account of the Fall of Man:

1. **Sexual Orientation (and marriage):** *"And Adam said, this is now bone of my bones, and flesh of my flesh: she shall be called Woman, because she was taken out of Man. Therefore shall a man leave his father and his mother, and shall cleave unto his wife: and they shall be one flesh. And they were both naked, the man and his wife, and were not ashamed"* (2:23-25).

2. **Sexual Identity (two genders):** *"And God said, let us make man in our image, after our likeness: and let them have dominion over the fish of the sea, and over the fowl of the air, and over the cattle, and over all the earth, and over every creeping thing that creepeth upon the earth. So God created man in his own image, in the image of God created he him; male and female created he them"* (1:26-27).

3. **The Environment:** *"And God blessed them, and God said unto them, be fruitful, and multiply, and replenish the earth, and subdue it: and have dominion over the fish of the sea, and over the fowl of the air, and over every living thing that moveth upon the earth"* (1:28).

When it comes to the environment and the narrative we see being promoted by (in my view) the bad people who appear to be in control of the affairs of men, this is being done in order to instil fear in the masses, that there is a climate emergency that if not dealt with could result in the planet being destroyed. In order to address this, drastic measures are needed that involve people giving up their freedoms and giving more power to this evil cabal. These early chapters of Genesis provide answers to this, as they do to the Babylonian system this cabal is part of, including the story of the Tower of Babel in Genesis 11, which God destroyed along with scattering the people. When Noah's flood ended, God gave a promise that has not been rescinded: *"While the earth remaineth, seedtime and harvest, and cold and heat, and summer and winter, and day and night shall not cease"* Genesis 8:22.

Of particular significance, including how it impacts on priests and the priesthood, is that in these early chapters we gain important insights into the war going on between God and His angels and Satan and his angels, a war that continues right up to the time Jesus comes back to Earth. It is well to be mindful of Satan's devices and also his end: "*And the great dragon was cast out, that old serpent, called the Devil, and Satan, which deceiveth the whole world: he was cast out into the earth, and his angels were cast out with him*" Revelation 12:9, "*And he laid hold on the dragon, that old serpent, which is the Devil, and Satan, and bound him a thousand years*" Revelation 20:2 and "*And the devil that deceived them was cast into the lake of fire and brimstone, where the beast and the false prophet are, and shall be tormented day and night for ever and ever*" Revelation 20:10.

Three significant incidents are recorded in these first eleven chapters that relate to the ongoing conflict between God and Satan, good and evil, darkness and light. The first is seen in Chapter 3 in the temptation of Adam and Eve by the serpent in the Garden of Eden, to eat the forbidden fruit, which they yielded to, ending with their expulsion from the garden and the gulf that would necessitate priests and mediation. Secondly, there is the sexual liaison between heavenly beings and women in Chapter 6, giving rise to the Nephilim, which is pertinent to today's transhuman/transgender ideology, and was a key factor in God bringing about a worldwide flood. Thirdly, we see the building of the Tower of Babel in Chapter 11, where man set himself up in defiance of God, which can be seen as a precursor to the Babylonian system that is running human affairs today. God's purposes have ever been (since the Fall) to redeem humanity, with priests and the priesthood being an important part of that plan.

We must recall God's word to the serpent: "*And I will put enmity between thee and the woman, and between thy seed and her seed; it shall bruise thy head, and thou shalt bruise his heel*" Genesis 3:15. It is worth reflecting too that there has always been a godly line, which continued through Seth, born after Adam's righteous son, Abel, was slain by his brother, Cain: "*And to Seth, to him also there was born a son; and he called his name Enos: then began men to call upon the name of the Lord*" Genesis 4:26, and continued through until Abraham, through the line of Shem (one of Noah's three sons). Moreover, it was Jesus, a descendant of Abraham, who was the one that bruised Satan's head.

In ending this chapter and hammering home why an understanding of these early chapters of Genesis is worth having, we might do well to consider the "**Mystery of Babylon**", and its subsequent fall, which is prophesied in Revelation 17 and 18 (and that picks up on texts such as Isaiah 47:8-11 and Jeremiah 50). We read, for example: "*And he cried mightily with a strong voice, saying, Babylon the great is fallen, is fallen, and is become the habitation of devils, and the hold of every foul spirit, and a cage of every unclean and hateful bird. For all nations have drunk of the wine of the wrath of her fornication, and the kings of the earth have committed fornication with her,* *and the merchants of the earth are waxed rich through the abundance of her delicacies"* Revelation 18:2-3.

Babylon represents a long line of pseudo-spiritual, socio-economic entities, opposed to the true God and His people, yet wielding power and influence, going back to Nimrod, the Tower of Babel and Babylon, and relates to the system that controls human affairs that is aligned to Satan himself. I considered some of this in my **"Prophets of the Bible"** book and also "Chapter 47: *Bible Prophecy and Current Events*". My point is not to distract from our main subject by engaging in wild speculation but to challenge readers by writing as I do that we need to be awake to the world as it is and respond in appropriate ways, including taking seriously such warnings as: *"Come out of her (Babylon), my people, lest you share in her sins, and lest you receive of her plagues"* Revelation 18:4.

As for Genesis, the first of the five Books of Moses (Torah, Pentateuch), if I were to stick my neck out, it will come at the top of my list, after the Gospels, of books of the Bible a new Christian should read. Among other things, such as what it tells us about the origins of much that matters, including the conflict between God and that which opposes Him, it introduces the Abrahamic Covenant, an understanding of which is needed in order to understand the other four books of Moses, some of which can be admittedly heavy going and provides the right setting for our study of Priests. But more than that, it introduces us to God's great plan of salvation, which is right up there among the key messages of the Bible, which can be seen when we consider the Priests of the Bible and the Bible itself. Finally, in a world where lies like transgenderism, homosexuality and climate change are being pushed, which people are being pressurised to accept, the counter is understanding our origins as set out in the Book of Genesis, especially the first eleven chapters, the very ones many dismiss or rationalise.

Chapter 49: Leviticus – An Unlikely Bible Favourite

There was a preacher named David Pawson, who was well respected by many as an excellent Bible teacher, who I often refer to, and when asked what his favourite book of the Bible was, answered that it was the book he was studying at the time. I confess to being a little naughty for, if asked, I might be tempted to say it is Leviticus, knowing for some it is their least favourite (and read), yet given it is so relevant to the central themes of this book about priests of the Bible, and happily make it my current favourite. In preparing this chapter I am spoilt for choice when it comes to actual content. I found a number of commentators point out that those keen to study the Bible, starting from the beginning, give up when they get to Leviticus. Pawson, whose videos on Leviticus have also provided an important source for this chapter, has suggested three reasons why many struggle when it comes to Leviticus:

1. **Boring** – there are hardly any stories in it, and that is why someone embarking on reading the Bible from cover to cover may well come unstuck when they get to Leviticus.

2. **Unfamiliar** – Leviticus applies to a culture whose norms are a lot different from that of twenty first century Gentiles, and some of the rules laid down appear baffling and not applicable.

3. **Irrelevant** – as it is to do with the Law of Moses which supposedly doesn't apply to Christians who are not beholden to keep the non-moral aspects of the Law.

Another commentator has listed the following themes as to why Leviticus is relevant and merits study:

1. **Holiness of God** – interestingly the word "holy" is used over 70 times in this Book, more than in any other Book of the Bible. Holiness is a key, maybe the most important theme in the whole Bible, and one we do well to follow. After all, we are told: *"Follow peace with all men, and holiness, without which no man shall see the Lord"* Hebrews 12:14.

2. **Sinfulness of man** – while the Book is about not polluting clean things and profaning holy things, it recognises the sinfulness of man, while telling man how he can relate to God.

3. **Fullness of Christ** – the Book points to Christ and His once and for all sacrifice for mankind.

4. **Godliness of life** – this Book is concerned about every aspect of our

life and while a lot of the content may not apply to us today, many of its principles do and we do well to apply them.

The point of this chapter is NOT to provide an in-depth exposition of the contents of the Book of Leviticus, which would merit a whole book, but rather to place on record why this Book is important as it helps to provide us with a better understanding of the subject of Priests of the Bible.

By the time we get to Leviticus in our journey through the Bible, we will have already picked up a lot regarding Priests, which has helped inform Part 2 and especially Part 1 of this book, for example:

- The Law
- The Covenant
- The Aaronic Priesthood
- The Levites
- The Tabernacle
- Israel

But there is more and that is why a study of Leviticus matters. Of the five books of Moses, Genesis is particularly significant for reasons discussed already. After Leviticus, a case could be made for highlighting Exodus (that precedes it) and Numbers and Deuteronomy (that follow it). The best we can do here is discuss Leviticus because it impacts on each one of these and point out that in our earlier discussions on priests, these are all referred to. There is no one prescribed way to break down Leviticus, but what follows is one way and is offered because it reflects a beautiful symmetry, and right at the centre of this is the Day of Atonement pointing to Christ who is both Priest and Sacrifice. While there is a lot in Leviticus that may seem boring, unfamiliar and irrelevant, is should be anything but.

PART 1: JUSTIFICATION – the Way to God (Chapters 1-15)

Offerings and Sacrifices (Chapters 1-7)
- The Burnt Offering (Chapter 1).
- The Grain Offering (Chapter 2).
- The Fellowship Offering (Chapter 3).
- The Sin Offering (4:1-5:13).

- The Guilt Offering (5:14-6:7).
- Additional Regulations for the Offerings (6:8-7:38).

Priesthood (Chapters 8-10)

- The Ordination of Aaron and His Sons (Chapter 8).
- The Ministry of the Priests (Chapter 9).
- The Death of Nadab and Abihu and Attendant Regulations (Chapter 10).

Unclean and Clean (Chapters 11-15)

- Clean and Unclean Food (Chapter 11).
- Purification After Childbirth (Chapter 12).
- Regulations for Skin Diseases (13:1-46).
- Regulations for Mildew (13:47-59).
- Cleansing from Skin Diseases (14:1-32).
- Cleansing from Mildew (14:33-57).
- Discharges That Cause Uncleanness (Chapter 15).

DAY OF ATONEMENT (Chapter 16)

PART 2: SANCTIFICATION – Walk with God (Chapters 17-27)

Common and Holy (Chapters 17-22)

- Eating Blood Prohibited (Chapter 17).
- Unlawful Sexual Relations (Chapter 18).
- Various Laws for Holy Living (Chapter 19).
- Punishments for Sin (Chapter 20).
- Regulations for Priests (21:1-22:16).
- Acceptable and Unacceptable Sacrifices (22:17-33).

Worship (Chapters 23-25)

- The Annual Feasts (Chapter 23).

- Rules for Oil and Bread in the Tabernacle (24:1-9).
- Punishment for Blasphemy (24:10-23).
- The Sabbath and Jubilee Years (Chapter 25).

Sanctions and Vows (Chapters 26-27)

- Covenant Blessings and Curses (Chapter 26).
- Regulations for Offerings Vowed to the Lord (Chapter 27)

Leviticus is, as we have indicated, the third of the five books of Moses (Torah, Pentateuch), where God spoke to Moses (90% of Leviticus is about God speaking) over a one-month period while Israel was camped around Mount Sinai and, unlike most of the rest of the Old Testament, it focuses on one Tribe – the **LEVI**tes. It is interesting to note though that the Levites, as opposed to the Priests, are not much mentioned in the Book of Leviticus, although they are in Numbers, the next book in the Pentateuch.

The Book of Exodus ends with the words: "*Then a cloud covered the tent of the congregation, and the glory of the Lord filled the tabernacle. And Moses was not able to enter into the tent of the congregation, because the cloud abode thereon, and the glory of the Lord filled the tabernacle. And when the cloud was taken up from over the tabernacle, the children of Israel went onward in all their journeys: But if the cloud were not taken up, then they journeyed not till the day that it was taken up. For the cloud of the Lord was upon the tabernacle by day, and fire was on it by night, in the sight of all the house of Israel, throughout all their journeys*" Exodus 40:34-38.

The Book of Leviticus, recounting happenings no more than a month later, begins with the words: "*And the Lord called unto Moses, and spake unto him out of the tabernacle of the congregation, saying, Speak unto the children of Israel, and say unto them, If any man of you bring an offering unto the Lord, ye shall bring your offering of the cattle, even of the herd, and of the flock*" Leviticus 1:1-2.

We end Exodus with the glory of the Lord filling the Tabernacle such that no-one could enter. This is in contrast to the Lord speaking from the Tabernacle at the start of Leviticus, laying down the rules whereby priests were able to function, specifically through the prescribed sacrifices and offerings, but nevertheless an invitation to enter was first needed. Restrictions included only the Priests being able to enter the Holy Place and only the High Priest, and then only on one day in the year, the Day of Atonement, being able to enter the Most Holy Place (or Holy of Holies).

Much that is significant concerning the Tabernacle is discussed in Chapters 5 and 6, but it is no overstatement to say the Tabernacle, its detailed construction, its contents, and what took place inside it was the central feature of Israelite life. It represented something that God had always intended for His creation when placing Adam and Eve in the Garden of Eden, only to expel them due to their sin, which was to dwell in their midst. It is significant that when we reflect on the layout of the Camp, right at the centre was the Tabernacle, with Moses, Aaron and the Levites forming around it an inner circle and the remaining tribes of Israel an outer circle. Right at the centre of the Camp was the Tabernacle, and inside the Tabernacle were the Holy Place and the Holy of Holies. Inside that was the Ark of the Covenant and the Mercy Seat, which in a sense was where God resided, and was so important in the life of Israel between the Exodus and the Exile, which is discussed in Chapter 44.

If there is one verse that encapsulates what the Book of Leviticus is all about, it is the imperative that the people of God be holy: *"And ye shall be holy unto me: for I the Lord am holy, and have severed you from other people, that ye should be mine"* (20:26). While the distinction made in Leviticus between common and holy, clean and unclean, may be hard for the modern mind to fathom, it was necessary for the nation that was to be God's special people that they be set apart (which is the meaning of holiness) from other nations and these baffling rules would reinforce what was required. As far as the subject of Priests goes, Leviticus 21 to 22 is particularly relevant as it considers several rules that apply only to priests that needed to be followed when exercising the priestly office, often to do with holiness.

If we needed a solemn reminder of the consequences of approaching God in an inappropriate way then what happened to Nadab and Abihu, the sons of Aaron, illustrates what happens. They *"took either of them his censer, and put fire therein, and put incense thereon, and offered strange fire before the Lord, which he commanded them not. And there went out fire from the Lord, and devoured them, and they died before the Lord. Then Moses said unto Aaron, This is it that the Lord spake, saying, I will be sanctified in them that come nigh me, and before all the people I will be glorified. And Aaron held his peace"* (10:1-3). This incident occurred not long after the priests were ordained for the first time (Leviticus 8-9) making it so much more poignant. It is worth noting the higher standards that priests were required to adhere to, for example those who weren't priests could mourn, but not Aaron.

If there is one important image that reflects the Gospel message it is the Scapegoat that was released into the wilderness on the Day of Atonement by the High Priest after carrying out his other duties. He had earlier drawn lots concerning two goats and the other goat was offered as an atoning sacrifice. "*And Aaron shall lay both his hands upon the head of the live goat, and confess over him all the iniquities of the children of Israel, and all their transgressions in all their sins, putting them upon the head of the goat, and shall send him away by the hand of a fit man into the wilderness: And the goat shall bear upon him all their iniquities unto a land not inhabited: and he shall let go the goat in the wilderness* (16:21,22). This beautifully helps us to look forward to the coming of Jesus who died outside the city in order to atone for our sins. Jesus is the example we are exhorted to follow (the Scapegoat that was sent out into the wilderness is representative of Him).

When it comes to offerings and sacrifices and feasts and a whole set of practices centred around Tabernacle worship and the part played by priests there is much that can be said and constructively applied which is still significant for our times. Given the importance of Tabernacle worship and so much more that could be profitably said on the subject, it is why those details are covered elsewhere. Several subjects raised in Leviticus are covered in detail in a number of chapters in Part 1 of this book. If there is a teaching in Leviticus that is of practical significance for our own times it is concerning that of holiness because if we ignore that it is unlikely God will take us seriously. Even on subjects, seemingly irrelevant to the modern mind: Unclean and Clean (Chapters 11-15) and Common and Holy (Chapters 17-22), it was as much to do with concerns for holiness as for the Covenant blessings and curses (Chapter 26), that would be elaborated in the later chapters of Deuteronomy, holiness is a key theme.

Something that touches a chord in today's culture where indigenous ethnic populations are having to come to terms with the infiltration of foreigners, often as a result of war and socio-economic pressures that are being increasingly seen (for better and also arguably for worse), is the treatment of the foreigner: "*And if a stranger sojourn with thee in your land, ye shall not vex him. But the stranger that dwelleth with you shall be unto you as one born among you, and thou shalt love him as thyself; for ye were strangers in the land of Egypt: I am the Lord your God*" (19:33-34) and "*when ye reap the harvest of your land, thou shalt not wholly reap the corners of thy field, neither shalt thou gather the gleanings of thy harvest. And thou shalt not glean thy vineyard, neither shalt thou gather every grape of thy vineyard; thou shalt leave them for the poor and stranger: I am the Lord your God Leviticus*" 19:9-10. But what should not be missed in what has been a contentious and emotive issue in our own times, when it comes to letting foreigners into one's country, is that foreigners need also to respect the customs and obey the laws of that country: "*Ye shall have one manner of law, as well for the stranger, as for one of your own country: for I am the Lord your God*" Leviticus 24:22.

Back to this book, "**Priests of the Bible**", Leviticus provides the setting in which priests operated, who were to play a pivotal role, seeking to connect the chosen people of YHWH with YHWH Himself and His perfect will, and at the heart of this is the Day of Atonement, whereby sinful man would be able to relate to a holy God. This is not just a central feature of Leviticus but it is that of the whole Bible and, because it is the theme that Leviticus is constantly hammering home, it is a book worth studying.

Chapter 50: Chronicles – A Book Worth Studying

1 and 2 Chronicles in the Christian Bible and Chronicles in the Hebrew Bible (here it is treating it as one book), are often neglected compared with other books of the Bible and competes with the Book of Leviticus as books that are not read by even those who claim that understanding the Bible is something they deem to be important. But like Leviticus, Chronicles is especially relevant to our study of priests, and for several of our named priests it is the main source of information about their lives and work.

Differences between Samuel / Kings and Chronicles

Topic	Samuel / Kings	Chronicles
Period covered	500 years	Starts earlier, finishes later
When written	Soon after events	Long after events
Historical emphasis	Political	Religious
Viewpoint	Prophet - and looking back to what went wrong	Priest - and looking forward to the promised Messiah
Kingdoms covered	Northern and Southern	Southern
Human or Divine focus	Human failings	Divine faithfulness
Virtues or vices emphasis	Royal vices	Royal virtues
Positive or negative emphasis	Negative	Positive
Moral or spiritual emphasis	Moral - righteousness	Spiritual - ritual
Likely authorship	Prophet	Priest
Notable difference	More narrative	More genealogy and religion
Which section in the Bible	History (Christian) Prophets (Hebrew)	History (Christian - after Kings) Writings (Hebrew - at the end)
How many books	Both two (Christian Bible) Both one (Hebrew Bible)	Two (Christian Bible) One (Hebrew Bible)

While Chronicles includes the same period as covered by Samuel and Kings and many of the same events, there are significant differences as this table illustrates. We need to study all of Samuel, Kings and Chronicles to get a complete picture. Moreover, there are many exceptions to what the table suggests are differences, including Chronicles talking about the bad acts of otherwise good kings and Samuel/Kings talking about the good acts of otherwise bad kings, and where Chronicles discusses prophets and their acts that are not mentioned in Samuel/Kings, while Samuel/Kings discusses priests and their acts that are not mentioned in Chronicles. We do well if we study all three in tandem!

Given 1 and 2 Chronicles follows after 2 Kings in the Christian Bible and might appear to be a cut down version with some less interesting items added in to what can be found in the Books of Samuel and Kings and some of the more interesting ones left out, there is a temptation to ignore it. I suspect even among Bible savvy Christians, with the exception of verses like "*If my people, which are called by my name, shall humble themselves, and pray, and seek my face, and turn from their wicked ways; then will I hear from heaven, and will forgive their sin, and will heal their land*" 2 Chronicles 7:14, many would be hard pressed when it comes to even being able to quote from Chronicles. Barriers may be erected from the outset, since the first eight chapters are devoted to a never ending, so it seems, list of genealogies, and this is a feature seen throughout the Book. Even when we do come to narrative, there is a pre-occupation with religious ritual and temple worship, with many Christians not much interested in such matters, and if seeing in Jesus the embodiment of the Temple, might choose to ignore. Genealogy and religious ritual matter as God includes it in His book, and there is much else to ponder.

I would argue any dismissiveness is mistaken and could cause us to miss out. Chronicles is different from Kings for several reasons as indicated above, but rather than merely repeat, it complements it. It is notable that its position in the Hebrew Bible differs from that in the Christian Bible. While the Christian Bible has Kings and Chronicles next to each other in the section referred to as History, in the Hebrew Bible, Kings is included in the Prophets section, specifically Former Prophets as opposed to Later Prophets, which in the Christian Bible cover just those referred to as major and minor prophets.

Chronicles comes at the end of the Hebrew Bible, in a section known as the Writings, covering the whole period of Jewish history, starting from Adam and ending with the return from Exile. If there is a rationale behind writing the Book, it could be to inform Jews, especially those who returned from exile to their land, concerning where they were now at as a people, how they got there and where they are and could be heading as the people of God. Chronicles begins: "*Adam, Sheth, Enosh*" 1 Chronicles 1:1. At the end of the Book (2 Chronicles 36) we read of the end of Israel, or rather Judah, as a nation that is ruled by its own kings and with the ability to govern itself, as they are taken into captivity in Babylon.

Pertinent to our main theme (Priests) is what happened to the Temple. We read: "*And all the vessels of the house of God, great and small, and the treasures of the house of the Lord, and the treasures of the king, and of his princes; all these he brought to Babylon. And they burnt the house of God, and brake down the wall of Jerusalem, and burnt all the palaces thereof with fire, and destroyed all the goodly vessels thereof*" (36:18-19). Yet that is not the end, for at the very end of the Book we read a message of hope, following 70 years of captivity in Babylon (one that would be fully realised in Jesus, their promised Messiah); we read of Cyrus' decree that allowed them back into their land.

Given Chronicles was written centuries after Samuel and Kings, the content of which would have been well known to the readership and referred to by the author, possibly the priest, Ezra, one might ask what the intention was behind this writing. To understand this better, we should put ourselves in the shoes of the Jewish readership. They had returned from Exile to the Promised Land, it is true. But things were far from what might have been expected, as seen when reading through the books that cover the period following the Exile: Ezra, Nehemiah, Haggai, Zechariah and Malachi.

They were looking for the awaited descendant of David to come as Israel's Messiah, and to restore the land to its former glories and better, as had been prophesied. The Temple, that David was so involved in, even though he was not allowed to build it, represented the Messianic hope that God would dwell among His people and all the promises made, going back to Abraham, would be fulfilled. The lineage of David and the importance of Temple worship were two themes emphasised in Chronicles but not in Kings. The various offices of the priests, including the various activities of gatekeepers and musicians and the use of lots to decide who were to be on duty and when are among its outstanding features.

In my studies of Chronicles, I was blown away by gems that could so easily have been missed. In going through the first eight genealogy chapters, for example, I found these two nuggets: "*And Jabez was more honourable than his brethren: and his mother called his name Jabez, saying, Because I bare him with sorrow. And Jabez called on the God of Israel, saying, Oh that thou wouldest bless me indeed, and enlarge my coast, and that thine hand might be with me, and that thou wouldest keep me from evil, that it may not grieve me! And God granted him that which he requested*" 1 Chronicles 4:9-10. And "*The sons of Reuben, and the Gadites, and half the tribe of Manasseh, of valiant men, men able to bear buckler and sword, and to shoot with bow, and skilful in war, were four and forty thousand seven hundred and threescore, that went out to the war. And they made war with the Hagarites, with Jetur, and Nephish, and Nodab. And they were helped against them, and the Hagarites were delivered into their hand, and all that were with them: for they cried to God in the battle, and he was intreated of them; because they put their trust in him*" 1 Chronicles 5:18-20. It is easy for today's people of God to forget that the One they purport to serve is interested in what they do and is desirous to act for them.

While on the subject of genealogies, with the line of David as the most important, many other lines are listed in Chronicles, which if they weren't there we could easily overlook. Even while tempted to skip such passages, we cannot fail to be impressed at the detail of what is covered. We note other family lines, also encountered in our Old Testament journey, are provided, showing the readers that as far as God was concerned such families were important. In God's eyes families have always mattered.

As we have already noted, Chronicles is placed right at the very end of the Hebrew Scriptures, and for a good reason. It was written primarily to encourage the Jewish people, notably those returning from Exile. While they were God's specially chosen people, a "rooted, royal and religious" people, their situation upon return was often not a particularly happy one. While they, or at least the small remnant who had returned from exile by God's hand, were God's people, they were subject to a foreign power. From thenceforth this was the conundrum they had to deal with but in Chronicles they can find hope.

While the Persians were benevolent, the Greeks and Romans who took over were not and things were a far cry from what ought to have been (see Chapter 16). Moreover, when it came to zeal for God, their response was often topsy-turvy, with the last book of the Old Testament, Malachi, indicating that in many ways they had lost the plot and with God's call, "*Bring ye all the tithes into the storehouse, that there may be meat in mine house, and prove me now herewith, saith the Lord of hosts, if I will not open you the windows of heaven, and pour you out a blessing, that there shall not be room enough to receive it*" Malachi 3:10, there was a sense that Malachi's words had largely fallen on deaf ears.

The beautiful thing that comes from reading the Bible, is that it tells us what happened without being over preachy. This is true in the case of Chronicles. In the final chapter, we read about the final days of Judah under its kings, and it is sad reading, e.g.: "*Moreover all the chief of the priests, and the people, transgressed very much after all the abominations of the heathen; and polluted the house of the Lord which he had hallowed in Jerusalem*" 2 Chronicles 36:14. It says little regarding the 70 year exile but it concludes at the end of that exile: "*Thus saith Cyrus king of Persia, All the kingdoms of the earth hath the Lord God of heaven given me; and he hath charged me to build him an house in Jerusalem, which is in Judah. Who is there among you of all his people? The Lord his God be with him, and let him go up*" 2 Chronicles 36:23. The point to make again is that Chronicles ends on a message of hope and, given the priestly input and emphasis, it is centred around the Temple. How that turned out depended on God's sovereignty and how the people of God responded, but at least the Chronicler had done his job.

In the 400 year period between the Old and New Testaments, when their

Messiah did come, the story of Israel and how they came to be in the position they found themselves in, highlighted many concerns. They were having to live under foreign tyranny with the hopes raised under Abraham, Moses and David being a distant memory. But their history and how they were meant to live needed to be recalled and celebrated, along with the hope that the long-expected Messiah from the line of David would set up His everlasting Kingdom of righteousness, peace and justice. This is something the Book of Chronicles sets out to do. While Israel, the physical descendants of Abraham, needed to be reminded of these things, so do his spiritual descendants today (the Church) and why studying this book matters. We need to be thankful we have the Book of Chronicles to help remind us of these important truths.

The following is a suggested breakdown of the content of the Book of Chronicles:

Genealogies: Creation to Restoration (1 Chronicles 1-9)

• The Patriarchs (Chapter 1).

• The 12 Sons of Jacob/Israel (2:1-2).

• The Family of Judah (2:3-4:23).

• The Sons of Simeon (4:24-43).

• Reuben, Gad and the Half-Tribe of Manasseh (Chapter 5).

• Levi and Families (Chapter 6).

• Issachar, Benjamin, Naphtali, Manasseh, Ephraim and Asher (Chapters 7-9).

The Reign of David (1 Chronicles 10-29)

• Death of Saul (Chapter 10).

• Capture of Jerusalem; David's Power Base (Chapters 11-12).

• Return of the Ark; Establishment of David's Kingdom (Chapters 13-16).

• Dynastic Promise (Chapter 17).

• David's Conquests (Chapter 18-20).

• The Census (Chapter 21).

• Preparations for the Temple (Chapter 22).

• Organization of the Temple Service (Chapters 23-26).

- Administrative Structures of the Kingdom (Chapter 27).
- David's Final Preparations for Succession and the Temple (28:1-29:20).
- Succession of Solomon; Death of David (29:21-30).

The Reign of Solomon (2 Chronicles 1-9)
- The Gift of Wisdom (Chapter 1).
- Building the Temple (2:1-5:1).
- Dedication of the Temple (5:2-7:22).
- Solomon's Other Activities (Chapter 8).
- Solomon's Wisdom, Splendour and Death (Chapter 9).

The Schism, and the History of the Kings of Judah (2 Chronicles 10-36)
- Rehoboam (Chapters 10-12).
- Abijah (13:1-14:1).
- Asa (14:2-16:14).
- Jehoshaphat (17:1-21:3).
- Jehoram and Ahaziah (21:4-22:9).
- Joash (22:10-24:27).
- Amaziah (Chapter 25).
- Uzziah (Chapter 26).
- Jotham (Chapter 27).
- Ahaz (Chapter 28).
- Hezekiah (Chapters 29-32).
- Manasseh (33:1-20).
- Amon (33:21-25)
- Josiah (34:1-36:1).
- Josiah's Successors (36:2-14).
- Exile and Restoration (36:15-23).

Chapter 51: "Prophets of the Bible" and "Kings of the Bible"

"Prophets of the Bible" re-visited

The first edition of "Prophets of the Bible" was released in September 2020. I saw it as my "Corona Lockdown project" and it was the culmination of a lifetime reflecting on the subject and listening to preachers who had something to say, not just when it comes to reflecting on End Time events but what the prophets experienced and spoke concerning the times in which they were living. My assignment was to address the subject given by the title on the cover of the book – **"Prophets of the Bible and their prophecies... understanding God's ways"** and to consider not just every named prophet but the unnamed ones too and those who may only be seen as prophetic voices. My intention was to reflect on the life, work and legacy of the Prophets of the Bible (well-known, little-known, unknown and unrecognised), discussing the context and background in which these prophets operated and, while sometimes only able to scratch the surface, consider the content and significance of their prophecies.

The book was aimed at ordinary Bible readers, supporting them in their endeavours to understand the Scriptures, especially the prophetic ones. My main source was the Bible itself but there is much to consider that has been written on the subject, and a lot available on the Internet. I tried to check out what I found particularly helpful. It was a big challenge because so many Bible characters fitted the bill and so much of the Bible is prophecy. I was also mindful there are some that place too much store on prophecy, especially that which has not yet been fulfilled (which I argue covers many, but since a lot more has been fulfilled, often remarkably, we can be left in little doubt the rest will be in due course), and then there are those, maybe the majority, that place too little store on prophecy and this omission gives them a distorted view of what the Bible teaches. Then there is the conundrum I began to address that faces the church generally – that of ignoring the prophetic voice, and doing so to its detriment. Just as God is looking to raise up a priestly people who will reign on the earth, I believe He is also wanting to raise up a prophetic people, a people that respond to Jesus' call to watch and pray.

The second edition allowed me a second bite of the proverbial cherry. The changes I made were substantial and the size of the book grew by a third. It meant I could correct typos and other errors, improve presentation and include stuff I thought would be helpful, omitted first time round, and I added four new chapters, including on major Bible doctrines and characters, and some additional appendices. The main addition, however, and one that might be considered controversial since it went beyond pure exegesis, which is my favoured approach to Bible teaching, is that I sought to relate current events, Bible prophecy and modern-day prophecy, which I had already been doing as a blogger, and the results of which can be found on my website. This was completed in April 2021. Even then, I was not satisfied that I had written all that I ought to write on the subject and, while continuing to see huge changes taking place in the world and the church, come December 2021, I added one more chapter, in which I reflected further on some of these important issues.

It is unlikely that I will produce a third edition, despite learning a lot more about the prophets (both in Bible times and today) and what they prophesied further to what I wrote. I am conscious that I may not have done my subject true justice but hope it encourages readers to delve deeper and to search the scriptures for themselves, as well as consider what is happening around them and how the people of God need to respond. As for happenings in the world, these continue at an alarming rate. It is unclear how things will turn out in the short term although we know God wins in the end, because the Bible tells us so. I would argue that much of what we are now seeing ties in with Bible prophecy. Because of how significant these events are or should be to a priestly people, I decided to share my thoughts on what I see to be happening that is particularly significant, in the light of Bible prophecy, in Chapter 47.

A lot of the detail of what I want to say by way of ending this section is in Chapter 47, which remains very much work in progress given how rapidly we are seeing changes in world affairs that have a prophetic impact. When the seed was sown to write that book, it touched many chords, ranging from it being a significant subject that Christians I love and respect often are ignorant concerning yet needed to be informed of in order to be effective warriors in the Lord's army, given the onslaught of Satan's one, and my research, knowledge and insights were something I could bring to the proverbial party for those with ears to hear what I and those like me have to say. Not only was there the subject of Bible prophets and their prophecies, mainly to be found in the Old Testament, but there was today's situation in the light of Bible prophecy and what those, purported or acclaimed to be prophets, have to say. For all that – please read my book. One of the many ironies is that some of those who are labelled false prophets, whether or not they claim to be speaking for God, often understand better than most Christians what is going on around us and what might be the best way to respond.

These include, not just that category of "modern day prophet" I label as "a political prophet", but those demonised as conspiracy theorists, such as Alex Jones, David Icke and Charlie Ward, many of which I regularly check out as often reliable alternatives to what mainstream media has to say. Not that they are orthodox, "born again" Christians (likely they aren't) but they have an uncanny knack of identifying what is going on in the world and even predicting what will happen before it happens – and if I need an example: that which happened around the Covid plan/scam demic is one, and it got me going. In my blogs, I talk about the "Hegelian dialectic", which is about the bad guys (the people who largely run planet earth) creating a problem (whether Covid, climate change, racism, LGBT inclusion), get good people worked up as a result and come up with a solution (that furthers their nefarious agenda), which they had in mind all along. The tragedy, as I see it, is that Christians around me, ranging from woke evangelicals to fundamentalists have been sucked in and choose not to get involved, as well as most of humanity, who they should be setting an example to and leading to the Lord. I say this, not to get readers bitter, twisted or judgemental, but to alert them to what God might be saying to us. Just as **"Priests of the Bible"** is written to encourage us to be *"a Priestly People"*, **"Prophets of the Bible"** was written to encourage us to be a prophetic people. The world needs true priests and true prophets.

"Kings of the Bible" anticipated

With reference to the Preface, where I stated my earlier intention to write a trilogy of books: "Prophets of the Bible", "Priests of the Bible" and "Kings of the Bible", noting that consideration of prophets, priests and kings, besides having a nice ring about it, studying them individually they complemented one another and studying them all would be a profitable exercise, that would go a long way to augment our overall understanding of the Bible, especially the Old Testament. With the completion of this book on priests, I can declare I am two thirds of the way through completing the project and all that is left is to write **"Kings of the Bible"**. I say this advisedly, as one should not assume anything, especially in the case of kings, it seems quite evident that this too is going to be a big undertaking. [**Note***: I wrote this section to do with kings, rather late in the day, before embarking on writing a "Part 4" to this book, which might be seen as a slimmed down version of* **"Kings of the Bible"**.]

The reason for this is that there are a lot more kings to cover than prophets or priests and there are so many of them (check out Chapter 2, Figure 5, which lists all the kings just of Israel and Judah). Also, a lot has been written in the Bible, just about the kings of Israel and Judah, and we find there are plenty of lessons that can be usefully learned and applied to our current situation. While researching prophets and priests, I often touched on one or other king as they happened to interact with the prophets and priests I had been writing about. Moreover, I have now taught on a number of the kings and have written down my thoughts, some of which are now available on my website. What remains is investing the time and effort to bring together new and existing material, and present it all as a coherent whole, and, when all this is done, I will have finally completed my "prophets, priests and kings" project.

I use the term king in the broadest sense, as in Bible times the title could apply to rulers of cities, nations or empires, and these continually crop up throughout the biblical account, starting, arguably, with Nimrod in Genesis 11. There is also a tricky judgment needed in determining how much influence kings had on what was going on in their sphere of influence and to what extent they were merely reflecting what was going on or were controlled by others. It was almost 1000 years before Israel had its first king (Saul) but, as we read Israel's history, we come across many kings of varying impact that ruled over cities, nations and empires living in and around Israel. Most played some part in determining Israel's future and often Israel had to overcome kings in order to possess the land God had promised them. While many kings not of Israel or Judah were not well disposed toward Israel, some were, and it makes for a fascinating study as well as finding out how God raised up and put down kings.

The challenge faced was, having found out what I could, to then determine how significant each king was and if mentioned by name whether to write about them and how much. Concerning the kings of surrounding nations, there are many to speak of, with Syria, Egypt and Philistia, and nations Israel were meant to drive out, particularly significant in the early period, as well as other near neighbours, such as Moab, Ammon and Edom. Then we see the rise of empires. The Assyrians were behind taking the northern kingdom of Israel into exile, later followed by the Babylonians taking the southern kingdom of Judah into exile. This was followed by the Persians who conquered Babylon and allowed the exiles of Judah to return to their ancestral home. Then we must not forget the two other great empires in Bible times: Greece and Rome, which were prophesied but only appeared on the scene after the end of the Old Testament period, with Rome the dominant power at the time of the New Testament.

Once again, the vast majority of material to be included in this book about kings relates to the Old Testament as there were so many more kings mentioned in the Old than the New. Besides drawing out what I hope will be helpful lessons in this study, I intend to consider the subject of kingship and its theological implications, as well as how the people of God ought to deal with the "kings" who are around today and their impact on world events. Then we must consider the Antichrist, perhaps the final and worst of the kings, as well as Jesus, who has come but is coming again, who besides being a descendant of David, Israel's greatest king, is the "King of kings", and also a prophet and a priest.

The nice thing, as far as this book **"Priests of the Bible"** is concerned, is that I don't need to say more and I could easily have said less. When I began to write this section, over six months prior to handing over for publishing, I really did not expect that I would be in a position to write what has turned out to be an entirely new part (PART 4) that is devoted to Kings of the Bible, but circumstances have conspired to make it so. Readers are encouraged to turn to Chapter 61 in order to find out more. Just as we are called to be a priestly people and a prophetic people, we are also called to be a kingly people, noting that: *"If we suffer, we shall also reign with him"* 2 Timothy 2:12, *"And hast made us unto our God kings and priests: and we shall reign on the earth"* Revelation 5:10. But always we must look to Him who is prophet, priest and king, about Whom we end with yet another Isaac Watts' hymn.

1. Join all the glorious names
Of wisdom, love, and pow'r,
That ever mortals knew,
That angels ever bore:
All are too weak to speak His worth,
To poor to set my Savior forth.

2. Great Prophet of my God,
My tongue would bless Thy name,
By Thee the joyful news
Of our salvation came,
The joyful news of sins forgiv'n,
Of hell subdued, and peace with Heav'n.

3. Jesus, my great High Priest,
Offered His blood, and died;
My guilty conscience seeks
No sacrifice beside;
His pow'rful blood did once atone,
and now it pleads before the throne.

4. Thou art my Counselor,
My Pattern, and my Guide,
And Thou my Shepherd art;
Oh, keep me near Thy side;
Nor let my feet e'er turn astray
To wander in the crooked way.

5. My dear almighty Lord,
My Conqu'ror and my King,
Thy scepter and Thy sword,
Thy reigning grace I sing:
Thine is the pow'r; behold, I sit
In willing bonds beneath Thy feet.

6. Now let my soul arise,
And tread the tempter down;
My Captain leads me forth
To conquest and a crown:
A feeble saint shall win the day,
Though death and hell obstruct the way.

7. Should all the hosts of death,
And pow'rs of hell unknown,
Put their most dreadful forms
Of rage and mischief on,
I shall be safe, for Christ displays
Superior pow'r, and guardian grace.

Chapter 52: Israel – Yesterday, Today and Tomorrow

I offer this as one of the chapters of my book that I did not plan on writing, but in the light of the Hamas attack on Israel 7th October 2023 and with the eyes of the whole world now turned onto Israel, ranging from very pro- to very anti-, along with Israel's significance both relating to this book and end times prophecy, it was a 'no brainer' for me to want to write something. Israel goes right to the heart of the subject of this book that is mainly about Jewish priests of the Bible and, even though I am revisiting some of what I wrote originally, I am doing so in the light of new knowledge and fresh insights. I want to share what I am finding, notwithstanding there are those with a greater knowledge than I possess and with greater intellect and understanding of the ways of the Almighty etc., including some who possess that all important Jewish perspective that I lack, and may see some things differently to me.

My approach was to write soon after those attacks and return to the subject later since I knew there would be plenty of "fall out", notwithstanding after going to print there will almost certainly be a lot more by way of developments! Moreover, the theological considerations around Israel are huge and Christians, even those of the mostly doctrinally sound ilk, are far from agreed. While I would rather not enter the fray (and, besides, what are my credentials anyway?) I feel I needed to do so and that meant doing a lot more research and reflection. Hopefully, if readers do not agree with all that I come up with in this chapter, we can still agree to disagree and take this as at least food for thought on some complex issues, while at the same time recognising that only the God of Israel has all the answers.

I hope readers will therefore bear with me for sharing my thoughts on what is a profound and controversial subject and, from my reading of church history alone, I have found it is one that Christian leaders have long pondered and disagreed on. There is much we don't know (which is why I needed time to reflect and research further) but this is my stake in the ground, mindful as I am that there will be those, even in my own theological stable, who will not agree with all that I am about to say.

I should begin with the caveat that there is much I have not fully made up my mind on, as much due to not being in possession of all the facts and these pertain to subjects where those who purport or appear to know what they are talking about often have opposing views and take polarised positions. Since we are talking about what is tantamount to war, the old maxim applies that truth is the first casualty of war. I have reflected elsewhere that we are not helped when media, politicians, and societal elites lie, including withholding the essential truth we need to come to a fully rounded view.

One of these subjects is as a big as any biggie – what to make out of events related to Israel today? But before I get going on Israel, which is also a major topic that is more than touched on in my book, I would point out the Priests of the Bible were also Priests of Israel according to the Covenant God made with Abraham and then the one with Moses at Mount Sinai relating to the Aaronic priesthood, which Priests of Bible considers at length. (I will further consider, at the end of this chapter, the Covenants of the Bible, including the Sinai and Davidic Covenants and especially the Abrahamic Covenant, noting both their relevance and that this too is a subject where Bible believing Christians hold different views.)

I want to reiterate that the Bible is firstly a Jewish book that is best read through a Jewish lens and with a Jewish mindset. Accepting this will have a bearing on any discussion. But first, I want to lay out a number of subjects that have given rise to controversy, particularly among earnest Christians. While most Christians I have come across do not take one or other extreme position, and such is the ignorance that is sadly all too apparent, many do not even have a view other than that which might have been told to them by their ministers, but I would like to suggest where one stands on these subjects will have a bearing on our views on Israel, and what is, will be and should be happening.

These are the subjects I have in mind. Not a definitive list to be sure but it is one that covers many subjects that I see as important and where Christians have different views, and this impacts not just on how one views Israel but also happenings in the world and church. What I want to do is define all the terms I use. I often defer to Wikipedia, despite not being a source I would normally go to for deeper theological understanding. I will also share what I find and say why I believe as I do. Besides studying the Bible on these matters, I have read what Christian scholars with different (sometimes opposing) ideas have had to say and now is the time to set out my thoughts, yet without claiming any special authority. When it comes to taking views, we may see things in terms of shades of grey rather than black and white, so defining what is meant when it comes to the use of terminology is important and often it is not the case that if you don't believe one thing you inevitably have to believe the opposite.

1. Preterism versus Futurism.
2. Cessationism versus Continuationism.
3. Supersessionism versus Dispensationalism.
4. Calvinism versus Arminianism.
5. Anti-Zionist and Anti-Semitism.

6. Reformed and not Reformed.

7. A-, Post- or Pre-Millennialism.

8. Israel and Palestine.

9. Evangelical, Liberal and Catholic.

10. Tackling (or not) "social injustice".

1. Preterism versus Futurism

When it comes to Bible prophecy, there are some that hold the view that almost all Bible prophecy was fulfilled in Bible times and, if not the case, those prophecies where there has been no literal fulfilment should not be taken literally. This is the Preterist view point. The Futurist, however, and my study of the Bible leads me to taking this position, will identify many (500 or more) not yet fully fulfilled prophecies and given that the other, about 2,000, prophecies have already been fulfilled to the letter, we can expect the same for what remains, although often prophecy, e.g., the Abomination of Desolation, touched on by Daniel, Jesus in His Olivet discourse and Paul when talking about the Antichrist that is yet to come, and that concerning Immanuel, mentioned in Isaiah 7:14, can be fulfilled partly sooner and completely later. There are a number of other examples that could also be given.

Often the crunch question is whether to interpret future events as physical or spiritual happenings. One of the consequences of taking the position we do concerns how we view what is happening to Israel today, e.g., becoming an autonomous nation with Jews living in their historic homeland and concerning a wonderful future that is in prospect for them under their Messiah.

2. Cessationism versus Continuationism

Cessationists believe the gifts of the Spirit (notably the sign gifts, e.g., speaking in tongues and prophecy) are not for today and these died out, and were effectively made redundant, when the canon of scripture was complete. Continuationists dispute this, believing that the gifts are for now. I am a continuationist as I find nothing in the Bible to support the cessationist position and much to back up the notion that these gifts are for today's church (even if we don't see them manifest) so they can bless others, but with a degree of scepticism, having seen too many instances of counterfeit gifts on display, which many of my "cessationist friends" are often all too quick to point out are a sham.

This is pertinent when those purporting to be prophets claim this or that concerning Israel, not directly found in the Bible. However, I believe we are all the poorer because much of the church, including the charismatics (who often focus on individuals and what is going on in their set-up rather than the bigger picture), have neglected the prophetic and have not tried to find what God is saying when it comes to what is going on and how we ought to respond. Always, we must test and weigh what is prophesied.

3. Supersessionism versus Dispensationalism

According to Wikipedia: "*Supersessionism, also called replacement theology, is a Christian theological doctrine which describes the theological conviction that the Christian Church has superseded the nation of Israel assuming their role as God's covenanted people, thus asserting that the New Covenant through Jesus Christ has superseded or replaced the Mosaic covenant exclusive to Jews*" and that "*Dispensationalism is a theological framework of interpreting the Bible which maintains that history is divided into multiple ages or "dispensations" in which God acts with his chosen people in different ways ... They believe that there is a distinction between Israel and the Church, and that Christians are not bound by Mosaic law. They maintain beliefs in premillennialism, a future restoration of national Israel, and a rapture of the Church that will happen before the Second Coming of Christ, generally seen as happening before a period of tribulation*".

My observation is that Replacement Theology has been the majority view in the church down the ages, and this began even before Augustine and, while Dispensationalism is often presented as being a more recent phenomenon, there have always been Christians who have believed there continues to be a special place for the nation of Israel in God's plan, outside the Gentile dominated church, even though there have been differences in views concerning when the Rapture of the Church is to take place. While I have rejected Supersessionism, largely because of the many Old Testament scriptures that foretell a future for a literal Israel, who are the actual descendants of Abraham, yet I cannot be an ardent dispensationalist either, although their argument that we need to distinguish the Church's heavenly calling from Israel's earthly one shouldn't be ignored, especially if seeing End Times prophecy through a Futurist lens. My reservations include: I am not convinced on the pre-tribulation rapture of the Church, after which Israel is again at the fore, and then Jesus returns, and disagree that teachings on the Gospel of the Kingdom, found in Matthew's gospel, are for Israel only but not for the Church, as well as several other scriptures being applicable to either Israel or the Church, but not to both. I should add that while I admire J.N.Darby, who has been referred to as the father of dispensationalism, for reasons other than his eschatology, I am not a fan of his disciple Schofield. I consider a number of the references that are to be found in his popular Reference Bible are biblically unsound or suspect.

4. Calvinism versus Arminianism

My first "Google hit" when I typed in "Calvinism vs Arminianism" (reasonably) gave me *"In Calvinism, God's sovereignty is emphasized to the extent that God controls all events, including the election of individuals for salvation. In Arminianism, there's a balance between God's sovereignty and human responsibility. God's sovereign will works in harmony with human free will"*. Taking sides on which is right has been a contentious factor throughout church history, giving rise to many debates. The strength of feeling on the subject along with taking a position was brought home to me when, shortly prior to writing this, three Christians in the knowledgeable and earnest category left my church, not due to personally falling out but they felt the position taken by the "Leadership" was too Calvinist.

While I see myself as a moderate Calvinist, e.g., holding the view of the "Eternal Security of Every Believer", I believe preaching the Gospel to all and sundry must be a priority and that beliefs like divine predestination and human free-will when it comes to making a response should be held in tension and are something only God can altogether resolve, although I can see the validity of arguments from either side. When it comes to Israel, they are elect of God but individually they need to respond to God's offer of salvation, made possible because of the atoning sacrifice of *Yeshua Hamashiach*.

5. Anti-Zionist and Anti-Semitism

According to Wikipedia: *"Zionism is a nationalist movement that emerged in the 19th century to enable the establishment of a homeland for the Jewish people in Palestine, a region roughly corresponding to the Land of Israel in Jewish tradition"* and *"Antisemitism is a certain perception of Jews, which may be expressed as hatred toward Jews. Rhetorical and physical manifestations of antisemitism are directed toward Jewish or non-Jewish individuals and/or their property, toward Jewish community institutions and religious facilities"*. The history of the Jews has thrown up many cases of Anti-Semitism, and we are seeing this today in the aftermath of the Hamas led attacks on Israel on 7/10 (which I will get to). Hatred of Jews, as with hatred of any ethnic group, is wrong and is something to be challenged and has been especially seen throughout history. Without wanting to be too pedantic, strictly speaking the Semites are the descendants of Shem, following the Great Flood, and include some of the Arab nations.

I reiterate, Anti-Zionism is **not** the same as Anti-Semitism, and such is today's cancel culture that those who criticise Israel often unfairly suffer for doing so (even if their views may be wrong) and are often labelled as Anti-semites, due to powerful forces pushing Zionist ideology and legitimising the oppression of non-Jews who get in the way of their plans, and these are often supported by well-meaning Christians who are sympathetic to the Zionist cause. I do not agree with many of the positions taken by Jeremy Corbyn, James Galloway, David Icke and Stephen Sizer, but all have suffered (wrongly imho) being cancelled for their "Anti-Semite" views that on closer examination are not Anti-Semite.

Also, my reading is Zionism is **not** Judaism and my suspicion is that some of the leading Zionists (where most quite frankly couldn't care less about the God of Israel), that among other things have politicians in their paid pockets and control much of the mainstream media, are behind some of wickedness going on in the world, e.g., 9/11, where those who don't go along with or seek to expose it are then accused by a powerful Zionist lobby as being Anti-Semite, with untoward consequences to follow. But always, as has been argued throughout this book, God has a special love for Israel and this includes today's Jews who are presently deceived, having turned from Him, yet Jew hatred is always unacceptable.

6. Reformed and not Reformed

According to Wikipedia, "*The Reformation was a major theological movement in Western Christianity in 16th-century Europe that posed a religious and political challenge to the papacy and the authority of the Catholic Church ... the Reformation marked the beginning of Protestantism*". Earlier, I wrote a chapter in this "Priests" book titled: "*Jesus our Great High Priest*". This is significant because among the important doctrinal emphases of the Reformation, Jesus our Great High Priest was central; His atoning sacrifice for all humanity, as a result of His dying on the Cross, means that we can approach God through Him, without the need for any other priestly intermediary.

There were many important figures of the Reformation, many unknown to most. The two that are best known are Luther and Calvin, who both held to Replacement Theology and gave indications from what they said that they were Anti-Semite. It is true that, while among the many other Reformers, some who gave their lives for upholding the very doctrines those in my theological camp nowadays take for granted, many were deficient in their thinking on Israel (although it can be argued, throughout the history of the church, no movement completely understood everything), yet their contribution in helping today's believers to have a correct understanding of God and His Word, was monumental.

7. A-, Post- or Pre-Millennialism

The prospect of a future reign of Christ on earth is a subject (at least implied) in many Bible prophecies, besides the one concerning His 1000-year

Millennial reign that we read about in Revelation 20. Sound, learned and pious Christians have long been divided over what to make out of the Millennium. I can think of many good Christians down the ages whose views differ from my own and whose modern equivalent I would want to unite with but, as to whether this matters or not, I would argue that it does because it will affect how we see and respond to what is going on in the world and how this relates to Bible prophecy. There are three main scenarios that have been put forward to explain the Millennium: A-Millennialist – believing the scriptures referring to the Millennium are not to be taken literally; Post-Millennialist – believing we are already in the Millennium or about to be, i.e., before the personal return of Christ; Pre-Millennialist – believing the Millennium will happen immediately following Christ's return to planet earth and when Israel has an important part to play, as led by their Messiah. As for "Pan-Millennialist" (all will pan out in the end), I find that position to be lazy and intellectually dishonest. My research undertaken writing my books has led me to take the Pre-Millennialist position.

8. Israel and Palestine

Also, in my research into the Prophets and the Priests of the Bible, I was able to plot some of the history of Israel, beginning with the call of Abraham, through the Exodus until the Exile and post Exile until the first century CE. While there have been Jews living in the land of Israel ever since, before the twentieth century they were relatively few in number and they shared the land with non-Jews, typically those following Islam and, to a lesser extent, Christians. Jews began returning to Israel later in the nineteenth century with the advent of Zionism. Following the Balfour declaration in 1926, and even more in the aftermath of World War 2, that migration increased. Until Israel was given independence in 1948, Israel was under foreign occupation and rule (ever since the destruction of the First Temple in 586 BC).

The land of Israel has been referred to as Palestine, beginning with the Romans (even though some who are pro-Israel detest the use of the term). As for today's "Palestinian" people, these are best referred to as mostly Arabs, often from countries that are surrounding Israel, although ever since the Exile in the sixth century BCE there have been non-Jews living in the land, including the Edomites and Samaritans, which has been discussed earlier in this book. "*The Palestinian Question*" is a complex and controversial one, which has given rise to heated exchanges and much division, even among earnest Christians, and is one I confess I do not have an entirely satisfactory answer to, other than to suggest that when God is left out of the equation, as my studies have shown, confusion often follows.

Britain conquered Palestine from the Ottomans in 1917, toward the end of World War 1. Significant, and often referred to, is "the Balfour Declaration", which according to my first "Google hit" *"was a letter written by British Foreign Secretary Arthur Balfour to Lionel Walter Rothschild, in which he expressed the British government's support for a Jewish homeland in Palestine"*. British rule in Palestine was administered under a League of Nations Mandate until Israel became a sovereign state in 1948. It was aimed to lead the native population to self-government and independence. Britain allocated nearly 80% of Palestine to Transjordan, and this included the majority of Arabs that lived there. Even so, there are claims on behalf of the Arabs living in non-Jordan Palestine prior to this that they were cruelly driven out by Zionists intent on ridding the land of those who didn't fully go along with being subject to a Jewish state. That tension remains to this day, with those, dare I say, with their particular agenda (both sides), wanting to stir up trouble. A moot point is that the almost all entirely Arab nations surrounding Israel have not been forthcoming when it comes to welcoming Palestinians from Israel.

9. Evangelical, Liberal and Catholic

According to Professor Bebbington, such as in his often referred to seminal book: **"Evangelicalism in Modern Britain - a history from the 1730s to the 1980s**", the four characteristics which have marked Evangelicals are: Biblicism (emphasis on the authority of Scripture); Crucicentrism (centrality of the atonement); Conversionism (people need to be converted to Christianity); and Activism (e.g., in evangelism, on issues of social justice). From the get-go, I was in the Evangelical camp and I soon discovered that my early mentors were anti-Liberal for taking away from the Scriptures and anti-Catholic for adding to the Scriptures (and they were also suspicious of many other Evangelicals for not being doctrinally sound enough) and definitely anti-cult. Over the years, I have mixed with and positively engaged with folk from the Liberal, Catholic and "unsound" Evangelical camps and, while seeing the bad in all of them (and in my own camp come to that), I have seen a deal of good too. My convictions are still predominantly Evangelical and my desire, like St. Paul, is for all Israel to be saved.

10. Tackling (or not) "social injustice"

Over my sixty years of engaging in Christian circles, I have seen many different emphases coming to the fore on what was deemed as being important. I have seen the divisions that often went with it, some of which could/should have been avoided (if only people could have been more genuinely tolerant). In my later working life, when I embarked on a career as a community worker, I saw how important it was to tackle issues that were to do with what came to be labelled as social justice, because I believed that was consistent with what the Bible teaches. I have found that this is something that has increasingly exercised Christian consciences as they seek to respond. I have also seen the pitfalls, such as making these concerns override those of preaching the Gospel and going along with secular agendas that do not have a sound Biblical basis. Often secularists are happy to receive from and give support to Christians for their campaigns etc., but often, only on their terms.

I cover these challenges and concerns in my other writings and it is one that Christians have to deal with the world over, often differently. Whether we include "social" or not, justice should be a concern of all Christians (because God is just) and this includes responding to the legitimate concerns of today's social justice movement (while rejecting the illegitimate), without losing our nerve by neglecting the teaching that the Holy Spirit has been sent to convince the people of the world of sin, righteousness and judgement. Only then can we have a world full of justice that the prophets predicted will happen when the Jewish Messiah comes. While limited in what we can do in an unjust world, ignoring injustice is not an option; neither is neglecting to preach the true Gospel. Whether or not "Palestinians" have been/are being dealt with justly by the Israeli authorities, is a contentious yet pertinent matter. There are many non-Jews living outside Gaza and the West Bank who say they have been well-treated.

Back to Israel

As we consider the situation as it relates to Israel today, that longing for justice for all the parties involved should be our concern. But concern should also be tempered with reality, for in my lifetime I have seen many attempts at peace deals and, while such attempts may be laudable none have ended up with entirely satisfactory results. One of the temptations we all face is getting on our spiritual high horses and looking down on those who don't go along with our way of thinking. I have tried to explain in each of the headings given above what each term means and my reasons for taking the position I do, knowing there will be a high likelihood that some of my readers will see things differently.

While one might deduce that where one stands on the ten "*either/ors*" raised above will dictate how one sees world events and the position one might adopt on Israel, and while this is true it is only to an extent. The quandary we all face is we do not know all of the relevant facts, amid all sorts of disinformation and opinionated pundits and our own prejudices. Trying to understand the wide range of views on offer and deciding what is true and what isn't and seeking the heart and mind of YHWH, who is the Holy One of Israel, are some of the main challenges I believe we need to face up to. I write in the knowledge that strong Christian believing friends take radically different views on the rights and wrongs of what has happened, is happening and should happen, concerning Jews and Palestinians.

So I will continue, in the light of the above, with how I see things right now, mindful that when I later return to the subject there may well be momentous, unforeseen developments. What I will do is to set out my own thoughts, soon after the October 7th event occurred, and then returning to them six months later, along with what has come out of my further theological reflecting. While in a peaceful, nice setting (our Indian family home), I don't have the same access to wide ranging perspectives.

October 2023

My first observation is Israel is never long out of the news and that is consistent with how I understand Bible prophecy. The 7/10 attacks have been referred to as Israel's 9/11 and just like 9/11 are likely to prove a "game changer", perhaps leading eventually to some of the end time battles such as the Gog-Magog war prophesied in Ezekiel 38 and 39. I am loathe to speculate though, for at least three reasons – it is too early to do so and the situation is in a state of flux; when that particular war takes place, Israel will stand alone (not the case at present) and it is God who delivers them, and lastly, Russia (Gog) supported by Magog (Iran) are being held up as the bad guys when the irony is all the parties that have supported Zelensky and Ukraine are just as bad and, now that conflict is all but lost, this anti Putin/Russia alliance is now, without exception, supporting Netanyahu and Israel. I am sceptical too of the official Israeli claim that these atrocities took place WITHOUT Israel leaders' prior knowledge.

Claims have been made backed up by evidence that the Israeli leaders did know and by allowing the attacks makes them just as guilty of war crimes as Hamas, even before we get to happenings in Gaza. There are other claims of nefarious dealings by the Israeli leadership and I could write a long paper to examine "evidence" but suffice to say my suspicions are more than raised, including Hamas having been set up by the Israeli leadership in the first place to oppose the PLO – all for political ends and to push an insidious Zionist agenda that includes Israel world domination. But this is not the place!

While not a point many would raise, I see all sorts of related events. Before Israel, it was Ukraine; before Ukraine it was Covid; before Covid it was Trump; before Trump it was Brexit (and we can go on about issues that get folk, including Christians, worked up and coming to virtual blows) and as I reflect on Israel, the apple of God's eye, it was Israel more than any that pushed the Covid hoax with its draconian measures in making its citizens take the deadly shot while at the same time sanctioning all sorts of unrighteous acts that in the past led to God's judgement. While it is said Israel does not practise idolatry, abortion is the modern equivalent to sacrificing to Molech. I am mindful of the pre 7/10 Palestinian claims of human rights violations, and believe some at least may be justified. In moving on from making these points that will grate with some who love Israel, I hark back to God's words to Moses that remain forever true: "*The Lord did not set his love upon you, nor choose you, because ye were more in number than any people; for ye were the fewest of all people: But because the Lord loved you, and because he would keep the oath which he had sworn unto your fathers*" Deuteronomy 7:7-8.

There are some among the Christian pro-Israel camp that would point to scriptures like "*Who hath heard such a thing? who hath seen such things? Shall the earth be made to bring forth in one day? or shall a nation be born at once? for as soon as Zion travailed, she brought forth her children*" Isaiah 66:8 as proof of divine providence in establishing the land of Israel. Others have reservations, such as claims by Palestinians living in the land of being treated badly. Over recent years, I have heard many claims and counter claims and am yet to come to a firm view. If we are into quoting scripture: "*And the Lord shall scatter thee among all people, from the one end of the earth even unto the other; and there thou shalt serve other gods, which neither thou nor thy fathers have known, even wood and stone*" Deuteronomy 28:64 might still apply. Sacrifices to Baal and Molech, for example, continue, as seen by the number babies aborted in Israel and all sorts of sexual immorality being practised, something the prophets regularly rebuked, when God's judgement would be the eventual outcome.

My object is not to take sides or win arguments but in this as in every season we need to be seeking the Lord and His truth. If I have a plea to my Christian brothers and sisters, it is that they seek the truth and do not gravitate to those plausible voices that merely reinforce their prejudices – both pro-Israel and pro-Palestine. One piece of wisdom from my late father was "*two wrongs don't make a right*", and I can't help feeling that is what is happening, with each side claiming the moral high ground. Both sides of the Israel Palestine divide may point to wrongs perpetrated by the other side and I do not feel qualified to definitely say where the right-wrong balance lies – Israel or Palestine, simply because I do not have the intellectual capacity, nor am I in full possession of the facts to do so. What I do know is many innocent people have suffered in the conflict and, whether it is an Israeli Jew or a Palestinian Arab, both deserve to live in peace. I liked it when a church leader friend, when asked to put on his church prayer bulletin "*Pray for Israelis in their suffering*", wisely added "*and for Palestinians*".

It was the 7/10 Hamas terror attacks on Israeli civilians that got the world's media attention on Israel and the various related conflicts, and following that the civilian deaths as a result of Israeli forces going into Gaza in order to seek out and then destroy Hamas. Then there are the Stop the War protests all over the world. I get some of the arguments of both sides. For the protestors, it is the carnage, suffering and avoidable deaths of civilian casualties living in Gaza. As for Israel, they need to go after the terrorists. As for Hamas, they create bases in civilian centres and prevent folk leaving when the IDF warn them that they are going in for an attack. While a cease-fire and a negotiated peace settlement is desirable, I feel that it is an unrealistic hope as things presently stand. While I do not trust the authorities on the Israel side because they are beholden to their nefarious, Zionist cabal puppet masters, I trust Hamas even less with their demonic driven leadership and avowed aim to wipe Israel entirely off the map and bring in the Caliphate. As I write, this remains an unresolved conundrum.

Much has been said concerning the cease-fire marches. For some protestors, maybe most, their motive was to call for an end to the conflict where most of the victims were innocent civilians. As with any protest, there are those with other intentions, including stirring up hatred toward Israel and supporting Hamas, irrespective of their actions that sparked off the current conflict and their avowed aim to destroy Israel. I see the actions of Hamas and their supporters and the mealy mouthed, virtue signaling response by some of those in authority disappointing, disgraceful and yet unsurprising, as are those that support Israel irrespective of whether their actions are right or wrong. I am sure, when I return to the subject in four months' time, such will have been the developments my views may well change.

As I begin to wrap up, I want to reflect on two descendants in the Abrahamic line: Ishmael, Abraham's son, and Esau, Jacob's son. Ishmael is seen as the father of the Arab nations and the person Muslims, who are often among those most opposed to Israel, look up to. While some Muslims have been friendly toward Israel, others have called for its complete destruction. Then there has been a long Bible history of conflict between Israel and Edom, through characters like Doeg, Haman and Herod. The demise of Edom and God's anger at their rejoicing in Israel's demise, were among the main themes of the prophecy of Obadiah. Among those whose ideology is Zionism with their vision of a greater Israel, there may be descendants of the Edomites following the Babylonian exile, the Khazarian mafia, some of their Ashkenazi Jew descendants forming much of present-day Israel, including the Rothchild dynasty, those influenced by the Sabbateans and freemasonry, and other bad "Jewish" actors, including the modern equivalent of the Synagogue of Satan spoken of in Revelation 2:9 and 3:9.

One might go further and see a relationship with the "sons of god", Nephilim infiltration in Genesis 6 and the prophecy concerning the Fall of Babylon in Revelation 17-18, for it is the ancient Babylon system and its nefarious and occult practices that has gained major leverage in all main monotheistic religions: Judaism, Christianity and Islam. Interestingly, the judgement of the Great Harlot we read of in Revelation 18 is what precedes Christ returning on His White Horse. We should also take a long-term view. With reference to the prophet Isaiah, we read: *"In that day shall there be a highway out of Egypt to Assyria, and the Assyrian shall come into Egypt, and the Egyptian into Assyria, and the Egyptians shall serve with the Assyrians. In that day shall Israel be the third with Egypt and with Assyria, even a blessing in the midst of the land: Whom the Lord of hosts shall bless, saying, Blessed be Egypt my people, and Assyria the work of my hands, and Israel mine inheritance"* Isaiah 19:23-25.

Regarding Israel, they remain the apple of God's eye (Zechariah 2:8), not because they are better than anyone else (they aren't) but God always keeps His promises and, because God has not washed His hands of Israel, Satan continually contrives for Israel to be destroyed, and he has been unsuccessfully trying to do so ever since God gave His word to Abraham. One of the promises is to give the physical descendants of Abraham the physical land of Israel (far beyond its current borders). While some would want to replace physical with spiritual, and others claim that it would be unfair of God to favour one nation over another, as dear Job had to find out – you can't expect to win an argument with God.

What we are seeing is the continuation of the Seed War that began in Genesis 3, with the Fall of Adam, followed in Genesis 6 with the Great Flood and in Genesis 11 with the confusion of the languages at the Tower of Babel – all before Abraham received from God his Great Nation promise. As I argue elsewhere, this is part of an ongoing war between God and Satan, good and evil, light and darkness. I believe there is an evil underbelly to both Hamas and Zionism, even if good people support one or the other. Those who I feel for are the innocent civilians, especially children, both Israeli and Palestinian, many of which from both sides have died. What we are seeing is more than a conflict between Israel and Palestine etc., and it is one that will only be finally and fully resolved after Jesus returns to Earth.

Given the direction the world is heading, all humanity will soon be forced to decide which side they are on, if they haven't already done so: good or evil, light or darkness, God or Satan. While I hope there will be a Great Awakening, when good prevails over evil, I believe that we must first brace ourselves for a false light amidst Great Deception (and here the Antichrist fits the bill) and the prospect of wickedness prevailing for a season. But God, who is not mocked, will have the last word. We know that in the end God wins (I know that to be so, for I have read to the end of His Book). We cannot sit on the sidelines. We must choose sides. It is not one between Israel or Palestine or any other choice of opposites, but it is God's side and it is to Him I turn and I would urge my readers to do so too. As for peace (shalom), that will only entirely happen when the Prince of Peace is reigning – from Zion!

March 2024

I confess that by leaving a four-month gap to reflect, research and watch how the Israel-Gaza conflict pans out I had expected more developments than I am seeing, including a wider escalation of the war. There is still time of course and the "war" along with threats and claims and counter threats and counter claims that are far from over continues to develop and is reported on in the news, although in checking out the main news stories there is much else going on to attract news reporting attention.

While the BBC is not my favoured news reporting outlet, it is the first I check out while on the road, and after that (from a British perspective) UK Column or GB News and (from a wider one) Bitchute and Rumble. There is little to demonstrate that the far wider escalation I had expected has yet happened. Instead, I find, as I check recent news, the BBC reporting stories like the Israeli admitted assassination of a Hamas leader in a foreign country and the outraged responses from the normal suspects. I confess that besides news stories, what I find are opinions voiced ranging from very pro- to very anti-Israel.

Whether any of this will be the trigger for the likes of Iran, Syria and Hezbollah to become more involved we cannot yet tell. Then there are happenings involving other powers in the region that I have not touched on. I suspect the USA, Russia and even China, the UK and the NATO alliance are playing their part as interested onlookers seeing this as part of a wider conflict that they all have a big stake in. There is also the part played by the UN and its agencies that are meant to be honest brokers and peace makers, but as I reflect elsewhere, they are not to be trusted as much as we might want to. I note a recent BBC report begins: *"Israeli Defence Minister Yoav Gallant has outlined proposals for the future governance of Gaza once the war between Israel and Hamas is over. There would, he said, be limited Palestinian rule in the territory. Hamas would no longer control Gaza and Israel would retain overall security control, he added"*.

Another BBC report begins *"Of all the priorities for US Secretary of State Antony Blinken on his fourth visit to the Middle East in three months, there is one message above all others that he wants to deliver. His main mission on this trip is to ensure the Israel-Gaza war does not spread into a regional conflict"*. I am sceptical, given my antipathy toward the current US administration, while recognising the laudable agendas include not creating a refugee crisis, not allowing the war to escalate, and peace. I confess I am suspicious of UN involvement. For one thing, the UN isn't an "honest broker". Then there is the part Yemen might play in the conflict, given recent Red Sea attacks and retaliation. One recent report is titled: "*Strikes on Houthi targets in Yemen show war in Gaza has already spread*" and sounds ominous in terms of what to expect, knowing the situation could quickly change.

What the Israeli action does confirm, not that there is a lack of other reasons to come to such a view, is the intent of the Israeli leadership to go after and destroy Hamas wherever it can be found, including if elements are to be found in the relative safety of another country. Checking past reports, we learn how Israel has attacked from the air and gone into Gaza with the avowed intent to destroy Hamas but with, as a result, enormous civilian casualties, and one wonders where it will all end? While there have been widespread calls for cease fires to allow access for humanitarian aid, the effect of such is limited. While I suspect, many looking on from the sidelines, do so in consternation at what they are seeing.

I know I will upset my pro-Israel friends by saying this but, as sympathetic as I am to the "Israel project" for reasons I have given, I cannot ignore the Israeli actions I am seeing as tantamount to genocide, with the intention to take over Gaza completely and displace its Palestinian inhabitants, despite claims it is all about going after the bad guys and the collateral civilian deaths, injuries and loss of homes and livelihood (which is proportionately very high) is what always happens in times of war. There are reports pushing both narratives and as one would expect the Israeli authorities denying they had done anything wrong and that the disputable number of civilian casualties are the inevitable result of what comes from any war, but the UK Column report I watched recently, claiming worse, I found disturbing. Obviously, propaganda plays a part. I suspect Hamas' claims of numbers of deaths include combatants who are well adept at mingling with the civilian population. Sadly too, the level of indoctrination among children for example has unnaturally heightened Jew hatred among Gazan citizens.

As I set out at the beginning of this chapter, I write neither as one who is pro-Israel, nor as one who is pro-Palestine, at least in the "which side I am on" sense, and it would be over-pious to claim that instead I am pro-God. If I have a concern, besides that of the innocent suffering, it is to echo the desire of those on both sides that want to live in peace but find for reasons beyond their control that is not possible and, for understandable reasons, meaningful, respectful dialogue while attempted on many occasions does not happen. My views on the Israeli leadership and the ungodliness seen among the people in Israel, which would have made the Hebrew prophets of old wince, are far from positive. I also sense that, while many Israeli citizens truly want to live in peace and to do the right thing, that many of the Israeli key and powerful influencers are those who have an ungodly agenda. That is just as true for the Gazan citizens who call themselves Palestinians, who are victims of the troubles, and their leaders who also have an ungodly agenda. I watch feeling helpless but trusting in Him who is holy.

As I keep repeating, as much as I would like to come to a fully rounded view, I cannot. Before my pro-Israel friends, who I suspect will be those most interested in priests of the Bible, disown me, in my quest to find right balance, I checked out and mostly accept the thoughts of two people providing a mainly pro-Israel perspective. The first is Melanie Phillips, who plausibly argues there is widespread antisemitism in all strata of society and that Israel is fighting for civilisation in a world where the so-called civilised nations are becoming increasingly uncivilised. The second is Colonel Richard Kemp who, reflecting on the military aspects of the current Gaza conflict, argues that the Israel defence forces have acted entirely appropriately. I am conscious that most of what I read comes with a bias, one way or another, requiring me to take this into account in trying to come to a rounded view.

I cannot subscribe to the views of modern day "Replacement Theologians" that there is nothing special about today's Israel in terms of attracting divine favour and any claims to sovereignty in the land they lay claim to cannot be sustained on biblical grounds. I beg to differ and believe Israel and the Jewish people are special and unique for all sorts of reasons. It is why I now turn to the Abrahamic Covenant. Yet, just like Gentile sinners, Israel needs to repent and the most loving thing we can do is to tell them the Gospel that is all about the Messiah, their Holy Book anticipates, and is at the heart of this book.

I close this section with a sense of disquiet that I may not have got the balance right amidst a plethora of perspectives on offer, a good deal of information on what is going on and even more that is hidden from us. The BBC headline shortly before I wrote this "*Gaza ceasefire vote: Commons debate descends into chaos*" is pertinent to this section for, despite the politicking we are seeing, it also highlights the anti-Israel sentiment we can now see that is afoot, the pressure being put on MPs to adopt an anti-Israel position and a deficient perspective among UK Parliamentarians and that going down such a path will unlikely resolve the matter of peace and security for Jew and Arab alike. I deplore the rise of true antisemitism (as opposed to anti Zionism). Not touched on much in this book is the nature and often overlooked impact of radical Islam and jihadism as well as Zionism on these and related matters.

I regularly check out newsfeeds, both "pro" and "anti" when it comes to presenting views on Israel's leadership. Just prior to writing this, an acrimonious debate took place between two people putting forward different views on what needs to happen: *"You're A MONSTER!" Cenk Uygur vs Douglas Murray On Israel-Palestine War With Piers Morgan"* making me realise that a middle ground is far from being agreed. I also note from checking out various newsfeeds that the overwhelming sentiment worldwide seems to be anti-Israel (although I suspect such is the cultural climate we live in, those who are pro-Israel dare not say so) and that has been the most notable change since the October 7th attacks. The reality of what is happening, who is right and who is wrong (and to what extent), and what now needs to happen is a complex one that many have sought to resolve without success, not least because the main players, including the Israeli ones, are beholden to agendas that are not that of the God of Israel. I don't claim to even being close to having all the answers, other than what I have laid out in this book, not that I can affect what is happening even if I had. Meanwhile, the yet to be revealed Antichrist is waiting in the wings with his peace deal to come, along with his opposition to the true Christ, ready to be welcomed by Jew and Gentile alike. The first seal opened in Revelation 6, kicking off "the Tribulation", suggests a short season of peace. Yet God who is ever just remains on His Throne and has not relinquished control.

The Abrahamic Covenant

In several places in "Priests of the Bible", we have referred to one or other covenant. The one most referred to is the Mosaic (Sinai) Covenant, which was, as is the case with most covenants, an agreement between two parties, here: YHWH and Israel. God said He would bless Israel provided they kept His Law. The fact they didn't, despite being given many chances to do so after failing the previous times and despite many warnings by the prophets, meant they finally ended up being sent into Exile as part of God's judgement. One of the prophets, Jeremiah, who saw what was happening in the final days of the Kingdom of Judah (the Kingdom of Israel had ceased to exist long before for the same reason) and Judah being sent into Babylonian Captivity, wrote about a new covenant concerning Israel.

This would be better than the one they had broken and while we have seen glimpses, it is still to happen: *"the days come, saith the Lord, that I will make a new covenant with the house of Israel, and with the house of Judah. Not according to the covenant that I made with their fathers in the day that I took them by the hand to bring them out of the land of Egypt; which my covenant they brake, although I was an husband unto them, saith the Lord: But this shall be the covenant that I will make with the house of Israel; After those days, saith the Lord, I will put my law in their inward parts, and write it in their hearts; and will be their God, and they shall be my people"* Jeremiah 31:31-33.

Going back to Moses, we have hints about a new covenant: "*And the Lord thy God will circumcise thine heart, and the heart of thy seed, to love the Lord thy God with all thine heart, and with all thy soul, that thou mayest live*" Deuteronomy 30:6. This is also spoken about in Ezekiel: "*A new heart also will I give you, and a new spirit will I put within you: and I will take away the stony heart out of your flesh, and I will give you an heart of flesh. And I will put my spirit within you, and cause you to walk in my statutes, and ye shall keep my judgments, and do them*" Ezekiel 36:26-27. When Jesus celebrated his final Passover meal, we read: "*And he took bread, and gave thanks, and brake it, and gave unto them, saying, This is my body which is given for you: this do in remembrance of me. Likewise also the cup after supper, saying, This cup is the new testament in my blood, which is shed for you*" Luke 22:19-20.

The writer to the Hebrews picks up concerning the New Covenant, which he argues is better in all sorts of ways to that of the Old Covenant, when discussing Jesus who is the Great High Priest, the one who made it all possible: "*Behold, the days come, saith the Lord, when I will make a new covenant with the house of Israel and with the house of Judah: Not according to the covenant that I made with their fathers in the day when I took them by the hand to lead them out of the land of Egypt; because they continued not in my covenant, and I regarded them not, saith the Lord. For this is the covenant that I will make with the house of Israel after those days, saith the Lord; I will put my laws into their mind, and write them in their hearts: and I will be to them a God, and they shall be to me a people: And they shall not teach every man his neighbour, and every man his brother, saying, Know the Lord: for all shall know me, from the least to the greatest. For I will be merciful to their unrighteousness, and their sins and their iniquities will I remember no more. In that he saith, A new covenant, he hath made the first old. Now that which decayeth and waxeth old is ready to vanish away*" Hebrews 8:8-13.

Another Covenant, also touched on in several places in this book, is The Davidic Covenant, which refers to God's promises to David and is found in 2 Samuel 7 and later summarised in 1 Chronicles 17:11-14 and 2 Chronicles 6:16. This is an unconditional covenant made between God and David through which God promises David and Israel that the Messiah (Jesus Christ) would come from the lineage of David and the tribe of Judah and would establish a kingdom that would endure forever. It is worth noting that Jesus is referred to ten times as "the Son of David" in Matthew's Gospel. While some may want to spiritualise what this "kingdom" is about, most references link it to Israel and Jerusalem. But the one covenant we want to focus on for the rest of this chapter is the Abrahamic Covenant, as it has an important bearing on the future of Israel and is a subject where different views have been put forward.

One of the first things we note that is so remarkable is that Abram, as he was called then, was an idol worshipper (or at least his family were), yet he had been specially selected by God for what would become one of the main themes of the Bible, which was to call a whole nation to Himself and how the relationship progressed, and when he was called, Abram responded. The Abrahamic Covenant is an unconditional covenant, which we first come across in Genesis 12: "*Now the Lord had said unto Abram, Get thee out of thy country, and from thy kindred, and from thy father's house, unto a land that I will shew thee: And I will make of thee a great nation, and I will bless thee, and make thy name great; and thou shalt be a blessing: And I will bless them that bless thee, and curse him that curseth thee: and in thee shall all families of the earth be blessed ... And the Lord appeared unto Abram, and said, Unto thy seed will I give this land: and there builded he an altar unto the Lord, who appeared unto him*" Genesis 12:1-3, 7. There are several important points to consider here, not least from our perspective: *in thee shall all families of the earth be blessed.* The Abrahamic Covenant is repeated several times in Genesis, firstly to Abraham (Chapters 15, 17, 22) as well as to Isaac (26:3-5) and then to Jacob (28:13-15).

Genesis 15 is particularly significant, not just because of the powerfully pertinent points it brings out, including to do with the Abrahamic Covenant, but it is one that is often neglected by those preaching and teaching on Abraham. It comes between two other remarkable chapters: Chapter 14 to do with the battle between the four kings against the five, the part Abram had to play and his important meeting with Melchizedek and Chapter 16 when Abraham tries to help God out regarding having the all-important heir needed for fulfilling God's promise, by sleeping with Hagar. While the product of that union, Ishmael, was himself to become a great nation, he was not part of the Promise God gave.

While over many years God's appearances to Abraham seem to be far and few between, they were always timely, as here: "*After these things the word of the Lord came unto Abram in a vision, saying, Fear not, Abram: I am thy shield, and thy exceeding great reward*" (15:1). He further reassures Abraham by telling him: "*Look now toward heaven, and tell the stars, if thou be able to number them: and he said unto him, So shall thy seed be*" (15:5). Abraham responds: "*And he believed in the Lord; and he counted it to him for righteousness*" (15:6). This response would be picked up by Paul, in order to support some of the arguments he makes that we will soon get to (Romans 4:3 and Galatians 3:6).

The ceremony recorded in 15:9-17 indicated the unconditional nature of the Covenant. When a covenant was dependent upon both parties keeping commitments, then it was tradition at that time and in that region for both parties to pass between the pieces of animals that had been previously slain and effectively cut in two. Here, God alone moved between the halves of the animals. Abraham was in a deep sleep. God's solitary action indicated that the Covenant was principally His promise, binding Himself to the Covenant. In this passage, two important topics are covered, discussed elsewhere in this book: the sins of the Amorites and the 400 years his descendants would be slaves.

The conclusion to Genesis 15 is also most important in that the matter of the land that God promised was also addressed: *"In the same day the Lord made a covenant with Abram, saying, Unto thy seed have I given this land, from the river of Egypt unto the great river, the river Euphrates: The Kenites, and the Kenizzites, and the Kadmonites, And the Hittites, and the Perizzites, and the Rephaims, And the Amorites, and the Canaanites, and the Girgash-ites, and the Jebusites"* (15:18-21).

Even 500 years later, after Joshua had conquered Caanan and allocated the land, and we read *"And the Lord have until Israel all the land He sware to give unto their fathers; and they possessed it, and dwelt therein"* Joshua 21:43, we also read at that time a lot of Caanan's land had not been entirely conquered: *"This is the land that yet remaineth ..."* Joshua 13:2 and even under David when Israel, territory and security wise were best placed, some of that land, in particular at the extremities of *"from the river of Egypt unto the great river, the river Euphrates"* had not been conquered. This begs the question if not then or between then and now, when? It questions those who say modern day Israel has forfeited any hope of future land or that the promises only apply spiritually or to spiritual Israel.

I do not know much about David Jeremiah, but what he has written well articulates my own understanding on this matter, and I quote: *"Of all God's covenant promises to Abraham, I believe the most amazing is His promise concerning the land. God told Abraham to leave his country, his family, and his father's house and go "to a land that I will show you" (Gen. 12:1). God then led Abraham to the land that would belong to his descendants forever. The land promised to Abraham and his descendants was described with clear geographical boundaries. It takes in all the land from the Mediterranean Sea as the western boundary to the Euphrates River as the eastern boundary. The prophet Ezekiel fixed the northern boundary at Hamath, one hundred miles north of Damascus (Ezek. 48:1), and the southern boundary at Kadesh, about one hundred miles south of Jerusalem (v. 28). If Israelis were currently occupying all the land that God gave to them, they would control all the holdings of present-day Israel, Lebanon, and the West Bank of Jordan, plus substantial portions of Syria, Iraq, and Saudi Arabia"*.

In Genesis 17, God again reaffirms the promises of the Covenant He first gave Abraham as well as establishing the rite of circumcision as the sign of that Covenant. All males in Abraham's line were to be circumcised and thus carry with them a lifelong mark in their flesh that they were part of God's physical blessing in the world. He also changed Abram's name (Exalted father) to Abraham (Father of a multitude): "*As for me, behold, my covenant is with thee, and thou shalt be a father of many nations. Neither shall thy name any more be called Abram, but thy name shall be Abraham; for a father of many nations have I made thee. And I will make thee exceeding fruitful, and I will make nations of thee, and kings shall come out of thee. And I will establish my covenant between me and thee and thy seed after thee in their generations for an everlasting covenant, to be a God unto thee, and to thy seed after thee. And I will give unto thee, and to thy seed after thee, the land wherein thou art a stranger, all the land of Canaan, for an everlasting possession; and I will be their God*" (17:4-8).

The big test for Abraham came when God told Abraham to sacrifice his son, Isaac, through whom the promise had been made and this after a long wait and an amazing miracle, all of which was to be undone at the end, or so it seemed. The point here is not to go through this amazing story, which we discuss elsewhere, but consider what Abraham was told at the end, which is all about the Covenant: "*And the angel of the Lord called unto Abraham out of heaven the second time, And said, By myself have I sworn, saith the Lord, for because thou hast done this thing, and hast not withheld thy son, thine only son: That in blessing I will bless thee, and in multiplying I will multiply thy seed as the stars of the heaven, and as the sand which is upon the sea shore; and thy seed shall possess the gate of his enemies; And in thy seed shall all the nations of the earth be blessed; because thou hast obeyed my voice*" (22:15-18). Other than mention again similar words that would be given to the children of that Promise, Isaac and Jacob, we leave the Old Testament for the time being and switch to the New.

"*Abraham was the first Hebrew patriarch and a figure revered by the three great monotheistic religions—Judaism, Christianity, and Islam*" (Britannica). We turn to the second of these religions: Christianity. The word "Abraham" appears 70 times in the New Testament and is mentioned in 11 of the books. The Abrahamic Covenant is specifically discussed in Galatians 3 but first we will consider what John the Baptist and then Jesus said. Both attracted the anger of the Jewish religious authorities because of what they said when taking them to task about being the physical descendants of Abraham and thinking that being descended from Abraham gave them some sort of entitlement in God's eyes. John said: "*And think not to say within yourselves, We have Abraham to our father: for I say unto you, that God is able of these stones to raise up children unto Abraham*" Matthew 3:9. Jesus said:

"Your father Abraham rejoiced to see my day: and he saw it, and was glad … Jesus said unto them, Verily, verily, I say unto you, Before Abraham was, I am" John 8:56, 58, doing so after accusing the Jews that they were children of the Devil rather than those of Abraham.

We mentioned earlier two instances of Paul quoting from Genesis that Abraham was imputed as righteous because of his faith. Paul develops the theme in Romans 4, in the context of explaining how we as believers in Jesus can be justified by faith. After dealing with some of the great doctrines concerning salvation in Romans 1-8, and before considering some of the implications of that teaching in Chapters 12-16, Paul turns his attention to a topic we could label as "the Israel conundrum". The question begged with an attempt made to answer it, is what to make out of Israel with whom some of the Covenants had been made, and given their present unbelief where it would lead them. This is a huge subject and not one I will attempt to consider in greater depth but instead I turn to Galatians 3.

Paul's epistle to the Galatians was written to address the thorny and contentious issue at the time of whether those Gentiles who had embraced the Christian faith needed to also obey what was written in the Old Testament Law, i.e., become Jews before becoming Christians, doing what the Mosaic Covenant required. In order to make his point that this was not a requirement, Paul cited Abraham as an example and specifically referred to the Abrahamic Covenant, in Galatians 3: *"Know ye therefore that they which are of faith, the same are the children of Abraham. And the scripture, foreseeing that God would justify the heathen through faith, preached before the gospel unto Abraham, saying, In thee shall all nations be blessed. So then they which be of faith are blessed with faithful Abraham"* (3:7-9).

He then makes the point concerning the use of the word "seed" and since the seed that was being looked forward to was Jesus, all those who believe in Him (Jew and Gentile) are beneficiaries: *"That the blessing of Abraham might come on the Gentiles through Jesus Christ; that we might receive the promise of the Spirit through faith. Brethren, I speak after the manner of men; Though it be but a man's covenant, yet if it be confirmed, no man disannulleth, or addeth thereto. Now to Abraham and his seed were the promises made. He saith not, And to seeds, as of many; but as of one, And to thy seed, which is Christ. And this I say, that the covenant, that was confirmed before of God in Christ, the law, which was four hundred and thirty years after, cannot disannul, that it should make the promise of none effect"* (3:14-17). Paul wraps up this particular argument thus: *"There is neither Jew nor Greek, there is neither bond nor free, there is neither male nor female: for ye are all one in Christ Jesus. And if ye be Christ's, then are ye Abraham's seed, and heirs according to the promise"* (3:28-29).

Before we move on, we need to raise an important "context" point. The word generally translated "seed" in the KJV is translated "offspring" in the ESV and "descendant" in the NIV and Amplified versions of the Bible. The Hebrew word, according to Strong (H2233), is "**zera**" and can take all these meanings, where seed might also be translated as semen. Interestingly, when the KJV uses the word that it translates as seed in the New Testament, e.g., in Galatians 3, the Strong (G4690) Greek word "**sperma**", which is where we get the word "sperm" from, it takes on the same meanings as that found from the Hebrew text. I make this point because it is easy, having read Paul's explanation of "seed" in Galatians 3, to ignore the many Old Testament references to the Abrahamic Covenant as being to the physical land which Abraham's physical descendants (at least some of them) would eventually possess.

Not only had physical land been promised to Abraham's "seed", with this being repeated on several occasions, as has been cited in the references above, and without being fully fulfilled as far as we can tell, it is also something the prophets prophesied concerning what was to happen in the Messianic age that was yet to come (based on a Futurist rather than a Preterist understanding of prophecy), all of which pointed to physical rather than spiritual Israel, notwithstanding the clear Pauline teaching that Gentile believers in Jesus are also beneficiaries. How they fit into these apparently yet to be fulfilled promises is a big subject, along with the claims of many Christian Zionists that today's Israel is entitled to the land simply because God said so in the Bible, and that which was written concerning Abraham and other heroes of faith: "*But now they desire a better country, that is, an heavenly: wherefore God is not ashamed to be called their God: for he hath prepared for them a city*" Hebrews 11:16.

It is appropriate we give the Hebrew prophets the last word. Since we are spoilt for choice, we only include the words of some "minor prophets" (there is much to be found in the "major prophets" too). I do not claim these are the only texts that concern a future Israel. I expect some will argue, either they have been fulfilled, e.g., after Judah returned from exile, or the correct understanding is to spiritualise what appears to be physical happenings, but I do so to in effect rest my case, declaring we have yet to see the final fulfilment of the Abrahamic Covenant and that fulfilment may well be a physical one.

"*For the sons of Israel will remain for many days without king or prince, without sacrifice or sacred pillar and without ephod or household idols. Afterward the sons of Israel will return and seek the Lord their God and David their king; and they will come trembling to the Lord and to His goodness in the last days*" Hosea 3:4-5.

"*Then the Lord will be zealous for His land And will have pity on His people. The Lord will answer and say to His people, "Behold, I am going to send you grain, new wine and oil, And you will be satisfied in full with them; And I will never again make you a reproach among the nations. "But I will remove the northern army far from you, And I will drive it into a parched and desolate land, And its vanguard into the eastern sea, And its rear guard into the western sea. And its stench will arise and its foul smell will come up, For it has done great things"* Joel 2:18-20.

"Also I will restore the captivity of My people Israel, And they will rebuild the ruined cities and live in them; They will also plant vineyards and drink their wine, And make gardens and eat their fruit. "I will also plant them on their land, And they will not again be rooted out from their land Which I have given them," Says the Lord your God" Amos 9:14-15.

""In that day," declares the Lord, "I will assemble the lame And gather the outcasts, Even those whom I have afflicted. "I will make the lame a remnant And the outcasts a strong nation, And the Lord will reign over them in Mount Zion From now on and forever" Micah 4:6-7.

"Behold, I am going to deal at that time With all your oppressors, I will save the lame And gather the outcast, And I will turn their shame into praise and renown In all the earth. "At that time I will bring you in, Even at the time when I gather you together; Indeed, I will give you renown and praise Among all the peoples of the earth, When I restore your fortunes before your eyes"" Zephaniah 3:19-20.

"Thus says the Lord of hosts, 'Behold, I am going to save My people from the land of the east and from the land of the west; and I will bring them back and they will live in the midst of Jerusalem; and they shall be My people, and I will be their God in truth and righteousness' ... "It will come about in all the land," Declares the Lord, "That two parts in it will be cut off and perish; But the third will be left in it. "And I will bring the third part through the fire, Refine them as silver is refined, And test them as gold is tested. They will call on My name, And I will answer them; I will say, 'They are My people,' And they will say, 'The Lord is my God'" Zechariah 8:7-8, 13:8-9.

Not that it matters what my views are on the current conflict, but it might be helpful to say what these are if readers haven't managed to figure this out for themselves. I suppose it would be some 45 years ago when I had dealings with a godly lady who had served as a missionary headmistress in Lebanon and we used to discuss the Israel Arab conflict. Given some of those who influenced me most were pro-Israel, I would put forward arguments they made. She would counter with pro-Arab arguments, often based on first-hand experience. I recall her making the point that the Israelis were adept at self-righteous propaganda (although I am sure the same is true on the Arab side). I have often dreamt of Jews and Arabs being able to put their cases in an atmosphere of mutual respect and finding, as is now happening on a small scale, the two parties coming together united in the one who died for both.

We continue to see good Christian folk arguing in favour of either side, with people like me sitting on the fence, despite believing God has promised physical descendants of Abaham "the land" and has a special place for Israel based on statements like: *"Since thou wast precious in my sight, thou hast been honourable, and I have loved thee"* Isaiah 43:4, *"I have loved thee with an everlasting love"* Jeremiah 31:3, and *"He shall choose our inheritance for us, the excellency of Jacob whom he loved"* Psalm 47:4. I suspect most Israelis are no better and no worse than any other ethnic group. But sadly, Israel has been infiltrated by bad people (Synagogue of Satan) and they are calling the shots. It seems to me that my Zionist leaning Christian friends not only do not see it but oppose Israel-loving Christians who do.

And this on top of all those prophecies cited earlier predicting a wonderful future for Israel under its coming King – and we have barely touched on what the major prophets have had to say on the subject. At the same time, the God I worship is a just God, yet many Arab supporters continually claim Israel is perpetrating injustice. As I see it, it is not a matter of one side is clearly right and the other side is clearly wrong; it is a lot more complicated than that, and as much I would like to come down on one side or the other, I can't because I don't know enough. If that is a lonely position to take then so be it.

One is spoilt for choice when it comes to an apt Israel related scripture to end with, but let us cite the words of Paul: *"For I would not, brethren, that ye should be ignorant of this mystery, lest ye should be wise in your own conceits; that blindness in part is happened to Israel, until the fulness of the Gentiles be come in. And so all Israel shall be saved: as it is written, There shall come out of Sion the Deliverer, and shall turn away ungodliness from Jacob: For this is my covenant unto them, when I shall take away their sins"* Romans 11:25-27. The big question continues to be begged: who then is true Israel?

As we have been considering Abraham, we do well to end with a hymn about the God of Abraham, for methinks the best we can do for now is to watch and pray, and praise and worship the God of Abraham:

1. *The God of Abraham praise,*
who reigns enthroned above;
Ancient of Everlasting Days,
and God of Love;
Jehovah, great I AM!
by earth and heaven confessed;
I bow and bless the sacred name
forever blest.

2. *The great I AM has sworn;*
I on this oath depend.
I shall, on eagle's wings upborne,
to heaven ascend.
I shall behold God's face;
I shall God's power adore,
and sing the wonders of God's grace
forevermore.

3. *The heavenly land I see,*
with peace and plenty blest;
a land of sacred liberty,
and endless rest.
There milk and honey flow,
and oil and wine abound,
and trees of life forever grow
with mercy crowned.

4. *The God who reigns on high*
the great archangels sing,
and "Holy, holy, holy!" cry
"Almighty King!

Who was, and is, the same,

and evermore shall be:

Jehovah, Lord, the great I AM,

we worship thee!"

Epilogue

This is one section I did not reckon on writing. I have already devoted an unexpectedly large amount of space to the subject of Israel and, while a lot more could be said, this is not the place to elaborate on themes that warrant a book in their own right. Besides which, while not going into detail, I have tried to consider alternative perspectives, aware of the folly of taking polarised positions while being exposed to widespread propaganda and cajoled to take sides. Yet there are reasons for saying more, brought about by a combination of factors. Firstly, writing my book has taken longer than I planned up to the point of publication when no further changes can be made. Secondly, there have been significant developments relating to the situation that has arisen following the October 7th Hamas-Gaza attacks on Israel since I last wrote, which warrant at least a mention. Thirdly, I have become increasingly aware that I have managed to unintentionally upset both the pro-Palestinian lobby and the pro-Israel lobby (whose theological perspective often more closely aligns with my own) with the views expressed in this chapter. While I like to think that anyone beholden to the truth should not be overly concerned at the danger that comes as a result of walking in the middle of the road, I am also mindful of texts to do with blessed are the peacemakers and the benefits arising out of brothers dwelling together in unity.

The main focus of this book remains on what the Bible teaches rather than what this or that pundit has to say (and, truly, I continue to find myself checking out what those presenting widely different and often opposing views come out with without necessarily taking sides). For having taken more of an interest in Bible end time prophecy in recent years, not just to indulge the whims of an old man who has been put out to pasture but I would like to think taking a leaf out of the Children of Issachar's book by helping the people of God know how best to respond. I hope readers will find these final thoughts and those that preceded them helpful. I am thinking of the Iran drone attacks on Israel (as well as from many allied countries), which I first found out about when checking my newsfeed on 13th April 2024, and the response of Israel and the various major global players. Of course, we wait for developments including, in a worst-case scenario, a world war. My point here is not to articulate on what happened, take sides or suggest what should happen next but note this could be part of the escalation expected following the October 7th attacks, leading to the end time events I have discussed, for example with reference to Daniel 7 onwards and Revelation 6 onwards. While I have argued that the quietist response of my early spiritual mentors is not altogether the right one, I am also conscious that we still don't have all the necessary facts to hand and even if we did what can we usefully do? But respond we must (check out the end of Chapter 47 for thoughts on what this response ought to be).

Let us conclude with two further thoughts: Firstly, the people caught up in the current conflict, and since our attention has been drawn to Iran where there is a spiritual revival of the right sort going on, we start there followed by most Jews and Arabs, are good people or at least no worse than anyone else and have no interest in violent conflict. Iran, Israel and much of the Arab world, along with many powerful nations who have an interest, happen to be led by bad people. Secondly, while rejecting the "rose tinted" view of Israel put forward by some of my pro-Israel friends, I stand by my belief that the Covenant with Abraham, which we first read of in Genesis 12:1-3 (verses I quote elsewhere), still stands: "*Now the Lord had said unto Abram, Get thee out of thy country, and from thy kindred, and from thy father's house, unto a land that I will shew thee: And I will make of thee a great nation, and I will bless thee, and make thy name great; and thou shalt be a blessing: And I will bless them that bless thee, and curse him that curseth thee: and in thee shall all families of the earth be blessed*". Moreover, we do well if we "*pray for the peace of Jerusalem*", for "*they shall prosper that love thee*" Psalm 122:6. Going back to numerous end time prophecies concerning Israel, the final outcome is a wonderful one. As has often been said: we live in interesting days, and we have only touched the surface. Perplexing things are happening around us at an alarming rate. Much is happening on earth that we don't see and can barely fathom, but there are even more unseen goings on in the spiritual realm we definitely can't see. But we can be confident; not only is God in control and He wins but He has already won.

Chapter 53: The Books of Wisdom

Before we get going on the rationale behind this chapter, and then follow it up with content, let us begin by quoting some Bible verses that have an important bearing on this subject of wisdom:

"Doth not wisdom cry? and understanding put forth her voice? She standeth in the top of high places, by the way in the places of the paths. She crieth at the gates, at the entry of the city, at the coming in at the doors. Unto you, O men, I call; and my voice is to the sons of man. O ye simple, understand wisdom: and, ye fools, be ye of an understanding heart. Hear; for I will speak of excellent things; and the opening of my lips shall be right things. For my mouth shall speak truth; and wickedness is an abomination to my lips. All the words of my mouth are in righteousness; there is nothing froward or perverse in them ... For wisdom is better than rubies; and all the things that may be desired are not to be compared to it ... The fear of the Lord is the beginning of wisdom: and the knowledge of the holy is understanding" Proverbs 8:1-8, 11, 9:10.

"And I gave my heart to seek and search out by wisdom concerning all things that are done under heaven: this sore travail hath God given to the sons of man to be exercised therewith ... I communed with mine own heart, saying, Lo, I am come to great estate, and have gotten more wisdom than all they that have been before me in Jerusalem: yea, my heart had great experience of wisdom and knowledge. And I gave my heart to know wisdom, and to know madness and folly: I perceived that this also is vexation of spirit. For in much wisdom is much grief: and he that increaseth knowledge increaseth sorrow." Ecclesiastes 1:13, 16-18.

"But where shall wisdom be found? and where is the place of understanding? Man knoweth not the price thereof; neither is it found in the land of the living ... No mention shall be made of coral, or of pearls: for the price of wisdom is above rubies. The topaz of Ethiopia shall not equal it, neither shall it be valued with pure gold. Whence then cometh wisdom? and where is the place of understanding? ... And he said to the human race, The fear of the Lord — that is wisdom, and to shun evil is understanding" Job 28:12-13, 18-20, 28.

... followed by some definitions ...

Fear (Hebrew: **yare**) can be translated by anything from respect to dread but is commonly understood by learned commentators to mean reverence and awe.

Knowledge (Hebrew: **yada**) goes beyond being intellectually informed and includes notions of perceiving, learning, understanding, performing, and experiencing.

Understanding (Hebrew: **binah**) relates to comprehension, discernment, apprehension, realisation, grasp, savvy, wit etc.

Wisdom (Hebrew: **chokmah**) enables us to skilfully apply knowledge gained, to understand life from God's perspective and have the ability to do the right thing at the right time.

In the Christian Bible, the Old Testament is often seen in four sections: Law, History, Prophets and Poetry (which comprises the Books of Job, Psalms, Proverbs, Ecclesiastes and Song of Solomon). The Jewish Bible comprises three sections: Law, Prophets and Writings. A central theme of the Poetry (Writings) books is wisdom, often coupled with the fear of the Lord. It has been said: the wisdom of Proverbs describes how godly character generally leads to success. Ecclesiastes tempers this by warning that rewards are not guaranteed, as a kind of "crookedness" has come into our world. The book of Job goes further by exploring how righteous people may suffer for no obvious reason.

All three agree – getting wisdom along with knowledge and understanding must be a priority for the godly and it all begins with the fear of God. While wisdom may not be the main themes in the Song of Solomon and Psalms, it is important when we consider the notion of *"love as strong as death"* (Song of Solomon) and the praise of the one who is truly worthy of praise – the Lord God of Israel (Psalms). Significantly, the word "fear" crops up 134 times and "wisdom" 109 times in our five wisdom books.

What I would like to do is to consider, albeit all too briefly, the Wisdom books in the order: Job, Psalms, Song of Solomon, Proverbs and Ecclesiastes. There is much that can be said about each of these books. Psalms is probably the book where most can be said and if one were to write on the Psalms, it would warrant a whole long book with sections dedicated to each of the 150 Psalms – but I am going to say relatively little, even though I have often quoted from the Psalms throughout this book – and for good reason. In 2021, I produced my book "**Song of Songs, Proverbs and Ecclesiastes – Meditations from Solomon's three books**", where I gave a more in-depth exposition on each of those books of the Bible. Along with Job and Psalms, much can be said about these three books, but we will keep it short.

Since I could easily stray from the main themes of this book, I will be mindful of these when I am tempted to stray and reflect on the notion that if we are to be a priestly people then gaining wisdom is very important. Part 3 of this book is about how a priestly people should conduct themselves in the light of what we learn in Part 1 about the priesthood and Part 2 about priests. In Part 3, we consider three of the more neglected books of the Bible: Leviticus, Chronicles and Hebrews. Besides going some way to redress that imbalance, each of these books has a lot to say about priests and the priesthood and warrants further consideration for that reason alone. As for Genesis, which arguably, besides Melchizedek, has not much to say about priests, a brief consideration of its contents is worth having as it provides the seedbed for the rest of the Bible and gives us insights into the conflicts and background in which priests operated: God versus Satan, good versus evil, light versus darkness.

Job

Dominating the Book of Job are discourses of a more philosophical nature, especially concerning suffering, between Job and his "friends", all enshrined in beautiful poetry. Other than the prologue and epilogue (which is prose), the rest of the book is poetry, with vivid imagery, deep reflection and debate on points made. I don't recall preachers preaching much on those middle chapters, at least in terms of verse-by-verse exposition. What is more common is to hear sermons based on how we may come to terms with the reality of innocent suffering and some stand out verses from the book, such as *"Though he slay me, yet will I trust in him"* (Job 13:15) and *"For I know that my redeemer liveth, and that he shall stand at the latter day upon the earth"* (Job 19:25). I suspect few readers can give more than a basic account of the differing often subtle arguments of Eliphaz, Bildad and Zophar (Job's three friends, known as Job's comforters) and the young chap who pops up toward the end, Elihu, who disagreed with all of them, along with telling Job off for not answering his friends' questions, or on how these players interacted and how the arguments are developed in the three rounds of discourse.

Job is an unusual book of the Bible for many reasons. Firstly, it is one of oldest, even though in it Job and his friends identify the one who is almost certainly the God of the Bible, despite likely predating even Moses and the Exodus. Secondly, it is not a Jewish book *per se*, and is possibly the only Old Testament book that isn't, which is apt since it deals with themes that have been raised by all humankind ever since the beginning of time and something akin to the "Job experience" discussed in ancient literature. Thirdly, while not overtly so, it touches on New Testament themes, such as the Sermon on the Mount and the afterlife, and other themes like that of wisdom, as developed in Proverbs and Ecclesiastes, and elements of the Torah, including the notion of blessings following the righteous and cursing the wicked, a central theme that Job and his three friends debated throughout their exchanges. Then there is a key underlying theme of the Bible that we get glimpses of – the plans of God and Satan's attempts to thwart them, something that, even when all is restored to him, Job is barely aware of. As for whether the events and dialogue in the book really happened, notwithstanding the poetic licence (after all, who holds discussions in poetry), my understanding is that they really did!

Job complements the other wisdom literature and helps us to make sense of all sorts of modern-day craziness. One stand out theme is that there is a redeemer, ever ready to plead the cause of those whom He has redeemed. Job's friends have been given a bad press and at the end were rebuked by God for not speaking rightly concerning Job. But they did sit with Job during his suffering, when others ignored or turned against him. Most of what they said was true and they only spoke in response to what Job said first. They clearly had a high view of God but fell short when claiming God always blesses the righteous. Besides not speaking the way one should speak to someone who is suffering, they fell into the all too familiar trap of dogmatism. Even if the rule is that God blesses the righteous (which Job was in God's eyes) and He punishes the unrighteous, there are exceptions, something that Job noted as in his turmoil he tried to figure this out. It not only covers "why me", for Job despite what his friends said had lived a good life and his appearance of being a righteous person was in fact the reality, but touches on the conundrum of why bad people get away with being bad rather than being dealt with as they deserve and why good people do not always get rewarded and are even penalised in their attempts to do good, and the question that has long vexed many: why do the innocent suffer?

There are all sorts of contradictions in the world we might want to identify, along with all sorts of injustices, including good and innocent people suffering, but it is good to know as we begin our journey with the first of our wisdom books that these questions have already been asked and, while not always fully answered, we do well to apply God's rebuke of Job to ourselves: *"Who is this that darkeneth counsel by words without knowledge?"* Job 38:2. As for what had been happening in Job's case, there was a perspective that overrode any other and this was missed by all parties – that of the unseen God, whose ways are beyond finding out, something in the end Job came to recognise. We do well to recognise that such is the case as we look around with consternation seeing every day cases of evil rewarded and good not so; the innocent suffering and the guilty prospering. While, at the end, there was a wonderful turnaround in Job's fortunes in that he was rewarded according to his righteousness, we can only look around us and historically to see this is not always the case, and there we leave it.

Part of the big unseen picture was that there was, in effect, a wager made between God and Satan to prove whether or not Job revered God, merely because he had been blessed by God and that is why Job had prospered – a wager that God won! If there is a lesson we can take away from the story of Job, it is that God knows and does what is best, despite how dire things appear. True wisdom is highly desirable and something that we do well to seek after. It is not something that can be found through the natural world or in searching out the hidden depths of the earth where much that is of value can be found. It begins with the fear of God and in humbly recognising how little we truly know.

Psalms

It is a quite remarkable fact that right across the ecclesiological spectrum Psalms continue to feature much in Christian worship, if for no other reason their words and sentiments are conducive and relevant. The first thing worth pointing out is just as Psalms continue to be read (and sometimes sung) and be pondered on in Christian worship and teaching, this was also the case in Jewish worship, whether in the Temple or the synagogue. We believe half of the Psalms were penned by David and some were written with the express intention they should be sung in Temple worship. It is likely the Psalms were penned over a longish period, a number of centuries, but before we get to the period of the New Testament it was agreed what to include, which the Christians were happy to go along with.

Before we continue with the Psalms, it is well to reflect on the qualifications of the author of half of them – David. The most well-known of his Psalms is 23, which begins *"The Lord is my shepherd; I shall not want"* 23:1, where, as in many of his psalms, David was writing from personal experience. He was a shepherd boy who became a warrior king, Israel's greatest king, with whom kings that came after him were compared. He was an accomplished musician and poet, as evidenced in his psalms. He wasn't without faults and, when he sinned, he did so big time. But he was also a man after God's own heart.

The purpose of the Psalms was primary to support worship, something the people of God are always encouraged to do, irrespective of their circumstances in life and their mental and spiritual state, which could be anything between despondency and jubilation. While the Psalms were written in quite different times to our own, the Psalmist's experience is not dissimilar. God is worth worshipping simply because He is God and, ever since the Psalms appeared, before the Christian era, they have been used to support that very purpose. I am sure far more lucid explanations can be given for why we should study the Psalms than I am giving, but the fact that I quote from the Psalms throughout this book and its companion to do with Prophets at least shows how significant I find Psalms to be, not least the number that we regard as Messianic (e.g., 2, 22, 45 and 110) that tell us much about the coming Messiah, which we can find fulfilled in the New Testament.

What also stands out is the Psalms reflect every aspect of the human experience, even to the extent that the Psalmist may argue with God on subjects such as why the baddies do come off better than the goodies, e.g., *"Fret not thyself because of evildoers, neither be thou envious against the workers of iniquity. For they shall soon be cut down like the grass, and wither as the green herb. Trust in the Lord, and do good; so shalt thou dwell in the land, and verily thou shalt be fed. Delight thyself also in the Lord: and he shall give thee the desires of thine heart. Commit thy way unto the Lord; trust also in him; and he shall bring it to pass"* Psalm 37:1-5. The Psalms are brutally honest when it comes to the struggles and conundrums we often face, but also in telling us what God requires. Yet invariably the Psalmist comes round to seeing things from God's perspective, realising He is in control and does all things well and all the Psalmist has to do is fall in line with God's plans and purposes, and be blessed. I will resist the temptation of quoting too much from the Psalms here but many who are reading this could cite Psalms that have blessed and challenged them; but allow me to share from ten of them.

"Blessed is the man that walketh not in the counsel of the ungodly, nor standeth in the way of sinners, nor sitteth in the seat of the scornful. But his delight is in the law of the Lord; and in his law doth he meditate day and night. And he shall be like a tree planted by the rivers of water, that bringeth forth his fruit in his season; his leaf also shall not wither; and whatsoever he doeth shall prosper" (1:1-3).

"Lord, who shall abide in thy tabernacle? who shall dwell in thy holy hill? He that walketh uprightly, and worketh righteousness, and speaketh the truth in his heart" (15:1-2).

"The law of the Lord is perfect, converting the soul: the testimony of the Lord is sure, making wise the simple. The statutes of the Lord are right, rejoicing the heart: the commandment of the Lord is pure, enlightening the eyes. The fear of the Lord is clean, enduring for ever: the judgments of the Lord are true and righteous altogether. More to be desired are they than gold, yea, than much fine gold: sweeter also than honey and the honeycomb. Moreover by them is thy servant warned: and in keeping of them there is great reward" (19:7-11).

"The Lord is my light and my salvation; whom shall I fear? the Lord is the strength of my life; of whom shall I be afraid? When the wicked, even mine enemies and my foes, came upon me to eat up my flesh, they stumbled and fell. Though an host should encamp against me, my heart shall not fear: though war should rise against me, in this will I be confident. One thing have I desired of the Lord, that will I seek after; that I may dwell in the house of the Lord all the days of my life, to behold the beauty of the Lord, and to enquire in his temple. For in the time of trouble he shall hide me in his pavilion: in the secret of his tabernacle shall he hide me; he shall set me up upon a rock" (27:1-5).

"I will bless the Lord at all times: his praise shall continually be in my mouth. My soul shall make her boast in the Lord: the humble shall hear thereof, and be glad. O magnify the Lord with me, and let us exalt his name together. I sought the Lord, and he heard me, and delivered me from all my fears. They looked unto him, and were lightened: and their faces were not ashamed" (34:1-5).

"God is our refuge and strength, a very present help in trouble. Therefore will not we fear, though the earth be removed, and though the mountains be carried into the midst of the sea; Though the waters thereof roar and be troubled, though the mountains shake with the swelling thereof. Selah. There is a river, the streams whereof shall make glad the city of God, the holy place of the tabernacles of the most High. God is in the midst of her; she shall not be moved: God shall help her, and that right early" (46:1-5).

"He that dwelleth in the secret place of the most High shall abide under the shadow of the Almighty. I will say of the Lord, He is my refuge and my fortress: my God; in him will I trust. Surely he shall deliver thee from the snare of the fowler, and from the noisome pestilence. He shall cover thee with his feathers, and under his wings shalt thou trust: his truth shall be thy shield and buckler" (91:1-4).

"I will lift up mine eyes unto the hills, from whence cometh my help. My help cometh from the Lord, which made heaven and earth. He will not suffer thy foot to be moved: he that keepeth thee will not slumber. Behold, he that keepeth Israel shall neither slumber nor sleep. The Lord is thy keeper: the Lord is thy shade upon thy right hand" (121:1-5).

"O lord, thou hast searched me, and known me. Thou knowest my down-sitting and mine uprising, thou understandest my thought afar off. Thou compassest my path and my lying down, and art acquainted with all my ways. For there is not a word in my tongue, but, lo, O Lord, thou knowest it altogether ... Search me, O God, and know my heart: try me, and know my thoughts: And see if there be any wicked way in me, and lead me in the way everlasting" (139:1-4, 23-24).

"Praise ye the Lord. Praise God in his sanctuary: praise him in the firmament of his power. Praise him for his mighty acts: praise him according to his excellent greatness. Praise him with the sound of the trumpet: praise him with the psaltery and harp. Praise him with the timbrel and dance: praise him with stringed instruments and organs. Praise him upon the loud cymbals: praise him upon the high sounding cymbals. Let every thing that hath breath praise the Lord. Praise ye the Lord" (150:1-6).

While what the Psalms say about priests and the priesthood is limited, it often harks back to the Law, the very thing priests were required to teach and be exemplars of (e.g., *"Blessed are the undefiled in the way, who walk in the law of the Lord. Blessed are they that keep his testimonies, and that seek him with the whole heart. They also do no iniquity: they walk in his ways"* (119:1-3)). One of the recurring themes of both Priests and Kings of the Bible is God's righteous judgements. The word "judgement" (judgment) crops up 61 times in the Psalms, 17 times in Psalm 119, and each time this was in the context of something we need to pay attention to, e.g., *"My soul breaketh for the longing that it hath unto thy judgments at all times ... At midnight I will rise to give thanks unto thee because of thy righteous judgments ... Righteous art thou, O Lord, and upright are thy judgments"* (119:20, 62, 137).

The Psalms are full of wisdom on how a priestly people should live in what are often tumultuous times, when the innocent and righteous are afflicted and evil doers seem to do well, including reflecting on the fact of God being utterly trustworthy and how blessed we are to be His people. When it comes to wisdom, we find an emphasis that true wisdom should result when trusting the Lord, honouring Him and worshiping Him, and is good reason why Psalms should be used in praise and prayer (private and public), meditated upon and memorised, forming a basis for individual and congregational worship.

We often associate the Psalms with David and understandably so for he wrote half of them, but what about Asaph, a Levite, set apart for God's service, unable to acquire land and income independence, who among other things led worship in the Temple and wrote Psalms? According to **Got Questions**: *"There were a number of Levites that King David assigned as worship leaders in the tabernacle choir, according to 1 Chronicles 6:31-32. Asaph was one of these men (1 Chronicles 6:39). Asaph's duties are described in detail in 1 Chronicles 16. According to 2 Chronicles 29:30, both Asaph and David were skilled singers and poets. Asaph is also mentioned as a "seer" or prophet. The "sons of Asaph" are mentioned in 1 Chronicles 25:1, 2 Chronicles 20:14, and Ezra 2:41. The sons of Asaph were likely a guild of skilled poets and singers, modeling themselves musically after Asaph, their master. The church musicians of our day can be considered spiritual "children of Asaph." Psalms 50 and 73-83 are called the "Psalms of Asaph" because his name appears in the superscription at the head of those psalms. Regarding Asaph's role as a prophet, of particular interest is the imprecatory Psalm 83, which deals with God's judgment of Israel's enemies: Edom, the Ishmaelites, Moab, the Hagarites, Gebal, Ammon, the Amalekites, Philistia, Tyre, and Assyria. If we examine the psalms written by Asaph, we can see that all of them have to do with the judgment of God, and many involve the prayers of the people at the prospect or moment of a particular event. Asaph was* *a gifted individual. He understood where the gift came from, and he used his music to praise the Lord and communicate His Word to a needy world".*

As I revisit this section on the Psalms for the last time, I do so having recently listened to a preacher expound on one of Asaph's Psalms (Psalm 73) and was excited because this was not a Psalm I have considered in this book thus far or even much in my regular meditating, and yet is so pertinent to the theme of priests, not just of the Bible but also believer-priests: "*Truly God is good to Israel, even to such as are of a clean heart. But as for me, my feet were almost gone; my steps had well nigh slipped. For I was envious at the foolish, when I saw the prosperity of the wicked. For there are no bands in their death: but their strength is firm. They are not in trouble as other men; neither are they plagued like other men. Therefore pride compasseth them about as a chain; violence covereth them as a garment. Their eyes stand out with fatness: they have more than heart could wish. They are corrupt, and speak wickedly concerning oppression: they speak loftily. They set their mouth against the heavens, and their tongue walketh through the earth. Therefore his people return hither: and waters of a full cup are wrung out to them. And they say, How doth God know? and is there knowledge in the most High? Behold, these are the ungodly, who prosper in the world; they increase in riches. Verily I have cleansed my heart in vain, and washed my hands in innocency. For all the day long have I been plagued, and chastened every morning. If I say, I will speak thus; behold, I should offend against the generation of thy children. When I thought to know this, it was too painful for me; Until I went into the sanctuary of God; then understood I their end. Surely thou didst set them in slippery places: thou castedst them down into destruction. How are they brought into desolation, as in a moment! they are utterly consumed with terrors. As a dream when one awaketh; so, O Lord, when thou awakest, thou shalt despise their image. Thus my heart was grieved, and I was pricked in my reins. So foolish was I, and ignorant: I was as a beast before thee. Nevertheless I am continually with thee: thou hast holden me by my right hand. Thou shalt guide me with thy counsel, and afterward receive me to glory. Whom have I in heaven but thee? and there is none upon earth that I desire beside thee. My flesh and my heart faileth: but God is the strength of my heart, and my portion for ever. For, lo, they that are far from thee shall perish: thou hast destroyed all them that go a whoring from thee. But it is good for me to draw near to God: I have put my trust in the Lord God, that I may declare all thy works*" (73:1-28).

This Psalm, as with many Psalms, begins and ends on a high note. It begins by reflecting on God's goodness and ends by declaring how good it is to draw near to God and trust in Him, along with the great privilege of "*I may declare all thy works*". In between, Asaph rues his folly because of his envying of the bad, clearly identifiable, people who seem to live charmed and care free lives, whereas he was committed to the service of God and did not appear to be rewarded for doing so. But then he realises their end and the rewards of staying true to God despite having to endure troubles. If nothing else, this Psalm, like many Psalms, encourages the people of God to keep pressing on concerning the service of God. While I can identify with Asaph, having felt similarly and come to similar conclusions, we should take note that as a Levite, dedicated to the service of God, he was dependant on others for his support and without property or a paid job "on the side" he was in a vulnerable position, especially on seeing the wicked prosper. This Psalm serves a warning to the ungodly that their demise will be swift and terrible, as was realised when Jonathan Edwards preached on "*Sinners in the Hands of an Angry God*".

Song of Solomon

I confess – the Song of Solomon has been, for me, perhaps the book of the Bible that has intrigued me most during my Christian life. Harking back to when I was a teenager attending a traditional Brethren Breaking of Bread meeting, where the focus was on Christ and especially His atoning death, I recall many a meditation shared from this sublime song, all of which had to do with the glories of Christ. I agree with the Rabbi who declared: "*Heaven forbid any man in Israel ever disputed that the Song of Songs is holy. For the whole world is not worth the day on which the Song of Songs was given to Israel, for all the Writings are holy and the Song of Songs is holy of holies*" Rabbi Akiba (circa 100 AD).

I came to learn there were other views of the Song, besides those expressed by my early Brethren mentors. Like many in the church down the ages, they saw it more in terms of a picture of Christ and His Church, just as Jewish folk before then may have seen it in terms of YHWH and Israel. Other commentators, especially the modern ones, often see it as a poem mostly to do with sexual ethics, not so dissimilar to the sort of love poetry that had been written outside Israel 3000 years ago when Solomon wrote his Song and often dismiss claims it is depicting the love that ought to be present (if God has His way) in the divine/human relation. I have no problem with the notion that sex is good if done in the way God intended, and God wants us to know this to be the case and is why He inspired the writer of the Song to write in the way he did. I take that writer to be Solomon, David's son, just as I do when it comes to the writer of Proverbs (mostly) and Ecclesiastes (which we will get to).

I have come to a view (and not one I wish to impose on readers but rather share here by way of food for thought) that, when it comes to interpreting the Song, we can incorporate notions of it being both a holy sex manual and a beautiful love story of how it can be with any one of us and our blessed Lord Jesus Christ, with real life experiences including many of the ups and downs, joys and sorrows, triumphs and disasters, we might see in any lasting marriage relationship, written about in the Song explicitly and such that this can be seen both in an enduring relationship between a man and his wife. It is what God had always intended since He declared: "*Therefore shall a man leave his father and his mother, and shall cleave unto his wife: and they shall be one flesh*" Genesis 2:24. The Song can be taken as relating to a man/woman with his/her wife/husband, as well as that with their heavenly spouse. What is just as compelling is that this love story also records both the trials and triumphs of true love.

When it comes to controversial books of the Bible, where even the holy and learned often see things very differently, the Song of Solomon could well match what we find in the Book of Revelation. This is perhaps understandable given the Song is so rich in imagery, which may be best understood in terms of the Hebrew culture and mindset relating to the times when the Song was written. One area of contention has been the identity of the main characters. I am happy to accept the lover as being Solomon himself, albeit in a shepherd's disguise, and his beloved was a simple village girl he met and fell in love with when visiting his kingdom, perhaps far away from where he normally resided, and perhaps she was his one true love (he did write 1005 songs maybe one for each wife – but this was his Song of Songs), noting that Solomon eventually ended up having 700 wives and 300 concubines.

I would like to end this section on the Song of Solomon with a few of its stand out verses that have blessed me, all of which I have reflected on in my "Solomon" book that I referred to earlier:

- "*The song of songs, which is Solomon's.*" (1:1).
- "*Behold, thou art fair, my love; behold, thou art fair; thou hast doves' eyes.*" (1:15).
- "*He brought me to the banqueting house, and his banner over me was love.*" (2:4).
- "*The voice of my beloved! behold, he cometh leaping upon the mountains, skipping upon the hills.*" (2:8).
- "*My beloved spake, and said unto me, Rise up, my love, my fair one, and come away.*" (2:10).
- "*Take us the foxes, the little foxes, that spoil the vines: for our vines have tender grapes.*" (2:15).
- "*My beloved is mine, and I am his: he feedeth among the lilies.*" (2:16).

- *"By night on my bed I sought him whom my soul loveth: I sought him, but I found him not".* (3:1).

- *"Thou hast ravished my heart, my sister, my spouse; thou hast ravished my heart with one of thine eyes, with one chain of thy neck."* (4:9).

- *"Awake, O north wind; and come, thou south; blow upon my garden, that the spices thereof may flow out. Let my beloved come into his garden, and eat his pleasant fruits."* (4:16).

- *"My beloved is white and ruddy, the chiefest among ten thousand."* (5:10).

- *"Thou art beautiful, O my love, as Tirzah, comely as Jerusalem, terrible as an army with banners."* (6:4).

- *"I am my beloved's, and his desire is toward me."* (7:10).

- *"Set me as a seal upon thine heart, as a seal upon thine arm: for love is strong as death; jealousy is cruel as the grave: the coals thereof are coals of fire, which hath a most vehement flame."* (8:6).

- *"Many waters cannot quench love, neither can the floods drown it: if a man would give all the substance of his house for love, it would utterly be contemned."* (8:7).

- *"Make haste, my beloved, and be thou like to a roe or to a young hart upon the mountains of spices."* (8:14).

Proverbs

We come now to *"The proverbs of Solomon the son of David, king of Israel"* (1:1). Some, maybe most, of the proverbs were known before Solomon, and Solomon merely did a sifting job to make these available to those who would read them later. While, in writing Proverbs, Solomon may have had his sons in mind (who may have largely later ignored their father's counsel) and paid particular attention to things like avoiding loose women and not getting drunk, the book is rich in wisdom such that now that I am in my dotage I can reflect on "what if" (I had taken this advice seriously throughout my life).

Some proverbs are referred to as the sayings of the wise (22-24), suggesting these at least were not originated by Solomon. Not known of course but it would be interesting to know how many of the *"three thousand proverbs"* (1 Kings 4:32) Solomon wrote ended up in the Book of Proverbs. Some 350 years later, in the reign of King Hezekiah (715 to 686 BC), others did a further editing and compiling job, perhaps removing some of the inevitable repetition Solomon had introduced in order to make what we now see set before us all the more readable. Some, maybe many, proverbs were known already in the ancient world and originated by those who were from outside Israel, e.g., Egypt, including the followers of gods other than YHWH. It is perhaps a good example of common grace, that wisdom can come from unlikely sources. One may infer that part of Solomon's wisdom was to recognise the wisdom in others. We know of two named persons who contributed: Agur and Lemuel.

We also read from the outset the purpose of writing: "*To know wisdom and instruction; to perceive the words of understanding; To receive the instruction of wisdom, justice, and judgment, and equity; To give subtilty to the simple, to the young man knowledge and discretion. A wise man will hear, and will increase learning; and a man of understanding shall attain unto wise counsels: To understand a proverb, and the interpretation; the words of the wise, and their dark sayings*" (1:2-6). To complete the prologue, it is worth mentioning a statement that is central to the whole book, as it introduces two themes we do well to apply in our own lives, repeatedly referred to in Proverbs: wisdom is better than foolishness and that the fear of the Lord is what should govern our lives: "*The fear of the Lord is the beginning of knowledge: but fools despise wisdom and instruction*" (1:7).

A lot of the Book of Proverbs is pretty down to earth and, as one friend put it, "downright obvious". It covers all sorts of subjects, often very practical and matter of fact, and is good sound common-sense advice to help us follow the way of wisdom. Refreshingly, while God features big time, it is not particularly religious (which some find quite appealing) and covers all sorts of topics that could raise the eyebrows of those who are. It can be seen as advice parents (mother as well as father) would want their sons to take heed of, which given universal experience does not always happen, as lessons are often learned from the mistakes made by not taking heed of what one is taught. Proverbs seemed to be directed at men rather than women, because men were looked upon as the ones taking the lead, including in the family, although what is advised applies to us all, even today, 3000 years later, irrespective of all the cultural differences we now see. One amusing thought concerns the duties of a good wife (31:10-31) since I don't know any, even among the best, doing all that is written here.

Interestingly, sayings from the Proverbs are not just often quoted in the New Testament but many find themselves being referred to in everyday life. My own experience as a preacher and hearer of many sermons is that, unlike Solomon's other books, Proverbs does not usually feature as the main sermon subject, but specific examples are often referred to. Not only that, but in real life application, including what people write on social media, by some who are unaware they are quoting from the Bible. The English translators of

Proverbs, e.g., in the KJV, have done a creditable job given the limitations of translating breath-taking Hebrew poetry into a form that modern readers can easily identify with.

What is so thrilling is the practicality of what is said by someone who had lived long enough to have experienced life in the raw (been there, done that and got the tee shirt), yet wisdom from on High is needed to make sense of much of life, whether disciplining children, the value of hard work, the art of the deal, how to treat women, being honest in business, the power of the tongue, maintaining one's own counsel – and so much more. To cite my NIV Study Bible: these proverbs range widely across the broad spectrum of human situations, relationships and responsibilities; offering insights, warnings, instructions and counsels, along with frequent motivations to heed them.

In a variety of situations and relationships, the reader is exhorted to honesty, integrity, diligence, kindness, generosity, readiness to forgive, truthfulness, patience, humility, cheerfulness, loyalty, temperance, self-control and the prudent consideration of consequences that flow from attitudes, choices and/or actions. Anger should be held in check, violence and quarrelsomeness shunned, gossip avoided, arrogance repudiated. Drunkenness, gluttony, envy and greed should all be renounced. The poor are not to be exploited, the courts are not to be unjustly manipulated, legitimate authorities are to be honoured. Parents should care for the proper instruction and discipline of their children, and children should duly honour their parents and ensure they bring no disgrace upon them. Human observation and experience have taught the wise that a certain order is in place in God's creation. To recognise such leads to known positive effects; to deny it leads only to unhappy consequences. Life should be lived in conscious awareness of the unfailing scrutiny of the Lord and in reliance on His generous providence. All these are good reasons why we should study the Book of Proverbs!

Ecclesiastes

Ecclesiastes should be seen as a book for all ages – for the older generation making sense out of this world and having learned from the school of hard knocks that what it says makes sense; for the younger, as a sober warning of what is to come and why they should *"remember now thy Creator in the days of thy youth"*, as well as the in-betweeners, being a useful foil to Proverbs with its hopeful message of the way of wisdom, and to Song of Songs with its recurring theme of love that conquers all. The main thrust of Ecclesiastes is the meaninglessness of *"life under the sun"*, and it does well to complement the messages of the importance of the way of wisdom (Proverbs) and that of the power of love (Song of Songs). The notions of vanity (or pointlessness), referred to 29 times in Ecclesiastes, and of life under the sun, 31 times, is indicative of the author's central themes. Vanity (Hebrew: *hebel* – vapor, breath) appropriately sums up what life under the sun is like as far as the author is concerned. Realising this to be the case helps us to make sense of life.

No doubt the position Solomon found himself in (having time, power, wealth etc.), as well as wisdom from above, gave him ample opportunity to reflect as he did. One can't help wondering, though, why this same person, who began his reign so well, with every good intention, ended it so badly, by not practising what he preached. One of the good things to come out of his falling away toward the end is that Solomon better understood the consequences of where such actions might lead. If there is a salutary lesson here – we can be cynical and correct but it makes little difference to how we live. The whole point of getting to know the brutal truth as we do here is we can then respond appropriately.

Reading through Ecclesiastes leaves us in little doubt the author had lived a long and full life, experiencing for himself and seeing it in others – highs and lows, triumphs and disasters, joy and sorrow, justice and injustice; from the very good to the very bad etc., suggesting by the time he got to write he was getting old. Reading Ecclesiastes leaves one with the impression that here was someone who had experienced many aspects of life but now he could no longer summon up much enthusiasm, being unimpressed, having seen it all, along with a sense of world weariness. If we are to come up with an alternative, Ecclesiastes could show how "life under the sun" could be.

What the Preacher has learned includes:

1. Humans cannot by all their striving achieve anything of ultimate or enduring significance. Nothing appears to be going anywhere (1:5-11), and people cannot by all their efforts break out of this caged treadmill (1:2-4; 2:1-11); they cannot fundamentally change anything (1:12-15; 6:10; 7:13). Hence, they often toil foolishly (4:4,7-8; 5:10-17; 6:7-9). All their striving *"under the sun"* (1:3) after unreal goals leads only to disillusionment.

2. Wisdom is better than folly (2:13-14; 7:1-6, 11-12,19; 8:1,5; 9:17-18; 10:1-3, 12-15; 12:11) – it is God's gift to those who please him (2:26). But it is unwarranted to expect too much from having such wisdom – to expect that human wisdom is capable of solving all problems (1:16-18) or of securing for itself enduring rewards or advantages (2:12-17; 4:13-16; 9:13-16).

3. Experience confronts humans with many apparent disharmonies and anomalies that wisdom cannot unravel. Of these, the greatest

is human life, which comes to the same end as that of the animals – death (2:15; 3:18-19; 7:15; 8:14; 9:1-3; 10:5-7).

4. Although God made humankind upright, people have gone in search of many "schemes" (to get ahead by taking advantage of others; see 7:29; cf. Psalm 10:2; 36:4; 140:2). So even humans are a disappointment (7:24-29).

5. People cannot know or control what will come after them, or even what lies in the more immediate future. Therefore, all their efforts remain balanced on the razor's edge of uncertainty (2:18; 6:12; 7:14; 9:2).

6. God keeps humans in their place (3:16-22).

7. God has ordered all things (3:1-15; 5:19; 6:1-6; 9:1), and a human being cannot change God's appointments or fully understand them or anticipate them (3:1; 7; 11:1-6). But the world is not fundamentally chaotic or irrational. It is ordered by God, and it is for humans to accept matters as they are by God's appointments, including their own limitations. Everything has its "time" and is good in its time.

He therefore counsels:

1. Accept the human state, as it is shaped by God's appointments and enjoy the life you have been given as fully as you can.

2. Don't trouble yourself with unrealistic goals – know the measure of your human capabilities.

3. Be prudent in all your ways – follow wisdom's leading.

4. "*Fear God and keep his commandments*" (12:13), beginning in your youth before the fleeting days of life's enjoyments are gone and "*the days of trouble*" (12:1) come when infirmities of advanced age vex you and hinder you from tasting, seeing and feeling the good things of life. While no kill joy, the Preacher stresses the need to fear God and to start young.

5. Ecclesiastes provides plentiful instruction on how to live meaningfully, purposefully and joyfully within the theocratic arrangement – primarily by placing God at the centre of one's life, work and activities, by contentedly accepting one's divinely appointed lot in life, by making sound life decisions and by reverently trusting in and obeying the Creator-King.

Finally

With these thoughts in mind, we complete our short consideration of the five books of Wisdom, and with it express the hope that this has whetted the appetite of the reader to check these out and do the very things that the texts we have cited have encouraged those of us who are a priestly people to do. That is to get wisdom (as long as it is the wisdom which is derived from our infallible God rather than that of fallible man) and thereby be able to skilfully apply the knowledge we gain, to understand life from God's perspective and have the ability to do the right thing at the right time. Let us too remember God's invitation and promise "*If any of you lack wisdom, let him ask of God, that giveth to all men liberally, and upbraideth not; and it shall be given him*" James 1:5. Having recognised the desirability of wisdom, we should rejoice at the examples of people who acted wisely in the Bible and ourselves be exemplars of it: "*Who is a wise man and endued with knowledge among you? let him shew out of a good conversation his works with meekness of wisdom. But if ye have bitter envying and strife in your hearts, glory not, and lie not against the truth. This wisdom descendeth not from above, but is earthly, sensual, devilish. For where envying and strife is, there is confusion and every evil work. But the wisdom that is from above is first pure, then peaceable, gentle, and easy to be intreated, full of mercy and good fruits, without partiality, and without hypocrisy. And the fruit of righteousness is sown in peace of them that make peace*" James 3:13-18.

We end with two hymns. Both concern the importance of wisdom and, as wisdom is a subject that also interests New Testament writers, some thoughts of the Apostle Paul, which bring out the point that the wisdom we need is godly wisdom rather than the wisdom of the world. Such wisdom should interest all devoted followers of Jesus, as it should have done with those living in ancient Israel:

1. Be thou my vision, O Lord of my heart;
naught be all else to me, save that thou art.
Thou my best thought, by day or by night,
waking or sleeping, thy presence my light.

2. Be thou my wisdom, be thou my true word;
I ever with thee, and thou with me, Lord.
Born of thy love, thy child may I be,
thou in me dwelling and I one with thee.

3. Be thou my buckler, my sword for the fight.
Be thou my dignity, thou my delight,
thou my soul's shelter, thou my high tow'r.
Raise thou me heav'nward, O Pow'r of my pow'r.

4. Riches I heed not, nor vain empty praise;
thou mine inheritance, now and always.
Thou and thou only, first in my heart,
Ruler of heaven, my treasure thou art.

4. High King of heaven, my victory won
May I reach heaven's joys, O bright heaven's sun
Heart of my own heart, whatever befall
Still be my vision, O ruler of all

And

1. Immortal, invisible, God only wise,
In light inaccessible hid from our eyes,
Most blessed, most glorious, the Ancient of Days,
Almighty, victorious, Thy great name we praise.

2. Unresting, unhasting, and silent as light,
Nor wanting, nor wasting, Thou rulest in might;
Thy justice like mountains high soaring above
Thy clouds which are fountains of goodness and love.

3. To all life Thou givest, to both great and small;
In all life Thou livest, the true life of all;
We blossom and flourish as leaves on the tree,
And wither and perish, but nought changeth Thee.

4. Great Father of Glory, pure Father of Light

Thine angels adore Thee, all veiling their sight;

All laud we would render, O help us to see:

'Tis only the splendor of light hideth Thee.

"*For the preaching of the cross is to them that perish foolishness; but unto us which are saved it is the power of God. For it is written, I will destroy the wisdom of the wise, and will bring to nothing the understanding of the prudent. Where is the wise? where is the scribe? where is the disputer of this world? hath not God made foolish the wisdom of this world? For after that in the wisdom of God the world by wisdom knew not God, it pleased God by the foolishness of preaching to save them that believe. For the Jews require a sign, and the Greeks seek after wisdom: But we preach Christ crucified, unto the Jews a stumblingblock, and unto the Greeks foolishness; But unto them which are called, both Jews and Greeks, Christ the power of God, and the wisdom of God. Because the foolishness of God is wiser than men; and the weakness of God is stronger than men. For ye see your calling, brethren, how that not many wise men after the flesh, not many mighty, not many noble, are called: But God hath chosen the foolish things of the world to confound the wise; and God hath chosen the weak things of the world to confound the things which are mighty; And base things of the world, and things which are despised, hath God chosen, yea, and things which are not, to bring to nought things that are: That no flesh should glory in his presence. But of him are ye in Christ Jesus, who of God is made unto us wisdom, and righteousness, and sanctification, and redemption: That, according as it is written, He that glorieth, let him glory in the Lord*" 1 Corinthians 1:18-31.

Chapter 54: Relating Old and New Testaments

"For the prophecy came not in old time by the will of man: but holy men of God spake as they were moved by the Holy Ghost" 2 Peter 1:21.

"All scripture is given by inspiration of God, and is profitable for doctrine, for reproof, for correction, for instruction in righteousness: That the man of God may be perfect, thoroughly furnished unto all good works" 2 Timothy 3:16.

"These (Bereans) were more noble than those in Thessalonica, in that they received the word with all readiness of mind, and searched the scriptures daily, whether those things were so" Acts 17:11.

As with "**Prophets of the Bible**", "**Priests of the Bible**" contains far more references, concerning what we need to know about those subjects, from the Old Testament rather than from the New. The reason for this is simple – just as there were far more prophets (and prophecies) written about in the Old Testament than in the New, there were also far more priests (and priestly activities) written about in the Old Testament than in the New Testament. Yet together, the two Testaments, besides both being of paramount importance when it comes to discerning the will of God and understanding His ways, contain God's written Word, and that is reason enough for our needing to study them both.

With reference to the three verses given at the beginning of this chapter, the first is do with prophecy that originated from God and can all be found in the Old Testament, with the fulfilment of some to be found in the New Testament, some since then and some yet to be fulfilled, but they will be by the time of Jesus' Second Coming, His Millennial reign and the bringing in of the New Heaven and the New Earth. The second text provides several good reasons why the Scriptures need to be studied and, given the full New Testament was not available then, the Scriptures Paul would have had in mind would have been found in the Old Testament. Regarding the third text, this was in the context of the response of Jews that Paul met on his missionary journeys, when it was his practice to reason with them out of the Scriptures, a challenge the Bereans enthusiastically responded to and were commended for.

I recall as a young man listening to the person who helped to sow the seed for my interest in Bible priests, coming out with the saying: *"the New is in the Old concealed; the Old is in the New revealed"*. He was spot on and he was simply expressing why Old and New Testaments are complementary and why we need both to fully understand either. That same brother taught the young people, over several sessions, lessons arising from the Wilderness wanderings of the Children of Israel, following their Exodus from Egypt, and these lessons generally had some New Testament application. As for this book, when it comes to priests and the priesthood, much of the basics concerning those subjects can be found during that period. The same principles apply to all the books of the Old Testament.

Without overstating the obvious, the God of Israel in the Old Testament is the same God of followers of Jesus (Jews and Gentiles) in the New: "*I am the Lord, I change not*" Malachi 3:6, and given the notion of the Trinity (Father, Son and Holy Ghost) is to be found from right at the beginning of the Bible: "*Jesus Christ the same yesterday, and today, and for ever*" Hebrews 13:8. While it is true that the central focus in the Old concerned the Covenant God made with Israel on Mount Sinai, the principles laid down are for all of us to learn from. The Old Testament, especially the books following the Torah (Law), also looked forward to the coming Messiah that Christians believe were fulfilled in Jesus. As for the New Testament, the Messiah has been revealed in the person of Jesus and also the New Covenant in His blood – but, to explore more deeply all the ramifications of this, we need to refer back to the Old.

When advising a new Christian where to begin when studying the Bible, my standard response is to begin with one or more of the four Gospels – but what next? Understandably, they might be encouraged to stay in the New Testament before delving into the Old, beginning with Genesis and Exodus, until it stops being primarily story telling. But to gain a full understanding of God's revealed word and will, they need to study all the Bible and, while not the practice of most, read the whole Bible in a year and do so every year because always they will find things not previously seen.

One good reason to study the Old Testament is it helps us understand the New. The Books of Matthew, and Hebrews spring to mind as ones containing many references to the Old Testament and, not surprisingly, these were aimed firstly at Jewish believers but also contain those nuggets of truth we all need. We find somewhere between two and three hundred quotations from the Old Testament in the New Testament. Beyond this, there is a great amount of allusive material, some of which is deliberate, and some is unconscious, although nevertheless real. The New Testament writers were thoroughly immersed in the Old Testament. They lived and breathed the content of those writings, particularly God's saving activity on behalf of Israel and the Covenant promises concerning Israel.

When they were confronted with the ministry of Jesus, His proclamation by word and deed of the reality of the Kingdom, they understood it to be the consummation of God's saving activity and the fulfilment of the Covenant promises, although it wasn't until Jesus had risen from the dead that they truly understood what this was. When they came to narrate the story of Christ in the Gospels and the meaning of that story in the epistles, these writers continually made use of the Old Testament to show that what had so recently taken place in their midst was the fulfilment of Old Testament expectation. As for the one book that is mainly prophecy, Revelation, this is best interpreted in the light of the Old Testament as so much refers to it. Often too their interpretation of the scriptures they cited may not be ones that occur to the modern Gentile mind, thus making it even more pertinent.

When Paul engaged with Jews who knew the Hebrew Scriptures, he used those same scriptures to prove his case, as noted earlier with the Bereans. We may be no Paul, and unlike Paul, we do have the whole of the New Testament (including Paul's writings) from which we can make our case, and how more powerfully can we do so if drawing upon both Testaments. The reality is that while there are Jewish believers in Yeshua their Mashiach, they are a minority and this has been the case after the first century CE. While the Gospel is for the Jew first, a day is coming when all Israel shall be saved and the challenge remains to present the Gospel to Israel (and best if we can use their Book). The Bible is a book full of truth and in order to get anything approaching the full truth, and in order to fully grasp the whole counsel of God, which should be the goal of all believers, we need both Testaments.

A powerful argument as to the truth that Christians claim concerning Jesus is the fulfilment of Old Testament prophecy, such as Isaiah 53 that is to do with the Suffering Servant. Many scriptures can be cited: Genesis 3:15, Genesis 12:3, Psalm 2:6, Psalm 22:16, Psalm 45:6-7, Psalm 110:4, Isaiah 7:14, Isaiah 9:1-2, Isaiah 50:6, Daniel 2:44, Daniel 7:13-14, Hosea 11:1, Micah 5:2, Zechariah 9:9, Zechariah 11:12, Zechariah 12:10 are all worth checking out, and there are many more. It should be realised that when the Hebrew prophets prophesied, they often did not see the long (more than 2000 years) time gap between the two comings. As believers, we are told to "*be ready always to give an answer to every man that asketh you a reason of the hope that is in you with meekness and fear*" 1 Peter 3:15. The fulfilment of Old Testament prophecy, among other things, may be cited as reasons for that hope.

One of the motivations behind my writing "**Priests of the Bible**" is a desire to reach out to Jews, especially those who do not accept Yeshua (Jesus) as being their Mashiach (Messiah). I am conscious many better than I have tried to do the same down the millennia with often, it seems, little result from their efforts. We can cite the example of Jesus, after He rose from the dead, as the type of approach attempted in this book. We read of when Jesus walked with two God fearing Jews along the Emmaus Road; their hopes that Jesus might be the real deal, the very Messiah they had been waiting for, had been dashed when He ended up dying that shameful death upon the Cross. Having let them get off their chests their concerns, without revealing His identity, we find Jesus responding: *"Then he said unto them, O fools, and slow of heart to believe all that the prophets have spoken: Ought not Christ to have suffered these things, and to enter into his glory? And beginning at Moses and all the prophets, he expounded unto them in all the scriptures the things concerning himself"* Luke 24:25-27. We read at the end: *"And their eyes were opened, and they knew him; and he vanished out of their sight. And they said one to another, Did not our heart burn within us, while he talked with us by the way, and while he opened to us the scriptures?"* Luke 24:31-32.

Over the years, I have enjoyed friendly relations with many Jews (as well as Muslims) and the best I can do now, besides maintaining friendship and developing new ones, is to declare, as did John the Baptist: *"Behold the Lamb of God, which taketh away the sin of the world"* John 1:29. While much could be said about approaches and attitudes toward Jews (and Muslims); Christians, Jews and Muslims are *"People of the Book"* or Ahl al-kitāb, which is an Islamic term referring to followers of those religions which Muslims regard as having been guided by previous revelations, generally in the form of a scripture. This ought to spur on Christians to know their Book (Old and New Testaments).

Some commentators have had a field day going through every book of the Old Testament saying why in each of these books we can see types and shadows of, if not references to, the Christ that is to come. I will focus on the first five books and affirm my belief that these are more than merely tenuous links:

Genesis, specifically 22:1-19, relates to God telling Abraham that he needed to sacrifice his son, Isaac. When Isaac asked: *"Behold the fire and the wood: but where is the lamb for a burnt offering?"* (v7), Abraham responded *"My son, God will provide himself a lamb for a burnt offering: so they went both of them together"* (v8). In the end, Isaac earned a reprieve, just before the knife came down, and a ram caught in a thicket was sacrificed instead. At the Cross of Calvary, God did sacrifice His own Son and, like Isaac, Jesus obeyed His Father. *"For God so loved the world, that he gave his only begotten Son, that whosoever believeth in him should not perish, but have everlasting life"* John 3:16.

Exodus, specifically 12:1-51, tells us what happened on the first Feast of Passover, just before the Children of Israel left Egypt in order to journey to the Promised Land. The central act was each Israelite family sacrificing a lamb and applying the blood from the lamb to the door posts and the key text is *"when I see the blood, I will pass over you"* (12:13). That night every firstborn Egyptian son was slain. We read in the New Testament, Jesus celebrating the Passover with His disciples just prior to going to the Cross: *"the Lord Jesus the same night in which he was betrayed took bread: And when he had given thanks, he brake it, and said, Take, eat: this is my body, which is broken for you: this do in remembrance of me. After the same manner also he took the cup, when he had supped, saying, this cup is the new testament in my blood: this do ye, as oft as ye drink it, in remembrance of me. For as often as ye eat this bread, and drink this cup, ye do shew the Lord's death till he come"* 1 Corinthians 11:23-26.

Leviticus, specifically 16:1-19, details what took place on the day of Atonement. In part, it was the tale of two goats. One goat was sacrificed for the sin of the people and its blood sprinkled by the High Priest over the Mercy Seat situated in the Holy of Holies to atone for the sins of the people. The other goat (the Scapegoat) had the High Priest's hands laid on it whereby the sin of the people would be transferred onto the goat, before it was released into the Wilderness. We are reminded that Jesus is both the Priest and also the sacrifice for sin (our sin): *"Wherefore Jesus also, that he might sanctify the people with his own blood, suffered without the gate"* Hebrews 13:12.

Numbers, specifically 21:4-9, is the account of God sending a plague of snakes in response to the Israelites complaining during their wilderness journey, but there was a solution: *"And the Lord said unto Moses, Make thee a fiery serpent, and set it upon a pole: and it shall come to pass, that every one that is bitten, when he looketh upon it, shall live. And Moses made a serpent of brass, and put it upon a pole, and it came to pass, that if a serpent had bitten any man, when he beheld the serpent of brass, he lived"* 21:8-9. In Jesus' discourse with Nicodemus, He recalled that incident and applied it to himself and the lesson that one needed to look to Jesus in order to live: *"And as Moses lifted up the serpent in the wilderness, even so must the Son of man be lifted up"* John 3:14.

Deuteronomy, specifically 21:22,23, is where we learn *"And if a man have committed a sin worthy of death, and he be to be put to death, and thou hang him on a tree: His body shall not remain all night upon the tree, but thou shalt in any wise bury him that day; (for he that is hanged is accursed of God;) that thy land be not defiled, which the Lord thy God giveth thee for an inheritance"*. We learn in the New Testament that Jesus took that curse on our behalf by taking upon Himself our sin and being forsaken by His Father as a result: *"Christ hath redeemed us from the curse of the law, being made a curse for us: for it is written, Cursed is every one that hangeth on a tree"* Galatians 3:13.

As important as types and shadows in the Old Testament are when it comes to relating to many of the major themes of the New Testament, even more important is the number of prophecies that were later fulfilled in the time of Jesus and many yet to be fulfilled. In my book "**Prophets of the Bible**" I considered many of these prophecies. We are spoiled for choice when it comes to finding examples to cite that are pertinent concerning "**Priests of the Bible**" but we will do so here with respect to the Book of Isaiah. There are many prophecies from Isaiah quoted by the New Testament writers and it is sometimes said that Isaiah can be seen to be a fifth gospel, where many of the Gospel themes can be found. Isaiah may be viewed in two halves: Chapters 1-39 that are particularly to do with judgement and Chapters 40-66 that are particularly to do with salvation.

One commentator remarked that the whole gospel narrative can be found in this second half, starting with John the Baptist in Chapter 40, the voice in the wilderness preparing the way of the Lord, and ending with the final judgement and new heaven and new earth in Chapter 66. Of particular interest here are the Servant Songs that the New Testament writers believed were about Jesus. The details given were a powerful presentation of His life and ministry, 700 years before He was born. It could be said that the central theme of the New Testament is that we are sinners needing to be saved and Jesus is that saviour and, pertinent to our consideration of the sacrificial system as a key element of the Levitical Priesthood, Jesus is that sacrificial lamb.

According to **Got Questions**: "*There are four "Servant Songs" of Isaiah that describe the service, suffering, and exaltation of the Servant of the Lord, the Messiah. All four songs show the Messiah to be God's meek and gentle Servant. He is a royal figure, representing Israel in its ideal form; He is the high priest, atoning for the sins of the world. Isaiah predicts that this Servant of the Lord would deliver the world from the prison of sin. In the royal terminology of the ancient Near East, a servant was a "trusted envoy," a "confidential representative," or "one who is chosen." The Servant Songs are found in Isaiah 42:1-9; Isaiah 49:1-13; Isaiah 50:4-11; and Isaiah 52:13-53:12. Isaiah initially identifies God's servant as Israel (41:8; 44:1–2), who serves as God's witness (43:10) and as a light to the Gentiles. Yet Israel could not fulfill this mission: Israel was deaf, blind (42:19), and in need of God's forgiveness (44:21-22). Israel failed again and again. By contrast, God's Servant, the Messiah, faithfully completes all the work He is given to do (cf. Luke 13:32; John 17:4). The Servant of the Lord is God's faithful and true witness to humanity*". We will focus here on the fourth song: Isaiah 52:13-53:12, quoted several times in the New Testament and precisely fulfilled in Jesus. It was the very passage that Philip referred to when he explained the Gospel before leading the Ethiopian eunuch to Christ (Acts 9:26-40).

Quoting from "**Prophets of the Bible**", this is how detailed and exact the Isaiah 52:13-53:12 prophecy was concerning what Jesus did and accomplished as a result of dying on the Cross:

- He shall be exalted and extolled (52:13).
- His visage was so marred more than any man (52:14).
- So shall He sprinkle many nations (52:15).
- The kings shall shut their mouths at him (52:15).
- What he did was beyond belief (53:1).
- There is no beauty that we should desire him (53:2).
- He is despised and rejected of men (53:3).
- A man of sorrows, and acquainted with grief (53:3).
- We hid as it were our faces from him (53:3).
- He was despised, and we esteemed him not (53:3).
- He hath borne our griefs, and carried our sorrows (53:4).
- Yet we did esteem him stricken, smitten of God, and afflicted (53:4).
- He was wounded for our transgressions, bruised for our iniquities (53:5).
- With his stripes we are healed (53:5).
- All we like sheep have gone astray (53:6).
- The Lord hath laid on him the iniquity of us all (53:6).
- He was oppressed, and he was afflicted (53:7).
- He opened not his mouth (53:7).
- He is brought as a lamb to the slaughter (53:7).
- As a sheep before her shearers is dumb, so he openeth not his mouth (53:7).
- For he was cut off out of the land of the living (53:8).
- For the transgression of my people was he stricken (53:8).
- He made his grave with the wicked (53:9).
- And with the rich in his death (53:9).
- Yet it pleased the Lord to bruise him (53:10).
- Thou shalt make his soul an offering for sin (53:10).
- The pleasure of the Lord shall prosper in his hand (53:10).
- He shall see of the travail of his soul, and shall be satisfied (53:11).
- By his knowledge shall my righteous servant justify many (53:11).
- He shall bear their iniquities (53:11).

- He will be given a portion with the great (53:12).

- He poured out His soul unto death (53:12).

- He was numbered with the transgressors (53:12).

- He bare the sin of many, and made intercession for the transgressors (53:12).

If it comes to having to choose between studying the Old or the New Testament, I would refuse to do so. I suspect, I may be unusual among Christians who preach, as I often go off the beaten track when choosing unusual Old Testament subjects to preach on. This has obviously been the case covering the subject of Priests of the Bible. Besides my curiosity and the fact that these subjects are often otherwise neglected by those who teach from the Bible, I often find myself remonstrating with God over matters like His ordering the annihilation of whole people groups and ordering the stoning of those committing what in these days would be seen as minor misdemeanours, and a whole set of dos and don'ts that don't make sense to modern minds, yet were mandated on people, especially His chosen people, Israel. As I further reflect, I find myself concurring with the Psalmist: "*The statutes of the Lord are right, rejoicing the heart: the commandment of the Lord is pure, enlightening the eyes. The fear of the Lord is clean, enduring for ever: the judgments of the Lord are true and righteous altogether*" (19:8-9).

All this appeared to bear little relevance to the situation seen at the time, let alone today's situation. On top of that, there are a whole string of objections to believing in the Jewish/Christian God, often based on the Old Testament caricature of a cruel and vindictive God as opposed to the New Testament one of a kind and loving God, which many, including nominal Christians, are happy to go along with. Another objection goes back to the first eleven chapters of the Bible, especially the first one, that talks about God creating the world in six days, and how do we reconcile that with what science teaches if we are to take the Bible literally and deduce that Earth cannot be more than 10,000 years old?

Having been confronted with these various objections, both as a result of questions I have raised in my going deeper than most in my studies of the Old Testament and from listening to what other people say, especially if their questions are sincere and they are not merely seeking to bait or it is an excuse that stops them doing what they know they need to do, i.e., repent, the best I can come up with is my conviction, that the Bible, both Old and New Testaments, is entirely true, and God who repeatedly reveals Himself to be holy is entirely righteous in His actions and what He requires of human kind.

I would love to talk about the sins of the Amorites and God's plan for dealing with it, as discussed with Abraham in Genesis 15, and the fact that

God owns the planet and can do what he wants with it, allocating land to those He chooses, favouring one nation (the Jews) above all others, that God is holy beyond measure and nothing is too difficult for God. These are subjects for another day and another book. While all these perceived to be problematic features of the Old Testament are sufficient reasons for many of today's priests/ministers to avoid preaching on anything other than the "easy bits", I would argue that studying the "hard bits" would lead one to a fuller understanding of God and His ways.

While much "Christian" teaching is best laid out in the New Testament and it is that which is within people's comfort zones, teaching that benefits any who wish to be disciples of Jesus is to be found in both Testaments and both are needed for a full understanding. Not to study both means we will miss out. We need to *study to shew thyself approved unto God, a workman that needeth not to be ashamed, rightly dividing the word of truth*" 2 Timothy 2:15. We must remember "*All scripture is given by inspiration of God, and is profitable for doctrine, for reproof, for correction, for instruction in righteousness*" 2 Timothy 3:16. While there is a lot more to the Christian life than studying the Old and New Testament and knowledge of the scriptures is no substitute for obedience to God and being good people, if we are to know what God requires of us and arrive at a true balance as to what is needed, there is no better place to begin than with the Bible, and that includes both Old and New Testaments.

As for responding to this knowledge in an appropriate way, we might begin by understanding the true meaning and purpose of worshipping the Lord and become first and foremost worshippers of Him ahead of self-gratification or propensity to do our "own thing" (something directed first to me, before any of my readers): "*O come, let us worship and bow down: let us kneel before the Lord our maker. For he is our God; and we are the people of his pasture, and the sheep of his hand. Today if ye will hear his voice, Harden not your heart, as in the provocation, and as in the day of temptation in the wilderness ... Give unto the Lord the glory due unto his name: bring an offering, and come into his courts. O worship the Lord in the beauty of holiness: fear before him, all the earth*" Psalm 95:6-8, 96:8-9.

In conclusion, the God Moses knew and spoke concerning is the same God spoken of by Peter, Paul and John in the New Testament, who all proclaimed: "*Give ear, O ye heavens, and I will speak; and hear, O earth, the words of my mouth. My doctrine shall drop as the rain, my speech shall distil as the dew, as the small rain upon the tender herb, and as the showers upon the grass: Because I will publish the name of the Lord: ascribe ye greatness unto our God. He is the Rock, his work is perfect: for all his ways are judgment: a God of truth and without iniquity, just and right is he*" Deuteronomy 32:1-4.

Chapter 55: Hebrews – The New Testament Book About Priests

" *God, who at sundry times and in divers manners spake in time past unto the fathers by the prophets, Hath in these last days spoken unto us by his Son, whom he hath appointed heir of all things, by whom also he made the worlds; Who being the brightness of his glory, and the express image of his person, and upholding all things by the word of his power, when he had by himself purged our sins, sat down on the right hand of the Majesty on high"* Hebrews 1:1-3.

I love the way the Book of Hebrews begins, and especially when expressed in the KJV. Hebrews may be to the New Testament what Leviticus is to the Old (at least in the eyes of many modern Gentile readers) in that it is one least studied. Understandably, new Christians may begin with one or more of the four Gospels and then move on to the Acts and some of the epistles (Paul, John, Peter, James and Jude, possibly in that order) and, depending on how their church views end times prophecy, Revelation. That leaves Hebrews! Going back to the preacher who was asked what his favourite book of the New Testament was, wisely replying it was the one he was currently studying, I can think of two reasons to reply – Hebrews, besides the fact that it teaches more about the priests and the priesthood than any other New Testament book and is particularly relevant to **"Priests of the Bible"**. Firstly, in terms of doctrinal richness and coverage it matches that of the Book of Romans, for example. Secondly, in terms of memorable verses, Hebrews is full of them. These are some I can recall from my youth:

1. The verses we started this chapter with (1:1-3).

2. *"But we see Jesus, who was made a little lower than the angels for the suffering of death, crowned with glory and honour; that he by the grace of God should taste death for every man"* (2:9).

3. *"For the word of God is quick, and powerful, and sharper than any twoedged sword, piercing even to the dividing asunder of soul and spirit, and of the joints and marrow, and is a discerner of the thoughts and intents of the heart"* (4:12).

4. *"For we have not an high priest which cannot be touched with the feeling of our infirmities; but was in all points tempted like as we are, yet without sin"* (4:15).

5. *"Wherefore he is able also to save them to the uttermost that come unto God by him, seeing he ever liveth to make intercession for them"* (7:25).

6. *"And as it is appointed unto men once to die, but after this the judgment"* (9:27).

7. *"Having therefore, brethren, boldness to enter into the holiest by the blood of Jesus, by a new and living way, which he hath consecrated for us, through the veil, that is to say, his flesh"* (10:19-20).

8. *"Not forsaking the assembling of ourselves together, as the manner of some is; but exhorting one another: and so much the more, as ye see the day approaching"* (10:25).

9. *"But without faith it is impossible to please him: for he that cometh to God must believe that he is, and that he is a rewarder of them that diligently seek him"* (11:6).

10. *"Looking unto Jesus the author and finisher of our faith; who for the joy that was set before him endured the cross, despising the shame, and is set down at the right hand of the throne of God"* (12:2).

11. *"Jesus Christ the same yesterday, and today, and for ever"* (13:8).

12. *"Wherefore Jesus also, that he might sanctify the people with his own blood, suffered without the gate. Let us go forth therefore unto him without the camp, bearing his reproach. For here have we no continuing city, but we seek one to come"* (13:12-14).

Before we consider (albeit all too briefly) some of the content of the Book of Hebrews, it is worth considering how it is laid out. One suggestion, based on what my NIV Study Bible presents, is:

Prologue: God's New Revelation is better (Hebrews 1:1-4)

Christ is better than leading figures under the Old Covenant (Hebrews 1:5-7:28)

Christ is better than the Angels (1:5-2:18).

- Scriptural proof of his superiority (1:5-14).
- Exhortation not to ignore the revelation of God in his Son (2:1-4).
- Jesus was made a little lower than the angels (2:5-9).
- Having been made like us, Jesus was enabled to save us (2:10-18).

- Christ Is better than Moses (3:1-4:13).
- Demonstration of Christ's superiority (3:1-6).
- Exhortation to enter salvation-rest (3:7-4:13).

Christ Is better than the Aaronic Priests (4:14-7:28).

- Jesus is the great high priest (4:14-16).
- Qualifications of a priest (5:1-10).
- Exhortation to press on toward maturity (5:11-6:12).
- The certainty of God's promise (6:13-20).
- Christ's superior priestly order (7:1-28).

The Sacrificial Work of Our High Priest is better (Hebrews 8:1-10:18)

- A New Sanctuary and a New Covenant (8:1-13).
- The Old Sanctuary (9:1-10).
- The Better Sacrifice (9:11-10:18).

A Call to Follow Jesus Faithfully and with Perseverance (Hebrews 10:19-12:3)

- As in the past, so in the future (10:32-39).
- Faith and its many outstanding examples (11:1-40).
- Jesus, the supreme example (12:1-3).

Encouragement to Persevere in the Face of Hardship (Hebrews 12:4-12:29)

- Exhortation to Holy Living (12:4-17).
- Crowning Motivation and Warning (12:18-29).

Conclusion (Hebrews 13:1-25)

- Rules for Christian Living (13:1-17).
- Request for Prayer (13:18-19).
- Benediction (13:20-21).
- Personal Remarks (13:22-23).
- Greetings and Final Benediction (13:24-25).

Another, shorter yet helpful breakdown, is based on Stuart Kimber's "A Pathway into the Bible":

1. Jesus – God's Final Revelation (Ch. 1-2).
2. Moses, Creation and the High Priest (Walk on beyond the Old Covenant) (Ch. 3:1-6:20).
3. Jesus – High Priest of the New Covenant (Walk on into the New Covenant) (Ch. 7:1-10:39).
4. All those who walked this way before us (Walk on with Jesus) (Ch. 11-13).

As with the earlier overviews of books of the Bible (Genesis, Leviticus, Chronicles and the Wisdom books) this one, concerning Hebrews, is going to be short, even though much can be profitably drawn from its contents and better Bible teachers than me have written large volumes expounding the lessons it teaches. Mine, besides providing an overview to encourage students of the Bible, has a particular emphasis on how the arguments etc., that the writer to the Hebrews sets out in his letter relate to the subject of this book (priests and the priesthood). We have already considered one of the core themes of Hebrews, that of Jesus being the Great High Priest of the Order of Melchizedek (Chapter 20), but it will also be noted that other chapters of this book draw on Hebrews as a source.

We say "writer to the Hebrews" because we don't know who it is, although in the Christian set-up I was part of as a young believer, some assumed it was Paul, or at least wished it were so. Most commentaries will take up space considering the possibilities, often without coming up with a certain statement of who the writer is, arguably not that it matters. Some intriguingly suggest the writer could have been a woman and that is why I refer to him/her as "the writer". Also, unlike every other letter in the New

Testament that was either addressed to an individual or a church or group of churches, we don't know who the writer was writing to. The audience is not identified in the letter, unlike in all the other New Testament letters. Few would argue the title "Hebrews" is inappropriate because the intended audience were Jewish believers, although where they were based we cannot say for sure.

There is plenty of evidence as to why the writer referred back so much to what was written in the Old Testament, starting with its use of types and shadows, to an extent that is far in excess of that of any other New Testament book. With reference to Chapter 54, Hebrews is a prime example of relating Old and New Testaments. It is unlikely that the modern Bible lover would have made the sort of associations with Old Testament imagery that the writer of the Hebrews did and if one were to study a range of commentaries on Hebrews from writers that are not quite in one's own theological stable we would find a range of views and this is yet another reason readers are urged to study Hebrews.

We find there is an extraordinary number of quotations taken from the Old Testament and the writer assumes a thorough knowledge of the Old Testament. It is a good reason why anyone wanting to understand the New Testament should study the Old Testament. In the first chapter of Hebrews alone, the writer quotes seven Psalms, and the Books of Deuteronomy, Samuel, Chronicles and Isaiah. As with most New Testament writers, the author quotes from the (Greek) Septuagint version of the Old Testament, rather than a translation from the Hebrew, that most readers today are familiar with. These are: Ch. 1:5: Psalm 2:7, 2 Samuel 7:14; Ch 1:6: Deuteronomy 32:43, Psalm 97:7; Ch. 1:7: Psalm 104:4; Ch. 1:8-9: Psalm 45:6-7; Ch. 1:12: Psalm 102:25-27; Ch. 1:13: Psalm 110:1.

Then the arguments presented are typically Jewish and not ones that Gentiles might resonate with, brought up with a Greek way of thinking. For example, the argument that Melchizedek was better than Aaron on the basis that Aaron was a descendant of Levi, who was a descendant of Abraham, who gave tithes to Melchizedek, shows why the Melchizedek priesthood, of which Jesus is a member, is superior to that of the Aaronic priesthood, and such is more in line with the Jewish way of thinking.

A more pertinent question may be, why was the Book of Hebrews written in the first place? While verses can be cited along the lines of exhorting the readers to keep the faith as revealed in Jesus, rather than return to Judaism and thus deny Christ, to provide reasons, the answer might also be derived from reading between the lines. A lot of what is written would appeal to the Jewish mind, familiar with Jewish traditions. While relevant to Gentiles to gain understanding of the whole counsel of God, such a presentation may not be so compelling to them as to those who are steeped in Judaism. One difference between Jewish and Gentile believers was in declaring the latter were not required to become a Jew and thus keep the whole Law before becoming Christian. It is notable that a good portion of the writer's argument was that Jesus is better than anything found in the Old Testament – better in terms of what has been revealed through Jesus, and the argument continues when declaring Jesus is better than angels, better than Moses and better than the Aaronic priests.

It is likely there was great pressure being placed on the Hebrew believers to ditch following Christ and turn back to Judaism, because by doing so they would likely escape the anticipated persecution of those who followed Jesus. Some of the wording even implies that by turning back those who do so might lose their salvation, for example *"For it is impossible for those who were once enlightened, and have tasted of the heavenly gift, and were made partakers of the Holy Ghost, And have tasted the good word of God, and the powers of the world to come, If they shall fall away, to renew them again unto repentance; seeing they crucify to themselves the Son of God afresh, and put him to an open shame"* (6:4-6). While I tend to the Calvinistic belief of the eternal security of all (true) believers (yet noting someone like David Pawson, whose commentaries on the Bible, including Hebrews, I found to be helpful in writing this book, would cite texts from Hebrews to argue that the opposite is the case).

The Book of Hebrews is strong on matters like the fear of God, e.g., *"Let us therefore fear, lest, a promise being left us of entering into his rest, any of you should seem to come short of it"* (4:1), *"It is a fearful thing to fall into the hands of the living God"* (10:31) and *"Wherefore we receiving a kingdom which cannot be moved, let us have grace, whereby we may serve God acceptably with reverence and godly fear"* (12:28) and the importance of holiness *"For they verily for a few days chastened us after their own pleasure; but he for our profit, that we might be partakers of his holiness"* (12:10) and *"Follow peace with all men, and holiness, without which no man shall see the Lord"* (12:14). This important emphasis on godly fear and reverential holiness is often missing in today's "Christian set-ups" and is therefore another reason why we should be encouraged to study the Book of Hebrews.

Hebrews is a practical book as it urges readers to walk on with Jesus and the importance of godly discipline and fellowship with other believers. One memorable passage is that of the "Hall of Faith" Chapter 11, where the writer urges the life of faith, despite all sorts of challenges and obstacles to overcome, the costs of living the life of faith but with ultimate rewards, using as example several Old Testament figures. The chapter begins *"Now faith is the substance of things hoped for, the evidence of things not seen. For by it the elders obtained a good report"* (11:1-2) and ends *"And these all, having obtained a good report through faith, received not the promise: God having provided some better thing for us, that they without us should not be made perfect"* (11:39-40).

The writer rounds this off by considering Jesus, urging us not just to walk on but race on, looking to the one we should be following who has gone before us: *"Wherefore seeing we also are compassed about with so great a cloud of witnesses, let us lay aside every weight, and the sin which doth so easily beset us, and let us run with patience the race that is set before us, Looking unto Jesus the author and finisher of our faith; who for the joy that was set before him endured the cross, despising the shame, and is set down at the right hand of the throne of God. For consider him that endured such contradiction of sinners against himself, lest ye be wearied and faint in your minds* (12:1-3).

As we draw this chapter to an end, it is worth reflecting on a short passage found toward the end of Hebrews, which begins with a verse that defines my own community activism (detailed in Chapter 56) and an exhortation that governed the thoughts and motivations of my PB mentors of yesteryear, when it comes to having heavenly as opposed to earthly pre-occupations. This also returns us to an essential theme when we consider the subject of Priests of the Bible – that of sacrifice: *"Let us go forth therefore unto him without the camp, bearing his reproach. For here have we no continuing city, but we seek one to come. By him therefore let us offer the sacrifice of praise to God continually, that is, the fruit of our lips giving thanks to his name. But to do good and to communicate forget not: for with such sacrifices God is well pleased"* Hebrews 13:13-16.

We might ask why is praising God a sacrifice and why is it something that is urged upon us to do? The word "sacrifice" (Greek, *"thusia"*) comes from the root *thuo*, a verb meaning *"to kill or slaughter for a purpose."* Praise often requires that we "kill" our pride, fear, sloth etc., anything that threatens to diminish or interfere with our worship of the Lord. And isn't that the central point if we are serious when it comes to being a priestly people. As Jesus told the Samaritan woman at the well: *"But the hour cometh, and now is, when the true worshippers shall worship the Father in spirit and in truth: for the Father seeketh such to worship him"* John 4:23. To do this we need to do what Paul urged on the church at Rome: *"I beseech you therefore, brethren, by the mercies of God, that ye present your bodies a living sacrifice, holy, acceptable unto God, which is your reasonable service. And be not conformed to this world: but be ye transformed by the renewing of your mind, that ye may prove what is that good, and acceptable, and perfect, will of God"* Romans 12:1-2. All of which ties in with a key theme of **"Priests of the Bible"** – the need to offer right sacrifices to God.

We close this short reflection with the final benediction that reflects the writer of Hebrew's desire for the readers to be Christ centred and for God to be glorified: *"Now the God of peace, that brought again from the dead our Lord Jesus, that great shepherd of the sheep, through the blood of the everlasting covenant, make you perfect in every good work to do his will, working in you that which is well pleasing in his sight, through Jesus Christ; to whom be glory for ever and ever. Amen"* (13:20-21).

Praise to our joyful man of sorrows

While *"Looking unto Jesus the author and finisher of our faith; who for the joy that was set before him endured the cross, despising the shame, and is set down at the right hand of the throne of God"* Hebrews 12:2, we are also reminded that Jesus, the subject of Hebrews, was also the Man of Sorrows.

1. Man of sorrows what a name
for the Son of God, who came
ruined sinners to reclaim:
Hallelujah, what a Saviour!

2. Bearing shame and scoffing rude,
in my place condemned he stood,
sealed my pardon with his blood:
Hallelujah, what a Saviour!

3. Guilty, helpless, lost were we;
blameless Lamb of God was he,
sacrificed to set us free:
Hallelujah, what a Saviour!

4. He was lifted up to die;
"It is finished" was his cry;
now in heaven exalted high:
Hallelujah, what a Saviour!

5. *When he comes, our glorious King,*
all his ransomed home to bring,
then anew this song we'll sing:

Hallelujah, what a Saviour!

Chapter 56: "Outside the Camp" Revisited

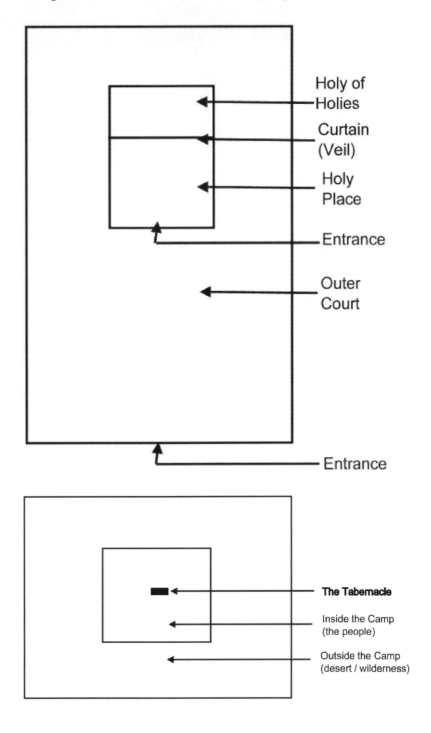

The images on the previous page relate to a major theme of this book – The Tabernacle in the Wilderness. They also relate to a theme that was closely linked to my experience of going outside the camp. I associate this with the non-colour reproduction of the painting: "The Scapegoat" by William Holman Hunt, found in Chapter 2, Figure 15. Besides being a fan of Holman Hunt, the Scapegoat, along with the previous image (Inside and Outside the Camp), relates to an important theme of this book (Priests of the Bible) as well as to my earlier work (Outside the Camp), which is to go into the world as Christ's representatives, even when it means having to face opposition and embrace hardships.

We learn in Leviticus 16 how the High Priest drew lots concerning two goats on the Day of Atonement, one being offered as a sacrifice for sin, with the High Priest entering the Holy of Holies and applying the blood to the Mercy Seat, and one designated to be the Scapegoat (all of which is discussed in Chapter 10). After the High Priest had laid hands on the Scapegoat in order to transfer the sins of the people, it was then released "outside the camp" (into the wilderness) bearing the sins of the people. Holman Hunt clearly regarded the Scapegoat as a type of Christ, e.g., "*Surely he hath borne our griefs, and carried our sorrows: yet we did esteem him stricken, smitten of God, and afflicted*" Isaiah 53:4.

In 2012, I wrote my book "**Outside the Camp**" and produced a second edition in 2014, along with four further books that related, in order to incorporate updates to what I was doing as a community worker and offer further analysis and reflections (all can be freely downloaded from my website). A synopsis begins: "*"Outside the Camp – Reflections of a Community Activist" and contains the author's own "inside" story of his wide-ranging, full-time activities in the community, in the town in which he was born and grew up, over a period of more than ten years, in the latter part of his working life*".

I also included thoughts on two hot topics for me at that time: homosexuality and mental health, having had many instances when I have engaged with gay folk and those experiencing mental health issues and it being quite an eye-opener for me to view the world from their point of view. Concerning homosexuality, I was finding myself increasingly in meaningful contact with gay folk, noting opposing tendencies in the church to become either too "gay friendly" or entrenched homophobia and of a culture that has switched from penalising gay folk to penalising those seen as "anti-gay". I wanted to find the right balance. As for mental (ill) health, this is something I have tended toward for much of my life and, as evidenced by my Growing Together/ Trust Links involvement, arising out of the realisation that unmet mental health related needs in society were rife, along with, as has historically often been the case, people of faith leading the way to address the needs. I wanted also to better understand the issues so that I could better help those experiencing mental ill health and help others to understand. Not unrelated were issues to do with addiction, e.g., alcohol, drugs, gambling and pornography.

I mentioned two key texts, both of which are quoted elsewhere in this book and have much to do with Priests of the Bible. "*Having therefore, brethren, boldness to enter into the holiest by the blood of Jesus, by a new and living way, which he hath consecrated for us, through the veil, that is to say, his flesh*" Hebrews 10:19-20 and "*Wherefore Jesus also, that he might sanctify the people with his own blood, suffered without the gate. Let us go forth therefore unto him without the camp, bearing his reproach. For here have we no continuing city, but we seek one to come*" Hebrews 13:12-14.

Regarding my story as a community worker/activist, I refer readers to the book. There is a certain irony behind the story because, while my PB background attached significant store to going inside the Veil and then outside the Camp, community activism beyond being a good neighbour and serving the community as part and parcel of gospel outreach, evidenced for example in the setting up of schools, hospitals and orphanages in overseas mission, was not something that was much encouraged – in fact, working alongside those who were not Christians was often discouraged. While going inside the Veil was seen to be a good thing as part of the prayer life of the believer, going outside the camp was better associated with Holman Hunt's forlorn looking Scapegoat, having been cast out all alone into the wilderness, but it was where believers were meant to be, as they looked forward to the return of Jesus.

My own philosophy was to do with community engagement, encompassing all faiths and none, with the idea of working in a partnership paradigm to promote the common good and, if need be, putting aside differences when it comes to beliefs and approaches in doing so. As a result, I was able to engage with the six strands to do with equality and diversity that were what was being widely encouraged at the turn of the millennium when I began my third career, following that of a teacher and software engineer. Those strands were: age, disability, race, religion, sexual identity and sexual orientation. I recognised there were areas of potential conflict with those whose world view was different to my own, yet was able to accomplish a good deal in what I regarded as being positive. When "equality and diversity" was flavour of the month (and to an extent that remains the case) I even found myself co-opted onto committees and such, in looking into the issues arising and doing my bit to combat discrimination, and at times it struck my sense of humour given my own fundamentalist background.

My activities included supporting a wide range of community groups, organising community events, helping set up and manage a mental health charity (Trust Links), advocating on behalf of asylum seekers, engaging with different faith groups on community matters, working with "Turning Tides" (a government initiative to bring together and empower different sections of the community), helping black and minority ethnic (BME) groups, involvement with initiatives that empower the socially disadvantaged, research concerning local community needs and opportunities, chairing my local resident association, becoming a Street Pastor and various homelessness related activities. Concerning homelessness, I found myself helping to set up and chair an organisation (SHAN) to bring together those wanting to help, chairing a "Soup Kitchen" (Street Spirit), managing a homeless night shelter, and coming along side homeless folk as opportunities arose, and helping with inter-church initiatives serving the wider community. Some of what I did was by way of paid employment but some of it was as a volunteer, especially in the later years. I was happy to call myself a "gospel preaching, community activist", and in later years as I moved toward retirement and could pick and choose what I did, I added "watchman on the wall" to that title as I reflected on world events and warned of their implications.

I have many positive memories from my "all faiths and none" community engagement, including with groups whose core beliefs were at odds with my own Christian faith. If I have any regrets, I feel it was my not always being the shining light I should have been, I may have missed opportunities for sharing my faith. I sometimes fell into the trap of putting aside my faith in order not to upset those who wanted to exclude faith. But as I consider my involvement, I see several positive outcomes. Perhaps one main highlight was the positive associations I had and friendships I developed with members of my local Muslim community as well as understanding better the hopes and concerns of LBGT folk. But I see my early involvement in mental health and later in homeless related issues, as being the most significant.

I feel I should say something more about politics, a subject I touched on in my book. As a newly converted 15-year-old, I was very interested in politics and it happened to be of the left leaning variety, for I was attracted by the idea that the "haves" should be made to help the "have nots" and that could only be brought about if government got involved. My PB mentors, despite some of them being closet conservatives, dissuaded me from political activism and what could have turned into a promising political career never transpired. That didn't dampen my interest in things political, however, and I have been a politics watcher ever since. I have usually voted and usually for who I thought was the best candidate, regardless of party. These days I oscillate somewhere in the middle between right and left, coming to a view that the solutions that are needed should not be about right or left politics.

While my interest has mostly been UK politics, now with my watchman remit I look at politics across the world and, given the emergence of one Donald J Trump and the evident shenanigans of US politics, I take as much interest in the USA as I do the UK. I confess I have also been intrigued at the shifts seen between globalism and nationalism and, what is becoming increasingly apparent, the external, hidden influences that evidently drive politicians. As part of my own awakening, I have seen and been disturbed by the amount of deception and apathy as well as hopeful that at least some are awake. This is accentuated in the light of so many seemingly unrelated happenings that are in fact related and driven by what the "conspiracy theorist" David Icke calls "the hidden hand", whose agenda is anything but altruistic. While my "leftie" youth naivety has long ago dissipated, much due to my mistrust of government to deliver, I am neither convinced that being a "rightie" is the way to go, simply because I have come to see that there is no guarantee when allowing people to keep their wealth and allowing them the choice to do what they want with it, that it would help the worse off in our society.

I have found though, having become a community activist and recognising one's limitations when dealing with issues such as homelessness and mental health that we cannot ignore political solutions altogether. For that reason, I have engaged and have often been on good terms with politicians of all shades of left and right in order to get things done. Speaking concerning the UK, although I suspect this could apply more generally, I find today's political scene depressing and lament what I perceive to be a lack of quality among political leaders. I find I cannot support any of the main parties. I feel all the main parties are barking up the wrong trees and hear too few voices coming from those parties to bring to the attention of decision makers what needs doing. Noting the UK system does not encourage minority parties, I find I cannot support, or at least not fully, any of the alternatives either.

Nevertheless, I would not want to dissuade people who are rightly motivated from getting involved politically (and have often found myself encouraging, advising and working with those who do – albeit mostly locally), including some who are Christians, for while one may be limited in what one is able to do in what I have come to see as a much-flawed system, one can still make a difference. One difference I have found that a conscientious politician can make is to effectively advocate on behalf of those he/she represents. Those who do so, regardless of their politics, more often than not earn my respect.

A lot of water has gone under the proverbial bridge since I wrote my "second edition" and, while I have had to cut down on my community involvement, and am selective when it comes to choosing what I participate in, not just because I am officially retired but due to other priorities, including writing books like this one, as well as slowing down due to old age and disability, I am still involved, e.g., helping the homeless as a volunteer and finding ways to support the next generation of community activists, irrespective of faith but especially those who do share my faith to become closer to God and effective in their activism. I do not intend producing a third edition of "**Outside the Camp**" but, if I were to do so, I might be tempted to re-write the book, not just to bring it up-to-date with what has since taken place in the nearly ten years since I wrote the second edition, but to reflect on the significant changes concerning my perspectives on life as they relate to matters of faith and community involvement. I have found Christian involvement is not a matter of being in the domain of the woke lefties identifying neo-Marxism with compassion, with rabid righties not getting a look in as uncaring, for I have found community involved Christians with a range of political and theological views, but how to go about it?

While I still believe my earlier PB influencers were wrong to take the view of not getting involved, I can now look back and see many of their concerns were valid. To cut to the chase, and having seen many good Christians get involved in community activism, I can see how it can be a distraction to what they should be doing: "*Go ye therefore, and teach all nations, baptizing them in the name of the Father, and of the Son, and of the Holy Ghost: Teaching them to observe all things whatsoever I have commanded you*" Matthew 28:19-20a. While it is true that many an opportunity to serve a community has been lost through a lack of activism by the church, it has also been true that the people of God have lost their nerve by allowing those who have no time for the God of the Bible to set the agenda, expecting Christians to comply while unwilling themselves to make compromises. While I like it when churches act in a partnership paradigm and resist the temptation of being at the centre, I again urge caution.

Looking back to the early days when engaging with the wider community became my almost full-time occupation, I see how I could have done certain things differently, having made many mistakes, yet I do not regret my third career despite going from being a highly paid computer consultant running my own business to being a lowly paid community worker that often had to eat humble pie in order to realise my common good goals. I was often amazed and encouraged by the efforts of those who did not share my faith in order to help others with no expectation of any reward. Seeing people of all faiths and none succeed in making a difference in their communities, along with their need for the Gospel, is enough to convince this old codger that this is not the time to sit back and relax, and do nothing.

This is especially so, as often appears to be the case, when Christians who should be taking the lead, have lost their nerve, seen by their ditching faith inspired principles in order not to upset those who might take offence if they did not. I commend any Christian group seizing the opportunity to serve the community, including working with other statutory and voluntary groups, but regret it when I see faith principles compromised. I hope I have made a difference, although I have not always done what I have argued for in this chapter, but it will be for God and others to determine how well I have done. In the meantime, I try to learn from my mistakes and press on doing what I can and in encouraging others!

I have found in life that one can go around in a full circle, sometimes more than once. I have noted elsewhere there is nothing new under the sun, and we do well to learn lessons from past mistakes, something I can now hold my hands up to concerning my early community activism. While I have come to appreciate the power of community coming together and playing a small part in making this possible, I can also see ways I could have done better and avoided foolish mistakes. Now I am old, I have had time to observe what is happening to others, especially Christians, and reflect on my past actions. It is not a matter of not getting involved in community activism because of the consequences of upsetting secular entities or God, if we don't preach the Gospel, or getting involved because we feel we can and must make a difference, but rather we need to choose wisely and be prepared to adjust.

There is no simple solution, especially if our wanting to help goes beyond what can be done just in the confines of the local church and especially so when our church has, as many do, a very limited view of what can be done. Often it comes down to not just what the Bible tells us is right but also what our conscience tells us. Hard decisions sometimes have to be made, although I can't help noting in recent history how many charities that began with high Christian ideals have ditched them for the sake of expediency. While I recognise that charity ought not come with strings attached, neither can it ignore faith values for the sake of political correctness, the very thing today's western culture is telling us we must conform to. Wisdom and winsomeness in this matter are important. I can see many examples of worthwhile charity endeavours, but those I admire most are faith led and do so without ostentation.

While I can't turn the clock back for myself, and am too old to start again in the light of what I now know, I can do what I can to support Christians that go outside the camp, into the Wilderness, in order to serve the needy. I should also add that I have seen much division among real Christians on these and related matters. This is one reason why I have written on Christian unity. Having been convicted about my own sinfulness, I suggest this is not the time to get on our holy high horses on these matters. The fact that there are many I know, who do share my Christian beliefs, that have gone out of their way to serve the poor and needy without any hidden agenda, also gives me hope.

Before I do close, I would like to ponder a little more on what is meant by going "*outside the camp*". It was a term I picked up in the early days of my community activism. Besides being a phrase that struck me when I first heard it used by my mentors from my youth, it seemed applicable to what I was trying to achieve as a community activist. When the Hebrews' writer uses the phrase "*without the camp*" (13:13), he/she precedes it with the words "*let us go forth therefore unto him*" and follows up with the words "*bearing his reproach*". When I did a "Google search" to find out what Bible commentators had to say, I found a range of interpretations, none of which I found entirely satisfactory, although I was mindful that the Book of Hebrews was aimed at those who had converted from Judaism to Christianity and were having to pay the price, which was what Jesus did when He died on the Cross (outside the camp) and what the forlorn looking goat in Holman Hunt's painting had to do in carrying Israel's sins.

I mention all this to touch on another subject that is also to do with going outside the camp, which is that of suffering and especially that which is to do with persecution. I confess, I cannot recall any time getting close to being killed for my faith, nor even physically beaten up, although I know those who have been. But I have suffered. Part of my own journey, I touch on when I share my testimony, in Chapter 57, concerns trauma with the seeds being sown in my childhood, some of which I see as faith related. And before some get dismissive, because like many who "suffer" some of it at least is a product of one's own foolishness, this has been a huge deal for me and, even in my old age I have experienced flashbacks, despite preaching on verses in the Bible like those to do with God's new creation.

But in a strange way I have come to thank God for those experiences because one of the positive outcomes of suffering can be the end product: "*we glory in tribulations also: knowing that tribulation worketh patience; And patience, experience; and experience, hope: And hope maketh not ashamed; because the love of God is shed abroad in our hearts by the Holy Ghost which is given unto us*" Romans 5:3-5. I can also identify with Paul when he wrote: "*Who comforteth us in all our tribulation, that we may be able to comfort them which are in any trouble, by the comfort wherewith we ourselves are comforted of God. For as the sufferings of Christ abound in us, so our consolation also aboundeth by Christ*" 2 Corinthians 1:4-5. Surely, being able to "*comfort*" (hearten, refresh) is a desirable outcome.

The reality is that many of my brothers and sisters across the world are experiencing tribulation due to their faith. I write this in the comfortable setting of our home in South India where I enjoy the same freedoms as I do in the UK. Only a couple of days ago, I had a conversation with a missionary that ministers in North India, where things are quite different and when going outside the camp, doing what Christians are meant to be doing – sharing the Good News of the Gospel, means to suffer for one's faith. Even as I write, another brother with a ministry in South India was able to share stories of those who have experienced horrendous suffering simply for converting to Christianity. Yet another brother has shared that some "church" attendees have stopped attending meetings in "free Kerala" because if they do attend they forgo rights and privileges as a result of doing so. One of my sources of information comes from the **Barnabas Fund**, which serves the persecuted church across the world. Every day it sends out prayer requests concerning some situation where Christian believers are having to suffer because of their faith. Even in the UK, with its supposed religious freedom, we find people having been arrested for preaching the Gospel. My point is that going outside the camp has all sorts of ramifications, one of which is the willingness to suffer for/with Christ as the situation necessitates.

If I could go back and change things, not only were there opportunities to make a difference by going outside the camp that I had missed, often as a consequence of paying too much attention to personal priorities, perspectives or pain; even more, I should have spent more time inside the Veil, for I am convinced the closer we are to God the more we can help our fellow man. But I am glad that despite present limitations due to age, circumstances and disability, I am still able to make a difference. As I look around me, I can see more than ever ways the people of God can serve their communities. While preaching the Gospel and making disciples should be our priorities, so should loving our neighbours.

I close with a hymn that intriguingly makes the connection between "*inside the veil*" where we must begin our community activist journey and "*outside the camp*" where we must end it. I suspect when it comes to dealing with LBGT activists, visiting the local mosque and encouraging and working with politicians of all flavours, these activities would not have been the sort of things the hymn writer had in mind, who instead saw being outside the camp as a place of isolation, but at least we can agree that our place as believer-priests is to be both "*inside the veil*" and "*outside the camp*" and, while that inevitably attracts opposition and can be challenging, we can make a significant difference if that is what we do. While critical of LBGT lifestyles, radical Islam and mainstream politics, and the way many/most have been sucked in by these agendas, I have often found engaging with and befriending some of those associated with those groups to be positive. I have also loved working among those on the fringes of society, often disempowered and rejected, notably as a part of my homeless activism.

Notwithstanding, we must not lose sight that we need to live holy lives, love our neighbour and preach Christ. May we be found in both places, seeking to find a right balance, void of ostentation and pride, loving our Christian brothers and sisters and non-Christian detractors who may see things differently.

1. Through Thy precious body broken
Inside the veil;
O what words to sinners spoken
Inside the veil!
Precious as the blood that bought us,
Perfect as the love that sought us,
Holy as the Lamb that brought us
Inside the veil!

2. When we see Thy love unshaken
Outside the camp;
Scorned by man, by God forsaken,
Outside the camp;
Thy loved cross alone can charm us,
Shame need now no more alarm us,
Glad we follow, naught can harm us
Outside the camp.

3. Lamb of God, through Thee we enter
Inside the veil;
Cleansed by Thee, we boldly venture
Inside the veil;
Not a stain; a new creation;
Ours is such a full salvation;
Low we bow in adoration
Inside the veil.

4. Unto Thee, the homeless stranger
Outside the camp,
Forth we hasten, fear no danger
Outside the camp.
Thy reproach, far richer treasure
Than all Egypt's boasted pleasure;
Drawn by love that knows no measure,
Outside the camp.

5. Soon Thy saints shall all be gathered
Inside the veil;
All at home, no more be scattered,
Inside the veil.
Naught from Thee our hearts shall sever;
We shall see Thee, grieve Thee never;
Praise the Lamb! shall sound for ever
Inside the veil!

Chapter 57: A Personal Testimony

A few months back, my wife and I were asked to share our testimonies in the church we belong to. What follows is my testimony with some minor modifications plus an extra section that was not shared at the time due to time limitations. Besides which, some of what I have added here may not have been appropriate for that occasion and setting. As many readers may not know some of the names I give below, Jolly is the name of my wife; Matthew is the name of my son and Roger and Ray were the two elders that were serving at the time we joined that church. So here goes …

Thank you for giving us this opportunity to share our testimonies. In mine, I would like to focus on three aspects of my life: how I became a Christian, how I met Jolly and meeting today's challenges.

I grew up in the newly built Blenheim Park council estate, during the 50s and 60s. My parents might be described as nominal Christians but they insisted that my sister and I attend Sunday School held at the nearby Blenheim School. It was led by a formidable lady named Doris Rafan, helped by her mostly spinster assistants. Miss Rafan's day time job was as a school headmistress and she had all the attributes we might expect. She was strict but fair and had a heart of gold. She loved the Lord, the children and what became a recurring theme throughout my life, the Bible, and she taught us well.

When aged 12, we moved to the east side of Southend. It happened that the parents of a boy in my class at school attended Coleman Street Gospel Hall (later renamed Chapel and which now hosts the Potters House). Around age 13 or 14, my class mate invited me to the Covenanter group held at the Hall. Covenanters combined Bible Class and Youth Club activity and was led by Bryn Jones, who had been an army sergeant during the War. I was a somewhat disruptive influence and by rights I should have been expelled from the group but Mr Jones believed the Lord had told him that he needed to persist with me. When aged 15, I attended a Christian youth camp in Dorset. It was there I became a Christian. This was in 1966 and it was during the week the English football team won the World Cup.

I then became involved with the Chapel throughout the rest of my schooling, when home from university and college and during my first career, which was as a teacher. While the Chapel had its funny ways, I recognised that many of its members were committed to faithfully following the Lord, were resolved to find out and be beholden to what the Bible taught, and saw preaching the Gospel and home and overseas mission to be important, all defining factors in my own Christian journey. One significant occurrence upon leaving school was joining Operation Mobilisation for a summer crusade.

In 1977, I moved from Southend to Poole in order to pursue my second career, which was that of a software engineer with the Plessey Company. I joined Longfleet Baptist Church where I became actively involved in church life, especially its youth work: Bible class, youth clubs and Boys Brigade, and served as a deacon. In 1983, I moved back to Southend for a new job and to be near my recently widowed Mum. Before that, I indulged my passion as a world traveller. I decided to do India! I recall the culture shock upon arriving at Bombay airport in the middle of the night: the humid heat, the smells and grime, the sight of seeing many living on the streets next to opulent looking housing – but I was to fall in love with this land I found to be of great contrasts, which has become my second home.

Soon upon arrival I was faced with making what was a momentous decision, whether to continue my travels by taking a train heading north or to head south. I decided on south and after a two-day train journey ended up in Trivandrum city. I had been given the address of the brother of the husband of a friend of a friend and arrived at his doorstep and was invited to stay. Soon after, an eccentric livewire, named Varghese Matthai, turned up at the house. I found he was a Brethren evangelist. I told him of my plans to explore India, ideally off the tourist trail, and I let it be known that I was a Christian who had Brethren roots. He invited me to stay with him in his village some 30 miles away and I accepted.

Visiting his humble home felt a bit like going back in time. There was, for example, no electricity and few of the amenities we take for granted here. It felt like I was the first white man to set foot in his village. I was treated to splendid hospitality and my host became a great encourager and friend. I appreciated the simplicity of village life, for it seemed the people often had what really mattered. I got to meet many people, helped by those who could translate for me. My evangelist host even got me preaching in the open air. After staying a few days, I continued on my journey to explore India, guided by O.J.John, a friend of my host. I was to return to India many times after that and got involved in preaching and teaching activities. Some years later, I was to marry Jolly, the daughter of my host.

When I moved back to Southend, I continued to work as a software engineer, including running my own business for 12 years. I did try out a number of churches but was unable to settle and was encouraged to rejoin Coleman Street Chapel, now with far less numbers. I helped in its preaching and teaching activities, serving as an elder and missionary secretary. During that time Jolly came to Southend and we married. Soon after the turn of the millennium, I embarked on my third career – that of a community worker with a particular interest working with Southend's diverse community and in the areas of mental health and homelessness. My mantra was *"Wherefore*

Jesus also, that he might sanctify the people with his own blood, suffered without the gate. Let us go forth therefore unto him without the camp, bearing his reproach" Hebrews 13:12-13. I felt it right to engage with the wider community for the sake of the common good, noting how often Christians, when doing so, compromise on matters concerning true faith and, as for me, I needed, but did not always find a right balance.

Regarding this text, I had in mind not just Jesus suffering outside the city gates for our sins, the only way any of us can be reconciled to a holy God, but also that of the High Priest, who on the Day of Atonement, took two goats, drawing lots as to which would be sacrificed and which set free. One goat was killed and its blood was sprinkled on the Mercy Seat situated inside the Holy of Holies. The other, the Scapegoat, was released into the wilderness having first had hands laid on it by the High Priest, transferring the sins of people. I felt my calling was both to go inside the veil and outside the camp in my service here, describing myself as a *"gospel preaching, community activist"*. I later added the term *"watchman on the wall"*, taking up Jesus' call to *"watch and pray"*. These are the Last Days and the people of God are being deceived. We need to be warned and prepare for Jesus' Coming.

Around 10 years ago, it was decided to close the work at Coleman Street Chapel and we needed to find somewhere else in order to fellowship. It eventually came down to a two horse-race, with me and our then 15-year-old son assigned to checking out each candidate. One fellowship lost out because it was too happy clappy (for Matthew) and too lightweight in its preaching (for me). It all then came down to Providence, which got Matthew's thumbs up, partly because it was closer to what he was used to and he had good memories when he attended the Bible club that Roger led as a junior. It got my approval as I was quite taken with Roger's expository, forensic preaching approach (he had just begun a 2+ year journey on the Book of James). I knew Ray, who sometimes preached at Coleman Street, and I could remember Providence's strictness and its own set of funny ways from back in my youth, when I was at school with Pastor Tait's son. But I could see at Providence three qualities that in my dotage I have come to realise are particularly important: kindness, godliness and faithfulness. In the end, it was a unanimous family decision and we joined Providence, and we are still here today!

I want to end by reflecting on the question *"what about now"*? and want to consider a song, another inspirational text (and here we are spoiled for choice) and finish up with a final song. My first song is neither Christian nor theologically sound yet, besides liking the song, some of its lyrics resonate with me, especially as the one who is singing it and myself see ourselves as coming to the end of our lives and we are both wanting to look back on what we have done in our lives. The song is "My Way", made famous by Frank Sinatra. One phrase stood out: "*Regrets, I've had a few but then again too few to mention*". Here I disagree, as naturally speaking I have too many regrets. While I have been let down, ridiculed, hurt etc., by some, my biggest regret is not responding as I ought and not allowing God to do His work in me, making me the person He wants me to be, and not making the most of the opportunities that have come my way. The other stand out phrase in the song is: "*I did it my way*". Due to my own make up and circumstances and not wanting to follow the herd, I often tried to do things my way. While God has given us freedom of choice and we differ in temperaments, giftings and circumstances, in looking back, I see mine was not always the best way or what God had intended. It would have been better if I had done more God's way, despite finding God has always been faithful.

But there is good news – and it is what the Gospel we preach is all about. Ever since Genesis 1:1, God has been in the creation business. While humankind has mucked up God's wonderful creation by sin, we read "*Therefore if any man be in Christ, he is a new creature: old things are passed away; behold, all things are become new. And all things are of God, who hath reconciled us to himself by Jesus Christ, and hath given to us the ministry of reconciliation; To wit, that God was in Christ, reconciling the world unto himself, not imputing their trespasses unto them; and hath committed unto us the word of reconciliation. Now then we are ambassadors for Christ, as though God did beseech you by us: we pray you in Christ's stead, be ye reconciled to God. For he hath made him to be sin for us, who knew no sin; that we might be made the righteousness of God in him*" 2 Corinthians 5:17-21.

It means I can put aside regrets because I am God's new creation. Besides which, I have found that even though we might in the past have failed Him who matters most, God's purposes are greater and so is His grace. As the hymn writer put it: "*God works in mysterious ways*". As Paul wrote: "*by God's grace, I am what I am*". He can use any one of us if we let Him. As for the right or wrong way, I will let God and others be the judge of what I have done in the past but, as for now onwards, I must prioritise "*the ministry of reconciliation*" and being "*an ambassador for Christ*". Two lovely thoughts arise out of this: it ought to free us from distractions and from caring too much what others think.

I come now to my final song. I first heard it sung at the Christian camp at the time I was saved.

I have decided to follow Jesus;

I have decided to follow Jesus;

I have decided to follow Jesus;

No turning back, no turning back.

Tho' none go with me, I still will follow,

Tho' none go with me I still will follow,

Tho' none go with me, I still will follow;

No turning back, no turning back.

The world behind me, the cross before me,

The world behind me, the cross before me;

The world behind me, the cross before me;

No turning back, no turning back.

It was sometimes sung in Christian services I attended in the UK and India, for it was in India the song originated. The words "*I have decided to follow Jesus*", "*Tho' none go with me, I still will follow*" and "*The world behind me, the cross before me*" were coined by a missionary whose endeavours in a remote tribal area, preaching the Gospel, resulted in several souls saved, much to the consternation of the tribal chief. The missionary was brought before the chief, who threatened to have him killed, but offered to spare his life and those of his family, but only if he undertook to stop preaching and to renounce Christ. These words were his response and as a result that threat was carried out.

One of my favourite films is "**It's a Wonderful Life**". The hero was George Bailey, who had come to the end of his tether, wished he hadn't been born and wanted to end it all. It took an angel to show George how things would have been if he hadn't been born because, through his dogged persistence, he was able to do a great deal of good, helping many. In the few days that remain for me, what truly matters is to make a positive difference and doing what the words of this song says I ought to be doing.

Addendum

The phrase that often comes back to me is one coined from William Cowper's hymn – "*The Lord works in mysterious ways*". I see that is so, looking back over my life. While tempted to despair because of bitter disappointments and having come to the realisation I am a bit of an odd ball, God has kept me around *"for such a time as this"* and as I look back over my life, including when I got it wrong as well as right, I see God's hand. Having seen many of my peers, some much better than me, departing from this scene, I conclude God has spared me for a purpose and my work on planet earth is not yet complete. There have been many times in my depressive state when I have woken up wishing I was dead. Besides hurts and frustrations, like being ostracised by some, including Christian leaders taking exception to my robustly expressed but not generally accepted views, because I cannot remain silent when seeing the Lord's people duped or patronised, because I fall into that category of person that may be labelled a "loner" rather than a herd follower and finding my own church going along with official but false narratives e.g., regarding Covid, and having been let down by those who I trusted.

Then there are my many failures when, on one hand, I have sought to be out and out for God; but on the other, I have done things that are incompatible with how a man of God should be, including when I have sought solace from pain and anguish in ways not fitting for a believer or shown a lack of character when under pressure but, as I have found out the hard way, we mustn't *"halt between two opinions"* and, if we do, there will be consequences. One "regret" besides letting God down, who I am meant to love and serve, is all too often not following the Golden Rule: *"Ask yourself what you want people to do for you, then grab the initiative and do it for them"* Matthew 7:12 (The Message).

But rather than end on a gloomy, downbeat note, I'd rather end on one of optimism and hope, and declare with the Psalmist *"my cup runneth over"*, mindful that God has been ever patient with me despite the fact He cannot be mocked and He will have His way. His intention has ever been to use me for His glorious purposes provided I let Him, and I am thankful. It is true, while I have done things to advance the Kingdom, I have also missed many opportunities, but I must not rest on any laurels. Nor must I wallow in self-pity. My God *"restores what the locusts have eaten"* and sends His *"refining fire"* in order to bring out pure gold. The one thing no one can take away is I am a child of God, loved by Him, yet I am also His *"unprofitable servant"* needing to go about doing what is my duty to do, without expectation of reward. Yet by *"the grace of God, I am what I am"* and *"I am but a brand plucked out of the fire"* and *"a sheep that once was lost but now is found"*. Acceptance by God is what truly matters.

Having attended many and even taken some funerals, I can see besides needing to be right with God before my time is up, the importance of leaving a worthwhile legacy, and that includes passing on to those I leave behind that which is of value as opposed to that which isn't. While there is a long list of physical ailments that have restricted me in recent years that have logical explanations, I can't help feeling one good reason for this is that God has wanted to get my attention, including getting me to be a whole hearted, faithful, consistent follower of Jesus. While it is true, the best is yet to come (heaven); methinks, while I remain in this earthly scene, He has a work for me to do. I am at an age when I regularly learn of the deaths of many people (my peers and nowadays many who are younger), including those who are dedicated servants of the Lord. When I ask, why not me, the answer quickly comes back that God still has things for me to do and only then can it be my time. It is my privilege and sacred duty to commend my Lord and Saviour to those reading this and invite all and sundry to follow Him. I conclude with two well-loved hymns that tie in with all these thoughts ...

1. There's a work for Jesus, ready at your hand,
'Tis a task the Master just for you has planned.
Haste to do His bidding, yield Him service true;
There's a work for Jesus none but you can do.

[Refrain]
Work for Jesus, day by day,
Serve Him ever, falter never; Christ obey.
Yield Him service loyal, true,
There's a work for Jesus none but you can do.

2. There's a work for Jesus, humble though it be,
'Tis the very service He would ask of thee.
Go where fields are whitened, and the lab'rers few;
There's a work for Jesus none but you can do. [Refrain]

3. There's a work for Jesus, precious souls to bring,
Tell them of His mercies, tell them of your King.
Faint not, nor grow weary, He will strength renew;
There's a work for Jesus none but you can do. [Refrain]

The Vow of the Nazirite

According to Wikipedia: "*In the Hebrew Bible, a Nazirite or a Nazarite (Hebrew: Nāzīr – separate, consecrated, devoted) is a man or woman who voluntarily took a vow which is described in Numbers 6:1–21. This vow required the Nazirite to:*

- *Abstain from wine and all other grape products, such as vinegar and grapes.*

- *Refrain from cutting the hair on his head.*

- *Not become ritually impure by contact with corpses or graves, even those of family members.*

After following these requirements for a designated time period (which would be specified in the individual's vow), the Nazirite would offer a specific animal sacrifice; along with it, the Nazirite's hair was to be shorn and burned."

Readers may think it strange that I should include a section on the Nazirite vow in a book that is about Priests of the Bible, and at the end of a chapter where I have shared my testimony. In fact, these late in the day thoughts on Nazirite vows could have been included in a number of places or even its own chapter. For example, what we read in Wikipedia also relates to what priests had to do concerning their being especially set apart to God, in having to make offerings on behalf of themselves besides others and being required to keep away from dead bodies and, as I thought about it, could have been included in what I wanted to share in "Chapter 43: What I would like to say to the Next Generation".

Making and keeping vows, concerning which the Nazirite vow was what we find mostly referred to, appeared to have been a big deal when we study the Old Testament. When it came to making vows, it was something that needed to be taken seriously by the one making the vow, given its binding nature, for we read: "*When thou vowest a vow unto God, defer not to pay it; for he hath no pleasure in fools: pay that which thou hast vowed. Better is it that thou shouldest not vow, than that thou shouldest vow and not pay*" Ecclesiastes 5:4-5. A good example of someone who made a vow and took it seriously, although it was offered foolishly, was Jephthah, one of the Judges of Israel: "*And Jephthah vowed a vow unto the Lord, and said, If thou shalt without fail deliver the children of Ammon into mine hands, Then it shall be, that whatsoever cometh forth of the doors of my house to meet me, when I return in peace from the children of Ammon, shall surely be the Lord's, and I will offer it up for a burnt offering.... And it came to pass at the end of two months, that she returned unto her father, who did with her according to his vow which he had vowed: and she knew no man*" Judges 11:30-31, 39.

While we only have two references to vows being taken in the KJV New Testament, both involved the Apostle Paul (likely a Nazirite one) (Acts 18:18; 21:23). Jesus words are worth taking to heart though: "*Again, ye have heard that it hath been said by them of old time, Thou shalt not forswear thyself, but shalt perform unto the Lord thine oaths: But I say unto you, Swear not at all; neither by heaven; for it is God's throne: Nor by the earth; for it is his footstool: neither by Jerusalem; for it is the city of the great King. Neither shalt thou swear by thy head, because thou canst not make one hair white or black. But let your communication be, Yea, yea; Nay, nay: for whatsoever is more than these cometh of evil*" Matthew 5:33-37. We also read "*But above all things, my brethren, swear not, neither by heaven, neither by the earth, neither by any other oath: but let your yea be yea; and your nay, nay; lest ye fall into condemnation*" James 5:12. But that is no reason for ignoring the significance of Nazirite vows.

In my study of the Bible, I have come across many amazing characters, and these included: Samson, Samuel and John the Baptist. All these were Nazirites, not just for a period but for all of their lives. It appeared they had little choice in the matter. In the case of Samson and John, the messenger from God (angel) instructed their parents that this was to be so, and in Samuel's case, it was something his mother vowed when she prayed for a son. Remarkably, all three were born to hitherto barren women. Moreover, it can be no coincidence that there was a special anointing that could clearly be seen in the lives of all three of these men and each of them had taken the Nazirite vow. Because I perceive there to be a monumental lack of genuine Holy Ghost power in the church, I am drawn to the Nazirites.

When we consider the requirements of being a Nazirite, none of them would likely be on the top of our lists if we were to make a Nazirite equivalent vow today, yet are remarkably pertinent:

- Abstinence from strong drink – self-control, discipline to prevent addictions.
- Avoid defilement from a corpse – integrity, staying pure, holy living.
- Uncut hair – refusal to let image and what others think influence you.

All three: Samson, Samuel and John the Baptist had extraordinary ministries. Samson was a carnal man despite being set aside by God. For much of his life, he blew whatever opportunities came his way and yet God used him mightily to deal with the Philistines that were oppressing God's chosen people, Israel. Toward the end of his life, after he had reneged on his vow by having his hair cut and thereby losing the remarkable strength God had given him, it appeared he was done for, but not with God, for after the now blinded Samson was brought out as an object of ridicule by his Philistine captors, we read at the very end of his life, he achieved his greatest feat: "*And Samson called unto the Lord, and said, O Lord God, remember me, I pray thee, and strengthen me, I pray thee, only this once, O God, that I may be at once avenged of the Philistines for my two eyes. And Samson took hold of the two middle pillars upon which the house stood, and on which it was borne up, of the one with his right hand, and of the other with his left. And Samson said, Let me die with the Philistines. And he bowed himself with all his might; and the house fell upon the lords, and upon all the people that were therein. So the dead which he slew at his death were more than they which he slew in his life*" Judges 16:28-30.

What applications and words of wisdom, especially as relating to my testimony, would I want to pass on to those who read this? As I see it, good people from my own Christian background were not much into making vows (in the light of those off-putting verses we quoted) but when I think of singing that song that made such an impact when I became a Christian: "*I have decided to follow Jesus ... Tho' none go with me, I still will follow ... The world behind me, the cross before me ...*" I had in effect made a vow. While like Samson, I may have "blown it" on countless occasions, God who will not be mocked and is ever faithful has kept me to that vow I made as a 15-year-old, amidst the ensuing years: failure, disappointment, stubbornness, rejection and pain to myself and others, and yet He blesses. Today, perhaps more than anything else, we need extraordinarily, ordinary Christians that take seriously the vow of the Nazirite. They won't just move the pillars; they will move the world for God.

The point about "A Priestly People", and why the Priesthood and Priests matter, is that we should be such a people. But as well, just as there was a call for a prophetic people in the forerunner to this book, there is a call for modern day Nazirites, albeit not ones taking vows laid out in Numbers 6. While today's church may object to being compared with the Israelites of Amos' day, when he took them to task: "*And I raised up of your sons for prophets, and of your young men for Nazarites. Is it not even thus, O ye children of Israel? saith the Lord. But ye gave the Nazarites wine to drink; and commanded the prophets, saying, Prophesy not*" Amos 2:11-12, the truth of the matter is that the church does too little to encourage prophets and Nazirites when God does raise up such persons. When God does, we should be those who surround them in prayer because we know they will be targets of Satan's attacks.

There have been countless believer-priests from all sorts of backgrounds, circumstances etc., down the ages. We get a glimpse of some of them in the Revelation 5 scene when there were multitudes gathered around God's Throne and all were worshipping God, for they had been redeemed to God by Christ's blood *"out of every kindred, and tongue, and people, and nation"*. My own observation has been that among the many of the Lord's people I have come across, who could rightly be described using adjectives like 'lovely', 'dedicated', 'sincere', and even useful, and irrespective of doctrinal differences, there have been all too few with the sort of extraordinary anointing that was to be found on the Old Testament Nazirites: Samson and Samuel and on the New Testament Nazirite, John the Baptist and for a short period, the Apostle Paul. Would that this were to happen in our day!

Those that have such an anointing could often be placed in the unlikely category that Paul talks about when he wrote concerning God's wisdom: *"For ye see your calling, brethren, how that not many wise men after the flesh, not many mighty, not many noble, are called: But God hath chosen the foolish things of the world to confound the wise; and God hath chosen the weak things of the world to confound the things which are mighty; And base things of the world, and things which are despised, hath God chosen, yea, and things which are not, to bring to nought things that are: That no flesh should glory in his presence"* 1 Corinthians 1:26-29. It is for such persons (actual and potential) that I am writing concerning the Nazirites of today who we need to support and encourage. Part of my testimony is what could have been but wasn't, but I am glad God has not given up on me, nor has He on you!

In conclusion

Concerning the main reason for this chapter, which was to share my testimony, I would like to offer these final thoughts. I have already stated that I am **not** a priest, other than being a believer-priest, in the commonly understood sense of being a member of the clergy or leadership team. Neither would I claim to be a prophet since neither God nor man has told me I am one and I make no claim to being able to foretell the future, although I do claim to be a "watchman on the wall" albeit, if my detractors are to be believed, a self-appointed one. What then about "Nazirite", which from my reading of the Bible is something that is open to anyone, providing they did what was required of any Nazirite (as could arguably be translated into a modern set of equivalent requirements)?

If I am, it would be more in the Samson mould (although if that were so, I wish I had had his strength to dispose of the bullies in my youth) rather than that of Samuel. The only thing one can fault Samuel for, from what I read in the Bible record, is he did not discipline his sons. With Samson, it is a matter of where do we begin? But the wonderful thing in the Samson story is when everyone thought he was done for, toward the end of his life, having "blown it" on several occasions beforehand, he achieved more then than he had with anything he did prior to that. And with such a prospect, especially for those folk who, like me, are sometimes despondent and tempted to feel they have been a failure in life, I end this chapter with the exhortation to keep pressing on for God, for He is at work, irrespective of how bad you might have been, wanting to bless you and others through you.

Triumph and tragedy are two extremes that could be seen as two sides of the same coin that is life. Like many (most), my life has oscillated between the two without touching either extreme. It has taken me a long time to realise this but the lessons learned from that which tends toward tragedy have been the more valuable. It has enabled me to best identify with the great range of experiences found among those whom I am called to serve, especially when it comes to being hurt or let down, and feelings of coming to the end of one's tether. Having heard many testimonies, it is easy to come away with the impression that before conversion it tended more to tragedy and after more to triumph. If I were to give that impression, it would be misleading, for it is tragedy that has often stood out, despite thinking that "In Christ" it ought to be triumph. Having said that, we are called to victorious Christian living, to be beholden to the truth and to be overcomers. Whilst this has not always been my experience, I have tasted and seen that the Lord is good and gracious and I know that the end of life will be glorious.

Talking about two opposites of a spectrum, joy and sorrow, success and failure also feature in my testimony, and while tragedy, sorrow and failure are all painful, yet with God good can come out of it all. Since giving this testimony is an intrinsic part of writing this book, especially when it comes to the practical implications of being a priestly people, I hope readers will find these thoughts, by way of saying how it has been, helpful. We could also add trials and tribulations and suffering to complement knowing the truth that sets us free, living as true disciples of Jesus, and God's precious gift of "Shalom" and His full, free salvation. Let us end with these words, and take heart: "*All praise to the God and Father of our Master, Jesus the Messiah! Father of all mercy! God of all healing counsel! He comes alongside us when we go through hard times, and before you know it, he brings us alongside someone else who is going through hard times so that we can be there for that person just as God was there for us. We have plenty of hard times that come from following the Messiah, but no more so than the good times of his healing comfort – we get a full measure of that, too*" 2 Corinthians 1:3-5 (The Message).

1. When we walk with the Lord
in the light of his word,
what a glory he sheds on our way!
While we do his good will,
he abides with us still,
and with all who will trust and obey.

[Refrain]
Trust and obey, for there's no other way
to be happy in Jesus, but to trust and obey.

2. Not a burden we bear,
not a sorrow we share,
but our toil he doth richly repay;
not a grief or a loss,
not a frown or a cross,
but is blest if we trust and obey. [Refrain]

3. But we never can prove
the delights of his love
until all on the altar we lay;
for the favor he shows,
for the joy he bestows,
are for them who will trust and obey. [Refrain]

4. Then in fellowship sweet
we will sit at his feet,
or we'll walk by his side in the way;
what he says we will do,
where he sends we will go;
never fear, only trust and obey. [Refrain]

Chapter 58: Christians who have Influenced me for the Better

Of all the chapters in this book, this might appear to be the one that has least to do with priests. Yet those Christians who I identify as having influenced me for the better that I have chosen (they needed to be dead to qualify), who I am about to name and give a brief description concerning, are good examples of the priestly people we are meant to be. Regarding my list, the first nine are people who I once had day to day dealings with and it was their life as much as anything that influenced me. The remaining seven were known more widely and it was their ministries especially that attracted me.

Most in this second group are people I first came across when they were young, active firebrands but then they kept going right up to the end, including re-inventing themselves according to circumstances etc., ending up as somewhat mellowed, wise, older statesmen. One can't help noting too that life really is transient and ephemeral and we will not be here after a breath. Each one has impacted me, but I should add that in every case there were things about them I disagreed with. However, the accolade they and we should desire at the end is the Lord's *"well done good and faithful servant"*, which I believe they received. There are others I could name, who are Christians (and indeed some non-Christians) who influenced me for good, and I can't help feeling there are a large number of worthy "unknowns" (to all but God) but I have to leave it there. May we be those who will do likewise, serving Him, and remember that God is not calling us to be anything other than ourselves, living in fellowship with Him.

Doris Rafan

Miss Rafan, whose day time job was headmistress at a school, was in charge of the Sunday School serving the Council Estate in Leigh, where I lived the first 12 years of my life. She was a formidable lady with a heart of gold and was clearly on a mission. My Mum and Dad sent me and my sister along to her Sunday School, where the seed was sown for my later embracing the faith she clearly lived.

Bryn Jones

Bryn Jones was my Covenanter leader, when aged 13-14 I attended his Bible Class/Boys Club. I was a naughty boy and should have been kicked out, but he patiently persisted with me. He was a stuffy man. He had served as an army sergeant during the War. He did lighten up when he got zapped with the Spirit later on, but it was his godly influence and sense of duty and honour that inspires me still.

Dorothy Wetton

Dorothy Wetton served much of her working life as a missionary nurse in Nigeria. When returning to the UK and living in my locality, she was keen to enthuse young people in missionary endeavour (this was how we met). When she saw the dire state of the church, she joined the Charismatic Movement, desirous to wake up the church. She was a woman of prayer, an encourager and a mother in Israel.

Len Ladd

Len Ladd was an elderly gentleman, a retired grocer, who attended the church I joined as a teen, and remained a member of until recently. I recall him as a gentle, gracious, humble man, who loved the Lord and knew His Word and was adept in sharing it, and did so without being judgmental. As I went through various ups and downs, he provided much needed and appreciated, kindly, wise counsel.

Winston Chilcraft

I first encountered Winston Chilcraft in my early Christian life. I recall, when attending the mid-week Bible study for the first time, the message he shared – it was on Elijah and Naboth's vineyard. I got to know him better later in life, including his love for the Hebrew prophets. He was his "own man" and a "character". His role model was Jeremiah. Winston became a role model to me, noting he was often "sacked" due to his forthright preaching, and that became a consolation when I experienced similar.

Iris Naish

Iris Naish had served as a missionary in Lebanon, where she was a headmistress. She was a stalwart, with a strong sense of duty, in the church I joined when I first moved away from home for work reasons. I recall her steadfast faithfulness and her priority for prayer. I recall our conversations on the "Israel situation", which continue to guide my thoughts on the subject. Behind a stern appearance was a kindly soul who cared. I appreciated her wise counsel and friendship during that transition time.

Varghese Mathai

I met Varghese Mathai almost by chance when I visited India for the first time in 1983, and then met up with him on several return visits, right up to the time of his death. He was a caring man who lived simply yet trusted the Lord to provide for his family's needs and those he cared for. He was a Brethren evangelist who took his job to "win souls" seriously. He took me under his wing and encouraged me when it came to doing what mattered most, the work of the Lord. I was later to marry his daughter.

Ron Wright

I first met Ron as a young, mischievous teenager, when my Covenanter group attended an event run at the church that hosted his Covenanter group. We had many interactions from then on. For a period, I was at the church Ron was a member of and got involved in the young people's work that he led. His dedication to doing the Lord's work, along with his can-do attitude and ability to think outside the box, were outstanding and he was dependable. He was involved right up to the end in all sorts of ventures.

Babu Henry

It has been my privilege to meet many fine Christians on my India visits and Babu was one of them. I met him when I was preaching at a church and he invited me to his home to preach. I was impressed by his warmth and bubbly character and dedication to the Lord, something often confirmed to me, including his willingness to suffer for the cause of the Gospel. I generally tried to visit him whenever I went to India and found him to be a simple, humble brother who did the work of an evangelist.

Alex Buchannan

Alex Buchannan combined being a member of the Plymouth Brethren with becoming recognised as a respected prophet (but not in most PB circles). I loved his Christ centred preaching, which combined gentleness and forthrightness with grace and humility. He once prophesied a word over me, early in my Christian life, when I was at a low ebb. It was a word I am seeing being worked out today. We live in times when even the charismatics don't always get prophecy. I am glad I got to meet the real deal.

Geoff Carr

Geoff Carr was an evangelist based in my county, who my church had associations with for much of the period I was involved, and where he would regularly visit to preach. I recall the time I was one of Geoff's helpers at one of his evangelistic campaigns when I was a university student. What I loved about Geoff was his winsome and encouraging nature, his warmth and humour, his creative approach to evangelism, his uncompromising gospel presentation and his desire to bring people to the Lord.

David Pawson

David Pawson is best known as a Bible teacher of international renown. He was as thorough as any I have come across in his understanding and exposition of the Bible and, while spurned by some for holding controversial views, I found his teaching, especially his "Unlocking the Bible" series, incisive and helpful. Of all non-Bible sources referred to while writing this book, his words may have had the most impact. We need people to dig deep into the Scriptures. This man was a fine example of such.

Jim Packer

I don't put any Christian teacher on a pedestal these days but, if I were to, it might be Jim Packer, whose writings I first came across when I was at university. I found him to be a sound and balanced teacher, in the Reformed tradition, who appreciated the Puritan writers. I found he was a humble and gracious man, who earnestly contended for the truth in the midst of all manner of false teaching. There are many voices purporting to be doctrinally sound, but I rate Jim to be near the top of my list.

George Verwer

A major influence on my earlier Christian life was Operation Mobilisation (OM). It was one that was to continue, especially when it came to authentic Christian discipleship and world mission. George is credited as being the founder OM, which to this day has a worldwide ministry, where sharing the Gospel is its main focus. I joined an OM crusade upon leaving school. It was there I came across George. I found his teaching, perspectives, vision, humour, example and servant heart to be inspirational.

Gerald Coates

Gerald is the one person on my list who I have never met, although we have corresponded. He came to my notice when I had a friend at university who belonged to Gerald's fellowship, who told me I reminded him of Gerald. It was at a time I was questioning my earlier Brethren influences, as did Gerald, who left the Brethren and started his own house church. While I was amused by the way he irreverently exposed Christian double standards, I was to find later how much he loved the Church.

Roger Forster

There is a lot Roger and Gerald have in common, such as associating with the Brethren, challenging the status quo concerning how church should function, founding networks of churches described as charismatic house fellowships. I came across both when I was at university, and found both diligently serving the Lord 50 years later, after having been effective in bringing many to real faith. I recall back in the day hearing Roger preach three-hour sermons that at the time gripped and inspired me.

1. *I know not why God's wondrous grace*
To me He hath made known,
Nor why, unworthy, Christ in love
Redeemed me for His own.

[Refrain]
But "I know Whom I have believed
And am persuaded that He is able
To keep that which I've committed
Unto Him against that day."

2. *I know not how this saving faith*
To me He did impart,
Nor how believing in His word
Wrought peace within my heart. [Refrain]

3. *I know not how the Spirit moves,*
Convincing men of sin,
Revealing Jesus through the Word,
Creating faith in Him. [Refrain]

4. *I know not what of good or ill*
May be reserved for me,
Of weary ways or golden days,
Before His face I see. [Refrain]

5. I know not when my Lord may come,
At night or noon-day fair,
Nor if I'll walk the vale with Him,
Or "meet Him in the air." [Refrain]

Chapter 59: Holiness – Without which no Man shall see the Lord

"Holiness, without which no man shall see the Lord"
Hebrews 12:14b

Writing **"Priests of the Bible"** has been part of a long journey with many, often unexpected, twists and turns. As I have already indicated, perhaps the greatest revelation, a surprise even, was to re-discover the importance attached to the fact that God is holy and He requires not just the priests but all of His people to live a life that is holy, to the extent that a fundamental explanation of why what God made to happen or allowed to happen was with this end in mind. A lot of consideration and change occurred when setting out the chapter headings for this book, and this was almost the last of the 66 chapters I eventually decided upon and represents a strand of thought that can be seen throughout the book.

One of my favourite sayings, found in the first line of William Cowper's hymn are the words *"God moves in mysterious ways His wonders to perform …"* and I can't help feeling that has been the case when it came to deciding what to include (and exclude) from this book and one reason why it has taken me a lot longer that I had anticipated. At the time the penny dropped that I needed to include this chapter on holiness, noting as our opening text reminds us, without it none of us can see God, it thus makes this a subject of great importance, Paul Slennet, the owner of our local Southend Christian Bookshop announced on his Facebook page that he was virtually giving away copies of J.C.Ryle's classic **"Holiness – Its Nature, Hinderances, Difficulties and Roots"** which is a collection of some of the sermons by this great man of God relating to this subject. I recall reading his writings in my youth and to my shame I have not responded anywhere nearly as consistently enough to the exhortation to pursue holiness.

I was taken with a comment by the Bookshop owner that the take up on the offer may serve as a barometer as to how ready the Church is for revival. As I began to re-read the book, which is not light reading, and in my dotage it is now not one I am likely to read from beginning to end, I was reminded again of the relevance and practical importance of Bishop Ryle's seminal work. This would be the case, even if I were not considering the subject of **"Priests of the Bible"**. Even so, when I read the first two chapters to do with justification and sanctification and seeing how these two subjects relate and have an important bearing on the third chapter "Holiness", my mind went back to the Tabernacle, the Altar and the Laver and how these relate to the subject of holiness. The Priest had to sacrifice an animal (at the Altar) and be washed (at the Laver) (as well as anointed) before he could enter the Holy Place.

I have found in life there are few truly original thinkers. Even those who might have a claim to being such will likely have been influenced by others as well as by personal circumstances, experiences, interests and temperament. I make this point, not just because it is relevant to our approach to the Holy, but I wanted to refrain from sharing the thoughts of others, despite many being in the precious category. But the one thing that has powerfully struck me is that when we talk about a Holy God, it is about One who is unlike any other and exhibits all the manifold attributes we associate with Him. One of the many mysteries we can only at best touch on is that He wants fellowship with His rebellious human creation but it is on His terms. In a nutshell, it is we who must be like Him or, at least, follow His ways and, notwithstanding our individual characteristics, be godly (or Christlike) in our characters.

One plagiarised nugget is in the Lord's (disciple's) prayer which forms a part in regular worship in some churches but not in others, but includes the phrase *"Hallowed be Thy Name"* that links to many prayers prayed in the Bible, and is the right setting for whenever we pray. The one original nugget I offer though that I have not spotted amidst the many I uncovered when re-searching this subject is: *"My beloved is white and ruddy, the chiefest among ten thousand"* Song of Solomon 5:10. My point is: my beloved (Jesus) is spotless, pure, righteous in every way, yet He loved life, would relate to the dregs of society, give all that he had in order to bless humanity, and ultimate-ly His Life. That is what holiness is about!

Another, and related to the subject of this book, is what Isaiah wrote: *"… I saw also the Lord sitting upon a throne, high and lifted up, and his train filled the temple … And one cried unto another, and said, Holy, holy, holy, is the Lord of hosts: the whole earth is full of his glory"* Isaiah 6:1, 3. The realisation of God's holiness, in contrast to his own sinfulness, was a trans-formational experience for Isaiah that later had a profound effect on his life and ministry. May it be so for us!

There is so much else one could say about holiness that is pertinent and helpful. As I trawl the Internet and other writings, I am amazed at the many profitable insights (if we were to take them on board) that are on offer, lead-ing me to the view that speaking about that which pertains to holiness and learning profound lessons on this subject while good, better still is to do holi-ness! Rather than spend time figuring out the perfect ending for this chapter, I will first adapt what I wrote on the subject in my Prophets of the Bible book, which is just as applicable when it comes to Priests of the Bible …

One of the major recurring themes of the Bible that the Hebrew prophets continually referred to was the holiness of God, and along with that was God's demand that His people be holy: *"And ye shall be unto me a kingdom of priests, and a holy nation. These are the words which thou shalt speak unto the children of Israel"* Exodus 19:6 and *"Speak unto all the congregation of the children of Israel, and say unto them, Ye shall be holy: for I the Lord your God am holy"* Leviticus 19:2. A major reason for God's displeasure with His people and for their demise was they were not living as holy people. An important principle and purpose in God's dealings with His people is to make them holy.

For modern minds, an emphasis on holiness can often be looked on with suspicion because of negative connotations, such as concentrating on the inconsequential things some insist on doing and ignoring consequential things they may refrain from doing, and a feeling of foreboding because "holy" people often come across as judgmental, "holier than thou" and not nice people. There is also the claim that such folk are joyless and legalistic, too heavenly minded to be any earthly good, and that some who supposedly attach importance to holiness are sanctimonious and out of touch. In God's eyes, holiness, at least in the biblically held sense, is a very good thing. While I don't have as many examples to illustrate my point as I would like, it seems to me that those who are most holy are also those who are the happiest and most useful, despite what popular culture would have us believe. To be holy is not just worth pursuing but it is essential. The same command given to the Israelites applies to the Church: *"Follow peace with all men, and holiness, without which no man shall see the Lord"* Hebrews 12:14.

There is a wide discrepancy among churches when it comes to how holiness is taught. For some, it is a matter of lots of dos and don'ts, often ignoring what it means to truly love thy neighbour, and has negative implications or it is taught at the expense of other important Bible doctrines. For others, it is something that is ignored because it is seen to be divisive, intolerant and judgmental, so as not to put off the assorted group of sinners who might take umbrage. Then there are some whose focus is solely on getting people saved such that what comes after and responding to the call to live a holy life and the encouragement to do so is easily overlooked. Some take a view that holiness will automatically follow once saved and talk of it is downplayed. Yet holiness remains of paramount importance and is a subject that any preacher worth his salt should be preaching on, and with truth and balance.

While not perfect correlations or synonyms to the word holiness as used in the Bible, the following are near matches: *set-apartness, separateness, devotedness, godliness, righteousness, piety, virtue, consecration, sacredness, sinlessness, sanctification.* Yet none do full justice to this important aspect of God's character that we are called to emulate as part of our own act of devotion and worship. It may involve ritual cleanliness and manifests itself, especially in Jewish religion, in the way God was worshipped and the things people did or did not do, but more importantly it is a matter of the heart:

"Who shall ascend into the hill of the Lord? or who shall stand in his holy place? He that hath clean hands, and a pure heart; who hath not lifted up his soul unto vanity, nor sworn deceitfully. He shall receive the blessing from the Lord, and righteousness from the God of his salvation. This is the generation of them that seek him, that seek thy face," (Psalm 24:3-6).

In preparing for this section on holiness, besides checking out what Old Testament prophets and New Testament writers said, e.g., Paul, Peter, John, I checked out what great men of God in the past, whose insights I particularly respect, wrote about holiness: Jonathan Edwards, John Owen, John Wesley, C.H. Spurgeon and J.C. Ryle, as well as what people who have lived during my lifetime have written: A.W. Tozer, Derek Prince, David Wilkerson, David Pawson and J.I. Packer (to name just a few). Jim Packer's book, titled: **"A Quest for Godliness – the Puritan Vision of the Christian Life"** makes many pertinent points concerning the importance of holiness made by the Puritans better than I ever could. In all these cases, I was blown away, not so much because of the gravity of what they shared but because what they shared was so important, making me realise that I still have a way to go, but it is worth it.

As I look around me and ponder on God's dealing with humankind, past and present, the more I can see that a significant factor when it came to outcomes was God's holiness. It is true that God deals with us in judgment and mercy, but it is also to vindicate His holy name and He desires to make us His holy people. As we look with consternation at world events and try to make sense out of it all, it is worth bringing to that mix the notion that God, as has ever been the case, is seeking a holy people. To reiterate, perhaps the most significant lesson arising out of our study of Priests and the Priesthood is the importance of holiness and that it is our duty and privilege to worship (serve) a holy God.

Before rounding off by quoting a few of the many significant verses of the Bible that contain the word "holy" or "holiness", bearing in mind there are many more texts where those words are not mentioned that are equally relevant, I would like to offer the following thoughts:

Ten holiness thoughts

1. An important theme of the prophets is the Salvation of God. For those of us who believe, we have been saved (justification); we are being saved (sanctification) and we shall be saved (glorification), intrinsic in all this is the need to depart from sin and pursue holiness.

2. It is a grave truth: heaven is a holy place; if you are not interested in being holy on earth, it is unlikely you will experience the joys of heaven or the presence of a holy God.

3. Anyone serious about God will want to be holy, because they want to please and honour Him. It is not just for those we call saints but it is something for all true children of God.

4. Those who are truly saintly are invariably those most concerned about overcoming sin.

5. Becoming holy is not something that occurs overnight. We come to God as sinners and while there should be a desire and expectation to overcome sin, it is a lifelong undertaking.

6. A holy person is as much concerned with doing the right thing (e.g., in our dealings with others, such as the poor and those who are suffering) as things that might cause us to drift away from God, and is why cultivating good habits and not doing those things that might lead us into temptation is important.

7. A holy person is more concerned about being holy rather than being happy, with the praise of God rather than that of men, doing the right thing rather than being successful. Often the person who takes the call to holy living seriously will do so when no-one is looking and (as I have observed) true happiness often follows when people follow holiness.

8. While a holy person may possess an aura of the presence of God and a sense of "the other", often those who are truly holy are among the most empathetic, wholesome, down to earth and productive examples of humanity.

9. A holy person grieves for the sin that is all too apparent in those around them (as well as their own) and desires and wants to help such people to be saved and holy.

10. A holy person, above everything else, seeks to please God. Holiness is his/her watchword, and reason for living. Often it is the most unlikely people who are the most holy, although it is the Lord alone who can pass judgement as to how holy any of us are.

Ten holiness texts

1. Exodus 15:11: "*Who is like unto thee, O Lord, among the gods? who is like thee, glorious in holiness, fearful in praises, doing wonders?*"

2. Exodus 28:36: "*And thou shalt make a plate of pure gold, and grave upon it, like the engravings of a signet, Holiness to the Lord.*"

3. Psalm 29:2: "*Give unto the Lord the glory due unto his name; worship the Lord in the beauty of holiness.*"

4. Isaiah 35:8: "*And an highway shall be there, and a way, and it shall be called The way of holiness; the unclean shall not pass over it; but it shall be for those: the wayfaring men, though fools, shall not err therein.*"

5. Obadiah 1:17: "*But upon mount Zion shall be deliverance, and there shall be holiness; and the house of Jacob shall possess their possessions.*"

6. 2 Corinthians 7:1: "*Having therefore these promises, dearly beloved, let us cleanse ourselves from all filthiness of the flesh and spirit, perfecting holiness in the fear of God.*"

7. Ephesians 4:24: "*And that ye put on the new man, which after God is created in righteousness and true holiness.*"

8. 1 Thessalonians 3:13: "*To the end he may stablish your hearts unblameable in holiness before God, even our Father, at the coming of our Lord Jesus Christ with all his saints.*"

9. Hebrews 12:10: "*For they verily for a few days chastened us after their own pleasure; but he for our profit, that we might be partakers of his holiness.*"

10. Hebrews 12:14: "*Follow peace with all men, and holiness, without which no man shall see the Lord:*"

Ten holy texts

1. Exodus 19:6: "*And ye shall be unto me a kingdom of priests, and an holy nation. These are the words which thou shalt speak unto the children of Israel.*"

2. 1 Samuel 2:2: "*There is none holy as the Lord: for there is none beside thee: neither is there any rock like our God.*"

3. Psalm 15:1: "*Lord, who shall abide in thy tabernacle? who shall dwell in thy holy hill?*"

4. Psalm 103:1: "*Bless the Lord, O my soul: and all that is within me, bless his holy name.*"

5. Isaiah 6:3: "*And one cried unto another, and said, Holy, holy, holy, is the Lord of hosts: the whole earth is full of his glory.*"

6. Habakkuk 2:20: "*But the Lord is in his holy temple: let all the earth keep silence before him.*"

7. Romans 12:1: "*I beseech you therefore, brethren, by the mercies of God, that ye present your bodies a living sacrifice, holy, acceptable unto God, which is your reasonable service.*"

8. Ephesians 5:27: "*That he might present it to himself a glorious church, not having spot, or wrinkle, or any such thing; but that it should be holy and without blemish.*"

9. 1 Peter 2:5, 9: "*Ye also, as lively stones, are built up a spiritual house, an holy priesthood, to offer up spiritual sacrifices, acceptable to God by Jesus Christ ... But ye are a chosen generation, a royal priesthood, an holy nation, a peculiar people; that ye should shew forth the praises of him who hath called you out of darkness into his marvellous light.*"

10. Revelation 22:11: "*He that is unjust, let him be unjust still: and he which is filthy, let him be filthy still: and he that is righteous, let him be righteous still: and he that is holy, let him be holy still.*"

We end with two hymns which are about the holiness of God and how to respond:

1. Holy, holy, holy! Lord God Almighty!
Early in the morning our song shall rise to Thee;
Holy, holy, holy! merciful and mighty!
God in three Persons, blessed Trinity!

2. Holy, holy, holy! all the saints adore Thee,
casting down their golden crowns around the glassy sea;
cherubim and seraphim, falling down before Thee,
which wert and art and evermore shalt be.

3. Holy, holy, holy! though the darkness hide Thee,
though the eye of sinful man Thy glory may not see;
only Thou art holy, there is none beside Thee,
perfect in pow'r, in love, and purity.

4. Holy, holy, holy! Lord God Almighty!
All Thy works shall praise Thy name, in earth and sky and sea;
Holy, holy, holy! merciful and mighty!
God in three Persons, blessed Trinity!

And

1. *Take time to be holy, speak oft with thy Lord;*
Abide in Him always, and feed on His Word.
Make friends of God's children, help those who are weak,
Forgetting in nothing His blessing to seek.

2. *Take time to be holy, the world rushes on;*
Spend much time in secret, with Jesus alone.
By looking to Jesus, like Him thou shalt be;
Thy friends in thy conduct His likeness shall see.

3. *Take time to be holy, let Him be thy Guide;*
And run not before Him, whatever betide.
In joy or in sorrow, still follow the Lord,
And, looking to Jesus, still trust in His Word.

4. *Take time to be holy, be calm in thy soul,*
Each thought and each motive beneath His control.
Thus led by His Spirit to fountains of love,
Thou soon shalt be fitted for service above.

Chapter 60: A Hymn, a Psalm and some Final Thoughts

If you have managed to read the preceding 59 chapters, dear reader, then congratulations!

This final 60th chapter, unlike many before it that just emerged out of the wood work, was planned from the get-go, and the idea was to write a fitting conclusion and say anything needing to be said that had not been said already. While the idea behind this chapter was to suitably wrap up, it has turned out that what I want to say now was not what I had thought from the beginning, for such has been my journey with its amazing eye-opening highlights on the way, which while not expected have delighted in surprising ways. While Priests of the Bible is a subject I can go on and on about, and the longer I delay getting it published the more thoughts come my way, but as I write, I reckon I have said all that needs saying for now other than a few thoughts about my journey while writing this book.

Going back to before the beginning, I had this bright idea (dare I say it, something the Lord laid on my heart) that having written "**Prophets of the Bible**" I need to follow it up with "**Priests of the Bible**" and "**Kings of the Bible**". It was a toss-up which came first and Priests that won out. The biggest surprise to me was that this book turned out a lot differently to what I had envisaged and, to what extent it has been for the good, is for readers to decide although, as I said in the case of Prophets, if it gets readers thinking about the subject and, even more importantly, closer to God, then I reckon it would be job done. What I am in no doubt about is this subject of Priests of the Bible is far more important, and has many more implications and applications than I had thought when I first embarked on this journey.

Perhaps, less surprising, was my previous ignorance on the subject, despite wanting to give a shout out for my early PB mentors, who paid a lot of attention to the subject of priests and the priesthood, and in a way I have not seen in other church set-ups other than perhaps those labelled messianic. I am still learning. Not only could I benefit from reading through yet again the relevant scriptures but also studying the contextual material I urged readers to do in Chapter 2. But an end has to come some time and this is it. As for lessons learned, there are many, but among the most important is the significance of being a Priestly People, the Glory of God and the Holiness of God. Besides being a gospel preaching, community activist, watchman on the wall, I have been reminded I needed to be a worshipper of God.

I had imagined, as a hymn to end with, selecting one recently sung at the funeral of one of the Lord's faithful servants, since it gets right to the heart of our subject and I wouldn't mind if it were to be sung at my funeral also! But we have already ended "Chapter 19: Jesus our Great High Priest", appropriately, with that hymn: "*Before the throne of God above ...*". Instead, I have chosen another golden oldie. Whilst it is one of the less well-known ones by that great English hymn writer, Isaac Watts, yet it encapsulates some of the major themes of this book and gets to the heart of the matter regarding the reason why studying Priests of the Bible is a worthwhile undertaking, and why we ought to give thanks for, praise to and marvel concerning Jesus, who is forever our Great High Priest:

1. Alas! and did my Savior bleed,
and did my Sovereign die!
Would he devote that sacred head
for sinners such as I?

2. Was it for crimes that I have done,
he groaned upon the tree?
Amazing pity! Grace unknown!
And love beyond degree!

3. Well might the sun in darkness hide,
and shut its glories in,
when God, the mighty maker, died
for his own creature's sin.

4. Thus might I hide my blushing face
while his dear cross appears;
dissolve my heart in thankfulness,
and melt mine eyes to tears.

5. But drops of tears can ne'er repay
the debt of love I owe.
Here, Lord, I give myself away;
'tis all that I can do.

Given the importance of David when we consider the Bible and priests, it is worth mentioning his end-of-life prayer as he prepared to hand over the kingship to his son, Solomon, notably to do with building the Temple. These words became part of Psalm 105, one of the Psalms sung at the Temple:

"Wherefore David blessed the Lord before all the congregation: and David said, Blessed be thou, Lord God of Israel our father, for ever and ever. Thine, O Lord is the greatness, and the power, and the glory, and the victory, and the majesty: for all that is in the heaven and in the earth is thine; thine is the kingdom, O Lord, and thou art exalted as head above all. Both riches and honour come of thee, and thou reignest over all; and in thine hand is power and might; and in thine hand it is to make great, and to give strength unto all. Now therefore, our God, we thank thee, and praise thy glorious name" 1 Chronicles 29:10-13.

When it comes to appropriate verses from the Bible to end with, we are spoiled for choice, all throughout the Bible, and especially in the Psalms with some, like Psalm 105, written specifically for use in Temple worship, and often used in church worship down the ages, and even today. But I have chosen David's Psalm 30, sung at the dedication of the Temple, noting that truly worshipping God was a top priestly priority, and in doing so I break my KJV rule and quote from "The Message":

1 *I give you all the credit, God – you got me out of that mess, you didn't let my foes gloat.*

2-3 *God, my God, I yelled for help and you put me together. God, you pulled me out of the grave, gave me another chance at life when I was down-and-out.*

4-5 *All you saints! Sing your hearts out to God! Thank him to his face! He gets angry once in a while, but across a lifetime there is only love. The nights of crying your eyes out give way to days of laughter.*

6-7 *When things were going great I crowed, "I've got it made. I'm God's favorite. He made me king of the mountain." Then you looked the other way and I fell to pieces.*

8-10 *I called out to you, God; I laid my case before you: "Can you sell me for a profit when I'm dead?   auction me off at a cemetery yard sale? When I'm 'dust to dust' my songs and stories of you won't sell. So listen! and be kind! Help me out of this!"*

11-12 *You did it: you changed wild lament into whirling dance; You ripped off my black mourning band and decked me with wildflowers. I'm about to burst with song; I can't keep quiet about you. God, my God, I can't thank you enough.*

As I said in the Preface, I wanted this book to be more about God than anything else, notably concerning His glory and holiness, along with His desire to engage with His people, specifically through the Priesthood and the Priests. Methinks there is no better way to end than on a note of worship to the God most of the priests we have discussed were dedicated to serve. As we have shown, worship, including through song, was the principal activity of Priests of the Bible. Especially for those readers more into modern songs rather than deep, dignified hymns as were regularly sung in bygone days, I would like to share six examples that make points I would like to be made better than I could, and upon coming across them, since when I was a young Christian, have blessed me and hope will bless you too:

"*Within the veil I now would come, into the holy place to look upon Thy face. I see such beauty there, no other can compare, I worship Thee, my Lord, within the veil*".

"*Our God is an awesome God He reigns from Heaven above with wisdom power and love Our God is an awesome God.*"

"*Thou art worthy, Thou art worthy, Thou art worthy, O Lord. Thou art worthy to receive glory, Glory and honor and power. For Thou hast created, hast all things created, For Thou hast created all things. And for Thy pleasure they are created; Thou art worthy, O Lord*".

"*Majesty, Worship His Majesty, Unto Jesus Be Glory Honour And Praise, Majesty, Kingdom, Authority, Flows From His Throne, Unto His Own, His Anthem Raise. So Exalt, Lift Upon High, The Name Of Jesus, Magnify Come Glorify, Christ, Jesus The King*"

"*His Name Is Wonderful; His Name Is Wonderful, His Name Is Wonderful; Jesus My Lord, He Is The Mighty King; Master Of Everything, His Name Is Wonderful; Jesus My Lord, He's The Great Shepherd; The Rock Of All Ages, Almighty God Is He.*"

"*We Bring The Sacrifice Of Praise, Unto The House Of The Lord. And We Offer Up To You, The Sacrifices Of Thanksgiving; And We Offer Up To You, The Sacrifices Of Joy*".

Let me be a bit personal as I come almost to the end. I am sure I am not the only one that has felt embarrassed when encountering folk that are fully caught up in worshipping the Lord, but then that was more likely than not to my shame. I indicated earlier that what particularly struck me on my journey that I hadn't fully expected was to be overwhelmed by thoughts on the holiness of God and that He wanted His people to be holy, whether the Children of Israel as they journeyed through the desert or today's church in its many different manifestations and pre-occupied over a variety of church related matters. But close behind, besides thoughts on glory and beauty, like that on show in the Tabernacle, which Priests were meant to convey to the people, was that of worship, in which Priests were meant to encourage the people. God wants His people to be spirit and truth worshippers of Him.

A book dedicated to the subject of worship could easily turn out to be as big as this one on the subject of priests, but that is not my intention and neither is it to talk about something we should be doing anyway, without being told how or when etc. One preacher said: *"worship is giving to God in secret without anyone knowing that which is costly; giving up, sacrificing, denying oneself"*. I have come across worshippers, singing yesterday's profound, solemn hymns and today's happy-clappy choruses, as well as those, maybe the majority, and I include myself, who merely go through the motions, which brings me to the beautiful story we read about in John 4 of Jesus' meeting with the Samaritan Woman at the Well, with her colourful past, who was told how she would be able to get living water for herself.

Toward the end of the conversation, the subject got onto worship. For the woman, it was, as is the case with many, about the mechanics of worship, e.g., (for her) where to worship, but for Jesus it was more to do with one's attitude to worship: *"Jesus saith unto her, Woman, believe me, the hour cometh, when ye shall neither in this mountain, nor yet at Jerusalem, worship the Father. Ye worship ye know not what: we know what we worship: for salvation is of the Jews. But the hour cometh, and now is, when the true worshippers shall worship the Father in spirit and in truth: for the Father seeketh such to worship him. God is a Spirit: and they that worship him must worship him in spirit and in truth"* John 4:21-24. My point is that another reason for studying "Priests of the Bible", besides helping us to have a deeper understanding of God's holiness, is that we become true worshippers of God. I sense it has been something many of us may have missed out on, but is so important that we need to be doing it.

It could be said that today's people of God are, like the Children of Israel, also journeying through a wilderness and there will be times when to worship is easier said than done, but what is important to remember is the destination: *"And they sung a new song, saying, Thou art worthy to take the book, and to open the seals thereof: for thou wast slain, and hast redeemed us to God by thy blood out of every kindred, and tongue, and people, and nation; And hast made us unto our God kings and priests: and we shall reign on the earth. And I beheld, and I heard the voice of many angels round about the throne and the beasts and the elders: and the number of them was ten thousand times ten thousand, and thousands of thousands; Saying with a loud voice, Worthy is the Lamb that was slain to receive power, and riches, and wisdom, and strength, and honour, and glory, and blessing. And every creature which is in heaven, and on the earth, and under the earth, and such as are in the sea, and all that are in them, heard I saying, Blessing, and honour, and glory, and power, be unto him that sitteth upon the throne, and unto the Lamb for ever and ever. And the four beasts said, Amen. And the four and twenty elders fell down and worshipped him that liveth for ever and ever"* Revelation 5:9-14.

Which nicely brings us back again to the Psalms, which more than in any other place presents us with the call to worship and a wide plethora of subjects and reasons that could/should inspire us in our worship. In considering one more suitable Psalm with which to end, I could think of none better than the final Song of Ascent (Psalm 134), last of the 15 Psalms pilgrims would have sung as they ascended the hill in order to worship God in His holy Temple and as they thought about those priests and Levites whose daily business and great privilege it was to worship the Lord (night as well as day) in His Temple:

1 Behold, bless ye the Lord, all ye servants of the Lord, which by night stand in the house of the Lord.

2 Lift up your hands in the sanctuary, and bless the Lord.

3 The Lord that made heaven and earth bless thee out of Zion.

So that's it – we have done prophets and now we have done priests. The temptation remains to add more but we really have to wind things up. Moreover, the author has rather pushed it by bringing in stuff which is only loosely priest related, which he thinks is important and wanted to share with his readers, and this was the best vehicle to do so. Just as he missed out some relevant thoughts and insights regarding prophets, no doubt the same will later be seen to be the case with priests. Whilst we might imagine this to be the END, there is another part, quite unexpected and unplanned for, to come, concerning Kings of the Bible – so please read on! We can afterwards really end, with the author having got nearly all of what was on his heart off his chest in our prophets, priests and kings trilogy!

But let us end the Priest section of this book with "the Priestly blessing": *"Speak unto Aaron and unto his sons, saying, On this wise ye shall bless the children of Israel, saying unto them, The Lord bless thee, and keep thee: The Lord make his face shine upon thee, and be gracious unto thee: The Lord lift up his countenance upon thee, and give thee peace. And they shall put my name upon the children of Israel, and I will bless them"* Numbers 6:23-27, and we follow it with a better-known Isaac Watts hymn that puts what being a priestly people entails into a right perspective as we survey the wondrous cross:

1. When I survey the wondrous cross
on which the Prince of glory died,
my richest gain I count but loss,
and pour contempt on all my pride.

2. Forbid it, Lord, that I should boast
save in the death of Christ, my God!
All the vain things that charm me most,
I sacrifice them through his blood.

3. See, from his head, his hands, his feet,
sorrow and love flow mingled down.
Did e'er such love and sorrow meet,
or thorns compose so rich a crown?

4. Were the whole realm of nature mine,
that were an offering far too small.
Love so amazing, so divine,
demands my soul, my life, my all.

Part 4
Kings of the Bible

Chapter 61: Introducing Kings of the Bible

Having completed writing "**Prophets of the Bible**", after attempting to cover every prophet that is to be found in the Bible (unknown, unnamed and unrecognised, as well as the named prophets that are commonly recognised as prophets) it made sense to do something similar concerning priests and kings and thus end up with a trilogy of books, one each for prophets, priests and kings. Chapters 1 through 60 was our attempt at priests. While no particular order is required, if readers have read the book to do with prophets and Parts 1 – 3 of this book, they will find it helps as we come to studying the kings.

As will become apparent to readers, writing these books covering prophets and priests respectively were considerable undertakings, albeit (it is hoped) worthwhile ones. In now turning our attention away from priests and to kings, we are faced with the seemingly daunting prospect that writing "**Kings of the Bible**" could be just as challenging and also turn out to be a long drawn-out exercise, as was the case with both prophets or priests, if for no other reason than there are many more kings than prophets and priests mentioned in the Bible and there are a large number of instances where much has been written concerning kings that is relevant and worthy of study. This presents us with a writing challenge that is compounded, given that in the case of kings not of Israel a lot more is told about the kingdoms than the kings, and often the kings of those kingdoms are hardly ever mentioned by name.

The term "king" is used somewhat loosely in the Bible and could equally apply to rulers of cities or regions (partly explaining why there were so many of them), nations and empires. Yet, as far as the most significant nation mentioned in the Bible is concerned, i.e., Israel, it was not God's purpose for them to be ruled by earthly kings. But as we will see, rule through pure theocracy in Israel's case only lasted for a period before God gave in to their request and gave them kings. Later, due to their disobedience when it came to following false gods etc., and despite many warnings, Israel was made subject to foreign rule, which lasted from the time of their Exile until the modern era, when Israel became an independent state once again, not ruled by a king but (supposedly) through a democracy.

We find, for example, with reference to Chapter 2, Figure 21, concerning the kingdoms that were surrounding Israel in the time of the prophet Amos, while many of these kingdoms (or their main cities) are mentioned by name, the kings that ruled the kingdoms often were not or they were barely mentioned. We read words to the effect *"For three sins of <insert name of kingdom>, even for four, I will not turn back my wrath because <insert reason>"*, which are repeated several times while specifying *name of* *kingdom* and *reason*: Amos 1:3 – Damascus, Amos 1:6 – Gaza, Amos 1:9 – Tyre, Amos 1:11 – Edom, Amos 1:13 – Ammon, Amos 2:1 – Moab, before addressing Judah and Israel.

Part of the consideration of **"Prophets of the Bible"** was not just the particular focus of the prophets on Israel and Judah but we find they also turned their attentions to other kingdoms, especially those surrounding Israel and Judah, who God warns and judges. God also specifically raises up kings, including bad ones, for a purpose, and just as easily puts them down as part of His sovereign will. We find examples in many of the "writing prophets". We find that the prophecies found in the Books of Daniel, Obadiah, Jonah and Nahum are more to do with these other nations, and as for the rest, these also have a lot to say. This thought is developed in the chapters that follow, especially Chapter 66.

As often happens in life, compromise is needed. It applies in the author's case, faced with the choice between ending up with something fully comprehensive or somewhat more basic. The idea of this "PART 4" came late in the day, as it was the intention to include the content that follows as part of a much larger work that he imagined **"Kings of the Bible"** to be, should such a book ever be written. It was to become obvious to the author, however, that writing such a book, given current circumstances etc., would likely be too steep a hill to climb, and therefore the reader's understanding is valued.

The compromise is that in what follows we have the outline (and sometimes more) of what the author would have liked to have covered if that more ambitious project he had previously set his heart on were to have happened and hopes what is offered here will nevertheless provide a sound framework for readers who wish to delve more deeply into the subject of kings of the Bible and that it will at least go some way to answer the question that has already been begged: how did what kings did tie in with what the prophets and priests did? We have ended up (as a result) with:

Chapter 61: Introducing Kings of the Bible (this chapter).

Chapter 62: Kings of the Bible before Israel had its own King, where we consider the kings that crop up in the first seven books of the Christian Bible (Genesis – Judges).

Chapter 63: Kings of Israel – the United Kingdom (Saul, David, Solomon), where we consider the transition from the time when Israel had no king until it had Saul, David and Solomon as its kings.

Chapter 64: Kings of Judah – Rehoboam to Zedekiah, having seen Israel split between the Northern Kingdom under Jeroboam (still referred to as Israel) and the Southern Kingdom under Rehoboam (after referred to as Judah) we turn our attention to all the kings of Judah, following that division.

Chapter 65: Kings of Israel – Jeroboam to Hoshea, where we turn our attention to all the kings of the divided kingdom of Israel, following the division of the Kingdom between the ten (northern) tribes of Israel (referred to thereafter as Israel) and two (southern) tribes of Judah and Benjamin.

Chapter 66: Kings of the Bible, not of Israel or Judah, this is a "catch-all", where we consider those remaining kings that have not been dealt with to a sufficient enough extent in the previous chapters, and also touches upon what the prophets have to say concerning these kings.

In order to carry out this exercise, a forensic study is preferred, primarily of the Old Testament, and to a large extent this is what has been attempted. While Chapter 62 focuses on the first seven Books of the Christian Bible (eight if you count Ruth), the remaining chapters focus on the rest of the Old Testament – the Books of Samuel for Chapter 63, the Books of Kings for Chapters 64 and 65, and books like Daniel, Ezra, Nehemiah and Esther for Chapter 66. In all these cases, reference is also made to the Books of Chronicles, to the Books of Wisdom and to those of various Prophets when applicable.

We have deliberately omitted kings of the New Testament, partly because of time limitations but also because the kings that crop up are mostly either Roman emperors, starting from Caesar Augustus, or their puppets from the Herodian dynasty, starting with Herod the Great, and we have discussed these already in our Chapters 16 and 17. But there is one king that cannot be omitted because He is the King of kings, who was prophesied as being Israel's Messiah in the Old Testament and revealed as Lord and Saviour for Jews and Gentiles alike in the New Testament, who one day will return to earth.

We keenly anticipate the time: *"And I saw heaven opened, and behold a white horse; and he that sat upon him was called Faithful and True, and in righteousness he doth judge and make war. His eyes were as a flame of fire, and on his head were many crowns; and he had a name written, that no man knew, but he himself. And he was clothed with a vesture dipped in blood: and his name is called The Word of God. And the armies which were in heaven followed him upon white horses, clothed in fine linen, white and clean. And out of his mouth goeth a sharp sword, that with it he should smite the nations: and he shall rule them with a rod of iron: and he treadeth the winepress of the fierceness and wrath of Almighty God. And he hath on his vesture and on his thigh a name written, KING OF KINGS, AND LORD OF LORDS"* Revelation 19:11-16. It is with wonder that we contemplate Jesus of Nazareth, who was crucified and then rose again, who is not only King of kings but He is also prophet, priest and king, wonderfully combining all of these offices. He is the one of whom the Psalmist wrote:

"My heart is inditing a good matter: I speak of the things which I have made touching the king: my tongue is the pen of a ready writer. Thou art fairer than the children of men: grace is poured into thy lips: therefore God hath blessed thee for ever. Gird thy sword upon thy thigh, O most mighty, with thy glory and thy majesty. And in thy majesty ride prosperously because of truth and meekness and righteousness; and thy right hand shall teach thee terrible things. Thine arrows are sharp in the heart of the king's enemies; whereby the people fall under thee. Thy throne, O God, is for ever and ever: the sceptre of thy kingdom is a right sceptre. Thou lovest righteousness, and hatest wickedness: therefore God, thy God, hath anointed thee with the oil of gladness above thy fellows" Psalm 45:1-7.

Besides Rome, we have also deliberately left out Greece. Other than what was written about Greece by Daniel the Prophet, including the Antichrist figure, Antiochus (IV) Epiphanes (prophesied in Daniel 11), named kings of Greece do not feature in the Bible, yet they played an important part, not just by being what came between Persian and Roman rule over Israel, but in extending Greek influence, beginning with Alexander the Great, (prophesied in Daniel 8) who laid the foundation of the Greek empire, as well as Antiochus Epiphanes, whose oppression of Jews who sought to follow the Law of Moses knew no bounds. Such influence, e.g., the imposition of Greek thinking, continues today! See Chapter 16 for more information concerning the Bible related significance of kings of Greece.

Besides asking how kings of the Bible fitted in with priests of the Bible and prophets of the Bible and what lessons we can draw as a result of these interactions, as well as lessons drawn from what the Bible tells us about these kings, there are many questions that could reasonably be asked concerning today's kings and how we should approach living under their rule. For example:

- How do we apply Romans 13 when it comes to submitting to authority, which was an issue of contention among earnest Christians during the "Corona Pandemic", while living under regimes that are far from godly and even anti-God, as is the case with many "kings" today?

- Are there instances when civil disobedience may be justified on conscience grounds, such as seen more recently in those movements led by Mahatma Gandhi and Martin Luther King?

- What applications can we draw from texts like *"honour the king"* 1 Peter 2:17 and a number of texts that are to do with kings, that can be found in the Book of Proverbs, e.g., Proverbs 8:15, 14:35, 16:13, 22:11, 29:4, 12, 14?

- Isaiah looked forward to a day when *"a king shall reign in righteousness"* Isaiah 32:1; in what ways should such a prospect give us encouragement and hope?

- Should Christians go to war or take up arms for kings and, if so, under what circumstances?

- What ought to be entailed when it comes to praying for those who are in authority, as we are exhorted to do in 1 Timothy 2:1-2?

- How can we reconcile it with God's sovereignty when, as is often the case, it is the bad people that seem to get to be in charge and the good people seem to hardly get a look in, and what hope and advice can we offer those who are forced to endure under oppression?

- To what extent are today's kings puppets of those often hidden yet nefarious forces acting behind the scenes, intent on enslaving and harming humanity, despite claims that most countries operate as democracies and rulers are meant to be answerable to the people?

- Often kings in Bible times achieved power through stealth or force and were autocratic in their rule, more often than not serving their interests and those of their close circle rather than those of the people. In what ways does this differ from today's supposed democracies?

- Concerning living in a democracy, is there a case for Christians partaking in the political process and what should happen if we cannot in all conscience join any political party?

- Often kings in Bible times were nationalist leaning, despite forming alliances. How does this compare to today's trend toward globalism, with the prospect of a Great Reset and a New World Order being bandied around, along with moves toward a one world government?

- While looking around at today's kings (rulers of nations) can be a depressing exercise, can we still see the hand of God when it comes to the raising up and putting down of kings, and does God warn and judge nations today as He clearly did in Old Testament times?

- Christians are divided when it comes to what to make out of God's purposes for Israel, its part (good or bad) in world events today and subjects like the Abrahamic, Sinai and Davidic Covenants and of not yet fulfilled prophecy; what does the Bible have to say on the subject?

- Given an overriding umbrella for this "prophets, priests and kings project" has been the exploration of how these three offices interacted, the question that might be reasonably asked is when in the Bible, if ever (besides Jesus), has this been done successfully?

All these and more are questions that may cross the reader's mind, if theirs are anything like the author's, and no doubt studying kings of the Bible will provide certain insights. One piece of advice though; having seen good Christians divide when it comes to what are the right answers to these questions – any debate ought to be done intelligently, relevantly, respectfully and with humility. It is noteworthy that in certain cultures people are free to criticise kings and their emissaries and enjoy relative freedom, in others that is far from being the case, and is one reason why this study is pertinent.

While the author has views (see his blogs) on these questions, often at odds even with Christians found in a similar theological stable to his (which is one reason why he asked them besides deeming these important and food for thought), this (PART 4) is not the place to push them, but rather we will now turn our attention to our subject – Kings of the Bible, what we can find out about them in terms of what they did and why they did what they did and lessons we can learn from their lives and reigns.

But given the number of kings mentioned, and our remit is merely to provide a concise account of kings of the Bible, we will concentrate on the more significant kings and miss out some we deem to be less significant. Again, reader forbearance is requested, for as with our prophets' book and no doubt the same will apply in the case of priests, some kings may not get the mention they deserve.

Picking up on Chapter 41, where we discussed the subject of the Priesthood of All Believers, it is worth adding those same believers are also to exercise a kingly role: "*But ye are a chosen generation, a royal priesthood, an holy nation, a peculiar people; that ye should shew forth the praises of him who hath called you out of darkness into his marvellous light*" 1 Peter 2:9 and "*and hast made us unto our God kings and priests: and we shall reign on the earth*" Revelation 5:10.

While the chapters that follow are all to do with human kings, it is worth ending this chapter by once again considering Him who was and still is the King of kings and the one who we crown and worship:

1. King of my life, I crown Thee now,

Thine shall the glory be;

Lest I forget Thy thorn-crowned brow,

Lead me to Calvary.

[Refrain]
Lest I forget Gethsemane;
Lest I forget Thine agony;
Lest I forget Thy love for me,
Lead me to Calvary.

2. Show me the tomb where Thou wast laid,
Tenderly mourned and wept;
Angels in robes of light arrayed
Guarded Thee while Thou slept. [Refrain]

3. Let me like Mary, through the gloom,
Come with a gift to Thee;
Show to me now the empty tomb,
Lead me to Calvary. [Refrain]

4. May I be willing, Lord, to bear
Daily my cross for Thee;
Even Thy cup of grief to share,
Thou hast borne all for me. [Refrain]

5. Fill me, O Lord, with Thy desire
For all that know not Thee;
Then touch my lips with holy fire,
To speak of Calvary. [Refrain]

And

1. O worship the King all-glorious above,
O gratefully sing his power and his love:
our shield and defender, the Ancient of Days,
pavilioned in splendor and girded with praise.

2. O tell of his might and sing of his grace,
whose robe is the light, whose canopy space.
His chariots of wrath the deep thunderclouds form,
and dark is his path on the wings of the storm.

3. Your bountiful care, what tongue can recite?
It breathes in the air, it shines in the light;
it streams from the hills, it descends to the plain,
and sweetly distills in the dew and the rain.

4. Frail children of dust, and feeble as frail,
in you do we trust, nor find you to fail.
Your mercies, how tender, how firm to the end,
our Maker, Defender, Redeemer, and Friend!

5. O measureless Might, unchangeable Love,
whom angels delight to worship above!
Your ransomed creation, with glory ablaze,
in true adoration shall sing to your praise!

Chapter 62: Kings of the Bible before Israel had its own King

We now begin our trawl through the Bible to find out what is relevant and interesting to include in this more modest attempt at covering as many as we can of the kings of the Bible. If we were to take a more literalist approach and adopt the view that Bishop Usher was right, that the world we live in is not much older than 6000 years, we will see it was only at the halfway point that Israel operated under its first king. Therefore, this chapter needs to cover the first half of earth time (according to Usher) when there were many kings, many we might place in the unknown or unnamed category, and a good number of these are at least alluded to in the Bible.

Whilst to cover these might still be a profitable exercise, the approach we will adopt in this chapter and, in a modified way, in the chapters that follow, is to go through the Christian Bible, book by book, mindful that events are often not set out in time order, there are many gaps and finding out about kings was only something done as part of God's purpose to show us what He saw as important. Given our period is covered by the Books of Genesis, Exodus, Leviticus, Numbers, Deuteronomy, Joshua and Judges (and, as it happens, in that order) we will deal with each book in turn, beginning with Genesis.

Genesis

We could begin with the first son (Cain) of the first man (Adam). After killing his brother (Abel) and being given a mark by God by way of protection, he relocated to the land of Nod, where he married a wife, had a son and built a city. Several questions are begged though, such as what did this mark look like and do, where did Cain's wife come from and who helped build the city? One can't help but imagine that there would have been some form of government from that time and that Cain would have been the king of that city and, given the various occupations of his descendants, different civilisations might well have arisen, as well as what might have arisen out of the more "godly line" of Seth.

But we cannot say for sure and it was not until the aftermath of Noah's flood that we can begin to name kings with certainty. Following the Flood, we find in Genesis 10, a "Table of Nations" (see Chapter 2, Figure 15) arising from Noah's sons: Japheth, Ham and Shem, with Shem being the father of the Semites, which included Abraham and his descendants (see Chapter 2, Figure 17). There have been those who have studied this table in depth and see it as helping to explain the nations we have today. The only named king in that Table of Nations was Nimrod, of whom it was written that he was a *"mighty hunter before the Lord"*. Many have speculated what this means and whether Nimrod was a good or bad person. It is likely he was a baddie though and was responsible for building the Tower of Babel (Genesis 11) that was built in defiance of God, which God in his judgement destroyed. Notably, Nimrod was involved in setting up kingdoms around Babylon and Assyria, about which more could be said, with extra-biblical texts suggesting he was a formidable baddie, although a lot of it is not fully proven.

The major interest for Bible students is the call of Abraham (Abram) and the setting up of the nation of Israel. We read: *"Now the Lord had said unto Abram, Get thee out of thy country, and from thy kindred, and from thy father's house, unto a land that I will shew thee: And I will make of thee a great nation, and I will bless thee, and make thy name great; and thou shalt be a blessing: And I will bless them that bless thee, and curse him that curseth thee: and in thee shall all families of the earth be blessed"* Genesis 12:1-3. That line was to continue through Isaac and Jacob, although Abraham had another son – Ishmael and Isaac had another son – Esau. The Arab nations, through the line of Ishmael, and the Edomites through the line of Esau, along with those who ruled over those nations, were to play an important part in our later consideration of kings of the Bible. The same can be said of Moab and Ammon that descended from Lot, Abraham's nephew, who had accompanied him on his journey.

Abraham was to have dealings with Pharoah (Egypt) and Abimelech (Philistine). Both Egypt and the Philistines, along with their kings (Pharoah and Abimelech) were also to have a significant part to play in our story. Of particular fascination was the war between the five kings and the four, discussed in Genesis 14, where Abraham got involved as he found himself needing to rescue Lot, who had been caught up in that war and taken captive. Having succeeded in doing the rescue (remarkably, given what he was up against), Abraham then gets to meet Melchizedek, King of Jerusalem, as well as being a priest of the Most High God, who has already been an important feature of our book.

Following these incidents and looking ahead some 500 years, God revealed to Abraham what He was to do: *"In the same day the Lord made a covenant with Abram, saying, Unto thy seed have I given this land, from the river of Egypt unto the great river, the river Euphrates: The Kenites, and the Kenizzites, and the Kadmonites, And the Hittites, and the Perizzites, and the Rephaims, And the Amorites, and the Canaanites, and the Girgashites, and the Jebusites"* Genesis 15:18-21.

While clearing the land of its inhabitants was to take place over a long period of time, it did happen and, along with it, interactions, mostly hostile, with various kings. There would be a delay caused by Israel's frequent disobedience, as well as the sin of the Amorites having not reached its peak. Those nations were allowed by God to stay longer in the land than might otherwise have been the case. It would first mean Israel relocating to Egypt during a time of famine. Egypt was then under the rule of a sympathetic Pharoah. Moses, 400 years later, led them out of Egypt to possess the Promised Land.

Exodus

A lot of Exodus and the Books of the Bible that will be considered in this chapter concern Israel driving out those nations mentioned in Genesis 15. We note God's word to Abraham: *"And he said unto Abram, Know of a surety that thy seed shall be a stranger in a land that is not theirs, and shall serve them; and they shall afflict them four hundred years; And also that nation, whom they shall serve, will I judge: and afterward shall they come out with great substance. And thou shalt go to thy fathers in peace; thou shalt be buried in a good old age. But in the fourth generation they shall come hither again: for the iniquity of the Amorites is not yet full"* Genesis 15:13-16.

Some of the accounts are bloody and defy human sensibilities conditioned to being outraged when coming across reports that are tantamount to acts of genocide. Partly in mitigation (not that we need to apologise for God) the Amorites, and other people groups that would be dealt with, were extraordinarily wicked and we have the archaeological evidence to prove it. But this is what often happened when Israel conquered some of these nations. Yet we are reminded that God is one who also judges. His timing is always perfect, including allowing time for those down to be judged to repent.

Another area that may give cause for bafflement relates to giants and the Nephilim. Going back to Genesis 6 and the reason why God caused the Great Flood, for we read *"that the sons of God saw the daughters of men that they were fair; and they took them wives of all which they chose"* Genesis 6:2. The result of the union was giants, referred to as the Nephilim, and fully opposed to what God intended for humankind. Seeing giants in the Promised Land made the Israelites fearful in attempting to overcome this obstacle to possessing it. Whether it was Caleb prepared to do battle with the giants to conquer his tiny portion of the Promised Land (Hebron) or Israel having to face King Og of Bashan, who from the Bible account was a giant, or other mentions of giants and the Nephilim, we cannot dismiss their presence or significance when it came to obstacles needing to be overcome.

Neither must we dismiss the possibility of there being Nephilim today, exhibiting anti-human traits, including lack of empathy, even though they appear to greater humanity as being 'normal'. We do so in the light of the transhuman agenda that is being aggressively pushed by those we might label as globalists or "the bad guys", such as Yuval Noah Harari, spokesman of the World Economic Forum (WEF), who promote the merging of man with machine, in a cultural climate that condemns those who maintain there can only be two genders: man and woman and, dare one say it, the matter of the Covid-19 "vaccine" with its possible DNA and human interfering properties. It is notable that there has been an increased expectation in recent years of an alien invasion and if that were to happen it could be to do with that which pertains to the Nephilim. While on the subject, we cannot dismiss the argument that such was God's abhorrence of fallen angels mating with humans that this was a factor in ordering the likes of Moses and Joshua to wipe out peoples where this had occurred. What is apparent from carefully studying the Bible is there are three orders of creation: angels, humans and beasts, and any sexual relationship across those orders is strictly forbidden, with dire consequences if transgressed.

As Bible students seeking to study God's word in a way that honours Him, we must not ignore or "explain away" those passages of the Bible that might be deemed problematical. Neither must we over dwell on them or come to conclusions that cannot be justified when, as we must, we undertake a true, comprehensive and balanced study of the Bible. Seeming acts of genocide ordered by God and Nephilim giants that defied God's intentions for humanity to procreate with other humans and then produce godly offspring are two relevant facts to be borne in mind as we contemplate the rest of this chapter, with its focus on Israel possessing the land that God had promised to Abraham many years prior and having to overcome kings and nations along the way, who stood in the way of God's plans.

We ended Genesis with a benevolent Pharoah allowing Jacob and his family (numbering 70) to settle in Egypt and be well treated. 430 years later that family had grown to two million and the Pharoah of the day was anything but sympathetic toward Israel but rather treated them as slaves. This was the time for Moses to enter the scene, and lead the Israelites out of Egypt until just before entering the Promised Land. From Exodus 19 through to Numbers 12, we find the Israelites camped around Mount Sinai for a year. We do not find further mention of their interactions with other nations or their kings.

The only encounter with nations (and one of many examples of the king that led them not being mentioned by name) can be found in Exodus 17. Between crossing the Red Sea in Exodus 14 and coming to Mount Sinai in Exodus 19, we read of the beginnings of Israel's journey in the Wilderness. Opposing them firstly and significantly were the Amalekites but, with God's help, Israel was able to prevail and win the first of many battles they were to fight against both God's and their enemies. The Amalekites were to play an important part in Israel's future, as will be shown when we read on in the Bible. But until they were to resume their journey after Sinai there would be no more battles.

But they had been forewarned there would be battles but it was God and His angels that would be leading the fight, and what they must do was to serve Him and not the gods of those they would come across: *"For mine Angel shall go before thee, and bring thee in unto the Amorites, and the Hittites, and the Perizzites, and the Canaanites, the Hivites, and the Jebusites: and I will cut them off. Thou shalt not bow down to their gods, nor serve them, nor do after their works: but thou shalt utterly overthrow them, and quite break down their images. And ye shall serve the Lord your God, and he shall bless thy bread, and thy water; and I will take sickness away from the midst of thee"* Exodus 23:23-25.

Starting with Moses as the Israelites moved from their Sinai location, along with their encounters with the kings of the lands they would pass through, or be close to as they passed, onto Joshua who led them into Caanan's land in order to possess it, we later read, when near the end of his life, Joshua declaring: *"And you went over Jordan, and came unto Jericho: and the men of Jericho fought against you, the Amorites, and the Perizzites, and the Canaanites, and the Hittites, and the Girgashites, the Hivites, and the Jebusites; and I delivered them into your hand"* Joshua 24:11.

Leviticus

The focus on the Book of Leviticus was the Tribe of Levi and the laws and rules that governed the priesthood and national life. Importantly, Leviticus was about establishing the religious life of the nation so they could face other nations. There is nothing further we can add here concerning kings.

Numbers

In Numbers 13, we read an account that is enormously significant when we consider Israel's journey through the Wilderness and God's dealings with them. It concerned the 12 spies that were sent out to explore the land Israel was to eventually possess and then to report back. All said it was a good land, but ten of the spies said taking it would be too big an undertaking, as there were giants in the land. The remaining two (Joshua and Caleb) said that they should go and possess the land since God was with them. But it was the counsel of the ten that prevailed, and part of God's judgement was that the Israelites would spend a further 38 years wandering in the Wilderness before they took possession of the Promised Land – but not before everyone, excluding Joshua, Caleb and the children, had died.

As a sequel to this particular story, the people decided to go and try and possess the land despite Moses telling them not to do so. "*Go not up, for the Lord is not among you; that ye be not smitten before your enemies. For the Amalekites and the Canaanites are there before you, and ye shall fall by the sword: because ye are turned away from the Lord, therefore the Lord will not be with you. But they presumed to go up unto the hill top: nevertheless the ark of the covenant of the Lord, and Moses, departed not out of the camp. Then the Amalekites came down, and the Canaanites which dwelt in that hill, and smote them, and discomfited them, even unto Hormah*" Numbers 14:42-45.

All of which brings us to the remainder of Israel's Wilderness wanderings, seeing them almost ready to enter the Promised Land at the end of the Book of Numbers. There was much happening that is noteworthy but, given our focus is on kings and kingdoms, we will concentrate on these and the interaction each had with Israel. Most took place after leaving Sinai.

Edom denies Israel passage (20:14-21): Part of the preferred route into the Promised Land involved going through the land of Edom but given family connections (Esau was Jacob's son), the Israelites were told by God not to be an instigator of any conflict with Edom. Moses' request to pass through their land was denied and it was backed up by Edom's army being made ready to go to war to stop them. Moses' response was to find an alternative and thus bypass Edom.

The Caananite king of Arad (21:1-3): Arad did attack the journeying Israelites, but He was defeated.

The Journey to Moab (21:10-20): Moab along with Ammon also had family links with Israel, both being descendants of Abraham's nephew, Lot, and as with Edom, Israel was instructed not to create any problems. But we read in Chapters 22-25 how the Moabite king, Balak, having decided Israel was a threat, instructed the "prophet for hire" Balaam to curse them. We find recorded here what happened when instead of cursing Israel, Balaam ended up blessing and prophesying over them.

Sihon king of the Amorites (21:21-32): The Israelites requested passage through the land of Sihon, with no intention to invade or attack, but Sihon's response was to go to war and he was defeated.

Og king of Bashan (21:33-35): Og was the next in line to attack Israel and he too was defeated. We read later "*For only Og king of Bashan remained of the remnant of giants; behold, his bedstead was a bedstead of iron; is it not in Rabbath of the children of Ammon? nine cubits was the length thereof, and four cubits the breadth of it, after the cubit of a man*" Deuteronomy 3:11.

Vengeance of the Midianites (31:1-24): The Midianites were those who caused Israel to sin by worshipping false gods and committing sexual immorality, and almost succeeded where Balak and Balaam had failed, and they too were defeated when they were attacked by the Israelites.

Deuteronomy

The Book of Deuteronomy is taken up with the words of Moses, spoken shortly before his death as he looked back on the past, sharing his thoughts with a new generation of Israelites, prior to them crossing the Jordan in order to possess the land that God had promised to give them. As with Leviticus, Deuteronomy does not tell us much that is new concerning kings and kingdoms, other than by way of recap and with a degree of elaboration concerning when Israel encountered various kings on that journey, and being reminded of what being God's Covenant people entailed, before going to possess the Land. The interest goes was back to one of Abraham's early encounters with God, when God tells Abraham that the promise of taking the Land would be delayed for over 400 years: *"for the iniquity of the Amorites is not yet full"* Genesis 15:16, begging the question what was meant? That encounter Abraham had with God concluded: *"On that day the Lord made a covenant with Abram, saying, "To your offspring I give this land, from the river of Egypt to the great river, the river Euphrates, the land of the Kenites, the Kenizzites, the Kadmonites, the Hittites, the Perizzites, the Rephaim, the Amorites, the Canaanites, the Girgashites and the Jebusites"* Genesis 15:18-20.

Of particular interest when it comes to kings that the Israelites had to overcome were two, who we read were kings of the Amorites and ones Moses had defeated (other Amorite kings and the iniquity we will discuss when we come to Joshua): *"Then we turned, and went up the way to Bashan: and Og the king of Bashan came out against us, he and all his people, to battle at Edrei. And the Lord said unto me, Fear him not: for I will deliver him, and all his people, and his land, into thy hand; and thou shalt do unto him as thou didst unto Sihon king of the Amorites, which dwelt at Heshbon. So the Lord our God delivered into our hands Og also, the king of Bashan, and all his people: and we smote him until none was left to him remaining. And we took all his cities at that time, there was not a city which we took not from them, threescore cities, all the region of Argob, the kingdom of Og in Bashan. All these cities were fenced with high walls, gates, and bars; beside unwalled towns a great many. And we utterly destroyed them, as we did unto Sihon king of Heshbon, utterly destroying the men, women, and children, of every city. But all the cattle, and the spoil of the cities, we took for a prey to ourselves. And we took at that time out of the hand of the two kings of the Amorites the land that was on this side Jordan, from the river of Arnon unto mount Hermon"* Deuteronomy 3:1-8.

Joshua

The Book of Joshua is a mainly upbeat account of Israel entering the Promised Land and taking it (albeit not entirely) from those occupants that God was intent on judging. Joshua followed Moses when it came to leading the Israelites, having served a long apprenticeship, but neither he nor Moses could be looked upon as kings, yet both had heard from God and led the people. When God told them to do something they did it, realising success was only possible with God's help. They were conscious that they were in effect God's mouthpiece and it was God who was granting them victory in the battles they fought. In order to make progress, the people needed to be obedient to God. Joshua became a respected leader and did not encounter the same opposition and backsliding as Moses did.

The Book of Joshua begins on a high with a gentle exhortation and promise that as leader Joshua would be able to do what Moses was not permitted to do, and that was to take possession of the Promised Land (something the people gladly endorsed): *"This book of the law shall not depart out of thy mouth; but thou shalt meditate therein day and night, that thou mayest observe to do according to all that is written therein: for then thou shalt make thy way prosperous, and then thou shalt have good success. Have not I commanded thee? Be strong and of a good courage; be not afraid, neither be thou dismayed: for the Lord thy God is with thee whithersoever thou goest"* Joshua 1:8-9.

A lot of the Book of Joshua is taken up with a series of military campaigns that Joshua led (see Chapter 2, Figure 38). Joshua is often portrayed as a brilliant military strategist, which is probably true, but it was an ability given to him by God. Moreover, it was God who gave the victory, aided in every case, but the one in which Israel was defeated, by the people's obedience. This included God doing extraordinary miracles, which were needed given the heavy odds being faced. One remarkable encounter Joshua had, before the first battle was fought, was with an armed man who turned out to be an angel who, upon being asked whose side he was on, introduced himself as the commander of the Lord's army. Some commentators refer to the account recorded in Joshua 5:13-15 as an example of a Christophany, a pre-incarnate appearance of Christ, although we cannot fully prove this belief.

But before any battle could begin the Israelites needed to cross the River Jordan. They had already managed to take the land east of the Jordan that had been allocated to three of the tribes, although the fighting men of those tribes were still required to help their brethren to take the land west of the river that would then be divided up and allocated by lot according to tribe once it had been taken. To cross the Jordan required another miracle comparable to that of the parting of the Red Sea, 40 years earlier. Led by Levites carrying the Ark, the people followed and they crossed on dry land, erecting a cairn of stones as a memorial. They camped at Gilgal, where the men were circumcised. They also celebrated the Passover. This is when manna from heaven stopped. They could now live off the land.

The first battle fought was that to take the city of Jericho they were to possess west of the Jordan, a strategic stronghold in the land. This followed two spies spying out the land and being given shelter in the city by Rahab, who was a prostitute, but one who feared the Lord. "*Joshua fought the battle of Jericho … and the walls came tumbling down*" is a chorus this author remembers from his youth but the important point here is, just as in battles fought in the past and those yet to be fought, victory could only be won with God's help. It was God who brought down these nigh impregnable walls, so Israel could sack the city, putting to death all inside it, except Rahab and her family, as God had said.

In Chapters 8 to 12, there are several battles Joshua and his army fought and won, continuing with the "Southern campaign" in Chapters 8 to 10 and then the "Northern campaign" in Chapter 11 and culminating in a list of vanquished kings in Chapter 12, followed by a description of the land that had not been taken in Chapter 13. But first there was a setback. After Jericho, the next city in line to be taken was Ai, which given the earlier success should have been a straightforward proposition, except that it wasn't. There was sin in the camp, through a man named Achan, and until that had been dealt with no further progress could be made, but once sin had been dealt with, as indeed it must in any situation when God's help is sought, Ai was taken, in Chapter 8, followed by the renewal of the Covenant at Mount Ebal, in accordance with the instructions that Moses had given just before he died.

After renewing the Covenant, including being reminded of the blessings that came from obedience and the curses from disobedience to God, found at the end of Deuteronomy, the Israelites were ready to resume their journey of conquest, doing so with resounding success, with fear coming upon all those who were in their way and despite different kings making alliances to withstand the Israelite onslaught. This included one of those who might have been among those conquered, the Gibeonites (who were an Amorite tribe), making a treaty with Israel and thus securing protection, by means of a ruse. This brings us to perhaps a turning point in all the campaigns, when an alliance of five Amorite tribes sought to attacked Gibeon because they had allied themselves with the enemy. But the Israelites were completely victorious thanks to two miracles: the sending of hailstones on the Amorite army and then the extending of daylight for a whole day (records of which can be found in non-biblical sources). While there was still a lot of land left that needed to be taken over which, with God's help would happen in due course, the main focus for the rest of the Book of Joshua, was dividing up the land that was taken among the remaining tribes of Israel. The Book ends with Joshua's farewell speech on an upbeat note similar to how his leadership began, emphasising the need to be faithful to God:

"Now therefore fear the Lord, and serve him in sincerity and in truth: and put away the gods which your fathers served on the other side of the flood, and in Egypt; and serve ye the Lord. And if it seem evil unto you to serve the Lord, choose you this day whom ye will serve; whether the gods which your fathers served that were on the other side of the flood, or the gods of the Amorites, in whose land ye dwell: but as for me and my house, we will serve the Lord. And the people answered and said, God forbid that we should forsake the Lord, to serve other gods" Joshua 24:14-16.

At the end of the Book of Joshua we read of the burials of three significant persons who feature in our story. Besides that of Joshua, there was Eleazar the High Priest who had died toward the end, and also the bones of Joseph were laid to rest, according to his request which we read of at the end of Genesis.

Judges

Following the leadership of Moses and Joshua, and Israel occupying those parts of the land that had been allocated according to tribe, Israel came under the leadership of the Judges, that one commentator has described as being types of trouble shooters, leading Israel or parts of Israel in such times when they were being oppressed by some foreign power, usually as a result of their sin, and turning toward false gods and then crying to God for help. Concerning that period, we read *"In those days there was no king in Israel, but every man did that which was right in his own eyes"* Judges 17:6.

We begin Judges where Joshua left off, with the Israelites having renewed their Covenant with God and wanting to do right in His eyes. It also involved continuing to taking the land from its occupants or, failing that, making them their subjects. In Judges 1, we find Judah and Simeon going after some of the Canaanites and Perrizites and making subjects of king Adoni-Bezek along with 70 other kings. This pattern continued with other victories by other Tribes of Israel but after that the Israelites were unable to remove more of the inhabitants, although they were able to make subjects of some of them.

Tragically, Israel then began to stray from God and early in this period an angel came and warned them of their unfaithfulness and its consequences (Judges 2:1-5), such as those not of Israel who were in the land beginning to impose themselves and subject Israel to tyranny, which caused a positive response although not for long. This is where the Judges came in. What we then see is a cyclical pattern played out under successive judges. Israel turns from God – Israel attacked by one or other nation – Israel calls on God to deliver them – God answers and Israel is rescued when led by a judge – Israel becomes secure once again. This same cycle then repeats itself under another judge.

At the end of this Chapter, we will reflect on the parts played by the nations/tribes that turn out to be important "players" in our story, specifically the Philistines, Egypt and Syria, but at the beginning of Judges we are left in no doubt that this would be significant, as is the case with the inhabitants repeatedly mentioned in the Bible narrative and as indicated in Chapter 2, Figure 37. While Israel was largely successful in defeating the Amorites under Joshua, although the Gibeonites and the oath made with them would still play a part, other of the Caananite inhabitants, along with their kings, would be around for some time to come and as we will see in the rest of Judges, significantly impacted on the nation of Israel. A lot has been written about these tribes occupying Caanan as a result of historical and archaeological studies, independent of what can be found in the Bible, often regarding their way of life, practice of idolatry and how "advanced" they were as civilisations, but this is not the subject for this book, although readers are encouraged to check this out for themselves.

"Now these are the nations which the Lord left, to prove Israel by them, even as many of Israel as had not known all the wars of Canaan; Only that the generations of the children of Israel might know, to teach them war, at the least such as before knew nothing thereof; Namely, five lords of the Philistines, and all the Canaanites, and the Sidonians, and the Hivites that dwelt in mount Lebanon, from mount Baalhermon unto the entering in of Hamath. And they were to prove Israel by them, to know whether they would hearken unto the commandments of the Lord, which he commanded their fathers by the hand of Moses. And the children of Israel dwelt among the Canaanites, Hittites, and Amorites, and Perizzites, and Hivites, and Jebusites: And they took their daughters to be their wives, and gave their daughters to their sons, and served their gods. And the children of Israel did evil in the sight of the Lord, and forgat the Lord their God, and served Baalim and the groves. Therefore the anger of the Lord was hot against Israel, and he sold them into the hand of Chushanrishathaim king of Mesopotamia: and the children of Israel served Chushanrishathaim eight years" Judges 3:1-8. "Chushanrishathaim king of Mesopotamia" is widely associated with that of Syria (Aram).

What we will do for the remainder of this section on Judges is to list each judge that is named in the Book and state if they had dealings with any king or kingdom, whether inside or outside the land Israel occupied, along with who these were and what was the outcome.

Othniel (3:7-11): Here the oppressor was Cushan Rishathaim, king of Aram Naharaim, and this as a result of Israel serving Baal but then being rescued when they cried out to the Lord.

Ehud (3:12-30): Here the oppressor was Eglon king of Moab with the help of Ammonites and Amalekites, because Israel had done evil, and their rescuer this time was Ehud, a left-handed man.

Shamgar (3:31): All we know of this man was that he killed 600 Philistines with an ox goad.

Deborah (4:1-5:31): Jabin a king of Caanan was the oppressor and it was Sisera who led his army. Deborah, a prophetess, was Israel's judge at the time (the only woman who served as judge) and she called on the services of Barak to go fight Sisera's army. Barak's army prevailed but it was Jael, a woman, that delivered the final death blow by driving a tent peg through the temple of a sleeping Sisera.

Gideon (6:1-9:57): Here the Midianites were the oppressors and Gideon the reluctant rescuer, who with his whittled down army was able to secure victory against far superior forces, including killing Zebah and Zalmunna, kings of the Midianites. While much else could be said concerning Gideon, we note one of his son's, Abimelech, tried to become king, by first killing his 70 brothers. It was another woman that finally saved the day by dropping a millstone from a tower onto Abimelech's head.

Tola (10:1-2): No kings or nations mentioned.

Jair (10:3-5): No kings or nations mentioned.

Jephthah (10:6-12:7): Here we have yet another unlikely leader raised up to get Israel out of a dilemma of their own making as once again they served Baals. The oppressors this time were the Philistines and Ammonites. Jephthah was a societal misfit and had been rejected by his brothers because his mother was a prostitute, but he was also a warrior who had gathered around him a group of adventurers. He was called upon as the people's hope for deliverance and he prevailed in battle and thus was able to free the people. There are other interesting aspects to the Jephthah story, such as his unwise vow *"then it shall be, that whatsoever cometh forth of the doors of my house to meet me, when I return in peace from the children of Ammon, shall surely be the Lord's, and I will offer it up for a burnt offering"* Judges 11:31, and this turned out to be his daughter, but we find nothing else to do with kings.

Ibzan (12:8-10): No kings or nations mentioned.

Elon (12:11-12): No kings or nations mentioned.

Abdon (12:13-15): No kings or nations mentioned.

Samson (13:1-16:31): We come to our last named judge, famous for his long hair, a result of him taking the vow of the Nazarite. He was blessed with extraordinary strength as a result and used that strength to single hand-edly fight groups of Philistines and prevail. It appeared that they had the last word when through the guile of his mistress, Delilah, they cut his hair, captured him and gouged out his eyes. But the tables were once again turned at the end, after his hair grew. We read at the end: "*And Samson took hold of the two middle pillars upon which the house stood, and on which it was borne up, of the one with his right hand, and of the other with his left. And Samson said, Let me die with the Philistines. And he bowed himself with all his might; and the house fell upon the lords, and upon all the people that were therein. So the dead which he slew at his death were more than they which he slew in his life*" Judges 16:29-30. Samson was a carnal man, yet he was one the Lord powerfully used.

In the final chapters that follow these stories centred around judges (17-21), we find accounts of various harrowing episodes in the life of Israel, in-cluding idolatry, murder, rape and civil war, and two of these involved Levites: "Micah and the Levite" (17-18) and "a Levite and his concubine" (19-21). As none had to do with kings or foreign invaders, we will not dwell on them. The ending of the Book of Judges repeats what has been the case throughout the period covered by the Book of Judges: "*In those days there was no king in Israel: every man did that which was right in his own eyes*" Judges 21:25.

Yet always there is hope and accounts of positive happenings to read about. The Book of Ruth, which follows the Book of Judges, and in the He-brew Bible is part of Judges, is a case in hand. The fact Ruth who willingly accompanied her mother-in-law from Moab back to her home town in Isra-el, who along with her eventual husband, Boaz, is the hero of a book bearing her name. That she was a virtuous Moabitess, the great grandmother of King David and Jesus' ancestor, all illustrate her importance.

Three "significant" kingdoms

As we come to the end of this section devoted to kings before Israel (and Judah) had a king and before we look at what is given by far the most cover-age in the Bible, let us consider three "kingdoms" that have already cropped up and will do so again, significantly, as we consider the kings of Israel and Judah.

Philistia: Abimelech (a title like "Pharoah") has already cropped up in our accounts of Abraham and Isaac. The one thing we can be sure of is he/they was/were Philistine(s). Other, than that they did not appear to play much of a part in our story, until after Israel was settled in their land under the Judg-es. We do read though: "*And it came to pass, when Pharaoh had let the peo-*

ple go, that God led them not through the way of the land of the Philistines,
although that was near; for God said, Lest peradventure the people repent
when they see war, and they return to Egypt" Exodus 13:17, indicating they
were a threat, and also noting this was part of the land God has promised to
Abraham. As far as Philistia is concerned, there were five main cities: Gaza,
Ashdod, Askelon, Gath, and Ekron, each ruled by its own king. The threat
posed by the Philistines has already been seen during the time of the Judges
and would continue during the time of Israel's kings, notably under Saul
and David. From what we can make out, the Philistines had migrated to
the land they were to occupy from across the sea, e.g., Crete, for reasons
unknown. The land they occupied was a key gateway joining Africa, Europe
and Asia. During the period of Israel's kings, they either were assimilated
along with other non-Israel entities or taken into exile by the Assyrians and
the Babylonians, never again to achieve nationhood or be significant. While
"Palestine" is derived etymologically from "Philistine", today's Palestinians
are not Philistines.

Egypt: We have already discussed Egypt, as a significant power and advanced civilisation (which can be readily verified from external sources),
from the time God called Abraham in Genesis 10 until Moses led the Israelites out of Egypt in Exodus 14 and 15. Egypt does not feature again until
the period of Israel's kings, when they interacted with the rulers of Egypt
on several occasions. King Solomon married the daughter of an Egyptian
king who is thought to be Pharaoh Siamun (1 Kings 9:16). While King Rehoboam reigned, the Egyptian King Shishak invaded both Israel and Judah
and ransacked the Temple and Royal Palace (1 Kings 14:25-26). Hezekiah
called upon the king of Egypt for help when the Assyrian army besieged him
in Jerusalem (2 Kings 18:21). Judah's King Josiah was killed when he tried to
stop Pharaoh Neco from passing along the coast to help the Assyrians. Neco
also deposed King Jehoahaz and made Jehoiakim king over Judah instead (2
Chronicles 36:2-4). It was at that time Egypt ceased to be a sovereign power,
coming under Babylon, Persia, Greece and then Rome. Egypt has a symbolic significance in the Bible. Israel's redemption from Egypt is a picture of
Christian believers' deliverance from sin and death through faith in Jesus
Christ (Galatians 3:13; 4:5; Titus 2:14). While initially seen as a place of
refuge in famine or threat, Egypt became a place of oppression and slavery.

Syria: This was where Rebecca (Isaac's wife) came from and where Jacob fled to when fleeing from his brother, Esau. Other than the Judges 3:8-
10 reference, already discussed, we do not read about Syria (or Aram) until
the time of Israel's kings, where more often than not they proved to be a
threat. During the times of the kings, the Arameans often fought against
Israel, especially in David's reign (2 Samuel 8:3-10; 10:6-8; 1 Chronicles 18:3-

4). Ben-Hadad, one of the more powerful rulers of Aram, fought against the northern kingdom of Israel, but he failed in his attack because the Lord promised to give the vast Aramean army into King Ahab's hands (1 Kings 20:12-13). Furthermore, it was at the hand of the Arameans that the wicked Ahab met his ruin, as the prophet Micaiah had prophesied (1 Kings 22:28, 37-38). Like Egypt, Syria relinquished its sovereign status to empires that would effectively swallow it up, in this case it was Assyria that would later succumb to the Babylonians. Syria would play a significant part in the early church, in cities such as Antioch and Damascus. Today, Syria, along with Egypt, occupy much of the land they occupied in Bible times, having regained their sovereignty. Both play a significant role in the affairs of modern Israel, particularly concerning some of its struggles. In much of the period since Israel became a sovereign state once again, they have been antagonists. It will be interesting to watch how things work out from now on, including fulfilment of Bible prophecy.

The Nephilim

According to Wikipedia: "*The Nephilim are mysterious beings or people in the Hebrew Bible who are described as being large and strong. The Hebrew word Nephilim is sometimes translated as "giants", and sometimes taken to mean "the fallen ones". Their origins are disputed. Some, including the author of the Book of Enoch, view them as offspring of fallen angels and humans. Others view them as offspring of the descendants of Seth and Cain.*"

Because the Nephilim is such a contentious subject among "Bible believing" Christians (and in the author's experience one that is hardly ever taught "in church", even when the Bible is given due prominence), it is one, when it is raised, that could put readers off, especially if what they are looking for is a straightforward account of a subject such as the one here pertaining to the kings of the Bible and, besides, mention of the Nephilim would seem to bear little relevance to such subjects. It might therefore seem better to ignore it altogether, but for the argument that a study of the Nephilim is both relevant to that concerning the kings, both those that were around before Israel had its first king and afterward, and even extending to end-time prophecy where kings continue to play an important part.

We begin our justification of including this subject by referring to two scriptures that, because of their importance, are cited elsewhere in this book. Firstly: "*And I will put enmity between thee and the woman, and between thy seed and her seed; it shall bruise thy head, and thou shalt bruise his heel*" Genesis 3:15. This is relevant because the seed war that began in the Garden of Eden continues until the time Satan is finally defeated. Secondly: "*And it came to pass, when men began to multiply on the face of the earth, and daughters were born unto them, That the sons of God saw the daughters of men that they were fair; and they took them wives of all which they chose. And the Lord said, My spirit shall not always strive with man, for that he also is flesh: yet his days shall be an hundred and twenty years. There were giants in the earth in those days; and also after that, when the sons of God came in unto the daughters of men, and they bare children to them, the same became mighty men which were of old, men of renown"* Genesis 6:1-4. This is relevant because it is the only place in the Bible where the Nephilim (as opposed to their descendants) are explicitly mentioned and, unlike those who explain away the obvious, i.e., of angels mating with humans, it is the author's contention that this is indeed what happened and it is likely this went back to soon after "The Fall" and certainly after Enoch's time.

While not part of the Bible canon, the Book of Enoch is informative when it comes to the back story behind the Genesis 6:1-4 account, for example regarding the "fallen angels", what they did and what their status is. Jude both alludes to and quotes verbatim from the Book of Enoch, which remarkably looks far into the future, beyond our own time: *"And the angels which kept not their first estate, but left their own habitation, he hath reserved in everlasting chains under darkness unto the judgment of the great day ... And Enoch also, the seventh from Adam, prophesied of these, saying, Behold, the Lord cometh with ten thousands of his saints, To execute judgment upon all, and to convince all that are ungodly among them of all their ungodly deeds which they have ungodly committed, and of all their hard speeches which ungodly sinners have spoken against him"* Jude 1:6, 14-15.

Moreover, Peter also referred to fallen angels: *"For if God spared not the angels that sinned, but cast them down to hell, and delivered them into chains of darkness, to be reserved unto judgment; And spared not the old world, but saved Noah the eighth person, a preacher of righteousness, bringing in the flood upon the world of the ungodly"* 2 Peter 2:4-5. It is evident that the New Testament writers, along with the Jews at that time, had knowledge of the Book of Enoch and other pertinent texts. Since we have argued that context is very important, theirs is an example we do well to follow. As to what our priorities ought to be in the light of all this, Peter is clear: *"Looking for and hasting unto the coming of the day of God, wherein the heavens being on fire shall be dissolved, and the elements shall melt with fervent heat? Nevertheless we, according to his promise, look for new heavens and a new earth, wherein dwelleth righteousness"* 2 Peter 3:12-13.

It would be easy to add the subject of "the Nephilim" to that box of "stuff" from the Bible that we know is there but, since we don't understand well enough what it means etc., we will ignore thereafter, especially if taking the view that any Nephilim that may have been around were wiped out in the Flood. Maybe so, but their descendants (and how we cannot say) the "*Anakim*" and the "*Rephaim*", both referred to several times in the Bible and both exhibiting Nephilim traits, e.g., giant stature, were not only around but featured prominently after the Flood. We refer to what we wrote earlier in this chapter concerning, for example, Nimrod (Genesis 6), the giants in the land that were seen by the 12 spies (Numbers 13) and Og, the Amorite king of Bashan (Numbers 21), one of possibly many Nephilim related kings that the Israelites encountered as they sought to conquer the Promised Land.

While Israel proved successful in that undertaking, as they partnered with God in wiping out these Nephilim successors, they did not do so entirely. Neither is there evidence that this happened when the Bible narrative moved on to considering the kings of Israel and after that. We read, for example: "*And at that time came Joshua, and cut off the Anakims from the mountains, from Hebron, from Debir, from Anab, and from all the mountains of Judah, and from all the mountains of Israel: Joshua destroyed them utterly with their cities. There was none of the Anakims left in the land of the children of Israel: only in Gaza, in Gath, and in Ashdod, there remained*" Joshua 11:21-22. We read in King David's time of confrontations with the Anakim, but whether they were wiped out then we cannot say for sure.

We cannot cite much by way of hard evidence of Nephilim infiltration within the Bible narrative from the Book of Samuel onward, other than the story of Goliath and at best scant references elsewhere in the Bible account. But a lot is spoken concerning angelic beings, often as being entirely different in appearance to humans, but also looking just like humans, including in End Times prophecy. Then there are demons. To cover this subject would require another book and is beyond the scope of this one. Going back to the "Seed War" that we first read about in Genesis 3:15, it is worth pausing for thought concerning Jesus, who is referred to when God spoke about Eve's seed defeating Satan's in that war.

We should also bring Mount Hermon into our thoughts. It is believed to be the place where the fallen angels descended to Earth before the Flood, as described in the book of Enoch. This event led to the corruption of humankind and eventual judgment by God. The mountain represents the intersection of the heavenly and earthly realms, signifying both divine revelation and human transgression. Some scholars believe Mount Hermon was the site of Jesus' transfiguration, a supernatural event in which Jesus appeared in His true glory as the Son of God, revealing His identity as Israel's Messiah and in fulfilling the Law and the Prophets (Matthew 17:1-8; see also 2 Peter 1:16-18). At the transfiguration, His disciples: Peter, James, and John, were eyewitnesses to their beloved leader's pre-existent glory.

Going back to our earlier "Nephilim" point and concerning the relevance of this subject as we study kings of the Bible, the author has already argued, e.g., in Chapter 47, that, regarding our current crop of (often "democratically elected" and seemingly inept) kings and their lieutenants, many/most of them are controlled by forces/entities that are hidden, often in plain sight, from the great majority of the human population and, from among which, the Antichrist is yet to emerge. The question is begged: "who are these hidden forces/entities"? The answer, may be that these are Nephilim related, noting the significance often attached to blood lines, secret societies, royal families and the like, and, as we dig deeper, and see the connecting up of Bible prophecy and what previously appeared as a set of random dots, this could be the only plausible explanation to what is happening, and help join the dots!

To argue the case (better than this author could), let us introduce readers to the seminal, thoroughly researched, very much "in-depth" and credible books by two authors that are worth checking out. Each has a title that is provocative in challenging commonly held beliefs, and well worth reading, even if one were to want to question much of the content: "**The Roots of the Federal Reserve: Tracing the Nephilim from Noah to the US Dollar**" by Laura Sanger and "**The Genesis 6 Conspiracy: How Secret Societies and the Descendants of Giants Plan to Enslave Mankind**" and "**The Genesis 6 Conspiracy Part II: How Understanding Prehistory And Giants Helps Define End-Time Prophecy**" by Gary Wayne.

Besides exploring what the Bible and extra biblical texts have to say on the subject, the authors argue for a significant "Nephilim" presence and influence in today's world, typically among those who appear to and do shape current events. How the Nephilim translates to any number of identifiable bad actors on the world stage is something both authors try to explain. We make these references not to critique, endorse or refute what either author has to say on the subject of the Nephilim or the part they play in today's world but rather to refer to them as having thoroughly studied the subject and who believe Nephilim infiltration is huge and significant, even if unrecognised by most Christians. It is the position this author takes, while recognising his study of the Nephilim is a work in progress. If readers want to know more than this author is able to offer in this short account of something he sees as highly relevant, these resources are worth checking out. But do so with an open mind and a health warning. Both make points that will take us out of our comfort zones and challenge our pre-conceptions.

Much more could be said, but we need to wind down our discussion on the Nephilim and move on to consider more kings of the Bible. But we before we do, it is worth re-iterating an underlying theme of the Bible: "*For we wrestle not against flesh and blood, but against principalities, against powers, against the rulers of the darkness of this world, against spiritual wickedness in high places"* Ephesians 6:12. We are warned: *"be sober, be vigilant; because your adversary the devil, as a roaring lion, walketh about, seeking whom he may devour"* 1 Peter 5:8, *"that old serpent, called the Devil, and Satan, which deceiveth the whole world"* Revelation 12:9, *"Satan himself is transformed into an angel of light"* 2 Corinthians 11:14, *"lest Satan should get an advantage of us: for we are not ignorant of his devices"* 2 Corinthians 2:11. When it comes to the angelic, as opposed to human and animal orders of creation, there is considerable variety to be found, including factions aligning with God and those with Satan. While some readers will still want to dismiss associating the Nephilim of Noah's time with the nefarious happenings and sinister actors in today's world, we should realise we are up against a formidable foe.

All this should be borne in mind when considering kings: past, present and future. Let us remember what Jesus had to say about the *"Days of Noah"* that we now live in (the very days when the Nephilim and the seed war was such an important factor): *"But as the days of Noah were, so shall also the coming of the Son of man be. For as in the days that were before the flood they were eating and drinking, marrying and giving in marriage, until the day that Noe entered into the ark"* Matthew 24:37-38. The fact Jesus likened our times to the *"Days of Noah"* is highly significant. But we take comfort in the thought of *"the coming of the Son of man"* and we ought to live in the light of that coming.

Chapter 63: Kings of Israel – The United Kingdom (Saul, David, Solomon)

We ended our previous chapter by considering Israel under the Judges and the interactions they had (mostly contentious) with various kings and nations, some found in the earlier books of the Bible and some that will crop up again. But we still have one more judge to consider – Samuel (three if we were to include his two sons) and along with him the ongoing conflicts with kings and kingdoms, in particular the Philistines. The story of Hannah (Samuel's mother) and her prayer to God for a son, along with her vow to dedicate any son she had as an answer to her prayer to the service of God. Then there was Samuel hearing the voice of God and sharing with Eli, the High Priest, who was also Samuel's mentor, what God told him, especially regarding judgement to come. We read: *"And Samuel grew, and the Lord was with him, and did let none of his words fall to the ground. And all Israel from Dan even to Beersheba knew that Samuel was established to be a prophet of the Lord"* 1 Samuel 3:19-20.

We considered Eli in Chapter 27. He is a tragic figure, given his evident qualities and what he could have done. His ending follows Israel fighting the Philistines and being defeated. While the news from the battle front was devastating, it was even more so insofar as Eli's two sons were killed and, worse still (for Eli), the Ark of the Covenant was taken: *"And it came to pass, when he made mention of the ark of God, that he fell from off the seat backward by the side of the gate, and his neck brake, and he died: for he was an old man, and heavy. And he had judged Israel forty years"* 1 Samuel 4:18.

The story moves on. Samuel's influence grows and he becomes Israel's last judge and one who is widely recognised as a prophet who hears from God, and all that time the Philistines continue to look for ways to oppress and subjugate Israel, but it was also a spur for the Israelites to turn to God, hoping for His deliverance in overcoming their enemies, after Samuel gave a typical prophet's message: *"And Samuel spake unto all the house of Israel, saying, If ye do return unto the Lord with all your hearts, then put away the strange gods and Ashtaroth from among you, and prepare your hearts unto the Lord, and serve him only: and he will deliver you out of the hand of the Philistines. Then the children of Israel did put away Baalim and Ashtaroth, and served the Lord only. And Samuel said, Gather all Israel to Mizpeh, and I will pray for you unto the Lord. And they gathered together to Mizpeh, and drew water, and poured it out before the Lord, and fasted on that day, and said there, We have sinned against the Lord. And Samuel judged the children of Israel in Mizpeh"* 1 Samuel 7:3-6.

While Israel was able to beat off their Philistine enemies under Samuel, it soon became evident the people were not fully dedicated to God. They told Samuel they needed a king to rule over them and to fight their battles. They wanted to be like the other nations, all of which had kings. One reason they gave, and it seemed a laudable one, was that the two sons of the now old Samuel, whom he had appointed as judges, were no good (which from the Bible account can be borne out). But as far as God was concerned, their request was more to do with Israel rejecting Him. Despite Samuel warning the Israelites that having a king would come at a high price, they still insisted, and God acquiesced to their request – 1000 years after the seed for the nation of Israel had been sown under Abraham.

The issue of Israel wanting and having a king was foreseen by God long before the time of Samuel, for part of Moses parting words to the Israelites, just before he died, and before their going to possess the land God had promised was what the people had to do when choosing a king, what qualities were needed and how kings should honour God: "*When thou art come unto the land which the Lord thy God giveth thee, and shalt possess it, and shalt dwell therein, and shalt say, I will set a king over me, like as all the nations that are about me; Thou shalt in any wise set him king over thee, whom the Lord thy God shall choose: one from among thy brethren shalt thou set king over thee: thou mayest not set a stranger over thee, which is not thy brother. But he shall not multiply horses to himself, nor cause the people to return to Egypt, to the end that he should multiply horses: forasmuch as the Lord hath said unto you, Ye shall henceforth return no more that way. Neither shall he multiply wives to himself, that his heart turn not away: neither shall he greatly multiply to himself silver and gold. And it shall be, when he sitteth upon the throne of his kingdom, that he shall write him a copy of this law in a book out of that which is before the priests the Levites: And it shall be with him, and he shall read therein all the days of his life: that he may learn to fear the Lord his God, to keep all the words of this law and these statutes, to do them: That his heart be not lifted up above his brethren, and that he turn not aside from the commandment, to the right hand, or to the left: to the end that he may prolong his days in his kingdom, he, and his children, in the midst of Israel*" Deuteronomy 17:14-20.

In the remainder of this chapter we will consider what happened next as Israel transitioned from supposedly being a theocracy under YHWH to a kingdom ruled by kings, until the one kingdom (Israel) would after be split into two kingdoms (Israel and Judah). There are three kings to consider: Saul, David and Solomon, all contrasting characters that God undertook to bless, but as we will see the blessing of God also required the kings to be obedient to Him. We will consider each king in turn:

Saul

How often seemingly unrelated events come together in the Bible! Samuel was tasked with appointing and anointing the next king without knowing who that was to be. Through this sequence of events it became apparent that it was to be Saul who we read was *"a choice young man, and a goodly: and there was not among the children of Israel a goodlier person than he: from his shoulders and upward he was higher than any of the people"* I Samuel 9:2. While he looked the part, and would have been the sort of person people would typically have seen as being king material, the question was whether he was what God was looking for – someone who was after His own heart. We would soon find out.

There was no question God wanted Saul to succeed and we see evidence that he had been anointed by God for the task from the outset. There were occasions when the Spirit came on him in great power. Saul was successful in many of his early assignments and this began soon after he came to power and he needed to come to the aid of a section of his people that had been cruelly threatened by an enemy. He won a number of battles against Israel's enemies, and it was all with God's help, including against Israel's old foe – the Philistines. However, there were two big tests, both of which he failed.

The first was when gathering his army to fight the Philistines and he was told to wait for Samuel to arrive. Getting impatient as some of his army began to dessert, he presumptuously offered sacrifices and, soon after when Samuel did arrive, he was duly rebuked. The second and sterner test was when he fought the Amalekites and won. God's instruction was to kill every person and every animal since that was His judgement but instead Saul spared the king and the best of the animals. It was at that point God rejected Saul from being king and upon telling Saul what God's verdict was, Samuel was instructed to seek for a replacement as king. Samuel was never to meet with Saul again, except after his death his spirit was called up when Saul had turned to the Witch of Endor in order to get guidance.

Saul was to hang on to power for many years after, but it was a tragic ending of a kingly career that began with so much promise and potential. We would see Saul often go off into fits of rage and jealousy. One example was the way he dealt with David who had been anointed to replace Saul, who initially he welcomed as his harpist to play soothing music and then later as being the one who had killed Goliath, who he soon after appointed to be in charge of a section of his army and to whom he gave his daughter in marriage, but later Saul sought to kill him, all because of his jealousy.

One of the terrible things Saul did was to order the killing of the High Priest at the time and all of his family, who had assisted David while he was on the run. Saul's story is a tragic one when compared with how he had begun and what could have been. His downward slide followed his rejection by God and his foolish response after having been rejected, with no sign of repentance. He eventually was killed, along with his sons, including Jonathan, while fighting one of Israel's battles against the Philistines. He was seriously wounded and decided to end it all by falling upon his sword. This let in the king that God, several years earlier, through Samuel, had anointed to serve in his place – David.

Chronicles provides a sombre ending to Saul's story: "*So Saul died for his transgression which he committed against the Lord, even against the word of the Lord, which he kept not, and also for asking counsel of one that had a familiar spirit, to enquire of it; And enquired not of the Lord: therefore he slew him, and turned the kingdom unto David the son of Jesse*" 1 Chronicles 10:13-14.

David

This was Samuel's second time of having been told to anoint a king of Israel. But this time it was to be the one God wanted and not the one who fitted the bill as being man's choice, for God was looking for a man after His own heart. All Samuel knew was that he was to go to the house of Jesse and anoint one of his sons to be king. When he met Eliab, the oldest, Samuel thought he had found his man, but it was not to be. "*But the Lord said unto Samuel, Look not on his countenance, or on the height of his stature; because I have refused him: for the Lord seeth not as man seeth; for man looketh on the outward appearance, but the Lord looketh on the heart*" 1 Samuel 16:7. And that was the case with each of the seven sons of Jesse, who were paraded before him in age order.

When Samuel enquired of Jesse if that was all the sons, he was told there was one more who happened to be out in the fields looking after the sheep. Jesse demanded he be brought in right away and, when Samuel saw him, the Lord told him that this was His choice. Samuel duly anointed David and after that appeared to play little further part in the story of David. It is gratifying to know God sees beyond what humans see, beyond the outward appearance and into the heart. There was a quality in David that even his own family did not see and one that made him stand out. While the story of David that follows includes the good, bad and ugly, we soon find out something about David that makes him special far beyond most of his peers. He not only goes on to be Israel's greatest king but establishes a dynasty culminating in the coming of Jesus, Israel's Messiah and the Saviour of the world.

There is a considerable amount of Bible narrative that is David related and given he was the most significant of all the kings of Israel and Judah, we may wish to devote a lot more space to David than to any of the others, but we must refrain from over doing it. It was later written concerning him: *"David did that which was right in the eyes of the Lord, and turned not aside from anything that he commanded him all the days of his life, save only in the matter of Uriah the Hittite"* 1 Kings 15:5.

Picking up on the theme of Israel possessing the land God had promised and subjugating those who were opposed to Israel, David continued what Moses and Joshua began and the kingdom of Israel was at its greatest and most secure under his kingship, because God was with him and ensured he had victory in the battles he fought to drive out Israel's enemies or at least was able to make those living in his kingdom vassals. As for surrounding kingdoms, many sought peace with Israel and unlike under future kings realised opposing Israel came at too great a cost. The establishment of the kingdom in such a manner was a formidable legacy to pass on, and one never again to be matched. Nevertheless, whilst Israel was greatest, territory wise, under David, it did not possess all the land God promised.

What we will do next is to view David's life, and some of the notable events in that time, through the lens of those persons with whom he had the most interaction:

David and Samuel: Samuel was by then very old when he discharged his last major duty – anointing David to be king. While there were dealings with David after this, these were minor.

David and Goliath: If we needed any evidence that David was a man after God's own heart, we need look no further than when the Philistine army was facing Israel's army and Goliath, the Philistine champion, challenged anyone from the Israel side to fight him in single-handed combat. No-one came forward to accept the challenge, out of fear – all except for the boy David, who took this to be an affront to God. David won his fight, and it is what widely marked him out as being someone special.

David and Saul: As we discussed earlier, one of the preoccupations of Saul in the latter part of his reign was to seek out David while he was on the run. Twice David had the opportunity to kill Saul but he refused to do so because as far as he was concerned Saul was the Lord's anointed, right up to his death.

David and Jonathan: Jonathan (Saul's son) and David were kindred spirits. They were both brave warriors, intent on fighting on behalf of the armies of Israel, something Jonathan did with honour and success. In the short time David was around Saul, he and Jonathan became firm friends, although one necessary duty for Jonathan was watching David's back and giving timely warnings, as Saul's hatred and wanting to kill him became evident. All too soon it became necessary for David to flee for his life and after some further exchanges we have no further record of the two ever meeting again.

David and Joab: Joab was David's army commander who could be depended on to carry out his orders, and was looked up to by the army he led, although he could be cruel and sometimes exceeded what was required of him, including by murder. After David's death, Joab was put to death by Solomon at David's request for the bad things he had done. Nevertheless, he was a mighty and fearless warrior.

David and his mighty men: David spent several years as an outlaw, on the run from Saul, and many came to join him. We read: "*and every one that was in distress, and every one that was in debt, and every one that was discontented, gathered themselves unto him; and he became a captain over them: and there were with him about four hundred men*" 1 Samuel 22:2. This included a group referred to as his mighty men (1 Chronicles 11), one of which was Uriah the Hittite, who David later had murdered. He and his band had many adventures during that time before David claimed the Throne.

David and his wives: From what we can make out, David had eight wives: Michal, Abigail, Ahinoam, Maakah, Haggith, Abital, Eglah and Bathsheba, and ten concubines. Besides Bathsheba, with whom he had an extra marital affair, who we know about from accounts of David's sins of adultery and murder and later exposure, the wives we know more about are Michal and Abigail. Michal was Saul's daughter who was given to David in marriage by her father, Saul. That relationship soured when Michal later criticised David after he had danced before the Lord. We first read of Abigail while David was foraging with his outlaw band and asked help from Nabal, pointing out that he had been protecting him. We read how he refused and treated David's men roughly, incurring David's anger, leading to his resolve to seek revenge. But for Abigail's wise and timely intervention, there could have been a bloody retribution. Soon after this episode, Nabal died and David then married his widow. We know little of David's other wives or concubines. As an example of how married life should be, David was not.

David and his sons: With so many wives we should not be surprised at the number of children he had, some of whom, besides Solomon his chosen heir, were to play significant parts in David's story. Some of these stories were far from salubrious. Ammon raped his step sister and was murdered by her brother, Absolom, in revenge. Later, Absolom tried unsuccessfully to steal the throne from David and Adonojah tried to do the same from Solomon and also failed. Both ended up having violent deaths. When it came to parenting skills, David was far from being the perfect example of a good father.

David and the prophets: Nathan and Gad were the two main prophets in

David's time, but to David's credit he listened to them even if it was words of rebuke. We discuss both in "**Prophets of the Bible**".

David and the priests: Abiathar and Zadok were the two main priests in David's time and David allowed them full freedom to carry out their priestly duties and supported them in every way. Both were loyal to David. We discuss Abiathar in Chapter 28 and Zadok in Chapter 29.

David and his friends: Ittai was a foreigner and a fighter who led part of David's army. In his hour of need, when having to flee from Absolam, David was grateful for Ittai's support, even though he told Ittai not to get involved for he had no stake in the outcome. Hushai alone was called the "king's friend" and was loyal to David throughout his life. He put his life on the line by going over to Absalom in his rebellion, pretending to switch allegiance, and in giving faulty counsel saved the day for David.

David and his enemies: Shimei was among those, at the time when David was at his most vulnerable, who cursed David when he was fleeing from Absalom. Sheba led further rebellion after David won victory over Absalom. Ahithophel was David's trusted counsellor who switched sides to Absalom in the civil war and used his knowledge to advise Absalom how to proceed. Shimei, Sheba, and Ahithophel were later to receive their comeuppance and all of them died violent deaths.

David and God: Of all the relationships David had, the most important one was with God. Other than the matter of murdering Uriah following David's adulterous affair with Bathsheba, Uriah's wife, there were arguably other examples of David's sinful dealings, such as calling for a census out of pride. Yet he remained, throughout his life, a man after God's own heart. Two examples of this are concerning the returning of the Ark to Jerusalem and his part in organising the building of the Temple, carried out under Solomon, discussed in Chapter 14. Most important, were the Psalms he wrote (it has been argued he wrote half of them), showing his deep knowledge of God, blessing many down the ages.

As David approaches his end, just prior to handing over the kingship to Solomon, he prays one remarkable last prayer that encapsulated much of what had been on his heart ever since he was a boy and what made him the king future kings would be compared to: "*Wherefore David blessed the Lord before all the congregation: and David said, Blessed be thou, Lord God of Israel our father, for ever and ever. Thine, O Lord, is the greatness, and the power, and the glory, and the victory, and the majesty: for all that is in the heaven and in the earth is thine; thine is the kingdom, O Lord, and thou art exalted as head above all. Both riches and honour come of thee, and thou reignest over all; and in thine hand is power and might; and in thine hand it is to make great, and to give strength unto all. Now therefore, our God, we thank thee, and praise thy glorious name. But who am I, and what is my people, that we should be able to offer so willingly after this sort? for all things come of thee, and of thine own have we given thee. For we are strangers before thee, and sojourners, as were all our fathers: our days on the earth are as a shadow, and there is none abiding. O Lord our God, all this store that we have prepared to build thee an house for thine holy name cometh of thine hand, and is all thine own. I know also, my God, that thou triest the heart, and hast pleasure in uprightness. As for me, in the uprightness of mine heart I have willingly offered all these things: and now have I seen with joy thy people, which are present here, to offer willingly unto thee. O Lord God of Abraham, Isaac, and of Israel, our fathers, keep this for ever in the imagination of the thoughts of the heart of thy people, and prepare their heart unto thee: And give unto Solomon my son a perfect heart, to keep thy commandments, thy testimonies, and thy statutes, and to do all these things* …" 1 Chronicles 29:10-19.

Of all the outstanding characters of the Bible, David is there at the top. As far as the biblical account goes, David was the best of all the kings of Israel and Judah for: *"David did that which was right in the eyes of the Lord, and turned not aside from any thing that he commanded him all the days of his life, save only in the matter of Uriah the Hittite"* 1 Kings 15:5. Future kings and how they performed would often be compared to David. In studying the Bible critically, we might think of things David did which were not right: the matter of calling for a census out of pride, his proneness to violence, not dealing with Joab justly after he murdered someone, his attitude toward women, and his indulgent attitude toward his sons are examples that spring to mind. But he was courageous, confrontational, competent and committed ahead of any king we might compare him with and, importantly, he had an extraordinary yearning for God and a desire for Him to be glorified, an example we do well to follow.

David is referred to in many places in the Bible, following his death, including 54 times in the New Testament. In Matthew's Gospel, Jesus is referred to 11 times as the *"son of David"*. The fact of the matter is God had made a covenant (discussed elsewhere), that there will always be someone from David's line on the Throne. That person is Jesus. In the Book of Revelation, we read in three places of Jesus associating Himself with David: *"he that hath the key of David"* (3:7), *"the Lion of the tribe of Judah, the Root of David"* (5:5) and *"the root and the offspring of David"* (22:16).

In the Book of Ezekiel we find references that look forward to a yet to happen future: *"David; he shall feed them"* (34:23), *"my servant David a prince among them"* (34:24) and *"David my servant shall be king over them*" (37:24). This is also the case concerning the prophecies of Jeremiah. Looking beyond our present time to the aftermath of the time of Jacob's trouble, we read: "*Alas! for that day is great, so that none is like it: it is even the time of Jacob's trouble, but he shall be saved out of it ... But they shall serve the Lord their God, and David their king, whom I will raise up unto them*" Jeremiah 30:7, 9. Looking forward to a time of Millennial peace and concerning the Lord's Eternal Covenant with David (and the part played by the Levites), we read: "*Behold, the days come, saith the Lord, that I will perform that good thing which I have promised unto the house of Israel and to the house of Judah. In those days, and at that time, will I cause the Branch of righteousness to grow up unto David; and he shall execute judgment and righteousness in the land. In those days shall Judah be saved, and Jerusalem shall dwell safely: and this is the name wherewith she shall be called, The Lord our righteousness. For thus saith the Lord; David shall never want a man to sit upon the throne of the house of Israel; Neither shall the priests the Levites want a man before me to offer burnt offerings, and to kindle meat offerings, and to do sacrifice continually. And the word of the Lord came unto Jeremiah, saying, Thus saith the Lord; If ye can break my covenant of the day, and my covenant of the night, and that there should not be day and night in their season; Then may also my covenant be broken with David my servant, that he should not have a son to reign upon his throne; and with the Levites the priests, my ministers. As the host of heaven cannot be numbered, neither the sand of the sea measured: so will I multiply the seed of David my servant, and the Levites that minister unto me*" Jeremiah 33:14-22.

Solomon

Besides being the king that succeeded David, who was David's choice (and also God's choice) to follow him, ahead of David's older sons, Solomon is credited with writing three books, discussed in the author's book: "Song of Songs, Proverbs and Ecclesiastes", with the central themes: Song of Songs – "*Love as Strong as Death*"; Proverbs – "*The Way of Wisdom*" and Ecclesiastes – "*Life under the Sun*". He also wrote some of the Psalms, e.g., 72 and 127. Also, he was seen as an authority on the natural world and could have written on this subject too. We are told Solomon wrote 3000 proverbs and composed 1005 songs. He was regarded by many, far and wide, as a man of extraordinary wisdom who was much sought after but, when we look at him in his older years, this was not matched by his conduct. All of this makes Solomon a significant person besides that of being a significant king.

But Solomon's reign was one that might never have happened if the coup instigated by his brother, Adonojah, to take the crown, while David was nearing his end, had succeeded. He was able to gather around him a formidable array of support, including Joab and Abiathar. But as soon as Nathan got wind to what was being planned, he was able to instigate a counter coup, with the assistance of the dying David and Bathsheba (Solomon's mother). Nathan, along with Zadok the priest, was able to anoint Solomon as king while Adonojah was prematurely celebrating his success along with those he expected would support him. On receiving this news, that support quickly dissipated. After that, Solomon was able quash any rebellion, including killing Joab, Adonojah and Shimei, as well as deposing Abiathar from exercising the office as High Priest. He could then be considered as sitting secure upon his throne.

His reign began well – very well. Early on God appeared to Solomon and asked him what he wanted from Him. While Solomon might have asked for riches and honour, instead he asked for wisdom in order to govern the people in the right way. Pleased with that response, God gave him both. He soon set about the most important project of them all – the construction of the Temple, based on the blueprints David had drawn up, and involving an enormous workforce, for example quarrying and shaping the stone needed for the Temple. Some of this work was undertaken through forced labour, by non Israelites. Mention is made of Hiram, king of Tyre. He was favourably disposed toward Solomon and supplied him with all the timber he needed. The project was completed and the Temple was magnificent. A fuller account of what was involved, including Solomon's amazing prayer when the Temple was dedicated, is given in Chapter 14, including God's response to that prayer and His promise to do all that Solomon had asked for. He would bless the people provided they kept His Covenant.

The picture painted, especially in Solomon's early years, was that of a nation that enjoyed prosperity, peace and contentment. Solomon continued to undertake numerous building projects and accumulate great wealth, including foreign trading missions assisted by a fleet of ships. He was able to undertake projects close to his heart, becoming, for example, an authority on the natural world. He continued to govern wisely and his wisdom was on show when he decided on a dispute between two women, after there had been a tragic accident when one woman laid on her baby, who died, and then swapped babies claiming the live baby was hers. Then there was what he told and showed the Queen of Sheba, who visited him. She was blown away by both Solomon's wisdom and the splendour of his kingdom.

The seeds of his demise were sown as he began to accumulated foreign wives, who often brought with them foreign gods, including those of Baal and Molech, and who were free to practise their religions, unchecked. This began early on in his reign when he married Pharoah's daughter, which was a means of strengthening alliances, as has happened in history many times after that and continued significantly under the kings that followed Solomon, starting with his son, Rehoboam. We also see the seeds of rebellion on a number of fronts including those linked with Israel's traditional enemies. Following Solomon's death, we find one that was initiated by Jeroboam, who was someone that was at first honoured by Solomon. Later, Jeroboam fell out of favour and was forced to live in exile. When he returned to the land, he successfully led a rebellion against Rehoboam, Solomon's successor as king.

The writers of both Kings and Chronicles detail the splendour of Solomon's kingdom even up to the end but only in Kings is it made clear what had gone wrong at the end after such a promising start, and where it would lead: "*And Solomon did evil in the sight of the Lord, and went not fully after the Lord, as did David his father. Then did Solomon build an high place for Chemosh, the abomination of Moab, in the hill that is before Jerusalem, and for Molech, the abomination of the children of Ammon. And likewise did he for all his strange wives, which burnt incense and sacrificed unto their gods. And the Lord was angry with Solomon, because his heart was turned from the Lord God of Israel, which had appeared unto him twice, And had commanded him concerning this thing, that he should not go after other gods: but he kept not that which the Lord commanded*" 1 Kings 11:6-10

As for where it would lead, we need to turn to the next two chapters, when turning away from God to gods becomes a regular recurring theme. While there would be high points in the kings that were to follow Solomon, the overall trajectory was downward. Idolatry and following false gods may not appear to be an issue in today's world compared with, for example atheism or religious indifference, and when idols are not the ones we, typically, can see – but IT IS and, if Solomon shows us anything, it is something anyone of us could succumb to, even subtly. If there is a challenge, it is to allow our hearts to be examined as to whether or not we are wholehearted when it comes to the worship of the true God. While there is much that can be commended in the life of Solomon, he is one of several examples, of kings that began well and full of promise and yet ended badly, and one we do well to avoid.

It is well to remember that we can persuade others we are dedicated God followers, but God looks on the heart. Let us end with a prayer of David, who understood more than any the importance of having the right heart: "*Search me, O God, and know my heart: try me, and know my thoughts: And see if there be any wicked way in me, and lead me in the way everlasting*" Psalm 139:23-24, and a hymn:

1. Search me, O God, and know my heart today;
Try me, O Savior, know my thoughts, I pray.
See if there be some wicked way in me;
Cleanse me from ev'ry sin and set me free.

2. I praise thee, Lord, for cleansing me from sin;
Fulfill thy Word, and make me pure within.
Fill me with fire where once I burned with shame;
Grant my desire to magnify thy name.

3. Lord, take my life and make it wholly thine;
Fill my poor heart with thy great love divine.
Take all my will, my passion, self, and pride;
I now surrender; Lord, in me abide.

Chapter 64: Kings of Judah – The Divided Kingdom (Rehoboam to Zedekiah)

We come now, following the death of Solomon, and with his son Rehoboam installed on the throne, to a kingdom about to divide – the two southern tribes (henceforth referred to as Judah) and the ten northern tribes (continuing to be referred to as Israel). Here, we will consider the kings of Judah.

We will do so with reference to Chapter 2, Figure 5. For both Judah and Israel, we will consider their kings up to the time of their respective exiles (586 BC – Judah; 722 BC – Israel). Following the death of Solomon in 930 BC, Judah had 20 kings and Israel had 19. In Israel's case there are many instances of one king bloodily ousting his predecessor. What Figure 5 also shows us are all the kings of Judah and Israel in chronological order, along with the dates of their reigns. The Figure also states, for each named king, whether they were deemed as good or bad. "Good" and "bad" are relative terms, although as far as the Bible authors were concerned it was mainly to do with the extent that they honoured God.

Even the best of kings had bad points and some bad kings had good points. Often, bad kings punished the prophets but there were several instances when the prophets were respected by them. Because kings had so much power and influence, it was often the case that people followed their examples, although it was also the case that kings merely reflected the state of the nation. There were cases of kings starting well and ending badly, as we have already seen with Saul and Solomon, and sometimes the opposite was the case when bad kings actually repented of their sin. In the end, it is for God to judge who is good or bad, and for those of us who read of their exploits to choose to be/do good, and apply the lessons arising out of their good and bad behaviour, doing so from God's perspective.

Often bad kings followed good kings and vice versa, and the fact that the father was good or bad didn't necessarily determine that this would be the case with the son who followed him. When it comes to matters of eternal destiny, the Old Testament gives little indication. Whether good or bad, we often find phrases along the lines of dead kings sleeping with their fathers. Mention was often made of where kings were buried, if for example in the tombs of the kings or not so for some bad kings. David was often the yardstick by which future kings were judged and with whom they were often compared.

During the reigns of the various kings, there were frequent interactions with kings of other nations. Some of these were positive and occurred by way of treaties and alliances. More were negative though, as seen by the number of wars, conflicts and invasions, often as a result of Judah's sin. Some of the nations that we came across in previous chapters, we come across here, but some are new in our story. Not only were there dealings with surrounding nations, like Aram (Syria) that was an emerging nation from early on but declined when conquered by Assyria. We also see the emergence (and also the fall) of some of the new empires, such as those of the Assyrians and Babylonians.

Often the fortunes of Judah and Israel (i.e., whether doing well and overcoming their enemies or doing badly and succumbing to their enemies) had something to do with where the king reigning at the time might be placed on the good to bad spectrum. We should also bear in mind the "blessing" and "cursing" chapters at the end of Deuteronomy as to why this was so. Then there was the relationship between kings of Judah and Israel and noting the fact that these overlap on our timeline. Sometimes, as at the time the division occurred, it was an acrimonious one. At other times, it was an amicable one.

Adopting idols and worshipping false gods (sometimes including child sacrifice) was a regular feature in the life of the Northern Kingdom, not having the Temple or the Levitical priests to turn to, but was also a recurring feature in the Southern Kingdom and often related to whether the king reigning was good or bad. One peculiar aspect, notable as it kept being mentioned, were "the High Places". Whether to YHWH or one of the false gods, it is not always easy to tell, but worship at such places was usually frowned upon. It was sometimes noted that with certain good kings, while they followed the true God, they also allowed the High Places to continue, for such was the attraction these held among the people and it was only those we might label as very good kings that took them down.

Significant too, right up to the end, was the part prophets played in encouraging kings. Sometimes they heeded what the prophets told them and sometimes they did not – and such instances are discussed in "**Prophets of the Bible**". Often prophets were treated well because they were looked upon as men of God, but we find many instances when this was not the case and they suffered. It has become evident with this particular trawl through the Bible that we earlier omitted pertinent information concerning the prophets (about which, the author apologises). Because of the approach taken with this prophets, priests and kings project, to get the full picture we need to refer to what we have already written concerning prophets and also priests. Levitical priests played an important part in the reigns of several kings of Judah, but not of Israel, as has been demonstrated in Part 2 of this book.

We should note too that it was not just David and Solomon who had more than one wife but many kings that followed them were polygamous and often this was done in order to strengthen ties with kings from other kingdoms, rather than for love. It begs the question to what extent the Bible ideal for marriage, e.g., *"therefore shall a man leave his father and his mother, and shall cleave unto his wife: and they shall be one flesh"* Genesis 2:24, and as set out in Solomon's Song of Songs and Paul's teaching on marriage found in Ephesians 5:22-33, was appreciated by the kings of Israel and Judah.

Interestingly too was how queens and especially the mothers of the kings often had significant sway and influence over what went on and could be seen as the power behind the throne. It is no coincidence that when we read about kings in the Bible, not only are their fathers named but often their mothers too. Except for a six-year period, following the death of King Ahaziah, when his mother, Athaliah, reigned as queen having tried to kill all male heirs, only kings reigned in Judah and Israel.

Another poignant and oft repeated point we discover in our survey of kings of Israel and Judah is how God, in His sovereignty, both raises up and deposes kings, including giving assignments to even the bad ones, especially in the case of Israel, often with the view to undo the damage done by their predecessors. The more we delve, the more we can reflect in awe and wonder how God was working his purposes out, often using as his instruments flawed humans, which the kings were. Going back to our Longfellow quote (Chapter 2, Figure 32) God may appear to take His time, but His timing is perfect.

As far as the approach taken with this chapter and the next one goes, we will list every king in the order they came to reign and say something about them, including (if applicable) their relationship with other kings. Some did a lot worthy of comment and about whom we can find much written in the Bible, with many lessons that could be learned from their lives and times. With others, the opposite was the case, often covered by statements along the lines that they did evil like a certain named king before them. Invariably, there may be a lot worthy of mention that we have left unsaid, but hopefully enough to enthuse readers to find out more. Since our intention has been on being succinct, as well as relevant, there is much material that may be of interest to readers that we have not addressed.

We have based our research on the Books of Kings, noting there is additional material to be found in the writings of the prophets, and the Books of Chronicles, as it looked way back, even to the beginning of creation, and considered the important question of how and why Israel, but especially Judah, came to be in the position they then found themselves, and as it looked forward to the coming of the promised Messiah and Israel's hope arising from the line of David (concerning which we can relate to what happened on the first Palm Sunday when Jesus rode into Jerusalem on a donkey as was prophesied in Zechariah 9:9, along with other Old Testament texts predicting the coming Messiah).

Chronicles has a lot to say about the kings of Judah (a lot less so with kings of Israel) that is not included in the "Kings" accounts, but they should be seen as complementary. Chapter 50 considers why differences between Kings and Chronicles exist. Sometimes we are faced with the challenge of reconciling the bad things said about a king in Kings with the good things that are said in Chronicles, realising the different (prophet and priest) perspectives. Sometimes we find God does not make sense but then we have to remember that the writers of both Kings and Chronicles were brutally honest and saw God as always being just and righteous. Sometimes, extra biblical texts and archaeological findings also have something to say about what went on and that is why what we write is a work in progress.

Rehoboam

Soon after Rehoboam came to the throne, he was faced with the strong possibility of a people's rebellion, which if responded to wisely might have been dealt with. What the people wanted was to have their load lightened. The old men advisors counselled to give the people what they wanted and come to some accord. The young men advisors, some Rehoboam had grown up with, counselled the very opposite. It was their advice that Rehoboam heeded and the upshot was a divided kingdom, with the ten northern tribes coming under Jeroboam and the two southern tribes under Rehoboam.

Rehoboam was all for going to war to re-assert his authority, but he was told not to, and he heeded that advice. Even so, we read *"there was war between Rehoboam and Jeroboam all their days"* 1 Kings 14:30. While Rehoboam took measures to secure his kingdom, he was unable to prevent the people drifting away from God. In the early days, Judah appeared to do well with the Levites and those whose devotion to God was greatest, who were living in the North, relocating to the South. As a result of turning away from God, Judah was invaded by King Shishak of Egypt. While a degree of repentance led by Rehoboam meant Judah did not suffer a worse fate, it did come under Egypt's thumb for a period.

Not much more can be said about Rehoboam and his reign other than the decline that had begun continued, and to add: *"And Judah did evil in the sight of the Lord, and they provoked him to jealousy with their sins which they had committed, above all that their fathers had done. For they also built them high places, and images, and groves, on every high hill, and under every green tree. And there were also sodomites in the land: and they did according to all the abominations of the nations which the Lord cast out before the children of Israel"* 1 Kings 14:22-24. Rehoboam never became a whole hearted follower of God and his, often adopted, pick and mix approach to religion continued.

Abijah

Abijah also was much in the same vein as his father when it came to devotion to God. We read *"And he walked in all the sins of his father, which he had done before him: and his heart was not perfect with the Lord his God, as the heart of David his father"* 1 Kings 15:3. He did so amidst self-righteous claims that he was on God's side, when faced with the threats coming from Jeroboam, whereas Jeroboam was not. Despite being outnumbered in the major battle that followed, Abijah and Judah won the day. It was noted: *"the children of Israel were brought under at that time, and the children of Judah prevailed, because they relied upon the Lord God of their fathers"* 2 Chronicles 13:18. We read after this Jeroboam did not regain power and was struck down by God, while Abijah grew in strength.

Asa

It was said of him: *"And Asa did that which was right in the eyes of the Lord, as did David his father … Asa's heart was perfect with the Lord all his days"* 1 Kings 15: 11, 14. The Chronicles' writer concurs: *"Asa's heart was fully committed to the Lord all his life"* 2 Chronicles 15:17, but as the Kings' writer recognised: *"he did not remove the high places from Israel"*. We read about Asa both in 1 Kings 15 and 2 Chronicles 14-16. While both accounts cover many of the significant events in Asa's life, that of Chronicles provides a more comprehensive cover, especially furnishing more evidence that despite being a good king he was also a good king who in later life became bad (or did bad) and giving details of two major military conflicts that took place, showing Asa in firstly a good and later a bad light.

There is no doubt Asa began his reign well, in particular removing some of the rampant idolatry, including that of his own grandmother. He made good decisions that benefitted the people, such as public works projects and building up defences to help ensure security. And he needed it – Judah was attacked by an even more formidable army from the South (Cush) and, despite his preparations, humanly speaking Judah was no match. His response was to call upon the Lord, who delivered them. This pleased God who sent His prophet to encourage Asa and remind him of His Covenant with them and the consequences of obedience and disobedience. Asa responded positively, continuing to clean house and the Lord blessed Asa and Judah (who also responded) and it was evident to all, including some from the northern tribes choosing to settle in Judah, that unlike in Israel, God was honoured.

It seems it went well until 36 years into Asa's reign. The conflict between the northern and southern kingdoms that began under Jeroboam and Rehoboam continued and reached a high point when Israel under its king, Baasha, created an embargo such that people could not enter or leave Judah, and he did so in alliance with neighbouring Aram (Syria) under its king, Ben-Hadad. Unlike before when Judah was attacked and he called on the Lord to help, Asa took treasure from the Temple and gave it to Ben-Hadad as a bribe so that he would switch sides. The move worked to a point but it was at a price.

The Lord sent Hanani, a prophet, to rebuke Asa and tell him as a result of his foolishness he would be at war. For his pains Hanani was imprisoned and Asa also began to oppress some of his own people. Three years later, Asa was afflicted with a severe disease in his feet but he did not seek the Lord. When he died, Asa was given a splendid funeral but there was no indication he had turned back to the Lord.

Jehoshaphat

Putting David aside, Jehoshaphat was arguably one of the best among all of the kings. We certainly get that impression reading the Book of Chronicles, which says a lot more about Jehoshaphat than does the Book of Kings and portrays him in an even more glowing light, yet still pointing out his faults.

As far as the Book of Kings was concerned, Jehoshaphat was a good king but one, reading between the lines at least, who had several flaws. For example, when he allied himself with King Ahab of Israel and later when he joined forces with Ahab to fight the King of Syria in a battle God did not intend, he was rebuked. Kings also omits interesting details only to be found in Chronicles, such as (and relevant when considering priests of the Bible) the part played by the Levites in teaching the people and in administering justice. Moreover, other of Jehoshaphat's dealings were also bound up with the accounts given of the kings of Israel, with which he had many dealings, sometimes unwisely so.

While the Kings' account of Jehoshaphat's reign, where he is the main character, is short, it provides a good, concise summary from a neutral onlooker perspective: "*Jehoshaphat was thirty and five years old when he began to reign; and he reigned twenty and five years in Jerusalem. And his mother's name was Azubah the daughter of Shilhi. And he walked in all the ways of Asa his father; he turned not aside from it, doing that which was right in the eyes of the Lord: nevertheless the high places were not taken away; for the people offered and burnt incense yet in the high places. And Jehoshaphat made peace with the king of Israel*" 1 Kings 22:42-44.

In the account of Jehoshaphat defeating Moab and Amon, we read how he called upon God for help when all the odds seemed stacked against him: *"O our God, wilt thou not judge them? for we have no might against this great company that cometh against us; neither know we what to do: but our eyes are upon thee"* 2 Chronicles 20:12, and when we read in response: *"And when he had consulted with the people, he appointed singers unto the Lord, and that should praise the beauty of holiness, as they went out before the army, and to say, Praise the Lord; for his mercy endureth for ever. And when they began to sing and to praise, the Lord set ambushments against the children of Ammon, Moab, and mount Seir, which were come against Judah; and they were smitten"* 2 Chronicles 20:21-22. The thought of a successful army being led by a worshipping choir may seem strange but for the fact that God won the battle. Then following that victory we read: *"And the fear of God was on all the kingdoms of those countries, when they had heard that the Lord fought against the enemies of Israel. So the realm of Jehoshaphat was quiet: for his God gave him rest round about"* 2 Chronicles 20:29-30.

While he ended well, just as he began, the Chronicler couldn't resist pointing out his failings when Jehoshaphat *"rested with his fathers"*. We read at the end: *"And he walked in the way of Asa his father, and departed not from it, doing that which was right in the sight of the Lord. Howbeit the high places were not taken away: for as yet the people had not prepared their hearts unto the God of their fathers ... And after this did Jehoshaphat king of Judah join himself with Ahaziah king of Israel, who did very wickedly: And he joined himself with him to make ships to go to Tarshish: and they made the ships in Eziongeber. Then Eliezer the son of Dodavah of Mareshah prophesied against Jehoshaphat, saying, Because thou hast joined thyself with Ahaziah, the Lord hath broken thy works. And the ships were broken, that they were not able to go to Tarshish"* 2 Chronicles 20:32-33, 35-37.

Jehoram

Yet again, we see a very bad king following a very good king, doing so because he was the eldest son. One of his early acts was to kill all his brothers. Whilst the kingdom was secure under his father, under Jehoram it was attacked from many quarters and in some cases Judah came off worst. Part of God's judgement was that his family would be killed and he would die a lingering and painful death. We also read the incredibly sad statement upon his death that there was no-one left to mourn his passing.

Ahaziah

Ahaziah was the only surviving son of Jehoram and he too was bad and died a tragic death following his short reign. He joined forces with King Joram of Israel to wage war with the Syrians and came off worst. When he visited Joram, it was when Jehu was going about killing all that was left of the family of Ahab, including Joram. Ahaziah got caught up in this and he and some of his relatives were killed.

Athaliah

"And when Athaliah the mother of Ahaziah saw that her son was dead, she arose and destroyed all the seed royal. But Jehosheba, the daughter of king Joram, sister of Ahaziah, took Joash the son of Ahaziah, and stole him from among the king's sons which were slain; and they hid him, even him and his nurse, in the bedchamber from Athaliah, so that he was not slain. And he was with her hid in the house of the Lord six years. And Athaliah did reign over the land" 2 Kings 11:1-3. Here we read of the one and only queen to reign in Israel or Judah. We discussed what happened next, following the rescue of Jehu, because of the actions of Jehosheba and Jehoiada, the High Priest, in Chapter 30. It resulted in a counter coup, cleverly led by Jehoiada, in which wicked Queen Athaliah was executed, much to the delight of the people, and the boy, Joash, being safely installed and crowned as king.

Joash

"In the seventh year of Jehu Jehoash began to reign; and forty years reigned he in Jerusalem. And his mother's name was Zibiah of Beersheba. And Jehoash did that which was right in the sight of the Lord all his days wherein Jehoiada the priest instructed him. But the high places were not taken away: the people still sacrificed and burnt incense in the high places" 2 Kings 12:1-3.

Joash started well. We read, for example, his part in ensuring Temple repairs were made and that the prescribed worship took place. He did so under the mentorship of Jehoiada, but when he died things changed as Joash listened to his officials and abandoned the Temple and worshipped idols instead, doing so despite being warned by the prophets of God's displeasure. It is then Zechariah (Jehoiada's son) enters the frame and bravely denounces Joash publicly: *"And the Spirit of God came upon Zechariah the son of Jehoiada the priest, which stood above the people, and said unto them, Thus saith God, Why transgress ye the commandments of the Lord, that ye cannot prosper? because ye have forsaken the Lord, he hath also forsaken you. And they conspired against him, and stoned him with stones at the commandment of the king in the court of the house of the Lord. Thus Joash the king remembered not the kindness which Jehoiada his father had done to him, but slew his son. And when he died, he said, The Lord look upon it, and require it"* 2 Chronicles 24:20-22.

Joash's end was a tragic one, especially in the light of how he was rescued as a child from the clutches of wicked Athaliah and that he began well. After his mentor had died, he listened to foolish voices and despite being warned continued in his disobedience. He came up against the old enemy, the king of Aram, who he tried to buy off with treasures from the Temple and the Palace, who it seems later came again with inferior forces for more plunder, and fought and prevailed against the army of Judah, wounding Joash, who then was killed by some of his officials in revenge for killing Zechariah.

Amaziah

It was said of Amaziah *"he did that which was right in the sight of the Lord, but not with a perfect heart"* 2 Chronicles 25:2, reflecting an ongoing issue with many kings that on one hand they sought to serve the Lord, but on the other did what was wrong. He was not wholehearted and, as we seek to draw lessons and apply them to our own situation, we should reflect how important this is.

It is further said: *"Now it came to pass, when the kingdom was established to him, that he slew his servants that had killed the king his father. But he slew not their children, but did as it is written in the law in the book of Moses, where the Lord commanded, saying, The fathers shall not die for the children, neither shall the children die for the fathers, but every man shall die for his own sin"* 2 Chronicles 25:3-4. While we could sympathise with his father's assassins – after all, would that not be something we might want to do if we could, by way of revenge, if our loved one (in this case it was Zechariah the priest) had been murdered? But true to the approach of the writers of both Kings and Chronicles, not only do we read a frank account of what happened but a factor that is also important – Amaziah did not do what the Law of Moses forbade, and that was to kill children for the sin of their fathers.

Amaziah's reign was a messy one. He achieved a bloody victory against Edom with the Lord's help. He had hired Israelite mercenaries to help, but he was told by a prophet to send them home as they were not needed, which he did (although they wreaked havoc afterward). He took Edom's gods and bowed to them, threatening the prophet who rebuked him. He foolishly sought a fight with Jehoash, king of Israel and came off a lot worse. While he lived 15 more years after Jehoash died, his end was a sorry one for they (whoever they were) conspired to kill a fleeing Amaziah and were able to do so.

Uzziah

It was said concerning Uzziah (referred to as Azariah in Kings): *"And he did that which was right in the sight of the Lord, according to all that his father Amaziah did. And he sought God in the days of Zechariah, who had understanding in the visions of God: and as long as he sought the Lord, God made him to prosper"* 2 Chronicles 26:4-5. He won battles, subdued nations, undertook building, engineering, and agricultural projects. *"But when he was strong, his heart was lifted up to his destruction: for he transgressed against the Lord his God, and went into the temple of the Lord to burn incense upon the altar of incense"* 2 Chronicles 26:16. For what happened after he was confronted by a priest, read Chapter 31. Uzziah lived out his days as a leper, while his son, Jotham, ruled in his stead.

Jotham

It was said of Jotham: *"And he did that which was right in the sight of the Lord: he did according to all that his father Uzziah had done. Howbeit the high places were not removed: the people sacrificed and burned incense still in the high places. He built the higher gate of the house of the Lord".* 2 Kings 15:34-35. While this "High Place" blemish on Jotham's reign was one shared by many kings, he succeeded in battle to secure Judah, including exacting tribute from those he conquered. He successfully undertook a number of building projects. We read in Chronicles *"So Jotham became mighty, because he prepared his ways before the Lord his God"* 2 Chronicles 27:6. One commentator (F.B.Meyer) made the pertinent point: *"This story of Jotham is memorable if only for one sentence; that he became mighty because he ordered his way before the Lord his God. We should order our lives, as we order our prayers".*

Ahaz

Just as Jotham was good, so Ahaz, his son, was evil. This included worshipping Baal, sacrificing his sons and building High Places all over the place to sacrifice to other gods. We read of his battles with Israel and Aram (see under Pekah, king of Israel) with a devastating number of casualties, as well as with the Edomites and Philistines. He formed some sort of alliance with the King of Assyria, Tiglath-Pileser, at a high price, and it gained him a certain respite. One salutary tale was his taking a liking to the altar he saw in Damascus and instructing Uriah the priest to build something similar in the Temple, yet "just in case" keeping the Altar that was originally in the Temple if he needed to seek God's guidance. This is a good example of the sort of "hedge your bets" religion that was so prevalent in life under kings of Judah and Israel, that God found so abhorrent and that we must take careful heed to avoid.

Hezekiah

We are again spoiled for choice concerning King Hezekiah, because a lot had been written about him, and to get the full story we need to check out three different Bible passages:

- 2 Kings 18-20
- 2 Chronicles 29-32
- Isaiah 36-39

We are left in no doubt concerning his thoroughly good credentials, for we read: "*And he did that which was right in the sight of the Lord, according to all that David his father did. He removed the high places, and brake the images, and cut down the groves, and brake in pieces the brasen serpent that Moses had made: for unto those days the children of Israel did burn incense to it: and he called it Nehushtan. He trusted in the Lord God of Israel; so that after him was none like him among all the kings of Judah, nor any that were before him. For he clave to the Lord, and departed not from following him, but kept his commandments, which the Lord commanded Moses*" 2 Kings 18:3-6.

We are told "*in the third year of Hoshea son of Elah king of Israel, that Hezekiah the son of Ahaz king of Judah began to reign. Twenty and five years old was he when he began to reign; and he reigned twenty and nine years in Jerusalem*" 2 Kings 18:1-2. As for Hezekiah's father, Ahaz, who we discussed as being a bad king, an important part of what Hezekiah did was to reverse that evil legacy by removing idolatry and restoring the true worship of YHWH according to the Law and pertaining to the Temple. Looking throughout his reign, Hezekiah not only returned Judah (and some in Israel too) back to the true God, but he governed well, including public works projects, and God blessed his endeavours.

The big test for Hezekiah was concerning Assyria, which having conquered Israel then set its sights on Judah. It appeared Hezekiah was in two minds – stopping paying tribute to the king of Assyria and then as things looked ominous paying it again (including robbing the Temple of its treasures). But that was not enough and having taken towns in Judah, the Assyrian army sought to do the same with Jerusalem, making clear their demands to Hezekiah's representatives (including in a letter) and then shouting them out to the people in the City. For Hezekiah, not only was this a serious threat which he was unable to counter, but it was an insult to YHWH God. He laid the letter out before God and prayed.

What we have is one of the great prayers of the Bible. He prayed for God's help, ending appropriately with the words: "*Now therefore, O Lord our God, save us from his hand, that all the kingdoms of the earth may know that thou art the Lord, even thou only*" Isaiah 37:20. Isaiah the prophet played an important part during this time and, after Hezekiah had prayed, informed him that God had heard his prayer, and the answer would come quickly. That night, 185,000 of King Sennacherib's army were killed by the angel (just one) of the Lord (37:36), and soon after that Sennacherib was killed by his sons.

Sadly, after this, with peace and prosperity restored, Hezekiah grew proud and Isaiah came to him with a word from the Lord, to put his house in order and that he would die. And Hezekiah repented and God reversed His decision, added 15 years to Hezekiah's life and confirmed this with a remarkable miracle, which in effect was planet Earth rotating backwards for a period. But he was not done with his foolishness, for he gave the emissaries of the King of Babylon a guided tour of all his riches, only to be told (again by Isaiah) that all this (and some of his descendants) would one day be taken by Babylon.

Regarding Hezekiah, notwithstanding lapses (of which there were a number), he was a good king, indeed one of the best. There are many lessons we can take from the story of Hezekiah, such as the importance of God's glory and prayer and the need to live humbly before Him, not taking anything for granted. Concerning his end, we read: "*Now the rest of the acts of Hezekiah, and his goodness, behold, they are written in the vision of Isaiah the prophet, the son of Amoz, and in the book of the kings of Judah and Israel. And Hezekiah slept with his fathers, and they buried him in the chiefest of the sepulchres of the sons of David: and all Judah and the inhabitants of Jerusalem did him honour at his death. And Manasseh his son reigned in his stead*" 2 Chronicles 32:32-33.

Manasseh

Manasseh came to the throne of Judah, aged 12, and reigned for 55 years. His father was Hezekiah, who was reckoned to be one of the best kings and, as is so often seen, goodness (and badness) is not automatically passed down. The writer of Kings unequivocally condemned Manasseh, in whom he could see no redeeming features, and thus had nothing good to say about him. As far as he was concerned, Manasseh's evil character, his cruel acts, idolatry and awful legacy were self-evident:

"*And he did that which was evil in the sight of the Lord, after the abominations of the heathen, whom the Lord cast out before the children of Israel. For he built up again the high places which Hezekiah his father had destroyed; and he reared up altars for Baal, and made a grove, as did Ahab king of Israel; and worshipped all the host of heaven, and served them. And he built altars in the house of the Lord, of which the Lord said, In Jerusalem will I put my name. And he built altars for all the host of heaven in the two courts of the house of the Lord. And he made his son pass through the fire, and observed times, and used enchantments, and dealt with familiar spirits and wizards: he wrought much wickedness in the sight of the Lord, to pro-*

voke him to anger" 2 Kings 21:2-6.

The writer continues in similar vein about Manasseh's wicked reign and refers to warnings given by the prophets and God *"will forsake the remnant of mine inheritance, and deliver them into the hand of their enemies"* 2 Kings 21:14 and ending: *"Moreover Manasseh shed innocent blood very much, till he had filled Jerusalem from one end to another; beside his sin wherewith he made Judah to sin, in doing that which was evil in the sight of the Lord. Now the rest of the acts of Manasseh, and all that he did, and his sin that he sinned, are they not written in the book of the chronicles of the kings of Judah? And Manasseh slept with his fathers"* 2 Kings 21:16-18.

When we turn to the Book of Chronicles, much of what we will have picked up in Kings, concerning Manasseh's wickedness, is confirmed: *"But did that which was evil in the sight of the Lord, like unto the abominations of the heathen, whom the Lord had cast out before the children of Israel ... And he set a carved image, the idol which he had made, in the house of God, of which God had said to David and to Solomon his son, In this house, and in Jerusalem, which I have chosen before all the tribes of Israel, will I put my name for ever"* 2 Chronicles 33:2, 7.

But a new and positive aspect is brought out which we do not read about in Kings: *"Wherefore the Lord brought upon them the captains of the host of the king of Assyria, which took Manasseh among the thorns, and bound him with fetters, and carried him to Babylon. And when he was in affliction, he besought the Lord his God, and humbled himself greatly before the God of his fathers, and prayed unto him: and he was intreated of him, and heard his supplication, and brought him again to Jerusalem into his kingdom. Then Manasseh knew that the Lord he was God"* 2 Chronicles 33:11-13.

Manasseh would fit the bill as a bad king who became good, leaving us with hope. The Book of Chronicles ends up telling us of how Manasseh began to undo much of the evil he had initiated before being taken captive although it may have been too little, too late. When we read on, we see some of his evil legacy being passed down and the kingdom of Judah reaping the consequences.

Amon

Sadly, the reversal out from idolatry and false worship that Manasseh began at the end of his reign did not continue under his son, Amon, who went back to all the bad ways, and did a good deal of harm during his two-year reign. At the end he was assassinated by his own officials, who themselves were killed in revenge by the people, followed by them installing his son, the boy Josiah, as king.

Josiah

The Chronicler tells us (and the writer of Kings concurs) "*And he (Josiah) did that which was right in the sight of the Lord, and walked in the ways of David his father, and declined neither to the right hand, nor to the left*" 2 Chronicles 34:2. He set about the task of repairing the Temple, which was in a dilapidated state. During that time, the Book of the Law was found, under Hilkiah the priest (discussed in our Chapter 32), which brought out the spiritual state of the nation. When consulting with Huldah the prophetess, Josiah was left in no doubt concerning God's displeasure, but also because of Josiah's response the judgment that would happen would be after Josiah's death. The sad fact was that while what Josiah did what was right, the downward spiral the people were intent on could not be stopped.

Josiah continued in similar vein to how he began, starting with a public reading of the Law. He continued to clear out the idols and anything to do with false worship, which was a mammoth operation. This extended beyond Judah into Israel. He also fulfilled the prophecy given 300 years previously to Jeroboam I that he would destroy the altar erected at Bethel and burn the bones in the nearby tombs, but not those of the prophet that gave this prophecy. He also re-introduced the celebration of the Passover, which was a grand affair that had not been seen since the days of Solomon.

Josiah's ending was a disappointing one given he took part in a battle that he should have avoided. It was against the king of Egypt, Neco, who was passing through to join the king of Assyria in order to fight the Babylonians. Josiah died in that battle and not many years later both Egypt and Assyria were defeated by the Babylonians, who went on extending their empire, including conquering Judah.

Jehoahaz

Josiah's son, Jehoahaz, lasted only three months as king. We read he did evil and that Neco, king of Egypt carried him off to Egypt in chains, where he died.

Jehoiakim

Neco installed Jehoiakim as king in place of Jehoahaz and imposed on Judah a heavy levy. He too was evil, adopting the same practices as his predecessors. During that time there was a change in puppet master from Neco to Nebuchadnezzar who had defeated Egypt in battle and thereby put an end to Egypt's dominance in the region. After three years, Jehoiakim rebelled from being Nebuchadnezzar's vassal but then had to fight other invaders as well as Babylon as part of God's judgement for filling Jerusalem with innocent blood. Nebuchadnezzar also raided the Temple and took Jehoiakim in chains to Babylon. Jehoiachin his son succeeded him as king.

Jehoiachin

Jehoiachin too was evil and he also lasted only three months as king. He was taken to Babylon as a prisoner along with his family and officials, as well as treasures from the Palace and the Temple. Zedekiah, Jehoiachin's uncle was installed as king in his place. Jehoiachin's stay in Babylon was a long one and we read how many years later he was given a place of honour among his Babylonian captors.

Zedekiah

We come to the last of the evil quartet of kings following Josiah, who we might have thought would see where continuing on such a path could only end in disaster. When we consider the Book of Jeremiah, we find 48 references that mention Zedekiah by name. Most of these are to do with Jeremiah warning Zedekiah concerning the error of his ways and how he ought to respond, especially when coming to terms with the dictates of Judah's Babylonian captors, which he ignored as did his close circle, who sought ways to punish and suppress God's messenger. Toward the end of his reign, he rebelled against Babylon and the city of Jerusalem was under siege for a long period. In the end that siege was broken and many were killed, including Zedekiah's sons. Jerusalem, and notably the Temple, were destroyed and Zedekiah and those who were left were taken into captivity.

There we leave Kings of Judah, with the demise of its last king ever to have reigned. But as we see at both the end of Kings and Chronicles, it is not without hope. It is a topsy turvy tale, as has been the entire history of Israel, and one that continues to play out to this day, when God seeks a people that follow Him alone. If there is a short, sharp lesson to be learned, it is that if the people, ideally led by their king, obeyed God, it went well, and if not, it went badly.

The application that twenty first century students of Israel's history might want to consider is the same one that can be seen throughout the Bible, that there is a need for God's people to serve God fully and there would be a tragic outcome if that were not the case. Nowhere is this more illustrated than in the Book of Lamentations, written in the aftermath of the Fall of Jerusalem. We quote the very first and very last verse: *"How doth the city sit solitary, that was full of people! how is she become as a widow! she that was great among the nations, and princess among the provinces, how is she become tributary! ... But thou hast utterly rejected us; thou art very wroth against us"* Lamentations 1:1, 5:22. The problem too often seen in the situations of today's people of God is whether or not they are going to be whole hearted for God. The dilemma seen in Bible times and our own is of believers trying to accommodate both God and the ways of a world that is too often dead set against God, with dire consequences to follow (something this author has found to be the case in his own experience).

The Book(s) of Kings ends: "*And it came to pass in the seven and thirtieth year of the captivity of Jehoiachin king of Judah, in the twelfth month, on the seven and twentieth day of the month, that Evilmerodach king of Babylon in the year that he began to reign did lift up the head of Jehoiachin king of Judah out of prison; And he spake kindly to him, and set his throne above the throne of the kings that were with him in Babylon; And changed his prison garments: and he did eat bread continually before him all the days of his life. And his allowance was a continual allowance given him of the king, a daily rate for every day, all the days of his life*" 2 Kings 25:27-30.

Chronicles also ends on a positive and hopeful note – the decree of King Cyrus of Persia, bringing to an end the captivity. In doing so, it looks forward to the time of Israel's Messiah. On a related note, while we find when the captives do return, and only a small minority chose to take up that offer, their first governor is Zerubbabel, the grandson of King Jehoiachin, and part of the ancestral line that led to Jesus. Another often overlooked positive was that for 70 years, while the land was not worked, it enjoyed its sabbath rests, as required by the Law of Moses, which the people had previously ignored.

As far as the Old Testament is concerned a remnant of Judah and some from Israel who found their way back to the Promised Land, as a result of the "Cyrus edict", did return. While there were highlights such as the building of the Second Temple and short-lived periods of revival under the likes of Ezra and Nehemiah the types of blessings foretold by some of the prophets did not materialise and still have not done so. As we have reflected elsewhere, the Book of Malachi paints a sad picture of how it was at the end. While the Inter Testament period was to last 400 years, under the rule of foreign powers, i.e., Greece and Rome, that unlike Persia were unsympathetic toward Israel, the golden age that would be led by a descendant of David (Israel's Messiah), as shown in Jesus' genealogy, found in Matthew 1, did not happen, for the Messiah would be rejected. Given those prophecies concerning Israel living in a land that enjoyed peace and prosperity have yet to be fulfilled, we remain confident and hopeful and, other than what is written elsewhere in this book, that is a subject for another book.

1. Jesus shall reign where'er the sun
does its successive journeys run,
his kingdom stretch from shore to shore,
till moons shall wax and wane no more.

2. To him shall endless prayer be made,
and praises throng to crown his head.
His name like sweet perfume shall rise
with every morning sacrifice.

3. People and realms of every tongue
dwell on his love with sweetest song,
and infant voices shall proclaim
their early blessings on his name.

4. Blessings abound where'er he reigns:
the prisoners leap to lose their chains,
the weary find eternal rest,
and all who suffer want are blest.

5. Let every creature rise and bring
the highest honors to our King,
angels descend with songs again,
and earth repeat the loud amen.

Chapter 65: Kings of Israel – The Divided Kingdom (Jeroboam to Hoshea)

In this chapter, we will adopt the same approach as with the previous one, including making similar sorts of observations and applying similar principles that we set out at the start of that chapter. We will consider each Israel king in turn, noting most of the information we have comes from the Book of Kings (Chronicles says relatively little). We note with reference to Chapter 2, Figure 5, that all the kings of Israel were bad and this was related to Israel being more prone to backsliding than was Judah and lacking priests and Levites to teach them. With a number of Israel's kings, their reigns were short lived, often brought down by military coups, for such was the turmoil taking place during this period.

While the kings of Judah were usually sons of the kings that preceded them or at least were close relatives, and were all, following David, of the line of David, that was not so with the kings of Israel. The reason for the reigns being short was usually because one king was ousted by the king that replaced him in a bloody coup that usually bore some relationship to the wickedness of the deposed king. While none of the kings of Israel were good, a number we find, reading the words of the prophets, were raised up to kingship by God, often for a specific purpose. They might fulfil part of the reason for being appointed but generally they failed in other ways and this led to them being deposed. As we reflect on the sorry bunch of kings in today's world, we might want to reflect on this lesson and remember, God raises up and God puts down kings and by God kings reign (Proverbs 8:15).

While Israel was to end up in exile and thereafter their identity and uniqueness would be shrouded in mystery, we find God had not finished with them, evidenced by giving them prophets like those that appeared on the scene in Jeroboam's time and, more famously, Elijah and Elisha and, later still, Amos and Hosea. While, not long after, Israel was to go into exile under the Assyrians, 136 years before Judah went into exile under the Babylonians, and despite some from the Ten Tribes finding their way back to Judah, we mostly lose track of what happened to them after that, even though a promising future was prophesied, particularly in the Last Days with the return of Israel's Messiah.

Jeroboam I

One of the significant events concerning Jeroboam I, the first king of the divided kingdom of Israel, happened before he became king. A prophet of the Lord told him what would happen. God would take ten tribes and it was part of His judgement and will. Moreover, if Jeroboam were to do the right things God would establish a dynasty through him, in much the same way as he made happen with David. Jeroboam had served under Solomon with distinction, even gaining promotion. Then he rebelled and was exiled. How and why he managed to gain the kingdom is discussed in the previous chapter.

While there was ongoing hostility between Rehoboam and Jeroboam, it did not come to all-out war, but there was war later between Jeroboam and Rehoboam's successor, Abijah, and it was one in which Abijah decisively prevailed and inflicted many casualties on Israel's side. Early on, Jeroboam recognised Israel's religious sensibilities might be problematical to achieving his ambitions should the people decide to go to the Temple in Jerusalem to worship God. His solution was to set up High Places and two centres of worship, where he installed two golden calves he had made, at Bethel and Dan, and appointed his own priests. Concerning which, there was a remarkable prophecy about what Jeroboam did (discussed in **"Prophets of the Bible"**) that would be fulfilled over 200 years later under King Josiah. Despite the warnings and seeing God's power at work, Jeroboam persisted in his ways.

Later, at the time when his son lay dying, Jeroboam approached a prophet of the Lord, desirous to know what was going to happen. Through his wife, he approached the same prophet who had told him he would become king. The terrible nature of Jeroboam's sins, in God's eyes, were laid out. He was told that not only would his innocent son die but Jeroboam's male descendants would all be killed. Reading on, we find the whole prophecy being fulfilled. As is so often the case, there was a big gulf between what might have been, after a good start, to what actually happened.

Nadab

Nadab was Jeroboam's son. We don't know much about him beyond the fact he was bad and he lasted less than two years. He was assassinated by the king who succeeded him, Baasha, who then went about doing what the prophet said would happen, killing Jeroboam's male descendants.

Baasha

Baasha is another example of someone God raised up to be king and yet persisted in doing evil, and for this reason, just as with Jeroboam, his house was destined for destruction.

Elah

Elah was Baasha's son and was killed by Zimri, who replaced him.

Zimri

Zimri lasted 7 days but managed to kill off Baasha's whole family before

Omri laid siege to Zimri's palace which Zimri set fire to and he died as a result, and Omri took over as king.

Omri

There appears to have been a civil war over who was to be king, with the Omri faction prevailing. We read *"For he walked in all the way of Jeroboam the son of Nebat, and in his sin wherewith he made Israel to sin, to provoke the Lord God of Israel to anger with their vanities. Now the rest of the acts of Omri which he did, and his might that he shewed, are they not written in the book of the chronicles of the kings of Israel?"* 1 Kings 16:26-27.

Ahab

About Ahab, it is written: *"And Ahab the son of Omri did evil in the sight of the Lord above all that were before him. And it came to pass, as if it had been a light thing for him to walk in the sins of Jeroboam the son of Nebat, that he took to wife Jezebel the daughter of Ethbaal king of the Zidonians, and went and served Baal, and worshipped him ... Ahab did more to provoke the Lord God of Israel to anger than all the kings of Israel that were before him."* 1 Kings 16:30, 31, 33.

We are left in little doubt from the many times Ahab is mentioned in the Book of Kings that he was one of the worst of the kings of Israel. He will be forever associated with his queen, the ever-scheming Jezebel, who was the real power behind the throne, and could truly be described as wicked, and Jehu, a later king of Israel, who was anointed by God in order to drain the swamp that Ahab had left. Ahab's part in the story of Naboth's vineyard, including his weak nature, was rather telling.

Ahab is perhaps best known because he was married to the even more wicked, Jezebel, and for his encounter with the prophet Elijah, as detailed in 1 Kings 17 and 18, beginning with the words: *"And Elijah the Tishbite, who was of the inhabitants of Gilead, said unto Ahab, As the Lord God of Israel liveth, before whom I stand, there shall not be dew nor rain these years, but according to my word"* (17:1). Among other things: the judgment of God concerning Israel's idolatry, the successful plotting of Jezebel to kill the prophets and the showdown on the top of Mount Carmel, when the prophets of Baal received a mighty defeat by the hands of the Lord, we find Ahab saw first-hand God at work.

It is worth noting Ahab's part in the ongoing conflict between Israel and Syria, found in 1 Kings 20 and the words of an unnamed prophet promising Israel victory, which under Ahab they achieved on two separate occasions against King Ben-Hadad, king of Aram, accompanied by 32 kings and superior forces. This was achieved with God's help, but not entirely, inviting the Lord's rebuke via the prophet: "*And he said unto him, Thus saith the Lord, Because thou hast let go out of thy hand a man whom I appointed to utter destruction, therefore thy life shall go for his life, and thy people for his people. And the king of Israel went to his house heavy and displeased, and came to Samaria*" (20:42-43).

The story of Naboth's vineyard is told in 1 Kings 21, and brings out much concerning Ahab's weak and wicked character that was to invite a stinging rebuke by Elijah, leading to the deaths of Ahab and Jezebel (who master-minded the plot to kill Naboth and steal his vineyard) and the demise of Ahab's dynasty by way of God's judgement. What is of interest in this story was Ahab's response to the rebuke: "*And it came to pass, when Ahab heard those words, that he rent his clothes, and put sackcloth upon his flesh, and fasted, and lay in sackcloth, and went softly. And the word of the Lord came to Elijah the Tishbite, saying, Seest thou how Ahab humbleth himself before me? because he humbleth himself before me, I will not bring the evil in his days: but in his son's days will I bring the evil upon his house*" (21:27-29), and is indicative of how God responds to those who repent.

It would have been nice to place Ahab in the category of a bad king who came good in the end but sadly he remains in the category of bad kings and was the worst of the bad, albeit with this one act of repentance. When we read of yet another skirmish with the Syrians in 1 Kings 22, we read about more of Ahab's foolishness. He sought an alliance with (good) King Jehoshaphat of Judah to go and fight the Syrians. Ahab was even able to get the affirmation of 400 (approved) prophets, who told him what he wanted to hear – he would beat the Syrians if he went to war. Ahab put the one (unapproved) prophet (Micaiah) in prison. Micaiah was the only true prophet, who rightly counselled that such a move would be disastrous. Ahab suffered an ignoble end when he was hit by a stray arrow, when his chariot entered the field of battle, along with King Jehoshaphat, thus fulfilling the prophecy that spoke of his demise.

Before we move on to consider a succession of bad kings of Israel, it is worth exploring whether the people were also bad, and not just under the reign of particularly bad kings such as Ahab. When Elijah returned to Israel and met with Ahab, just before his showdown with the prophets of Baal on Mount Carmel, he met Obadiah, of whom we read "*Obadiah, which was the governor of his house. (Now Obadiah feared the Lord greatly)*" 1 Kings 18:3. Behind the king's back, Obadiah had been hiding 100 prophets while Jezebel was seeking them out to kill them. The fact that soon after this and just prior to Elijah's confrontation with the prophets of Baal, we read what summed up the dithering between God and Baal mentality of many of the ordinary people: "*And Elijah came unto all the people, and said, How long halt ye between two opinions? if the Lord be God, follow him: but if Baal, then follow him. And the people answered him not a word"* 1 Kings 18:21. Such "dithering" we too do well to avoid!

Later, after fleeing Jezebel, God caught up with Elijah on Mount Horeb and Elijah told God *"I have been very jealous for the Lord God of hosts: for the children of Israel have forsaken thy covenant, thrown down thine altars, and slain thy prophets with the sword; and I, even I only, am left; and they seek my life, to take it away"* 1 Kings 19:10, God responded: *"Yet I have left me seven thousand in Israel, all the knees which have not bowed unto Baal, and every mouth which hath not kissed him"* 1 Kings 19:18. The point we want to make here is that throughout history, even in the darkest, anti-God times, there has always been a despised or ignored remnant that has sought God despite the pressures not to do so, and always God has looked with favour upon such people, who would bow their knee to Him alone.

Ahaziah

We read that following Ahab's death, his son Ahaziah reigned. The verdict on his reign was a scathing one: *"Ahaziah the son of Ahab began to reign over Israel in Samaria the seventeenth year of Jehoshaphat king of Judah, and reigned two years over Israel. And he did evil in the sight of the Lord, and walked in the way of his father, and in the way of his mother, and in the way of Jeroboam the son of Nebat, who made Israel to sin: For he served Baal, and worshipped him, and provoked to anger the Lord God of Israel, according to all that his father had done"* 1 Kings 22:51-53. We read: *"And Ahaziah fell down through a lattice in his upper chamber that was in Samaria, and was sick: and he sent messengers, and said unto them, Go, enquire of Baalzebub the god of Ekron whether I shall recover of this disease"* 2 Kings 1:2 and would be told by Elijah *"Thus saith the Lord, Forasmuch as thou hast sent messengers to enquire of Baalzebub the god of Ekron, is it not because there is no God in Israel to enquire of his word? therefore thou shalt not come down off that bed on which thou art gone up, but shalt surely die. So he died according to the word of the Lord which Elijah had spoken"* 2 Kings 1:16-17.

Joram

We read concerning Joram (also given as Jehoram) *"Now Jehoram the son of Ahab began to reign over Israel in Samaria the eighteenth year of Jehoshaphat king of Judah, and reigned twelve years. And he wrought evil in the sight of the Lord; but not like his father, and like his mother: for he put away the image of Baal that his father had made"* 2 Kings 3:1-2.

In preparing this section, a note of caution is needed as certain inferences are made that were not explicit in the narrative, beginning with two names for the same person, references to kings without stating names and the tie in between King Jehoshaphat and his successor, also named Jehoram, and if this author has got some of it wrong, he apologises!

Following on from the quote above there was a war with Mesha, king of Israel, which involved Jehoshaphat as Israel's ally, which we will treat as different to another conflict involving Moab, detailed in 2 Chronicles 20, discussed under Jehoshaphat. When we consider the accounts under the title: "*Elisha Traps Blinded Arameans*" (2 Kings 6:8-23) and "*Famine in Besieged Samaria*" (2 Kings 6:24-7:20), we will take it that it is Joram being referred to when the king of Israel is mentioned.

As with so many of the wayward kings of Israel, Joram's ending was a tragic one, when allied with the latest king of Judah, he was killed by Jehu, who became king in his place, and was on a mission to track down and kill all who remained from the house of Ahab.

Jehu

When the prophet sent by Elisha came to anoint Jehu, he came with these words "*… I have anointed thee king over the people of the Lord, even over Israel. And thou shalt smite the house of Ahab thy master, that I may avenge the blood of my servants the prophets, and the blood of all the servants of the Lord, at the hand of Jezebel. For the whole house of Ahab shall perish: …*" 2 Kings 9:6-8. Jehu went on to do what he was told to do with remarkable swiftness and zeal, killing all of Ahab's family and many associated with him, all those he could find who promoted Baal worship and, of course, Jezebel.

But the verdict on his reign was a mixed one and Israel was overpowered by Hazael, king of Syria, who had also been anointed by God for a task. "*Thus Jehu destroyed Baal out of Israel. Howbeit from the sins of Jeroboam the son of Nebat, who made Israel to sin, Jehu departed not from after them, to wit, the golden calves that were in Bethel, and that were in Dan. And the Lord said unto Jehu, Because thou hast done well in executing that which is right in mine eyes, and hast done unto the house of Ahab according to all that was in mine heart, thy children of the fourth generation shall sit on the throne of Israel. But Jehu took no heed to walk in the law of the Lord God of Israel with all his heart: for he departed not from the sins of Jeroboam, which made Israel to sin. In those days the Lord began to cut Israel short: and Hazael smote them in all the coasts of Israel*" 2 Kings 10:28-32.

Jehu's story is another one of what might have been. Having done what God asked of him, he did something that we know (as no doubt Jehu did too) was not what God wanted and would have disastrous consequences. We read toward the end of his reign how Hazael, the king of Aram/Syria, the one anointed to be king by the young prophet sent by Elisha, overpowered Israel throughout their territory, and as with the anointing, it was God who enabled all this to happen. While Israel had some successes contending with this new foe, Syria/Aram continued mostly to be a formidable threat.

Footnote and warning: There are many unexpected yet important lessons that can be drawn from the accounts of kings such as Jehu (who was one of the three people, along with Elisha and Hazael, that God told Elijah he was to anoint, which we can look back and see was for a good reason). One such lesson is pertaining to a timely meeting Jehu had with someone who has been mostly overlooked. This was Jehonadab, and we read of the meeting in 2 Kings 10:15-16. We can reflect on reading that 200 years later, in Jeremiah 35:6-10, we find out how Jehonadab had founded a "God-fearing movement", important enough for Jeremiah to cite him as an example of how people ought to act.

According to **Got Questions**: "*The Rechabites were a nomadic people group known for their strict rules to abstain from wine, from building houses, from sowing seed, and from planting vineyards (Jeremiah 35:6-7). The Rechabites were faithful to abide by these rules through the generations, all the way from the time of Jehu (2 Kings 10:15) to the time of Jeremiah (Jeremiah 35:8-10) – over 200 years. The Rechabites were descendants of Rechab, a Kenite and thus related to the Midianites and Moses' family by marriage (see Judges 1:16). According to Jeremiah 35:6, the Rechabites' strict rules were put in place by a son (or descendant) of Rechab named Jehonadab (or Jonadab). This is the same Jehonadab who helped Jehu rid Israel of Baal-worship after the time of Ahab (2 Kings 10:15–27). Scholars have differing opinions as to why Jehonadab implemented the rules, but many believe he sought to preserve the primitive lifestyle of his nomadic forebears. God used the faithfulness of the Rechabites to teach an important lesson to His people*". The tragedy is, having begun well, Jehu adopted his own set of sins.

Many of these lessons we might easily miss in our shortened journey through the kings of Israel, and we will mention another one that this author believes is of particular importance. Part of this author's remit and interest, besides Bible exegesis, is as a watchman on the wall and observing how that all three of the "*Great Reset*", "*Great Awakening*" and "*Great Deception*" play out at the same time.

While he sees the danger of the world moving toward globalism, partly as it will lead to the emergence of the final Antichrist, he sees the danger of the nationalist backlash, and of setting up nationalist idols as replacements to globalist ones, such as represented by those pushing the New World Order.

We know too that while Satan is the Prince of Darkness, he is more effective and does most damage as an angel of light. Jehu may have taken down Jezebel, the Ahab dynasty and Baal (which is why God told Elijah to anoint him), but by way of a replacement he promoted another kind of idolatry, one paralleling certain aspects of the false light when relating to patriotism, nationalism, and New Ageism.

Besides *"watch and pray"*, we need to *"test and weigh"*, and take heed of the lessons we can draw from the life of King Jehu. There is another danger, including one that the author faces with his wanting people to read his "words of wisdom" and it all relates to the lure of idolatry that played such a significant part in the downfall of both Israel and Judah. While we may, rightly, refuse to take sides in the globalist versus nationalist debate, seeing flaws in both, just as we might in the left versus right debate as ways to sort out the problems in our world, we do well to recognise the dangers and keep our eyes focused on the Lord. While Baal images or golden calves may not be our problem, we have been warned: *"Little children, keep yourselves from idols"* 1 John 5:21, for we could easily succumb.

I write this having recently spoken with a wise Indian brother about the persecution now being seen throughout India, including where I am staying as I write, in different, sometimes subtle ways (a huge subject beyond the scope of this book), and the positive part (according to him) played by Prime Minister Modi, seen as not a friend to Christians (or Muslims come to that), helping to stem the tide, whereas others see his pro-Hindu administration that fails to tackle injustices as the reason for the troubles. Pertinent to the globalist versus nationalist debate is that, unlike many world leaders, Modi is nationalist leaning. Just as in Bible times, we are faced with the prospect of having a bad king (e.g., Jehu) or a very bad king (e.g., Ahab) and recognising, now as then, that kings come and go and God is the one who imposes and deposes kings in the world and we need to be continually intreating him.

I would imagine that most reading this book will be living in supposedly free western democracies, although this is increasingly coming under attack (as argued elsewhere) and many cannot comprehend situations outside their experience, e.g., India, a country where there still is considerable corruption and injustice. An argument that we could develop is that throughout the world people (of all faiths and none) often have to pay a huge price for pursuing truth and doing what is right (which is something that as believer-priests who should be acting according to our conscience we ought to see as of paramount importance), and while taking actions that can be seen as being political may be frowned upon in some circles (e.g., including those that are close to this author) when one is told to leave the sorting out to God, yet whoever is "in charge" does matter and this is not something to be ignored, for all are affected one way or the other and we are called to love our neighbour.

There is no simple, straightforward response to the state of affairs we have identified, but we can begin by heeding the words of St. Paul: "*I exhort therefore, that, first of all, supplications, prayers, intercessions, and giving of thanks, be made for all men; For kings, and for all that are in authority; that we may lead a quiet and peaceable life in all godliness and honesty*" 1 Timothy 2:1-2.

Jehoahaz

In following the sins of Jeroboam, which was about worshipping golden calves, as opposed to Baal worship, begun by Jehoahaz's father Jehu, we find it continued under Jehoahaz. King Hazael continued to exert power over Israel, followed by his son, Ben-hadad. We do read that Jehoahaz sought the Lord, who provided a measure of deliverance from Aram's oppression and a season of security for the people, although it did not cause Jehoahaz/Israel to turn from his/their sin.

Jehoash

Jehoash, Jehoahaz's son, continued in like fashion to his father. We read under Amaziah, king of Judah, how the two went to war, instigated by Amaziah, with Jehoash coming off better. We also read of an exchange he had with the dying Elisha (detailed in **"Prophets of the Bible"**) where he was promised victory over the King of Aram, but while it could and should have been a complete victory, it would only be a partial one, based on the passage: "*And he said to the king of Israel, Put thine hand upon the bow. And he put his hand upon it: and Elisha put his hands upon the king's hands. And he said, Open the window eastward. And he opened it. Then Elisha said, Shoot. And he shot. And he said, The arrow of the Lord's deliverance, and the arrow of deliverance from Syria: for thou shalt smite the Syrians in Aphek, till thou have consumed them. And he said, Take the arrows. And he took them. And he said unto the king of Israel, Smite upon the ground. And he smote thrice, and stayed. And the man of God was wroth with him, and said, Thou shouldest have smitten five or six times; then hadst thou smitten Syria till thou hadst consumed it: whereas now thou shalt smite Syria but thrice*" 2 Kings 13-18.

Jeroboam II

Jeroboam II, Jehoash's son again continued in similar vein as Jeroboam I, and it appeared that in his 41 years as king he saw Israel live securely, in prosperity, with Jeroboam achieving some notable victories against Israel's enemies, taking back territory that had been taken from them. We read "*For the Lord saw the affliction of Israel, that it was very bitter: for there was not any shut up, nor any left, nor any helper for Israel. And the Lord said not that he would blot out the name of Israel from under heaven: but he saved them by the hand of Jeroboam the son of Joash"* 2 Kings 14:26-27. It was around that time that Amos and Hosea prophesied and from what these prophets said, Israel despite this new found peace and prosperity, were complacent and continued to sin against God. While Jeroboam II turned out to be an effective deliverer for his people, beating back enemies besides Syria (Aram) that had been oppressing the people, and giving stability and security, these warnings were mostly ignored.

Zechariah

Zechariah, son of Jeroboam, had a short reign. He continued on the same evil path as his family before him and was assassinated, in front of the people, by Shallum, who succeeded him as king. Notably, the writer of Kings brings up the point of fulfilled prophecy, in that Jehu's descendants would sit on the throne until the fourth generation, just as the prophet had said would happen.

Shallum

Shallum's reign was for one month and he too was assassinated by the one who would succeed him.

Menahem

Mehahem was evil and did some horrendous crimes. We now find Assyria entering the frame as the new power emerging in the region, with its king, Pul, invading Israel, and being paid off from extra taxes levied on the people, so that he would (and did) withdraw.

Pekahiah

Pekahiah was Menahem's son. He too was evil and again his reign was short – two years. He was assassinated, by Pekah, one of his officials.

Pekah

Pekah lasted 20 years and was evil like his predecessors. Some of his land was taken from him by Tiglath-Pileser, king of Assyria. Deporting some of the people to Assyria, began at this time, and would continue when all of Israel came under Assyrian control. We read how Pekah fought Ahaz and prevailed with God's help, killing 120,000 Judaean soldiers in a day, taking many captives. It is a salutary thought *"For Pekah the son of Remaliah slew in Judah an hundred and twenty thousand in one day, which were all valiant men; because they had forsaken the Lord God of their fathers"* 2 Chronicles

28:6. A prophet told Pekah to return the prisoners, which is what he did. Soon after, Pekah, allied with Rezin, king of Aram, marched to fight Ahaz, king of Judah, but was not successful for Ahaz had as an ally the king of Assyria. Rezin was killed and it likely marked the end of the kingdom of Aram. At the end, Pekah was assassinated, by Hoshea, who took over as king, likely doing so with the help of Tiglath-Pileser.

A pertinent, often overlooked aspect of this Pekah/Rezin alliance going against Ahaz but failing is the prophesy Isaiah gave to Ahaz, who was faced with such a daunting prospect and despite his wayward hypocrisy God would help Judah and His judgement would prevail. This *"Behold, a virgin shall conceive, and bear a son, and shall call his name Immanuel"* Isaiah 7:14 goes far beyond the Christmas story and illustrates how God is in control of world events: *"So Isaiah told him, "Then listen to this, government of David! It's bad enough that you make people tired with your pious, timid hypocrisies, but now you're making God tired. So the Master is going to give you a sign anyway. Watch for this: A girl who is presently a virgin will get pregnant. She'll bear a son and name him Immanuel (God-With-Us). By the time the child is twelve years old, able to make moral decisions, the threat of war will be over. Relax, those two kings that have you so worried will be out of the picture. But also be warned: God will bring on you and your people and your government a judgment worse than anything since the time the kingdom split, when Ephraim left Judah. The king of Assyria is coming!"* (7:13-17 The Message).

Hoshea

We now come to Hoshea, the last of a series of the kings of Israel described as being evil. He had come to power having killed his predecessor and reaching an accord with the king of Assyria but was found to be a traitor and was taken prisoner as a result. The end for Israel was a sorry one as they were deported and replaced by people from nations that Assyria had conquered, each worshipping their own god. A strange occurrence was the Lord sending wild animals into the land to afflict the people newly installed there and in response the king of Assyria sending a Levite from among the Israelite captives to teach those in the land the requirements of the god of that land so that god could be appeased. All to no avail and the result was a mishmash of religious practices.

When we consider the Assyrian threat for both Israel and later Judah we might summarise that the first exile was the expulsion from the Kingdom of Israel (Samaria) begun by Tiglath-Pileser III of Assyria in 733 BCE. This process was completed by Sargon II with the destruction of the kingdom in 722 BCE, concluding a three-year siege of Samaria begun by Shalmaneser V.

The Assyrian siege of Jerusalem (circa 701 BCE) was an aborted siege, carried out by Sennacherib (discussed in the previous chapter under Hezekiah). The next experience of exile concerned Judah and this was the Babylonian captivity, in which portions of the population of the Kingdom of Judah were deported in 597 BCE and again in 586 BCE by the Neo-Babylonian Empire under the rule of Nebuchadnezzar II.

The Kings' writer, before turning his attention to Judah, who would experience a similar fate, gives a scathing summary of why this tragic end to the Northern kingdom. There is nothing new among the reasons given – Israel was exiled because of sin. The people had forsaken God and His Covenant, disobeying his commandments, worshipping other gods and following the practices of the nations, and despite numerous warnings, especially through the prophets, continued to act wickedly, often doing so secretly (but not to God). And as we have noted, the last set of Israel kings were particularly evil, turning from the true God who wanted to have a covenant relationship with His people.

We could go on, but let the writer of Kings have the last word: *"And there they burnt incense in all the high places, as did the heathen whom the Lord carried away before them; and wrought wicked things to provoke the Lord to anger: For they served idols, whereof the Lord had said unto them, Ye shall not do this thing. Yet the Lord testified against Israel, and against Judah, by all the prophets, and by all the seers, saying, Turn ye from your evil ways, and keep my commandments and my statutes, according to all the law which I commanded your fathers, and which I sent to you by my servants the prophets. Notwithstanding they would not hear, but hardened their necks, like to the neck of their fathers, that did not believe in the Lord their God. And they rejected his statutes, and his covenant that he made with their fathers, and his testimonies which he testified against them; and they followed vanity, and became vain, and went after the heathen that were round about them, concerning whom the Lord had charged them, that they should not do like them. And they left all the commandments of the Lord their God, and made them molten images, even two calves, and made a grove, and worshipped all the host of heaven, and served Baal. And they caused their sons and their daughters to pass through the fire, and used divination and enchantments, and sold themselves to do evil in the sight of the Lord, to provoke him to anger. Therefore the Lord was very angry with Israel, and removed them out of his sight: there was none left but the tribe of Judah only"* 2 Kings 17:11-18.

One might ponder – what then concerning the ten northern tribes of Israel, sometimes referred to as the "ten lost tribes"? It is beyond the scope of this book to try and follow their tracks after being taken captive by Assyria until now. At least with the two southern tribes of Judah we can follow what next when they went into exile and afterward, although even then most became part of the diaspora while remarkably maintaining their Jewish identity. Rather than figure out something greater minds than this author have researched and given thought to, we will leave the last word to Ezekiel who looks forward to a day yet to come when among other things Israel and Judah will be united under David their king:

"Moreover, thou son of man, take thee one stick, and write upon it, For Judah, and for the children of Israel his companions: then take another stick, and write upon it, For Joseph, the stick of Ephraim and for all the house of Israel his companions: And join them one to another into one stick; and they shall become one in thine hand. And when the children of thy people shall speak unto thee, saying, Wilt thou not shew us what thou meanest by these? Say unto them, Thus saith the Lord God; Behold, I will take the stick of Joseph, which is in the hand of Ephraim, and the tribes of Israel his fellows, and will put them with him, even with the stick of Judah, and make them one stick, and they shall be one in mine hand. And the sticks whereon thou writest shall be in thine hand before their eyes. And say unto them, Thus saith the Lord God; Behold, I will take the children of Israel from among the heathen, whither they be gone, and will gather them on every side, and bring them into their own land: And I will make them one nation in the land upon the mountains of Israel; and one king shall be king to them all: and they shall be no more two nations, neither shall they be divided into two kingdoms any more at all. Neither shall they defile themselves any more with their idols, nor with their detestable things, nor with any of their transgressions: but I will save them out of all their dwellingplaces, wherein they have sinned, and will cleanse them: so shall they be my people, and I will be their God. And David my servant shall be king over them; and they all shall have one shepherd: they shall also walk in my judgments, and observe my statutes, and do them" Ezekiel 37:16-24.

If only the Kings of Israel (and the people) had heeded the words given by perhaps their greatest prophet, Elijah, who heard from God, such as on the occasion alluded to in the hymn below, on Mount Horeb, and told the people what God's expectations were. It was he who challenged the people: *"And Elijah came unto all the people, and said, How long halt ye between two opinions? if the Lord be God, follow him: but if Baal, then follow him. And the people answered him not a word"* 1 Kings 18:21. May we be those who hear from God, just as Elijah did, speaking to us in that still small voice.

1. Dear Lord and Father of mankind,
forgive our foolish ways;
reclothe us in our rightful mind,
in purer lives thy service find,
in deeper reverence, praise.

2. In simple trust like theirs who heard
beside the Syrian sea
the gracious calling of the Lord,
let us, like them, without a word
rise up and follow thee.

3. O Sabbath rest by Galilee,
O calm of hills above,
where Jesus knelt to share with thee
the silence of eternity,
interpreted by love!

4. Drop thy still dews of quietness,
till all our strivings cease;
take from our souls the strain and stress,
and let our ordered lives confess
the beauty of thy peace.

5. Breathe through the heats of our desire
thy coolness and thy balm;
let sense be dumb, let flesh retire;
speak through the earthquake, wind, and fire,
O still, small voice of calm!

Chapter 66: Kings of the Bible, not of Israel or Judah

In our previous 'Kings' Chapters (61-65), we have considered many kings of the Bible, and especially their kingdoms, who were not of Israel and Judah and, in many/most cases, in order to keep Part 4 as short as we can, we are not going to elaborate further. There are certain kingdoms, however, that keep cropping up over a long period of time and in various contexts, and because of their importance to the Bible narrative, we may like to say more, along with those kings and kingdoms that up to now have not been mentioned. But we will desist from saying too much more about those kings already mentioned: Edom, Moab, Philistine, Syria and Egypt, unless there is something significantly new to say arising out of happenings between the time of Judah's exile until the end of the Old Testament.

While from the outset we recognised that there were many who were kings who only reigned over a city or region, we find as the Bible story developed, there were kings of the great empires who we would want to cover because they are mentioned in the Bible, notably those we can identify from Nebuchadnezzar's dream in Daniel 2: Babylon, Persia, Greece and Rome (the last two, for reasons given in Chapter 61, we will omit). Kingdoms come and kingdoms go, along with their kings, who God raises up and puts down according to His sovereign will, as borne out in the Bible narrative.

By the time we get to the New Testament, the various nations that occupied the Promised Land, along with surrounding nations, such as: the Philistines (ruled by its five kings (Gaza, Ashkelon, Ashdod, Ekron, Gath), Moab, Edom, Syria and other kingdoms that we have touched on in these earlier chapters, most appearing to be no longer anywhere near the force they once were when compared with their heyday. We read about their demise in prophecies like those of Jeremiah (and also contemporaries like Zephaniah and Habakkuk), discussed in **"Prophets of the Bible"**.

It might be worth further considering the fate of Edom though, which can be traced back to Esau, the brother of Jacob. At the time Judah was displaced from their land as part of the Babylonian exile, Edom was displaced from theirs and then came to occupy some of the land of Judea that had been vacated. Then after the Exile and the partial return of the exiled Jews, Edom co-existed to some extent with Israel and even got to exercise certain influence, e.g., through the Herodian dynasty.

While some, for example, David Pawson, whose writings have often been referred to in this book, claim we lose track of Edom after the destruction of the Temple in 70 AD, others, such as is argued in **"The Roots of the Fed-**

eral Reserve – Tracing the Nephilim from Noah to the US Dollar" by Laura Sanger, point to evidence showing that the Edomites further migrated, including into Eastern Europe, with some following the example of Herod, converting to Judaism for political gain. Today, there are those that argue they form a significant percentage of the population that live in the land of Israel, who claim to be Jews. Sanger also argues that these Edomite descendants, such as the Rothchild banking family, are among those nefariously controlling today's world events, including from Israel, and are also linked to the Nephilim. In Chapter 42 it was argued that there is a powerful, nefarious cohort of those going under the label "Jew", but the extent of this influence and whether Edom/Nephilim related is beyond the scope of this book. Edom is also a main focus of the Book of Obadiah, along with its stern criticism.

"For thy violence against thy brother Jacob shame shall cover thee, and thou shalt be cut off for ever. In the day that thou stoodest on the other side, in the day that the strangers carried away captive his forces, and foreigners entered into his gates, and cast lots upon Jerusalem, even thou wast as one of them. But thou shouldest not have looked on the day of thy brother in the day that he became a stranger; neither shouldest thou have rejoiced over the children of Judah in the day of their destruction; neither shouldest thou have spoken proudly in the day of distress" Obadiah 1:10-12.

As for nations seen to be the main parts of empires, such as Egypt, which we began to look at early in the story of Abraham, they keep cropping up, right to the end of the kings of the Southern Kingdom. As for Assyria, they became a significant force toward the end of the period of the Northern Kingdom and forcibly took over Israel, and then taking the Israelites into captivity and making them live in other parts of their empire. For the most part, we then lose track of the Ten Tribes, as they were replaced in the land they had previously occupied by captives from other nations that were put there.

Assyria is the main focus of two of the prophetic books of the Bible: Jonah and Nahum. As a result of Jonah's message that God was going to destroy Ninevah, upon hearing the message and as led by their king, they repented and God relented. When later Nahum gave a similar message, God's warning of judgment was carried out. While we get an inkling in the Bible account, beginning from reading how the reign of Josiah ended up, as well as from extra biblical sources, the newly emergent empire of Babylon conquered both Egypt and Assyria, who had itself previously conquered Syria. We read in Wikipedia: *"The Battle of Carchemish was fought around 605 BC between the armies of Egypt allied with the remnants of the army of the former Assyrian Empire against the armies of Babylonia, allied with the Medes, Persians, and Scythians. This was while Nebuchadnezzar was com-*

mander-in-chief and Nabopolassar was still king of Babylon. Nebuchad-nezzar became king after this battle."

Of the four kingdoms alluded to in Nebuchadnezzar's dream in Daniel 2, regarding the image Daniel saw in that dream, and which he was able to interpret, only Babylon had reached its peak in terms of power at the time. As far as the Bible accounts go the three other kingdoms were yet to become significant powers in terms of extending their empires: Persia, Greece and Rome. Only Rome was still a notable power when we come to the New Testament, although looking ahead to the End Times, we find mention of the revived Roman empire alluded to at the end of the dream and the fall of Babylon the Great, which is described in Revelation 17 and 18, and which has profound prophetic significance.

One empire arises and later falls to another empire, that then becomes the dominant power. As far as we can make out from the Bible accounts, empires like that of the Egyptians and Assyrians were overtaken by that of Babylon, and then by Persia, then by Greece, and then by Rome, leaving us at the end of the Bible with Rome being the major power. It too would eventually fall. With respect to Nebuchadnezzar's (Daniel 2) dream, while most commentators are agreed as to what the head (Babylon), breast (Persia), belly (Greece) and legs (Rome) of the statue represents, there is debate concerning the meaning of the feet and toes. Some see these as a revived Roman empire either historically or one that will come, e.g., an alliance of kings associated with the yet to emerge Antichrist: *"And the ten horns which thou sawest are ten kings, which have received no kingdom as yet; but receive power as kings one hour with the beast"* Revelation 17:12 (which we discuss further below).

Looking into the future, past the present day (how far we can't say), we read of a king still to come that some see as King Jesus who has yet to return: *"And in the days of these kings shall the God of heaven set up a kingdom, which shall never be destroyed: and the kingdom shall not be left to other people, but it shall break in pieces and consume all these kingdoms, and it shall stand for ever. Forasmuch as thou sawest that the stone was cut out of the mountain without hands, and that it brake in pieces the iron, the brass, the clay, the silver, and the gold; the great God hath made known to the king what shall come to pass hereafter: and the dream is certain, and the interpretation thereof sure"* Daniel 2:44-45.

While the Old Testament, from Genesis 12 to the end, is focused on Israel and when other nations (along with or often without their kings) are mentioned it is often because they had a part to play in Israel's story. It is worth noting that right from the outset when God called Abraham, from whom Israel came as a fulfilment of God's promise to him, we find God was interested in other nations for reasons other than their involvement with Israel and how they had treated God's specially chosen people.

There are many indications in the Old Testament of God's interest in nations besides that of Israel, for reasons besides having a part to play in Israel's story, for example, in the pronouncements by various Hebrew prophets. After all, *"the sins of the Amorites"* mentioned by God to Abraham in Genesis 15, and for which centuries later they would be judged, had little to do with Israel. God judges nations for their unrighteous acts, irrespective of whether or not they know about the God of the Bible. The mission for today's Church is both a solemn and an urgent one – to preach the Gospel to ALL nations.

Not just Amos, as mentioned in Chapter 61, but prophets like Jeremiah, which we will consider in this chapter, had much to say on the matter of God's dealings with nations outside of Israel and Judah. In the New Testament and afterward, the focus begins to switch from the Jews as part of a nation, albeit one under occupation, toward the Gentiles and the church, which brings in people from all nations. They, like this author, do not ignore the reality that we live in nations ruled by the modern equivalent of kings, many/most of which are not sympathetic to Christian belief – but that is for another book!

Jeremiah

As far as this chapter is concerned, we will focus on Babylon and Persia and two kings in particular: Nebuchadnezzar and Cyrus, followed by other named kings in their two empires. But firstly, we will consider Jeremiah, the prophet. We could choose from several other prophets to make our point that God is interested in nations other than Israel, sometimes acting in mercy but often in judgment; sometimes because of the way they treated Israel but also due to their own wickedness (reference *"the sins of the Amorites"*, discussed earlier). But we choose Jeremiah as he provides a commentary of the previous three chapters concerning kings of Israel and Judah, which while there were highlights of the people doing what was required of them concerning the Mosaic Covenant, too often they did the opposite and suffered the consequences. Jeremiah had an interest in those kings of nations other than Israel and Judah, in particular the surrounding nations, and when Israel and Judah had no king.

A lot of the Book of Jeremiah is about him warning Judah of the consequences of their sin and inviting them to turn back to God until the point came when it was too late. The Book tells us how he carried out what as a young man he was told by God to do: *"I have this day set thee over the nations and over the kingdoms, to root out, and to pull down, and to destroy, and to throw down, to build, and to plant"* Jeremiah 1:10, for a period of 40 years, during which time he saw it all. While a lot of Jeremiah's prophesying was directed to those living in Judah and it was a message of condemnation and judgment, there was a message of hope and mercy.

He also prophesied concerning surrounding nations and, extensively, the nation/empire that was going to be the instrument of God's judgment – Babylon. Chapters 46-51 records prophecies about the destruction of several nations surrounding Israel and why each would be destroyed. Jeremiah prophesied that Egypt (Chapter 46), Philistia (Chapter 47), Moab (Chapter 48), Ammon (Chapter 49:1–6), Edom (Chapter 49:7–22), Damascus (Chapter 49:23–27), Kedar (Chapter 49:28–29), Hazor (Chapter 49:30–33), Elam (Chapter 49:34–39), and Babylon (Chapter 50–51) would all be destroyed.

Jeremiah was a contemporary of Josiah (the last good king) and later lived under the reigns of Kings Jehoahaz, Jehoiakim, Jehoiachin and Zedekiah up to the time and just after Jerusalem was destroyed by the Babylonians when those, who were not yet already taken, were taken into Babylonian captivity. These kings all appear in the Book of Jeremiah, from which we can pick up more about their characters and events taking place. While Josiah was commended for acting in a righteous way, the others were condemned in the harshest of terms. Jeremiah is often portrayed as the prophet of doom and gloom.

When it comes to Josiah, other than to recognise Josiah as one of the good kings and composing a lament upon his death, which we no longer have access to, he does not have much more to say, perhaps realising that Josiah's best efforts were too little, too late. Jeremiah was opposed by prophets, priests and kings and suffered much by way of humiliation and imprisonment, which did not deter him.

That is not the case with the kings who followed. Jeremiah was devastating in his criticism of their acts that could be truly described as evil and breaking the Covenant agreed under Moses, and he would continue right until the end banging the drum concerning Israel's sin and God's forthcoming judgement (which all came to pass). He urged Judah's inhabitants to accept their fate rather than resist, which advice was largely ignored. Unsurprisingly, he would be well-treated by the Babylonians. His forthrightness did come at a price though, for he was treated abysmally by those same kings, and those close to them, including prophets and priests, and Jeremiah was barely able to escape with his life.

Jeremiah was far from alone when declaring God's displeasure and the consequences of continuing in a state of rebellion to God. We already read in Chapter 65 how Huldah had prophesied to Josiah what would happen. Then there was wise counsel in the light of some calling for Jeremiah's death, that under King Hezekiah, a prophet named Micah of Moresheth prophesied in a similar vein and it led Hezekiah to fear the Lord and seek His favour. Yet another prophet, Uriah, prophesied at the same time as Jeremiah and on similar lines, but he was hunted down and put to death. Also, two prophets who were contemporaries of Jeremiah: Zephaniah and Habakkuk, prophesied judgement. Then there was Ezekiel who had been exiled to Babylon some years prior to the final fall of Jerusalem. He too was prophesying concerning Judah and its sins, and in ways that complemented all of the above. It seems that God was going out of His way to ensure the people got the message, but it was all to little avail.

As with a number of the writing prophets, Jeremiah was not just concerned with what was going to happen to Israel or Judah but with other nations too, typically the ones they had dealings with. What is interesting in Jeremiah's case is that the nations he prophesied concerning had all played a part in our consideration of kings before Jeremiah appeared on the scene. Most were to fall, just like Judah, and some never to rise again. His final other nation prophesy concerns Babylon and it is a lot longer than all of the rest. Much we now know was fulfilled although how much also carries over to the Fall of Babylon described in Revelation 17 and 18 has to be a study for another day. What appears to be clear is that the spirit of Babylon, going back to the Tower of Babel in Genesis 11, continues to live on.

While Jeremiah is best known for prophesying what would happen to Judah because of their sin, he was also able to look into the future, not just immediately after their exile, but far into a future that is yet to happen, under their Messiah: "*Call unto me, and I will answer thee, and shew thee great and mighty things, which thou knowest not ... And I will cause the captivity of Judah and the captivity of Israel to return, and will build them, as at the first. And I will cleanse them from all their iniquity, whereby they have sinned against me; and I will pardon all their iniquities, whereby they have sinned, and whereby they have transgressed against me. And it shall be to me a name of joy, a praise and an honour before all the nations of the earth, which shall hear all the good that I do unto them: and they shall fear and tremble for all the goodness and for all the prosperity that I procure unto it ... Behold, the days come, saith the Lord, that I will perform that good thing which I have promised unto the house of Israel and to the house of Judah. In those days, and at that time, will I cause the Branch of righteousness to grow up unto David; and he shall execute judgment and righteousness in the land. In those days shall Judah be saved, and Jerusalem shall dwell safely: and this is the name wherewith she shall be called, The Lord our righteousness. For thus saith the Lord; David shall never want a man to sit upon the throne of the house of Israel*" Jeremiah 33: 3, 7-9, 14-17.

Nebuchadnezzar

Nebuchadnezzar II is mentioned by name 91 times in the Bible (2 Kings (8), 1 Chronicles (1), 2 Chronicles (5), Ezra (5), Nehemiah (1), Esther (1), Jeremiah (37), Ezekiel (5), Daniel (28)). There are also a good deal of secular history references to Nebuchadnezzar and his reign.

According to Wikipedia: *"Nebuchadnezzar II was the second king of the Neo-Babylonian Empire, ruling from the death of his father Nabopolassar in 605 BC to his own death in 562 BC. Historically known as Nebuchadnezzar the Great, he is typically regarded as the empire's greatest king. Nebuchadnezzar remains famous for his military campaigns in the Levant, for his construction projects in his capital, Babylon, and for the important part he played in Jewish history. Ruling for 43 years, Nebuchadnezzar was the longest-reigning king of the Chaldean dynasty. At the time of his death, Nebuchadnezzar was among the most powerful rulers in the world"*.

We have been reminded that God controls kings, even the bad ones, and King Nebuchadnezzar is an excellent example. As far as Jeremiah was concerned, he was God's instrument for judgement and while his counsel was shunned, things would have gone better if his counsel had been heeded. When we consider King Nebuchadnezzar in the first four chapters of the Book of Daniel, through the eyes of Daniel the prophet, who had been exiled to Babylon as a result of his land of Judah being conquered by Babylon, it is clear that what was going on around him was not something that could be ignored and nor was it something God was indifferent to. While as one of the upper echelons of Judean society taken into captivity, Daniel was limited in what he could do, we see in these chapters that Daniel did much to make a difference. Strangely enough, and despite our focus being on kings rather than prophets, that relationship between Daniel and Nebuchadnezzar changed the course of history.

We should remind ourselves that Nebuchadnezzar was probably the most powerful man on the planet during his reign. He had conquered both Assyria and Egypt, the empires that were Israel and Judah's greatest opposition (Israel, having already been conquered by Assyria). He was also responsible for some remarkable projects (not least one of the seven wonders of the ancient world – the Hanging Gardens of Babylon). From a human perspective, he could take pride in his achievements. While depicted as a cruel ruler, he could also show generosity and, from what we can make out, the Judean exiles in Babylon lived in relative peace. He selected four young Judeans: Daniel and his friends Shadrach, Meshach and Abednego, whose talents he recognised, to serve in his government, and they did so with distinction. These were also God-fearing men who rejected the gods of Babylon, and at the start made their intentions clear by refusing to eat food sacrificed to idols.

Nebuchadnezzars dream, which only Daniel could interpret under God's guidance, was a remarkable one concerning the rise and fall of kingdoms, starting with Babylon, with one everlasting kingdom still to come. The king, in recognising Daniel's extraordinary gifts, then promoted Daniel to a high position in his administration. It is a useful lesson, but Daniel, along with his three friends, was able to show how godly people can still serve and contribute even amidst ungodly rulers. Nevertheless, the resolve they showed was tested, when it would have been easier to make compromises. The evil nature of Nebuchadnezzar could be seen when he commissioned an image to be erected in his own likeness, which people were expected to bow down to and worship. Not so Shadrach, Meshach and Abednego, who were thrown into the fiery furnace for refusing to worship the image, from which God delivered them, with Nebuchadnezzar recognising He is God as a result.

Despite seeing the hand of God at work on two occasions, we later find recorded in Daniel 4, that Nebuchadnezzar was proud of his position and achievements, but God showed him through a dream that he had been found gravely wanting. Again, Daniel interpreted the king's dream, revealing what God thought and what He was going to do. Nebuchadnezzar needed to humble himself, or else he would experience personal calamity. Daniel's warning *"Wherefore, O king, let my counsel be acceptable unto thee, and break off thy sins by righteousness, and thine iniquities by shewing mercy to the poor; if it may be a lengthening of thy tranquillity"* (4:27) was ignored and 12 months later he heard the words *"O king Nebuchadnezzar, to thee it is spoken; The kingdom is departed from thee. And they shall drive thee from men, and thy dwelling shall be with the beasts of the field: they shall make thee to eat grass as oxen, and seven times shall pass over thee, until thou know that the most High ruleth in the kingdom of men, and giveth it to whomsoever he will"* (4:31-32) and it was so for seven years.

But there was to be a wonderful turnaround, Nebuchadnezzar recognised the true God and his kingdom was restored. It is best we end with Nebuchadnezzar's own words and then we can ponder their significance: *"And at the end of the days I Nebuchadnezzar lifted up mine eyes unto heaven, and mine understanding returned unto me, and I blessed the most High, and I praised and honoured him that liveth for ever, whose dominion is an everlasting dominion, and his kingdom is from generation to generation: And all the inhabitants of the earth are reputed as nothing: and he doeth according to his will in the army of heaven, and among the inhabitants of the earth: and none can stay his hand, or say unto him, What doest thou? At the same time my reason returned unto me; and for the glory of my kingdom, mine honour and brightness returned unto me; and my counsellors and my lords sought unto me; and I was established in my kingdom, and excellent majesty was added unto me. Now I Nebuchadnezzar praise and extol and honour the King of heaven, all whose works are truth, and his ways judgment: and those that walk in pride he is able to abase"* Daniel 4:34-37.

As an afterthought to this reflection on the life and significance of King Nebuchadnezzar, we might deduce, just from the Bible, that He was one of the worst of all the kings, yet God was not done with him. While he had to be truly chastened, there was a good ending for the king and for the world he influenced, for it brought about repentance and restoration. As we consider bad kings today, of which there are many, it is worth being reminded not just concerning God's judgement but also of His grace, and it is worth bearing in mind as we pray, as we are exhorted to do, for our rulers. And for us too, it may be that God may deal with us roughly because He wants to get our attention.

Excuse the use of the first person here, but after writing the above concerning Nebuchadnezzar, the pastor of my church preached concerning this king and he related the story that is outlined above to the subject of mental health, which is not a connection I had made previously, despite my interest in and insights into this subject. Few moderns who consider the subject of mental health would dispute that, during the period he had been deposed from his kingdom, Nebuchadnezzar had a mental health problem that went far deeper than with those we typically come across these days, such as depression. It is likely he was experiencing symptoms of schizophrenia. This touched a particular chord with me, not just because of my own mental health journey but a good deal of the work I did as a community activist (discussed in Chapter 56) was in the area of mental health.

In some cases, mental ill health is as a result of pride, arrogance and rebellion against God, just as it was with King Nebuchadnezzar, but likely not in most. Triggers, as I have argued in my earlier writings, are many and various and so are the cures and remedies. It does not surprise me when I come across many experiencing mental health problems today. Speaking personally, there is much going on around me that is not right and frankly, it blows my mind. If there is hope from our story, it is the lesson we learn that someone who had been experiencing mental ill health at its worse, when he acknowledged and turned to God, went on to experience mental good health at its best. I have long learned there are no simplistic solutions, especially as appears to be the case that many who "suffer" are Christians trying to come to terms with today's craziness, and we serve them best when we show compassion.

Some time later, toward the end of the exile period, when one of Nebuchadnezzar's descendants, Belshazzar, was king, we read an account (in Daniel 5) whereby this king displayed the same pride and arrogance that

Nebuchadnezzar had done. God showed his displeasure by the "writing on the wall", which Daniel alone was able to interpret that his kingdom was to be taken from him. That very same night that is what happened when King Darius entered the city and overran the Babylonians.

Between Nebuchadnezzar and Belshazzar, there was another king of Babylon mentioned in the Bible. This was Evilmerodach, who acted in an unexpectedly kind way toward the exiled king of Judah, Jehoiachin: *"And it came to pass in the seven and thirtieth year of the captivity of Jehoiachin king of Judah, in the twelfth month, on the seven and twentieth day of the month, that Evilmerodach king of Babylon in the year that he began to reign did lift up the head of Jehoiachin king of Judah out of prison; And he spake kindly to him, and set his throne above the throne of the kings that were with him in Babylon; And changed his prison garments: and he did eat bread continually before him all the days of his life. And his allowance was a continual allowance given him of the king, a daily rate for every day, all the days of his life"* 2 Kings 25:27-30.

Cyrus

Cyrus the Great had an enormous influence in bringing back the exiled Jews from Babylon to their ancestral home. According to Wikipedia: *"Cyrus II of Persia commonly known as Cyrus the Great, was the founder of the Achaemenid Persian Empire. Hailing from Persis, he brought the Achaemenid dynasty to power by defeating the Median Empire and embracing all of the previous civilized states of the ancient Near East, expanding vastly and eventually conquering most of West Asia and much of Central Asia to create the world's then-largest polity. The Achaemenid Empire's largest territorial extent was achieved under the rule of Cyrus' successor Darius the Great, whose rule stretched from the Balkans (Eastern Bulgaria–Paeonia and Thrace–Macedonia) and the rest of Southeast Europe in the west to the Indus Valley in the east ... Following the Achaemenid conquest of Babylon, Cyrus issued the Edict of Restoration, in which he authorized and encouraged the return of the Jewish people to the former Kingdom of Judah, officially ending the Babylonian captivity. He is described in the Hebrew Bible and left a lasting legacy on Judaism due to his role in facilitating the "return to Zion" of the Jews. According to Chapter 45:1 of the Book of Isaiah, Cyrus was anointed by the God of Israel for this task as a biblical messiah; Cyrus is the only non-Jewish figure to be revered in this capacity. Cyrus is also recognized for his achievements in human rights, politics, and military strategy, as well as his influence on the traditions of both the Eastern world and the Western world. Achaemenid influence in the ancient world would eventually extend as far west as Athens, where upper-class Athenians adopted aspects of the culture of the ruling class of Achaemenid Persia as their own. As the found-*

er of the first Persian empire, Cyrus has played a crucial role in defining the national identity of the Iranian nation; the Achaemenid Empire was instrumental in spreading the ideals of Zoroastrianism as far east as China. He remains a cult figure in modern-day Iran, with the Tomb of Cyrus serving as a spot of reverence for millions of the country's citizens".

Two hundred years earlier, Isaiah prophesied concerning Cyrus: *"Thus saith the Lord to his anointed, to Cyrus, whose right hand I have holden, to subdue nations before him; and I will loose the loins of kings, to open before him the two leaved gates; and the gates shall not be shut; I will go before thee, and make the crooked places straight: I will break in pieces the gates of brass, and cut in sunder the bars of iron: And I will give thee the treasures of darkness, and hidden riches of secret places, that thou mayest know that I, the Lord, which call thee by thy name, am the God of Israel. For Jacob my servant's sake, and Israel mine elect, I have even called thee by thy name: I have surnamed thee, though thou hast not known me. I am the Lord, and there is none else, there is no God beside me: I girded thee, though thou hast not known me: That they may know from the rising of the sun, and from the west, that there is none beside me. I am the Lord, and there is none else"* Isaiah 45:1-6.

The Book of Ezra begins at the same point the book of Chronicles ends and it was on an optimistic note: *"Now in the first year of Cyrus king of Persia, that the word of the Lord by the mouth of Jeremiah might be fulfilled, the Lord stirred up the spirit of Cyrus king of Persia, that he made a proclamation throughout all his kingdom, and put it also in writing, saying, Thus saith Cyrus king of Persia, The Lord God of heaven hath given me all the kingdoms of the earth; and he hath charged me to build him an house at Jerusalem, which is in Judah. Who is there among you of all his people? his God be with him, and let him go up to Jerusalem, which is in Judah, and build the house of the Lord God of Israel, (he is the God,) which is in Jerusalem. And whosoever remaineth in any place where he sojourneth, let the men of his place help him with silver, and with gold, and with goods, and with beasts, beside the freewill offering for the house of God that is in Jerusalem."* Ezra 1:1-4.

It is a great turn-around in the fortunes of those who had been exiled, demonstrating too how the prophecies of Isaiah and Jeremiah were able to be fulfilled, when Israel found itself in a predicament that appeared to have no way out. Cyrus was a remarkable figure, an enlightened king (as the extra-biblical accounts affirm) and one who can be truly said to have been anointed by God for a purpose and did what God wanted from him. He gave all the help that might be expected. It was a great opportunity to return to the land and rebuild; one that was taken up but only partially. As for Cyrus, the anointed of God, given the state of the world today, how much we wish for a modern-day Cyrus.

Not only was Cyrus a king who played an important and positive role in Israel's fortunes after he came to power, but the same can be said for other kings of Persia, who while sometimes fickle were often kindly disposed toward Israel, unlike the Greeks and Romans that followed. Much of what we read in the Bible ties in with the historical record. We list the relevant kings along with where they crop up in the Bible in Chapter 2, Figure 36. Pinning down actual kings to where in the Bible they crop up can be a debatable matter. We will do so according to where they appear in books of the Bible.

Daniel: The Persian king that Daniel had dealings with was Darius, following his taking over from Belshazzar. Darius recognised Daniel's qualities and promoted him to a high position within his administration. This caused jealousy among Daniel's contemporaries, who managed to persuade Darius to issue a decree that no prayer should be made other than to him, something Daniel refused to do, despite knowing he would be killed for not complying. This led Darius to reluctantly order Daniel to be cast into the lion's den. Miraculously, Daniel survived, much to the king's delight, who punished Daniel's accusers in the same way they had plotted for it to happen with Daniel.

At the end, we read of the king honouring the God of Daniel: "*I make a decree, That in every dominion of my kingdom men tremble and fear before the God of Daniel: for he is the living God, and stedfast for ever, and his kingdom that which shall not be destroyed, and his dominion shall be even unto the end. He delivereth and rescueth, and he worketh signs and wonders in heaven and in earth, who hath delivered Daniel from the power of the lions. So this Daniel prospered in the reign of Darius, and in the reign of Cyrus the Persian*" Daniel 6:26-28.

Ezra: Following the first set of returnees, we read in the Book of Ezra concerning the rebuilding of the Temple and of the social life, and how the Israelites were given the freedom and resources to do so under King Cyrus. Building work began with enthusiasm but then halted, partly due to those who were in opposition, who managed to stir up trouble with Kings Xerxes and Artaxerxes, the latter ordering work to stop. Later, another Persian king, Darius, reversed the order because of the decree of Cyrus, and the work resumed. Some 80 years after that first return, Ezra led a further return and was supported and given provisions by another king, Artaxerxes, to rebuild the religious life.

Esther: It is likely the story of Esther happened between these first and second returns of the Exiles from Babylon. She became the queen to King Xerxes after his former wife had displeased him, and what we read in the Book of Esther is a series of God incidences even though God is not mentioned. The most important one was her role, along with Xerxes and her uncle Mordecai, in preventing what might have been the total annihilation of the Jewish people if wicked Haman had had his way.

Nehemiah: He led the third set of returnees from Exile, and was responsible as governor for rebuilding the physical life, notably the wall. He was the cupbearer to King Artaxerxes, who gave his full support, after Nehemiah had informed the king on the sorry state of the exiles that had returned to Judah; support which was much needed given the opposition by some of the non-Jews in the land.

King of Tyre

Having made the point that Part 4 is meant, at best, to provide an introduction to kings of the Bible, and while there is a lot about nations other than Israel and Judah, and their kings, that could be said that we will not say as we do not want to make this longer than we ought, but we will make an exception in the case of Tyre (or Tyrus) and Sidon. We do so for various reasons and here are two: Firstly, circumstances and events around God's judgment of Tyre bear similarities to that concerning other nations, and are illustrative. Like many of these other nations, reasons for God's judgement included it being a response to both Tyre's own wickedness and its hostile attitude toward Israel. Secondly, there are a number of lessons we can draw, over and above God merely judging a nation, which are worth considering. Before we do so, we quote from an article titled "*What is the significance of the city of Tyre in the Bible?*" in **Got Questions**, giving us much by way of relevant background.

"Tyre is thought to be one of the oldest cities on the Phoenician coast, established long before the Israelites entered the land of Canaan. Isaiah affirms Tyre's ancient origins as "from days of old" (Isaiah 23:5-7). Tyre is situated on the Mediterranean coast directly north of Jerusalem between the mountains of Lebanon and the Mediterranean Sea, about 20 miles south of Sidon and 23 miles north of Acre. Neighboring Sidon is believed to be the oldest Phoenician city, but Tyre's history is more distinguished. The name Tyre (Tzor in Hebrew) signifies "a rock," an apt description for the rocky coastal fortress. In ancient times, Tyre flourished as a maritime city and a busy center for commercial trade. The area's most valuable export was its then world-famous purple dye.

Originally, the ancient city was divided into two parts: an older port city ("Old Tyre") located on the mainland and a small rocky island about a half-mile off the coast where most of the population resided ("New Tyre" or "insular Tyre"). The island has been connected to the mainland ever since Alexander the Great built a siege ramp to it in the fourth century BC. The causeway has widened over the centuries, creating Tyre's current-day peninsular formation.

The Bible first mentions Tyre in a list of cities that were part of the inheritance of the tribe of Asher (Joshua 19:24–31). Fortified with a wall, Tyre held an exceedingly strong position. It was the only city in the list described as "strong" or "fortified" (verse 29). Joshua was unable to capture Tyre (Joshua 13:3–4), and, evidently, it was never conquered by the Israelites (2 Samuel 24:7).

By the time of King David's reign, Israel had formed a friendly alliance with Hiram king of Tyre. David used stonemasons and carpenters from Tyre, along with cedars from that region to build his palace (2 Samuel 5:11). Peaceful relations with King Hiram continued into Solomon's reign, with the construction of the temple in Jerusalem relying heavily on supplies, laborers, and skilled artisans from Tyre (1 Kings 5:1–14; 9:11; 2 Chronicles 2:3).

Israel continued to share close ties with Tyre during King Ahab's reign. Ahab married the Phoenician princess Jezebel, daughter of Ethbaal, king of Sidon, and their union led to the infiltration of pagan worship and idolatry in Israel (1 Kings 16:31). Both Tyre and Sidon were notorious for their wickedness and idolatry, which resulted in numerous denouncements by Israel's prophets, who predicted Tyre's ultimate destruction (Isaiah 23:1; Jeremiah 25:22; Ezekiel 28:1–19; Joel 3:4; Amos 1:9–10; Zechariah 9:2–4). One of the most detailed prophecies of Tyre's demise is in Ezekiel: "They will destroy the walls of Tyre and pull down her towers; I will scrape away her rubble and make her a bare rock. Out in the sea she will become a place to spread fishnets, for I have spoken, declares the Sovereign Lord. She will become plunder for the nations" (Ezekiel 26:4–5).

After the restoration of Jerusalem in Nehemiah's time (c. 450 BC), the people of Tyre violated the Sabbath rest by selling their goods in the markets of Jerusalem (Nehemiah 13:16). In 332 BC, after a seven-month siege, Alexander the Great conquered Tyre, putting an end to Phoenician political control, but the city retained its economic power."

Tyre is also mentioned several times in the New Testament but we will focus here on what Ezekiel, Chapters 26-28, has to say. Up to this point in his prophecy, Ezekiel, who had come to Babylon as part of the Exile, was prophesying against Judah and Jerusalem. Before prophesying about Israel's future, from Chapter 33 onwards, he turns his attention to other nations, writing at the time of the Fall of Jerusalem in 586 BC: Amon, Moab, Edom, Philistia (Chapter 25) and Egypt (Chapter 29-32). Concerning Tyre, we can breakdown the relevant chapters into: "Prophecy Against Tyre" (Chapter 26), "A Lament Over Tyre" (Chapter 27) and "A Prophecy Against the King of Tyre" (Chapter 28).

We begin in Chapter 26 with Tyre taking delight in Jerusalem's demise and

God responding that He will destroy Tyre, which He does, beginning under King Nebuchadnezzar and later completed under Alexander the Great, much to the consternation of surrounding nations who had traded with the very prosperous Tyre. The prophecy regarding the destruction of Tyre that meant building a causeway from the mainland to the island is a remarkable one insofar this is not something that could have been humanly predicted. Chapter 27 builds on the fact that Tyre was a prosperous trading state and as such was proud of its achievements, power and wealth, but all this was going to be taken away. "*'As you crisscrossed the seas with your products, you satisfied many peoples. Your worldwide trade made earth's kings rich. And now you're battered to bits by the waves, sunk to the bottom of the sea, And everything you've bought and sold has sunk to the bottom with you. Everyone on shore looks on in terror. The hair of kings stands on end, their faces drawn and haggard! The buyers and sellers of the world throw up their hands: This horror can't happen! Oh, this has happened!'*" (27:33-36 The Message).

Chapter 28 is extraordinary in that it tells the story of two kings of Tyre. The first king (other translations has it as prince or ruler) is in 28:1-10. God does not mince words: "*Son of man, say unto the prince of Tyrus, Thus saith the Lord God; Because thine heart is lifted up, and thou hast said, I am a God, I sit in the seat of God, in the midst of the seas; yet thou art a man, and not God, though thou set thine heart as the heart of God ... Therefore thus saith the Lord God; Because thou hast set thine heart as the heart of God; Behold, therefore I will bring strangers upon thee, the terrible of the nations: and they shall draw their swords against the beauty of thy wisdom, and they shall defile thy brightness*" (28:2, 6-7).

The second king in 28:11-19, which many commentators take to be Satan (evidenced by e.g., "*Thou hast been in Eden the garden of God*" 28:13 and "*Thou art the anointed cherub that covereth*" 28:14) is the spiritual entity that controls and relates to the physical ruler. We read of a portrayal of one who was perhaps the most perfect of God's angelic creation but who chose to rebel against God but whose end is assured. For those of us trying to make sense of earthly rulers, both in Bible times and today, it is a salutary reminder that behind what we can see are evil angelic beings that we do not see but we are reminded in passages like these that they are real. Our job is to resist Satan and stand with God.

As we come to the end of Chapter 28, we first consider Sidon (28:20-23) and then Israel in the future (28:24-25). The verdict on Sidon and its end is much the same as that of Tyre. What is significant as far as this book is concerned, because it is a recurring theme, is that it brings together three aspects of God's character and shows yet again the way He deals with humanity: according to His holiness, His glory and His judgement. Along with Egypt, also a subject of Ezekiel's other nation prophecies, these were at the time among the two greatest powers, but both were proud, and their fates were sealed.

As for Israel in the future, it is a wonderful one. *"No longer will Israel have to put up with their thistle-and-thorn neighbors who have treated them so contemptuously. And they also will realize that I am God. God, the Master, says, "When I gather Israel from the peoples among whom they've been scattered and put my holiness on display among them with all the nations looking on, then they'll live in their own land that I gave to my servant Jacob. They'll live there in safety. They'll build houses. They'll plant vineyards, living in safety. Meanwhile, I'll bring judgment on all the neighbors who have treated them with such contempt. And they'll realize that I am God"* (28:24-26 The Message).

Significantly, as far as this book is concerned, is what we learn about the future of Israel. In Chapter 52: *"Israel – Yesterday, Today and Tomorrow"*, we do not let modern day Israel off the hook concerning what is going on as we write – and neither does God. Moreover, as heartwarming as our quoted text is, it was *not* fulfilled in its entirety when Israel returned from Exile and neither has it been completely fulfilled after Israel again became a sovereign state in 1948. But one day it will be, and we know that because 2500 years ago Ezekiel the prophet saw beyond what we see and wrote down what he saw.

Antichrist and Christ

We have deliberately focused on kings that were around when the Bible was written. Future kings are covered in **"Prophets of the Bible"** as this is to do with end times prophecy. Since Part 4 of this book is about Kings of the Bible, it would be remiss of us if we did not say something that is significant about two very important kings that are prophesied many times in the Bible as yet to come: the Antichrist and the Christ. For one reason, they are more significant than any of the kings covered so far. In the case of the Antichrist, he is the embodiment of all that is evil, matched with great power. In the case of the Christ, He is not only the final king of the Bible, He is also the best and, according to Christians, the third person of the Trinity and the King of kings who, when He comes (again), will rule over all.

It is tempting to write at length on the subject of the Antichrist but, other than providing a few thoughts, we will resist the temptation. Instead, we will provide a helpful quote from **Got Questions** in response to the question *"What is the Antichrist?"* and then add some "extra" thoughts.

"First John 2:18 speaks of the Antichrist: "Dear children, this is the last hour; and as you have heard that the antichrist is coming, even now many

antichrists have come. This is how we know it is the last hour." The specific term antichrist is used five times in Scripture, twice here in 1 John 2:18 and once in 1 John 2:22; 4:3; and 2 John 1:7. So, what is this Antichrist that the apostle John refers to?

The meaning of the term antichrist is simply "against Christ." As the apostle John records in First and Second John, an antichrist denies the Father and the Son (1 John 2:22), does not acknowledge Jesus (1 John 4:3), and denies that Jesus came in the flesh (2 John 1:7). There have been many "antichrists," as 1 John 2:18 states. But there is also coming the Antichrist.

Most Bible prophecy/eschatology experts believe the Antichrist will be the ultimate embodiment of what it means to be against Christ. In the end times/last hour, a man will arise to oppose Christ and His followers more than anyone else in history. Likely claiming to be the true Messiah, the Antichrist will seek world domination and will attempt to destroy all followers of Jesus Christ and the nation of Israel.

Other biblical references to the Antichrist include the following:

The imposing, boastful king of Daniel 7 who oppresses the Jews and tries to "change the set times and the laws" (verse 25).

The leader who establishes a 7-year covenant with Israel and then breaks it in Daniel 9.

The king who sets up the abomination of desolation in Mark 13:14 (cf. Daniel 9:27).

The man of lawlessness in 2 Thessalonians 2:1–12.

The rider on a white horse (representing his claim to be a man of peace) in Revelation 6:2.

The first beast—the one from the sea—in Revelation 13. This beast receives power from the dragon (Satan) and speaks "proud words and blasphemies" (verse 5) and wages war against the saints (verse 7).

Thankfully, the Antichrist/beast, along with his false prophet, will be thrown into the lake of fire, where they will spend all eternity in torment (Revelation 19:20; 20:10).

What is the Antichrist? In summary, the Antichrist is the end-times false messiah who seeks, and likely achieves, world domination so that he can destroy Israel and all followers of Jesus Christ."

We have referred to Nebuchadnezzar's dream in Daniel 2 more than once in this book. Most Bible scholars are agreed that the four kingdoms represented in the image the king saw in his dream were of the Babylonian, Persian, Greek and Roman Empires. Then there is the fifth empire, represented by the clay-and-iron feet of the statue. Various views have been put forward as to what this is. (One reason why this author did not select any image found on the Internet to use in this book was given those that might have been suitable often included annotated views on the identity with which he did not agree.)

It is worth making the point here that opinions among Christians on the subject of the Antichrist differ radically. Concerning the identity of a yet to come Antichrist (at least among those where views may be expected), the priority the subject is given in their thoughts and the actions concerning future events surrounding the Antichrist vary widely. Again, referring to Chapter 52, the author reflected on ten significant subjects where Christians hold different views and made the point: *"I would like to suggest where one stands on these subjects will have a bearing on our views on Israel"*. We can easily substitute "Antichrist" for "Israel" but here is what the author thinks:

Concerning the subject of *"clay-and-iron feet"*, the author is inclined to the view that the kingdom of the Antichrist will be a *"revived Roman Empire."* *"And the ten horns which thou sawest are ten kings, which have received no kingdom as yet; but receive power as kings one hour with the beast. These have one mind, and shall give their power and strength unto the beast. These shall make war with the Lamb, and the Lamb shall overcome them: for he is Lord of lords, and King of kings: and they that are with him are called, and chosen, and faithful"* Revelation 17:12-14. We read here how the Antichrist will lead a coalition of ten nations (which could be the statue's ten toes), but at the end Christ will defeat the Antichrist and his alliance, despite, as we write, the identity of the Antichrist and the ten kings remain shrouded in mystery. But then, after that, Jesus will set up His kingdom. The commentary on: *"the stone that smote the image* (in Nebuchadnezzar's dream) *became a great mountain, and filled the whole earth"* Daniel 2:35 could be: *"the kingdoms of this world are become the kingdoms of our Lord, and of his Christ; and he shall reign for ever and ever"* Revelation 11:15.

Rather than go down deep but pertinent rabbit holes by checking out what Daniel 7-12 and Revelation 6-19 have to say (which subject remains work in progress for this author), we will look at and end our consideration on matters pertaining to the Antichrist with Paul's teaching on the subject found in one of his letters, where the Antichrist is referred to as the *"man of lawlessness"*, who Paul speaks about in context with the *"Day of Christ"* – the time when the believer's struggles end and victory over sin and death is no longer a promise but a glorious reality – that Day we should all be keenly anticipating.

"Let no man deceive you by any means: for that day shall not come, ex-

cept there come a falling away first, and that man of sin be revealed, the son of perdition; Who opposeth and exalteth himself above all that is called God, or that is worshipped; so that he as God sitteth in the temple of God, shewing himself that he is God … For the mystery of iniquity doth already work: only he who now letteth will let, until he be taken out of the way. And then shall that Wicked be revealed, whom the Lord shall consume with the spirit of his mouth, and shall destroy with the brightness of his coming: Even him, whose coming is after the working of Satan with all power and signs and lying wonders, And with all deceivableness of unrighteousness in them that perish; because they received not the love of the truth, that they might be saved. And for this cause God shall send them strong delusion, that they should believe a lie" 2 Thessalonians 2:3-4, 7-11.

Concerning the Christ, let us first turn to a Jewish perspective, and typically one that does not believe Jesus is the Christ (Messiah), such as detailed in Wikipedia: *"In Abrahamic religions, a messiah 'the anointed one' is a saviour or liberator of a group of people. The concepts of mashiach, messianism, and of a Messianic Age originated in Judaism and in the Hebrew Bible, in which a mashiach is a king. Ha-mashiach often referred to as melekh mashiach ('King Messiah'), is to be a Jewish leader, physically descended from the paternal Davidic line through King David and King Solomon. He is thought to accomplish predetermined things in a future arrival, including the unification of the tribes of Israel, the gathering of all Jews to Eretz Israel, the rebuilding of the Temple in Jerusalem, the ushering in of a Messianic Age of global universal peace, and the annunciation of the world to come."*

There are many Old Testament references to Israel's coming king and there is little doubt many Jews at the time of Jesus were eagerly looking forward to the time when this would happen, no doubt accentuated by the fact that they were a land under occupation by an oppressive empire – the Romans, who could and would ruthlessly put down any rebellion. This was evidenced on "Palm Sunday", days before Jesus was crucified, when He was heralded by many as being the fulfilment of prophecy, including the one relating to the way he entered into Jerusalem that last time: *"Rejoice greatly, O daughter of Zion; shout, O daughter of Jerusalem: behold, thy King cometh unto thee: he is just, and having salvation; lowly, and riding upon an ass, and upon a colt the foal of an ass"* Zechariah 9:9. Many of those references, just as this example, were (according to Christians) remarkably fulfilled at Jesus' First Coming, and we can therefore be confident that the rest will be fulfilled at His Second Coming.

We could go through some of the large number of examples here but we won't. Please check out preceding chapters of this book, study the Hebrew Scriptures for yourself and check out from a selection of excellent resources to be found on the Internet to find out more. While the early church was comprised almost exclusively of Jewish believers, it was becoming evident by the time the New Testament had been completed that most Jews had rejected their Messiah. Fast forward to today: while there are Jewish believers in Jesus, they are in a minority. As for the rest (for the more spiritual) they would likely look for one that more closely aligns with that set out in our Wikipedia extract.

We have already said much about Jesus the King (of kings) and we could say a lot more, but we need to draw our thoughts to a conclusion and how better than to quote (once more) from two of those Old Testament messianic/kingly references: "*My heart is inditing a good matter: I speak of the things which I have made touching the king: my tongue is the pen of a ready writer. Thou art fairer than the children of men: grace is poured into thy lips: therefore God hath blessed thee for ever. Gird thy sword upon thy thigh, O most mighty, with thy glory and thy majesty. And in thy majesty ride prosperously because of truth and meekness and righteousness; and thy right hand shall teach thee terrible things. Thine arrows are sharp in the heart of the king's enemies; whereby the people fall under thee. Thy throne, O God, is for ever and ever: the sceptre of thy kingdom is a right sceptre. Thou lovest righteousness, and hatest wickedness: therefore God, thy God, hath anointed thee with the oil of gladness above thy fellows. All thy garments smell of myrrh, and aloes, and cassia, out of the ivory palaces, whereby they have made thee glad. Kings' daughters were among thy honourable women: upon thy right hand did stand the queen in gold of Ophir*" Psalm 45:1-9.

And since this book is about priests as well as kings, we conclude this section with our second reference. Here we quote a whole psalm that is often referred to in the New Testament: "*The Lord said unto my Lord, Sit thou at my right hand, until I make thine enemies thy footstool. The Lord shall send the rod of thy strength out of Zion: rule thou in the midst of thine enemies. Thy people shall be willing in the day of thy power, in the beauties of holiness from the womb of the morning: thou hast the dew of thy youth. The Lord hath sworn, and will not repent, Thou art a priest for ever after the order of Melchizedek. The Lord at thy right hand shall strike through kings in the day of his wrath. He shall judge among the heathen, he shall fill the places with the dead bodies; he shall wound the heads over many countries. He shall drink of the brook in the way: therefore shall he lift up the head*" Psalm 110:1-7.

Finally

We have come to the end of "**Kings of the Bible**" and the whole book. Some of what could have been said remains unsaid and the time has come to go with what we have. Much also has been said that readers may find surprising and might take them outside their comfort zones, e.g., when the author attempts to relate what any of us can find out about kings of the Bible just from a careful study of the Bible, applying the ten "context" points outlined in Chapter 2, but then, in trying to make sense of today's world, apply the lessons we have learnt when doing such a study. Readers are encouraged to find out things for themselves, and to not be afraid to ask questions and challenge the status quo, even when finding themselves in environments where that is not the done thing (but always exercising wisdom when or not to speak, doing so relevantly and respectfully, noting some may still not like it). Sometimes we have to hold our hands up and declare we don't know something or have been wrong (as has often happened to the author on this journey). But if what is written helps, then that is good!

When we began our prophets, priests and kings journey, it was to cover as far as was practicable every prophet, priest and king, whether named or not, to be found in the Bible and draw lessons from our investigations. For the author, it was something which he felt the Lord had laid on his heart that would be useful, and that earnest seekers after truth in these matters would find useful too, and it is now up to others to decide if that has been the case. With prophets, the task was more straightforward given it is pretty clear who the prophets were and, relatively speaking, there were not too many of them to deal with. With priests, it was a bit more challenging given there were more of them, more were unnamed and many appeared to do nothing more than exercise standard priestly functions. As for kings, besides this being a less ambitious project to that pertaining to prophets and priests, there were lots more of them, or so it seemed, and they kept cropping up, often as part of a bigger story, and even if kings were not mentioned by name, their kingdoms (whether cities, nations or empires) were.

We began our kings journey by considering general aspects concerning kings and why doing the study we were about to do would be a profitable exercise. Then we looked at the kings around before Israel (the main focus, after God, of the Bible) had a king. This meant considering a period of 3000 years, three quarters of the period covered by the Bible if we exclude prophecy that goes right up to the time we have a new heaven and a new earth, when kings (or at least their controllers) still play an important part in human affairs. We then devoted three chapters to the kings of Israel and, after the kingdom was divided, to the kings of Israel and Judah – that which is given greatest coverage in the Bible. Finally, we come to this chapter, by way of a mopping up exercise, albeit a selective one, when we consider the rest of the kings mentioned in the Bible, of cities, of nations and especially of empires. Of these empires, Egypt and Assyria featured in the earlier parts, Babylon and Persia in the later parts, and later still Greece and Rome. But Babylon, notably Nebuchadnezzar, and Persia, notably Cyrus, were our main focus. A lot of kings got scant or no mention, but that is what comes when one scales down.

Speaking now, personally, and reverting to the first person, I want to reiterate that what I set out to do has been what was said in the Preface. A lot of what I write (I hope) is sound Bible exegesis, but in some of it I venture a view. It is on a note of hope and encouragement that I would like to end. I am retired and feel I may be nearing my end. I do not need to earn a living and no longer care who I upset provided God is ok with it. Unlike some of my younger friends, I have less to lose if I say what I really think. If I have a wish, it is one that arose from studying priests, now followed by kings, and that is to leave a worthwhile legacy and quicken my readers. I am grateful I have a degree of freedom to pursue those things that interest me and, unlike my spiritual forefathers who were worthier than I am, besides the Bible, I have access to so much knowledge and opinion, although a lot of truth still remains hidden (even if some of it is in plain sight and needs to be discovered for ourselves). Besides which, being a watchman on the wall, understanding the times and suggesting to folk, especially Christians, how they ought to respond to happenings around them, are things I feel that I can bring to the proverbial party.

As I wrap up this chapter (and the Book as a whole) I would rather do so on a light, joyful and optimistic note (which I will do), and focus on God's love and that being the trigger for what we do here on earth, especially in reaching out in actions rather than words to the poor, vulnerable and hurting folk God would have us deal with. But one more serious and important point needs to be made before we do. Looking back to my "Prophets" book the characteristic of God that struck me as much as any concerns His wisdom. I have already said, concerning the "Priests" part of this book, it is His holiness. But what about kings? As I reflected on this part that is to with kings, I have to say it is His judgement, a recurring theme throughout our studies of Kings of the Bible and this applied to all nations (besides that of its and our main focus, Israel) and to individuals, some of whom were dealt with ever so severely. Included in this is the thought that not only is it kings that are being judged, but those who they ruled over often suffered as a result, such as the time when God punished Israel with a plague that killed 70,000 men, after God was angry with David for foolishly calling for a census, a decision that arose out of his pride.

Recently, I had an experience in my own city when a number of Christians I know, love and respect put on an outreach event. It seemed to me their preaching emphasis was on a God who was not angry with any of us when we do wrong since He is a God of love. I was disappointed to hear what was only half a gospel preached, and a perversion of it at that ("*God is angry with the wicked every day*", Psalm 7:11 relates). Which brings me back to what the Bible teaches concerning "*judgment*", a word that appears 408 times in the KJV Bible (including 79 references in the New Testament). I will leave you with three texts. Firstly, according to Jesus, the Holy Spirit's role is: "*And when he is come, he will reprove the world of sin, and of righteousness, and of judgment: Of sin, because they believe not on me; Of righteousness, because I go to my Father, and ye see me no more; Of judgment, because the prince of this world is judged*" John 16:8-11, Secondly, and harking back to the time when Moses received instructions from God on Mount Sinai (discussed earlier) and what people could see from a distance as being fire and it was awesome: "*Wherefore we receiving a kingdom which cannot be moved, let us have grace, whereby we may serve God acceptably with reverence and godly fear: For our God is a consuming fire*" Hebrews 12:28-29. Thirdly, considering the Day of Judgment we all have to face: "*And I saw a great white throne, and him that sat on it, from whose face the earth and the heaven fled away; and there was found no place for them. And I saw the dead, small and great, stand before God; and the books were opened: and another book was opened, which is the book of life: and the dead were judged out of those things which were written in the books, according to their works ... And whosoever was not found written in the book of life was cast into the lake of fire*" Revelation 20:11-13, 15.

I do not expect most of those who will be reading this to do the research I have done but I would counsel they be not ignorant of Satan's devices and to be faithful, noting the consequences, seen in our study of the kings, of being unfaithful. It is something we can and must do, even though, since we are sinners, we may fail and fail often – but God saves us fully by His grace and restores the penitent. We all have choices to make and we are not forced to choose one way or another. It is best though we choose to follow His Son, Jesus. God is ever faithful. There is a danger, of course, of falling into the deception of Adam and Eve – eating from the Tree of the Knowledge of Good and Evil (which is enticing but also forbidden), rather than eating from the Tree of Life (which is far more beneficial).

Finally, I urge readers, notwithstanding warnings to do with holiness and judgement, to choose life; seek truth; do what is right, find freedom, remember the poor, work for the King and look forward to King Jesus coming again: King of kings; Lord of lords, and to enjoy the words of an old gospel hymn:

1. Sing them over again to me,
Wonderful words of life;
Let me more of their beauty see,
Wonderful words of life;
Words of life and beauty
Teach me faith and duty.

[Refrain]

Beautiful words, wonderful words,
Wonderful words of life;
Beautiful words, wonderful words,
Wonderful words of life.

2. Christ, the blessed one, gives to all
Wonderful words of life;
Sinner, list to the loving call,
Wonderful words of life;
All so freely given,
Wooing us to heaven. [Refrain]

3. Sweetly echo the gospel call,
Wonderful words of life;
Offer pardon and peace to all,
Wonderful words of life;
Jesus, only Savior,
Sanctify forever. [Refrain]

About which gospel, a hymn the author remembers singing in his youth also applies:

1. *One day when heaven was filled with His praises,*
   One day when sin was as black as could be,
   Jesus came forth to be born of a virgin—
   Dwelt among men, my example is He!

[Refrain]

   Living, He loved me; dying, He saved me;
   Buried, He carried my sins far away;
   Rising, He justified freely forever:
   One day He's coming—O glorious day!

2. *One day they led Him up Calvary's mountain,*
   One day they nailed Him to die on the tree;
   Suffering anguish, despised and rejected;
   Bearing our sins, my Redeemer is He. [Refrain]

3. *One day they left Him alone in the garden,*
   One day He rested, from suffering free;
   Angels came down o'er His tomb to keep vigil;
   Hope of the hopeless, my Savior is He. [Refrain]

4. *One day the grave could conceal Him no longer,*
   One day the stone rolled away from the door;
   Then He arose, over death He had conquered;
   Now is ascended, my Lord evermore. [Refrain]

5. *One day the trumpet will sound for His coming,*
   One day the skies with His glory will shine;
   Wonderful day, my beloved ones bringing;
   Glorious Savior, this Jesus is mine! [Refrain]

And finally, let us meditate on yet another, perhaps less well-known Psalm (72), about the King who is to come, He who is our blessed hope, the Lord Jesus Christ:

"Give the king thy judgments, O God, and thy righteousness unto the king's son. He shall judge thy people with righteousness, and thy poor with judgment. The mountains shall bring peace to the people, and the little hills, by righteousness. He shall judge the poor of the people, he shall save the children of the needy, and shall break in pieces the oppressor. They shall fear thee as long as the sun and moon endure, throughout all generations … Yea, all kings shall fall down before him: all nations shall serve him. For he shall deliver the needy when he crieth; the poor also, and him that hath no helper. He shall spare the poor and needy, and shall save the souls of the needy. He shall redeem their soul from deceit and violence: and precious shall their blood be in his sight. And he shall live, and to him shall be given of the gold of Sheba: prayer also shall be made for him continually; and daily shall he be praised. There shall be an handful of corn in the earth upon the top of the mountains; the fruit thereof shall shake like Lebanon: and they of the city shall flourish like grass of the earth. His name shall endure for ever: his name shall be continued as long as the sun: and men shall be blessed in him: all nations shall call him blessed. Blessed be the Lord God, the God of Israel, who only doeth wondrous things. And blessed be his glorious name for ever: and let the whole earth be filled with his glory; Amen, and Amen. The prayers of David the son of Jesse are ended." Psalm 72:1-5, 11-20.

The Gospel – Bridging the Gap between God and Man

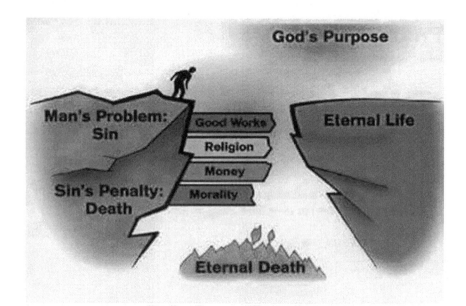

JESUS DIED IN YOUR PLACE

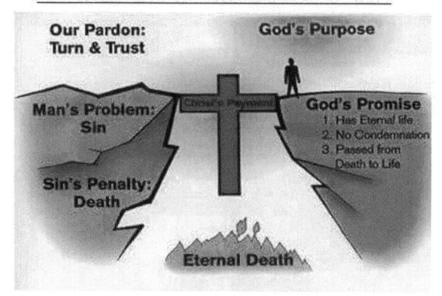

Throughout this book, we have frequently returned to the theme of the Gospel. While the subtitle of *"***Priests of the Bible***"* is *"Bridging the Gap between God and Man"*, and for a good reason, priests were not those who bridged the gap but rather, if they were doing what they were meant to be doing, they brought the message concerning how that gap can be bridged. What I would like to do as we approach the end of this book is to present the Gospel, simply, addressing some of the important what, why, who, when, where and how questions. Rather than write something new, I will reproduce in a slightly modified form a presentation that I last updated six years ago, and which can be found on my website:

"It's news I'm most proud to proclaim, this extraordinary Message of God's powerful plan to rescue everyone who trusts him, starting with Jews and then right on to everyone else!" Romans 1:16 (The Message).

Much of my website around that time related to issues around social justice and community action, where I expect there will be a good deal of agreement with those who do not share my faith. This I see as a positive thing because it helps create the possibility of doing something about such matters, sometimes together, as well as establishing some common ground, thus providing a springboard whereby I can point these and the folk we care about to my Lord and Saviour. I have argued that not only is the truth of the Gospel and making it known important but these other issues are too – humanly speaking and also from God's point of view. I see no incompatibility, for embracing the Gospel should inspire us to serve our communities and to deal with the difficult issues that together we might be able to address. I feel excited and exercised at the same time when people who disagree with my Christian views agree when it comes to matters like showing compassion toward the poor. One sticking point when trying to join forces is that obedience to God and giving Him pleasure has to be my main priority.

I turn to another of my passions, the righteousness of God and its implications, in particular the need to live accordingly and preach the Gospel, although to my shame I do not always hunger for righteousness as much as I should. While there may be different emphases in the two Testaments, they are entirely compatible. Many will see righteousness in moral terms or about obeying God and His laws, and both views are correct. Yet the Bible affirms that it is also about truth and justice along with blessing the poor. Put more simply, it is about doing what is right, but not what is right in our own or other people's eyes but what is right in the eyes of God, and it is a righteousness that covers and addresses all aspects of life. It is certainly not self-righteousness, for God requires from us a humble heart and contrite spirit. What matters is having righteousness imputed to us through faith in Christ.

While there is often broad agreement to do with matters relating to social justice, when it comes to the Bible message of righteousness I have found there is generally less and, from past experience, there is often hostile reaction. Yet I contend that from God's perspective social action and gospel proclamation are both important and connected. As a Christian (follower of Jesus) I am mandated to share the Gospel with all, which is why I have tackled this subject, as well as needing to enjoy Him. While my community activism means I work with those of all faiths and none, not imposing my beliefs on any, but not sharing the Gospel results in allowing people to go to their doom unwarned. I realise that besides needing righteousness imputed to us by faith in the One who died for our sins, the big challenge for us all is to live righteously. On the subject of us all being sinners, as far as God is concerned it isn't the type of sin that matters so much, for all sin is abominable, it is also that sinners rely on their own righteousness rather than God's and refuse to repent and submit to God's righteousness.

One of the important roles of the Holy Spirit, whose help Christians should be dependent upon for everything they do, is to *"reprove the world of sin, and of righteousness, and of judgment"* John 16:8, and part of the reason we are in a culture war is that many people resist and are offended by that message and react in such a way that those who proclaim it may end up suffering. While declaring the love of God is important, dealing with the matter of sin, righteousness and judgment is even more pressing as far as an unbeliever is concerned, even if for some this is a less palatable message to preach than that of love. Since God is righteous, He cannot allow anyone that is not righteous into His heaven, so something needs to change. I am in little doubt that when Jesus talked about the broad road that leads to destruction and the narrow road that leads to life, He knew this message would not be widely popular with many, although history shows us when people are at the end of their tether and find they have little to lose they often embrace this message, something God requires all of us to do.

Regarding opposition, I have no doubt that those who proclaim the message of righteousness and more significantly live accordingly, will be opposed by those outside the church and sadly even some who are in it who are seeking to accommodate the ways and agendas of the world. Sadly, today we see all sorts of anti-gospel teachings (even by some Christians). Jesus said: *"If the world hate you, ye know that it hated me before it hated you. If ye were of the world, the world would love his own: but because ye are not of the world, but I have chosen you out of the world, therefore the world hateth you"* John 15:18-19. But for those who believe, it is not merely about the things we refrain from doing but the things we do in reaching out to a lost world, take care of His creation (this world) despite its fallenness and love our neighbour, all of which those who follow Christ are compelled to do. Sadly, often the negative aspects are seen and not the positives but what ought to drive us is the practical implications of this Gospel of righteousness, irrespective of the revilement and ridicule we face.

According to the Bible, people tend to prefer unrighteousness to righteousness but they need to turn from their unrighteousness. Many people do much good but the bar is set high and our good is not good enough because we are sinners. *"For all have sinned, and come short of the glory of God"* Romans 3:23 and *"For the wages of sin is death; but the gift of God is eternal life through Jesus Christ our Lord"* Romans 6:23. I am compelled to share the Gospel with those who do not yet obey it, firstly by living out its message but also in words, albeit sensitive to the situation I find myself in. This is not done from a standpoint of moral superiority, self-satisfaction, or holier than thou sentiments but rather as a sinner saved by grace who has experienced struggles in overcoming sin, inviting hearers to repent and be saved. As a believer, I am called to overcome and to be righteous as this is how we get to please God.

The reason it is important to take heed of these matters is that God has always wanted to have an eternal relationship with us but given this disparity between God's righteous character and expectations and our own unrighteousness there is a quandary. We are in fact sinners, i.e., we do not live according to God's righteous precepts and, furthermore, however much we try to change we will remain sinners, meaning, until sin is dealt with, we remain separated from God. Therefore, having a relationship with Him cannot be possible, other than through the Gospel message. *"This is how much God loved the world: He gave his Son, his one and only Son. And this is why: so that no one need be destroyed; by believing in him, anyone can have a whole and lasting life"* John 3:16 – The Message, is likely one of the best-known, best-loved and most often quoted verses in the whole of the Bible.

The verses that follow though: *"God didn't go to all the trouble of sending his Son merely to point an accusing finger, telling the world how bad it was. He came to help, to put the world right again. Anyone who trusts in him is acquitted; anyone who refuses to trust him has long since been under the death sentence without knowing it. And why? Because of that person's failure to believe in the one-of-a-kind Son of God when introduced to him. This is the crisis we're in: God-light streamed into the world, but men and women everywhere ran for the darkness. They went for the darkness because they were not really interested in pleasing God. Everyone who makes a practice of doing evil, addicted to denial and illusion, hates God-light and won't come near it, fearing a painful exposure. But anyone working and living in truth and reality welcomes God-light so the work can be seen for the God-*

work it is" John 3:17-21 – The Message, are just as important, and it is important that we heed the warning that is given.

The good news (which is what "gospel" means) is that God has opened up a way whereby we can be saved – enjoy eternal life (as a result of our sins being forgiven), because of the gift of God's Son (Jesus) and upon our believing (trusting in, clinging to, relying on) him, forsaking our former unrighteousness. The bad news is we suffer eternal condemnation if we do not believe. The urgency for believers is to present the Gospel message to those who are unsaved and, call those who aren't believers, to respond before it is too late. The Gospel message is a simple one that can be grasped by the simplest among us, and just as equally, some of the most intelligent and sophisticated fail completely to get it. It is also a profound one that will never be fully grasped this side of eternity and it has enormous implications, such as how we view the world, how we are to respond to other people, how we are to live our lives, and importantly, where we spend eternity. It is a message that spans eternity since it goes back to the beginning of time when God had a plan and it will continue through the ages to come. It is a message of grace, which means that while we are called to righteousness, there is nothing we can do to earn our salvation. God's grace is such that He freely bestows His best gift on those who do not deserve it.

To find out what that plan is, we need to turn to the Bible, although why God should choose to create you and me we can't fully say for sure other than to take note that he did create humankind and right from the start He wanted to enjoy a loving relationship with those He had created. As far as recorded history goes, that story begins in the Garden of Eden when the first humans enjoyed living in paradise on earth and in perfect harmony along with their creator. When they disobeyed God by eating the forbidden fruit that relationship changed and they became estranged from God. But God still wanted to relate to His creation despite all humanity breaking His laws ever since then. Much of the Bible (and this book) is about how God went about doing this, culminating in sending His Son to earth to take the punishment for our sins: "*God, who at sundry times and in divers manners spake in time past unto the fathers by the prophets, Hath in these last days spoken unto us by his Son, whom he hath appointed heir of all things, by whom also he made the worlds; Who being the brightness of his glory, and the express image of his person, and upholding all things by the word of his power, when he had by himself purged our sins, sat down on the right hand of the Majesty on high*" Hebrews 1:1-3.

Much of the Old Testament is about God relating to a particular people, the Jews, who he wanted to bless, have a special (Covenant) relationship with and be his representatives here on earth (an important theme of this book), although there is plenty of evidence he wanted to relate to the Gentiles also – before Jesus was born. He gave the Jews a law to live by, although most Christians recognise that we are only beholden to the moral aspects today, typically that which is encapsulated in the Ten Commandments. Other aspects of the Law are helpful in understanding God and His purposes. When I wrote my book, "**Outside the Camp**", I deliberately chose to reflect Old Testament, non-moral law imagery, in particular that which related to what took place on the Day of Atonement (Yom Kippur), still celebrated by today's Jews. What originally took place that day is described in Leviticus 16.

The picture of the Scapegoat that appears on the cover of that book is of the goat that was released into the wilderness (outside the camp). Just prior, toward the end of the day's rituals, the High Priest had laid his hands on the goat in order to transfer the sins of the people onto it. The New Testament writers made something of the notion that we who follow Jesus need to identify with him by going outside the camp, just as Jesus (our scapegoat) did, "*bearing his reproach*" Hebrews 13:13. There was also another goat involved in the proceedings and lots had to be cast as to what the individual roles would be. The other goat was sacrificed for the sin of the people, whose blood was sprinkled before God, upon the Mercy Seat on top of the Ark of the Covenant, in the Holy of Holies.

I mention these matters for three reasons. Firstly, it ties in with my own community activist aspirations, which was the principle thrust of my work and of my website. Secondly, this is a picture of what was to come and pertinently points to what is in essence the Gospel message: "*Christ died for our sins according to the scriptures; and that he was buried, and that he rose again the third day according to the scriptures*" 1 Corinthians 15:3-4. Thirdly, this imagery reflects something of my own Christian background and heritage and the need to personally identify with Christ who can be seen both in the goat that was sacrificed and the Scapegoat that was released into the Wilderness.

Sacrificing an animal under the Old Testament law, and there were many examples of this happening, had limited value, yet showed there was a way for sinners to be reconciled with a righteous God. Such sacrifices could not take away all the sins of the people and were time limited (until the next time the people sinned). And besides which, God made it clear that he also required contrition and brokenness. Regarding sin, each and every one of us is a sinner and we thus incur the wrath of God. Because God is righteous and holy, He cannot live with that which is not. The quandary we find ourselves in is that we are helpless sinners who cannot save ourselves and we are in need of a saviour who can save.

But Jesus, when he died on the Cross and rose from the dead (and one day will return to this earth in triumph), is able to take away (atone for) all our sins for all time and completely save us (past, present and future). When Jesus said: *"I am the way, the truth and the life"* John 14:6, it was one of many unique, amazing claims that He made about himself. The great Christian philosopher C.S.Lewis came to the conclusion that Jesus had to be one of only three things: liar, lunatic or Lord. We need to ask ourselves which one, and if Lord, we need to respond accordingly. Moreover, it should be stated that Jesus is perfectly human and also divine (being one with the Father), for that is how He described himself. Moreover, the Bible is clear: *"Neither is there salvation in any other: for there is none other name under heaven given among men, whereby we must be saved"* Acts 4:12.

The good news is that we can have our sins forgiven and look forward to spending an eternity in God's heaven by trusting in Jesus to save us and making Him the Lord of our lives. While doing good works is important, as are things that Christians might encourage, like prayer, Bible study and church going, none of these can save us. Salvation is a central theme of the Bible and carries with it the notion of being rescued, delivered and set free. It is also to do with experiencing health, healing and wholeness. It is about the past, the present and the future. When a young boy once asked a wise bishop if he was saved, the answered came back that I have been saved (i.e., past sins have been forgiven), I am being saved (i.e., my life is being transformed in accordance with God's purposes) and I shall be saved (when sin and sickness will be left behind and I am truly able to be conformed to Christ's own image).

Looking back in history, we can see many great teachers, prophets and good people. But Jesus stands head and shoulders above them all, firstly because He was entirely sinless, secondly because only He can save us and thirdly because He is one with God (the only begotten Son of God). For our part, we must come to God as penitent sinners trusting through the merits of Christ alone and, when God does save us, we are (and can only be) saved by His grace alone. As Christ's followers, we are beholden to *"seek first the Kingdom of God and his righteousness"* Matthew 6:33, yet it is through the righteousness of Christ that is imputed to us by faith and by virtue of His atoning sacrifice that we can stand before Almighty God and enjoy the type of intimate relationship that Adam enjoyed before he fell.

This is in essence the Gospel message. The message is for all and, down the ages, men and women, boys and girls, from every circumstance, culture, creed etc., have responded to its call and their lives have been transformed. We can reflect that down the ages all sorts of people have responded to the Gospel message and have followed Jesus. I look forward to seeing them in the world to come and together worship our God. I invite you to embrace this message for yourself and do so now. I was told as a young Christian that becoming a Christian will not result in my living my life on a bed of roses despite offering true fulfilment – and so it has turned out; but in following Christ we will be able to enjoy what is most precious: a relationship with the One who is the Way, the Truth and the Life, a life with purpose, an eternal hope that is secure, and the ever-present help of God the Holy Spirit. Jesus said: "*I am come that they might have life, and that they might have it more abundantly*" John 10:10.

There are many verses from the Bible we can quote that relate to the Gospel message, but one that has brought me much hope and comfort in recent days is: "*Therefore if any man be in Christ, he is a new creature: old things are passed away; behold, all things are become new*" 2 Corinthians 5:17.

What next?

When Peter preached that famous sermon, on the Day of Pentecost when the church was effectively born, he told his listeners: "*Then Peter said unto them, Repent, and be baptized every one of you in the name of Jesus Christ for the remission of sins, and ye shall receive the gift of the Holy Ghost*" Acts 2:38, and many did that, 3000 people in fact. But the Christian life and the Gospel message does not end there; in fact it is where it begins. We are called to become like Christ and it means that with God's help our lives are gradually transformed. Much can be said about "what next" but it is interesting to note a few verses later what those who did become believers did: "*And they continued stedfastly in the apostles' doctrine and fellowship, and in breaking of bread, and in prayers*" Acts 2:42. While there is more to Jesus' teaching, such as taking up our cross, these cover four very practical things that we do well to attend to as we seek to live as disciples who follow in the footsteps of our Lord Jesus Christ:

While the apostles are no longer with us, their doctrine is and this is included in the Bible, which we do well to study and seek to apply since it contains the message both to guide us our daily dealings and God's purposes for us and humankind. One secular definition of fellowship is "*friendly association, especially with people who share one's interests*". While we could apply this to joining a church, sometimes sadly people who try to do this are put off because they find little in the way of real fellowship. Yet joining with other real Christians is important because by doing so we can encourage one another in our discipleship and are better placed to be able to serve others and tell them about Jesus. Breaking of bread is also known by other titles e.g., Eucharist, Communion and the Lords Supper. In this simple act of remembrance, we celebrate the Lord's death through partaking of the bread and the wine, it shows our oneness in Christ with other believers. Prayer is our essential lifeline to God. We talk to him and he talks to us. We can do so secretly or as part of a public gathering. It involves worship, praise, confession, supplication and intercession. It is an important way for us to become closer to God.

It is worth being reminded that God leaves us here on Earth to serve Him and through serving Him we are best able to serve others. There will be all sorts of challenges, including opposition, but Jesus has promised to always be with His followers. We should not forget, while doing good on earth, that our final destination is heaven and there we can look forward to the prospect of living with Him forever.

Testimony

While I was not brought up in an overtly Christian home, my parents did fear God to an extent and they sent me to Sunday School, where I was taught stories from the Bible. In my teens, I went along to a Christian Youth group, called the Covenanters, and, it was when I was 15 and attending a summer camp, I met God personally. I can trace my becoming a true Christian from that time. It was in 1966, the week the England football team won the World Cup! While my own Christian life has been a checkered one with lots of ups and downs, I can testify to the faithfulness of God and Him blessing some of my feeble efforts to serve Him. I am as the good book says: the Lord's unprofitable servant!

The Sacrificial Lamb

When I used the example of a goat earlier when referring to Old Testament sacrifices, it was in the context of relating this to my "Outside the Camp" book. A more common example of animal sacrifices is that of sheep, or more specifically: lamb. Going right back to the beginning we find Abel sacrificing from his flock (Genesis 4) and later we find Abraham sacrificing in lieu of his son, Isaac (Genesis 22). The particularly significant example relates to the feast of the Passover, for in order to escape the judgement God was about to inflict on the firstborn of every family, the children of Israel had to sacrifice a lamb without blemish and sprinkle the blood on the door posts of their homes in order to escape. At the back of the building of the church I attended for over half my life, there is the text: "*when I see the blood I will pass over you*" Exodus 12:13. I was told it was placed there deliberately to remind preachers, who saw it, that this was one aspect of their preaching that they must not neglect.

When Jesus celebrated the Passover with his disciples, just prior to his death, He gave it a new meaning: "*for this is my blood of the new testament, which is shed for many for the remission of sins*" Matthew 26:28, and ever since Christians have celebrated the Lords Supper (Communion) with this very act in mind. Going back to the Old Testament, we see the servant (who Christians believe refers to Jesus, despite being written 600 years before he was born) being led like a lamb to the slaughter (Isaiah 53). John the Baptist introduced Jesus by saying *"behold the Lamb of God, which taketh away the sin of the world"* John 1:29. When we get to the end of the Bible, in the book of Revelation, which is particularly about events yet to happen, we see the Lord Jesus Christ as the Lamb triumphant. He is the Lamb (that had been slain, i.e., on the cross) now seated on the Throne, worshiped by all heaven (Chapter 5). He is the Lamb that in the end overcomes, King of kings and Lord of lords (Chapter 17). He is the Lamb that joins His waiting bride, the Church (Chapter 19). He is the Lamb at the centre in the New Jerusalem (Chapter 22). This is the Lamb that we honour and Him I entreat you to follow!

For the Sceptic

Some folk who read thus far may point out, quite reasonably, that my urging them to accept the Gospel message is pointless if it isn't true or can't be proved to be true. I am sympathetic to such a position and have long ago gone on record as saying my being a committed Christian would be a waste of time and effort if Jesus is not who He says He is. Yet the issues are so important that they must not be dodged and must be checked out. I recognise four non-Christian categories (maybe there are others): the nominal Christian, i.e., one not truly following Christ despite taking upon him(her) self the label of Christian, the atheist and agnostic, the follower of another religion and the follower of no religion in particular yet who believes there is a spiritual dimension (whatever that happens to be).

I have addressed all four of these audiences in my writings. While opening up the subject, proving the case for the truth of the Christian message cannot be done in the few paragraphs we have here, but we can at least begin and I have more than done so in my writings. I do not wish to ignore those who doubt or do not believe. Indeed, I am instructed to *"be ready always to give an answer to every man that asketh you a reason of the hope that is in you with meekness and fear"* 1 Peter 3:15. I have spent many hours debating these matters with honest enquirers (and some less honest, who just like to bait, place red herrings in the way or merely argue for the sake of it) but am prepared to do so again.

I am mindful that there are those who rightly point out that there may be many who purport to having the truth who do not live accordingly, to which my response is invariably that what matters is the truth itself and of course we need to live in the light of that truth. I have heard it said that goodness and kindness is just as likely to be found in the local pub as in the local church. Whether or not this is true is not all that relevant. There are some who say that spirituality is important but it doesn't matter which religion we choose to follow as they all lead to God. Without knocking non-Christian religions (mindful there are many wonderful adherents of such beliefs), such a claim is not true. The crux issue is truth and that which is absolute rather than relative. Only Christianity passes the test. I recognise the need to exercise faith in the unseen, which in fact is what we all do every day of our lives, from when we get up and turn on the light switch expecting the light to come on or check the sun has risen.

The faith I'm talking about is reasonable as it is based on physical reality and evidence that stands up to scrutiny. It is where the subject of Christian apologetics comes into play. Books I have found helpful are those by C.S.Lewis: **"Miracles"**, Michael Green: **"Runaway World"** and Frank Morrison: **"Who Moved the Stone"**. There are undoubtedly many others. The bottom line as I see it is that while faith is important in what might be labelled as religious matters, as it is in any number of areas which touch our lives, the faith I am talking about is one that is based on fact and is the truth we need to embrace.

Internet

Click on *BibleGateway.com* for an online Bible (you can select your version – I often use King James but a modern version like Good News may serve you better). If you are going to read the Bible, it may be best to start with one of the Gospels e.g., Mark (the shortest). There are plenty of other links to dictionaries and commentaries etc. You can also listen to the whole of the Bible being read. If you do an Internet search on something like "*gospel presentations*" you will get a number of hits, some of which you may find helpful. There is a lot of sound Christian preaching to be found on the Internet.

Music

There is lots of Christian music such as will be found on You Tube. My favourite gospel hymns include: "Tell me the old, old story", "The old rugged cross", "When I survey the wondrous cross", "And can it be that I should gain", "Just as I am without one plea", "Thine be the glory risen conquering son", "Blessed assurance, Jesus is mine" and "Amazing grace". I would also recommend: Handel's Messiah. Not only do I love this music, and much more, but these examples also relate so much of the Gospel narrative. While these may reflect the tastes of an older person, there is much to inspire us in modern music too, and there is a tremendous amount of edifying modern music to be found on the Internet.

Books

Reading the Bible is the best place to start, particularly one of the four Gospels, as these recount the story of Jesus life and death, his works and his teachings. It is good to read a daily portion and there are many helpful reading aids. Two books that I have found especially helpful, which can be purchased online or from certain bookshops or borrowed from the local library, when finding out what the Gospel is all about, are: "**Mere Christianity**" by C.S.Lewis and "**Basic Christianity**" by John Stott. One smaller book that gives a graphical presentation of the Gospel message is: "**Journey into Life**" by Norman Warren. I have found reading the biographies of Christians down the ages can also be inspirational.

If you live in Southend

There exists Southend Christian Bookshop, where you can get hold of Bibles, and helpful books and other aids that relate to the Gospel. They even give Bibles freely to those who can't afford one. Obviously, the situation elsewhere will vary from place to place but there are plenty of outlets for getting hold of Christian literature, including online, and there are many who would love to assist you.

Wherever you live

While sadly many churches do not proclaim the Gospel, there will often be churches that do proclaim the Gospel message near to you, or at least real Christians who live for Christ. While some do so more effectively than others, some are more welcoming that others and some may present a better testimony than others, it is worth persisting in order to find out more concerning this great treasure. Having found other Christians, it will help you on your journey and you may help others. In following Christ, you will find a friend who will never leave or forsake you, even amidst trials and tribulations, but the Christian life is not to be lived in isolation but rather in fellowship with other Christians and, along with prayer, studying the Bible and serving others, you need to grow spiritually.

Finally

The Gospel message is not to be kept to yourself; it is the good news that needs to be shared with others.

1. O Lord my God! When I in awesome wonder
Consider all the works Thy hand hath made;
I see the stars, I hear the mighty thunder,
Thy power throughout the universe displayed

[Refrain]
Then sings my soul, my Saviour God, to Thee,
How great Thou art! How great Thou art!
Then sings my soul, my Saviour God, to Thee,
How great Thou art! How great Thou art!

2. When through the woods and forest glades I wander
And hear the birds sing sweetly in the trees;
When I look down from lofty mountain grandeur,
And hear the brook, and feel the gentle breeze: [Refrain]

3. And when I think that God, His Son not sparing,
Sent Him to die - I scarce can take it in:
That on the Cross, my burden gladly bearing,
He bled and died to take away my sin: [Refrain]

4. When Christ shall come with shout of acclamation
And take me home - what joy shall fill my heart!
Then shall I bow in humble adoration,
And there proclaim, my God how great Thou art! [Refrain]

And

1. From Heaven, You came helpless babe
Entered our world, your glory veiled
Not to be served but to serve
And give Your life that we might live

[Refrain]

This is our God, The Servant King
He calls us now to follow Him
To bring our lives as a daily offering
Of worship to The Servant King [Refrain]

2. There in the garden of tears
My heavy load he chose to bear
His heart with sorrow was torn
"Yet not My will but Yours", He said [Refrain]

3. Come see His hands and His feet
The scars that speak of sacrifice
Hands that flung stars into space
To cruel nails surrendered [Refrain]

4. So let us learn how to serve
And in our lives enthrone Him
Each other's needs to prefer
For it is Christ we're serving [Refrain]

A Closing Prayer

*L*ord, the God of Israel, enthroned between the cherubim, you alone are God over all the kingdoms of the earth. You raise up and put down rulers. You are sovereign over all things and your purposes will prevail. You are *worthy, our Lord and God, to receive glory and honour and power, for you have created all things, and by your will they were created and have their being.* May your glory fill all the earth as it does all of heaven. We come before you now in holy fear and in love, for you are great beyond all measure and have done great things for which we are glad. We are privileged to be called your people.

We are sorry when we have let you down but are thankful, in your mercy, you do not reject us and instead pick us up. We are thankful you gave us Jesus. Your Son is our great High Priest. Not only did He offer a sacrifice for our sin but He was that sacrifice, when He paid the penalty for our sins by dying for us on the Cross of Calvary. We rejoice that He intercedes on our behalf. Through Him, we enter into your presence and can do what the High Priest did when once a year he went into the Holy of Holies with the blood of animals sacrificed, where you dwell in glory, enthroned between the cherubim.

We know O Lord you have sought to have a relationship with those who you have created, but that relationship has been ruined because of sin, and there is a barrier, for you are a holy God and cannot abide sin in your presence. We read in your Word, from the beginning and right up to the end, that you have sought to restore that relationship. We are both enthralled by how you went about it and are appalled at the many times when people have spurned your overtures and have rebelled against you. Yet you are patient and ever gracious; your works are marvellous and we stand in awe of you.

We thank you that you are *the God, who at sundry times and in divers manners spake in time past unto the fathers by the prophets, hath in these last days spoken unto us by His Son, whom he hath appointed heir of all things, by whom also He made the worlds; who being the brightness of his glory, and the express image of his person, and upholding all things by the word of his power, when he had by himself purged our sins, sat down on the right hand of the Majesty on high.* We are so glad that your Son, Jesus, our Lord and Saviour and lover of our souls, is prophet, priest and king, and He is so much more.

We thank you for the prophets, priests and Nazirites that we read about in your Word. We thank you for those you raised up, ordinary and imperfect people, who still did exploits in your name. May we be a prophetic people, knowing more of your heart and mind concerning this world and those who live in it, and be discerning and courageous in making this known. May we be a priestly people and play our part in bridging the gap between heaven and earth in making you and your purposes known. May we be like the Nazirites, who were dedicated to your service, and prepared to pay the price to be so.

We thank you for your righteous judgements and when we are afflicted, we know your purposes are love. We thank you that when you humble us, it may be to get our attention and help us become more closely aligned with your will. We come to you as supplicants and intercessors because you invite us to come to you in this way. We pray for ourselves that we may not dishonour you and that we may live for your glory. We pray for our family, friends, neighbours and colleagues; some do not yet know you. You know all their situations. We ask you to deal graciously with them according to their many needs.

We pray for the church, your Church, bought with Jesus' own blood. We see it disturbed, deceived and disunited on every front and in so many ways. So many are not following you as they ought and it may include us. So many are suffering for your sake. Yet she is the glorious bride that one day will be re-united with your Son, her heavenly bridegroom. She remains your instrument to bring about your purposes in and your Gospel to our needy world. *In living power remake us, self on the cross and Christ upon the throne, past put behind us, for the future take us; Lord of our lives, to live for Christ alone.*

We pray for Israel, who are the apple of your eye. You promised to Abraham that his descendants will be your specially chosen people and you have not gone back on that promise. Today, we see Israel attacked on all sides and we know Satan is behind it. But your Word declares that while you keep all your promises you expect that those you make promises to do their part and often it has not been so. We rejoice some of Israel follow Jesus and sad most do not. We look forward to and pray all Israel will be saved. We thank you that much of what we learn about prophets, priests and kings is through Israel.

We pray for this world. Wherever we look there appears to be evil and turmoil. So much is happening that perplexes. There is much we do not know. We know Satan controls many in power but you are sovereign in allowing it to be so. We pray for world leaders. We pray for wisdom when it comes to our response. We thank you Lord that we see many acts of goodness, often done by those who do not know you. We pray that we will be good people. While there is much we do not understand and cannot change, may we live life in humility, kindness, faithfulness and godliness. Help us to be such a people.

We pray for those who read this book. May they not be put off because it appears to be too deep. May they learn from you rather than the author and may they see only you. May they learn more about priests and kings and how they went about their business and what they had to face and why they did what they did, but even more may we become the free from sin priests you desire, who will reign with Christ. We acknowledge Lord that even the best of us is deficient in all sorts of ways, but your mercy is more. May we be those who give you the honour and glory that is your due, especially if it costs us.

We join the throng in heaven, *redeemed from every kindred, and tongue, and people, and nation,* and those who overcame the evil one by *the blood of the Lamb, and by the word of their testimony,* and cry: *"worthy is the Lamb that was slain to receive power, and riches, and wisdom, and strength, and honour, and glory, and blessing. And every creature which is in heaven, and on the earth, and under the earth, and such as are in the sea, and all that are in them, heard I saying, Blessing, and honour, and glory, and power, be unto him that sitteth upon the throne, and unto the Lamb for ever and ever".*

"Glory be to the Father, and to the Son: and to the Holy Ghost; As it was in the beginning, is now, and ever shall be: world without end. Amen." Book of Common Prayer, 1662.

"Now unto him that is able to keep you from falling, and to present you faultless before the presence of his glory with exceeding joy, To the only wise God our Saviour, be glory and majesty, dominion and power, both now and ever. Amen." Jude 1:24-25.

1. *There is a fountain filled with blood*
Drawn from Immanuel's veins;
And sinners, plunged beneath that flood,
Lose all their guilty stains:
Lose all their guilty stains,
Lose all their guilty stains;
And sinners, plunged beneath that flood,
Lose all their guilty stains.

2. *The dying thief rejoiced to see*
That fountain in his day;
And there may I, though vile as he,
Wash all my sins away:
Wash all my sins away,
Wash all my sins away;

And there may I, though vile as he,

Wash all my sins away.

3. *Dear dying Lamb, Thy precious blood*

Shall never lose its power,

Till all the ransomed ones of God

Be saved, to sin no more:

Be saved, to sin no more,

Be saved, to sin no more;

Till all the ransomed ones of God,

Be saved to sin no more.

4. *E'er since by faith I saw the stream*

Thy flowing wounds supply,

Redeeming love has been my theme,

And shall be till I die:

And shall be till I die,

And shall be till I die;

Redeeming love has been my theme,

And shall be till I die.

5. *When this poor lisping, stammering tongue*

Lies silent in the grave,

Then in a nobler, sweeter song,

I'll sing Thy power to save:

I'll sing Thy power to save,

I'll sing Thy power to save;

Then in a nobler, sweeter song,

I'll sing Thy power to save.

List of Hymns included in "Priests of the Bible"

" *A*nd *be not drunk with wine, wherein is excess; but be filled with the Spirit; Speaking to yourselves in psalms and hymns and spiritual songs, singing and making melody in your heart to the Lord; Giving thanks always for all things unto God and the Father in the name of our Lord Jesus Christ"* Ephesians 5:18-20.

> *We bring the sacrifice of praise*
> *Into the house of the Lord*
> *We bring the sacrifice of praise*
> *Into the house of the Lord*
>
> *And we offer up to You*
> *The sacrifices of thanksgiving*
> *And we offer up to You*
> *The sacrifices of joy*

While the contents of this book are directed firstly toward our heads so that we might know our subject better, these are also aimed at the heart so that we can better appreciate and worship God. For this reason, we have included several hymns that have been written down the ages by writers coming from many different backgrounds. We list them here in the order that they appear in this book:

- Lord for the years your love has kept and guided
- Facing a task unfinished that drives us to our knees
- Oh the love that drew salvation's plan!
- Now thank we all our God
- In Christ alone, my hope is found
- Jesus, the Name high over all
- God moves in a mysterious way
- Sweet hour of prayer
- Guide me, O Thou great Jehovah
- Take my life and let it be

- No blood, no altar now
- O come, O come, Immanuel
- Sing we the King who is coming to reign
- Bless the Lord oh my soul
- Before the throne of God above
- O teach me what it meaneth
- My God, how wonderful Thou art
- Here comes Jesus, see Him walking on the water
- O Church of Christ, invincible
- The church's one foundation
- Jesus, Thine all-victorious love
- We are one in the Spirit, we are one in the Lord
- For the bread and for the wine
- This world is a wilderness wide
- When peace like a river attendeth my way
- O soul, are you weary and troubled?
- Join all the glorious names
- The God of Abraham praise
- Be thou my vision, O Lord of my heart
- Man of Sorrows what a name
- Through Thy precious body broken
- I have decided to follow Jesus
- There's a work for Jesus, ready at your hand
- When we walk with the Lord
- I know not why God's wondrous grace
- Holy, holy, holy! Lord God Almighty!
- Take time to be holy, speak oft with thy Lord
- Alas! and did my Savior bleed
- When I survey the wondrous cross
- King of my life, I crown Thee now
- O worship the King all-glorious above
- Search me, O God, and know my heart today

- Jesus shall reign where'er the sun
- Dear Lord and Father of mankind
- Sing them over again to me
- Living, He loved me; dying, He saved me
- O Lord my God! When I in awesome wonder
- From Heaven You came helpless babe
- There is a fountain filled with blood
- We bring the sacrifice of praise
- When the music fades and all is stripped away
- What kind of love is this that gave itself for me

Poems about Priests

Felix Randal by Gerard Manley Hopkins

Felix Randal the farrier, O is he dead then? my duty all ended,
Who have watched his mould of man, big-boned and hardy-
handsome
Pining, pining, till time when reason rambled in it, and some
Fatal four disorders, fleshed there, all contended?
Sickness broke him. Impatient he cursed at first, but mended
Being anointed and all; though a heavenlier heart began some
Months earlier, since I had our sweet reprieve and ransom
Tendered to him. Ah well, God rest him all road ever he offended!
This seeing the sick endears them to us, us too it endears.
My tongue had taught thee comfort, touch had quenched thy tears,
Thy tears that touched my heart, child, Felix, poor Felix Randal;
How far from then forethought of, all thy more boisterous years,
When thou at the random grim forge, powerful amidst peers,
Didst fettle for the great grey drayhorse his bright and battering
sandal!

The Deserted Village by Oliver Goldsmith (an extract)

The village preacher's modest mansion rose.
A man he was, to all the country dear,
And passing rich with forty pounds a year;
Remote from towns he ran his godly race,
Nor e'er had changed, nor wished to change his place;
Unpractised he to fawn, or seek for power,
By doctrines fashioned to the varying hour;
Far other aims his heart had learned to prize,
More skilled to raise the wretched than to rise.
His house was known to all the vagrant train,
He chid their wanderings but relieved their pain;
The long-remembered beggar was his guest,
Whose beard descending swept his aged breast;
The ruined spendthrift, now no longer proud,
Claim'd kindred there, and had his claims allowed;
The broken soldier, kindly bade to stay,
Sate by his fire, and talked the night away;
Wept o'er his wounds, or, tales of sorrow done,
Shouldered his crutch, and shewed how fields were won.
Pleased with his guests, the good man learned to glow,
And quite forgot their vices in their woe;
Careless their merits, or their faults to scan,
His pity gave ere charity began.
Thus to relieve the wretched was his pride,
And even his failings leaned to Virtue's side;
But in his duty prompt at every call,
He watched and wept, he prayed and felt, for all.
And, as a bird each fond endearment tries,
To tempt its new-fledged offspring to the skies;
He tried each art, reproved each dull delay,

Allured to brighter worlds, and led the way.

Beside the bed where parting life was layed,

And sorrow, guilt, and pain, by turns, dismayed

The reverend champion stood. At his control

Despair and anguish fled the struggling soul;

Comfort came down the trembling wretch to raise,

And his last faltering accents whispered praise.

At church, with meek and unaffected grace,

His looks adorned the venerable place;

Truth from his lips prevailed with double sway,

And fools, who came to scoff, remained to pray.

The service past, around the pious man,

With steady zeal, each honest rustic ran;

Even children followed, with endearing wile,

And plucked his gown, to share the good man's smile.

His ready smile a parent's warmth exprest,

Their welfare pleased him, and their cares distrest:

To them his heart, his love, his griefs were given,

But all his serious thoughts had rest in Heaven.

Feed My Sheep by author unknown

In fields of green and pastures wide,
The pastor walks with humble stride,
His heart filled with a burning flame,
To follow God's command, his only aim.
"Feed my sheep," the Lord did say,
And so the pastor treads the way,
To bring God's love to all who seek,
And give them food for soul and beak.
He tends his flock with love and care,
With words of hope, he's always there,
To guide and lead them through the night,
And show them the path that's right.
With every sermon, every prayer,
The pastor's words ring loud and clear,
His faith and love a shining light,
To help his sheep in darkest night.
Through trials, struggles, and pain,
The pastor's love will still remain,
A beacon of hope to all who weep,
For he obeys the Lord's command to "feed my sheep."
And when his work on earth is done,
And he's called to join the Heavenly Son,
He'll leave behind a legacy so grand,
Of a life well-lived, by God's command.

Some Thoughts from Past Blogs

I have sometimes referred to postings on my blog: jrbpublications.com/ blog over the past ten years on a wide variety of subjects including religion, politics and things that interest me. What follows are a few extracts from what I have written, just in the past year. I do not expect readers to agree with all that I write but I hope they will find these thoughts as a result of my *"watching on the wall"* helpful:

"Where to start? Whether people think I am self-appointed / talk twaddle or not, I do see one of my main roles in my twilight years is to be a watchman on the wall, accountable to God, since there are too few genuine watchmen around. While not knowing a lot of what is really going on around us and concentrating on being good Christians sounds piously attractive, for me (and may I say, for you too, dear reader) that is not a theologically sound option. Ignorance is no excuse, since we do need to know how to respond to what is going on and not hide behind Romans 13, even though we know so little, because the Unholy Trinity (media, politicians, societal elites), who are either fools or villains, misinform us and, even if we do know more, more likely than not, we can't do much about it other than to watch and pray and fight for truth, which if one were to think about it is still something pretty significant ..." Looking at the news; looking at the church; looking unto Jesus 26/11/23.

"They label us 'tin hat wearers', 'conspiracy theorists', 'lunatics', 'anti-vaxxers' 'climate deniers' 'anti-science' and even 'terrorists'! But who are we really? We are the ones that care more than others think is wise, the ones that risk more than others think is safe, that dream more than others think is practical and expect more than others think is possible. That is who we are. That is what separates us from the rest. And it all starts with the fact that we care. We care that we're being lied to by an entire system created for that purpose. We care that through the lies they have manipulated us to accept and perpetuate our own enslavement. We care that innocent people suffer daily because of this. We care that children are being mentally and physically abused. We care that we are being poisoned through the air, the food and the water. We care that medicine was hijacked by Big Pharma drug lords for making money, instead of healing. We care about human trafficking and child exploitation ..." Conspiracy theorists – the ones that care 28/10/23.

"... My blogs "How should Christians respond to conspiracy theories?" and "Tying up the loose ends – Truth" are two good "old gramophone record" examples, which while both written three years ago are remarkably relevant. "Conspiracy theory" is a pejorative term and something many thinking people who have influence go out of their way to distant them-

selves from, for fear of being ridiculed or rejected. Some conspiracy theories are bogus of course and others cannot be proven at the time (and is why they are theories); yet over time many prove to be facts. I regularly follow the likes of arch conspiracy theorists Alex Jones, David Icke and Charlie Ward, unashamedly, who may not always get it right but are often more spot on than mainstream media when it comes making sense of what is going on in today's crazy world, run largely by the evil cabal, yet are the very people who we are told we should avoid ..." Conspiracy theories, the truth and appropriate Christian responses 29/08/23.

"... Today this text was shared on my church WhatsApp page and people were encouraged. It also got me thinking about what I wrote six months ago. When I shared it was by way of an antidote to the dark happenings in today's world that I was keen to expose and see overturned, but there is another angle (there often is) to consider. According to the Book of Common Prayer and based on what the Bible teaches, we are up against the formidable foes of the world, the flesh and the devil often it seems acting in unison to turn us away from God. Instead of thinking about what is true, honest, just, pure, lovely and of good report, these entities seek to entice us to do the very opposite with the net result we turn away from God and influence others to do the same, and we are all the worse for it. While we mustn't be ostriches that bury their head in the sand when it comes to recognising, exposing and confronting evil, may we have the character, courage and discipline to make thinking on what is true, honest, just, pure, lovely and of good report our regular habit ..." Whatsoever things are true, honest, just, pure, lovely, of good report (2) 09/08/23.

"... Some things pertinent to that early project [Trust Links – Growing Together] *were difficult to predict. I recall we spent significant amounts of money ensuring our project was wheelchair assessable, yet I do not recall anyone in a wheelchair using our disabled toilet. Yet there are many other disabilities we ignored, some of which I have succumbed to. Given the project that we wrote policies for was helping those with mental health issues, we did make adjustments to help those with that disability but little thought was given to other disabilities, including my own muscle wasting condition affecting movement. The point about disability is those who have a disability can often achieve a lot although they may not always be easy to employ (except with a lot of support and flexibility that many employers can't give). There may be limitations on what the disabled person can offer or be offered, recognising too that certain disabilities may be hidden and may not be admitted. In my careers, firstly as a computer specialist and then as a community worker, I do not recall age being much of an issue. Yet now I am old myself, I can see examples of people being discriminated against,*

even subtlety and inadvertently, based on their age. Often older people are relatively high maintenance and have limited capacities, including mental and physical endurance. The temptation is to cast such people onto one side, sometimes arguing it is necessary to bring on the young. I have seen too many examples of old people being placed on the proverbial scrap heap and not only seeing the resultant depression it causes them but we lose out by not getting what they are able and willing to give ..." **Equal opportunities, old age and disability revisited** 01/08/23.

"*... I was bemused when good, sometimes godly, people went along with this false narrative and seeing Satan's divide and rule strategy in operation. While in the early days I vented my strong objections, sometimes falling out with those who dismissed my views or worse, I came to realise often one ought to maintain one's own counsel. Now we have come out of Covid, one wonders what next this often-hidden elite have in store to screw humanity, depopulate and make us slaves. While I have a good idea who some of the bad guys are, I suspect when it comes to who is at the top of the evil hierarchy led by Satan, these are unanswered questions. It is becoming clearer by the day that people have been conned by nefarious Covid and Climate Change hoaxes, lies behind the war in Ukraine, the election meddling in the US and elsewhere that has been covered up, who are truly the good and bad guys on the world stage and the woke agenda that has got so many nice people distracted and het up ...*" **How much longer will the masses be dumbed down?** 26/07/23.

"*... I was triggered to pen these thoughts following a conversation I had this past week with a friend that dear Charlie Ward would place in the fourth dimension. According to Charlie, those in the third dimension (the majority) believe what they are told by "The Unholy Trinity" (my term for the media, politicians and societal elites); those in the fourth dimension question what they are told but are not sure what to believe; those in the fifth dimension (including Charlie and I) not only refuse to believe what we are meant to believe by those in power, but believe we are being screwed by an evil, elite, powerful cabal intent on de-population and enslavement, including using the Corona crisis to achieve their ends, and because they are on the dark side (beholden to Satan) lack empathy with those who suffer. The challenge those of us face who are uncomfortable with the official narrative is that it is alright saying "go do your own research" but without a brain the size of the planet, unlike my favourite paranoid android, Marvin from "Hitchhikers Guide to the Galaxy", and with limited time and access to the facts, a lot is not easy to verify. Yet I smelt a rat when the "pandemic" was announced and now I am 99.9% certain ...*" **Corona revisited** 27/05/23.

Really Finally

Today, I hand over my manuscript to the person who will get it into a form that the likes of Ingram and Amazon can use in order to make the book available to potentially anyone, anywhere in the world, who wishes to acquire their own copy. We can do so using resources unimaginable not that long ago, thanks to the digital revolution and those devices that allow us to buy and sell over the Internet. I have been grateful to the person who has done a fantastic proof-reading job and has been patient throughout, especially given my propensity to change things whenever new thoughts come to mind. And always there are the lurking, subtle errors and inconsistencies that keep coming to light, and no doubt also after the book is published. But this is it, no more tinkering in order to accommodate the latest profound thought that has come my way – we have now reached the point of no return!

Am I satisfied with what I have written? Yes, because I have got an enormous amount off my chest, including stuff that is arguably nothing to do with the primary subject matter of this book, in this my almost certainly last bash writing project, and who knows any other project come to that. But also, no, because I know there is more that could be said. But then I am just a link in the proverbial chain and, as I keep reminding myself, merely an unprofitable servant who is trying to do his bit amidst all the challenges and conundrums of life. No doubt others will come after me who will say what needs to be said, including offering perspectives I glossed over or missed altogether, as well as those who remain on planet earth that have to come to terms with and respond to how things truly are, which happens to be a strange mixture of very good and very bad.

One of my burdens, and why I write as I do, is to help those who have to face the confusion and evil I am now seeing in the world, to recognise that is so and to respond in the right way, which is God's way. I have been half expecting something cataclysmic to happen so I could order "stop the press" but despite seeing disturbing happenings across the world, even new stuff as a result of checking out today's newsfeed, we await what comes with bated breath, yet with hope and confidence if we are following Him who we should be following. For me, there is my next project to ponder but before that I have to focus on being a good human being, recognising there are many opportunities to do good, especially, notwithstanding past failures etc., if I keep my eyes fixed on the One I claim to be serving, about whom I end with two final hymns that have blessed me and I hope and pray will bless you too:

1. When the music fades
And all is stripped away
And I simply come
Longing just to bring
Something that's of worth
That will bless your heart
I'll bring you more than a song
For a song in itself, is not what you have required
You search much deeper within
Through the way things appear
You're looking into my heart

[Refrain]
I'm coming back to the heart of worship
And it's all about you, it's all about you Jesus
I'm sorry Lord, for the thing I've made it
When it's all about you, it's all about you Jesus

2. King of endless worth
No one could express
How much you deserve
Though I'm weak and poor
All I have is yours
Every single breath
I'll bring you more than a song
For a song in itself, is not what you have required
You search much deeper within
Through the way things appear
Your looking into my heart [Refrain]

And

1. What kind of love is this
That gave itself for me
I am the guilty one
Yet I go free
What kind of love is this
A love I've never known
I didn't even know His name
What kind of love is this

2. What kind of man is this
Who died in agony
He who had done no wrong
Was crucified for me
What kind of man is this
Who laid aside His throne
That I might know the love of God
What kind of man is this

3. By grace I have been saved
It is the gift of God
He destined me to be His own
Such is His love
No eye has ever seen
No ear has ever heard
Nor has the heart of men conceived
What kind of love is this